SKU: PQ-PMP6-SW
20190321

D1790794

Table of Contents

Instructor name: _____

Instructor email: _____

Course Dates: _____

FOREWORD

I bought my first *PMBOK® Guide* in 1996, and it still sits in my office today. I remember the light bulb coming on the first time I really understood that there was a structure to project management and a way of thinking of my job as a series of interrelated processes. It was not only helpful; it was empowering!

Now that you have decided to pursue PMP® certification, you will find that there is often a steep initial learning curve. The way you do things may be different than the way that is presented in the *PMBOK® Guide*. Don't despair! Instead, think of all of these differences as opportunities to learn and grow within your profession.

As you prepare for certification, let me encourage you to never settle for the answer "it's just that way for the test" when seeking to understand why the material is presented the way it is. If you do, you'll shortchange yourself. Everything in the *PMBOK® Guide* is there for a reason, even if you don't agree with that reason. Seek to understand why the material is organized the way it is, and you will be better off for it.

PMP® certification is not easily attained, but the resources you have received with this class work. By investing the time to study, you'll be rewarded, not only with a valuable certification, but with a richer understanding of project management.

Good luck, and congratulations in advance!

Andy Crowe

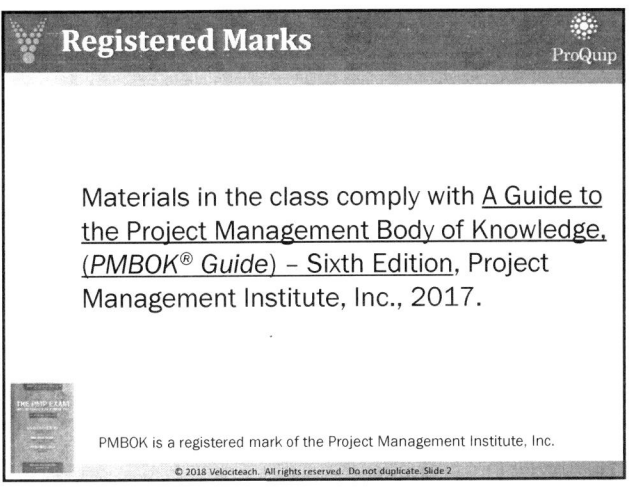

Registered Marks — ProQuip

Materials in the class comply with <u>A Guide to the Project Management Body of Knowledge, (*PMBOK® Guide*) – Sixth Edition</u>, Project Management Institute, Inc., 2017.

PMBOK is a registered mark of the Project Management Institute, Inc.

© 2018 Velociteach. All rights reserved. Do not duplicate. Slide 2

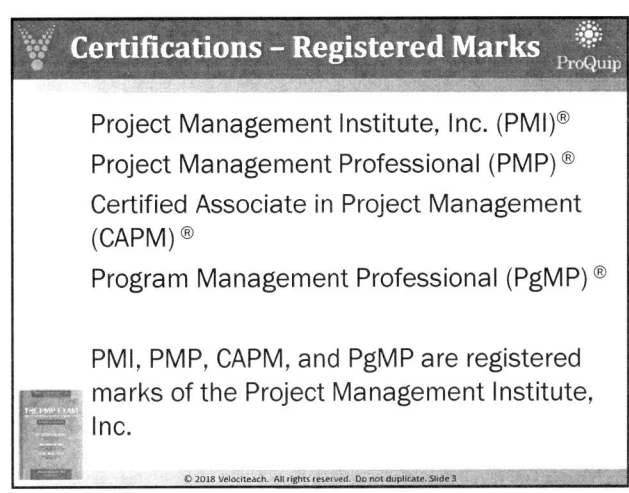

Certifications – Registered Marks — ProQuip

Project Management Institute, Inc. (PMI)®

Project Management Professional (PMP)®

Certified Associate in Project Management (CAPM)®

Program Management Professional (PgMP)®

PMI, PMP, CAPM, and PgMP are registered marks of the Project Management Institute, Inc.

© 2018 Velociteach. All rights reserved. Do not duplicate. Slide 3

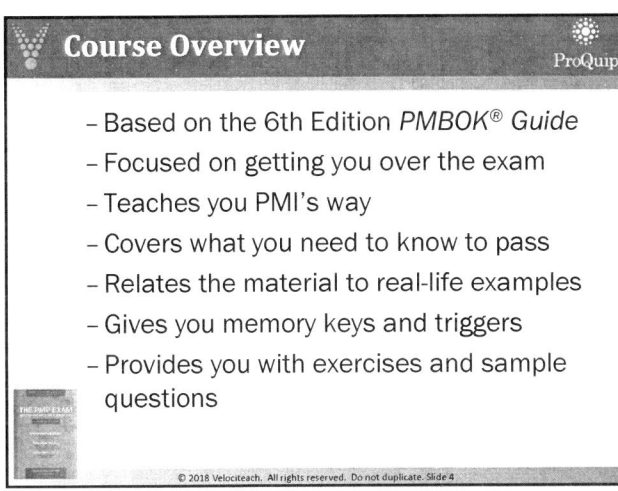

Course Overview — ProQuip

- Based on the 6th Edition *PMBOK® Guide*
- Focused on getting you over the exam
- Teaches you PMI's way
- Covers what you need to know to pass
- Relates the material to real-life examples
- Gives you memory keys and triggers
- Provides you with exercises and sample questions

© 2018 Velociteach. All rights reserved. Do not duplicate. Slide 4

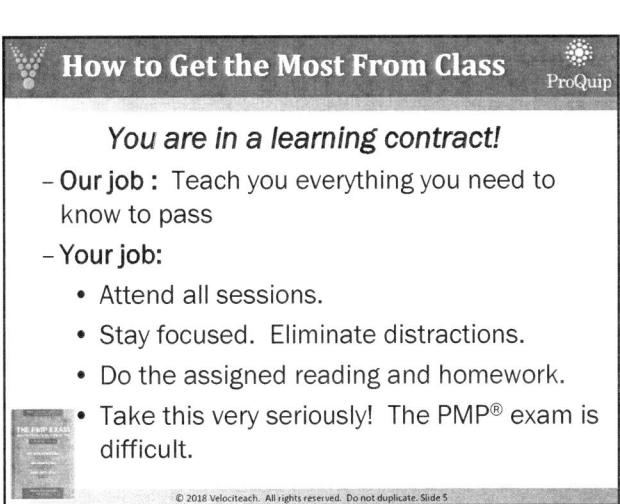

How to Get the Most From Class — ProQuip

You are in a learning contract!

- **Our job :** Teach you everything you need to know to pass
- **Your job:**
  - Attend all sessions.
  - Stay focused. Eliminate distractions.
  - Do the assigned reading and homework.
  - Take this very seriously! The PMP® exam is difficult.

© 2018 Velociteach. All rights reserved. Do not duplicate. Slide 5

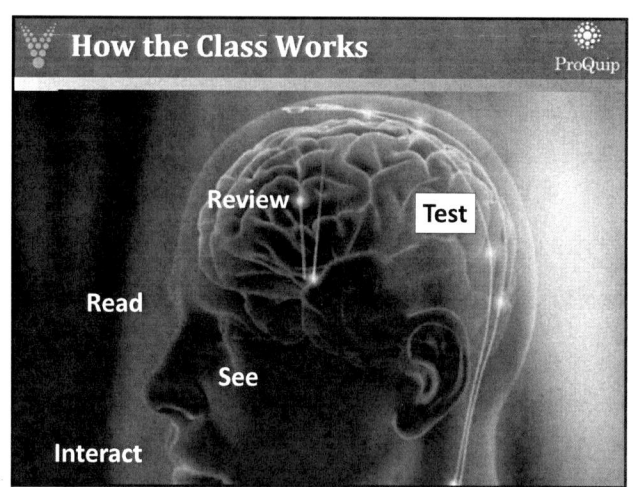

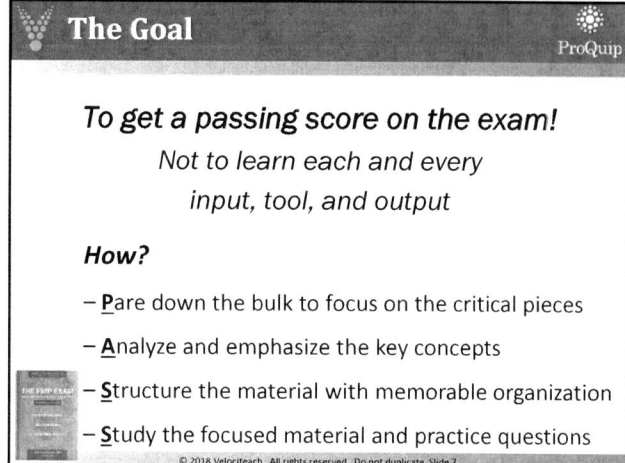

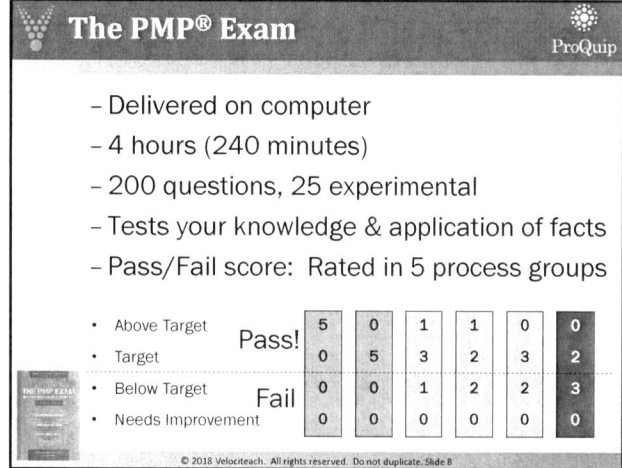

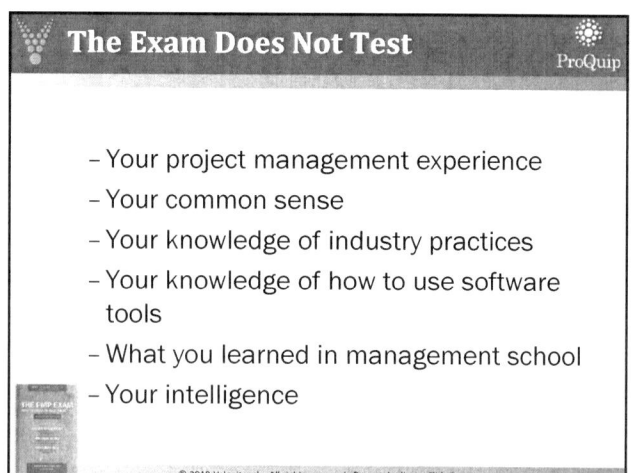

How the Class Works

Review

Test

Read

See

Interact

The Goal

To get a passing score on the exam!

Not to learn each and every input, tool, and output

How?

- **P**are down the bulk to focus on the critical pieces
- **A**nalyze and emphasize the key concepts
- **S**tructure the material with memorable organization
- **S**tudy the focused material and practice questions

© 2018 Velociteach. All rights reserved. Do not duplicate. Slide 7

The PMP® Exam

- Delivered on computer
- 4 hours (240 minutes)
- 200 questions, 25 experimental
- Tests your knowledge & application of facts
- Pass/Fail score: Rated in 5 process groups

• Above Target	Pass!	5	0	1	1	0	0
• Target		0	5	3	2	3	2
• Below Target	Fail	0	0	1	2	2	3
• Needs Improvement		0	0	0	0	0	0

© 2018 Velociteach. All rights reserved. Do not duplicate. Slide 8

The Exam Does Not Test

- Your project management experience
- Your common sense
- Your knowledge of industry practices
- Your knowledge of how to use software tools
- What you learned in management school
- Your intelligence

© 2018 Velociteach. All rights reserved. Do not duplicate. Slide 9

The Exam Does Test

- Your knowledge of PMI's processes
- Your understanding of the many terms used to describe the processes
- Your ability to apply the processes to situations
- Your ability to apply key formulas
- Your understanding of professional responsibility

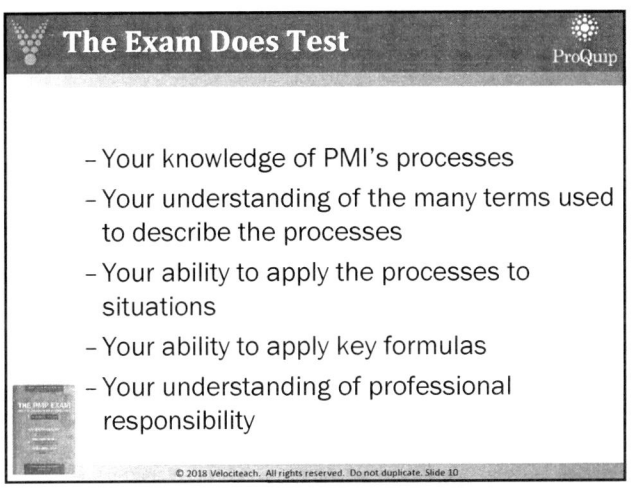

© 2018 Velociteach. All rights reserved. Do not duplicate. Slide 10

Wear Your PMI® Hat

Wearing your "Job Hat" of experience may have made you successful...

But put on the "PMI® Hat" for success on the PMP® exam!

© 2018 Velociteach. All rights reserved. Do not duplicate. Slide 11

What to Study

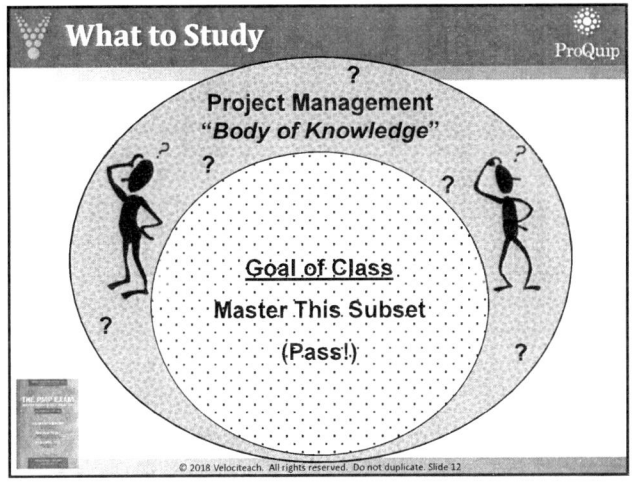

Project Management
"Body of Knowledge"

Goal of Class

Master This Subset

(Pass!)

© 2018 Velociteach. All rights reserved. Do not duplicate. Slide 12

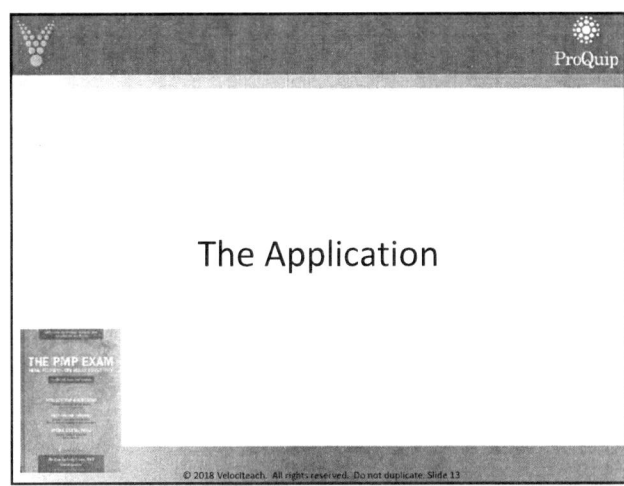

The Application

© 2018 Velociteach. All rights reserved. Do not duplicate. Slide 13

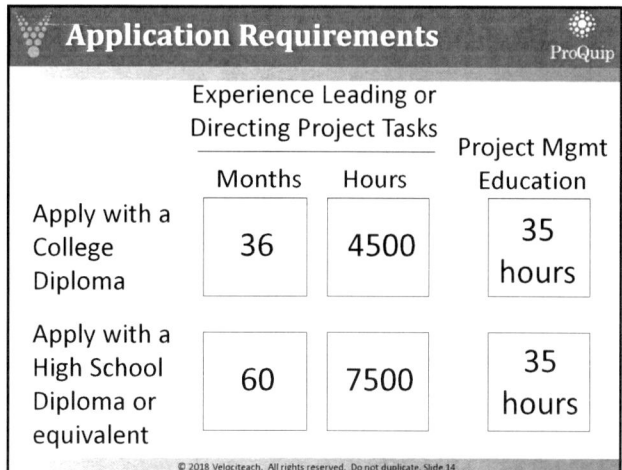

Application Requirements — ProQuip

| | Experience Leading or Directing Project Tasks | | Project Mgmt Education |
	Months	Hours	
Apply with a College Diploma	36	4500	35 hours
Apply with a High School Diploma or equivalent	60	7500	35 hours

© 2018 Velociteach. All rights reserved. Do not duplicate. Slide 14

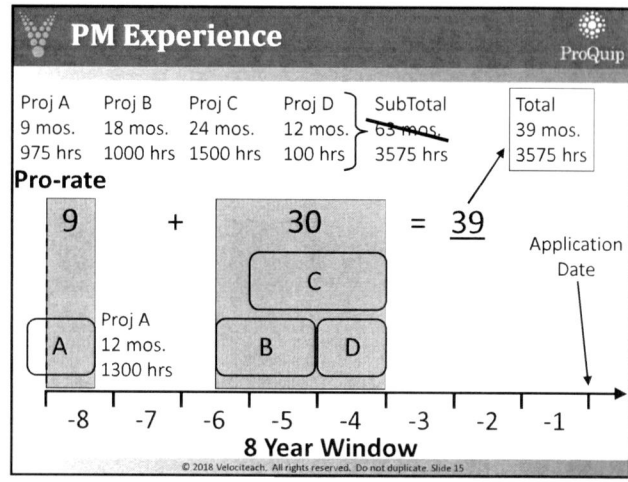

PM Experience — ProQuip

Proj A	Proj B	Proj C	Proj D	SubTotal	Total
9 mos.	18 mos.	24 mos.	12 mos.	63 mos.	39 mos.
975 hrs	1000 hrs	1500 hrs	100 hrs	3575 hrs	3575 hrs

Pro-rate

9 + 30 = 39

Application Date

C

A — Proj A 12 mos. 1300 hrs

B   D

-8 -7 -6 -5 -4 -3 -2 -1

8 Year Window

© 2018 Velociteach. All rights reserved. Do not duplicate. Slide 15

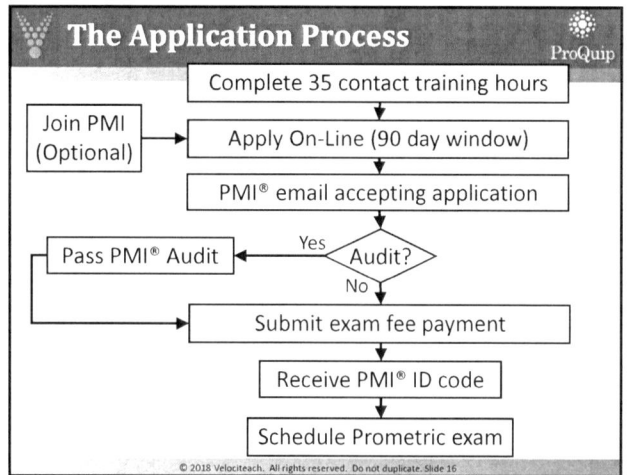

The Application Process — ProQuip

Complete 35 contact training hours

Join PMI (Optional) → Apply On-Line (90 day window)

PMI® email accepting application

Pass PMI® Audit ← Yes — Audit?

No

Submit exam fee payment

Receive PMI® ID code

Schedule Prometric exam

© 2018 Velociteach. All rights reserved. Do not duplicate. Slide 16

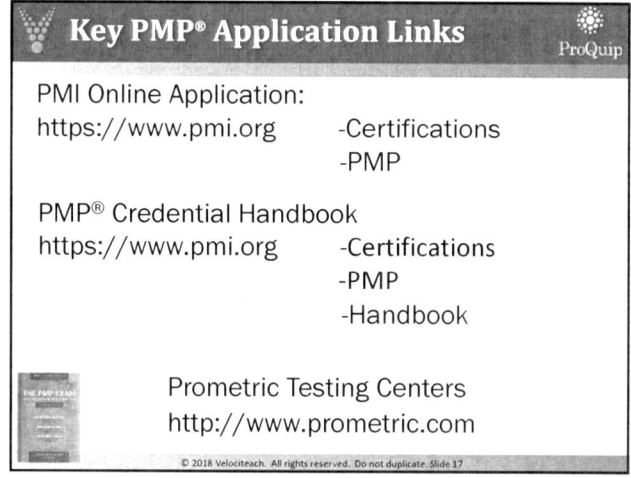

Key PMP® Application Links — ProQuip

PMI Online Application:
https://www.pmi.org   -Certifications
                       -PMP

PMP® Credential Handbook
https://www.pmi.org   -Certifications
                       -PMP
                       -Handbook

Prometric Testing Centers
http://www.prometric.com

© 2018 Velociteach. All rights reserved. Do not duplicate. Slide 17

Baseline Exam

25 Questions

Baseline Exam Instructions

- Complete the following 25 questions.

- Each question has only one BEST answer.

- Mark the one best answer on your answer sheet by filling in the circle next to A, B, C, or D.

- If you guess an answer, circle the **?** mark to remind you later that it was a guess.

- If you change an answer, circle the triangle to remind you later that you changed from your first answer choice.

- Upon completion of the exam, grade your exam using the Baseline Exam Answer Key.

Baseline Exam

1. The numbering system on a work package indicates:

    A. Whether the work package is decomposed to activity-level.
    B. To whom the work package is assigned.
    C. To which node on the work breakdown structure the work package belongs.
    D. The estimated duration of the work package.

2. If a team member is not performing well within a matrix organization, what is the first step the team member's project manager should take to address this situation?

    A. Talk with the team member directly.
    B. Talk with the team member's functional manager.
    C. Ask the human resources department for formal guidance.
    D. Document each infraction by the team member.

3. John has been asked to work on a project, reporting to the head of the research and development department. His job is to stay on top of all tasks, making sure they are completed as planned and reporting back to the head of research and development if they are not. John also makes sure spending is in line with budget, and if it is not, he reports that as well. Which would best describe John's role on this project?

    A. Project manager.
    B. Functional manager.
    C. Project controller.
    D. Project expediter.

4. Which of the following is the most important attribute or function of the project charter?

    A. It gives the project manager authority to work on the project.
    B. It authorizes the budget for the project.
    C. It becomes the main input into the project plan.
    D. It is signed by the customer.

5. The main function of the project management information system is:

    A. To distribute information in accordance with the communications management plan.
    B. To ensure that the project plan is clearly communicated and visible to the project team.
    C. To gather and disseminate the outputs of project management processes.
    D. To provide a system to manage information on project activity variance.

6. **You are the project manager on a construction project that is similar to a project performed by your company two years ago for the same customer. The previous project was very successful, being delivered ahead of schedule and under budget. The current project is on track for both time and budget; however, the customer is insisting on a scope change that will make the building more modern. What would be the first thing you do with this change?**

    A. Accept the change if it will not affect the schedule or cost.
    B. Accept the change if the customer agrees to the revised schedule and cost.
    C. Evaluate the change to understand its impact to the project.
    D. Submit the change to the change control board and abide by their decision.

7. **Which of the following activities is not performed in scope management?**

    A. Ensure that all of the work and only the work is performed on the project.
    B. Updating the scope baseline to include all approved scope changes.
    C. Creating the work breakdown structure for the project.
    D. Making certain that the project scope is communicated to the stakeholders.

8. **Which of the following is a tool that would be used in the creation of the work breakdown structure?**

    A. Decomposition.
    B. Alternatives analysis.
    C. Analogous estimates.
    D. Parametric tools.

9. **Using the table depicted at right, assuming the project begins on January 1 and work is performed 7 days per week, when will the project end?**

    A. January 18.
    B. January 26.
    C. January 27.
    D. February 5.

Task	Dependency	Duration
Start		0
A	Start	6
B	A, D	9
C	B	3
D	Start	7
E	B	1
F	B	10
Finish	C, E, F	0

10. **Which of the following is the best definition of quality?**

    A. The degree to which a set of characteristics fulfills requirements.
    B. The degree to which customer satisfaction is achieved.
    C. The degree to which the scope is completed.
    D. The number of defects as compared to the number of acceptable outputs.

11. Which of the following tools or techniques would be used in Control Quality?

    A. PERT charts.
    B. Benchmarking.
    C. Histograms.
    D. Quality audits.

12. Progressive elaboration is:

    A. A communications management technique.
    B. A resource management technique.
    C. Continuously improving and detailing a plan.
    D. A term describing the linear nature of projects.

13. The performance measurement baseline is used to:

    A. Measure whether a product, service, or result meets performance specifications.
    B. Document the plan and be measured against actual performance to show any variances.
    C. Measure the performance of both teams and individuals on the project.
    D. Create a baseline for subsequent measurements.

14. Contingency theory states:

    A. Employees like to work and may be trusted to contribute to the success of project.
    B. Team goals are contingent upon project's goals.
    C. Effectiveness is contingent upon the manager's style and the project environment.
    D. Loyalty is contingent upon project team members' basic needs being met by the performing organization.

15. Which of the following is not a risk management process?

    A. Perform Actuarial Risk Analysis.
    B. Perform Qualitative Risk Analysis.
    C. Perform Quantitative Risk Analysis.
    D. Implement Risk Responses.

16. What is the first step in project communications management?

    A. Create the communications management plan.
    B. Identify the stakeholders.
    C. Communicate the work results.
    D. Hold the kickoff meeting.

17. **Your company is in the middle of construction on an industrial power plant when you receive a change request from the customer. After detailed analysis, you estimate that the change will cost between $220,000 and $305,000, depending on weather conditions, but the customer asks you to "pad" your estimates to him by $50,000. What should you do?**

    A. Change your estimates to $270,000 to $355,000 as a lump sum.
    B. Find out why the customer thinks your estimates are too low.
    C. Distribute the $50,000 evenly across all sub-task line items and treat it as a reserve.
    D. Refuse to change your estimates.

18. **Make-or-buy analysis takes place during:**

    A. Plan Procurement Management.
    B. Collect Requirements.
    C. Conduct Procurements.
    D. Define Scope.

19. **A project was projected to cost $2,000,000 and take 8 months to complete. Two months into the project, the work is 50% complete, and you have spent $1,200,000. What is the Schedule Performance Index?**

    A. 1.0
    B. 1.2
    C. 2.0
    D. 2.4

20. **If there were 8 people on your project, how many channels of communication would there be?**

    A. 16
    B. 28
    C. 56
    D. 64

21. **Which choice below represents the correct sequence?**

    A. Project schedule, then work breakdown structure, then budget.
    B. Budget, then work breakdown structure, then project schedule.
    C. Work breakdown structure, then budget, then project schedule.
    D. Work breakdown structure, then project schedule, then budget.

©2018 Velociteach. All rights reserved.

22. Approximately what percentage of an effective project manager's time is spent communicating?

    A. 66%
    B. 75%
    C. 90%
    D. 95%

23. You are managing a project in a foreign country, and you are awaiting a critical piece of computer equipment to complete the project. Because the computer equipment is very high-tech and very new, it is taking considerable time to come through customs. A government official from the foreign country calls you at home and tells you that he can help you get the equipment the very next day if you will pay a $500 fee. What should you do?

    A. Investigate whether or not the fee is a bribe.
    B. Pay the $500 fee.
    C. Attempt to negotiate a fee less than $500.
    D. Refuse to pay the fee and report the official.

24. Which of the following types of organization is most like a functional organization?

    A. Projectized.
    B. Weak Matrix.
    C. Balanced Matrix.
    D. Strong Matrix.

25. The Work Breakdown Structure contains:

    A. An implicit benefit/cost analysis.
    B. A decomposition of the tasks critical to the project's success.
    C. All of the work and only the work to be completed on the project.
    D. Every available template from previous projects.

Score Sheet	**Baseline Exam**	 Velociteach

- Mark one answer: A, B, C, or D.
- Circle the '?' symbol if you are guessing at the answer.
- Circle the Δ symbol if you change your answer.

Total Correct: _____

% Correct: _____%

1.	A O	B O	C O	D O	?	Δ
2.	A O	B O	C O	D O	?	Δ
3.	A O	B O	C O	D O	?	Δ
4.	A O	B O	C O	D O	?	Δ
5.	A O	B O	C O	D O	?	Δ
6.	A O	B O	C O	D O	?	Δ
7.	A O	B O	C O	D O	?	Δ
8.	A O	B O	C O	D O	?	Δ
9.	A O	B O	C O	D O	?	Δ
10.	A O	B O	C O	D O	?	Δ
11.	A O	B O	C O	D O	?	Δ
12.	A O	B O	C O	D O	?	Δ
13.	A O	B O	C O	D O	?	Δ
14.	A O	B O	C O	D O	?	Δ
15.	A O	B O	C O	D O	?	Δ
16.	A O	B O	C O	D O	?	Δ
17.	A O	B O	C O	D O	?	Δ
18.	A O	B O	C O	D O	?	Δ
19.	A O	B O	C O	D O	?	Δ
20.	A O	B O	C O	D O	?	Δ
21.	A O	B O	C O	D O	?	Δ
22.	A O	B O	C O	D O	?	Δ
23.	A O	B O	C O	D O	?	Δ
24.	A O	B O	C O	D O	?	Δ
25.	A O	B O	C O	D O	?	Δ

This page left intentionally blank.

©2018 Velociteach. All rights reserved.

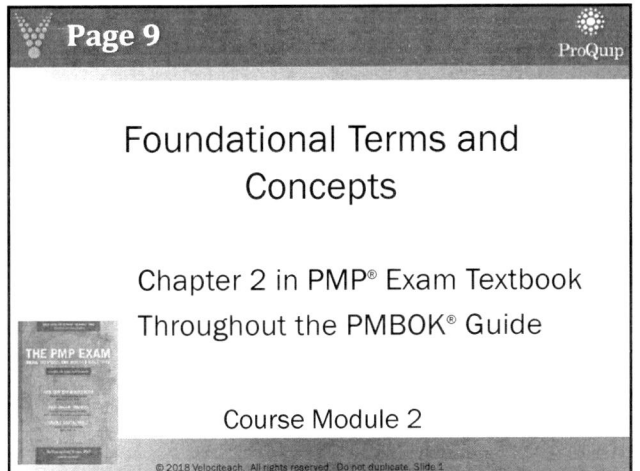

Page 9
ProQuip

Foundational Terms and Concepts

Chapter 2 in PMP® Exam Textbook
Throughout the PMBOK® Guide

Course Module 2

© 2018 Velociteach. All rights reserved. Do not duplicate. Slide 1

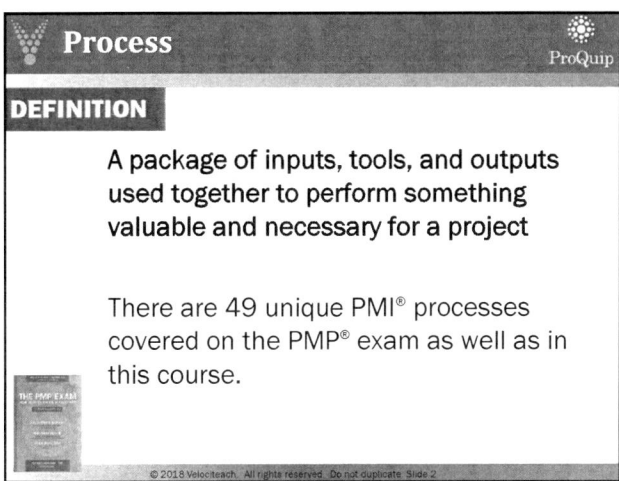

Process
ProQuip

DEFINITION

A package of inputs, tools, and outputs used together to perform something valuable and necessary for a project

There are 49 unique PMI® processes covered on the PMP® exam as well as in this course.

© 2018 Velociteach. All rights reserved. Do not duplicate. Slide 2

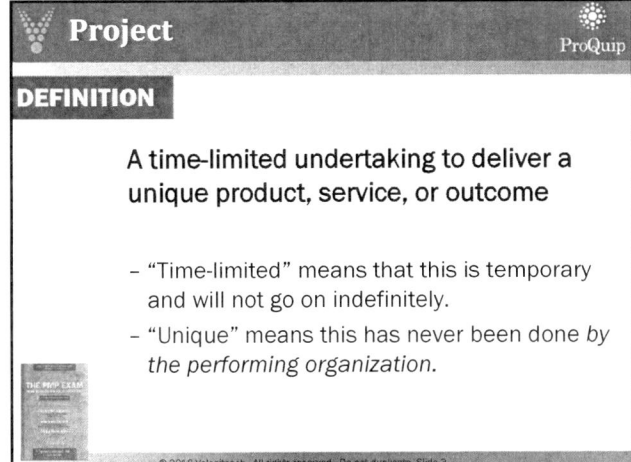

Project
ProQuip

DEFINITION

A time-limited undertaking to deliver a unique product, service, or outcome

– "Time-limited" means that this is temporary and will not go on indefinitely.
– "Unique" means this has never been done *by the performing organization*.

© 2018 Velociteach. All rights reserved. Do not duplicate. Slide 3

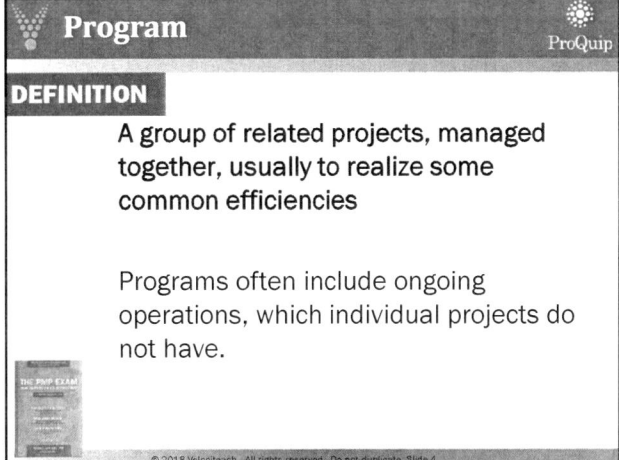

Program
ProQuip

DEFINITION

A group of related projects, managed together, usually to realize some common efficiencies

Programs often include ongoing operations, which individual projects do not have.

© 2018 Velociteach. All rights reserved. Do not duplicate. Slide 4

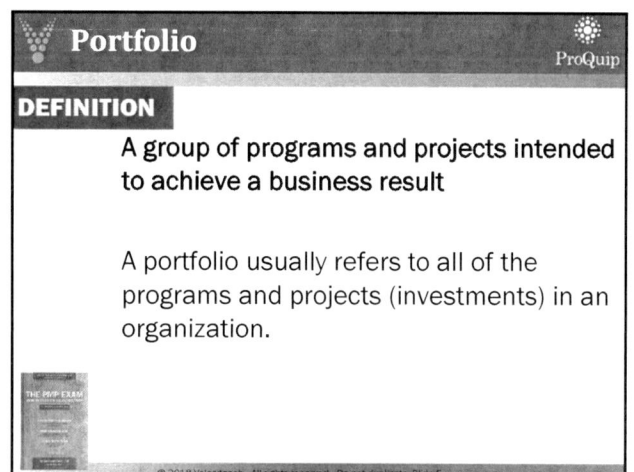

Portfolio
ProQuip

DEFINITION

A group of programs and projects intended to achieve a business result

A portfolio usually refers to all of the programs and projects (investments) in an organization.

© 2018 Velociteach. All rights reserved. Do not duplicate. Slide 5

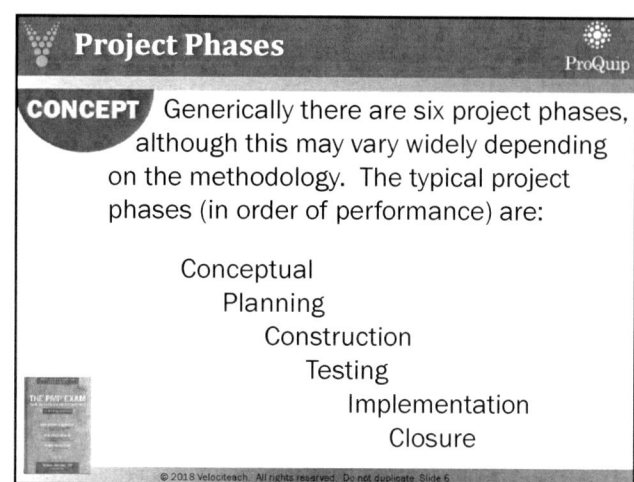

Project Phases
ProQuip

CONCEPT Generically there are six project phases, although this may vary widely depending on the methodology. The typical project phases (in order of performance) are:

Conceptual
Planning
Construction
Testing
Implementation
Closure

© 2018 Velociteach. All rights reserved. Do not duplicate. Slide 6

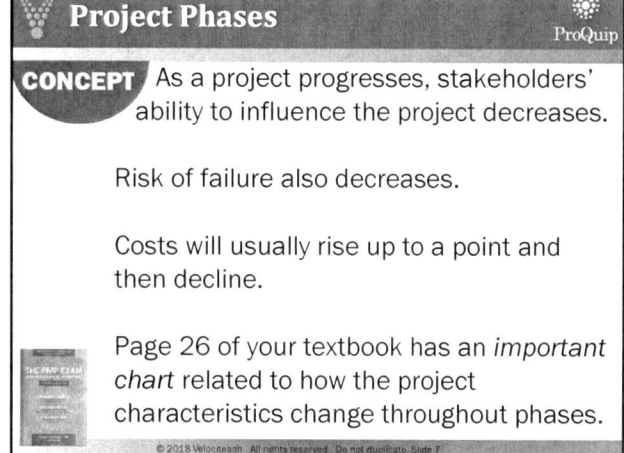

Project Phases
ProQuip

CONCEPT As a project progresses, stakeholders' ability to influence the project decreases.

Risk of failure also decreases.

Costs will usually rise up to a point and then decline.

Page 26 of your textbook has an *important chart* related to how the project characteristics change throughout phases.

© 2018 Velociteach. All rights reserved. Do not duplicate. Slide 7

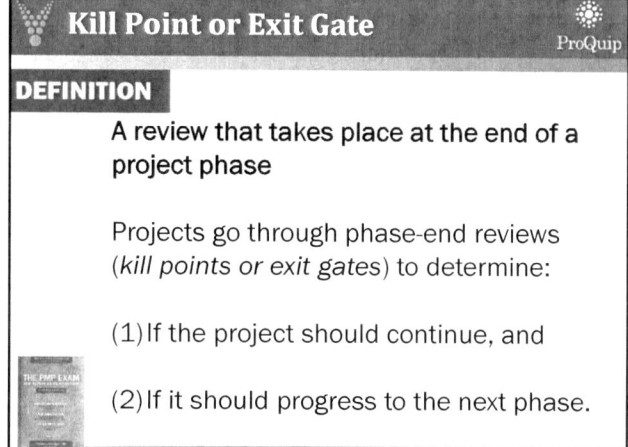

Kill Point or Exit Gate
ProQuip

DEFINITION

A review that takes place at the end of a project phase

Projects go through phase-end reviews (*kill points or exit gates*) to determine:

(1) If the project should continue, and

(2) If it should progress to the next phase.

© 2018 Velociteach. All rights reserved. Do not duplicate. Slide 8

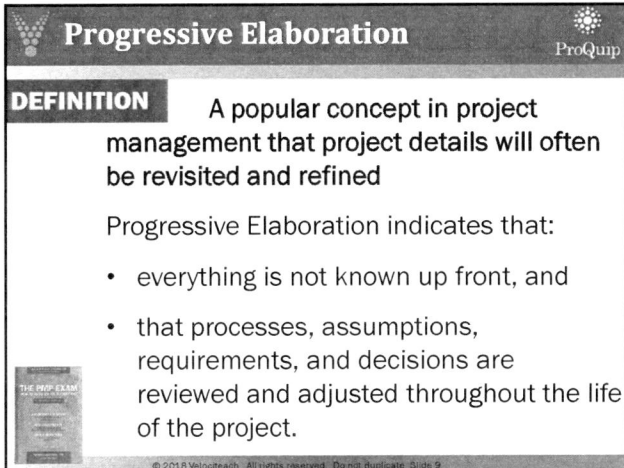

Progressive Elaboration

ProQuip

DEFINITION A popular concept in project management that project details will often be revisited and refined

Progressive Elaboration indicates that:

- everything is not known up front, and

- that processes, assumptions, requirements, and decisions are reviewed and adjusted throughout the life of the project.

© 2018 Velociteach. All rights reserved. Do not duplicate. Slide 9

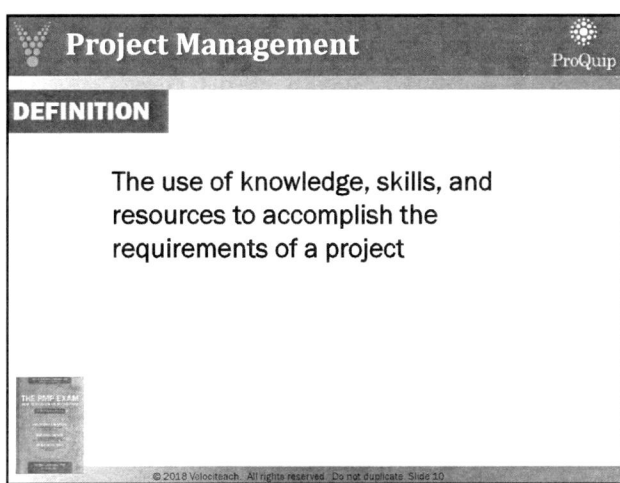

Project Management

ProQuip

DEFINITION

The use of knowledge, skills, and resources to accomplish the requirements of a project

© 2018 Velociteach. All rights reserved. Do not duplicate. Slide 10

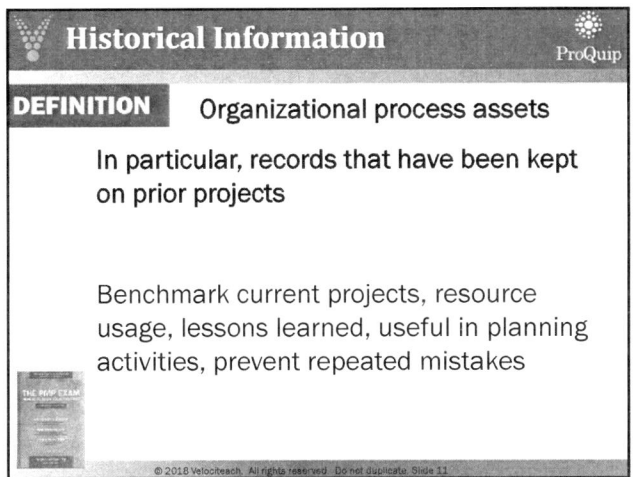

Historical Information

ProQuip

DEFINITION Organizational process assets

In particular, records that have been kept on prior projects

Benchmark current projects, resource usage, lessons learned, useful in planning activities, prevent repeated mistakes

© 2018 Velociteach. All rights reserved. Do not duplicate. Slide 11

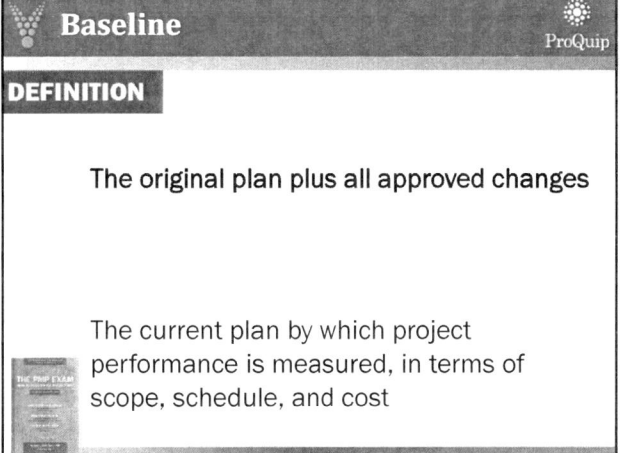

Baseline

ProQuip

DEFINITION

The original plan plus all approved changes

The current plan by which project performance is measured, in terms of scope, schedule, and cost

© 2018 Velociteach. All rights reserved. Do not duplicate. Slide 12

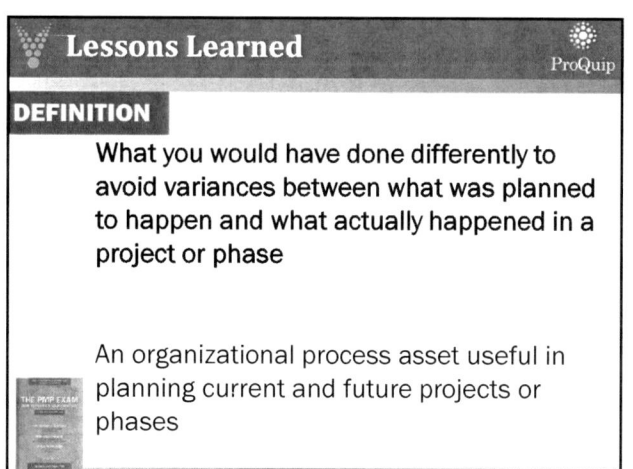

Lessons Learned — ProQuip

DEFINITION

What you would have done differently to avoid variances between what was planned to happen and what actually happened in a project or phase

An organizational process asset useful in planning current and future projects or phases

© 2018 Velociteach. All rights reserved. Do not duplicate. Slide 13

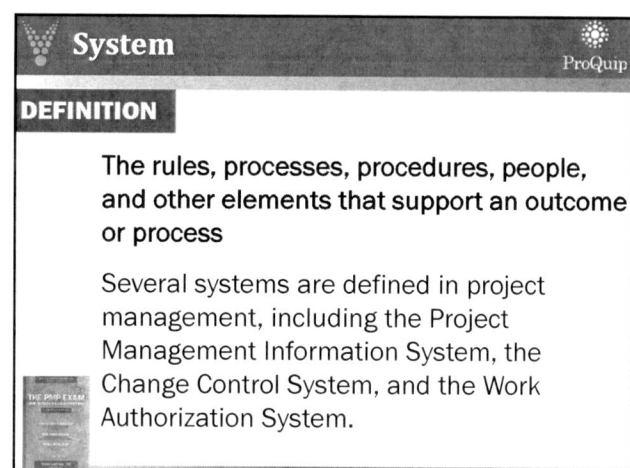

System — ProQuip

DEFINITION

The rules, processes, procedures, people, and other elements that support an outcome or process

Several systems are defined in project management, including the Project Management Information System, the Change Control System, and the Work Authorization System.

© 2018 Velociteach. All rights reserved. Do not duplicate. Slide 14

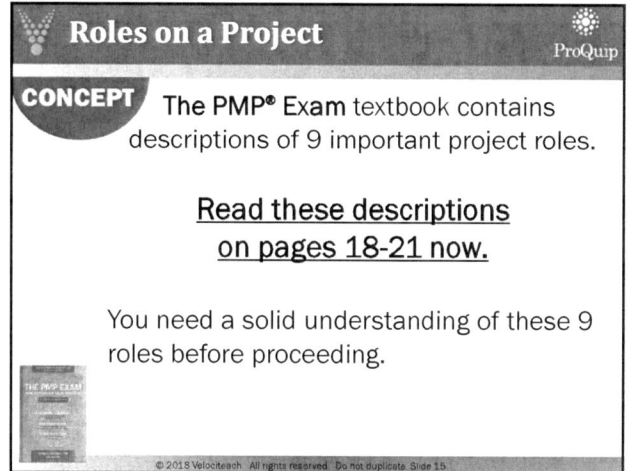

Roles on a Project — ProQuip

CONCEPT The PMP® Exam textbook contains descriptions of 9 important project roles.

<u>Read these descriptions
on pages 18-21 now.</u>

You need a solid understanding of these 9 roles before proceeding.

© 2018 Velociteach. All rights reserved. Do not duplicate. Slide 15

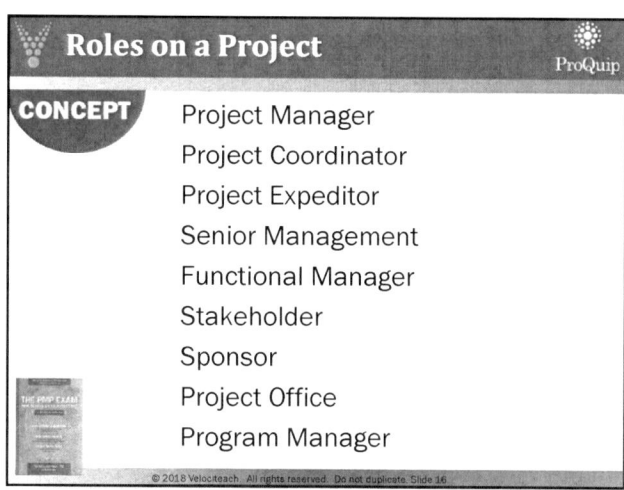

Roles on a Project — ProQuip

CONCEPT
- Project Manager
- Project Coordinator
- Project Expeditor
- Senior Management
- Functional Manager
- Stakeholder
- Sponsor
- Project Office
- Program Manager

© 2018 Velociteach. All rights reserved. Do not duplicate. Slide 16

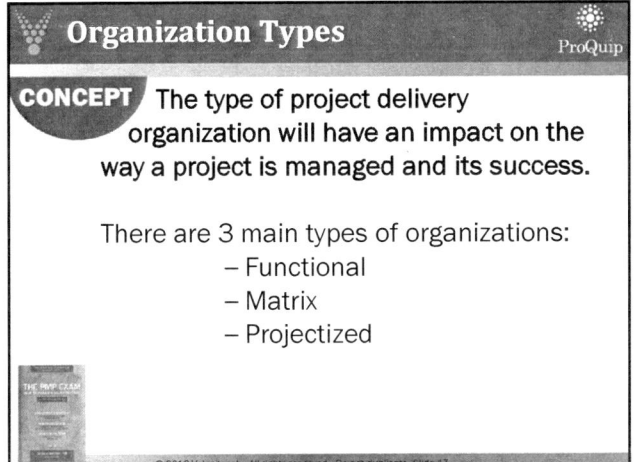

Organization Types — ProQuip

CONCEPT The type of project delivery organization will have an impact on the way a project is managed and its success.

There are 3 main types of organizations:
- Functional
- Matrix
- Projectized

© 2018 Velociteach. All rights reserved. Do not duplicate. Slide 17

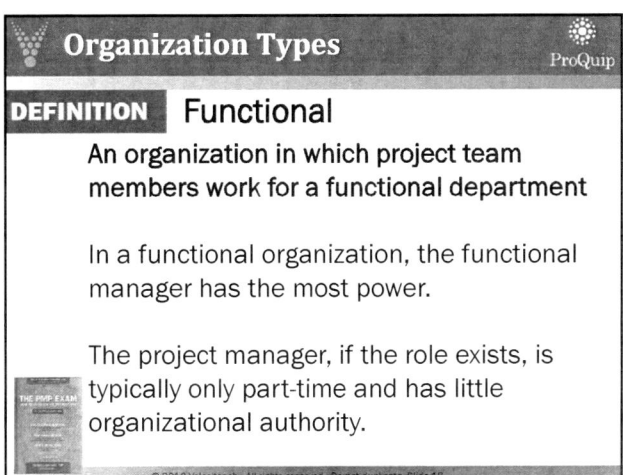

Organization Types — ProQuip

DEFINITION Functional

An organization in which project team members work for a functional department

In a functional organization, the functional manager has the most power.

The project manager, if the role exists, is typically only part-time and has little organizational authority.

© 2018 Velociteach. All rights reserved. Do not duplicate. Slide 18

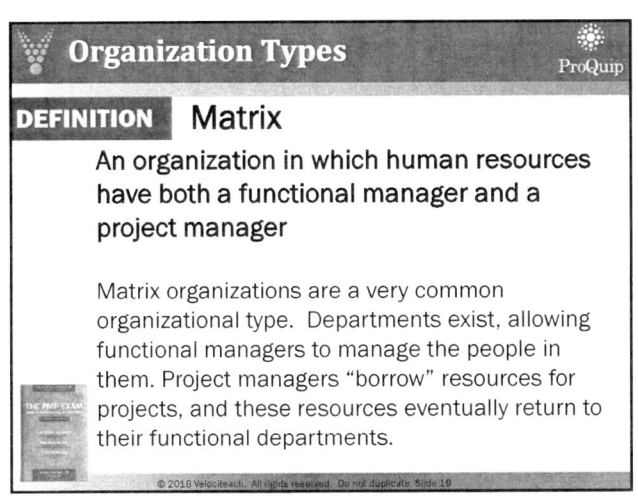

Organization Types — ProQuip

DEFINITION Matrix

An organization in which human resources have both a functional manager and a project manager

Matrix organizations are a very common organizational type. Departments exist, allowing functional managers to manage the people in them. Project managers "borrow" resources for projects, and these resources eventually return to their functional departments.

© 2018 Velociteach. All rights reserved. Do not duplicate. Slide 19

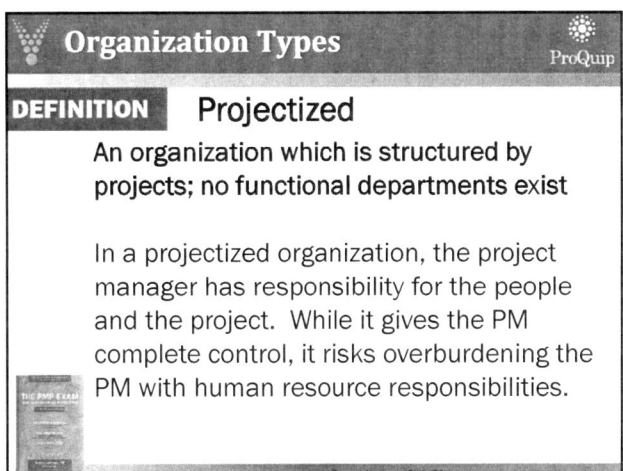

Organization Types — ProQuip

DEFINITION Projectized

An organization which is structured by projects; no functional departments exist

In a projectized organization, the project manager has responsibility for the people and the project. While it gives the PM complete control, it risks overburdening the PM with human resource responsibilities.

© 2018 Velociteach. All rights reserved. Do not duplicate. Slide 20

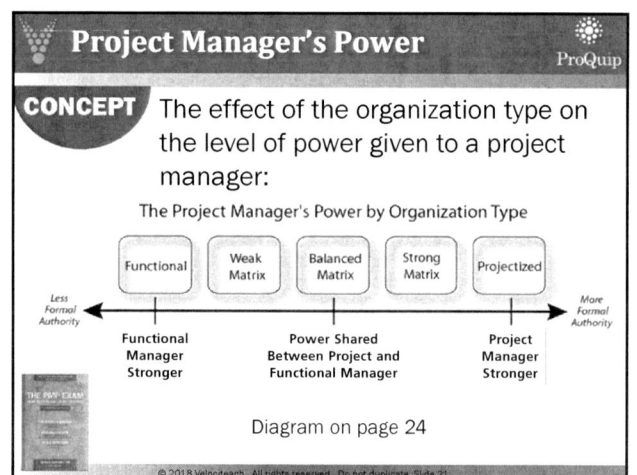

Project Manager's Power

ProQuip

CONCEPT The effect of the organization type on the level of power given to a project manager:

The Project Manager's Power by Organization Type

| Functional | Weak Matrix | Balanced Matrix | Strong Matrix | Projectized |

Less Formal Authority ←————————————————→ More Formal Authority

Functional Manager Stronger | Power Shared Between Project and Functional Manager | Project Manager Stronger

Diagram on page 24

© 2018 Velociteach. All rights reserved. Do not duplicate. Slide 21

PM's Management Skills

ProQuip

CONCEPT These skills will have a significant effect on projects; a project manager should have experience in:

• Technical skills:
  ▪ Focus, tailoring, planning and prioritization, managing

• Strategic and Business Management skills:
  • Knowledge of strategy, mission, goals, products, services, market, operations, competition

• Leadership skills:
  • Dealing with people, Communicating, Collaborating,

© 2018 Velociteach. All rights reserved. Do not duplicate. Slide 22

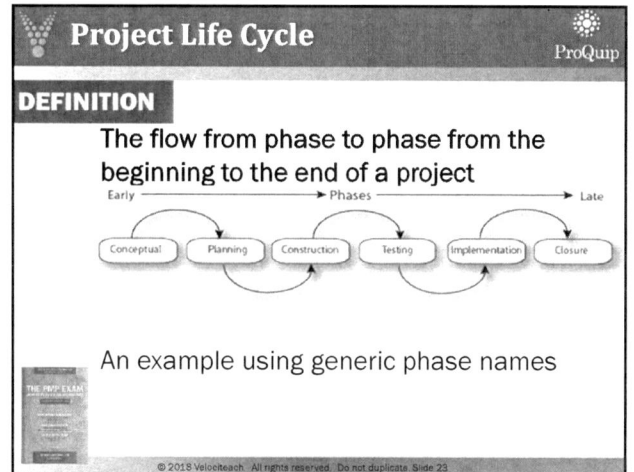

Project Life Cycle

ProQuip

DEFINITION

The flow from phase to phase from the beginning to the end of a project

Early ————→ Phases ————————→ Late

Conceptual → Planning → Construction → Testing → Implementation → Closure

An example using generic phase names

© 2018 Velociteach. All rights reserved. Do not duplicate. Slide 23

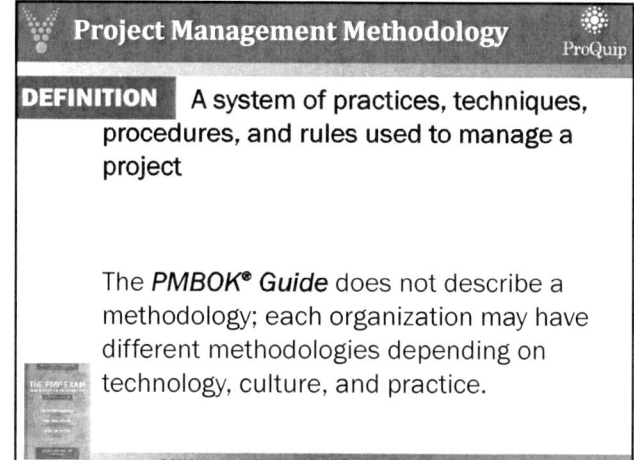

Project Management Methodology

ProQuip

DEFINITION A system of practices, techniques, procedures, and rules used to manage a project

The *PMBOK® Guide* does not describe a methodology; each organization may have different methodologies depending on technology, culture, and practice.

© 2018 Velociteach. All rights reserved. Do not duplicate. Slide 24

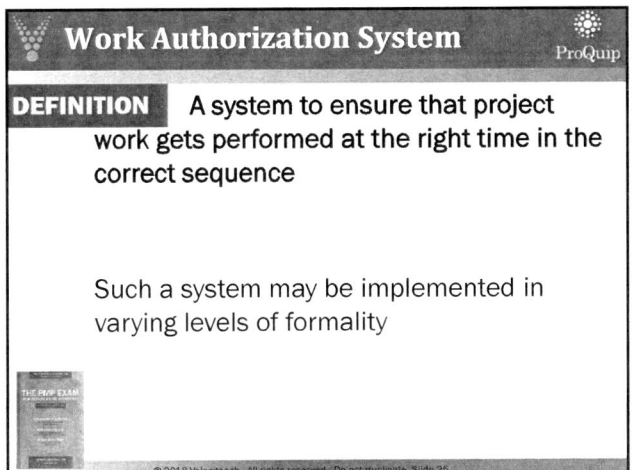

Work Authorization System

DEFINITION A system to ensure that project work gets performed at the right time in the correct sequence

Such a system may be implemented in varying levels of formality

© 2018 Velociteach. All rights reserved. Do not duplicate. Slide 25

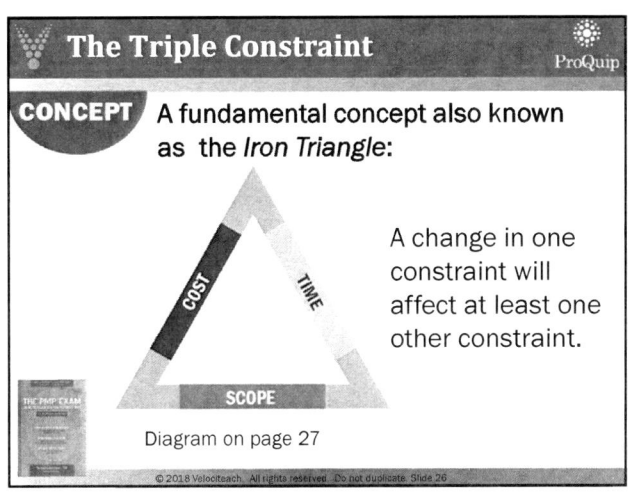

The Triple Constraint

CONCEPT A fundamental concept also known as the *Iron Triangle*:

A change in one constraint will affect at least one other constraint.

Diagram on page 27

© 2018 Velociteach. All rights reserved. Do not duplicate. Slide 26

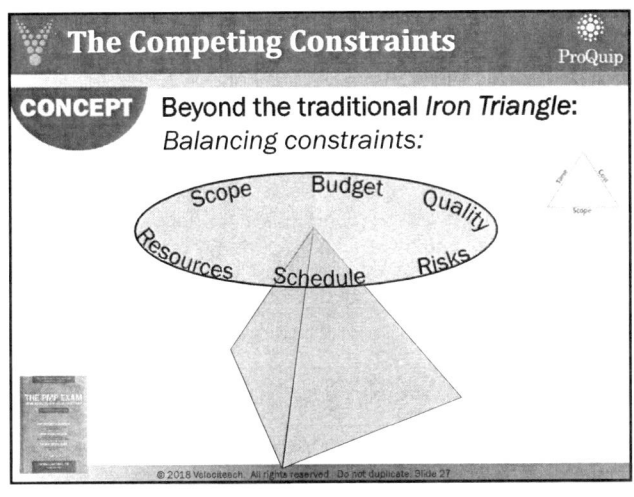

The Competing Constraints

CONCEPT Beyond the traditional *Iron Triangle*:
Balancing constraints:

Scope Budget Quality
Resources Schedule Risks

© 2018 Velociteach. All rights reserved. Do not duplicate. Slide 27

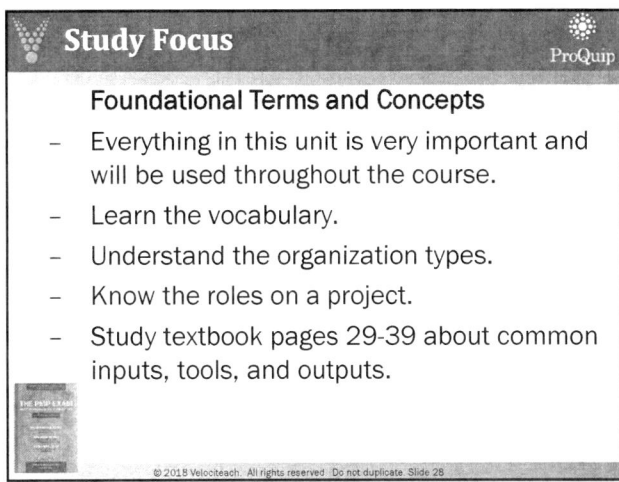

Study Focus

Foundational Terms and Concepts

- Everything in this unit is very important and will be used throughout the course.
- Learn the vocabulary.
- Understand the organization types.
- Know the roles on a project.
- Study textbook pages 29-39 about common inputs, tools, and outputs.

© 2018 Velociteach. All rights reserved. Do not duplicate. Slide 28

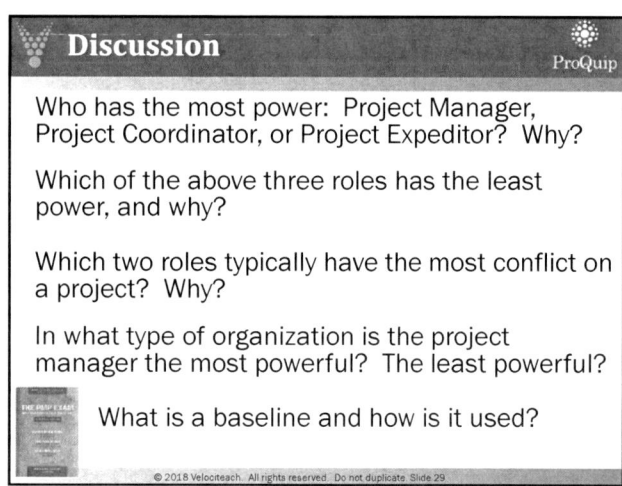

Discussion

Who has the most power: Project Manager, Project Coordinator, or Project Expeditor? Why?

Which of the above three roles has the least power, and why?

Which two roles typically have the most conflict on a project? Why?

In what type of organization is the project manager the most powerful? The least powerful?

What is a baseline and how is it used?

© 2018 Velociteach. All rights reserved. Do not duplicate Slide 29

ProQuip

Course Module 3

PMI's Process Framework

Chapter 3 in *PMBOK® Guide*

Chapter 3 in PMP® Exam Textbook

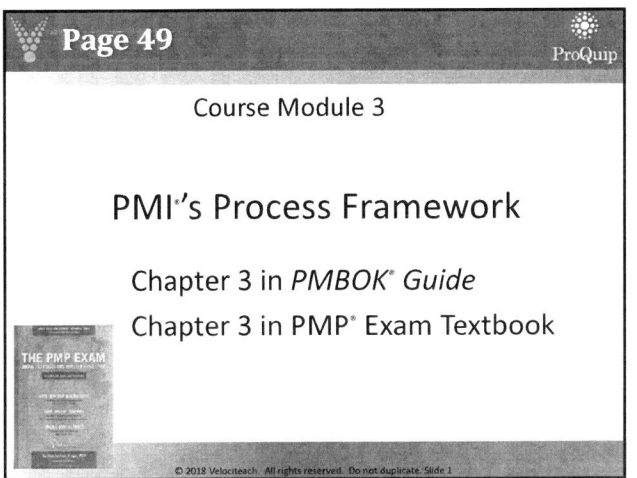

© 2018 Velociteach. All rights reserved. Do not duplicate. Slide 1

PMI's Process Framework

ProQuip

CONCEPT

The Project Management Institute has organized the *PMBOK® Guide* into a framework of processes, groups, and knowledge areas.

Master this organizational concept to structure and associate the remainder of your PMP® exam study.

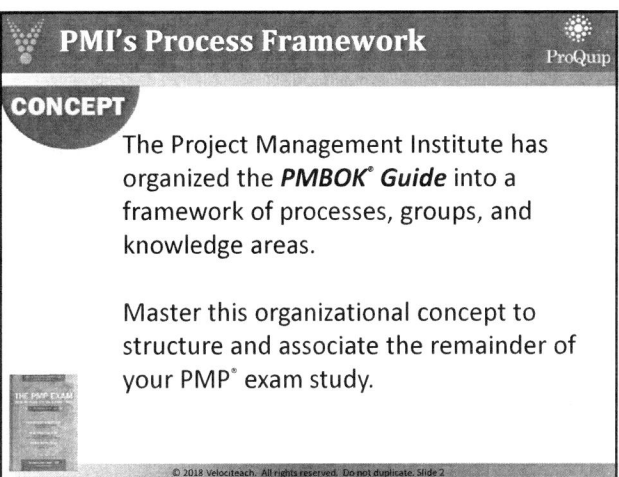

© 2018 Velociteach. All rights reserved. Do not duplicate. Slide 2

PMI's Process Framework

ProQuip

Key Points

- All project management work can be described by one of the 49 processes.
- Each process belongs to 1 of 5 Process Groups.
- Each process belongs to 1 of 10 Knowledge Areas.
- A process is defined by inputs, tools, and outputs.
- Every exam question will tie back to a process group.

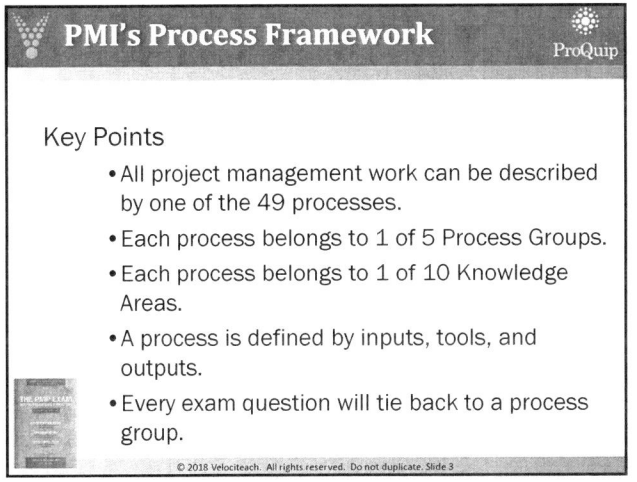

© 2018 Velociteach. All rights reserved. Do not duplicate. Slide 3

Process

ProQuip

DEFINITION PMI has described the discipline of Project Management by defining 49 "processes" of the discipline.

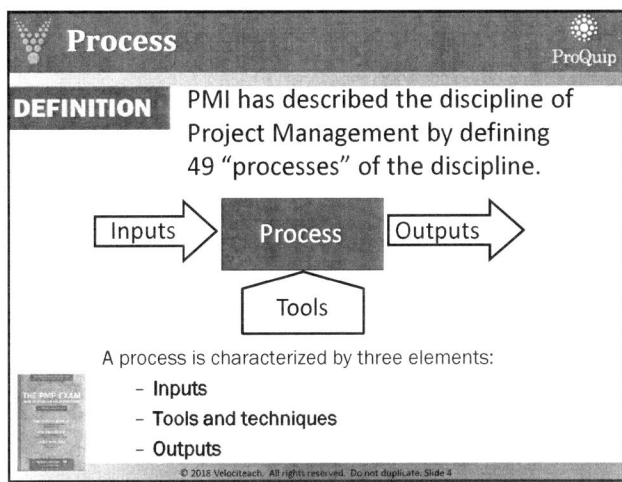

A process is characterized by three elements:
- Inputs
- Tools and techniques
- Outputs

© 2018 Velociteach. All rights reserved. Do not duplicate. Slide 4

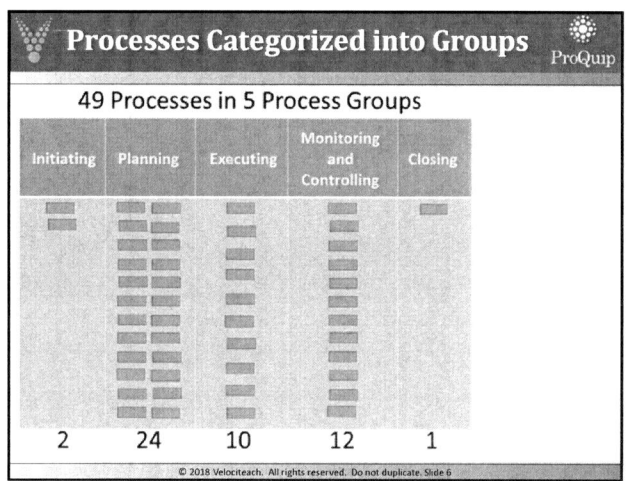

Processes Categorized into Groups

49 Processes in 5 Process Groups

Initiating	Planning	Executing	Monitoring and Controlling	Closing
2	24	10	12	1

© 2018 Velociteach. All rights reserved. Do not duplicate. Slide 6

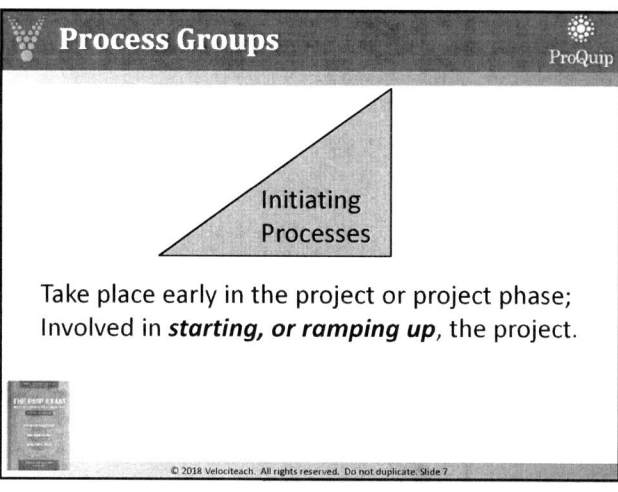

Process Groups

Initiating Processes

Take place early in the project or project phase; Involved in *starting, or ramping up*, the project.

© 2018 Velociteach. All rights reserved. Do not duplicate. Slide 7

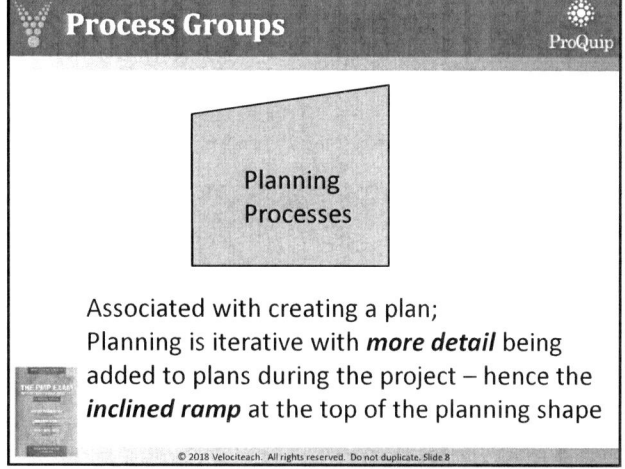

Process Groups

Planning Processes

Associated with creating a plan; Planning is iterative with *more detail* being added to plans during the project – hence the *inclined ramp* at the top of the planning shape

© 2018 Velociteach. All rights reserved. Do not duplicate. Slide 8

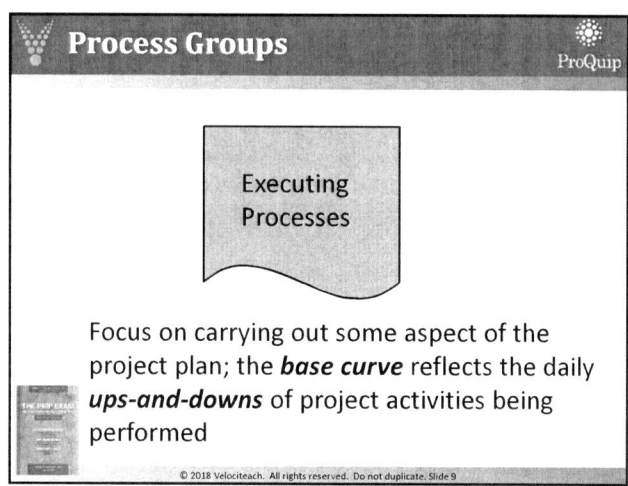

Process Groups

Executing Processes

Focus on carrying out some aspect of the project plan; the *base curve* reflects the daily *ups-and-downs* of project activities being performed

© 2018 Velociteach. All rights reserved. Do not duplicate. Slide 9

©2018 Velociteach. All rights reserved.

Process Groups

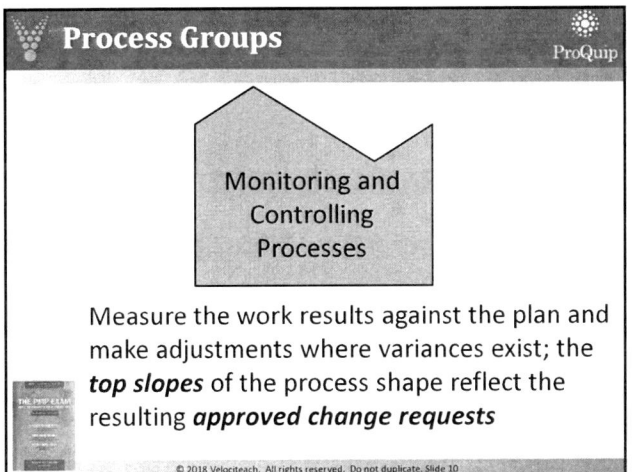

Monitoring and Controlling Processes

Measure the work results against the plan and make adjustments where variances exist; the *top slopes* of the process shape reflect the resulting *approved change requests*

© 2018 Velociteach. All rights reserved. Do not duplicate. Slide 10

Process Groups

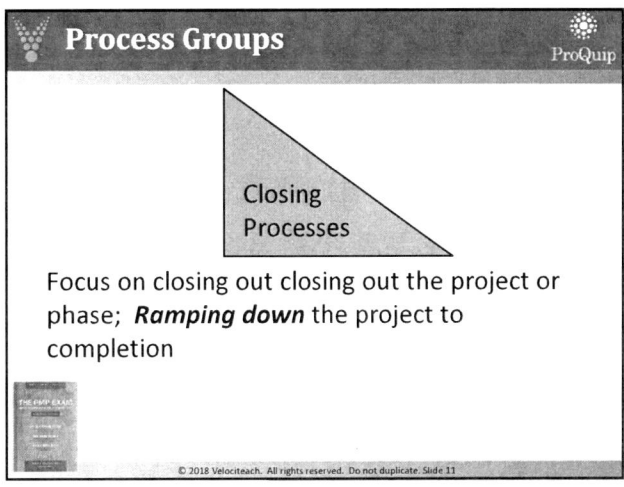

Closing Processes

Focus on closing out closing out the project or phase; *Ramping down* the project to completion

© 2018 Velociteach. All rights reserved. Do not duplicate. Slide 11

Process Group Flow

Process Groups are not performed in a serial, end-to-end, fashion –

They are *not the same as* Project Phases!

© 2018 Velociteach. All rights reserved. Do not duplicate. Slide 12

Process Group Flow

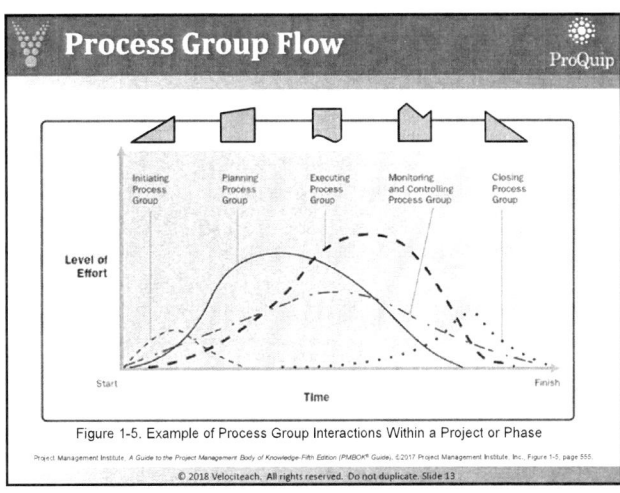

Figure 1-5. Example of Process Group Interactions Within a Project or Phase

Project Management Institute, *A Guide to the Project Management Body of Knowledge (PMBOK® Guide)*, ©2017 Project Management Institute, Inc., Figure 1-5, page 555.

© 2018 Velociteach. All rights reserved. Do not duplicate. Slide 13

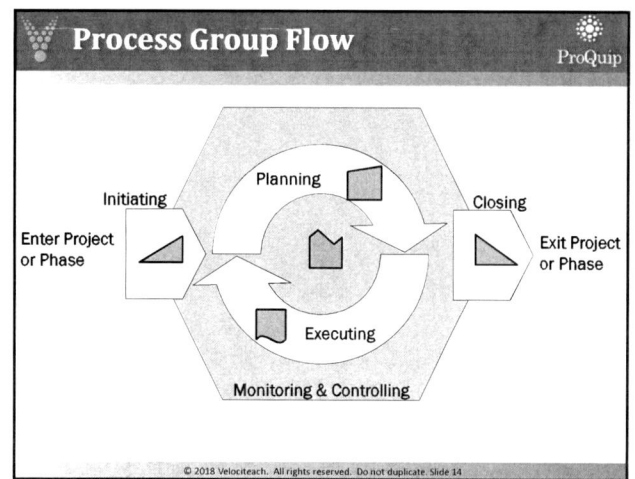

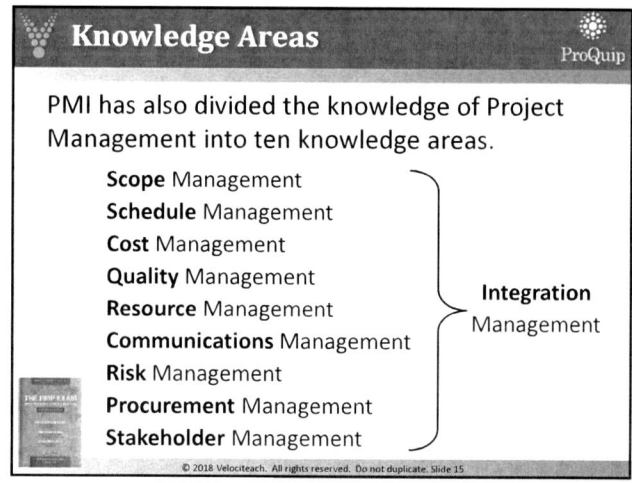

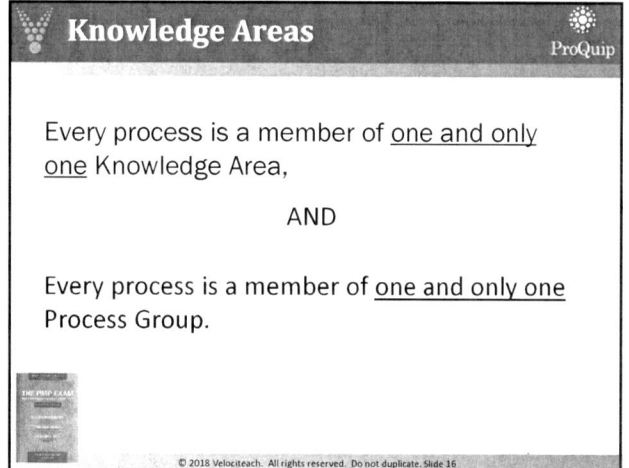

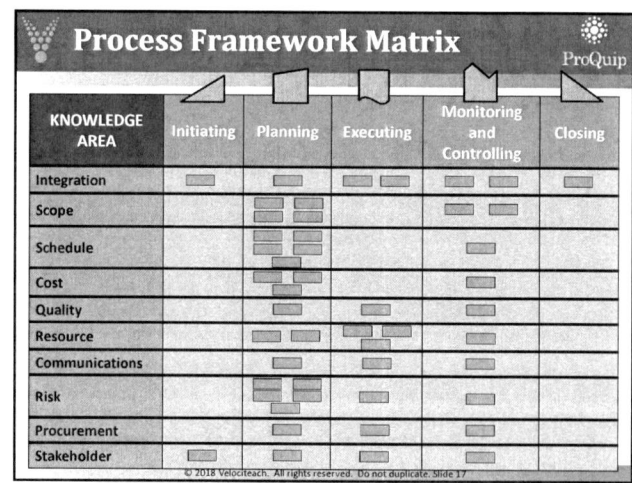

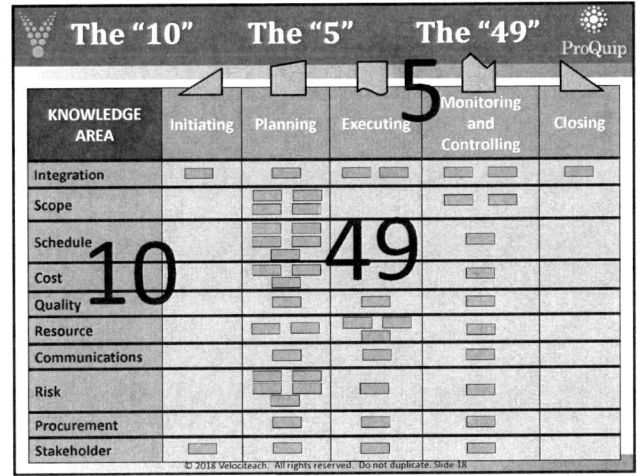

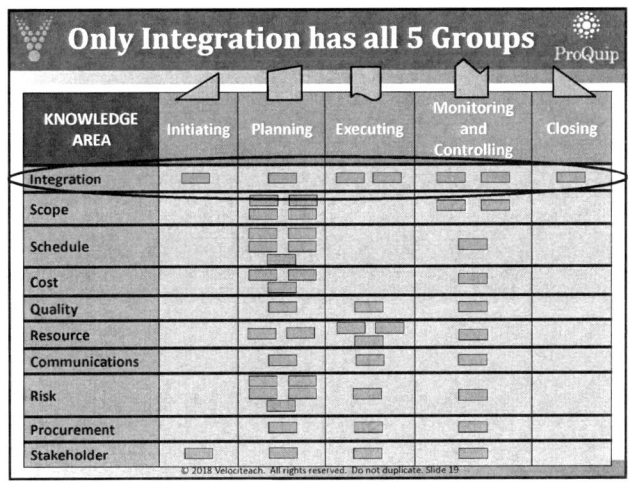

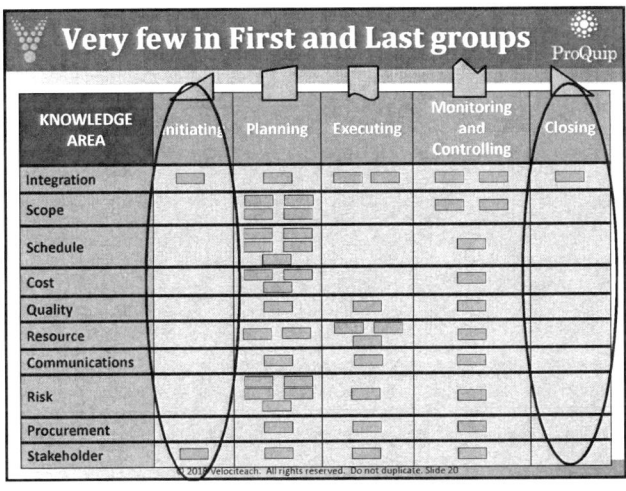

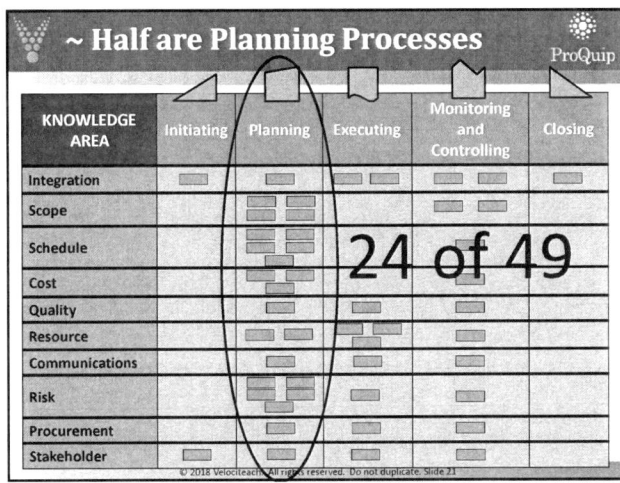

©2018 Velociteach. All rights reserved.

Detailed Framework

The *Process Framework Matrix* is documented on page 62 of __The PMP® Exam__ textbook, a great place for a bookmark!

Let's all turn to page 62 in the textbook.

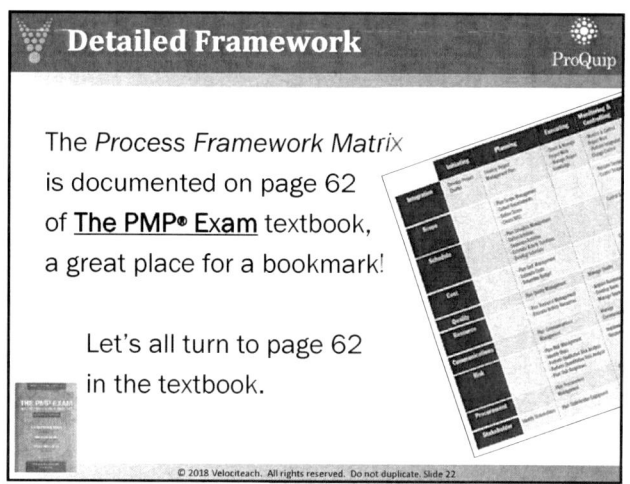

© 2018 Velociteach. All rights reserved. Do not duplicate. Slide 22

Project Management Processes

Draw in the respective shape for each process group:

Also note that the process matrix is on the back cover of the ProQuip Student Workbook.

Page 62

The 49 Processes of Project Management

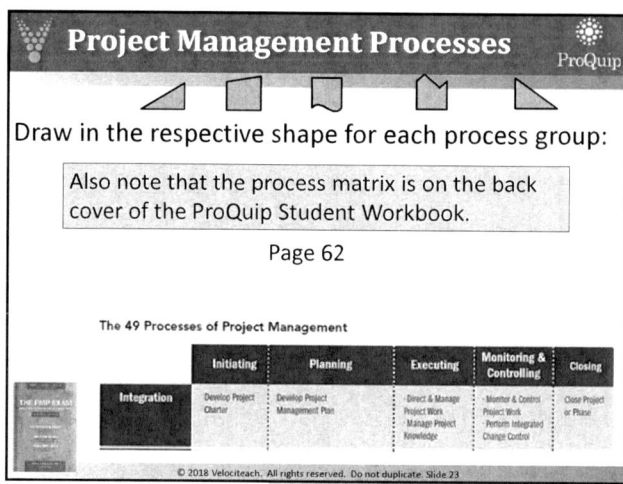

© 2018 Velociteach. All rights reserved. Do not duplicate. Slide 23

Framework Importance

The PMP® exam is _not just_ on the framework, but on the application of the knowledge contained in the framework!

Detailed coverage of each individual process will follow in this course, segmented by the ten Knowledge Areas.

Each Knowledge Area has a separate chapter in __The PMP® Exam__ textbook.

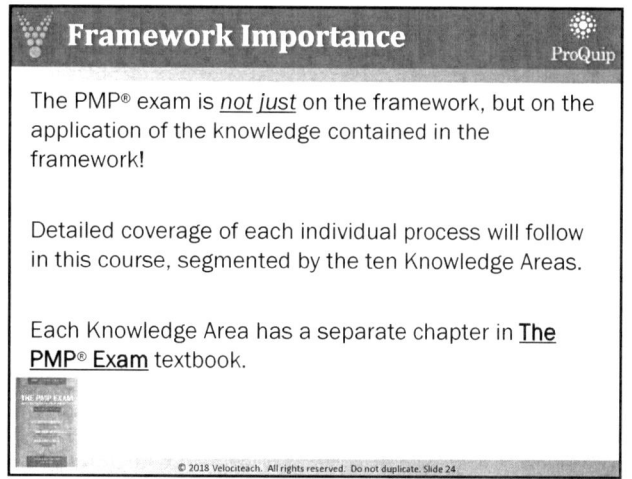

© 2018 Velociteach. All rights reserved. Do not duplicate. Slide 24

Common Inputs, Tools, & Outputs

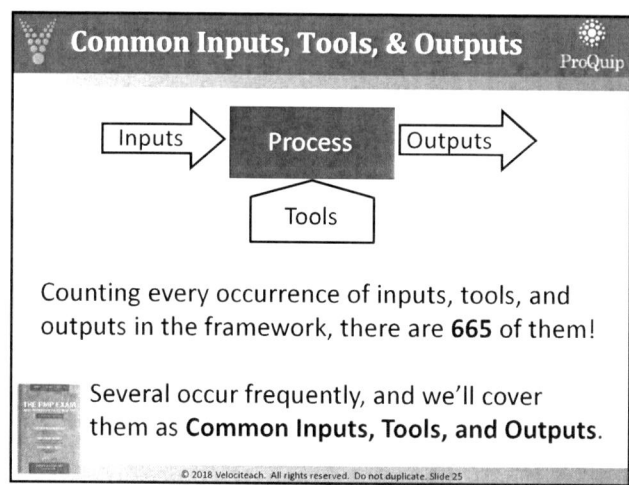

Counting every occurrence of inputs, tools, and outputs in the framework, there are **665** of them!

Several occur frequently, and we'll cover them as **Common Inputs, Tools, and Outputs**.

© 2018 Velociteach. All rights reserved. Do not duplicate. Slide 25

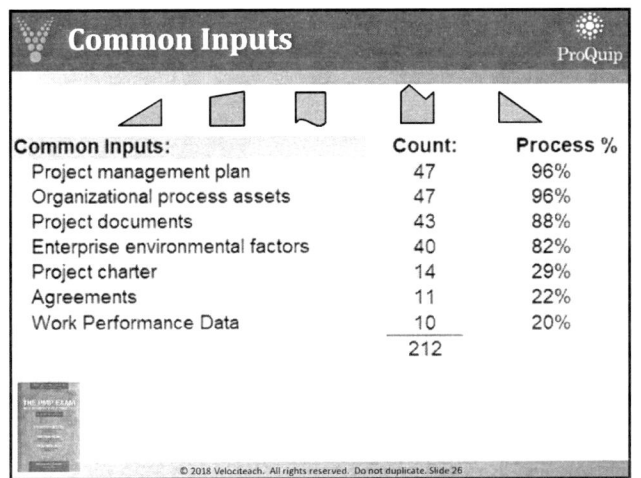

Common Inputs

Common Inputs:	Count:	Process %
Project management plan	47	96%
Organizational process assets	47	96%
Project documents	43	88%
Enterprise environmental factors	40	82%
Project charter	14	29%
Agreements	11	22%
Work Performance Data	10	20%
	212	

© 2018 Velociteach. All rights reserved. Do not duplicate. Slide 26

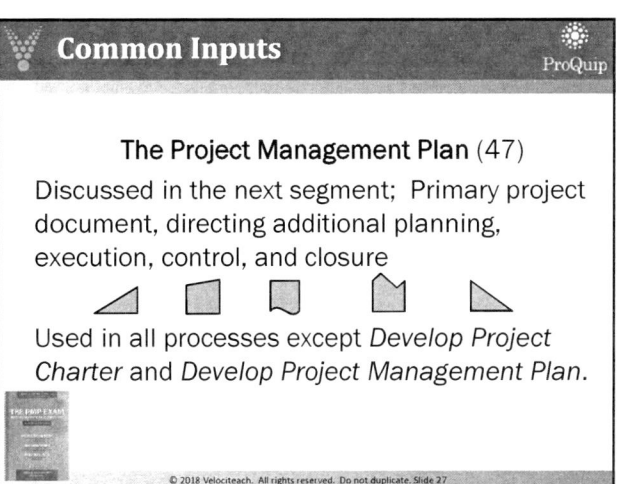

Common Inputs

The Project Management Plan (47)

Discussed in the next segment; Primary project document, directing additional planning, execution, control, and closure

Used in all processes except *Develop Project Charter* and *Develop Project Management Plan*.

© 2018 Velociteach. All rights reserved. Do not duplicate. Slide 27

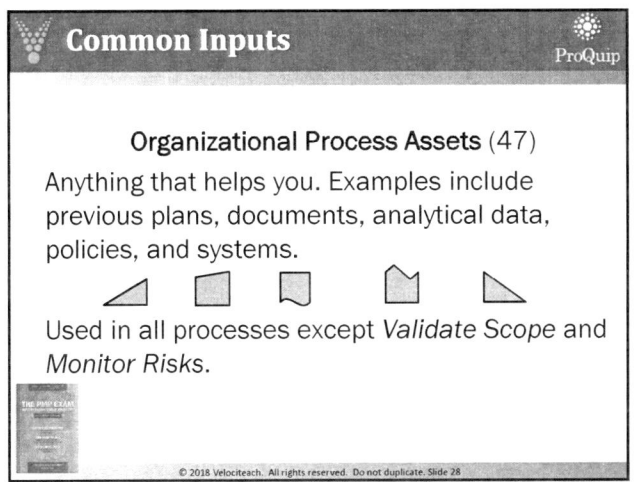

Common Inputs

Organizational Process Assets (47)

Anything that helps you. Examples include previous plans, documents, analytical data, policies, and systems.

Used in all processes except *Validate Scope* and *Monitor Risks*.

© 2018 Velociteach. All rights reserved. Do not duplicate. Slide 28

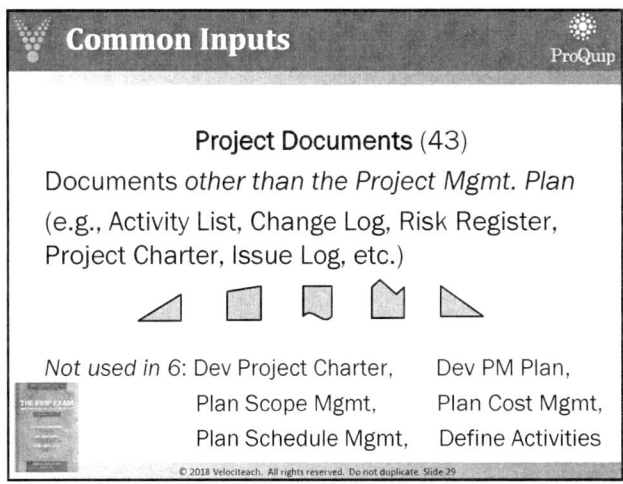

Common Inputs

Project Documents (43)

Documents *other than the Project Mgmt. Plan* (e.g., Activity List, Change Log, Risk Register, Project Charter, Issue Log, etc.)

Not used in 6: Dev Project Charter,   Dev PM Plan,
Plan Scope Mgmt,   Plan Cost Mgmt,
Plan Schedule Mgmt,   Define Activities

© 2018 Velociteach. All rights reserved. Do not duplicate. Slide 29

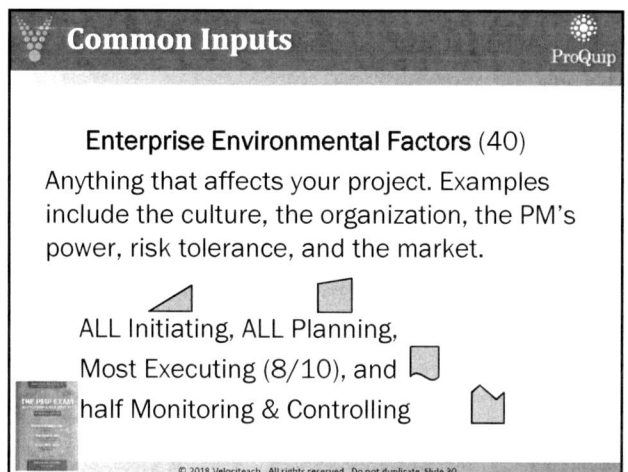

Common Inputs

ProQuip

Enterprise Environmental Factors (40)

Anything that affects your project. Examples include the culture, the organization, the PM's power, risk tolerance, and the market.

ALL Initiating, ALL Planning,
Most Executing (8/10), and
half Monitoring & Controlling

© 2018 Velociteach. All rights reserved. Do not duplicate. Slide 30

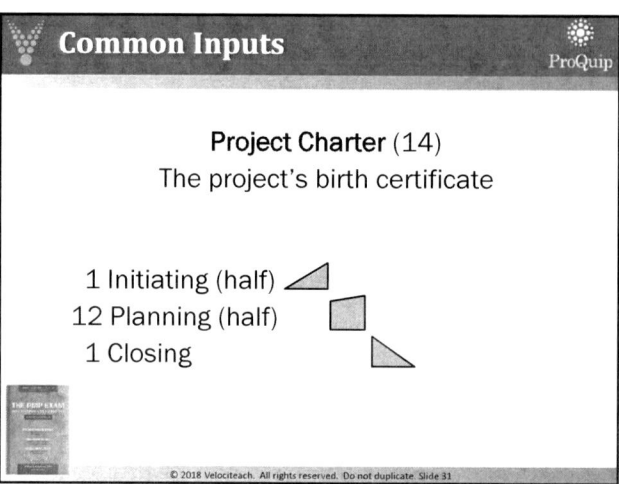

Common Inputs

ProQuip

Project Charter (14)

The project's birth certificate

1 Initiating (half)
12 Planning (half)
1 Closing

© 2018 Velociteach. All rights reserved. Do not duplicate. Slide 31

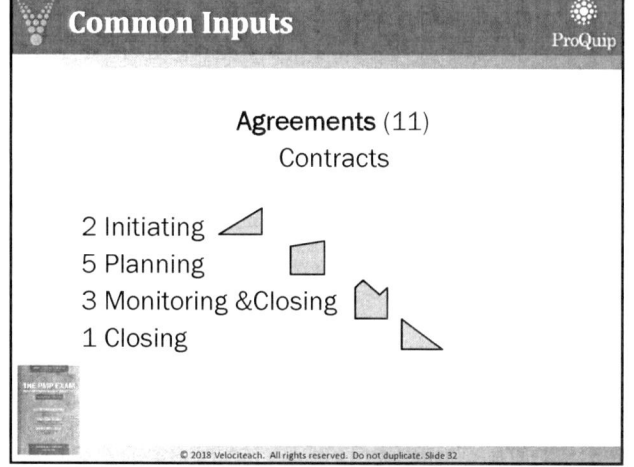

Common Inputs

ProQuip

Agreements (11)

Contracts

2 Initiating
5 Planning
3 Monitoring &Closing
1 Closing

© 2018 Velociteach. All rights reserved. Do not duplicate. Slide 32

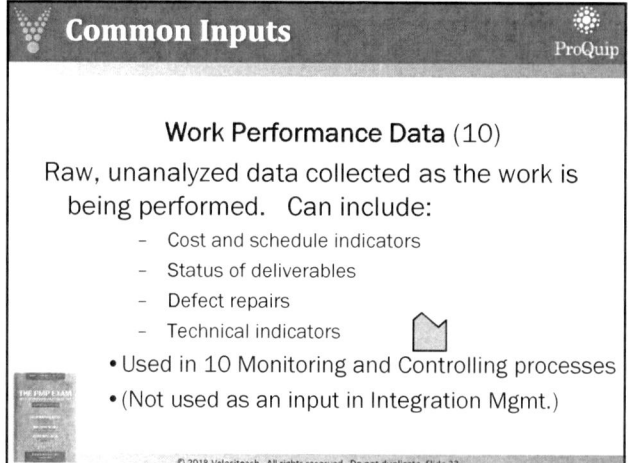

Common Inputs

ProQuip

Work Performance Data (10)

Raw, unanalyzed data collected as the work is being performed. Can include:

- Cost and schedule indicators
- Status of deliverables
- Defect repairs
- Technical indicators
- Used in 10 Monitoring and Controlling processes
- (Not used as an input in Integration Mgmt.)

© 2018 Velociteach. All rights reserved. Do not duplicate. Slide 33

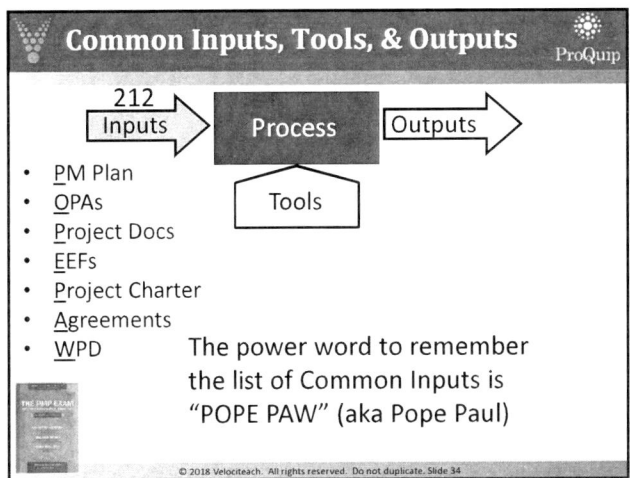

Common Inputs, Tools, & Outputs — ProQuip

212

Inputs → Process → Outputs

Tools

- PM Plan
- OPAs
- Project Docs
- EEFs
- Project Charter
- Agreements
- WPD

The power word to remember the list of Common Inputs is "POPE PAW" (aka Pope Paul)

© 2018 Velociteach. All rights reserved. Do not duplicate. Slide 34

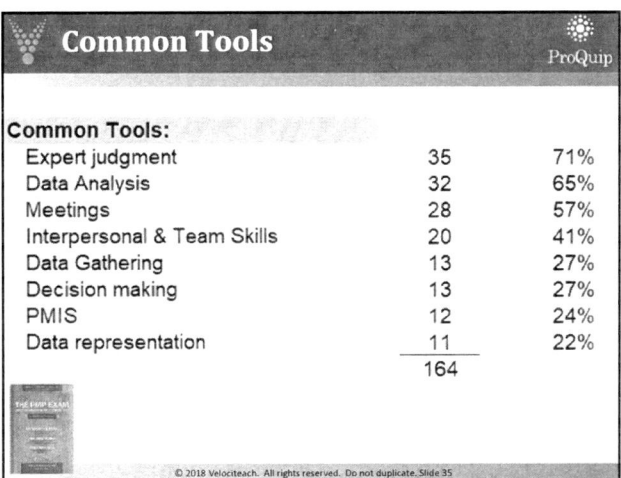

Common Tools — ProQuip

Common Tools:

Tool		
Expert judgment	35	71%
Data Analysis	32	65%
Meetings	28	57%
Interpersonal & Team Skills	20	41%
Data Gathering	13	27%
Decision making	13	27%
PMIS	12	24%
Data representation	11	22%
	164	

© 2018 Velociteach. All rights reserved. Do not duplicate. Slide 35

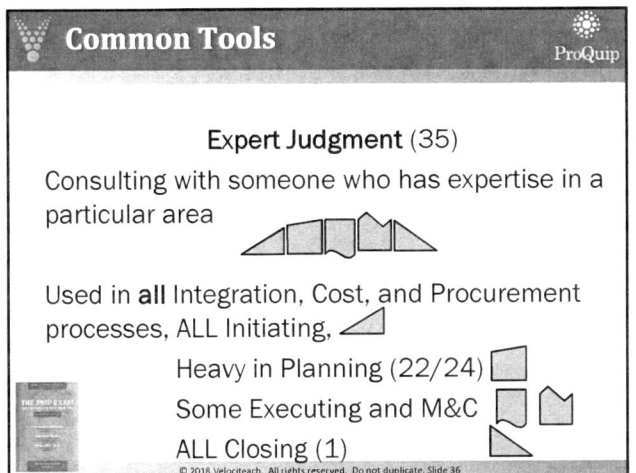

Common Tools — ProQuip

Expert Judgment (35)

Consulting with someone who has expertise in a particular area

Used in **all** Integration, Cost, and Procurement processes, ALL Initiating,

Heavy in Planning (22/24)

Some Executing and M&C

ALL Closing (1)

© 2018 Velociteach. All rights reserved. Do not duplicate. Slide 36

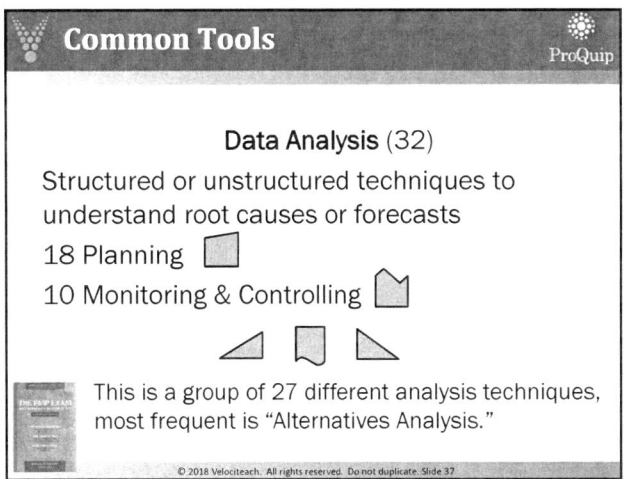

Common Tools — ProQuip

Data Analysis (32)

Structured or unstructured techniques to understand root causes or forecasts

18 Planning

10 Monitoring & Controlling

This is a group of 27 different analysis techniques, most frequent is "Alternatives Analysis."

© 2018 Velociteach. All rights reserved. Do not duplicate. Slide 37

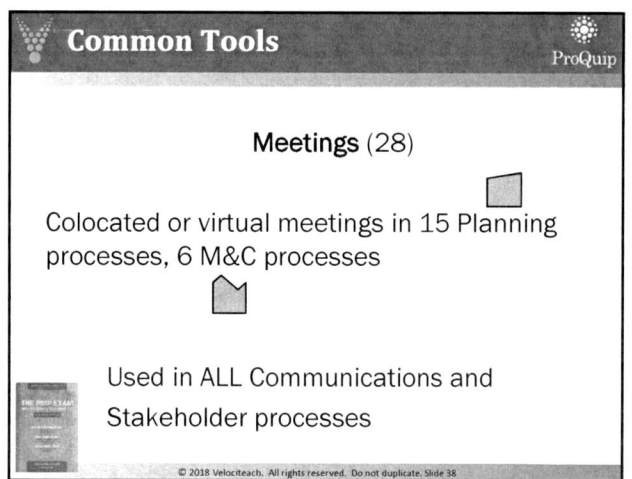

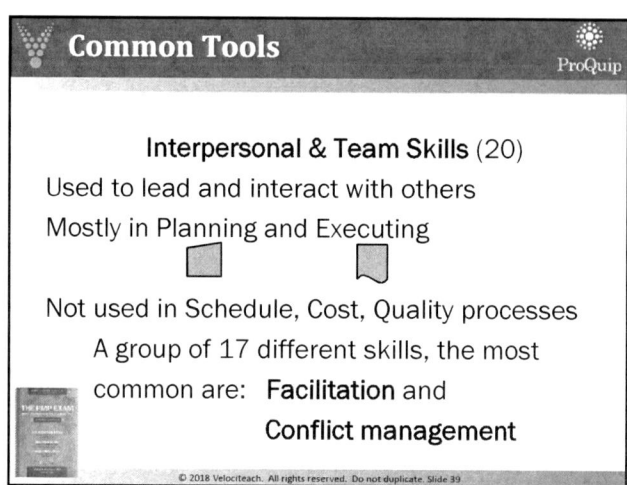

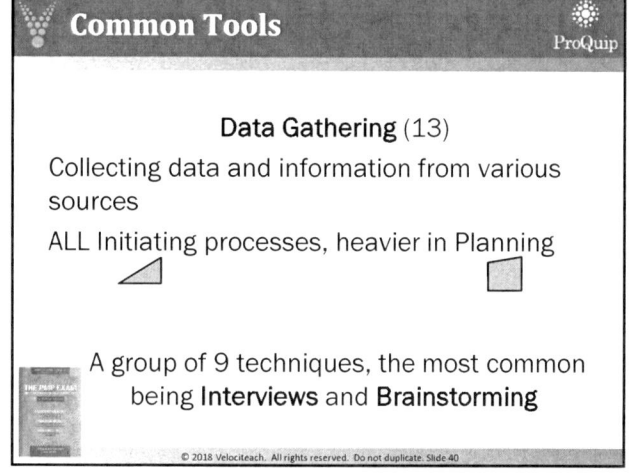

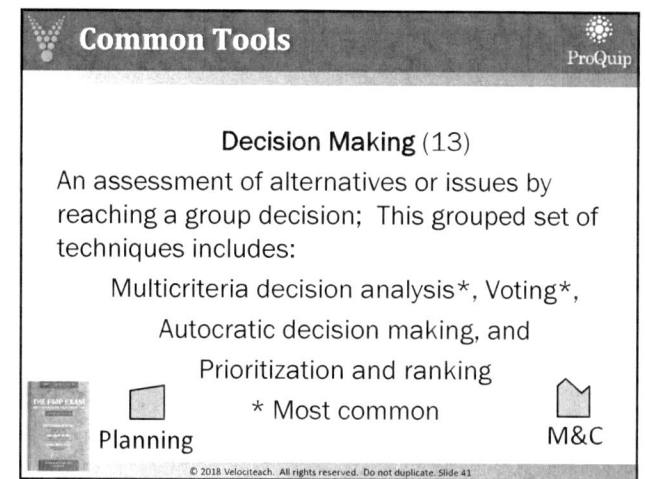

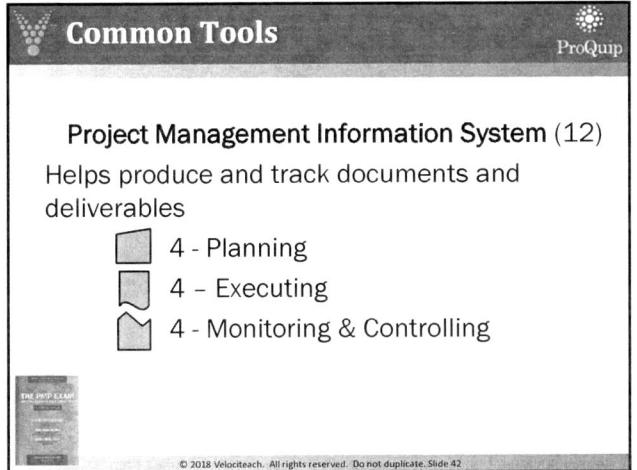

Common Tools

ProQuip

Project Management Information System (12)

Helps produce and track documents and deliverables

4 - Planning

4 – Executing

4 - Monitoring & Controlling

© 2018 Velociteach. All rights reserved. Do not duplicate. Slide 42

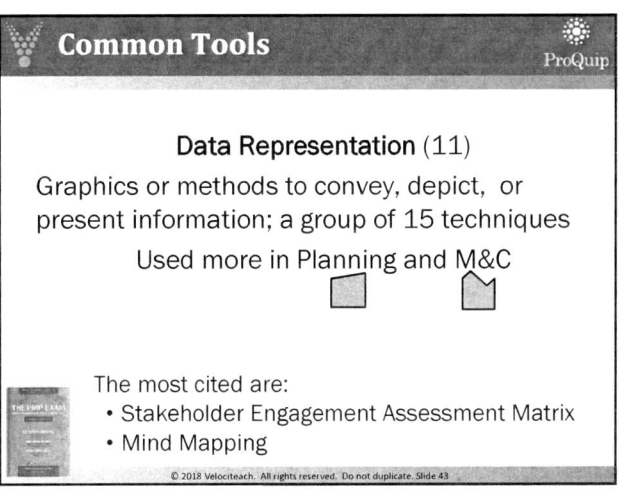

Common Tools

ProQuip

Data Representation (11)

Graphics or methods to convey, depict, or present information; a group of 15 techniques

Used more in Planning and M&C

The most cited are:
- Stakeholder Engagement Assessment Matrix
- Mind Mapping

© 2018 Velociteach. All rights reserved. Do not duplicate. Slide 43

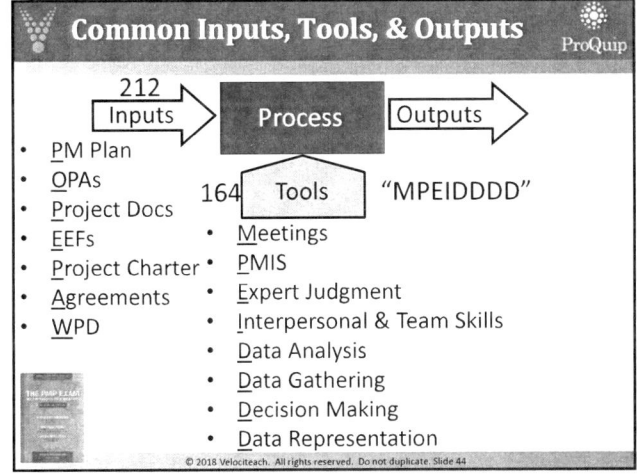

Common Inputs, Tools, & Outputs

ProQuip

212

Inputs → Process → Outputs

- PM Plan
- OPAs
- Project Docs
- EEFs
- Project Charter
- Agreements
- WPD

164 Tools "MPEIDDDD"

- Meetings
- PMIS
- Expert Judgment
- Interpersonal & Team Skills
- Data Analysis
- Data Gathering
- Decision Making
- Data Representation

© 2018 Velociteach. All rights reserved. Do not duplicate. Slide 44

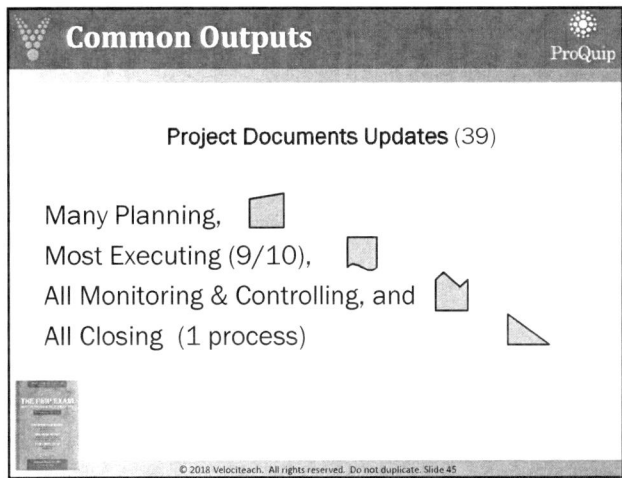

Common Outputs

ProQuip

Project Documents Updates (39)

Many Planning,

Most Executing (9/10),

All Monitoring & Controlling, and

All Closing (1 process)

© 2018 Velociteach. All rights reserved. Do not duplicate. Slide 45

©2018 Velociteach. All rights reserved.

Common Outputs

Project Management Plan Updates (26)

Few Planning,
Most Executing (9/10),
Most Monitoring & Controlling (11/12)

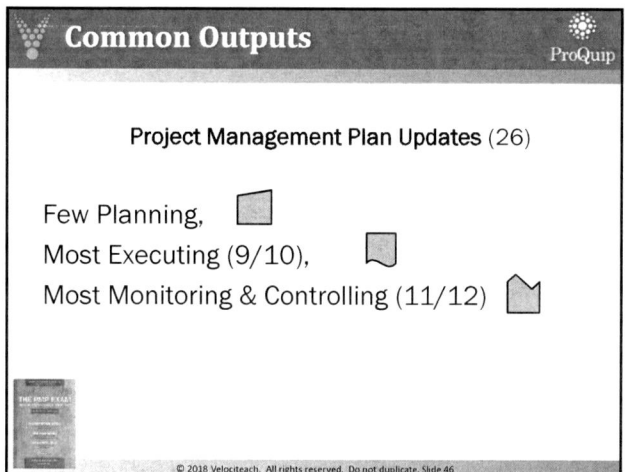

© 2018 Velociteach. All rights reserved. Do not duplicate. Slide 46

Common Outputs

Change Requests (24)
(Scope, Schedule, Budget, etc.)

Change the plan or how the work is being performed

- Corrective actions
- Preventive actions
- Defect repairs

Mostly Executing (8/10) and
Monitoring & Controlling (11/12)

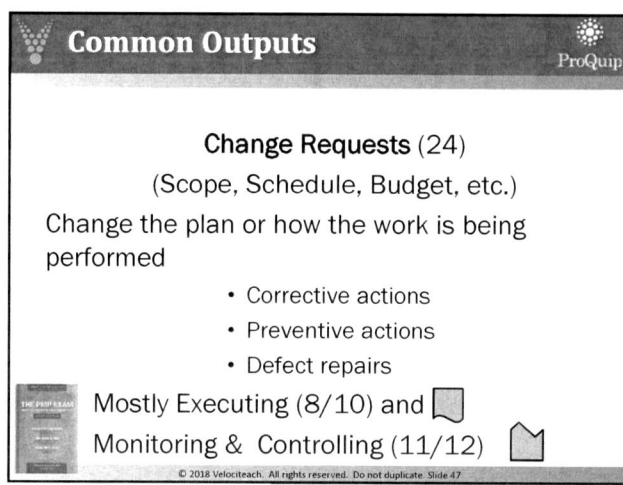

© 2018 Velociteach. All rights reserved. Do not duplicate. Slide 47

Common Outputs

Work Performance Information (10)

Result of analyzing/processing WPData

- Summary figures
- Statistics
- Percentages
- Lessons Learned

Most Monitoring & Controlling (10/12)
(not an output of Integration Mgmt.)

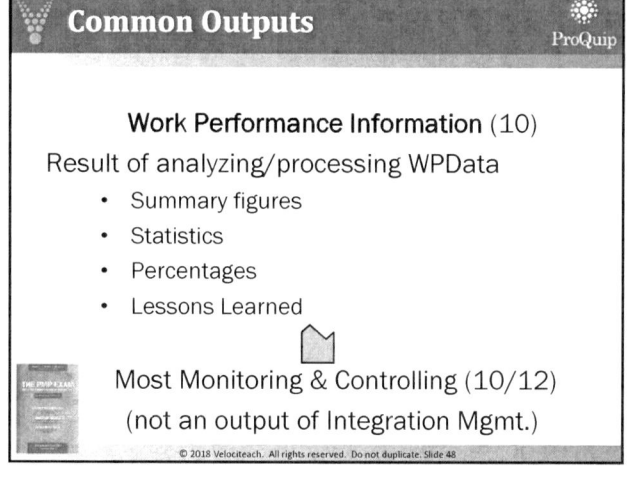

© 2018 Velociteach. All rights reserved. Do not duplicate. Slide 48

Common Outputs

Organizational Process Asset Updates (10)

Several Executing (6/10),
Some Monitoring & Controlling (2/12), and
Closing process

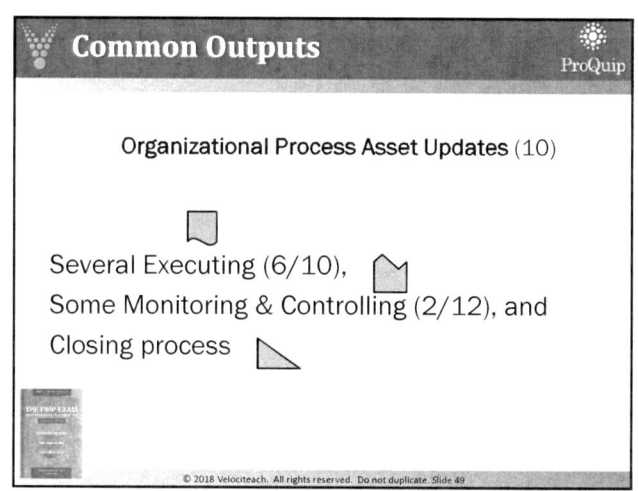

© 2018 Velociteach. All rights reserved. Do not duplicate. Slide 49

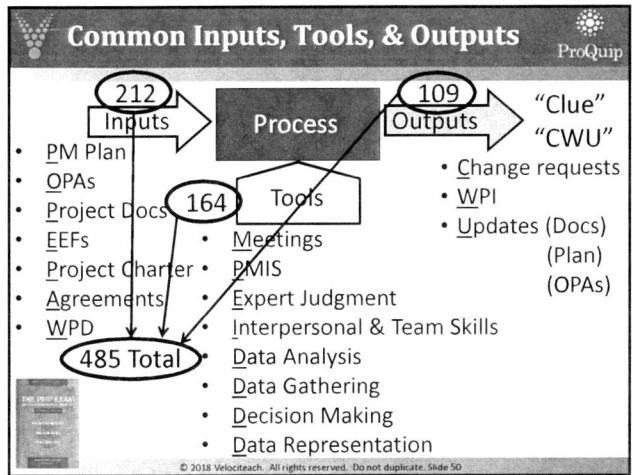

Common Inputs, Tools, & Outputs · ProQuip

212 Inputs → Process → 109 Outputs → "Clue" "CWU"

- PM Plan
- OPAs
- Project Docs — 164 Tools
- EEFs
- Project Charter
- Agreements
- WPD

485 Total

Outputs:
- Change requests
- WPI
- Updates (Docs) (Plan) (OPAs)

Tools:
- Meetings
- PMIS
- Expert Judgment
- Interpersonal & Team Skills
- Data Analysis
- Data Gathering
- Decision Making
- Data Representation

© 2018 Velociteach. All rights reserved. Do not duplicate. Slide 50

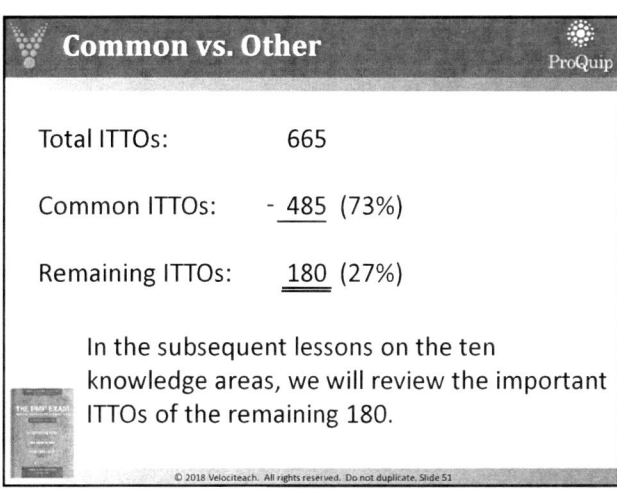

Common vs. Other · ProQuip

Total ITTOs:	665
Common ITTOs:	- 485 (73%)
Remaining ITTOs:	180 (27%)

In the subsequent lessons on the ten knowledge areas, we will review the important ITTOs of the remaining 180.

© 2018 Velociteach. All rights reserved. Do not duplicate. Slide 51

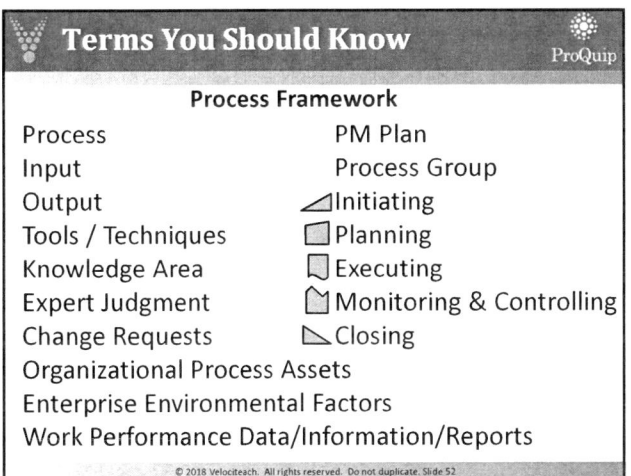

Terms You Should Know · ProQuip

Process Framework

Process	PM Plan
Input	Process Group
Output	◁ Initiating
Tools / Techniques	▢ Planning
Knowledge Area	▢ Executing
Expert Judgment	⬠ Monitoring & Controlling
Change Requests	◹ Closing

Organizational Process Assets
Enterprise Environmental Factors
Work Performance Data/Information/Reports

© 2018 Velociteach. All rights reserved. Do not duplicate. Slide 52

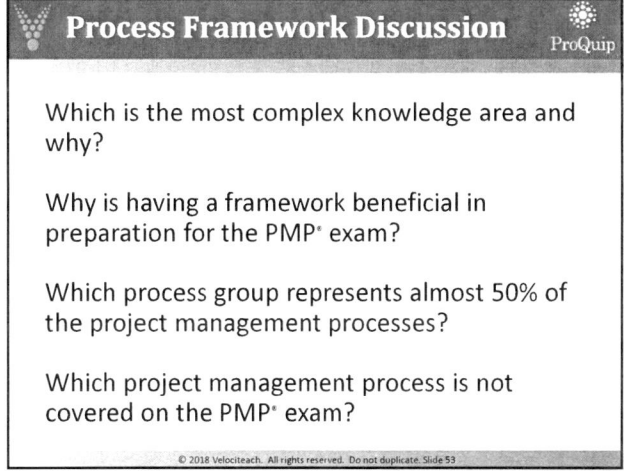

Process Framework Discussion · ProQuip

Which is the most complex knowledge area and why?

Why is having a framework beneficial in preparation for the PMP® exam?

Which process group represents almost 50% of the project management processes?

Which project management process is not covered on the PMP® exam?

© 2018 Velociteach. All rights reserved. Do not duplicate. Slide 53

ProQuip

Project Integration Management

Course Module 4

PMBOK® Guide Chapter 4

PMP® Exam Textbook Chapter 4

© 2018 Velociteach. All rights reserved. Do not duplicate Slide 1

Integration Management

ProQuip

What does this knowledge area involve?
- Maintaining the "big picture" of the project throughout the life of the project
- Coordinating every part of the project
- Balancing project priorities
- Starting, planning, executing, controlling, and closing the project

© 2018 Velociteach. All rights reserved. Do not duplicate Slide 2

PMI® Philosophy: Integration Mgmt

ProQuip

The Project Manager is the decision maker, keeping the project team focused on project execution.

Project management is not a serial progression of processes; much happens in parallel and in an iterative fashion. Integration coordinates and orchestrates order to project management.

© 2018 Velociteach. All rights reserved. Do not duplicate Slide 3

---

7 Processes of Integration

ProQuip

Memory Tip!
Integration Management is the *only* knowledge area involving *all five* Process Groups!

KNOWLEDGE AREA	Initiating	Planning	Executing	Monitoring and Controlling	Closing
Project Integration Management	Develop Project Charter	Develop Project Mgmt Plan	Direct & Manage Project Work	Monitor & Control Project Work	Close Project or Phase
			Manage Project Knowledge	Perform Integrated Change Control	

© 2018 Velociteach. All rights reserved. Do not duplicate Slide 4

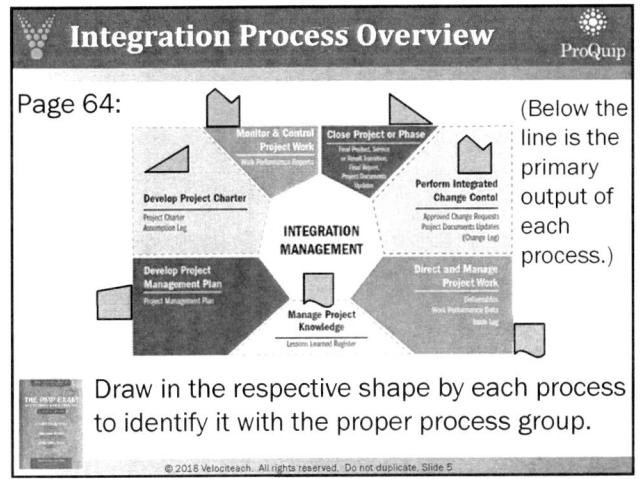

Integration Process Overview

Page 64:

Draw in the respective shape by each process to identify it with the proper process group.

(Below the line is the primary output of each process.)

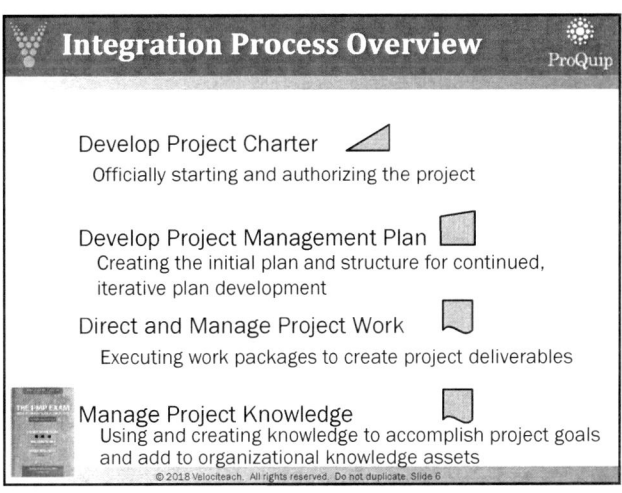

Integration Process Overview

Develop Project Charter
Officially starting and authorizing the project

Develop Project Management Plan
Creating the initial plan and structure for continued, iterative plan development

Direct and Manage Project Work
Executing work packages to create project deliverables

Manage Project Knowledge
Using and creating knowledge to accomplish project goals and add to organizational knowledge assets

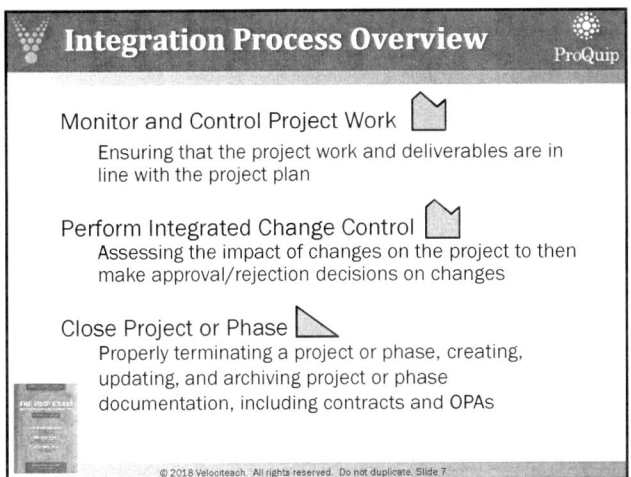

Integration Process Overview

Monitor and Control Project Work
Ensuring that the project work and deliverables are in line with the project plan

Perform Integrated Change Control
Assessing the impact of changes on the project to then make approval/rejection decisions on changes

Close Project or Phase
Properly terminating a project or phase, creating, updating, and archiving project or phase documentation, including contracts and OPAs

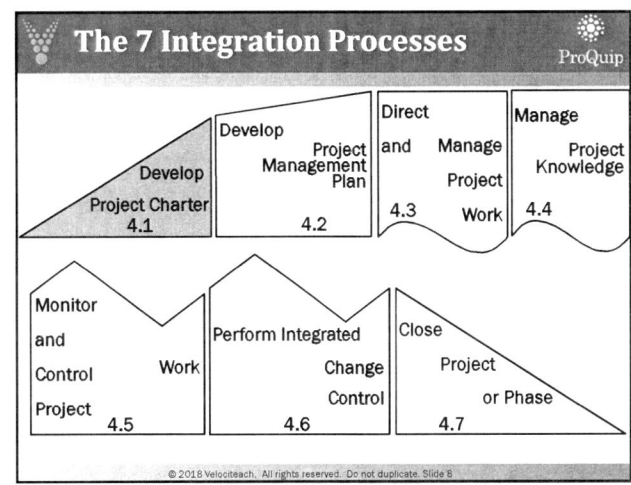

The 7 Integration Processes

Develop Project Charter 4.1

Develop Project Management Plan 4.2

Direct and Manage Project Work 4.3

Manage Project Knowledge 4.4

Monitor and Control Project Work 4.5

Perform Integrated Change Control 4.6

Close Project or Phase 4.7

©2018 Velociteach. All rights reserved.

Develop Project Charter   ProQuip

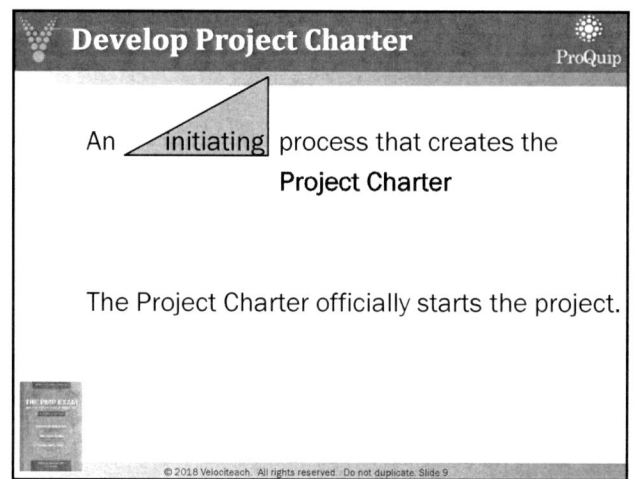

An initiating process that creates the
Project Charter

The Project Charter officially starts the project.

© 2018 Velociteach. All rights reserved. Do not duplicate. Slide 9

Develop Project Charter   ProQuip

Key Points
- Project is triggered by a need
- May be driven by an agreement (contract)
- Project is selected from many proposed projects based on financial and business priorities (Business case)
- The charter authorizes (empowers) and names the PM

© 2018 Velociteach. All rights reserved. Do not duplicate. Slide 10

Develop Project Charter   ProQuip

The *key* inputs in this process are:

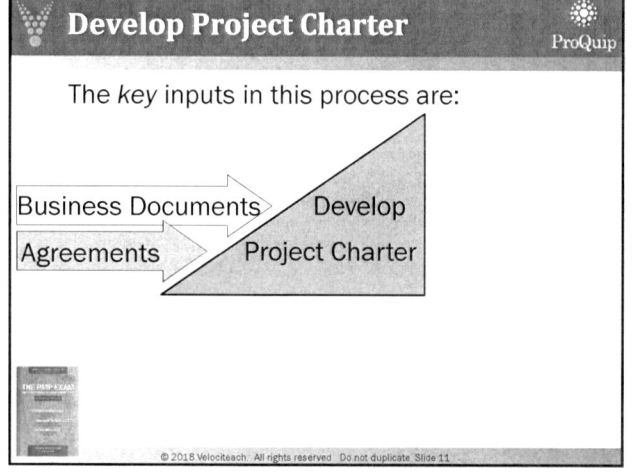

Business Documents → Develop
Agreements → Project Charter

© 2018 Velociteach. All rights reserved. Do not duplicate. Slide 11

PM Role *   ProQuip

Help stakeholders with feasibility study by assessing project parameters:
- Available information
- Lessons Learned (previous projects)
- Assumptions and constraints
- Proposed new deliverables

* Subject for scenario-based questions

© 2018 Velociteach. All rights reserved. Do not duplicate. Slide 12

Business Documents — ProQuip

Business Case: Project Triggers, page 68
- Market demand
- Organizational need
- Customer request
- Technological advance
- Legal requirement
- Ecological impact
- Social need

© 2018 Velociteach. All rights reserved. Do not duplicate. Slide 13

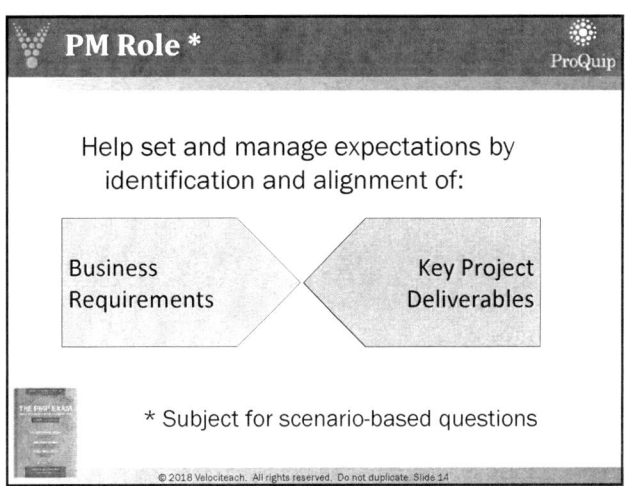

PM Role * — ProQuip

Help set and manage expectations by identification and alignment of:

Business Requirements	Key Project Deliverables

* Subject for scenario-based questions

© 2018 Velociteach. All rights reserved. Do not duplicate. Slide 14

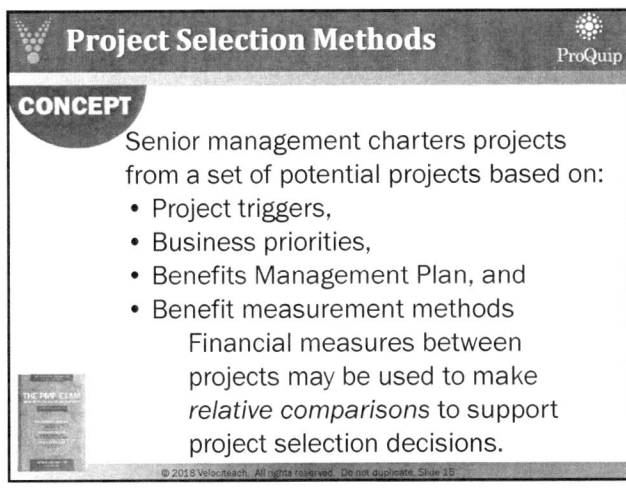

Project Selection Methods — ProQuip

CONCEPT

Senior management charters projects from a set of potential projects based on:
- Project triggers,
- Business priorities,
- Benefits Management Plan, and
- Benefit measurement methods
  Financial measures between projects may be used to make *relative comparisons* to support project selection decisions.

© 2018 Velociteach. All rights reserved. Do not duplicate. Slide 15

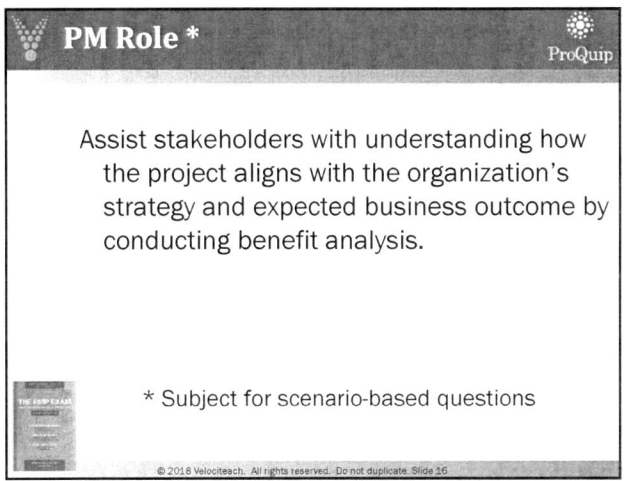

PM Role * — ProQuip

Assist stakeholders with understanding how the project aligns with the organization's strategy and expected business outcome by conducting benefit analysis.

* Subject for scenario-based questions

© 2018 Velociteach. All rights reserved. Do not duplicate. Slide 16

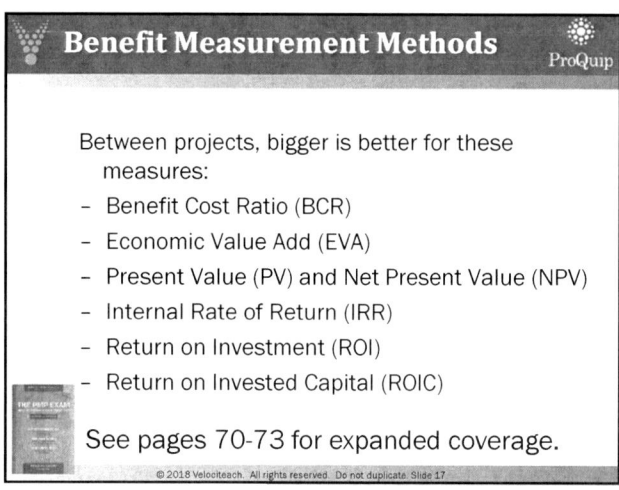

Benefit Measurement Methods

Between projects, bigger is better for these measures:
- Benefit Cost Ratio (BCR)
- Economic Value Add (EVA)
- Present Value (PV) and Net Present Value (NPV)
- Internal Rate of Return (IRR)
- Return on Investment (ROI)
- Return on Invested Capital (ROIC)

See pages 70-73 for expanded coverage.

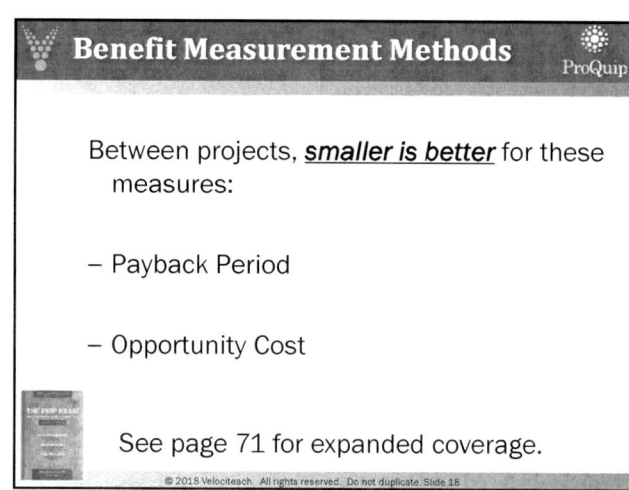

Benefit Measurement Methods

Between projects, *smaller is better* for these measures:

- Payback Period

- Opportunity Cost

See page 71 for expanded coverage.

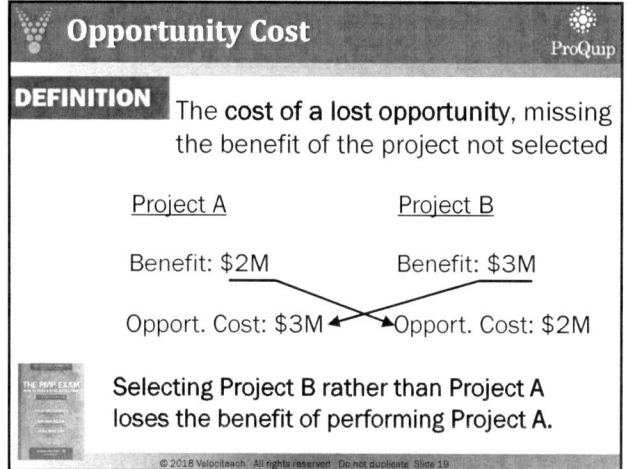

Opportunity Cost

DEFINITION The **cost of a lost opportunity**, missing the benefit of the project not selected

Project A	Project B
Benefit: $2M	Benefit: $3M
Opport. Cost: $3M	Opport. Cost: $2M

Selecting Project B rather than Project A loses the benefit of performing Project A.

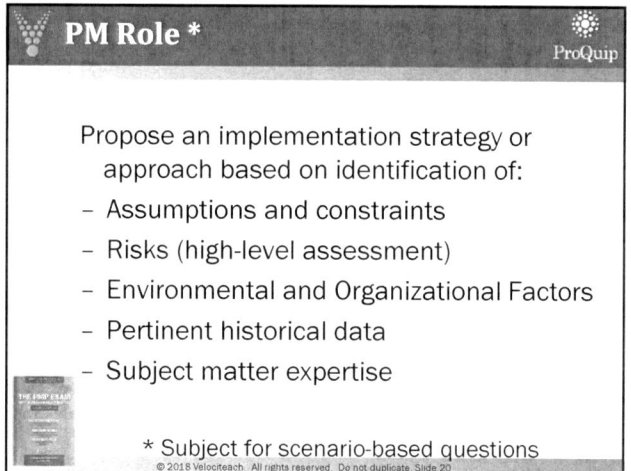

PM Role *

Propose an implementation strategy or approach based on identification of:
- Assumptions and constraints
- Risks (high-level assessment)
- Environmental and Organizational Factors
- Pertinent historical data
- Subject matter expertise

* Subject for scenario-based questions

© 2018 Velociteach. All rights reserved. Do not duplicate. Slide 17

© 2018 Velociteach. All rights reserved. Do not duplicate. Slide 18

© 2018 Velociteach. All rights reserved. Do not duplicate. Slide 19

© 2018 Velociteach. All rights reserved. Do not duplicate. Slide 20

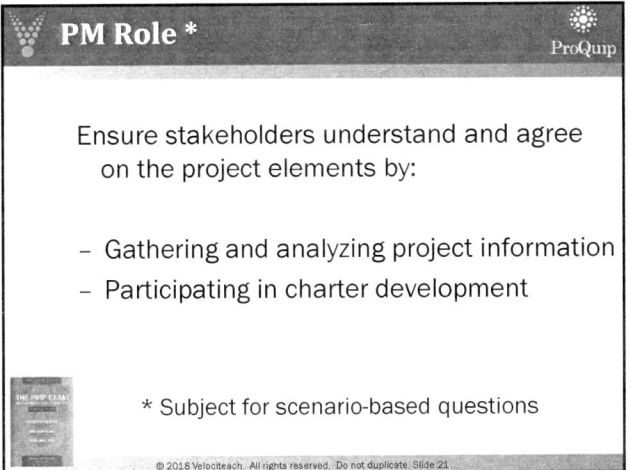

PM Role *

Ensure stakeholders understand and agree on the project elements by:

- Gathering and analyzing project information
- Participating in charter development

* Subject for scenario-based questions

© 2018 Velociteach. All rights reserved. Do not duplicate. Slide 21

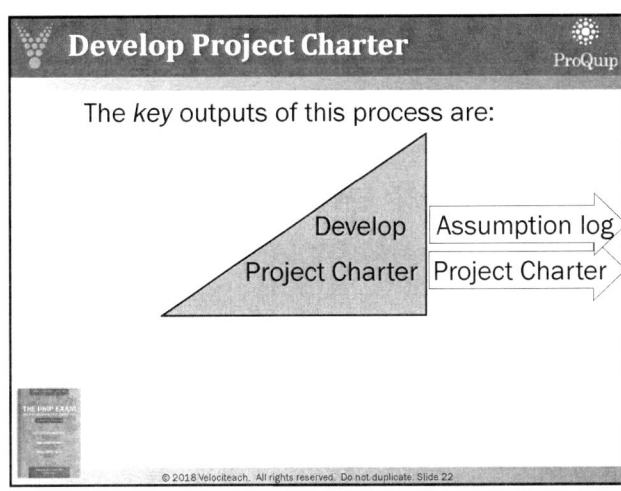

Develop Project Charter

The *key* outputs of this process are:

Develop Project Charter → Assumption log / Project Charter

© 2018 Velociteach. All rights reserved. Do not duplicate. Slide 22

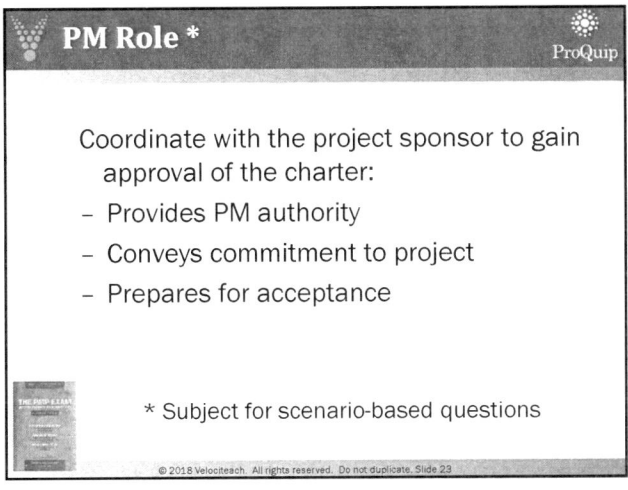

PM Role *

Coordinate with the project sponsor to gain approval of the charter:

- Provides PM authority
- Conveys commitment to project
- Prepares for acceptance

* Subject for scenario-based questions

© 2018 Velociteach. All rights reserved. Do not duplicate. Slide 23

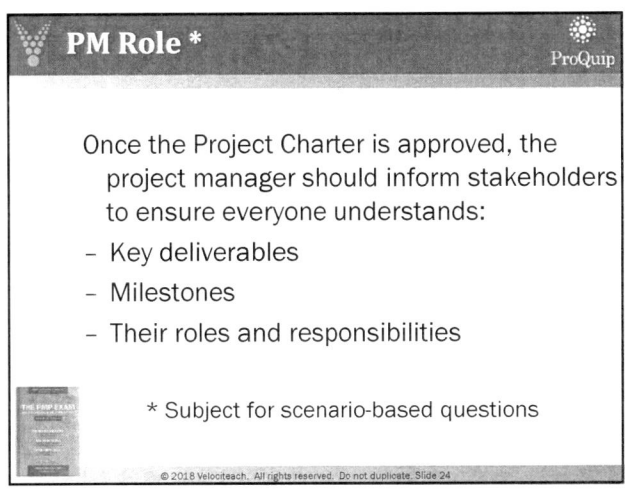

PM Role *

Once the Project Charter is approved, the project manager should inform stakeholders to ensure everyone understands:

- Key deliverables
- Milestones
- Their roles and responsibilities

* Subject for scenario-based questions

© 2018 Velociteach. All rights reserved. Do not duplicate. Slide 24

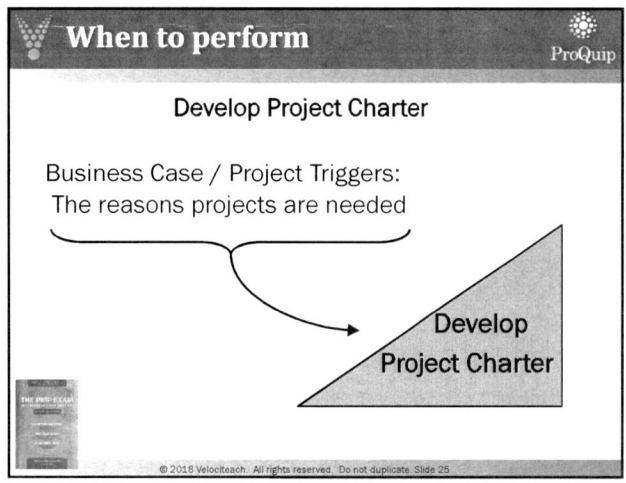

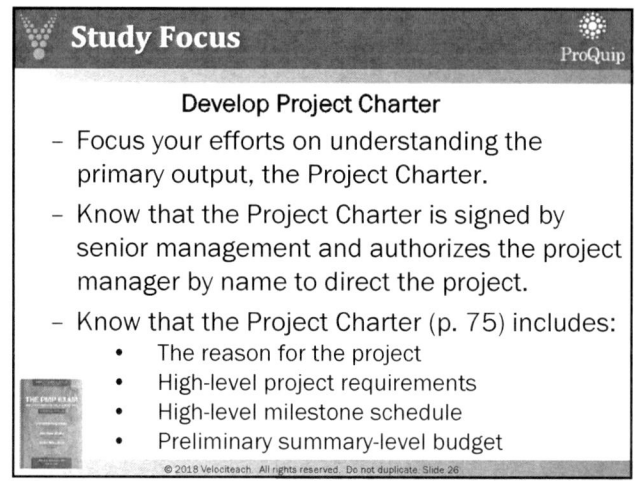

Review the ITTOs

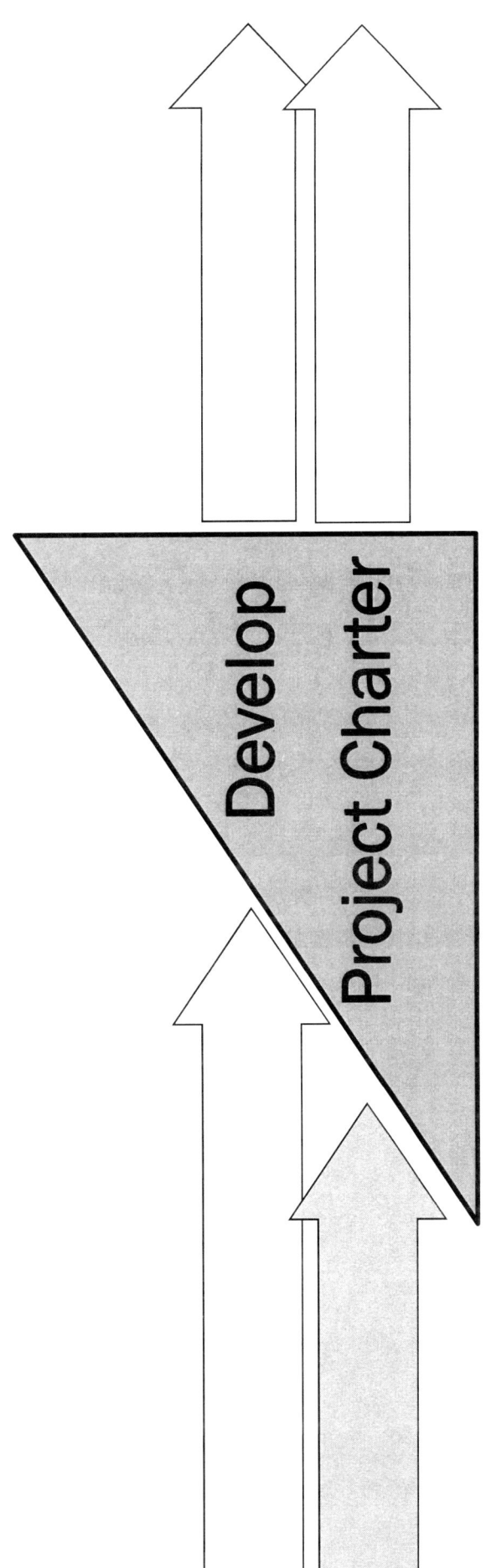

Develop Project Charter

© 2018 Velociteach. All rights reserved.

ProQuip

This page left intentionally blank.

©2018 Velociteach. All rights reserved.

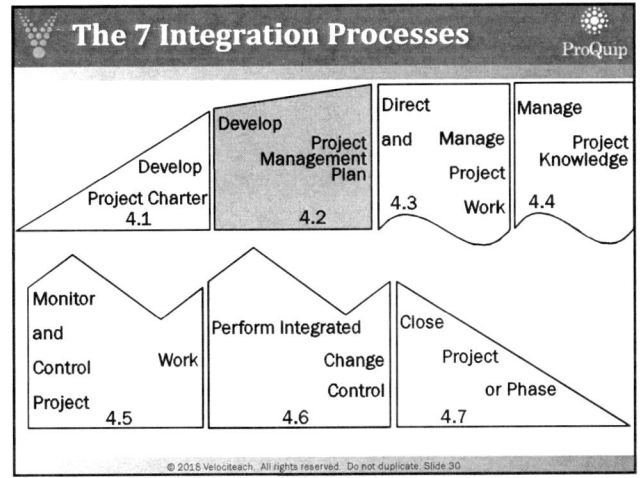

The 7 Integration Processes

ProQuip

Develop Project Charter 4.1

Develop Project Management Plan 4.2

Direct and Manage Project Work 4.3

Manage Project Knowledge 4.4

Monitor and Control Project Work 4.5

Perform Integrated Change Control 4.6

Close Project or Phase 4.7

© 2018 Velociteach. All rights reserved. Do not duplicate. Slide 30

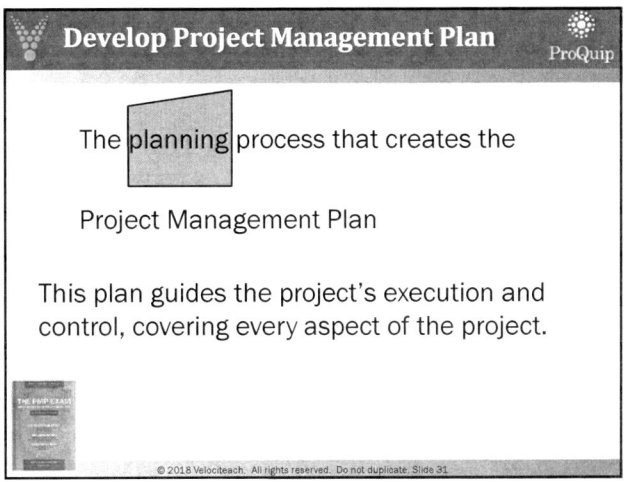

Develop Project Management Plan

ProQuip

The planning process that creates the

Project Management Plan

This plan guides the project's execution and control, covering every aspect of the project.

© 2018 Velociteach. All rights reserved. Do not duplicate. Slide 31

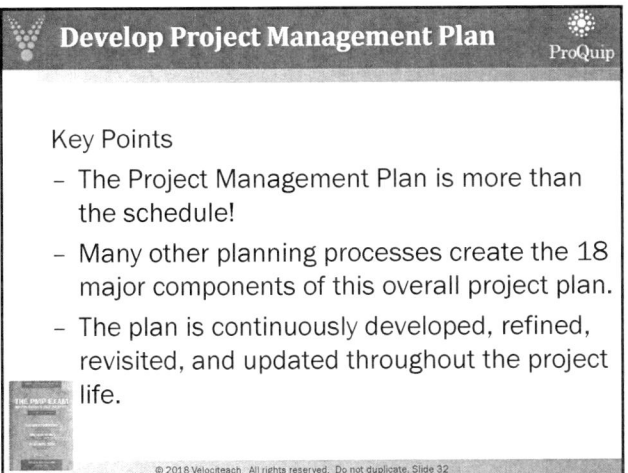

Develop Project Management Plan

ProQuip

Key Points
- The Project Management Plan is more than the schedule!
- Many other planning processes create the 18 major components of this overall project plan.
- The plan is continuously developed, refined, revisited, and updated throughout the project life.

© 2018 Velociteach. All rights reserved. Do not duplicate. Slide 32

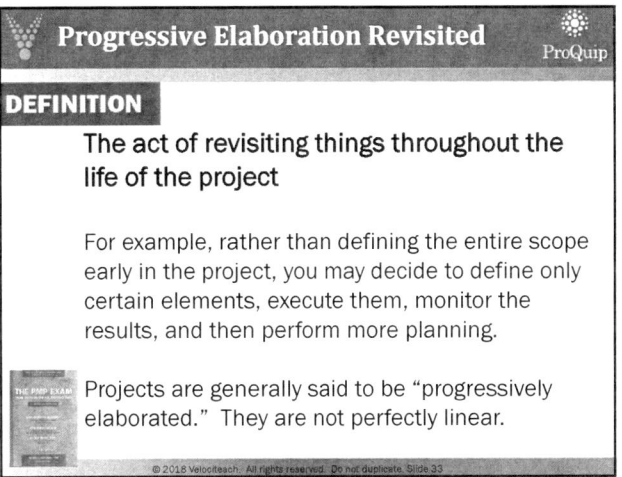

Progressive Elaboration Revisited

ProQuip

DEFINITION

The act of revisiting things throughout the life of the project

For example, rather than defining the entire scope early in the project, you may decide to define only certain elements, execute them, monitor the results, and then perform more planning.

Projects are generally said to be "progressively elaborated." They are not perfectly linear.

© 2018 Velociteach. All rights reserved. Do not duplicate. Slide 33

Develop Project Management Plan

The key input to this process is:

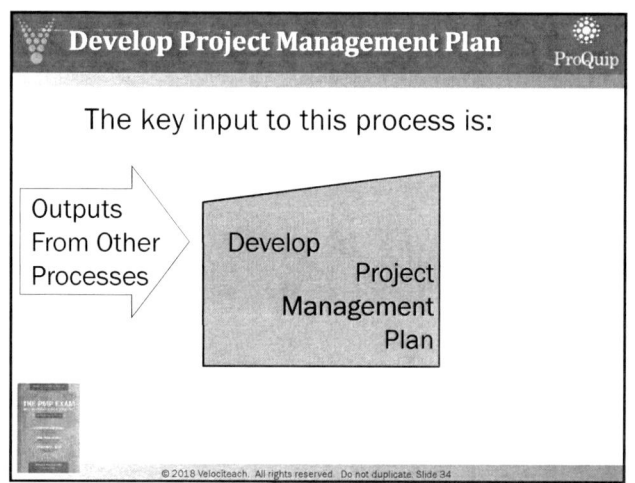

Develop Project Management Plan

The key output to this process is:

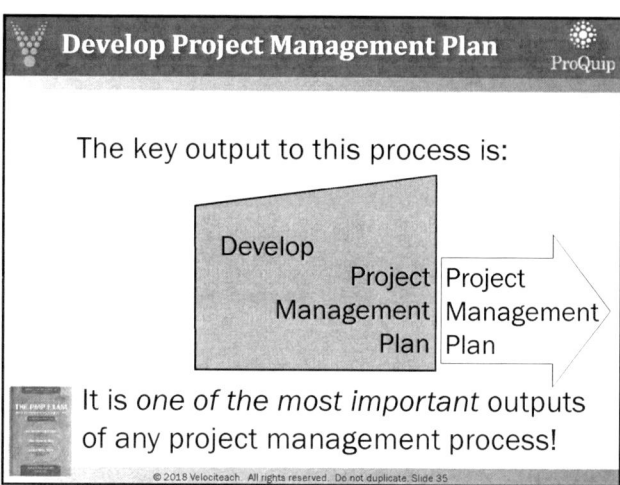

It is *one of the most important* outputs of any project management process!

PM Role *

Present the Project Management Plan to key stakeholders:

- Within organization's guidelines
- For approval to begin execution

* Subject for scenario-based questions

Project Management Plan

DEFINITION

How the project will be managed;

A formal, approved document composed of other planning documents

Also known as the "project plan" or "PM plan."

©2018 Velociteach. All rights reserved. Page 46

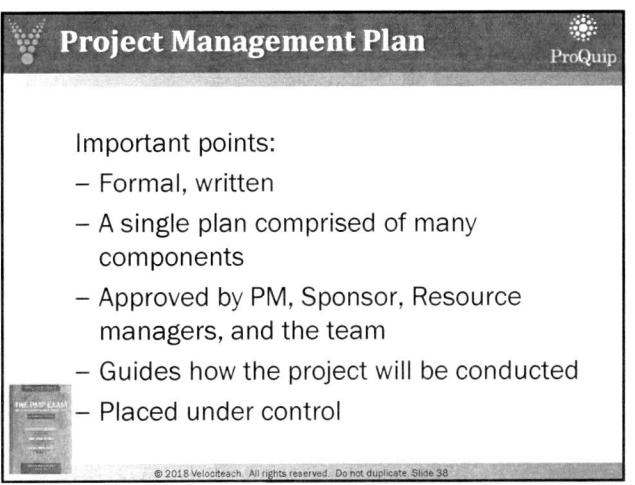

Project Management Plan

Important points:
- Formal, written
- A single plan comprised of many components
- Approved by PM, Sponsor, Resource managers, and the team
- Guides how the project will be conducted
- Placed under control

© 2018 Velociteach. All rights reserved. Do not duplicate. Slide 38

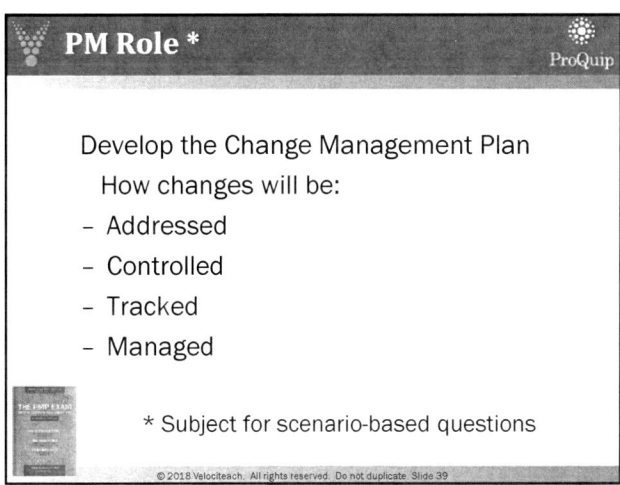

PM Role *

Develop the Change Management Plan
How changes will be:
- Addressed
- Controlled
- Tracked
- Managed

    * Subject for scenario-based questions

© 2018 Velociteach. All rights reserved. Do not duplicate. Slide 39

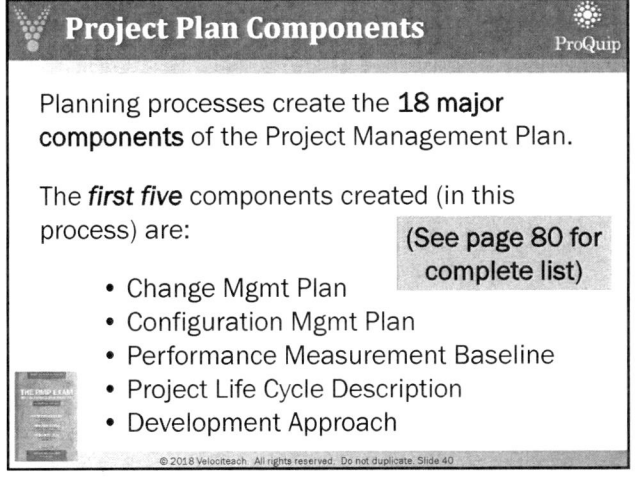

Project Plan Components

Planning processes create the **18 major components** of the Project Management Plan.

The *first five* components created (in this process) are:

(See page 80 for complete list)

- Change Mgmt Plan
- Configuration Mgmt Plan
- Performance Measurement Baseline
- Project Life Cycle Description
- Development Approach

© 2018 Velociteach. All rights reserved. Do not duplicate. Slide 40

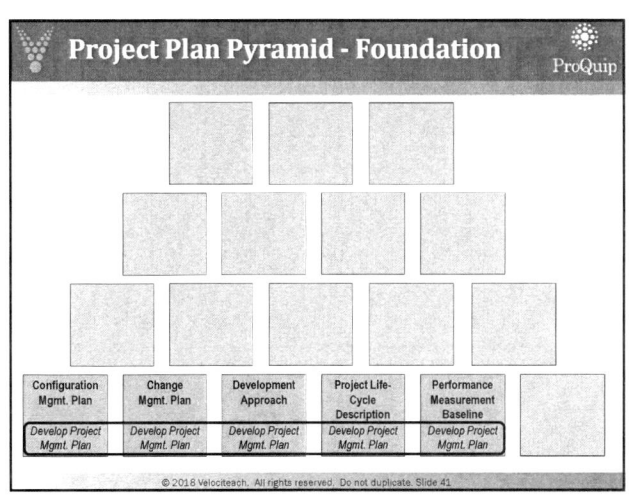

Project Plan Pyramid - Foundation

Configuration Mgmt. Plan	Change Mgmt. Plan	Development Approach	Project Life-Cycle Description	Performance Measurement Baseline	
Develop Project Mgmt. Plan	Develop Project Mgmt. Plan	Develop Project Mgmt. Plan	Develop Project Mgmt. Plan	Develop Project Mgmt. Plan	

© 2018 Velociteach. All rights reserved. Do not duplicate. Slide 41

When to perform

ProQuip

Develop Project Management Plan

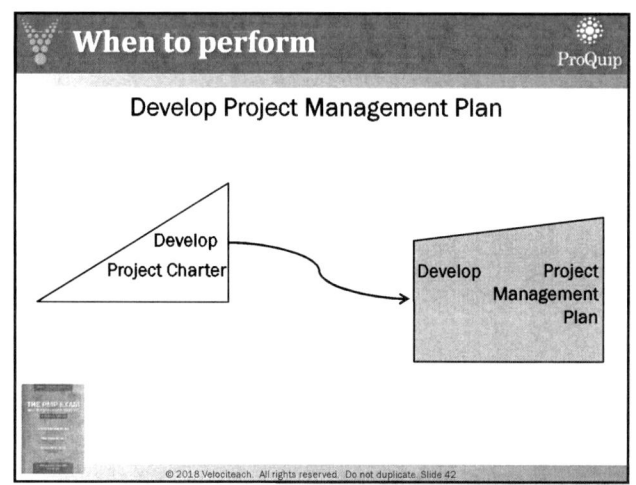

Study Focus

ProQuip

Develop Project Management Plan

- – Focus your efforts on understanding the output, the **Project Management Plan.**
- – Know that the Project Management Plan is the overall plan, not just the project schedule!
- – Know the 18 components and in which process they are created (see table, textbook page 80).
- – Know that the Project Plan continues to be developed *iteratively* until the project is closed.

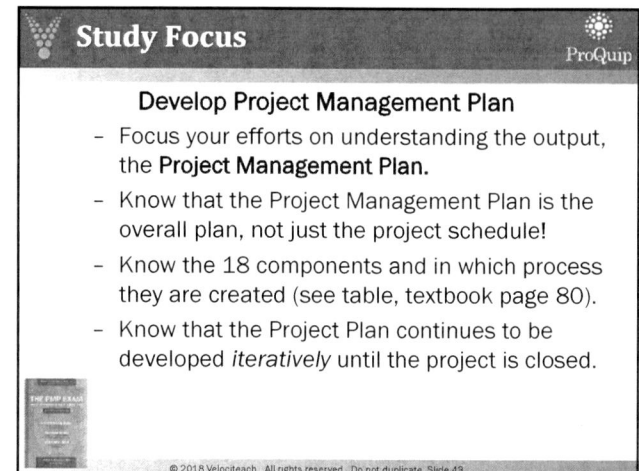

© 2018 Velociteach. All rights reserved. Do not duplicate. Slide 42

© 2018 Velociteach. All rights reserved. Do not duplicate. Slide 43

Review the ITTOs

Develop Project Management Plan

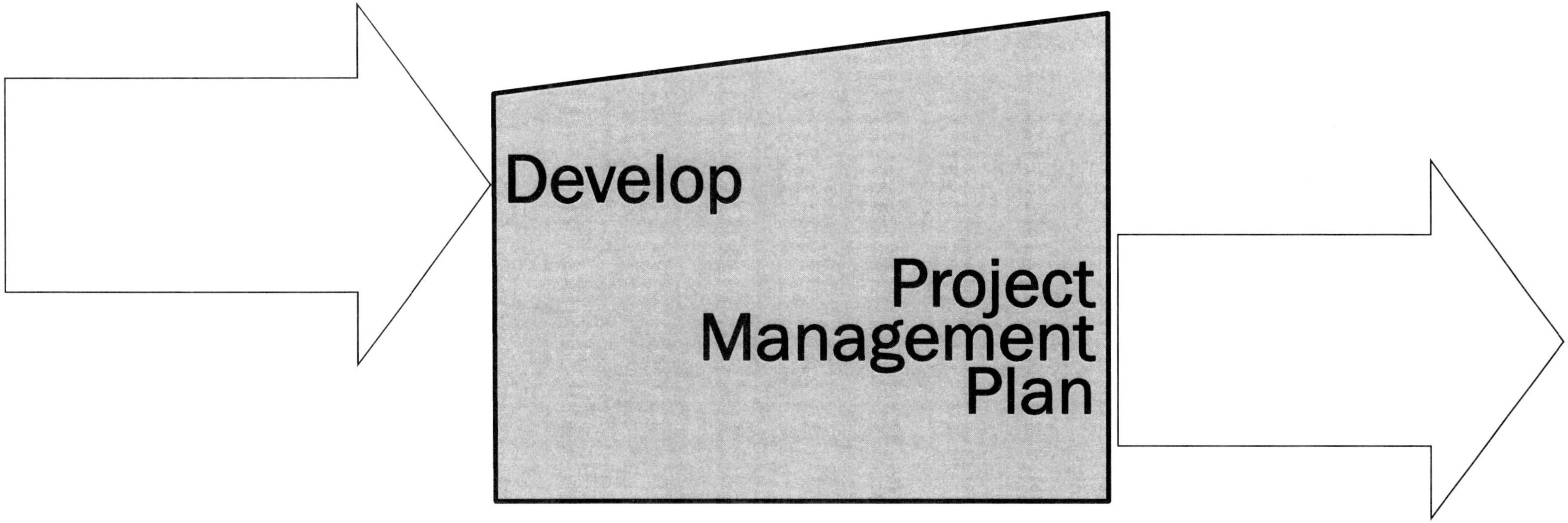

© 2018 Velociteach. All rights reserved.

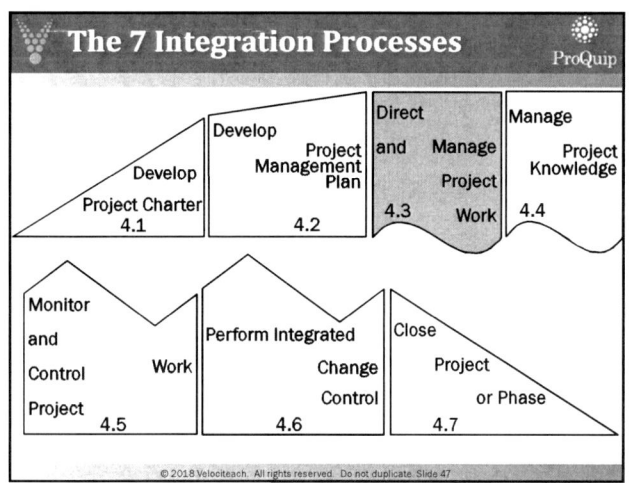

The 7 Integration Processes

- Develop Project Charter 4.1
- Develop Project Management Plan 4.2
- Direct and Manage Project Work 4.3
- Manage Project Knowledge 4.4
- Monitor and Control Project Work 4.5
- Perform Integrated Change Control 4.6
- Close Project or Phase 4.7

© 2018 Velociteach. All rights reserved. Do not duplicate. Slide 47

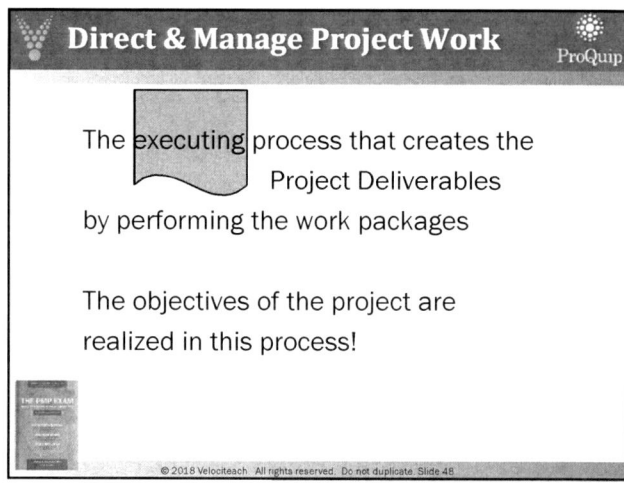

Direct & Manage Project Work

The executing process that creates the Project Deliverables by performing the work packages

The objectives of the project are realized in this process!

© 2018 Velociteach. All rights reserved. Do not duplicate. Slide 48

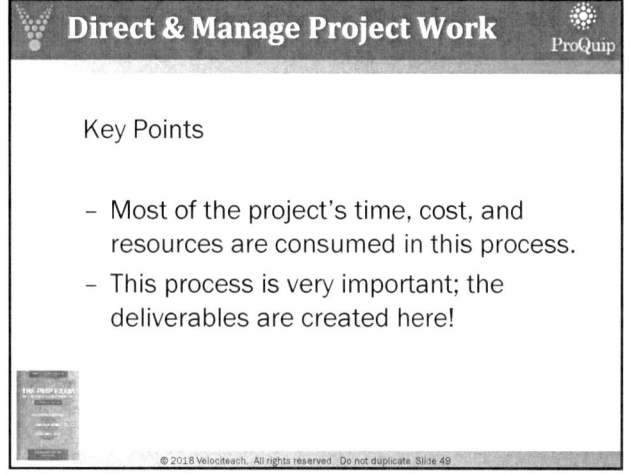

Direct & Manage Project Work

Key Points

- Most of the project's time, cost, and resources are consumed in this process.
- This process is very important; the deliverables are created here!

© 2018 Velociteach. All rights reserved. Do not duplicate. Slide 49

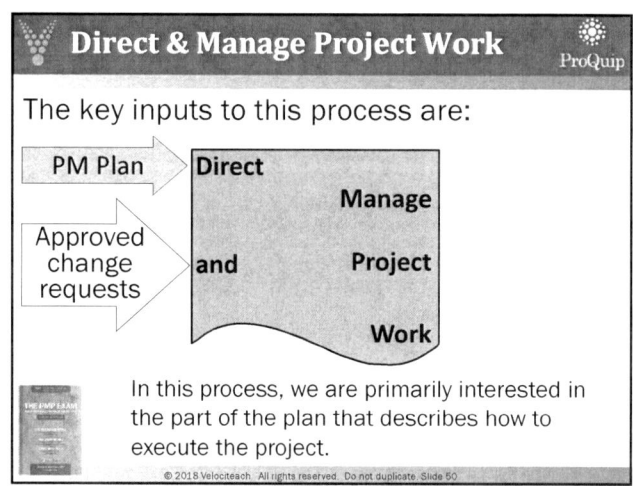

Direct & Manage Project Work

The key inputs to this process are:

- PM Plan
- Approved change requests

Direct and Manage Project Work

In this process, we are primarily interested in the part of the plan that describes how to execute the project.

© 2018 Velociteach. All rights reserved. Do not duplicate. Slide 50

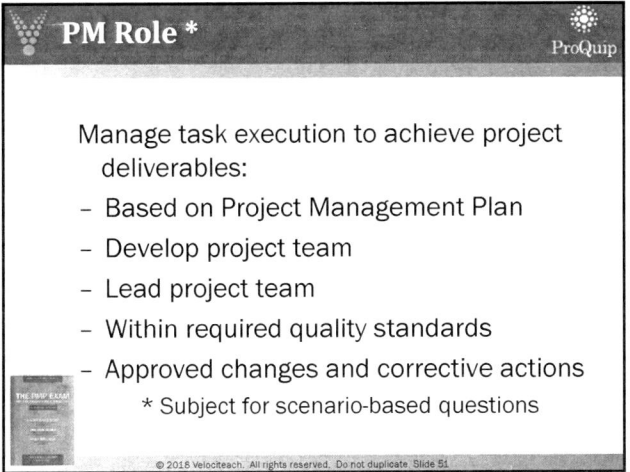

PM Role *

Manage task execution to achieve project deliverables:

- Based on Project Management Plan
- Develop project team
- Lead project team
- Within required quality standards
- Approved changes and corrective actions
  - * Subject for scenario-based questions

© 2018 Velociteach. All rights reserved. Do not duplicate. Slide 51

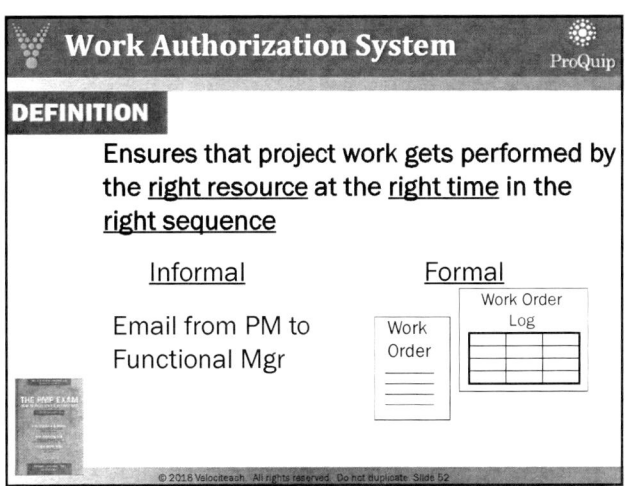

Work Authorization System

DEFINITION

Ensures that project work gets performed by the <u>right resource</u> at the <u>right time</u> in the <u>right sequence</u>

Informal

Email from PM to Functional Mgr

Formal

Work Order

Work Order Log

© 2018 Velociteach. All rights reserved. Do not duplicate. Slide 52

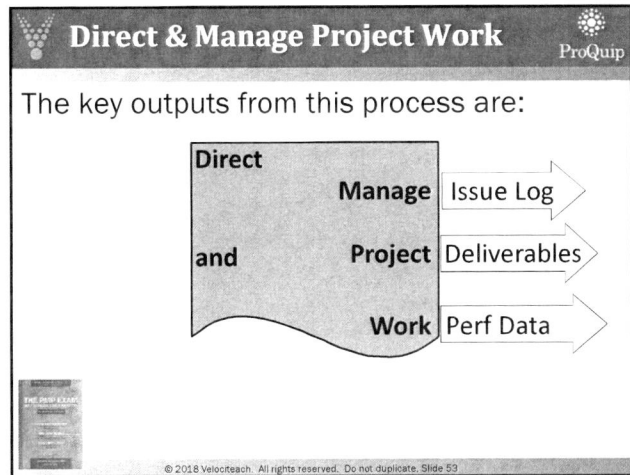

Direct & Manage Project Work

The key outputs from this process are:

Direct

Manage — Issue Log

and

Project — Deliverables

Work — Perf Data

© 2018 Velociteach. All rights reserved. Do not duplicate. Slide 53

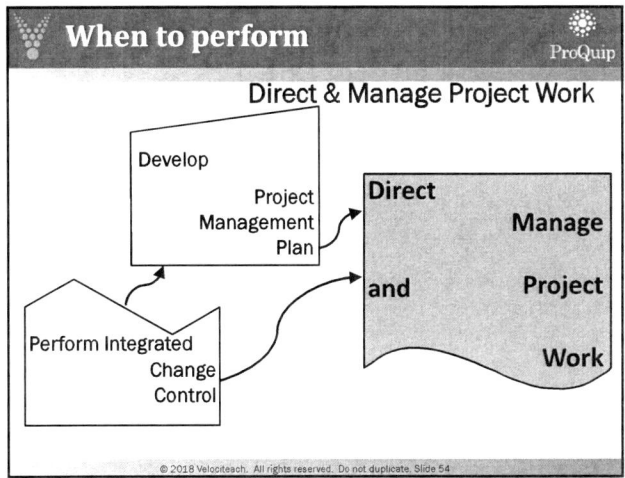

When to perform

Direct & Manage Project Work

Develop Project Management Plan

Perform Integrated Change Control

Direct

Manage

and

Project

Work

© 2018 Velociteach. All rights reserved. Do not duplicate. Slide 54

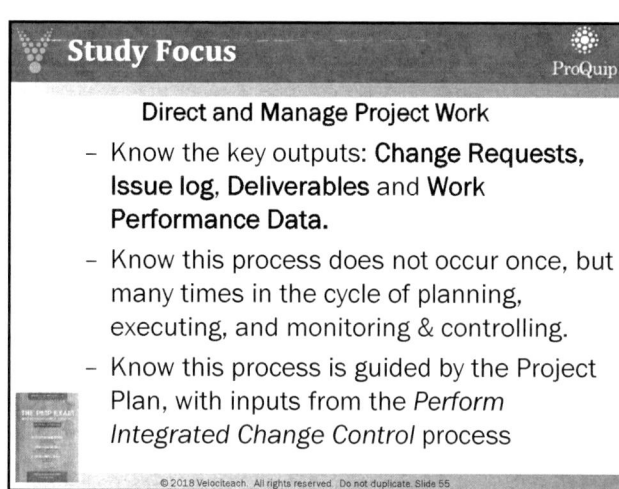

Study Focus

ProQuip

Direct and Manage Project Work

- Know the key outputs: **Change Requests, Issue log, Deliverables** and **Work Performance Data.**

- Know this process does not occur once, but many times in the cycle of planning, executing, and monitoring & controlling.

- Know this process is guided by the Project Plan, with inputs from the *Perform Integrated Change Control* process

© 2018 Velociteach. All rights reserved. Do not duplicate. Slide 55

Review the ITTOs

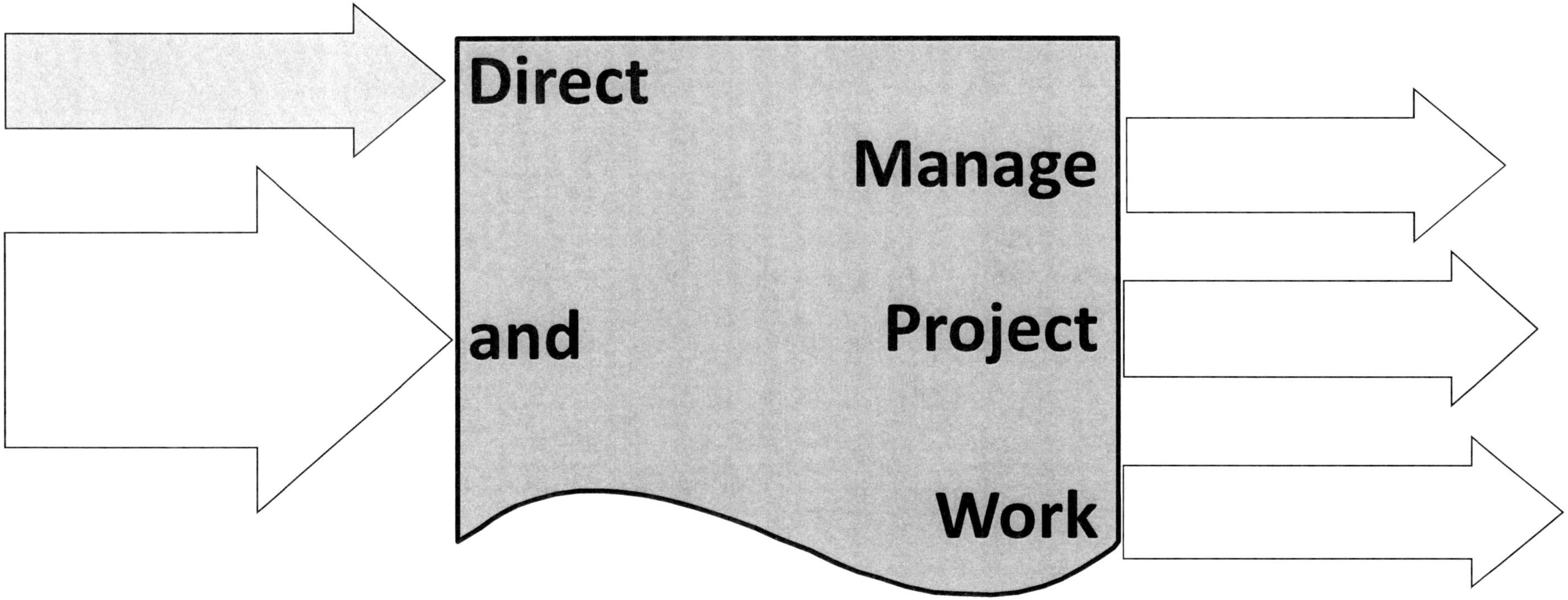

ProQuip

Direct and Manage Project Work

© 2018 Velociteach. All rights reserved.

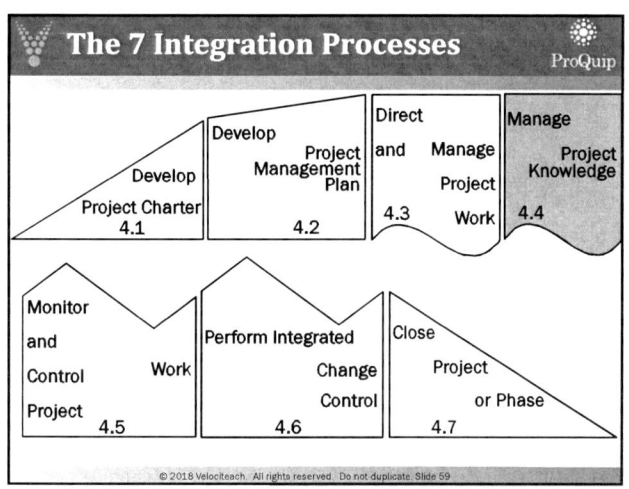

The 7 Integration Processes

Develop Project Charter 4.1

Develop Project Management Plan 4.2

Direct and Manage Project Work 4.3

Manage Project Knowledge 4.4

Monitor and Control Project Work 4.5

Perform Integrated Change Control 4.6

Close Project or Phase 4.7

© 2018 Velociteach. All rights reserved. Do not duplicate. Slide 59

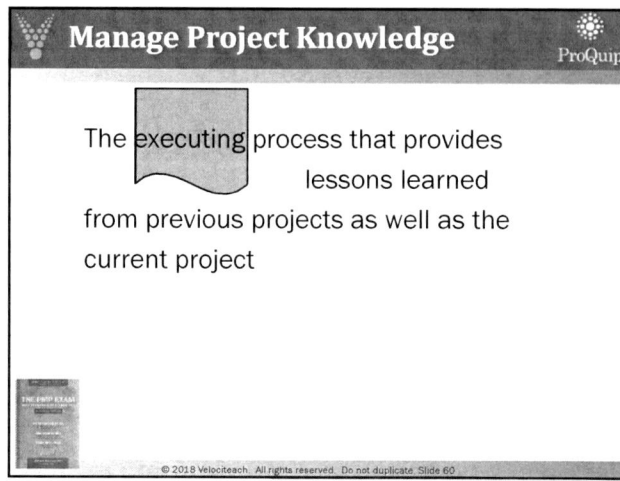

Manage Project Knowledge

The executing process that provides lessons learned from previous projects as well as the current project

© 2018 Velociteach. All rights reserved. Do not duplicate. Slide 60

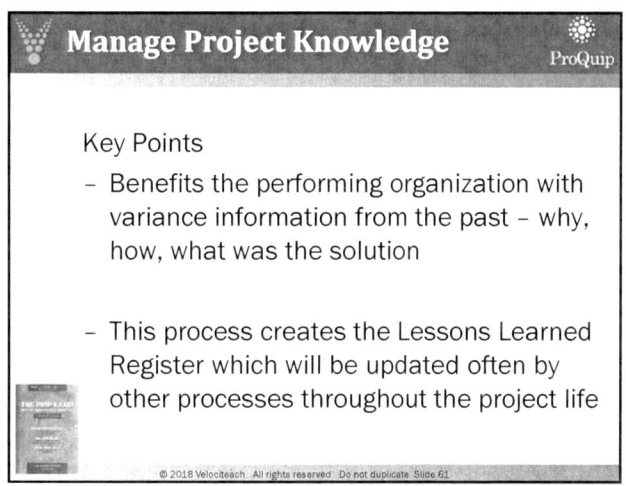

Manage Project Knowledge

Key Points

– Benefits the performing organization with variance information from the past – why, how, what was the solution

– This process creates the Lessons Learned Register which will be updated often by other processes throughout the project life

© 2018 Velociteach. All rights reserved. Do not duplicate. Slide 61

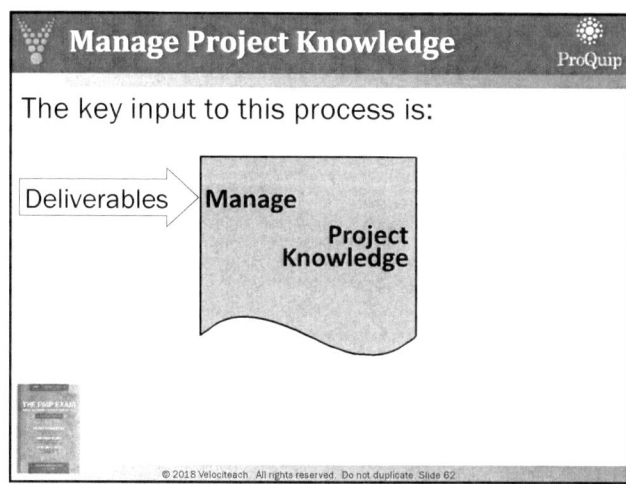

Manage Project Knowledge

The key input to this process is:

Deliverables → Manage Project Knowledge

© 2018 Velociteach. All rights reserved. Do not duplicate. Slide 62

©2018 Velociteach. All rights reserved.

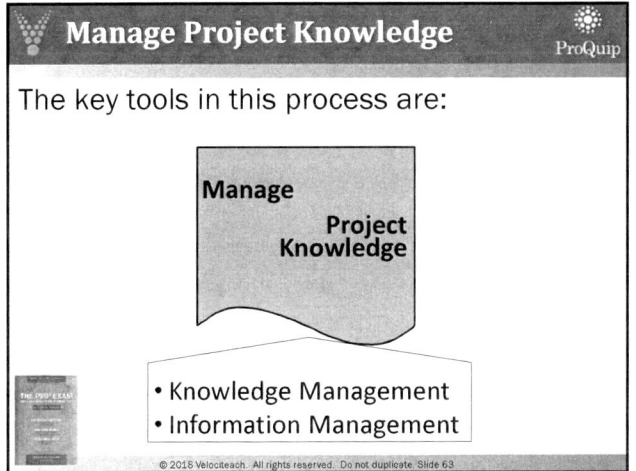

Manage Project Knowledge

The key tools in this process are:

Manage Project Knowledge

- Knowledge Management
- Information Management

© 2018 Velociteach. All rights reserved. Do not duplicate. Slide 63

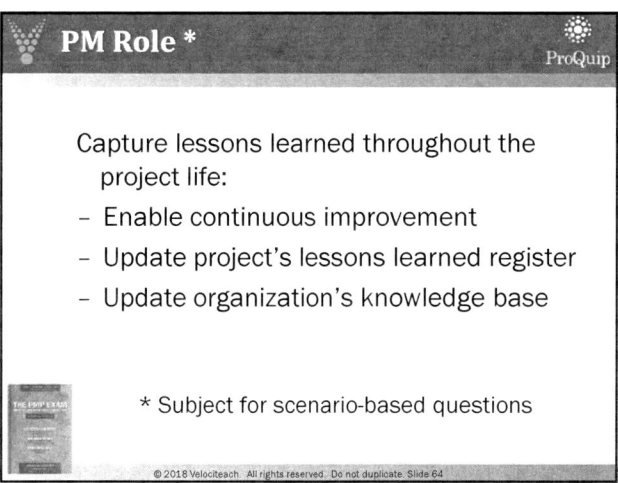

PM Role *

Capture lessons learned throughout the project life:

- Enable continuous improvement
- Update project's lessons learned register
- Update organization's knowledge base

* Subject for scenario-based questions

© 2018 Velociteach. All rights reserved. Do not duplicate. Slide 64

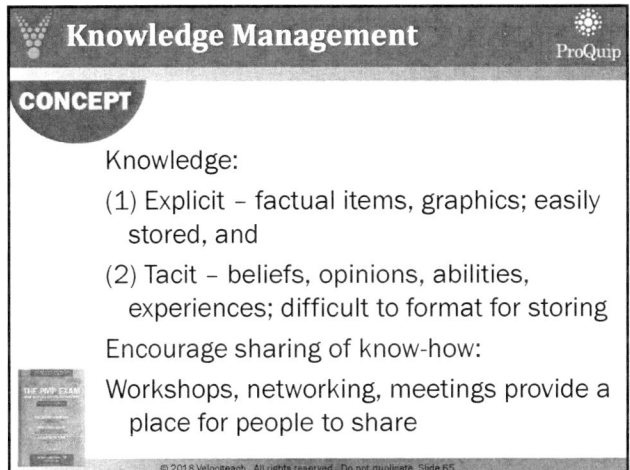

Knowledge Management

CONCEPT

Knowledge:

(1) Explicit – factual items, graphics; easily stored, and

(2) Tacit – beliefs, opinions, abilities, experiences; difficult to format for storing

Encourage sharing of know-how:

Workshops, networking, meetings provide a place for people to share

© 2018 Velociteach. All rights reserved. Do not duplicate. Slide 65

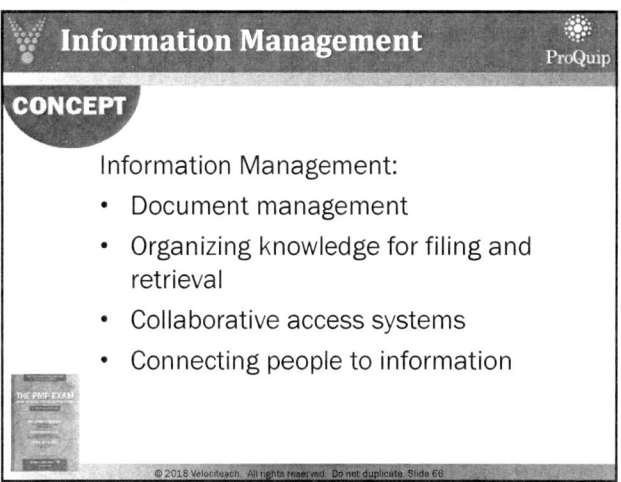

Information Management

CONCEPT

Information Management:

- Document management
- Organizing knowledge for filing and retrieval
- Collaborative access systems
- Connecting people to information

© 2018 Velociteach. All rights reserved. Do not duplicate. Slide 66

PM Role *

Develop project team's knowledge by:

– Promoting interaction and sharing

– Cross-training

– Workshops (connecting people)

– Sharing project lessons learned register

– Access to organization's knowledge base

* Subject for scenario-based questions

© 2018 Velociteach. All rights reserved. Do not duplicate. Slide 67

Manage Project Knowledge

The key output from this process is:

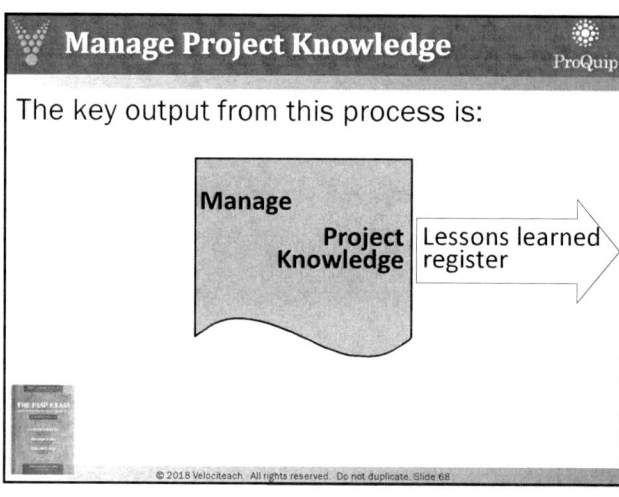

© 2018 Velociteach. All rights reserved. Do not duplicate. Slide 68

When to perform

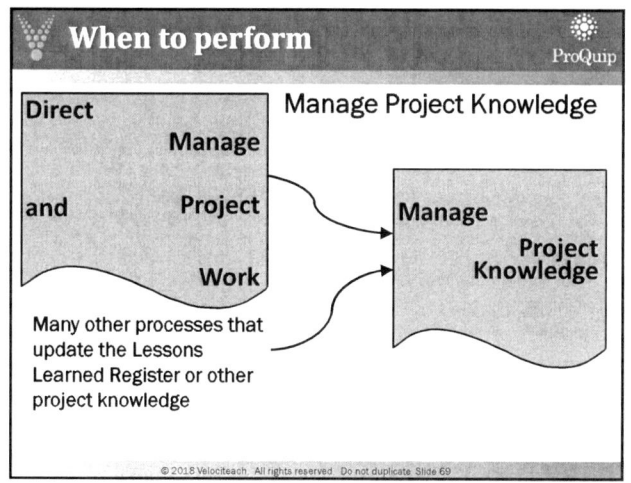

Many other processes that update the Lessons Learned Register or other project knowledge

© 2018 Velociteach. All rights reserved. Do not duplicate. Slide 69

Study Focus

Manage Project Knowledge

– Know the key output: Lessons Learned Register.

– Know this process does not occur once, but many times in the project life.

– Know the nuance between Knowledge Management and Information Management.

© 2018 Velociteach. All rights reserved. Do not duplicate. Slide 70

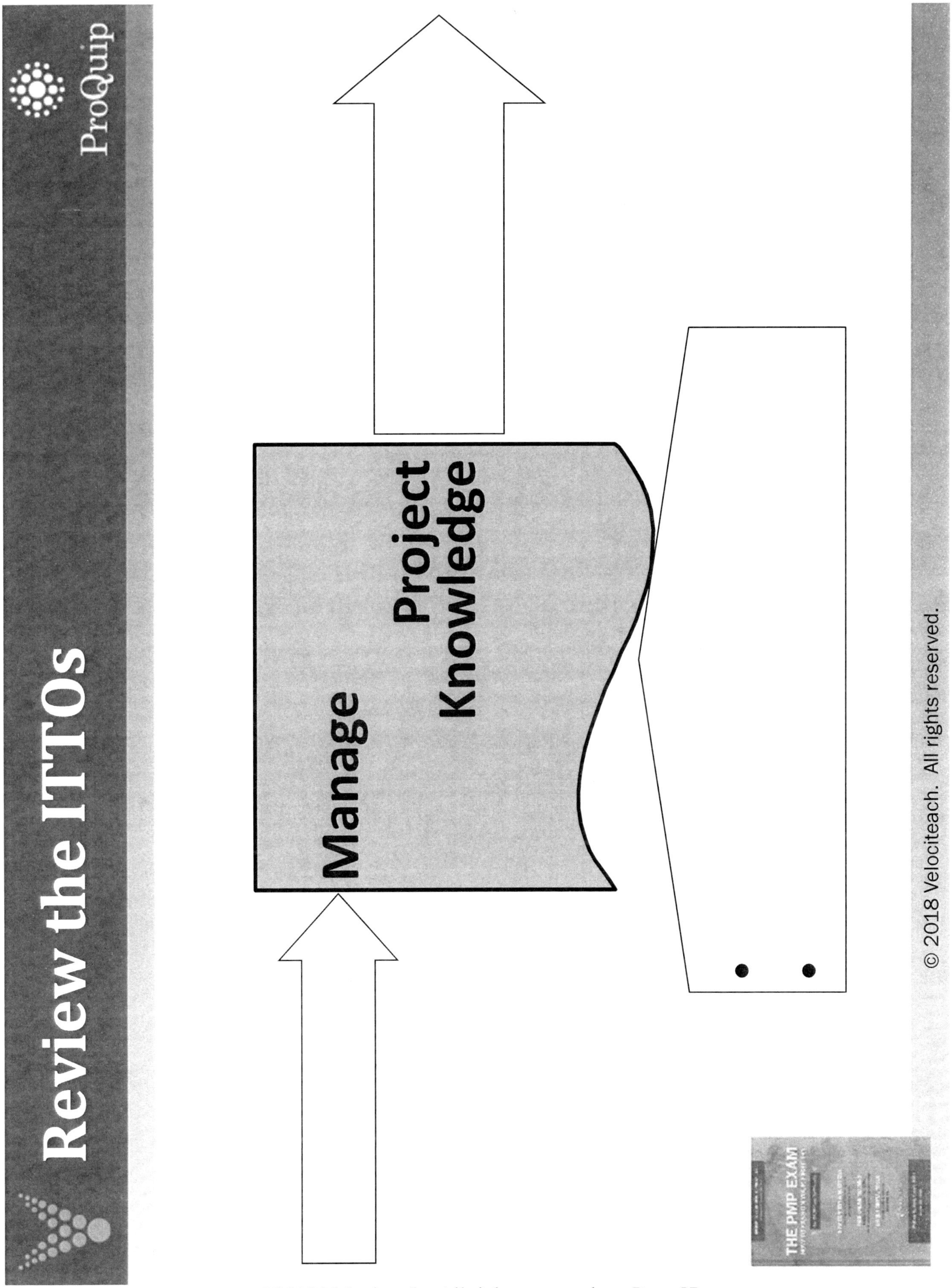

Review the ITTOs

Manage Project Knowledge

© 2018 Velociteach. All rights reserved.

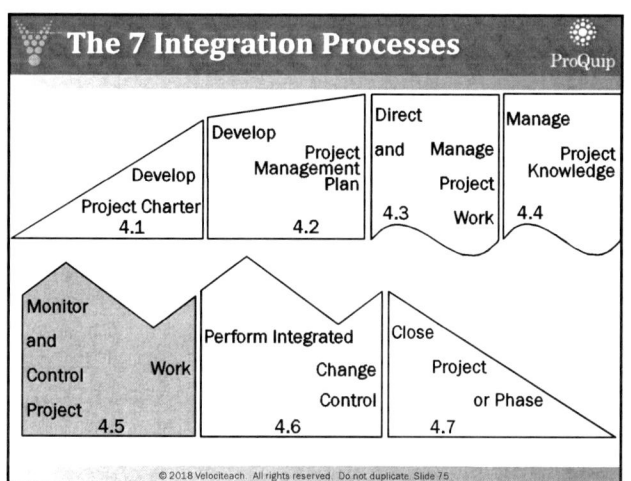

The 7 Integration Processes

Develop Project Charter 4.1

Develop Project Management Plan 4.2

Direct and Manage Project Work 4.3

Manage Project Knowledge 4.4

Monitor and Control Project Work 4.5

Perform Integrated Change Control 4.6

Close Project or Phase 4.7

© 2018 Velociteach. All rights reserved. Do not duplicate. Slide 75

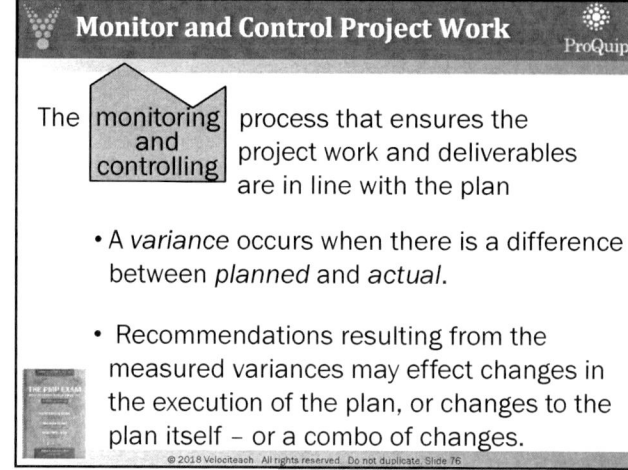

Monitor and Control Project Work

The monitoring and controlling process that ensures the project work and deliverables are in line with the plan

• A *variance* occurs when there is a difference between *planned* and *actual*.

• Recommendations resulting from the measured variances may effect changes in the execution of the plan, or changes to the plan itself – or a combo of changes.

© 2018 Velociteach. All rights reserved. Do not duplicate. Slide 76

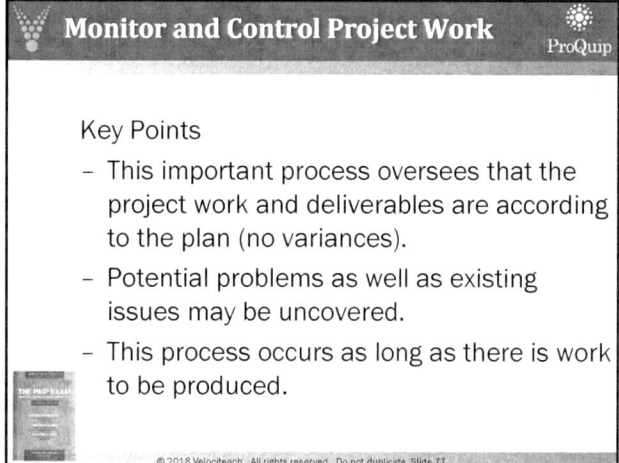

Monitor and Control Project Work

Key Points

– This important process oversees that the project work and deliverables are according to the plan (no variances).

– Potential problems as well as existing issues may be uncovered.

– This process occurs as long as there is work to be produced.

© 2018 Velociteach. All rights reserved. Do not duplicate. Slide 77

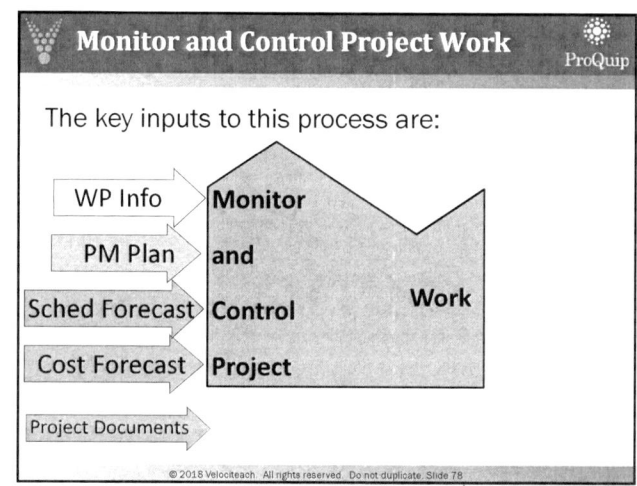

Monitor and Control Project Work

The key inputs to this process are:

WP Info

PM Plan

Sched Forecast

Cost Forecast

Project Documents

Monitor and Control Project Work

© 2018 Velociteach. All rights reserved. Do not duplicate. Slide 78

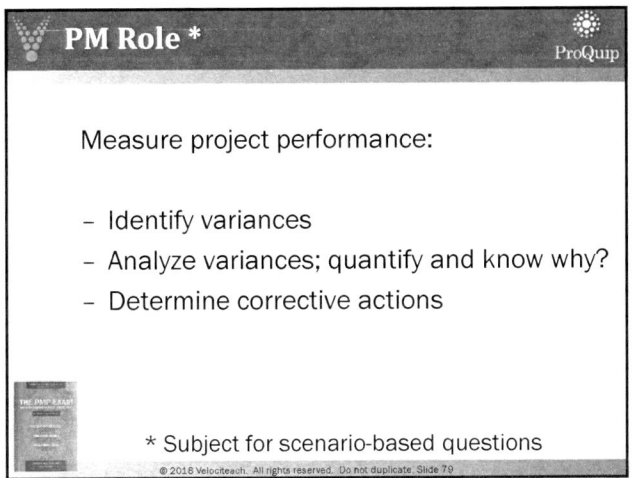

PM Role *

Measure project performance:

- Identify variances
- Analyze variances; quantify and know why?
- Determine corrective actions

* Subject for scenario-based questions

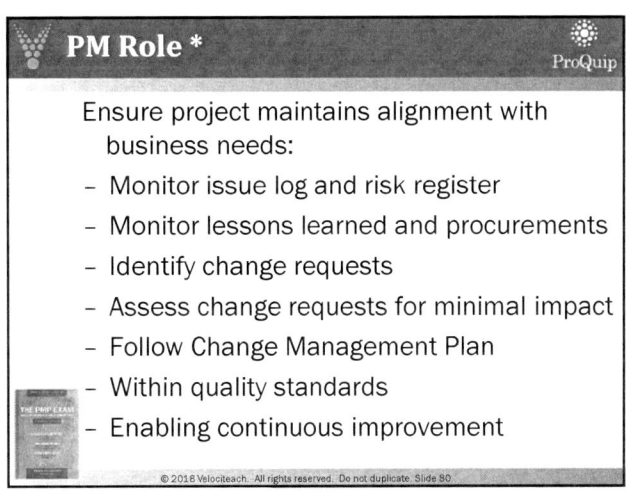

PM Role *

Ensure project maintains alignment with business needs:
- Monitor issue log and risk register
- Monitor lessons learned and procurements
- Identify change requests
- Assess change requests for minimal impact
- Follow Change Management Plan
- Within quality standards
- Enabling continuous improvement

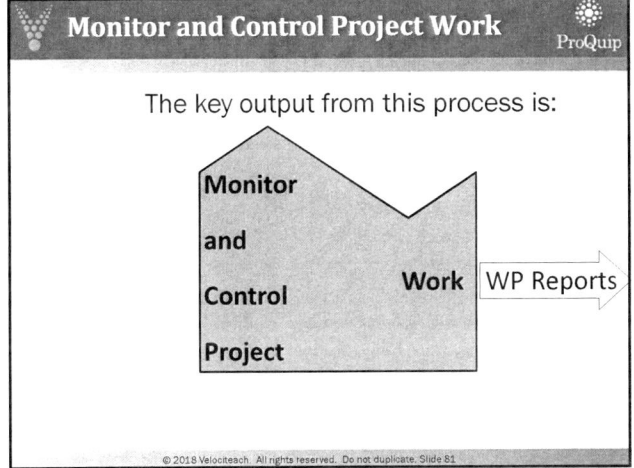

Monitor and Control Project Work

The key output from this process is:

Monitor and Control Project Work → WP Reports

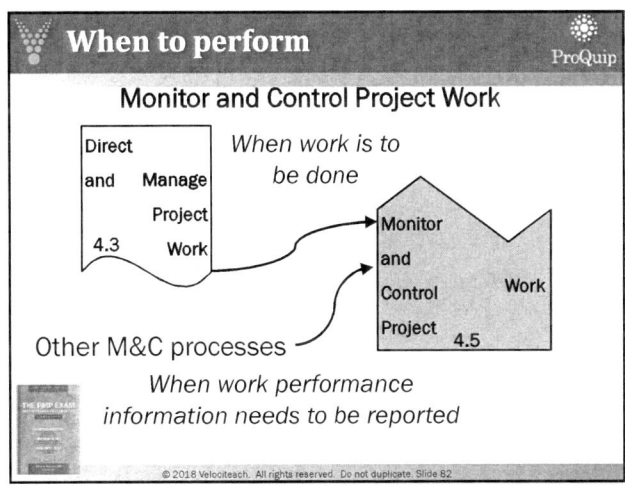

When to perform

Monitor and Control Project Work

Direct and Manage Project Work 4.3

When work is to be done

Monitor and Control Project Work 4.5

Other M&C processes

When work performance information needs to be reported

©2018 Velociteach. All rights reserved.

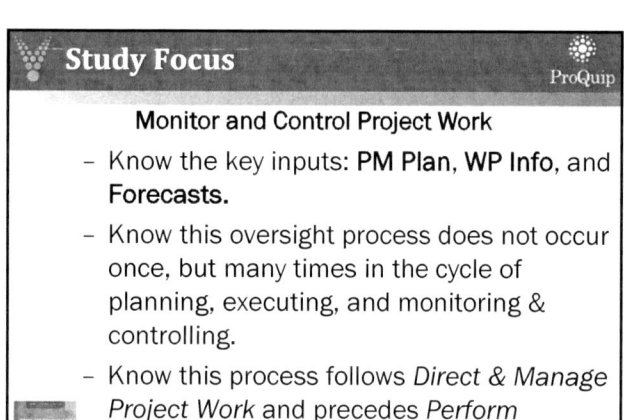

Study Focus

ProQuip

Monitor and Control Project Work

- Know the key inputs: **PM Plan, WP Info,** and **Forecasts.**

- Know this oversight process does not occur once, but many times in the cycle of planning, executing, and monitoring & controlling.

- Know this process follows *Direct & Manage Project Work* and precedes *Perform Integrated Change Control (next)*

© 2018 Velociteach. All rights reserved. Do not duplicate. Slide 83

Review the ITTOs

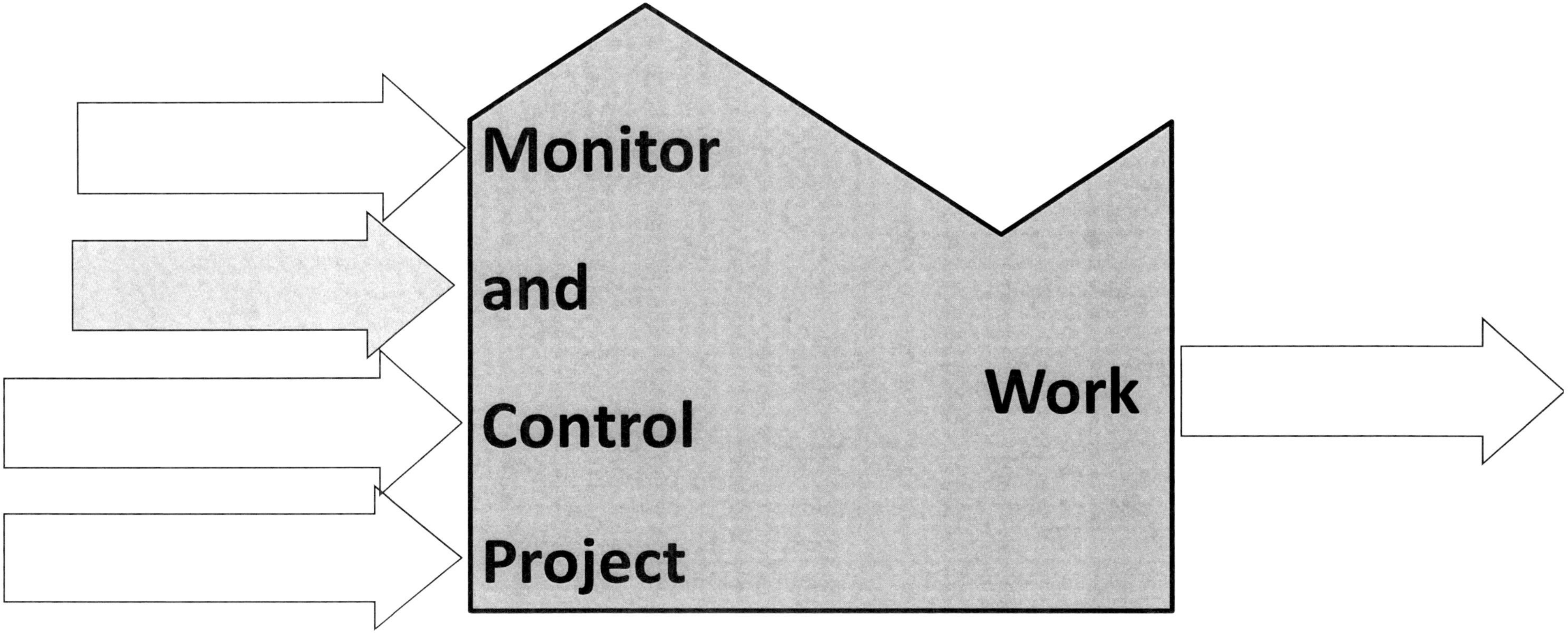

Monitor and Control Project Work

© 2018 Velociteach. All rights reserved.

This page left intentionally blank.

©2018 Velociteach. All rights reserved.

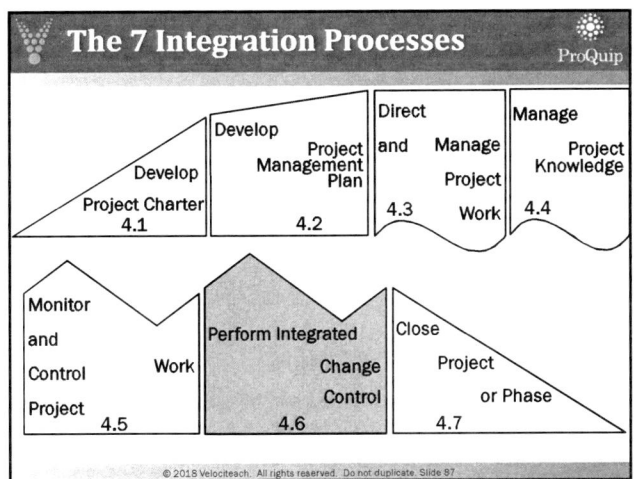

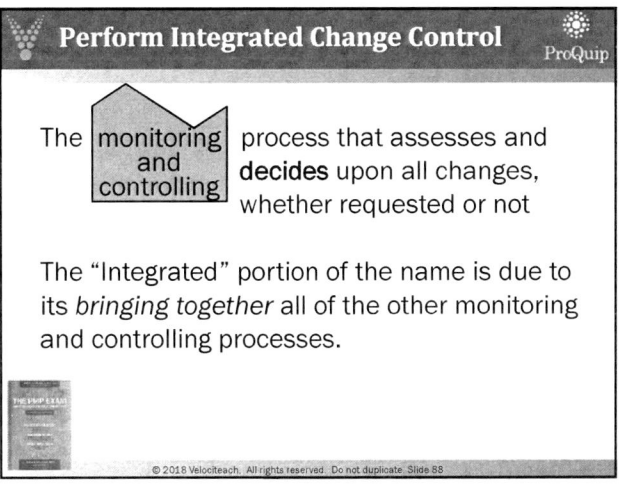

The 7 Integration Processes slide shows:
- Develop Project Charter 4.1
- Develop Project Management Plan 4.2
- Direct and Manage Project Work 4.3
- Manage Project Knowledge 4.4
- Monitor and Control Project Work 4.5
- Perform Integrated Change Control 4.6
- Close Project or Phase 4.7

Perform Integrated Change Control slide:

The monitoring and controlling process that assesses and **decides** upon all changes, whether requested or not

The "Integrated" portion of the name is due to its *bringing together* all of the other monitoring and controlling processes.

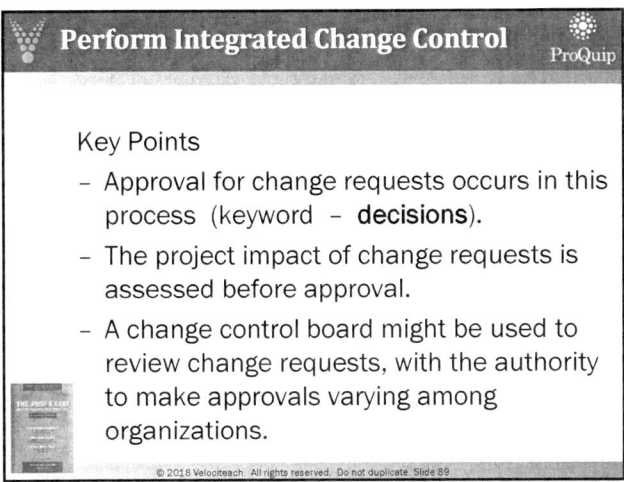

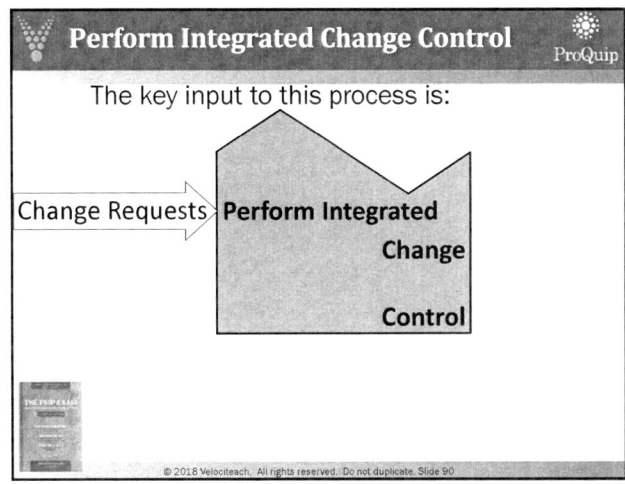

Perform Integrated Change Control

Key Points
- Approval for change requests occurs in this process (keyword – **decisions**).
- The project impact of change requests is assessed before approval.
- A change control board might be used to review change requests, with the authority to make approvals varying among organizations.

Perform Integrated Change Control

The key input to this process is:

Change Requests → **Perform Integrated Change Control**

© 2018 Velociteach. All rights reserved. Do not duplicate. Slide 87
© 2018 Velociteach. All rights reserved. Do not duplicate. Slide 88
© 2018 Velociteach. All rights reserved. Do not duplicate. Slide 89
© 2018 Velociteach. All rights reserved. Do not duplicate. Slide 90

PM Role *

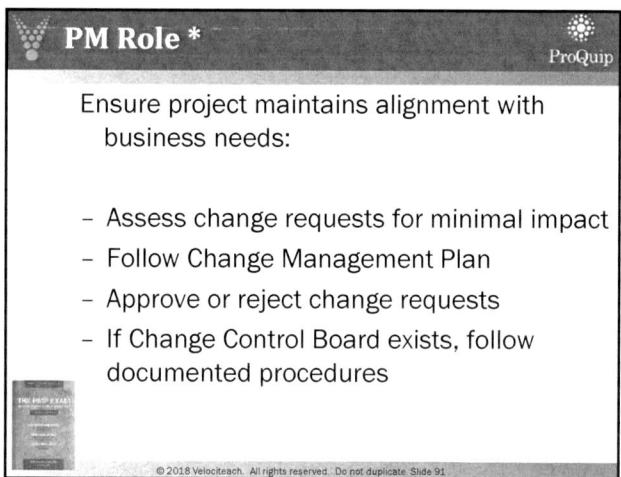

Ensure project maintains alignment with business needs:

- Assess change requests for minimal impact
- Follow Change Management Plan
- Approve or reject change requests
- If Change Control Board exists, follow documented procedures

© 2018 Velociteach. All rights reserved. Do not duplicate. Slide 91

Perform Integrated Change Control

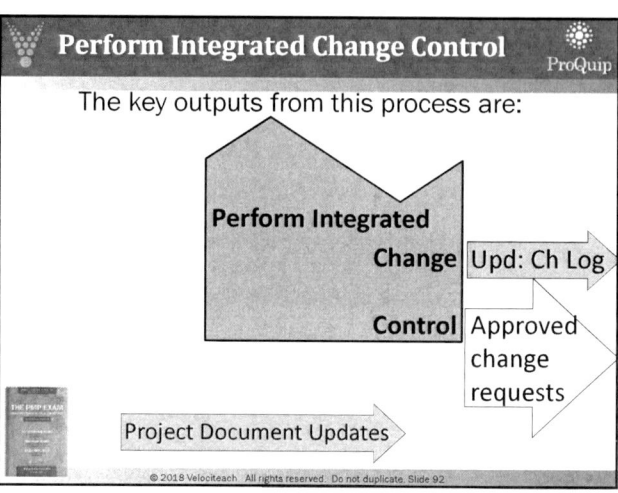

The key outputs from this process are:

Perform Integrated Change Control

Upd: Ch Log

Approved change requests

Project Document Updates

© 2018 Velociteach. All rights reserved. Do not duplicate. Slide 92

When to perform

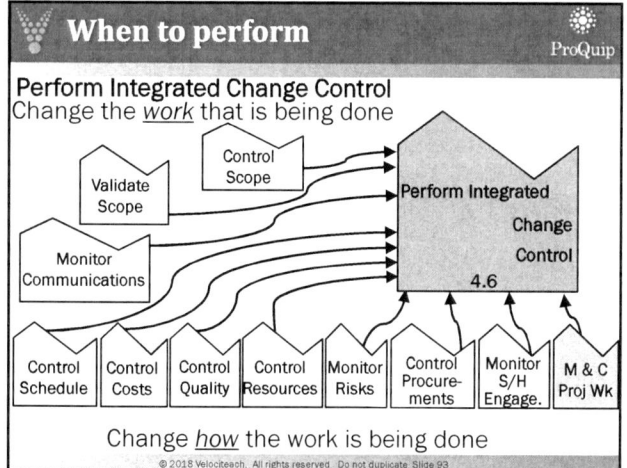

Perform Integrated Change Control
Change the *work* that is being done

Validate Scope

Control Scope

Monitor Communications

Perform Integrated Change Control 4.6

Control Schedule | Control Costs | Control Quality | Control Resources | Monitor Risks | Control Procure-ments | Monitor S/H Engage. | M & C Proj Wk

Change *how* the work is being done

© 2018 Velociteach. All rights reserved. Do not duplicate. Slide 93

Study Focus

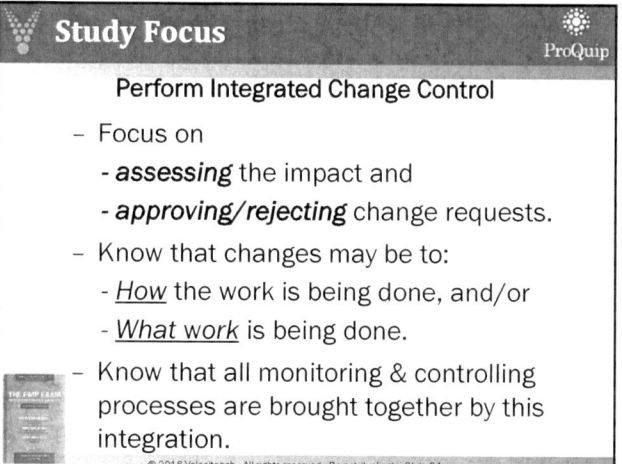

Perform Integrated Change Control

- Focus on
  - *assessing* the impact and
  - *approving/rejecting* change requests.
- Know that changes may be to:
  - *How* the work is being done, and/or
  - *What work* is being done.
- Know that all monitoring & controlling processes are brought together by this integration.

© 2018 Velociteach. All rights reserved. Do not duplicate. Slide 94

©2018 Velociteach. All rights reserved. Page 64

Review the ITTOs

Perform Integrated Change Control

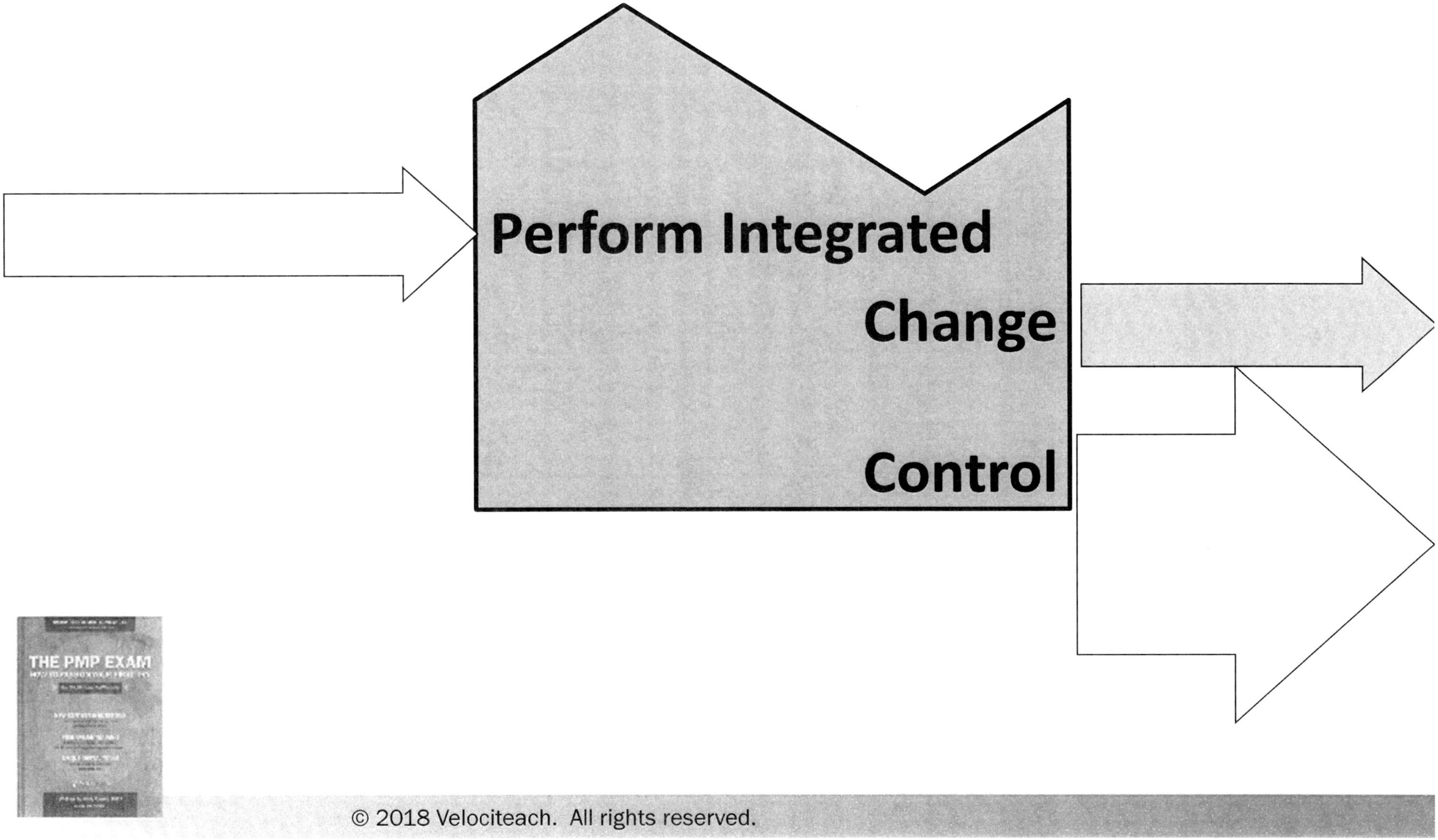

© 2018 Velociteach. All rights reserved.

This page left intentionally blank.

©2018 Velociteach. All rights reserved.

The 7 Integration Processes

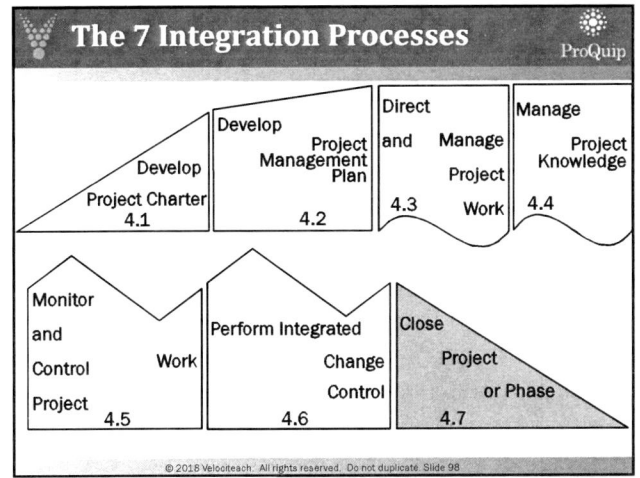

© 2018 Velociteach. All rights reserved. Do not duplicate. Slide 98

Close Project or Phase

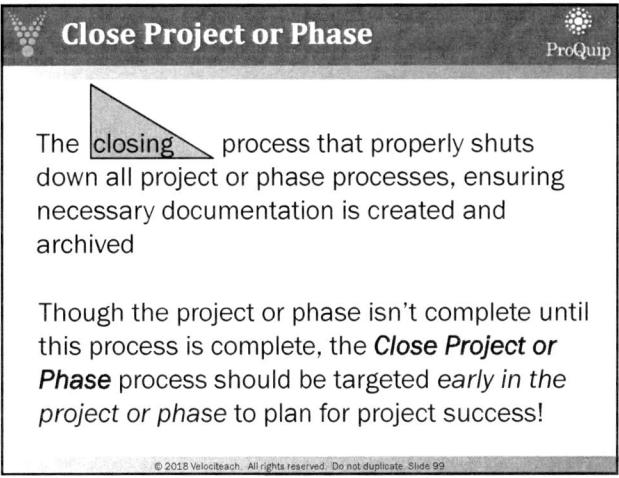

The closing process that properly shuts down all project or phase processes, ensuring necessary documentation is created and archived

Though the project or phase isn't complete until this process is complete, the *Close Project or Phase* process should be targeted *early in the project or phase* to plan for project success!

© 2018 Velociteach. All rights reserved. Do not duplicate. Slide 99

Close Project or Phase

Key Points
- This is always the last process to be completed.
- Finalize "Lessons Learned" to help prevent future projects or phases from similar mistakes.
- *Transition* of the ownership of the deliverable is key
- No more change requests!

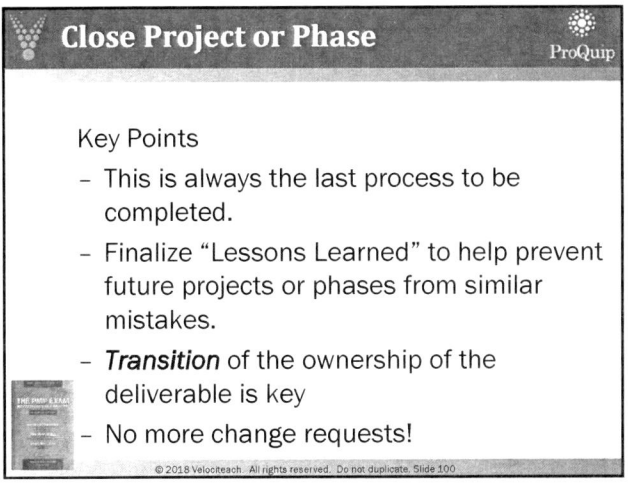

© 2018 Velociteach. All rights reserved. Do not duplicate. Slide 100

Close Project or Phase

The focal input to this process is:

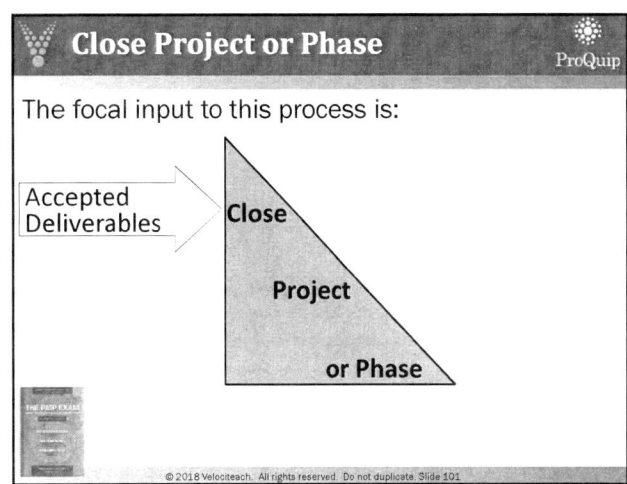

© 2018 Velociteach. All rights reserved. Do not duplicate. Slide 101

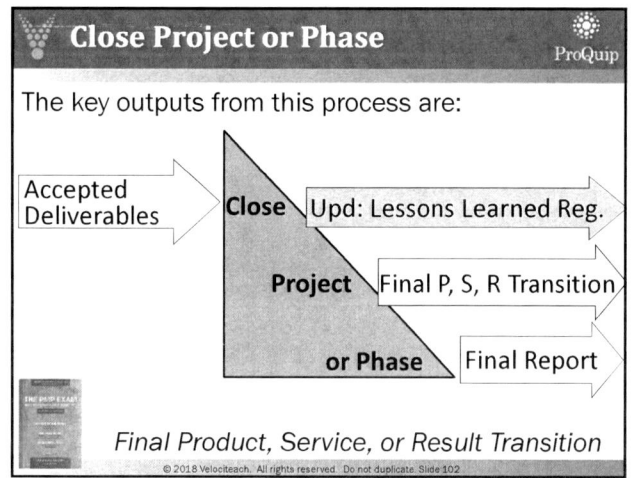

Close Project or Phase

The key outputs from this process are:

Accepted Deliverables → **Close** Upd: Lessons Learned Reg.

Project Final P, S, R Transition

or Phase Final Report

Final Product, Service, or Result Transition

© 2018 Velociteach. All rights reserved. Do not duplicate. Slide 102

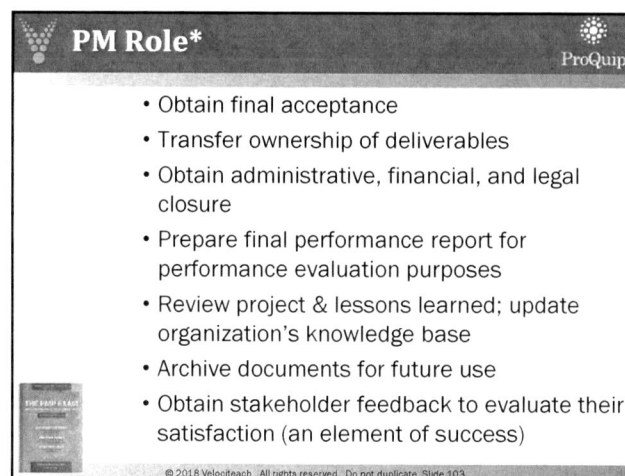

PM Role*

- Obtain final acceptance
- Transfer ownership of deliverables
- Obtain administrative, financial, and legal closure
- Prepare final performance report for performance evaluation purposes
- Review project & lessons learned; update organization's knowledge base
- Archive documents for future use
- Obtain stakeholder feedback to evaluate their satisfaction (an element of success)

© 2018 Velociteach. All rights reserved. Do not duplicate. Slide 103

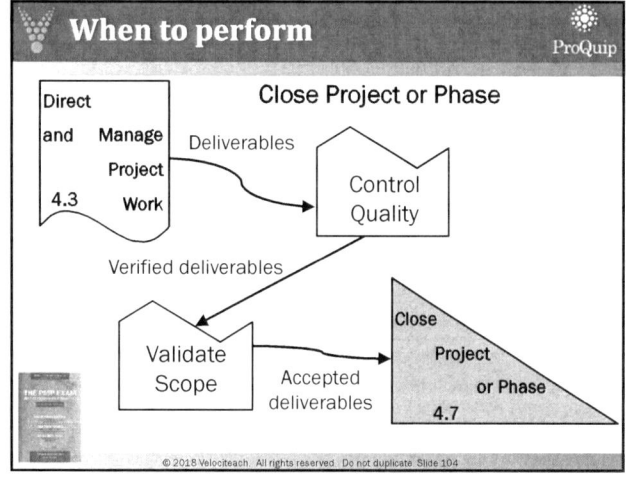

When to perform

Close Project or Phase

Direct and Manage Project 4.3 Work — Deliverables → Control Quality

Verified deliverables → Validate Scope — Accepted deliverables → Close Project or Phase 4.7

© 2018 Velociteach. All rights reserved. Do not duplicate. Slide 104

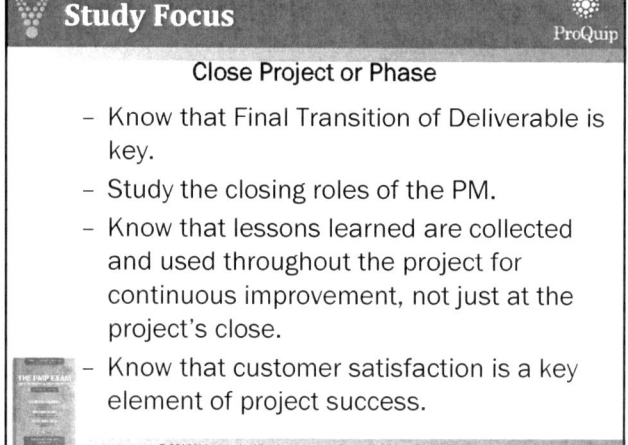

Study Focus

Close Project or Phase

- Know that Final Transition of Deliverable is key.
- Study the closing roles of the PM.
- Know that lessons learned are collected and used throughout the project for continuous improvement, not just at the project's close.
- Know that customer satisfaction is a key element of project success.

© 2018 Velociteach. All rights reserved. Do not duplicate. Slide 105

Review the ITTOs

Close Project or Phase

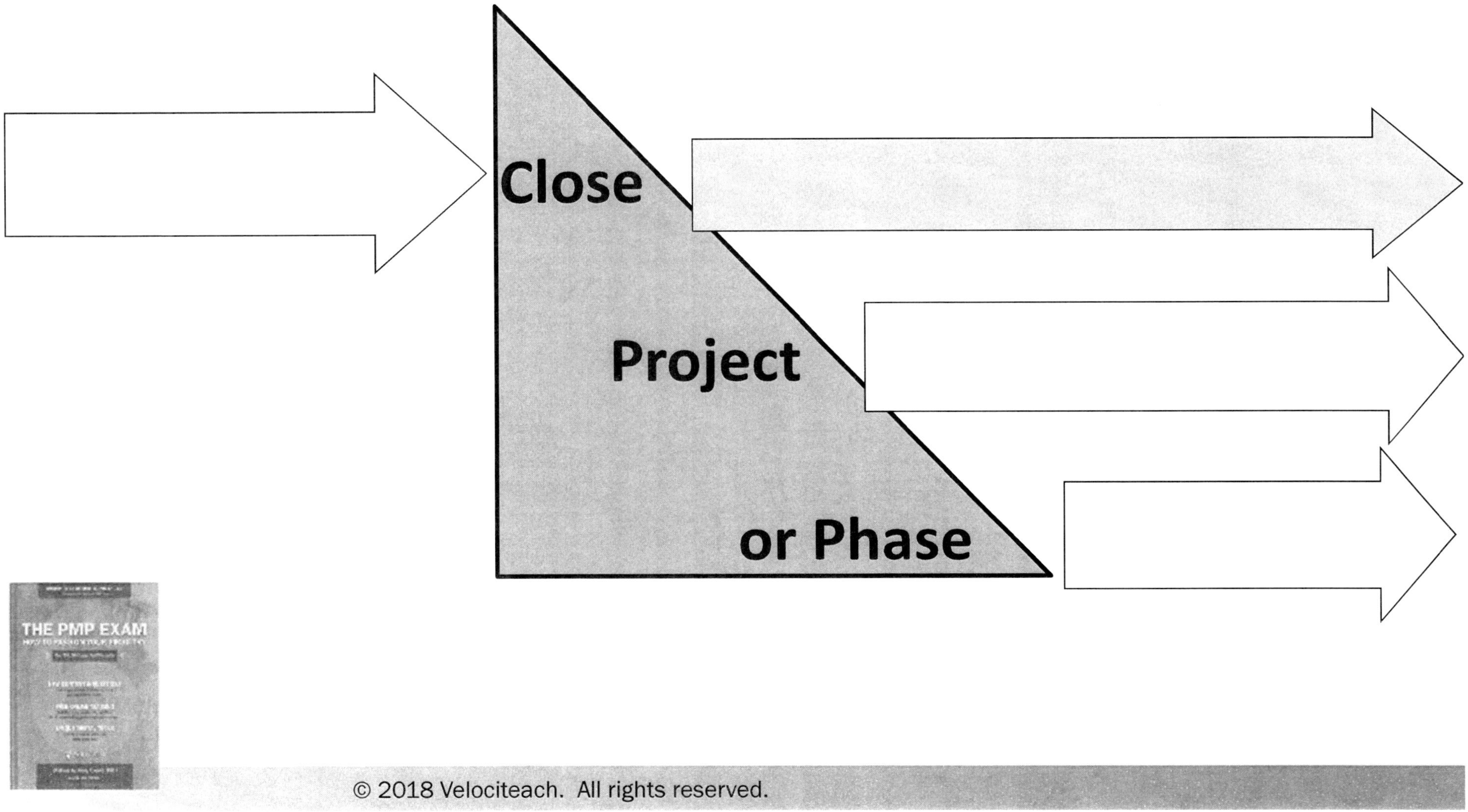

© 2018 Velociteach. All rights reserved.

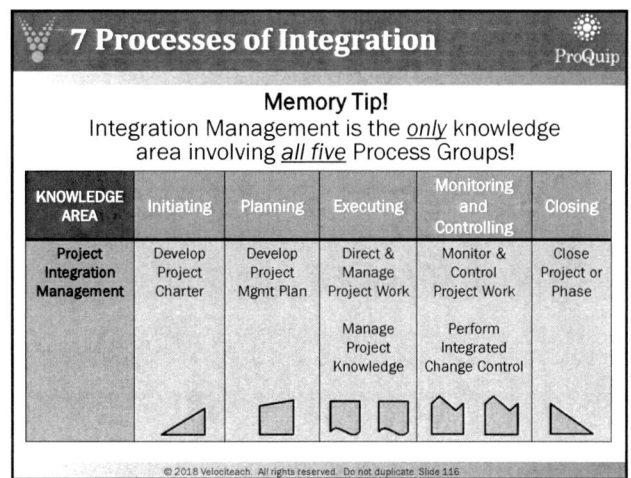

7 Processes of Integration

ProQuip

Memory Tip!
Integration Management is the *only* knowledge area involving *all five* Process Groups!

KNOWLEDGE AREA	Initiating	Planning	Executing	Monitoring and Controlling	Closing
Project Integration Management	Develop Project Charter	Develop Project Mgmt Plan	Direct & Manage Project Work	Monitor & Control Project Work	Close Project or Phase
			Manage Project Knowledge	Perform Integrated Change Control	

© 2018 Velociteach. All rights reserved. Do not duplicate. Slide 116

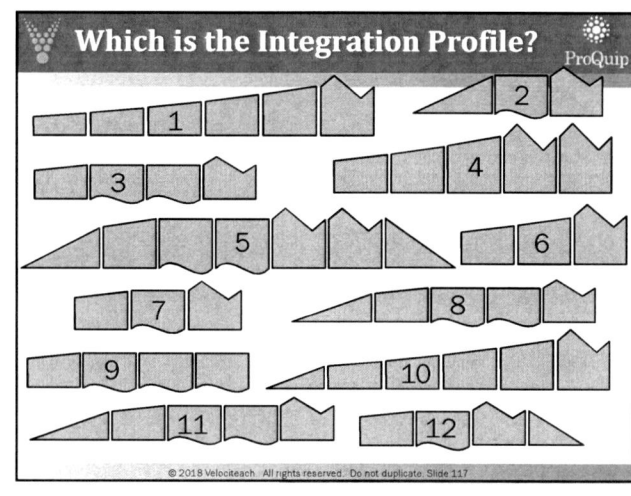

Which is the Integration Profile?

ProQuip

© 2018 Velociteach. All rights reserved. Do not duplicate. Slide 117

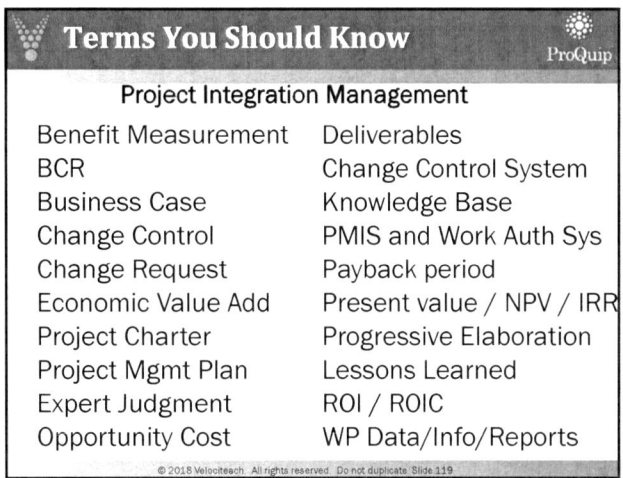

Terms You Should Know

ProQuip

Project Integration Management

Benefit Measurement	Deliverables
BCR	Change Control System
Business Case	Knowledge Base
Change Control	PMIS and Work Auth Sys
Change Request	Payback period
Economic Value Add	Present value / NPV / IRR
Project Charter	Progressive Elaboration
Project Mgmt Plan	Lessons Learned
Expert Judgment	ROI / ROIC
Opportunity Cost	WP Data/Info/Reports

© 2018 Velociteach. All rights reserved. Do not duplicate. Slide 119

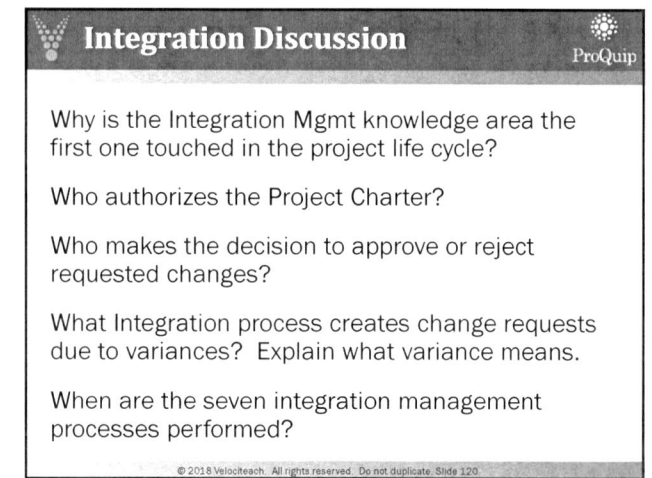

Integration Discussion

ProQuip

Why is the Integration Mgmt knowledge area the first one touched in the project life cycle?

Who authorizes the Project Charter?

Who makes the decision to approve or reject requested changes?

What Integration process creates change requests due to variances? Explain what variance means.

When are the seven integration management processes performed?

© 2018 Velociteach. All rights reserved. Do not duplicate. Slide 120

Summary

ProQuip

Knowledge Area

KNOWLEDGE AREA	Initiating	Planning	Executing	Monitoring and Controlling	Closing
Project Management					

©2018 Velociteach. All rights reserved.

Score Sheet	**Integration Mgmt Exam**	 Velociteach

- Mark one answer: A, B, C, or D.
- Circle the '?' symbol if you are guessing at the answer.
- Circle the Δ symbol if you change your answer.

Total Correct: _____

% Correct: _____%

1.	A O	B O	C O	D O	? Δ
2.	A O	B O	C O	D O	? Δ
3.	A O	B O	C O	D O	? Δ
4.	A O	B O	C O	D O	? Δ
5.	A O	B O	C O	D O	? Δ
6.	A O	B O	C O	D O	? Δ
7.	A O	B O	C O	D O	? Δ
8.	A O	B O	C O	D O	? Δ
9.	A O	B O	C O	D O	? Δ
10.	A O	B O	C O	D O	? Δ
11.	A O	B O	C O	D O	? Δ
12.	A O	B O	C O	D O	? Δ
13.	A O	B O	C O	D O	? Δ
14.	A O	B O	C O	D O	? Δ
15.	A O	B O	C O	D O	? Δ
16.	A O	B O	C O	D O	? Δ
17.	A O	B O	C O	D O	? Δ
18.	A O	B O	C O	D O	? Δ
19.	A O	B O	C O	D O	? Δ
20.	A O	B O	C O	D O	? Δ
21.	A O	B O	C O	D O	? Δ
22.	A O	B O	C O	D O	? Δ
23.	A O	B O	C O	D O	? Δ
24.	A O	B O	C O	D O	? Δ
25.	A O	B O	C O	D O	? Δ

Project Scope Management

Course Module 5

PMBOK® Guide Chapter 5

PMP® Exam Textbook Chapter 5

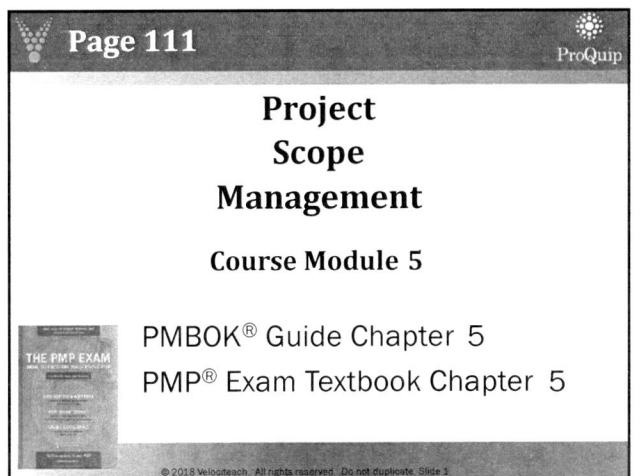

© 2018 Velociteach. All rights reserved. Do not duplicate. Slide 1

Scope Management

What does this knowledge area involve?
- Collecting the stakeholders' requirements
- Planning the scope of the project
- Understanding and documenting the scope
- Breaking the scope down into manageable components
- Controlling the scope for acceptance
- Eliminating "scope creep"

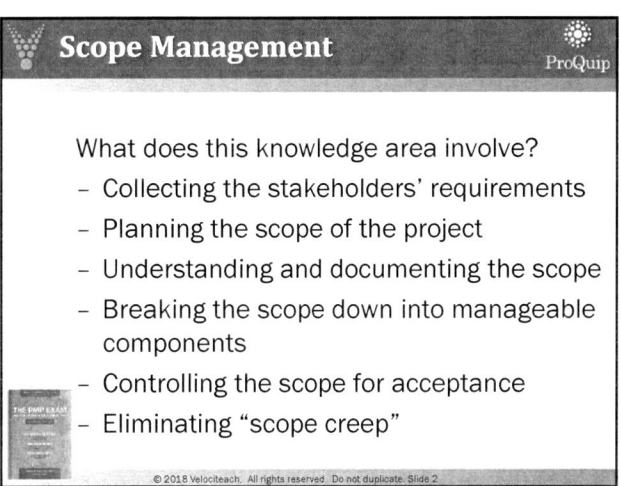

© 2018 Velociteach. All rights reserved. Do not duplicate. Slide 2

Scope Management

Project Scope Management processes:

plan, — the scope,

define, and — changes to the scope, and

manage — the acceptance of the project's product.

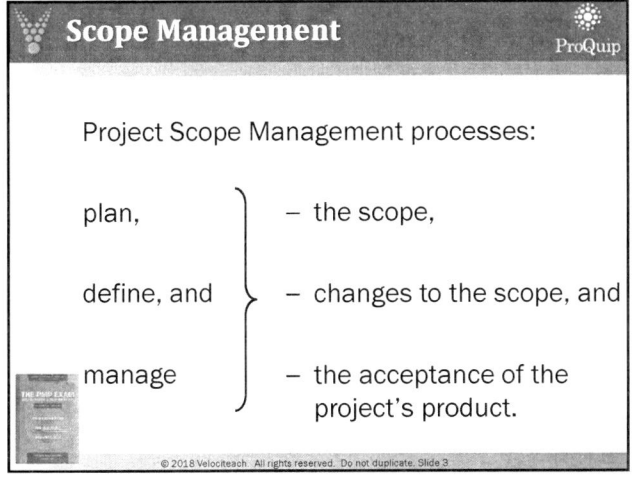

© 2018 Velociteach. All rights reserved. Do not duplicate. Slide 3

PMI® Philosophy: Scope Mgmt

1. The Project Manager must define and document the scope and manage the processes.

2. Changes should be handled in a structured and controlled manner.

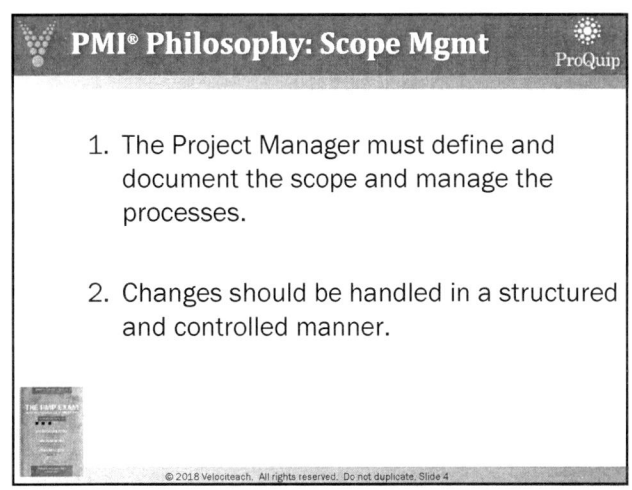

© 2018 Velociteach. All rights reserved. Do not duplicate. Slide 4

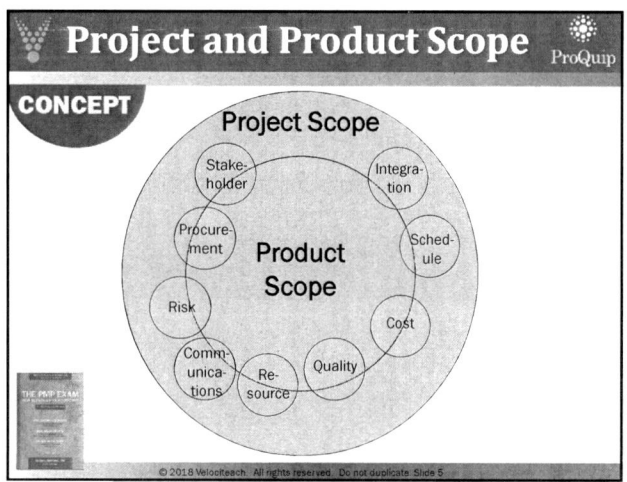

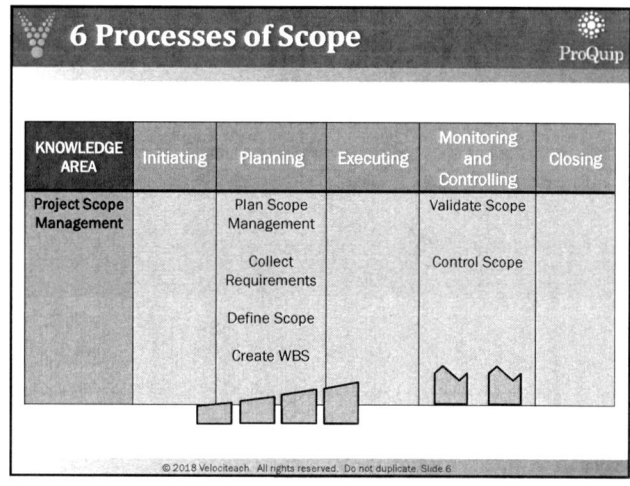

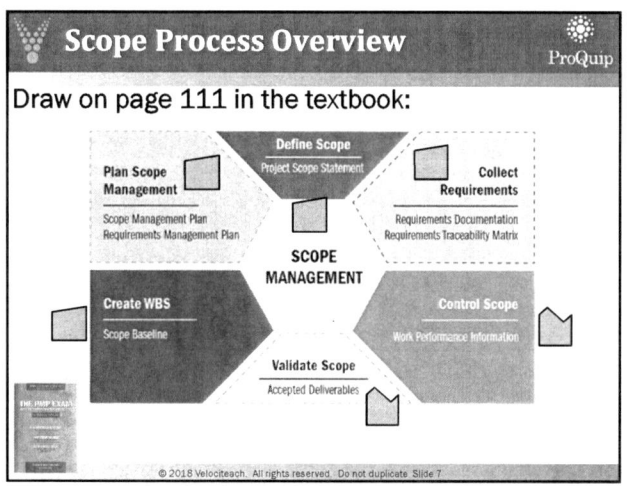

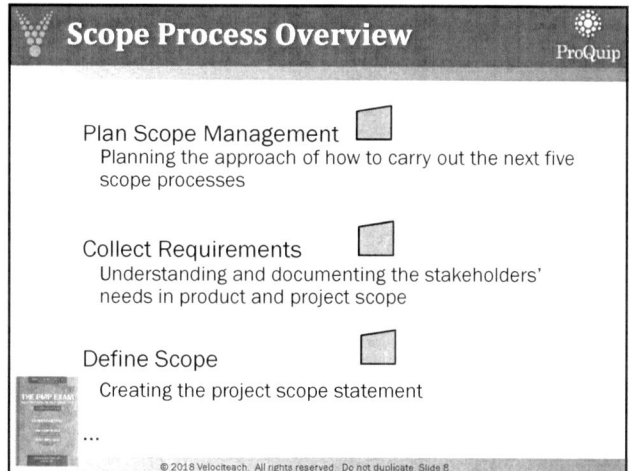

©2018 Velociteach. All rights reserved. Page 74

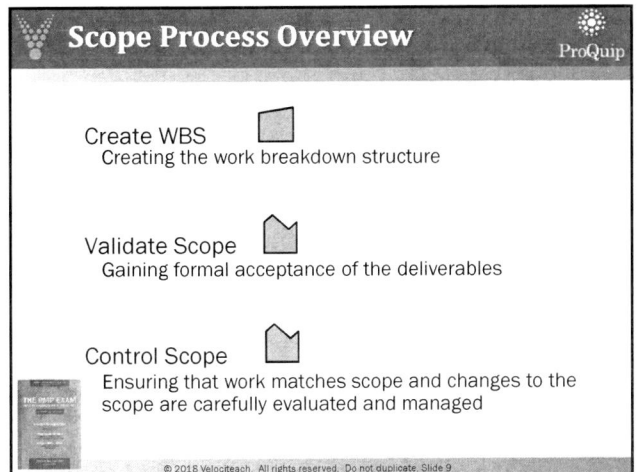

Scope Process Overview

Create WBS
  Creating the work breakdown structure

Validate Scope
  Gaining formal acceptance of the deliverables

Control Scope
  Ensuring that work matches scope and changes to the scope are carefully evaluated and managed

© 2018 Velociteach. All rights reserved. Do not duplicate Slide 9

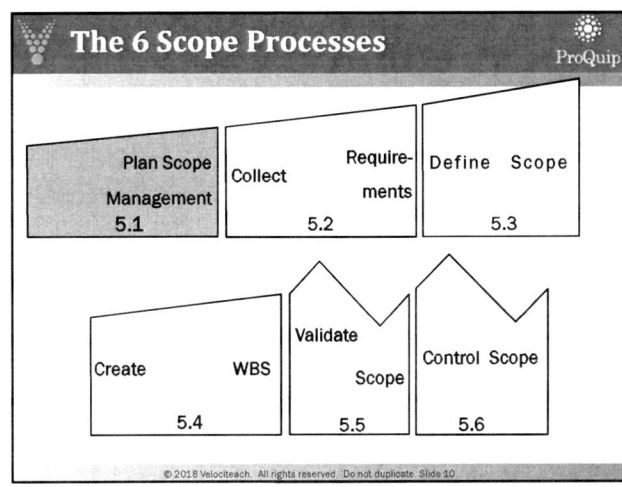

The 6 Scope Processes

| Plan Scope Management 5.1 | Collect 5.2 | Require-ments | Define Scope 5.3 |

Create WBS 5.4 | Validate Scope 5.5 | Control Scope 5.6

© 2018 Velociteach. All rights reserved. Do not duplicate Slide 10

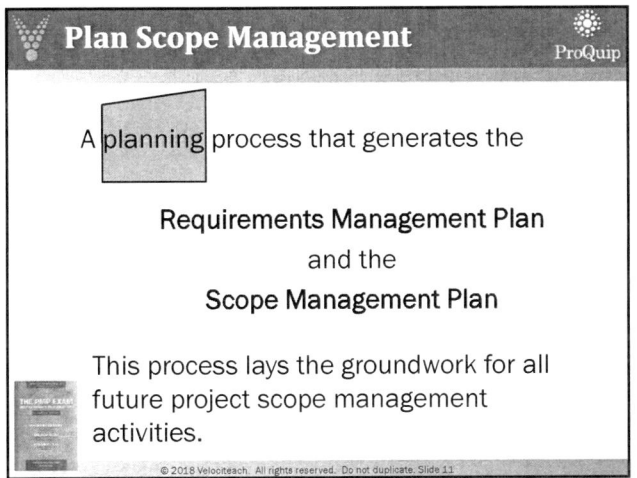

Plan Scope Management

A planning process that generates the

Requirements Management Plan
and the
Scope Management Plan

This process lays the groundwork for all future project scope management activities.

© 2018 Velociteach. All rights reserved. Do not duplicate Slide 11

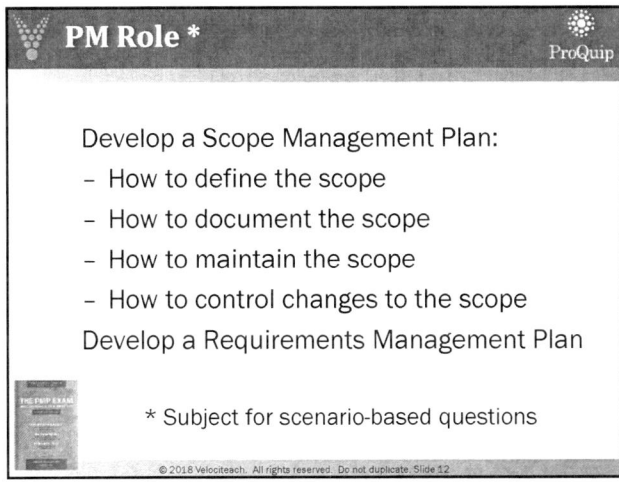

PM Role *

Develop a Scope Management Plan:
– How to define the scope
– How to document the scope
– How to maintain the scope
– How to control changes to the scope
Develop a Requirements Management Plan

* Subject for scenario-based questions

© 2018 Velociteach. All rights reserved. Do not duplicate Slide 12

©2018 Velociteach. All rights reserved.   Page 75

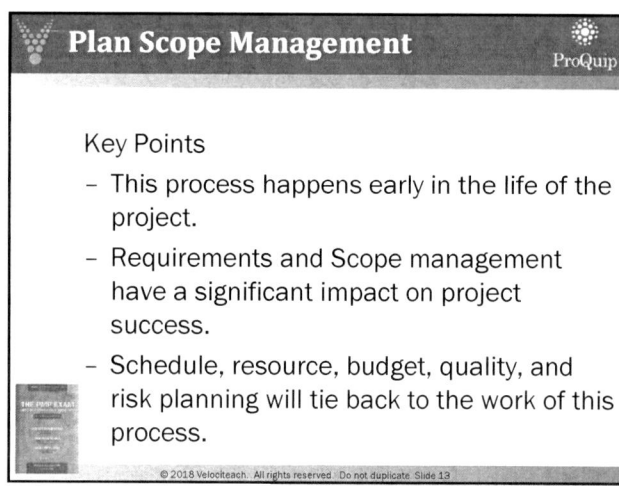

Plan Scope Management

Key Points

- This process happens early in the life of the project.
- Requirements and Scope management have a significant impact on project success.
- Schedule, resource, budget, quality, and risk planning will tie back to the work of this process.

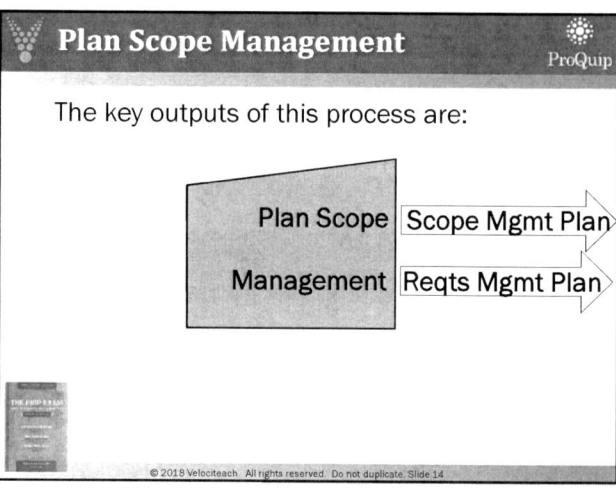

Plan Scope Management

The key outputs of this process are:

Plan Scope Management → Scope Mgmt Plan, Reqts Mgmt Plan

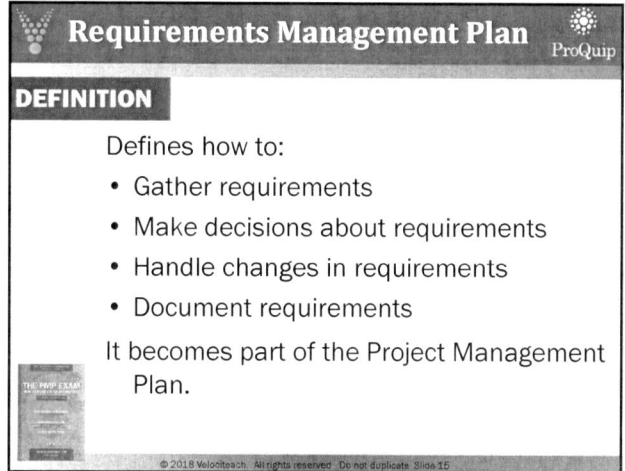

Requirements Management Plan

DEFINITION

Defines how to:

- Gather requirements
- Make decisions about requirements
- Handle changes in requirements
- Document requirements

It becomes part of the Project Management Plan.

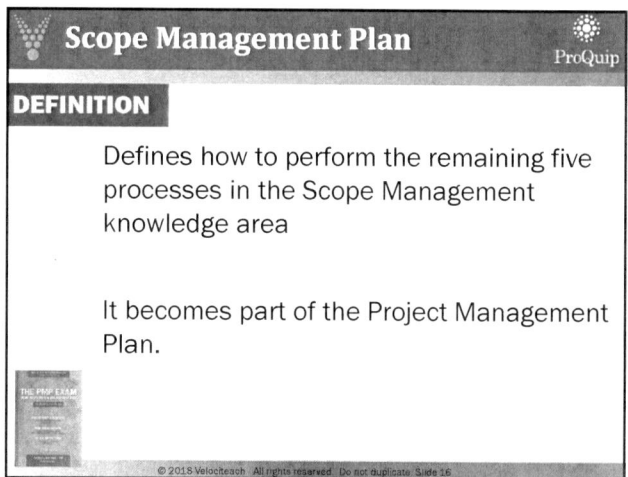

Scope Management Plan

DEFINITION

Defines how to perform the remaining five processes in the Scope Management knowledge area

It becomes part of the Project Management Plan.

©2018 Velociteach. All rights reserved.

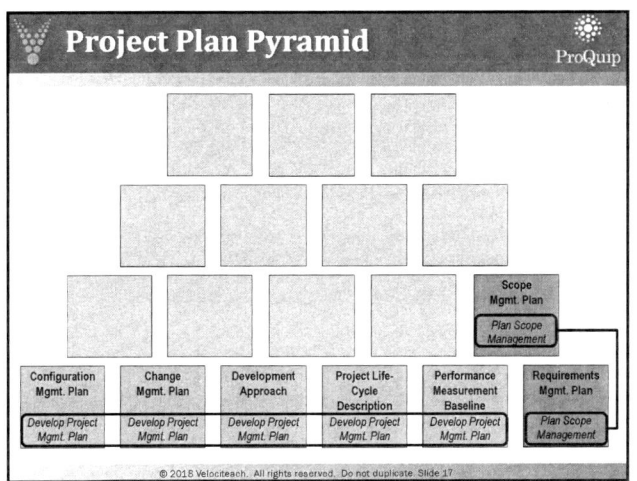

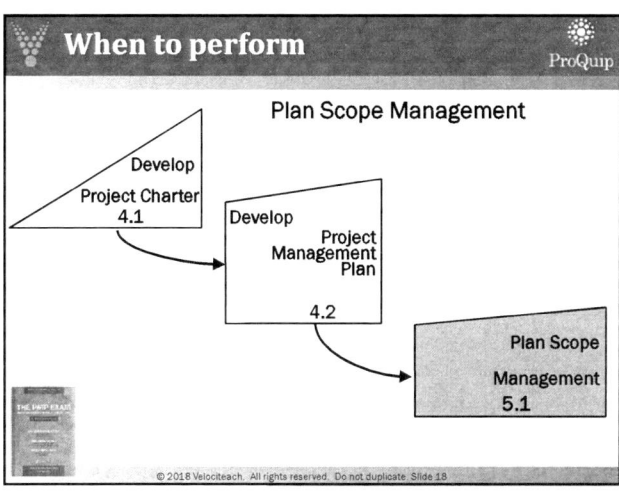

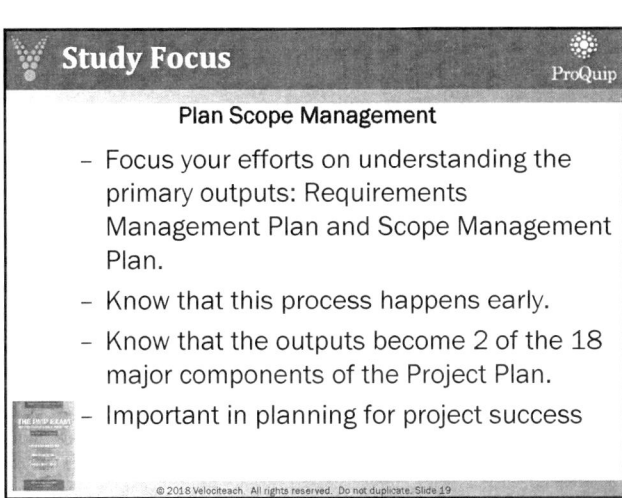

©2018 Velociteach. All rights reserved.

This page left intentionally blank.

©2018 Velociteach. All rights reserved.

Review the ITTOs

ProQuip

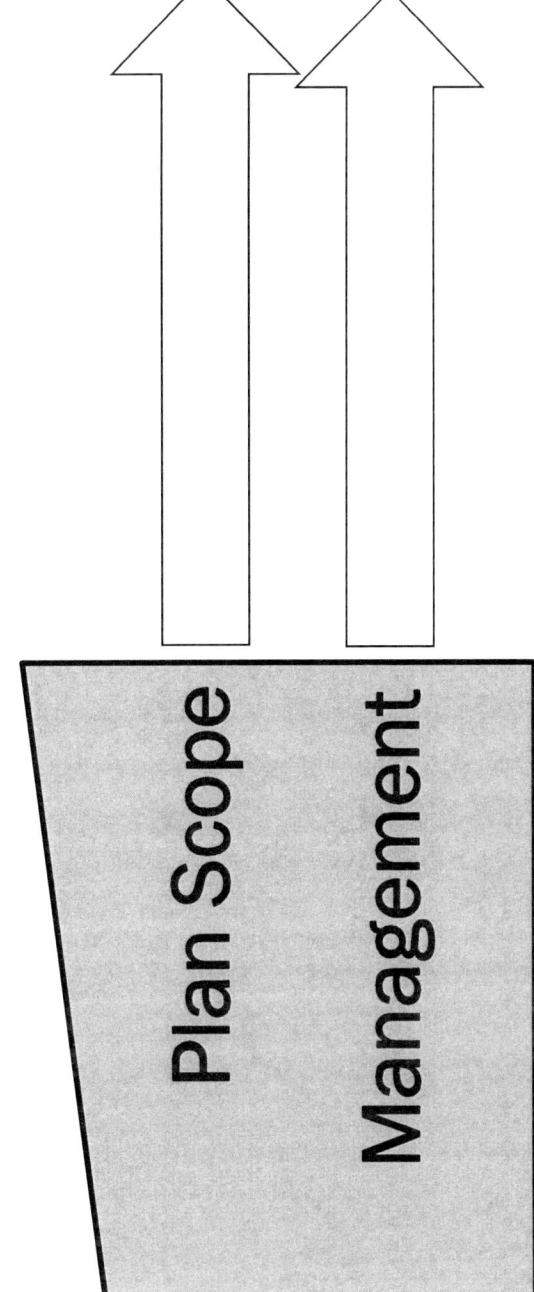

Plan Scope Management

© 2018 Velociteach. All rights reserved.

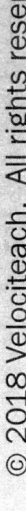

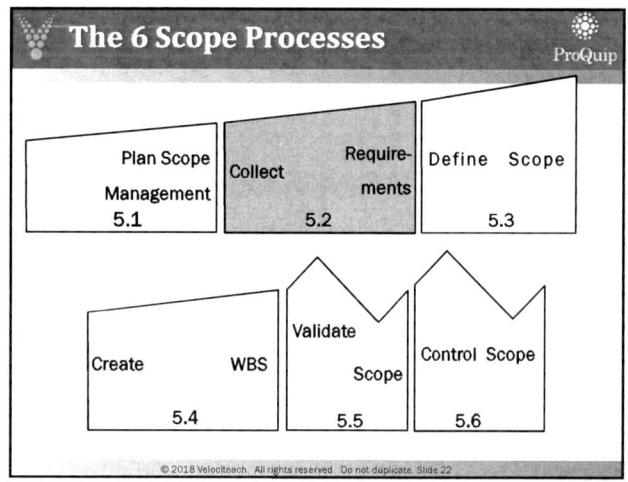

The 6 Scope Processes

- Plan Scope Management 5.1
- Collect Require-ments 5.2
- Define Scope 5.3
- Create WBS 5.4
- Validate Scope 5.5
- Control Scope 5.6

© 2018 Velociteach. All rights reserved. Do not duplicate. Slide 22

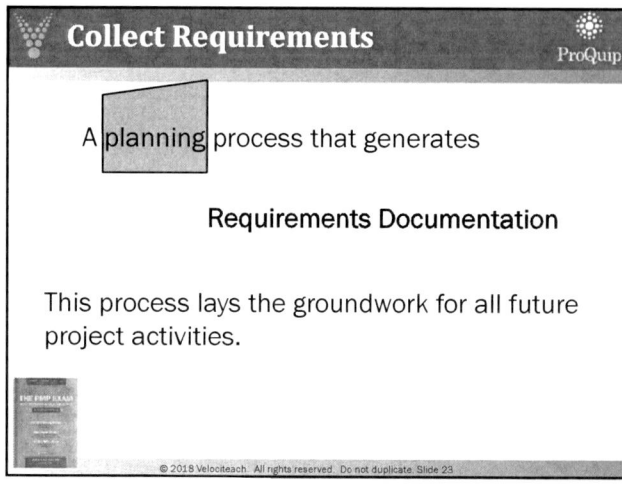

Collect Requirements

A planning process that generates

Requirements Documentation

This process lays the groundwork for all future project activities.

© 2018 Velociteach. All rights reserved. Do not duplicate. Slide 23

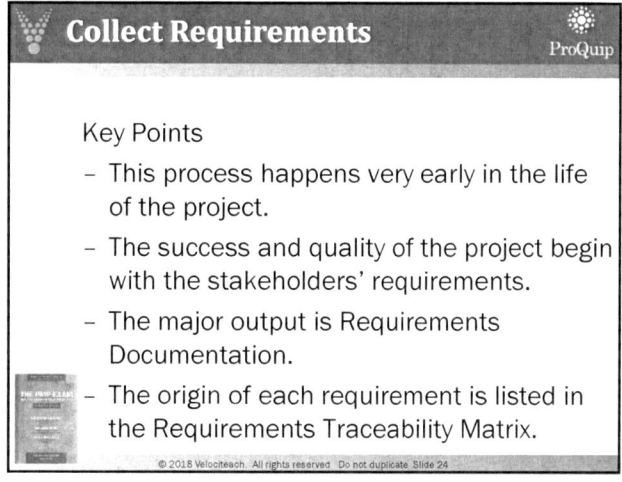

Collect Requirements

Key Points
- This process happens very early in the life of the project.
- The success and quality of the project begin with the stakeholders' requirements.
- The major output is Requirements Documentation.
- The origin of each requirement is listed in the Requirements Traceability Matrix.

© 2018 Velociteach. All rights reserved. Do not duplicate. Slide 24

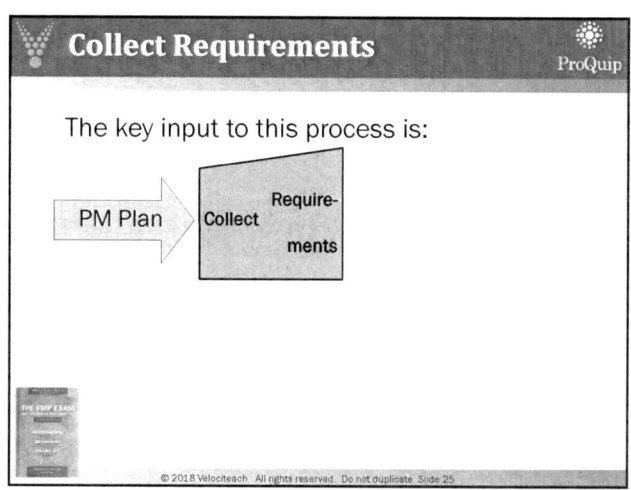

Collect Requirements

The key input to this process is:

PM Plan → Collect Require-ments

© 2018 Velociteach. All rights reserved. Do not duplicate. Slide 25

PM Role *

Review and assess with stakeholders:

– Detailed project requirements

– Assumptions and constraints

– Lessons Learned

Using Requirements Gathering Techniques

Establish Detailed Deliverables

* Subject for scenario-based questions

© 2018 Velociteach. All rights reserved. Do not duplicate. Slide 26

Collect Requirements

The key tools in this process are:

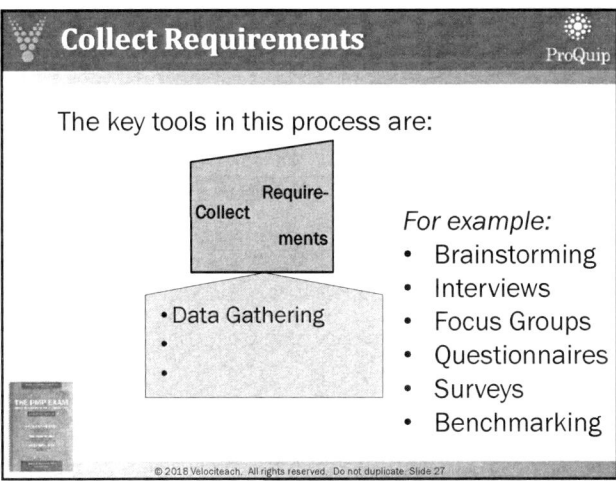

For example:
- Brainstorming
- Interviews
- Focus Groups
- Questionnaires
- Surveys
- Benchmarking

© 2018 Velociteach. All rights reserved. Do not duplicate. Slide 27

Collect Requirements

The key tools in this process are:

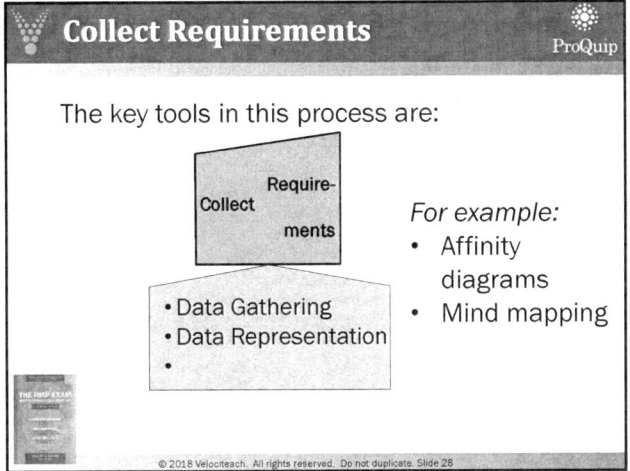

For example:
- Affinity diagrams
- Mind mapping

© 2018 Velociteach. All rights reserved. Do not duplicate. Slide 28

Collect Requirements

The key tools in this process are:

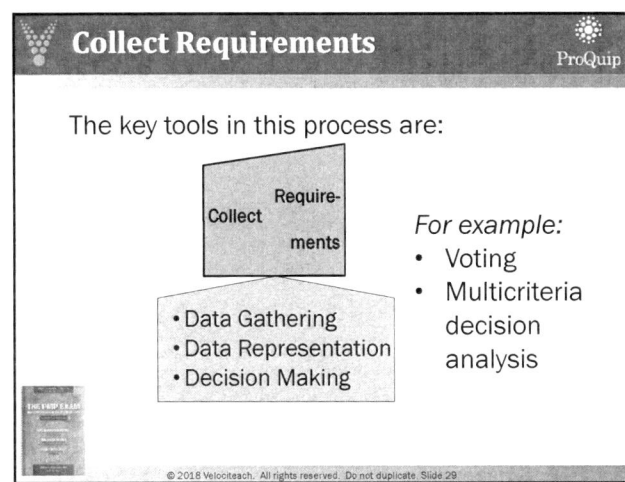

For example:
- Voting
- Multicriteria decision analysis

© 2018 Velociteach. All rights reserved. Do not duplicate. Slide 29

Collect Requirements

ProQuip

The key outputs from this process are:

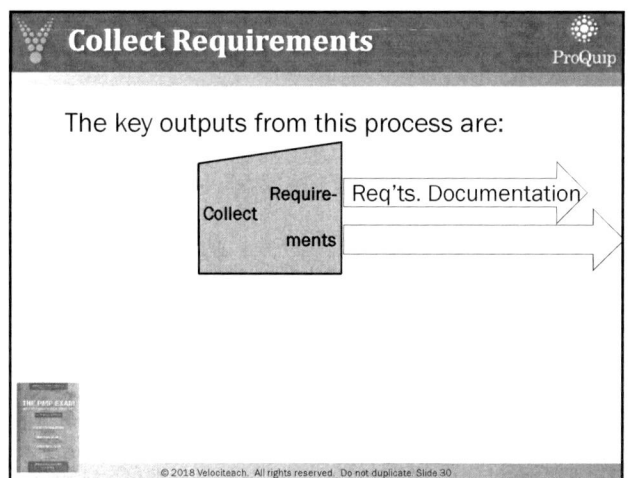

Collect Require-ments → Req'ts. Documentation

© 2018 Velociteach. All rights reserved. Do not duplicate. Slide 30

Requirements Documentation

ProQuip

- Root problem being solved

- Origin of requirement

- How the requirement solves the problem

- Measures and targets

- Constraints

- Interaction with other requirements

© 2018 Velociteach. All rights reserved. Do not duplicate. Slide 31

Collect Requirements

ProQuip

The key outputs from this process are:

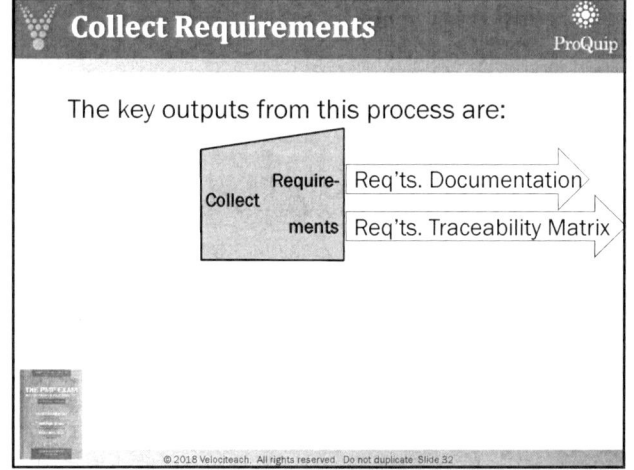

Collect Require-ments → Req'ts. Documentation
Req'ts. Traceability Matrix

© 2018 Velociteach. All rights reserved. Do not duplicate. Slide 32

Requirements Traceability Matrix

ProQuip

DEFINITION A table linking requirements to the source, tracking throughout the project life cycle

May include information such as:
- Description
- Why it is a requirement
- Origin
- Version
- Priority
- Status
- Acceptance criteria
- Business value

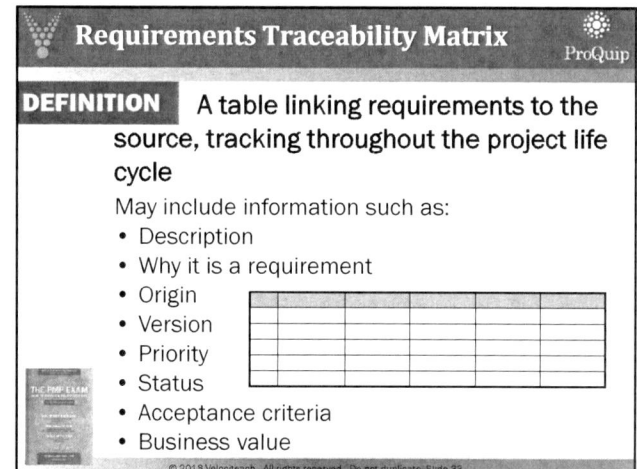

© 2018 Velociteach. All rights reserved. Do not duplicate. Slide 33

Collect Requirements

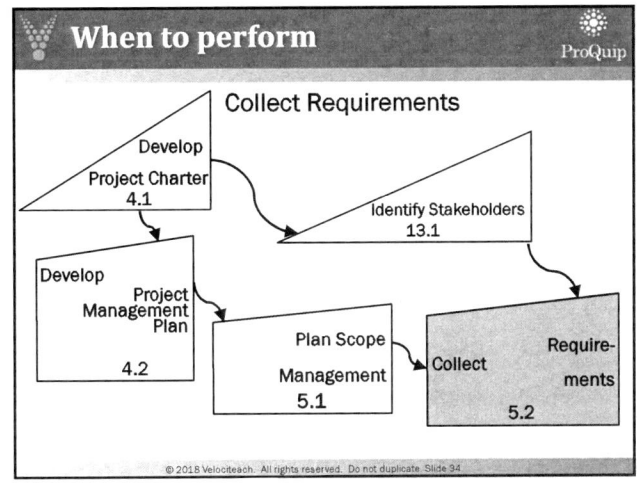

© 2018 Velociteach. All rights reserved. Do not duplicate. Slide 94

Collect Requirements

- Focus on understanding the primary outputs: Requirements Documentation and the Requirements Traceability Matrix.
- Know that this process happens early.
- Know that this process is significant in detailing the success of the project and stakeholder expectations.
- Know the key tools and example techniques under each tool group.

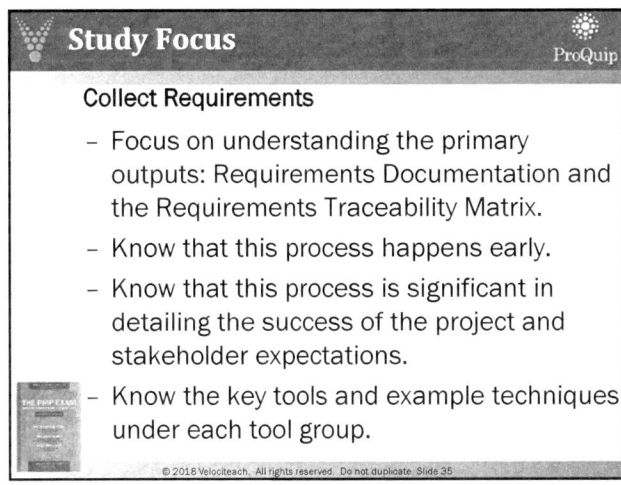

© 2018 Velociteach. All rights reserved. Do not duplicate. Slide 35

This page left intentionally blank.

©2018 Velociteach. All rights reserved.

Review the ITTOs

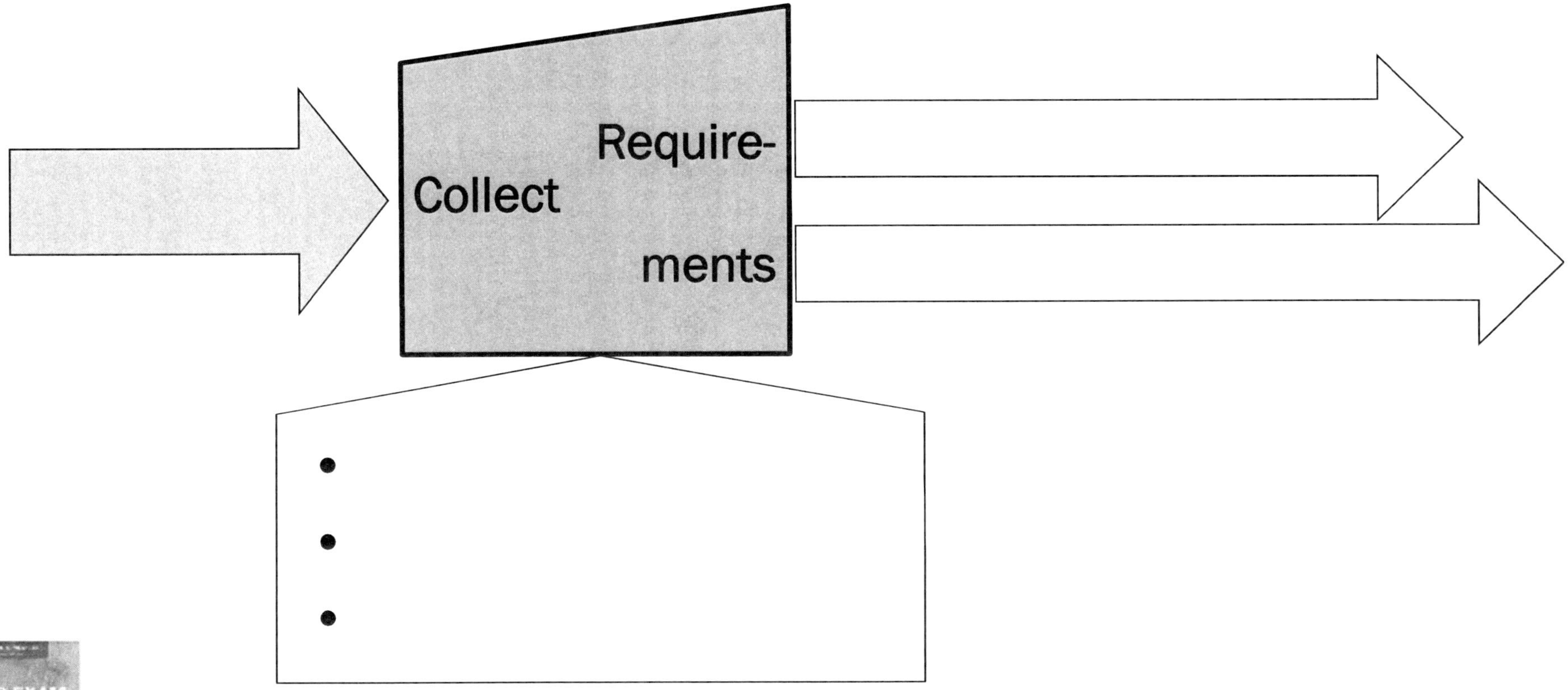

ProQuip

Collect Require-ments

© 2018 Velociteach. All rights reserved.

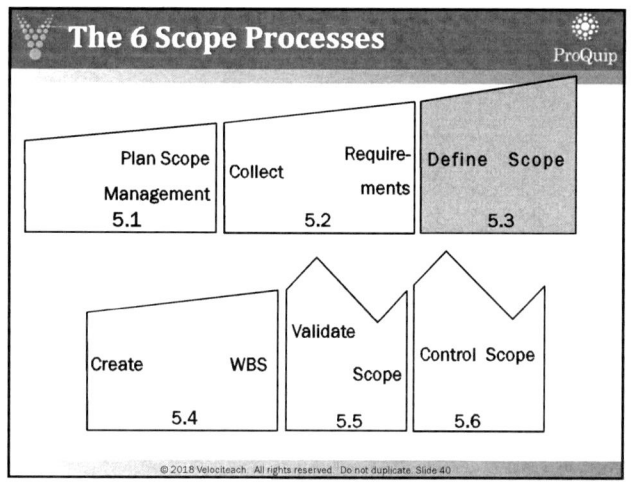

The 6 Scope Processes
ProQuip

Plan Scope Management 5.1 | Collect Require-ments 5.2 | Define Scope 5.3

Create WBS 5.4 | Validate Scope 5.5 | Control Scope 5.6

© 2018 Velociteach. All rights reserved. Do not duplicate. Slide 40

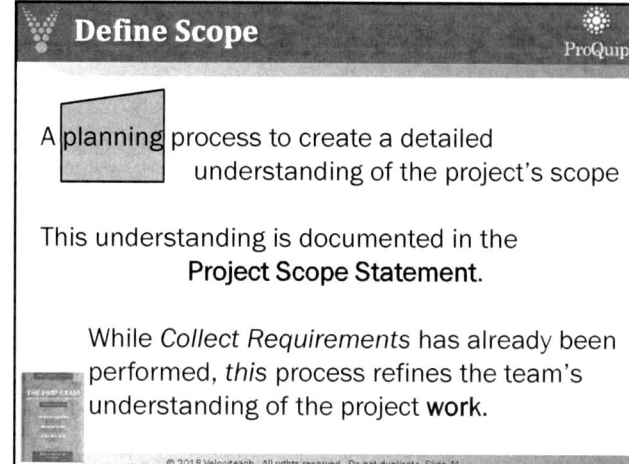

Define Scope
ProQuip

A planning process to create a detailed understanding of the project's scope

This understanding is documented in the **Project Scope Statement.**

While *Collect Requirements* has already been performed, *this* process refines the team's understanding of the project **work.**

© 2018 Velociteach. All rights reserved. Do not duplicate. Slide 41

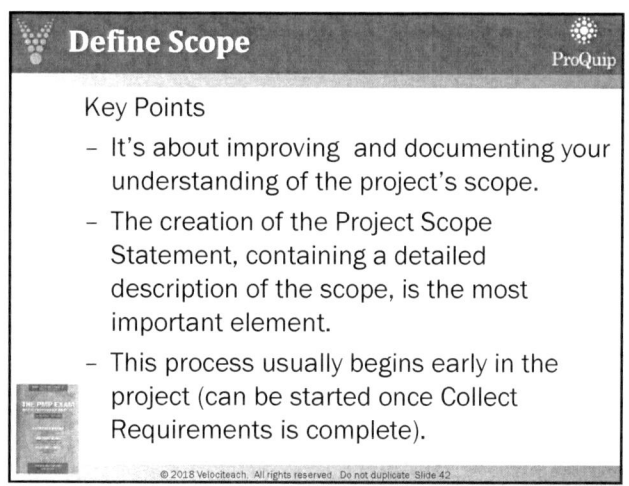

Define Scope
ProQuip

Key Points
- It's about improving and documenting your understanding of the project's scope.
- The creation of the Project Scope Statement, containing a detailed description of the scope, is the most important element.
- This process usually begins early in the project (can be started once Collect Requirements is complete).

© 2018 Velociteach. All rights reserved. Do not duplicate. Slide 42

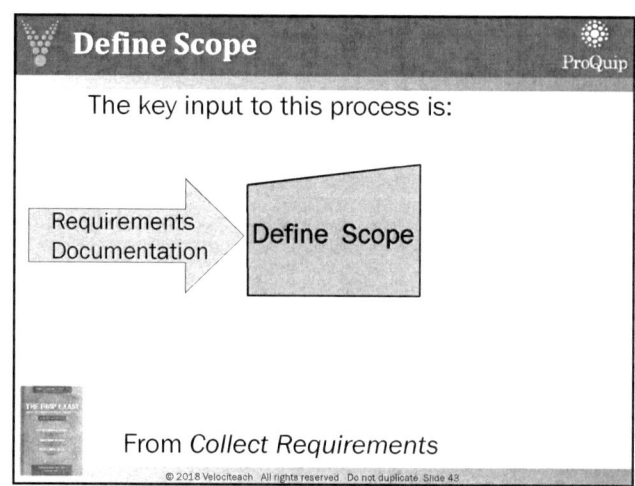

Define Scope
ProQuip

The key input to this process is:

Requirements Documentation → Define Scope

From *Collect Requirements*

© 2018 Velociteach. All rights reserved. Do not duplicate. Slide 43

©2018 Velociteach. All rights reserved.   Page 86

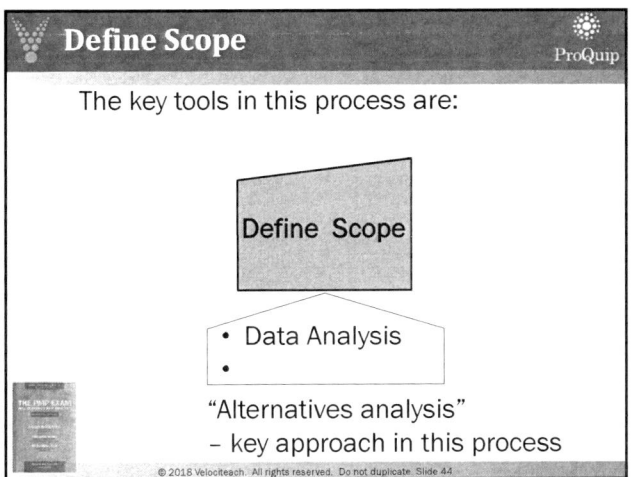

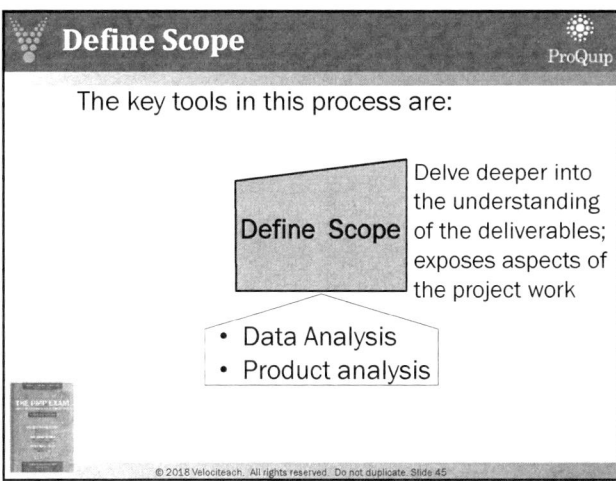

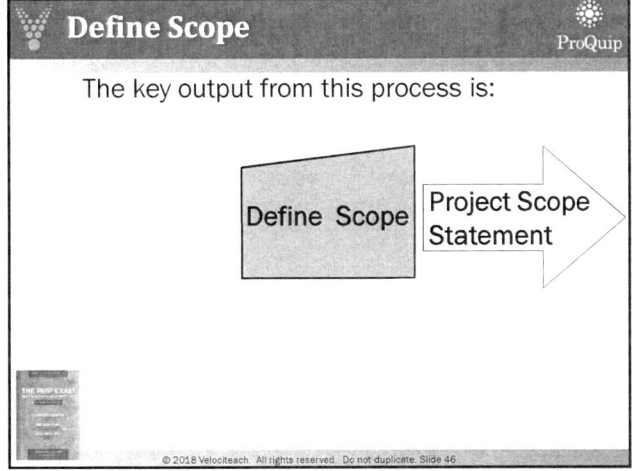

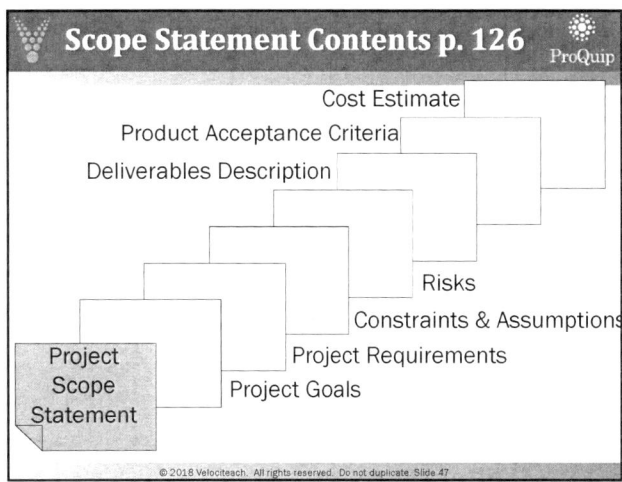

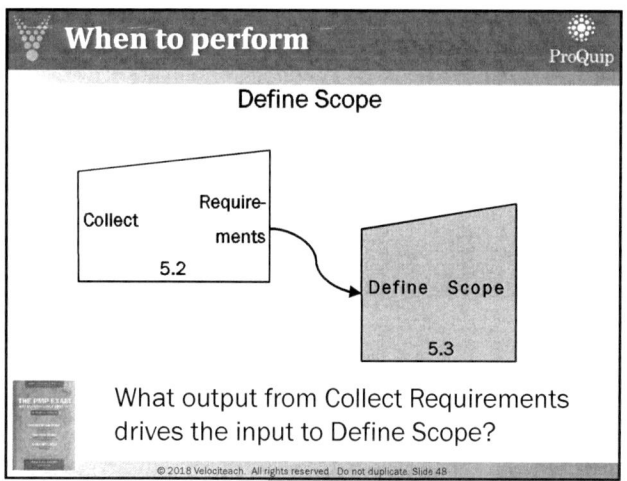

When to perform

Define Scope

What output from Collect Requirements drives the input to Define Scope?

© 2018 Velociteach. All rights reserved. Do not duplicate. Slide 48

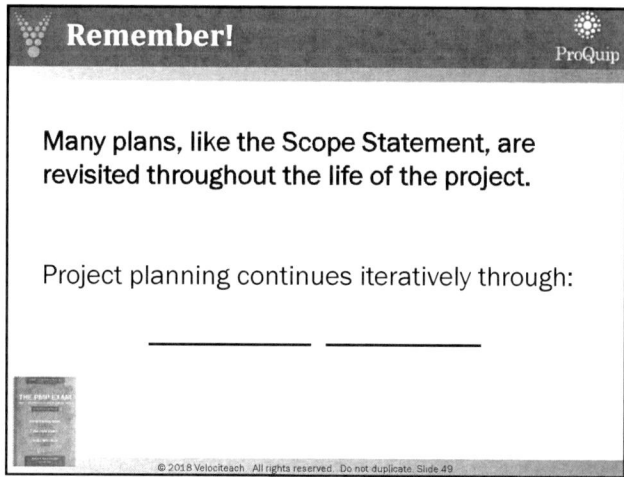

Remember!

Many plans, like the Scope Statement, are revisited throughout the life of the project.

Project planning continues iteratively through:

_____ _____

© 2018 Velociteach. All rights reserved. Do not duplicate. Slide 49

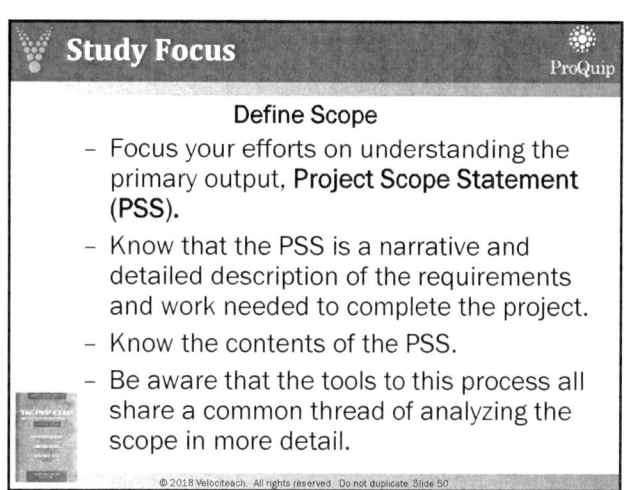

Study Focus

Define Scope

- Focus your efforts on understanding the primary output, **Project Scope Statement (PSS).**
- Know that the PSS is a narrative and detailed description of the requirements and work needed to complete the project.
- Know the contents of the PSS.
- Be aware that the tools to this process all share a common thread of analyzing the scope in more detail.

© 2018 Velociteach. All rights reserved. Do not duplicate. Slide 50

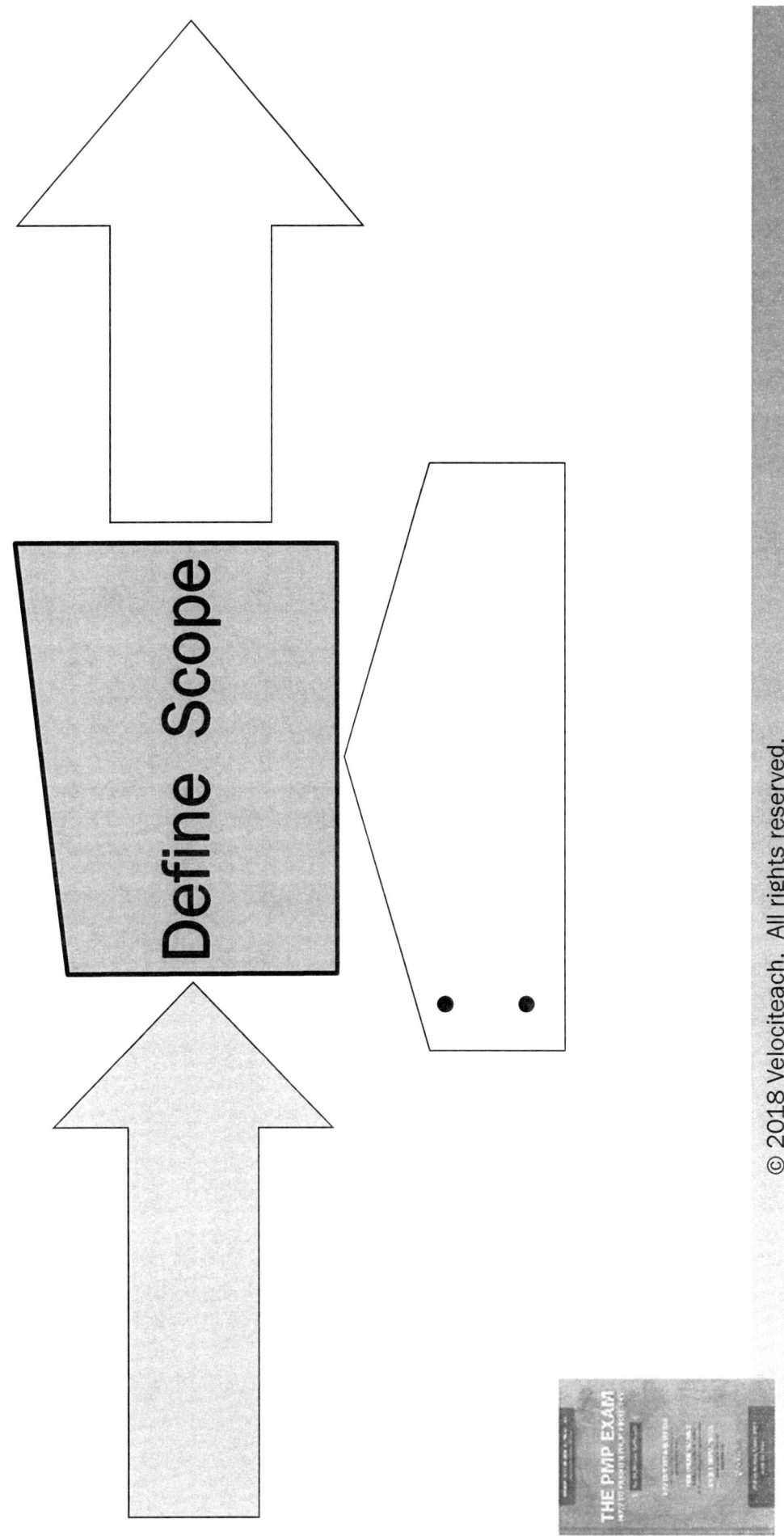

Review the ITTOs

ProQuip

Define Scope

© 2018 Velociteach. All rights reserved.

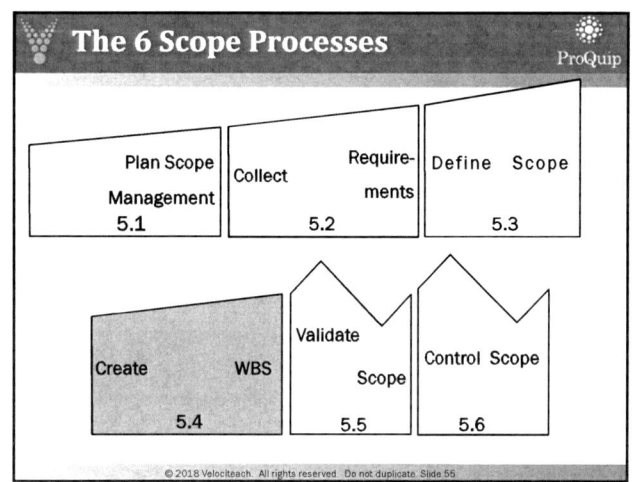

The 6 Scope Processes

ProQuip

| Plan Scope Management 5.1 | Collect Requirements 5.2 | Define Scope 5.3 |

Create WBS 5.4 | Validate Scope 5.5 | Control Scope 5.6

© 2018 Velociteach. All rights reserved. Do not duplicate. Slide 55

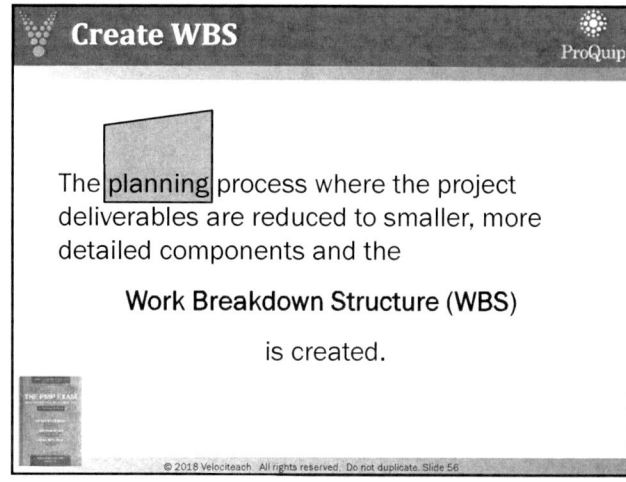

Create WBS

ProQuip

The planning process where the project deliverables are reduced to smaller, more detailed components and the

Work Breakdown Structure (WBS)

is created.

© 2018 Velociteach. All rights reserved. Do not duplicate. Slide 56

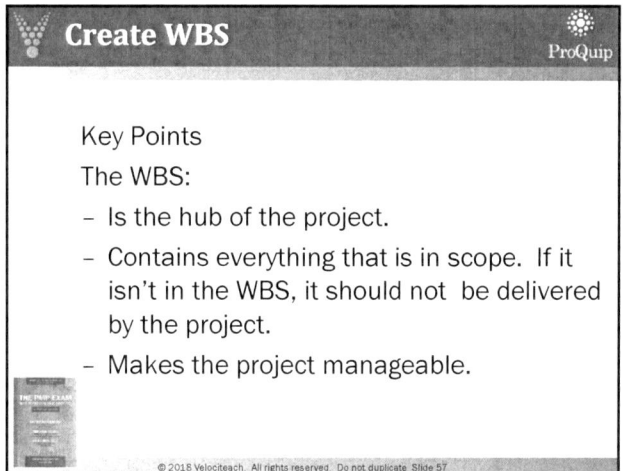

Create WBS

ProQuip

Key Points

The WBS:

– Is the hub of the project.

– Contains everything that is in scope. If it isn't in the WBS, it should not be delivered by the project.

– Makes the project manageable.

© 2018 Velociteach. All rights reserved. Do not duplicate. Slide 57

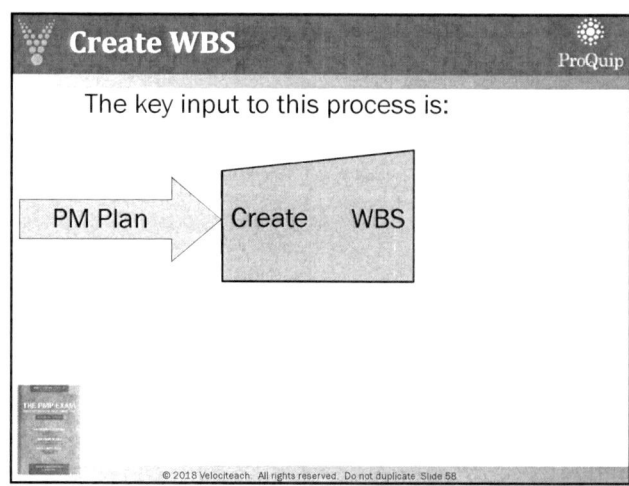

Create WBS

ProQuip

The key input to this process is:

PM Plan → Create WBS

© 2018 Velociteach. All rights reserved. Do not duplicate. Slide 58

©2018 Velociteach. All rights reserved.

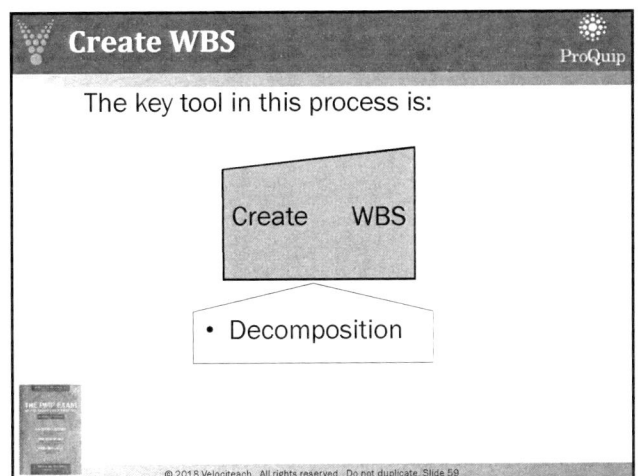

Create WBS

The key tool in this process is:

Create WBS

- Decomposition

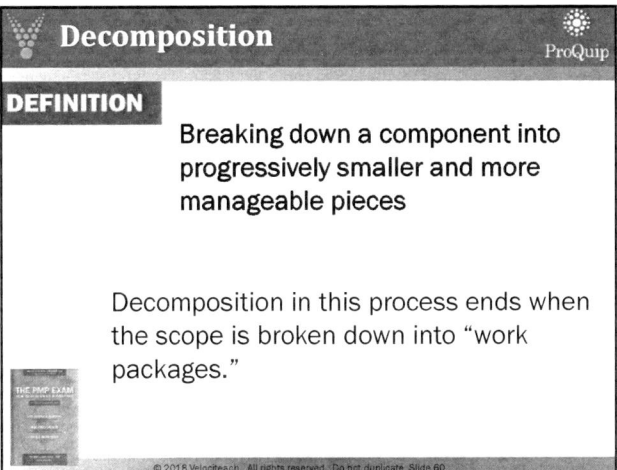

Decomposition

DEFINITION

Breaking down a component into progressively smaller and more manageable pieces

Decomposition in this process ends when the scope is broken down into "work packages."

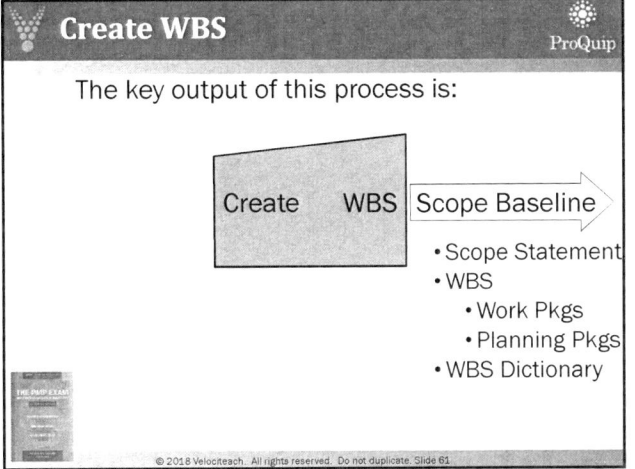

Create WBS

The key output of this process is:

Create WBS → Scope Baseline

- Scope Statement
- WBS
  - Work Pkgs
  - Planning Pkgs
- WBS Dictionary

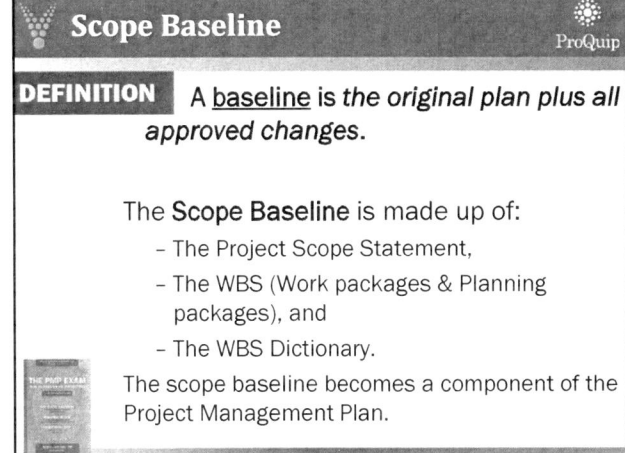

Scope Baseline

DEFINITION A <u>baseline</u> is *the original plan plus all approved changes.*

The **Scope Baseline** is made up of:
- The Project Scope Statement,
- The WBS (Work packages & Planning packages), and
- The WBS Dictionary.

The scope baseline becomes a component of the Project Management Plan.

©2018 Velociteach. All rights reserved. Page 91

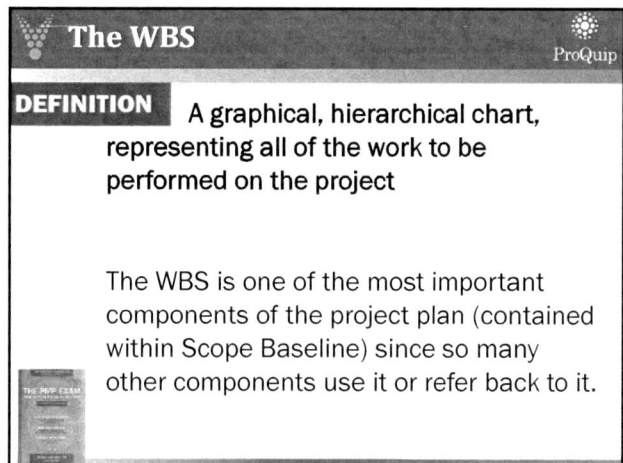

The WBS

ProQuip

DEFINITION A graphical, hierarchical chart, representing all of the work to be performed on the project

The WBS is one of the most important components of the project plan (contained within Scope Baseline) since so many other components use it or refer back to it.

© 2018 Velociteach. All rights reserved. Do not duplicate. Slide 63

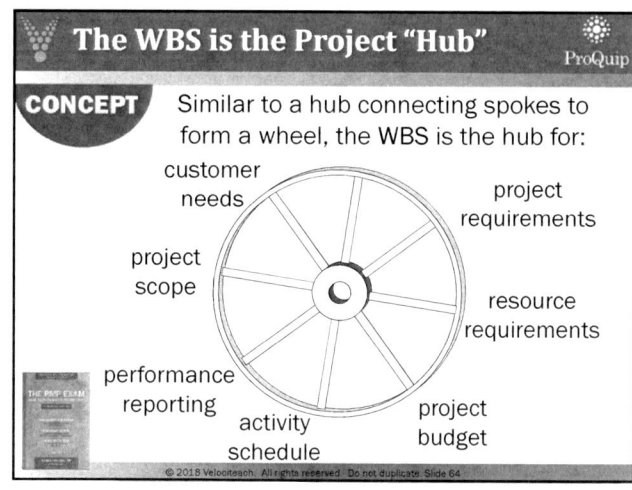

The WBS is the Project "Hub"

ProQuip

CONCEPT Similar to a hub connecting spokes to form a wheel, the WBS is the hub for:

customer needs

project requirements

project scope

resource requirements

performance reporting

activity schedule

project budget

© 2018 Velociteach. All rights reserved. Do not duplicate. Slide 64

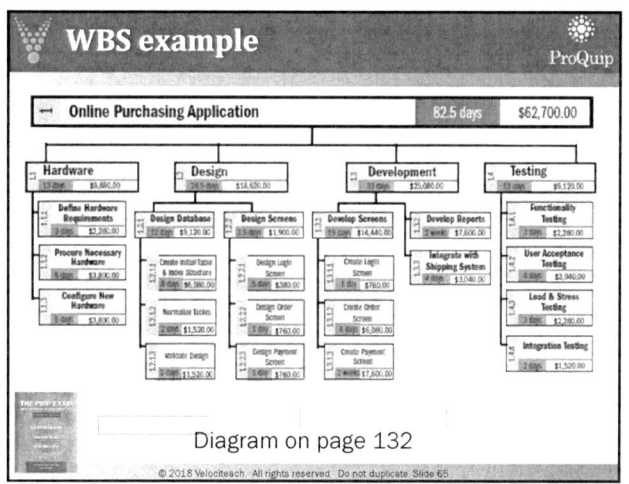

WBS example

ProQuip

Diagram on page 132

© 2018 Velociteach. All rights reserved. Do not duplicate. Slide 65

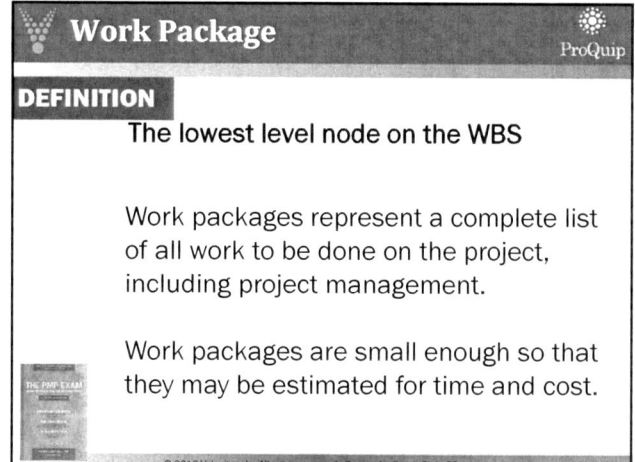

Work Package

ProQuip

DEFINITION

The lowest level node on the WBS

Work packages represent a complete list of all work to be done on the project, including project management.

Work packages are small enough so that they may be estimated for time and cost.

© 2018 Velociteach. All rights reserved. Do not duplicate. Slide 66

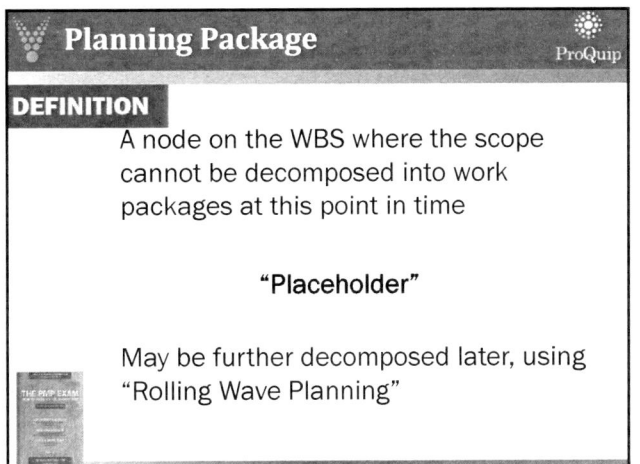

Planning Package

ProQuip

DEFINITION

A node on the WBS where the scope cannot be decomposed into work packages at this point in time

"Placeholder"

May be further decomposed later, using "Rolling Wave Planning"

© 2018 Velociteach. All rights reserved. Do not duplicate. Slide 67

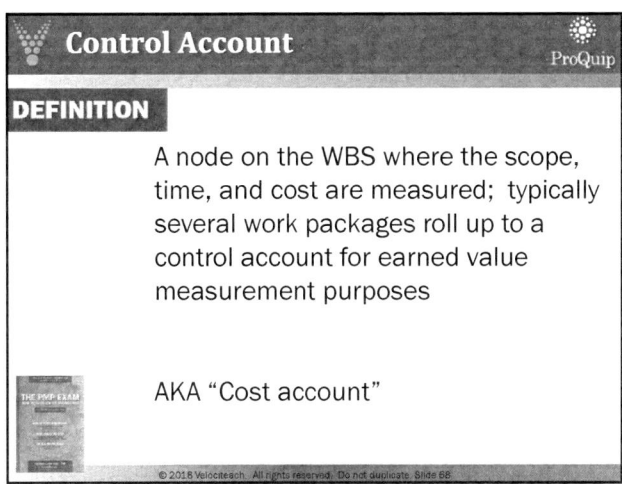

Control Account

ProQuip

DEFINITION

A node on the WBS where the scope, time, and cost are measured; typically several work packages roll up to a control account for earned value measurement purposes

AKA "Cost account"

© 2018 Velociteach. All rights reserved. Do not duplicate. Slide 68

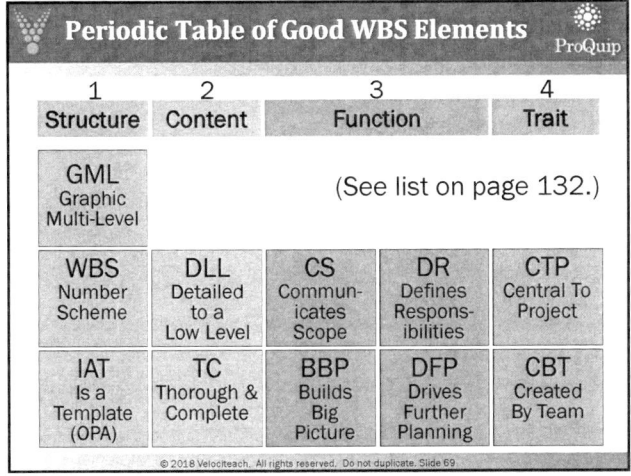

Periodic Table of Good WBS Elements

ProQuip

1 Structure	2 Content	3 Function		4 Trait
GML Graphic Multi-Level	(See list on page 132.)			
WBS Number Scheme	DLL Detailed to a Low Level	CS Commun- icates Scope	DR Defines Respons- ibilities	CTP Central To Project
IAT Is a Template (OPA)	TC Thorough & Complete	BBP Builds Big Picture	DFP Drives Further Planning	CBT Created By Team

© 2018 Velociteach. All rights reserved. Do not duplicate. Slide 69

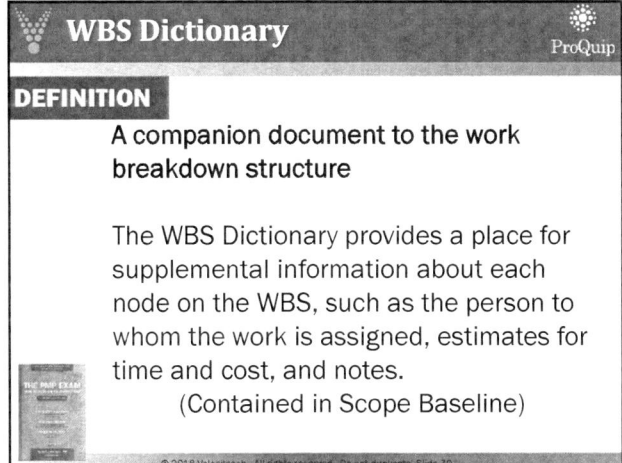

WBS Dictionary

ProQuip

DEFINITION

A companion document to the work breakdown structure

The WBS Dictionary provides a place for supplemental information about each node on the WBS, such as the person to whom the work is assigned, estimates for time and cost, and notes.
(Contained in Scope Baseline)

© 2018 Velociteach. All rights reserved. Do not duplicate. Slide 70

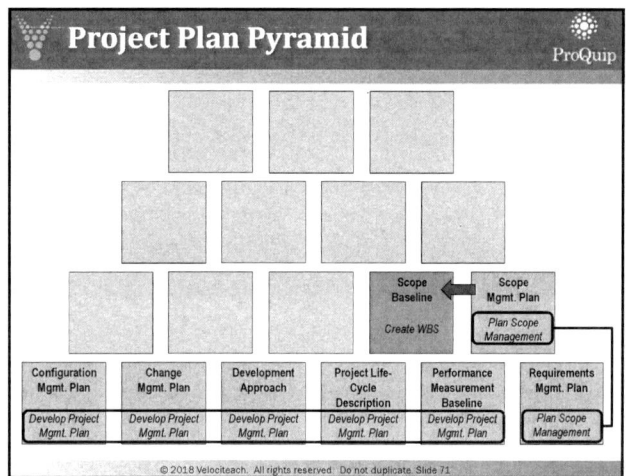

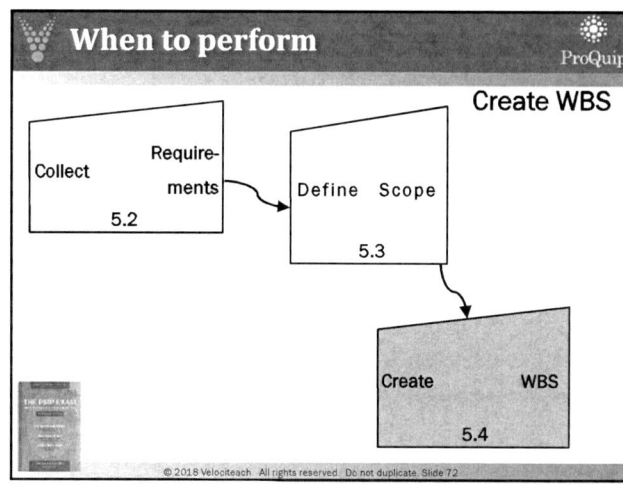

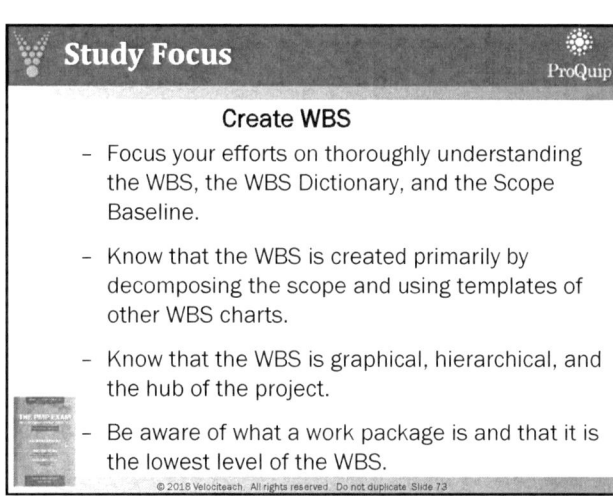

Review the ITTOs

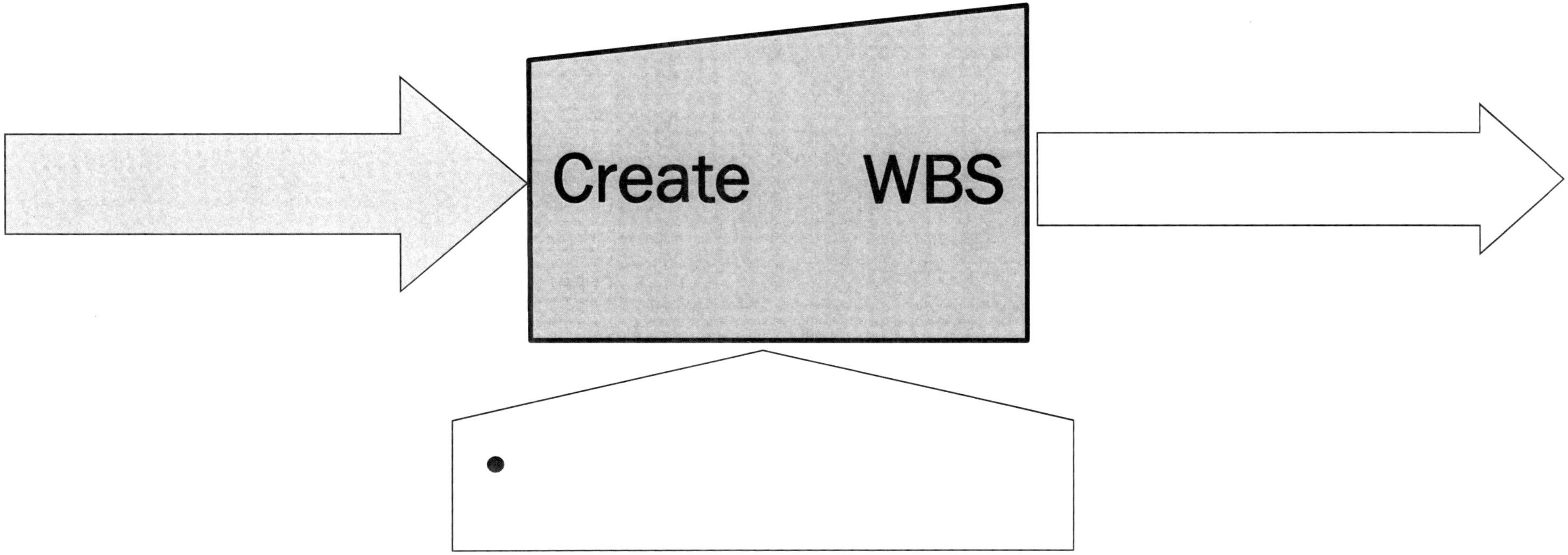

Create WBS

© 2018 Velociteach. All rights reserved.

This page left intentionally blank.

The 6 Scope Processes

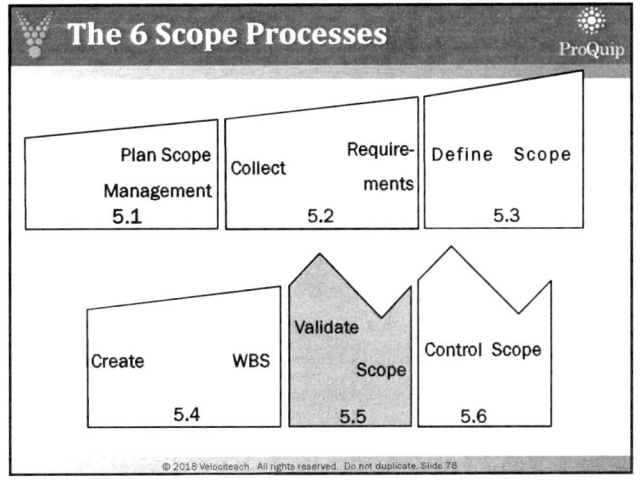

Plan Scope Management 5.1

Collect Requirements 5.2

Define Scope 5.3

Create WBS 5.4

Validate Scope 5.5

Control Scope 5.6

© 2018 Velociteach. All rights reserved. Do not duplicate. Slide 78

Validate Scope

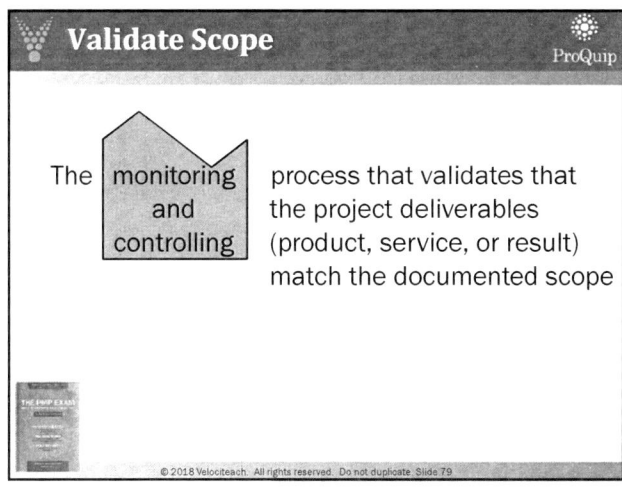

The **monitoring and controlling** process that validates that the project deliverables (product, service, or result) match the documented scope

© 2018 Velociteach. All rights reserved. Do not duplicate. Slide 79

Validate Scope

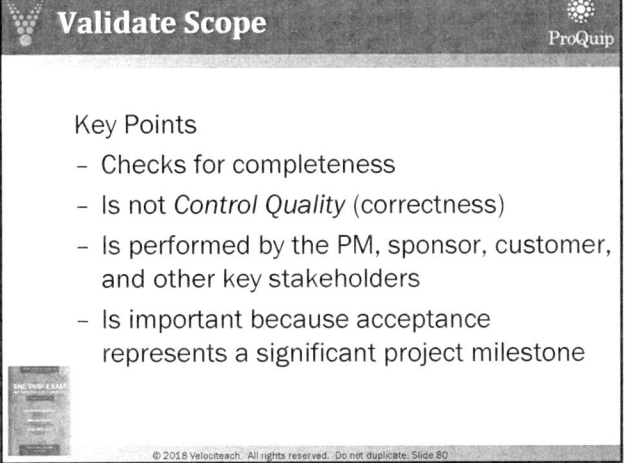

Key Points
- Checks for completeness
- Is not *Control Quality* (correctness)
- Is performed by the PM, sponsor, customer, and other key stakeholders
- Is important because acceptance represents a significant project milestone

© 2018 Velociteach. All rights reserved. Do not duplicate. Slide 80

Validate Scope

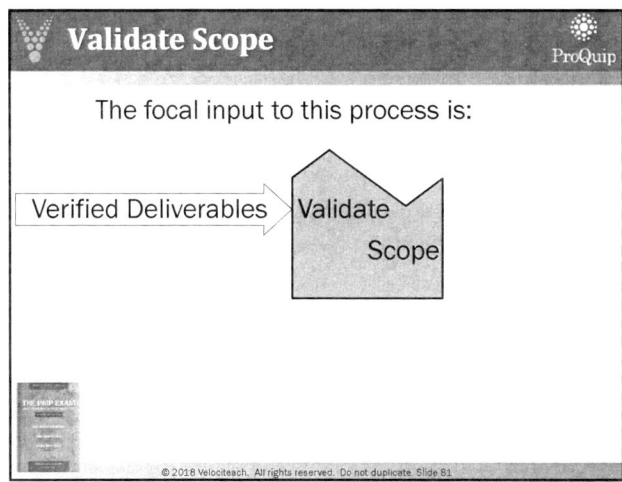

The focal input to this process is:

Verified Deliverables → Validate Scope

© 2018 Velociteach. All rights reserved. Do not duplicate. Slide 81

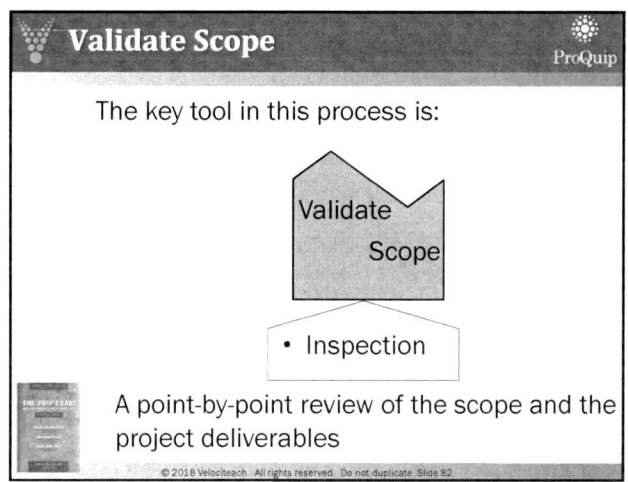

Validate Scope

The key tool in this process is:

Validate Scope

• Inspection

A point-by-point review of the scope and the project deliverables

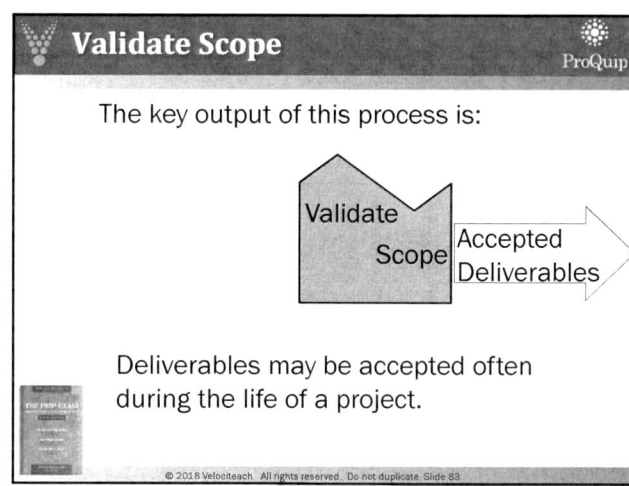

Validate Scope

The key output of this process is:

Validate Scope → Accepted Deliverables

Deliverables may be accepted often during the life of a project.

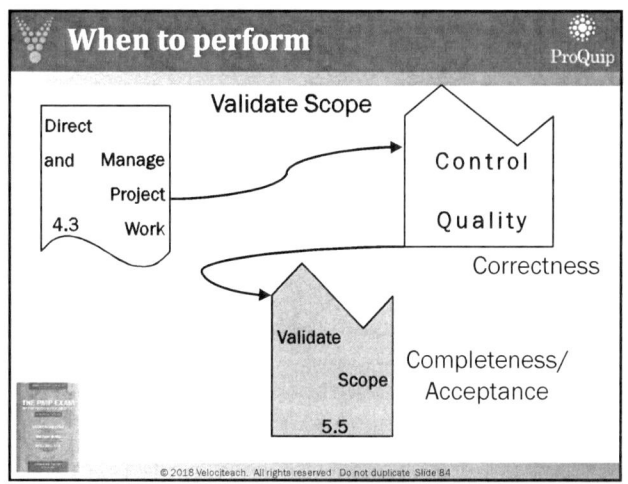

When to perform

Validate Scope

Direct and Manage Project Work 4.3 → Control Quality — Correctness

→ Validate Scope 5.5 — Completeness/ Acceptance

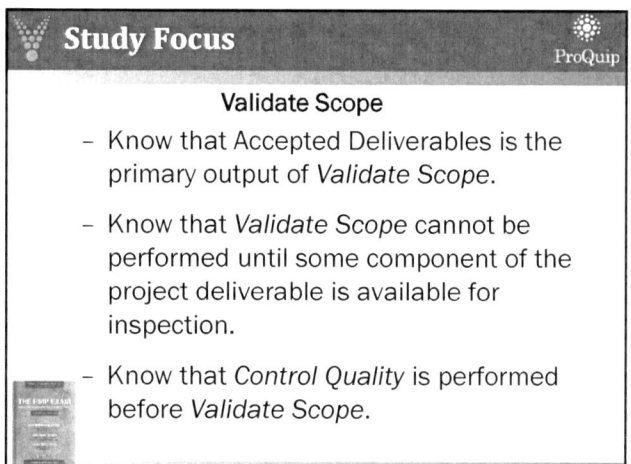

Study Focus

Validate Scope

- Know that Accepted Deliverables is the primary output of *Validate Scope*.

- Know that *Validate Scope* cannot be performed until some component of the project deliverable is available for inspection.

- Know that *Control Quality* is performed before *Validate Scope*.

©2018 Velociteach. All rights reserved. Page 98

ProQuip

Validate Scope

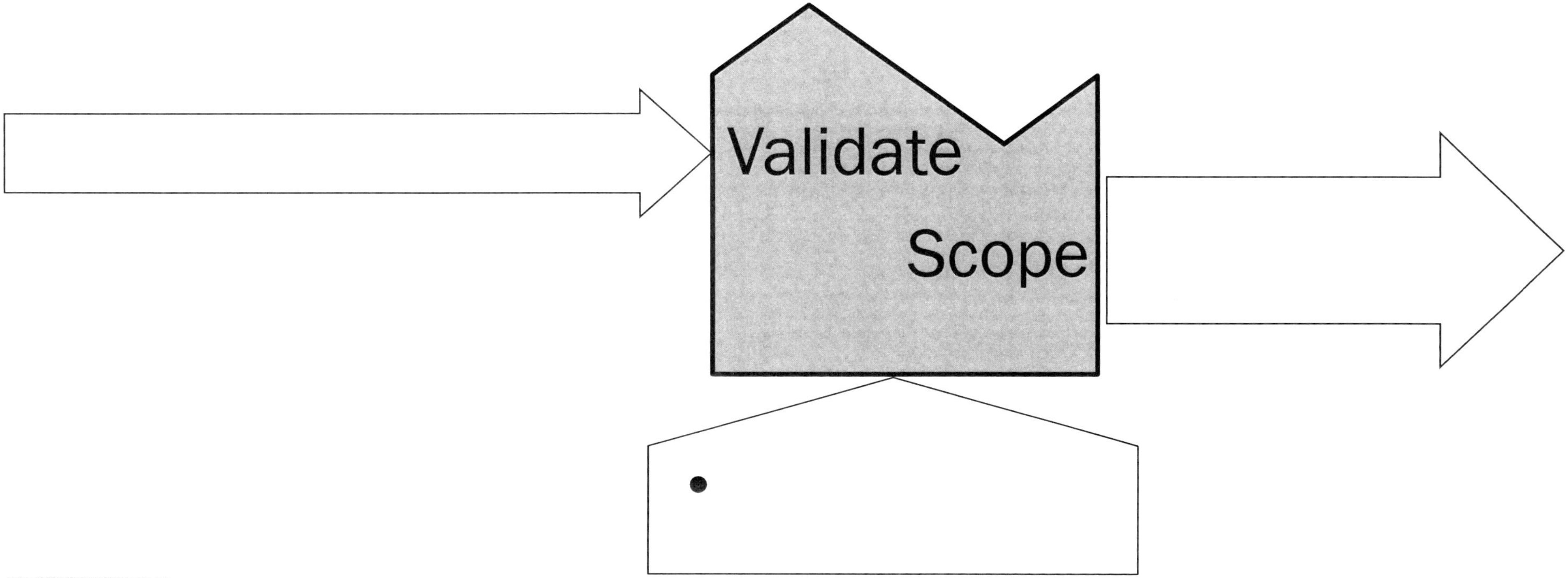

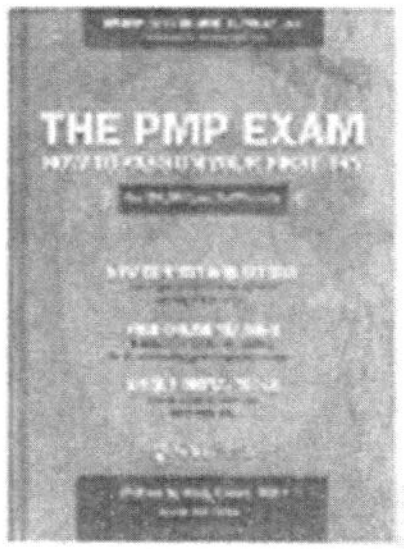

© 2018 Velociteach. All rights reserved.

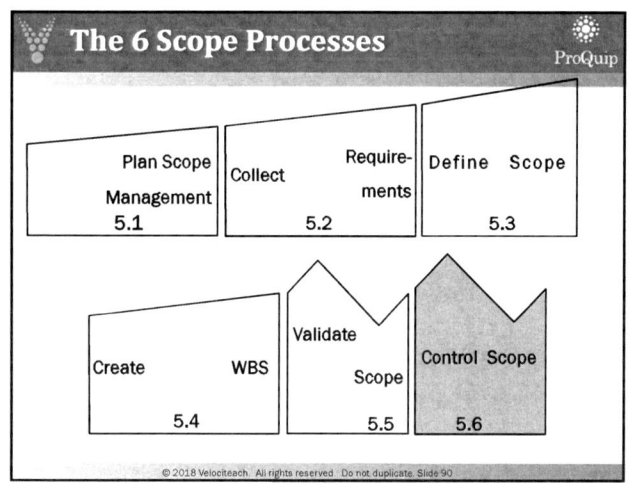

The 6 Scope Processes

- Plan Scope Management 5.1
- Collect Requirements 5.2
- Define Scope 5.3
- Create WBS 5.4
- Validate Scope 5.5
- Control Scope 5.6

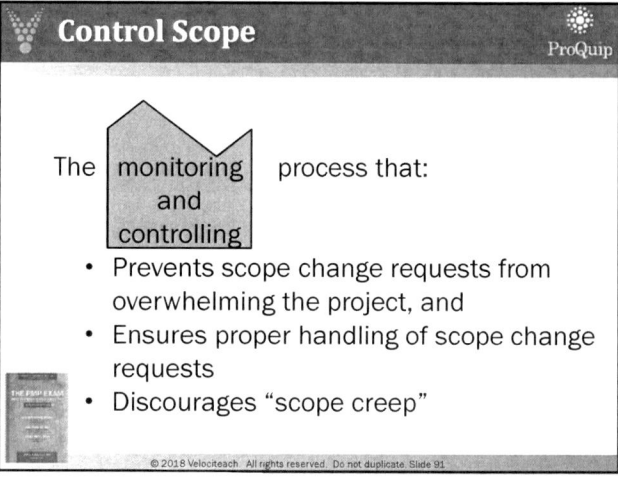

Control Scope

The **monitoring and controlling** process that:

- Prevents scope change requests from overwhelming the project, and
- Ensures proper handling of scope change requests
- Discourages "scope creep"

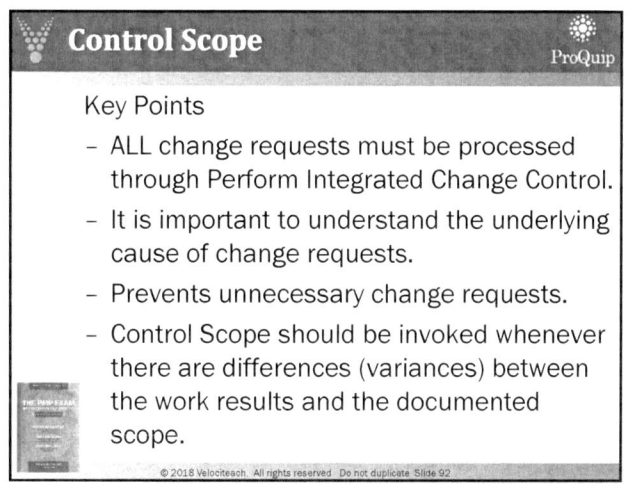

Control Scope

Key Points

- ALL change requests must be processed through Perform Integrated Change Control.
- It is important to understand the underlying cause of change requests.
- Prevents unnecessary change requests.
- Control Scope should be invoked whenever there are differences (variances) between the work results and the documented scope.

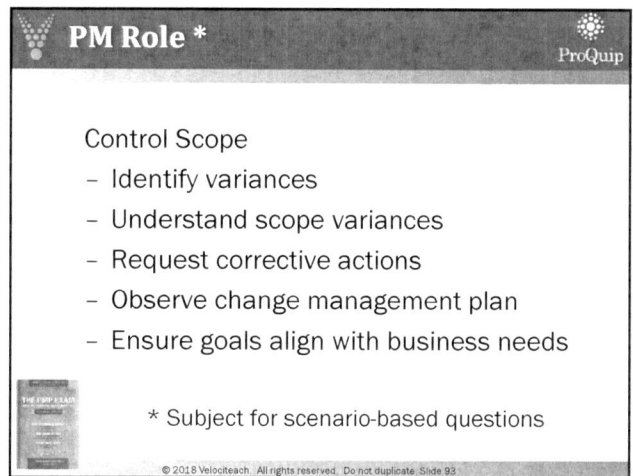

PM Role *

Control Scope

- Identify variances
- Understand scope variances
- Request corrective actions
- Observe change management plan
- Ensure goals align with business needs

* Subject for scenario-based questions

©2018 Velociteach. All rights reserved. Page 100

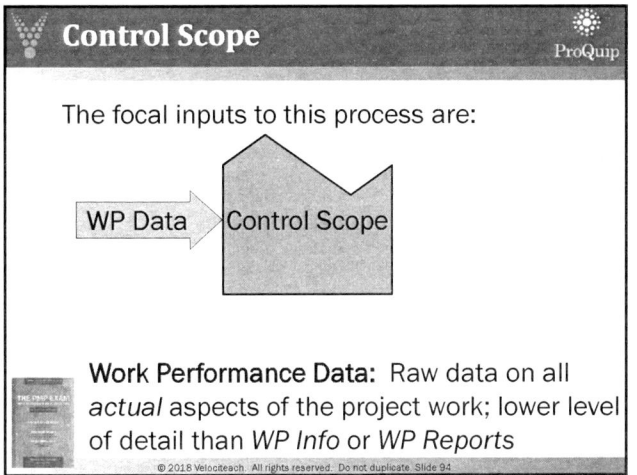

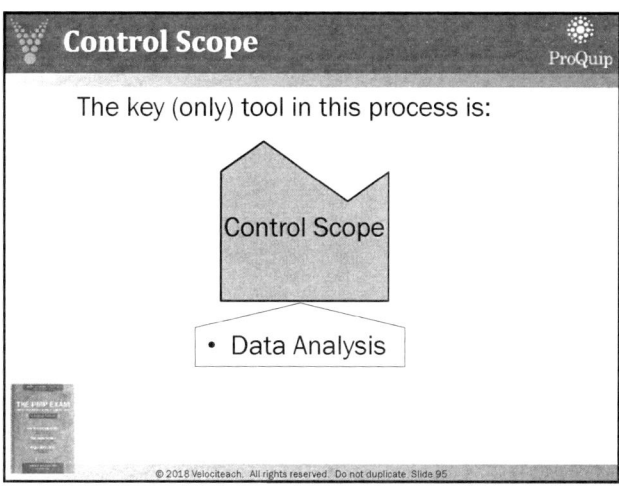

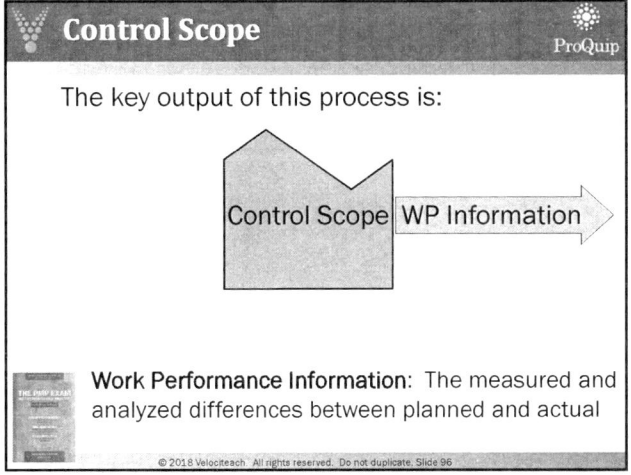

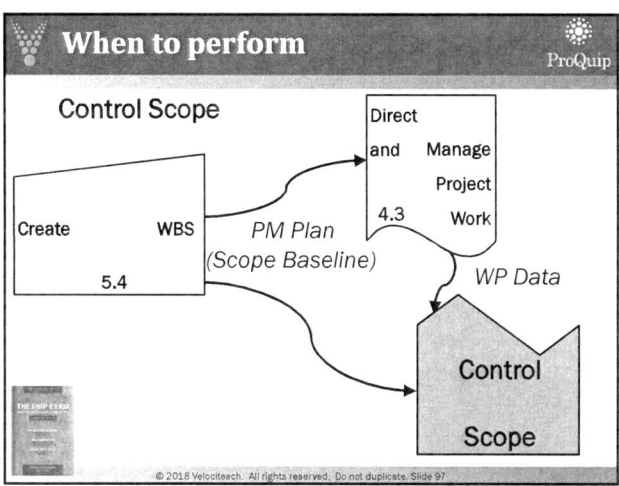

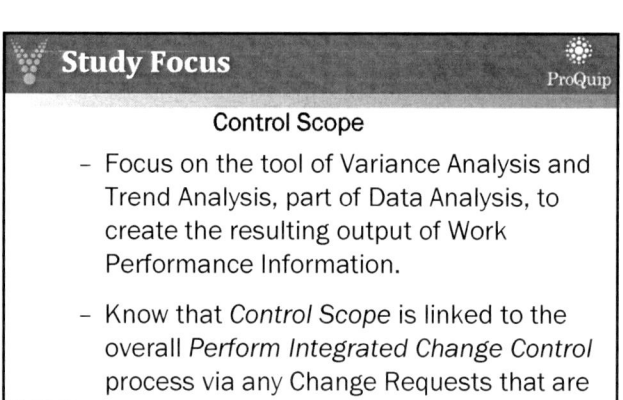

Study Focus

ProQuip

Control Scope

- Focus on the tool of Variance Analysis and Trend Analysis, part of Data Analysis, to create the resulting output of Work Performance Information.

- Know that *Control Scope* is linked to the overall *Perform Integrated Change Control* process via any Change Requests that are created here.

© 2018 Velociteach. All rights reserved. Do not duplicate. Slide 98

Review the ITTOs

Control Scope

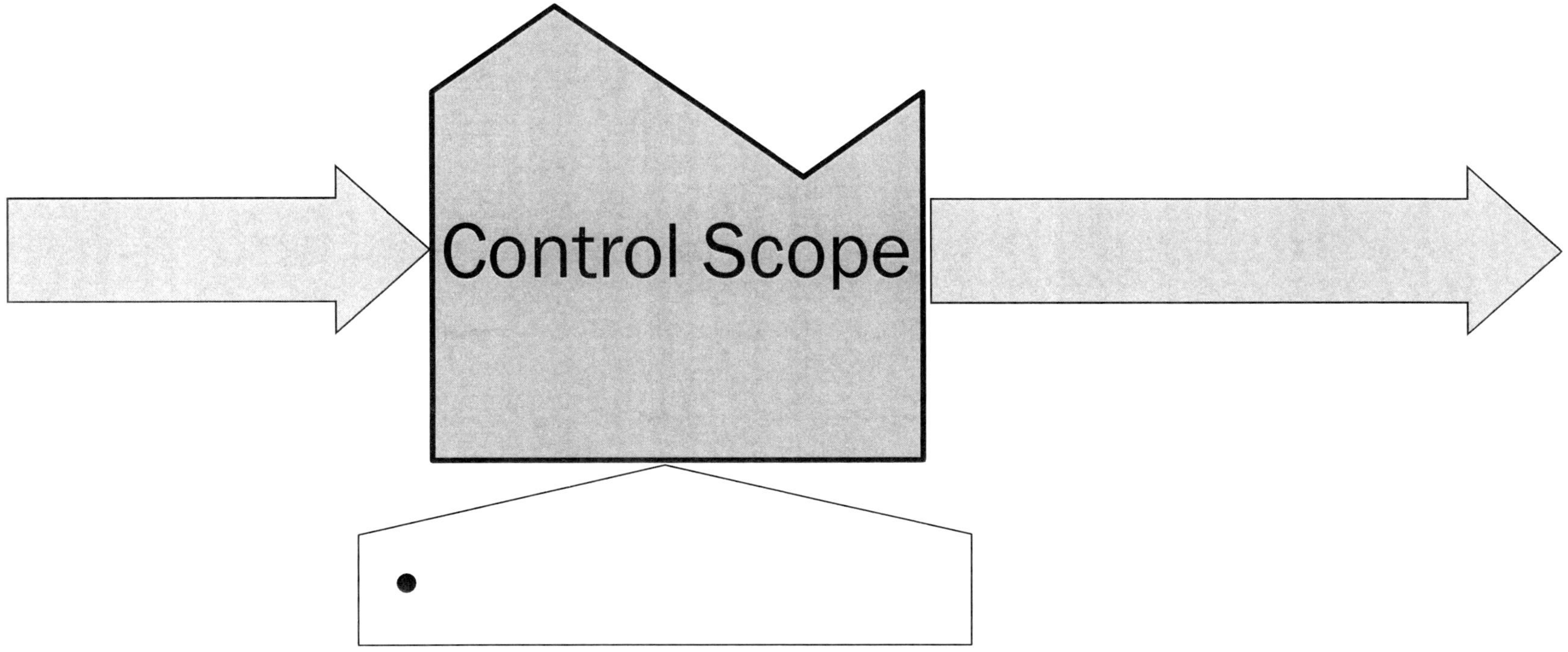

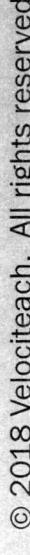

© 2018 Velociteach. All rights reserved.

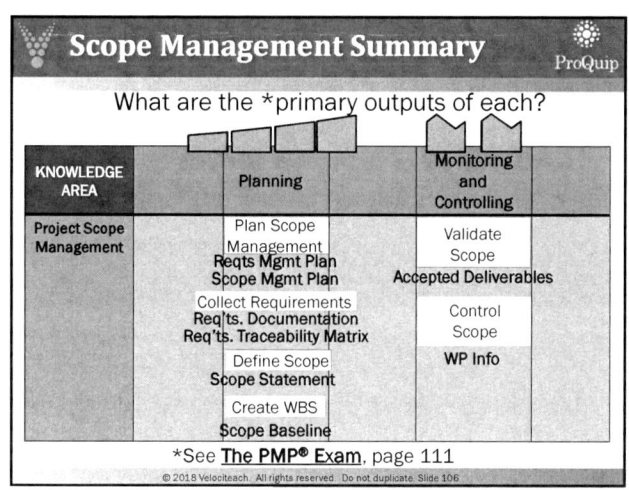

Scope Management Summary

What are the *primary outputs of each?

KNOWLEDGE AREA	Planning	Monitoring and Controlling
Project Scope Management	Plan Scope Management Reqts Mgmt Plan Scope Mgmt Plan	Validate Scope Accepted Deliverables
	Collect Requirements Req'ts. Documentation Req'ts. Traceability Matrix	Control Scope
	Define Scope Scope Statement	WP Info
	Create WBS Scope Baseline	

*See The PMP® Exam, page 111

© 2018 Velociteach. All rights reserved. Do not duplicate. Slide 106

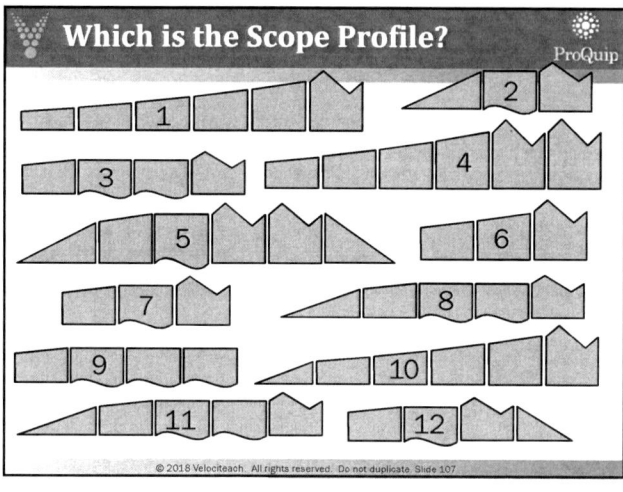

Which is the Scope Profile?

1 2 3 4 5 6 7 8 9 10 11 12

© 2018 Velociteach. All rights reserved. Do not duplicate. Slide 107

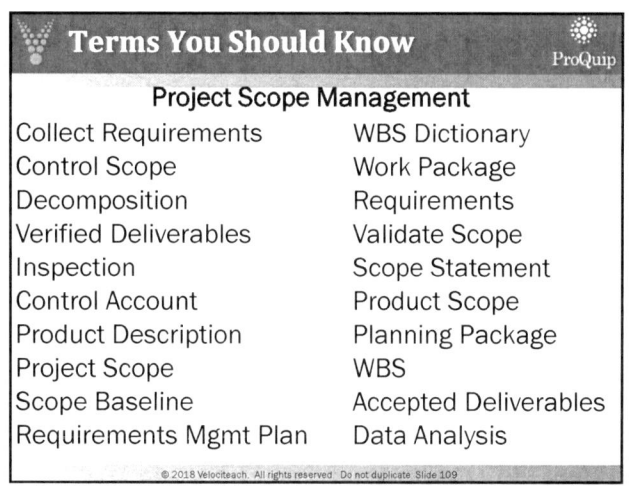

Terms You Should Know

Project Scope Management

Collect Requirements	WBS Dictionary
Control Scope	Work Package
Decomposition	Requirements
Verified Deliverables	Validate Scope
Inspection	Scope Statement
Control Account	Product Scope
Product Description	Planning Package
Project Scope	WBS
Scope Baseline	Accepted Deliverables
Requirements Mgmt Plan	Data Analysis

© 2018 Velociteach. All rights reserved. Do not duplicate. Slide 109

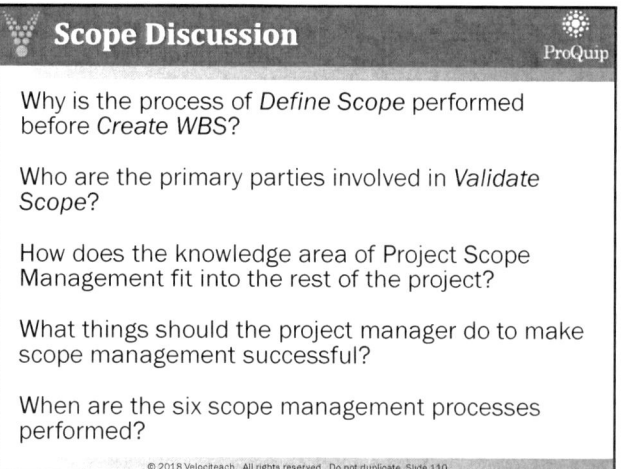

Scope Discussion

Why is the process of *Define Scope* performed before *Create WBS*?

Who are the primary parties involved in *Validate Scope*?

How does the knowledge area of Project Scope Management fit into the rest of the project?

What things should the project manager do to make scope management successful?

When are the six scope management processes performed?

© 2018 Velociteach. All rights reserved. Do not duplicate. Slide 110

Summary

Knowledge Area

ProQuip

KNOWLEDGE AREA	Initiating	Planning	Executing	Monitoring and Controlling	Closing
Project Management					

©2018 Velociteach. All rights reserved.

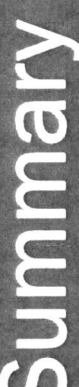

- Mark one answer: A, B, C, or D.
- Circle the '?' symbol if you are guessing at the answer.
- Circle the Δ symbol if you change your answer.

Total Correct: _____

% Correct: _____%

1.	A ○	B ○	C ○	D ○	? Δ
2.	A ○	B ○	C ○	D ○	? Δ
3.	A ○	B ○	C ○	D ○	? Δ
4.	A ○	B ○	C ○	D ○	? Δ
5.	A ○	B ○	C ○	D ○	? Δ
6.	A ○	B ○	C ○	D ○	? Δ
7.	A ○	B ○	C ○	D ○	? Δ
8.	A ○	B ○	C ○	D ○	? Δ
9.	A ○	B ○	C ○	D ○	? Δ
10.	A ○	B ○	C ○	D ○	? Δ
11.	A ○	B ○	C ○	D ○	? Δ
12.	A ○	B ○	C ○	D ○	? Δ
13.	A ○	B ○	C ○	D ○	? Δ
14.	A ○	B ○	C ○	D ○	? Δ
15.	A ○	B ○	C ○	D ○	? Δ
16.	A ○	B ○	C ○	D ○	? Δ
17.	A ○	B ○	C ○	D ○	? Δ
18.	A ○	B ○	C ○	D ○	? Δ
19.	A ○	B ○	C ○	D ○	? Δ
20.	A ○	B ○	C ○	D ○	? Δ
21.	A ○	B ○	C ○	D ○	? Δ
22.	A ○	B ○	C ○	D ○	? Δ
23.	A ○	B ○	C ○	D ○	? Δ
24.	A ○	B ○	C ○	D ○	? Δ
25.	A ○	B ○	C ○	D ○	? Δ

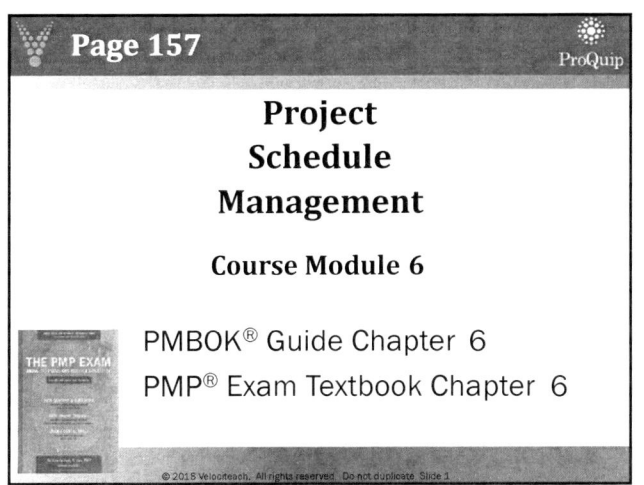

Page 157

ProQuip

Project Schedule Management

Course Module 6

PMBOK® Guide Chapter 6

PMP® Exam Textbook Chapter 6

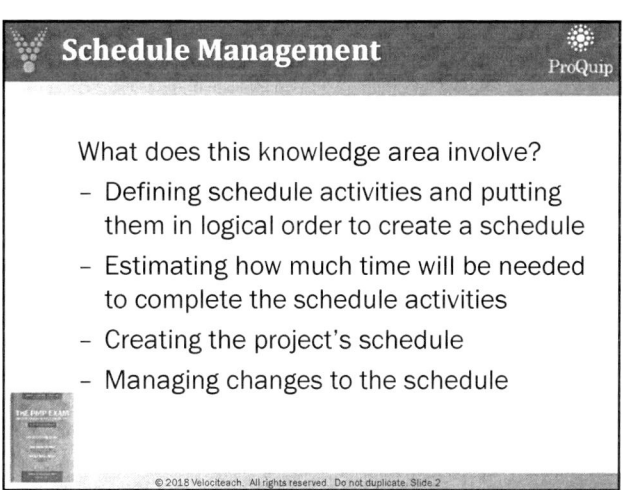

Schedule Management

ProQuip

What does this knowledge area involve?
- Defining schedule activities and putting them in logical order to create a schedule
- Estimating how much time will be needed to complete the schedule activities
- Creating the project's schedule
- Managing changes to the schedule

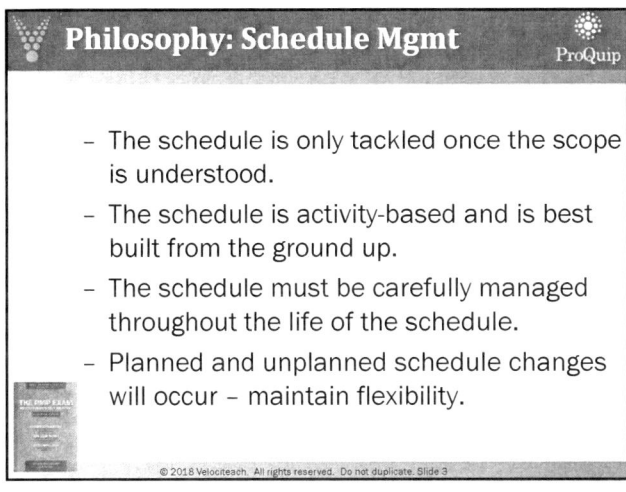

Philosophy: Schedule Mgmt

ProQuip

- The schedule is only tackled once the scope is understood.
- The schedule is activity-based and is best built from the ground up.
- The schedule must be carefully managed throughout the life of the schedule.
- Planned and unplanned schedule changes will occur – maintain flexibility.

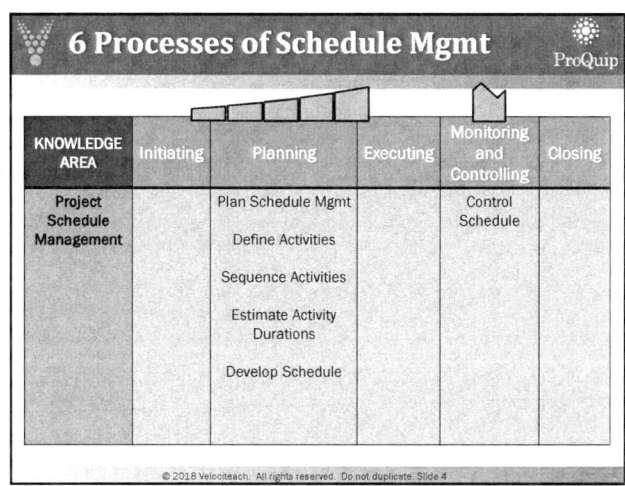

6 Processes of Schedule Mgmt

ProQuip

KNOWLEDGE AREA	Initiating	Planning	Executing	Monitoring and Controlling	Closing
Project Schedule Management		Plan Schedule Mgmt		Control Schedule	
		Define Activities			
		Sequence Activities			
		Estimate Activity Durations			
		Develop Schedule			

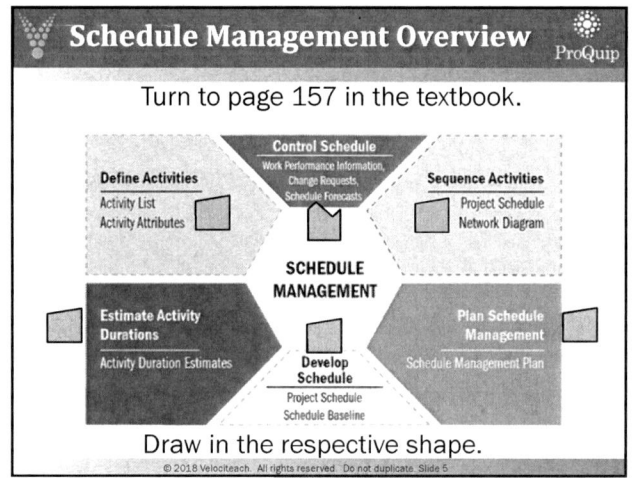

Schedule Management Overview

Turn to page 157 in the textbook.

Draw in the respective shape.

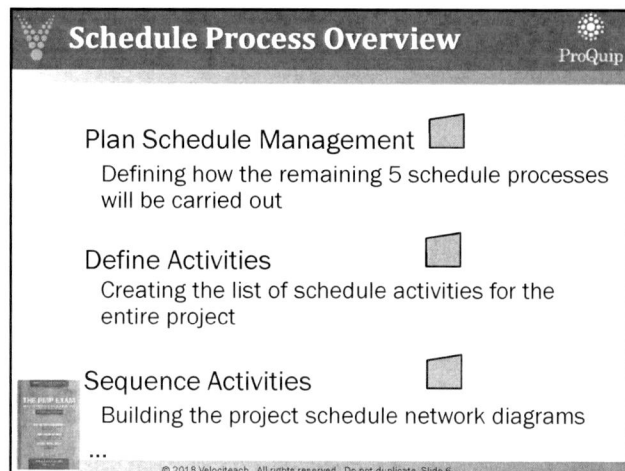

Schedule Process Overview

Plan Schedule Management
Defining how the remaining 5 schedule processes will be carried out

Define Activities
Creating the list of schedule activities for the entire project

Sequence Activities
Building the project schedule network diagrams
...

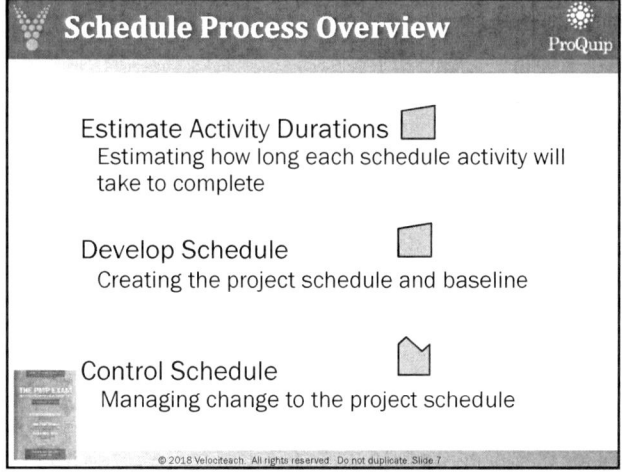

Schedule Process Overview

Estimate Activity Durations
Estimating how long each schedule activity will take to complete

Develop Schedule
Creating the project schedule and baseline

Control Schedule
Managing change to the project schedule

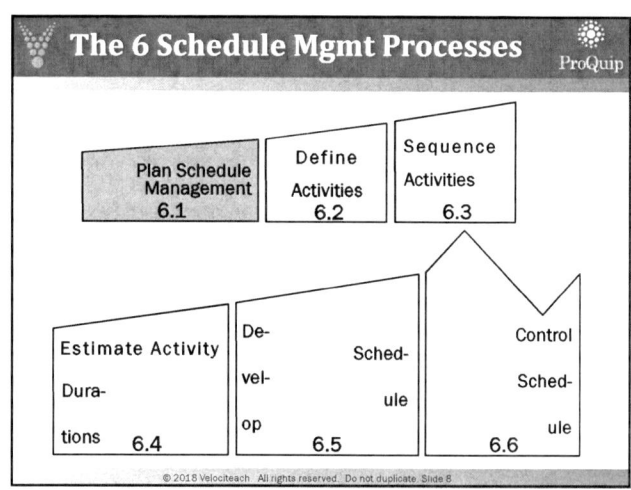

The 6 Schedule Mgmt Processes

Plan Schedule Management

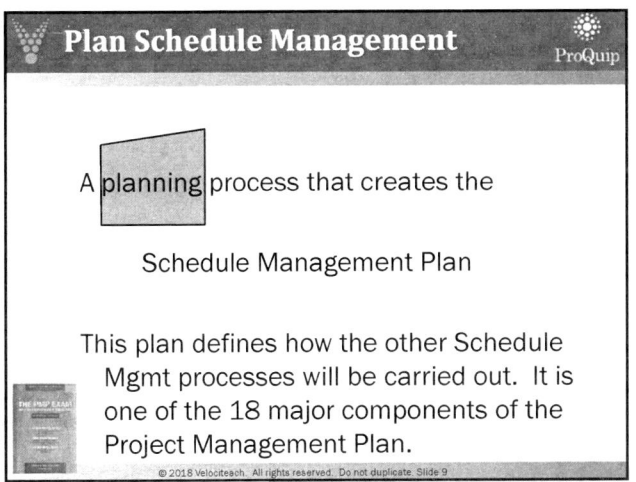

A planning process that creates the

Schedule Management Plan

This plan defines how the other Schedule Mgmt processes will be carried out. It is one of the 18 major components of the Project Management Plan.

© 2018 Velociteach. All rights reserved. Do not duplicate. Slide 9

PM Role *

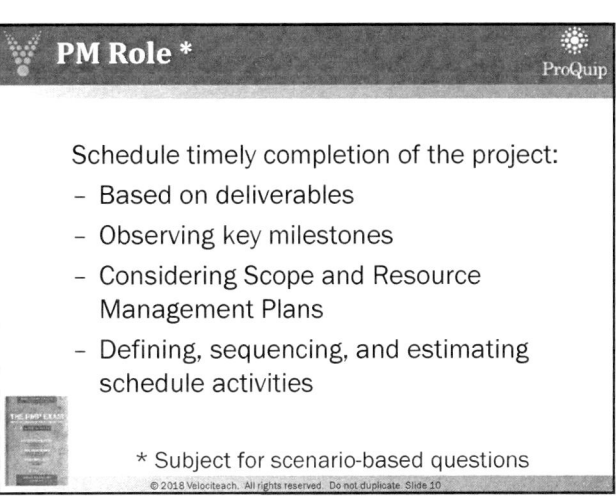

Schedule timely completion of the project:
- Based on deliverables
- Observing key milestones
- Considering Scope and Resource Management Plans
- Defining, sequencing, and estimating schedule activities

* Subject for scenario-based questions

© 2018 Velociteach. All rights reserved. Do not duplicate. Slide 10

PM Role *

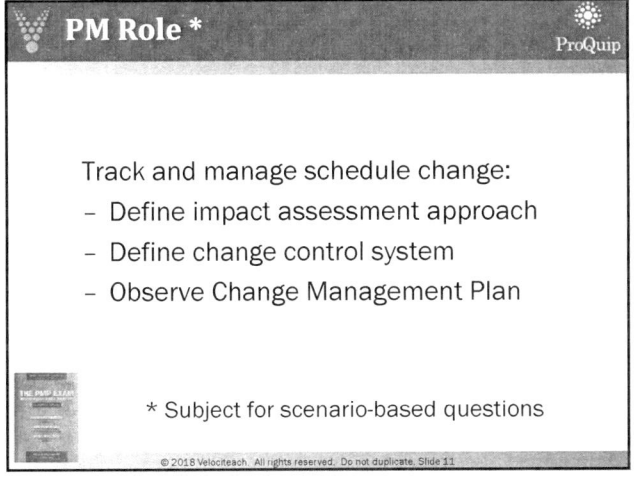

Track and manage schedule change:
- Define impact assessment approach
- Define change control system
- Observe Change Management Plan

* Subject for scenario-based questions

© 2018 Velociteach. All rights reserved. Do not duplicate. Slide 11

Plan Schedule Management

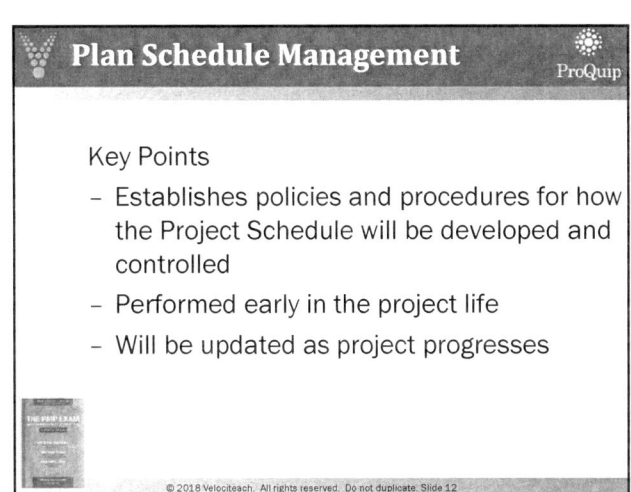

Key Points
- Establishes policies and procedures for how the Project Schedule will be developed and controlled
- Performed early in the project life
- Will be updated as project progresses

© 2018 Velociteach. All rights reserved. Do not duplicate. Slide 12

Plan Schedule Management

The key output of this process is:

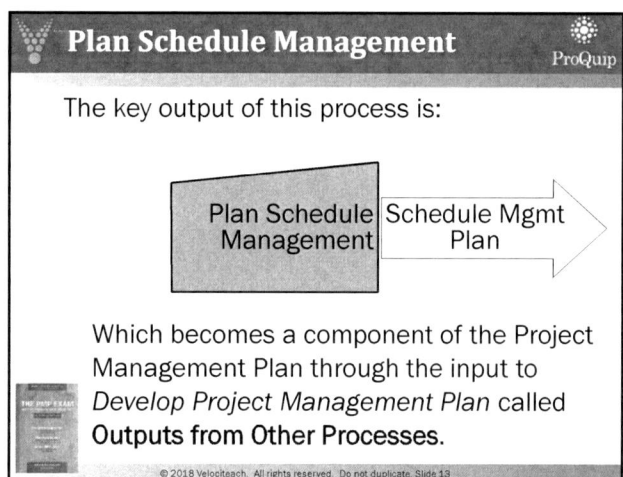

Which becomes a component of the Project Management Plan through the input to *Develop Project Management Plan* called **Outputs from Other Processes.**

© 2018 Velociteach. All rights reserved. Do not duplicate. Slide 13

Project Plan Pyramid

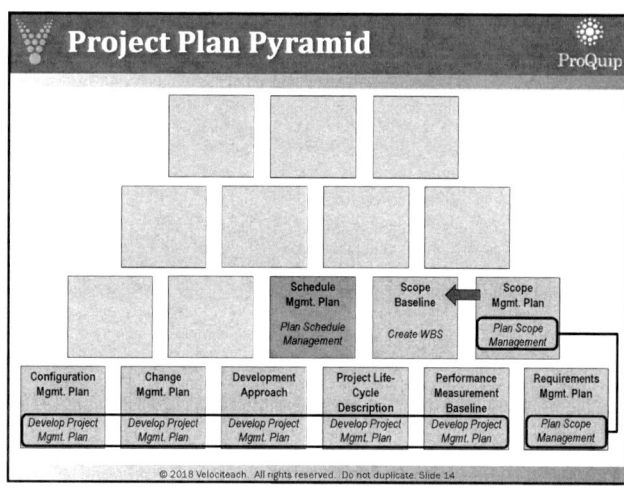

© 2018 Velociteach. All rights reserved. Do not duplicate. Slide 14

When to perform

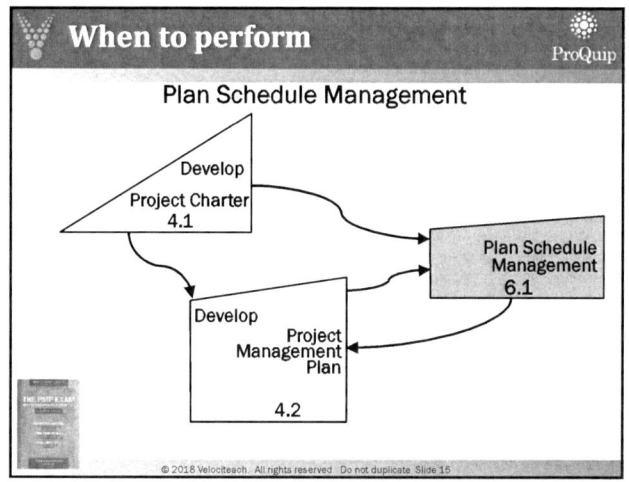

© 2018 Velociteach. All rights reserved. Do not duplicate. Slide 15

Study Focus

Plan Schedule Management
- Focus your efforts on understanding the primary output, the **Schedule Management Plan.**
- Know that this subsidiary plan becomes a component of the PM Plan from this process.
- Be aware that this process occurs early, but may be progressively elaborated.

© 2018 Velociteach. All rights reserved. Do not duplicate. Slide 16

Review the ITTOs

Plan Schedule Management

© 2018 Velociteach. All rights reserved.

The 6 Schedule Mgmt Processes

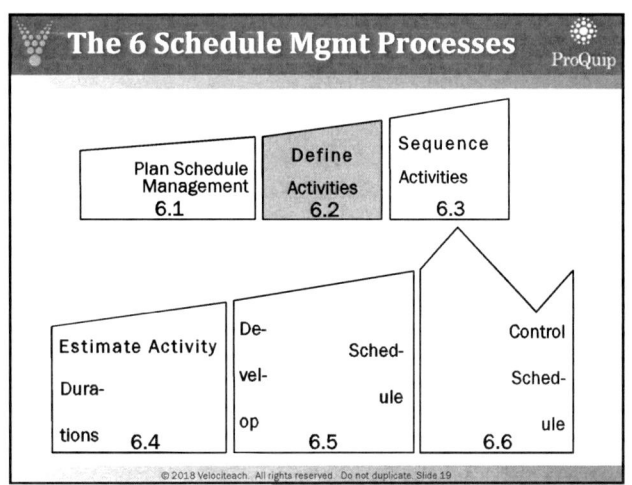

© 2018 Velociteach. All rights reserved. Do not duplicate. Slide 19

Define Activities

A | planning | process that creates a list of schedule activities called the

Activity List

The activity list contains all of the schedule activities that will (eventually) be used to create the schedule.

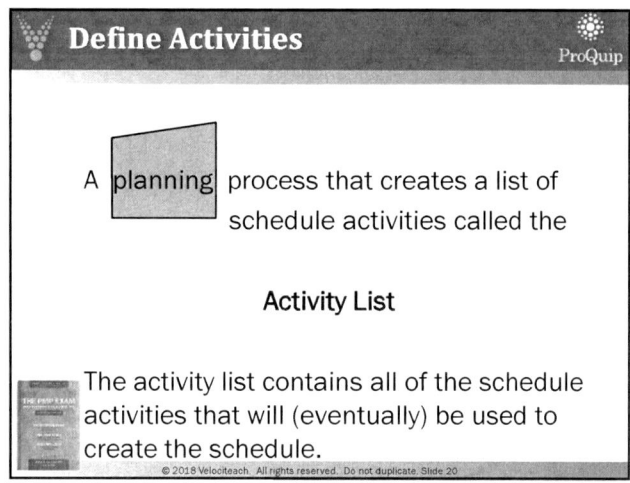

© 2018 Velociteach. All rights reserved. Do not duplicate. Slide 20

Schedule Activity

DEFINITION A task that must be performed in order to complete work on the project

Activities are created by further decomposing work packages. Schedule activities are first defined, then sequenced and estimated for duration.

One way schedule activities are represented is through the bars on a GANTT chart.

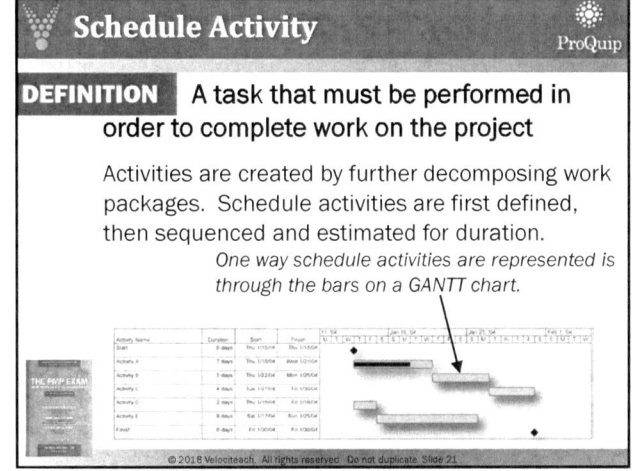

© 2018 Velociteach. All rights reserved. Do not duplicate. Slide 21

Define Activities

Key Points

– *Define Activities* flows from the WBS.

– WBS work packages are further decomposed into schedule activities.

– Schedule activities are small enough to estimate for time and cost and can be assigned to a single person or group.

– The main purpose of *Define Activities* is to create the activity list.

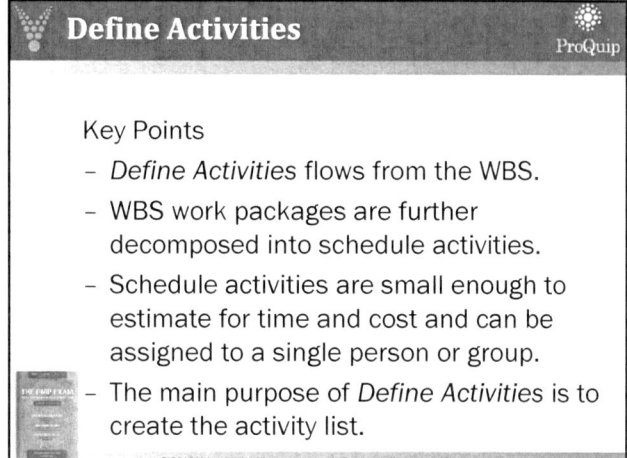

© 2018 Velociteach. All rights reserved. Do not duplicate. Slide 22

Define Activities

The key inputs to this process are:

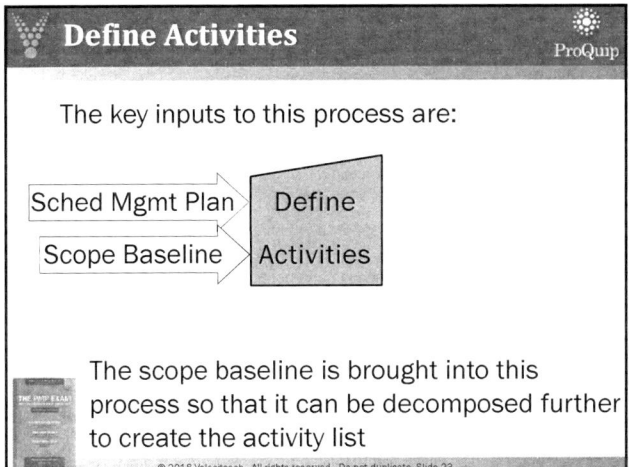

The scope baseline is brought into this process so that it can be decomposed further to create the activity list

© 2018 Velociteach. All rights reserved. Do not duplicate. Slide 23

Define Activities

The key tools in this process are:

• **Decomposition:** used to break down the work packages into schedule activities.

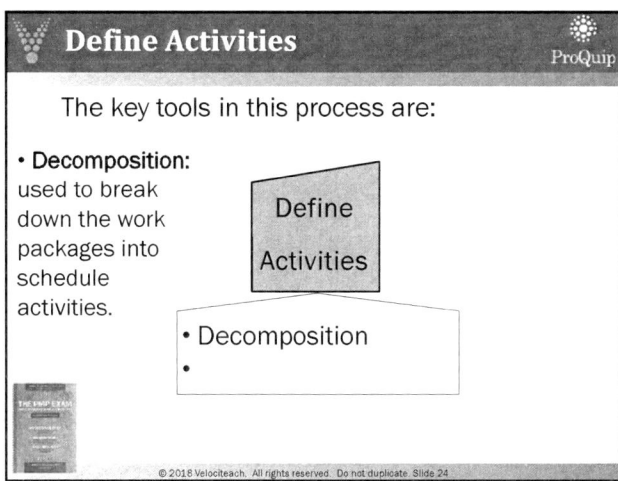

• Decomposition
•

© 2018 Velociteach. All rights reserved. Do not duplicate. Slide 24

Define Activities

The key tools in this process are:

• **Decomposition:** used to break down the work packages into schedule activities.

• **Rolling Wave Planning:** only plans imminent project activities in detail

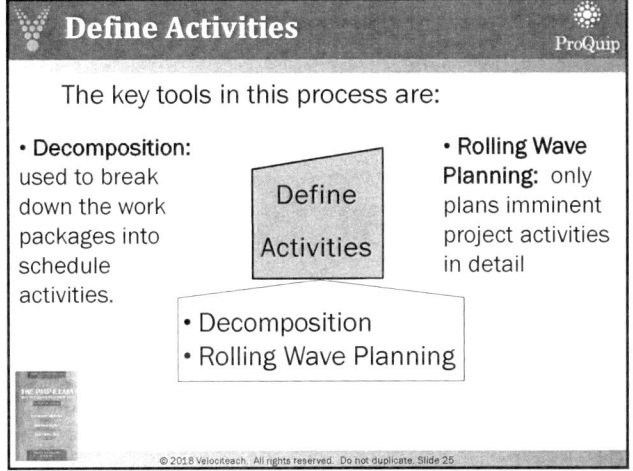

• Decomposition
• Rolling Wave Planning

© 2018 Velociteach. All rights reserved. Do not duplicate. Slide 25

Define Activities

The focal outputs of this process are:

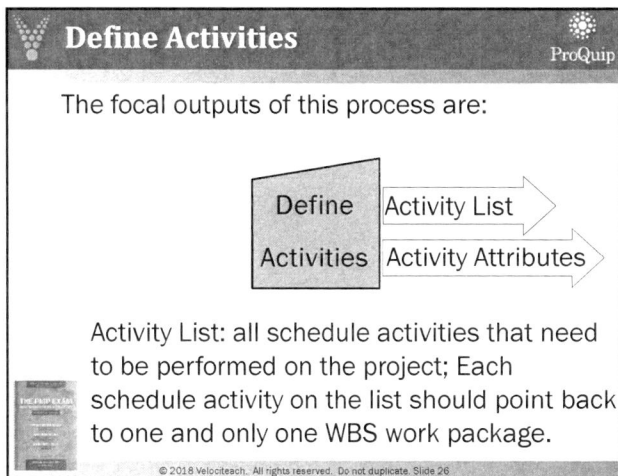

Activity List: all schedule activities that need to be performed on the project; Each schedule activity on the list should point back to one and only one WBS work package.

© 2018 Velociteach. All rights reserved. Do not duplicate. Slide 26

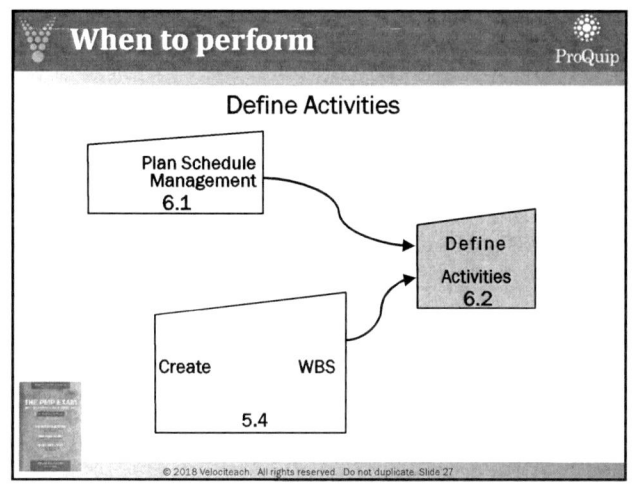

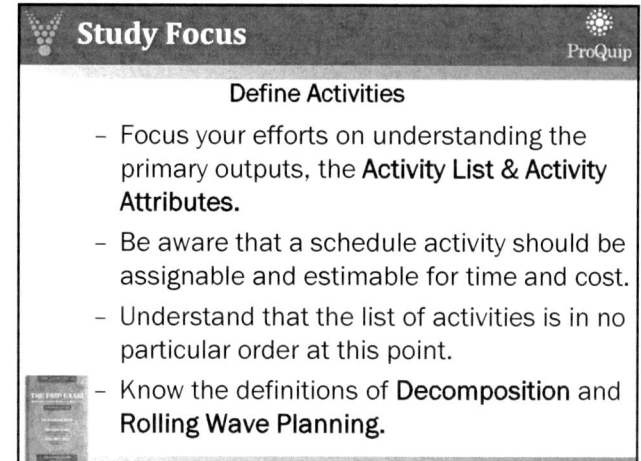

©2018 Velociteach. All rights reserved. Page 114

Review the ITTOs

ProQuip

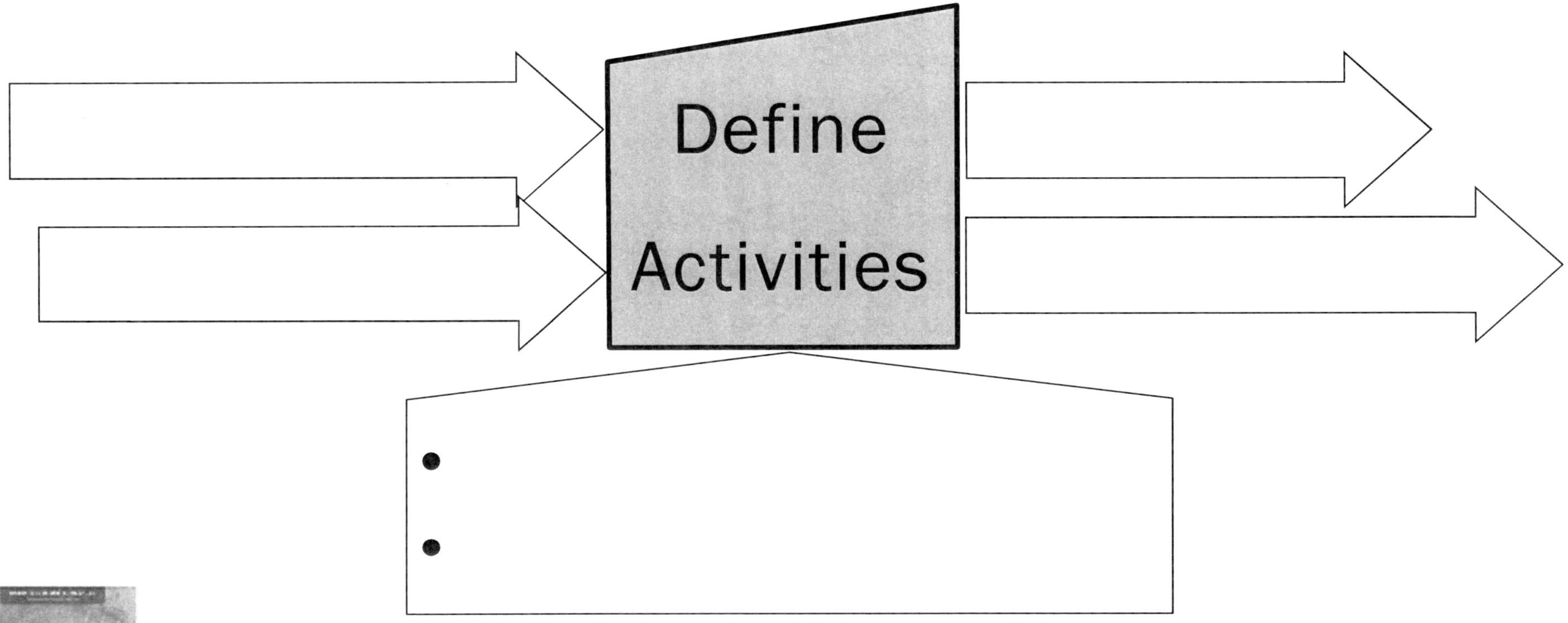

Define Activities

© 2018 Velociteach. All rights reserved.

This page left intentionally blank.

©2018 Velociteach. All rights reserved.

The 6 Schedule Mgmt Processes

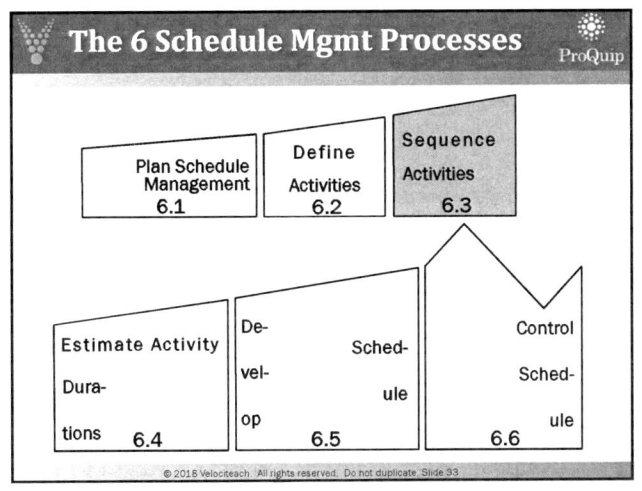

© 2018 Velociteach. All rights reserved. Do not duplicate. Slide 33

Sequence Activities

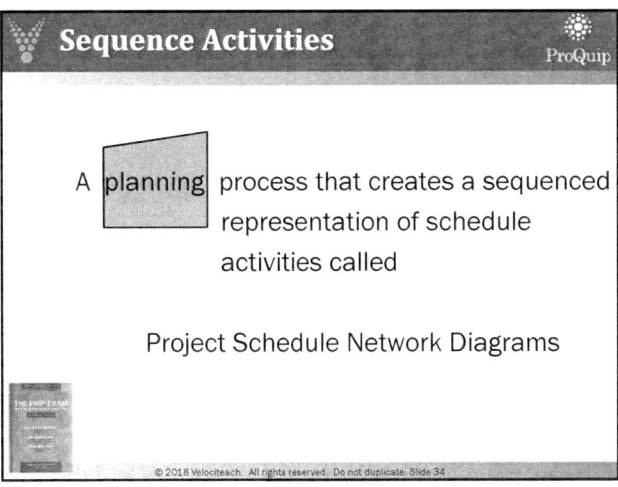

A planning process that creates a sequenced representation of schedule activities called

Project Schedule Network Diagrams

© 2018 Velociteach. All rights reserved. Do not duplicate. Slide 34

Sequence Activities

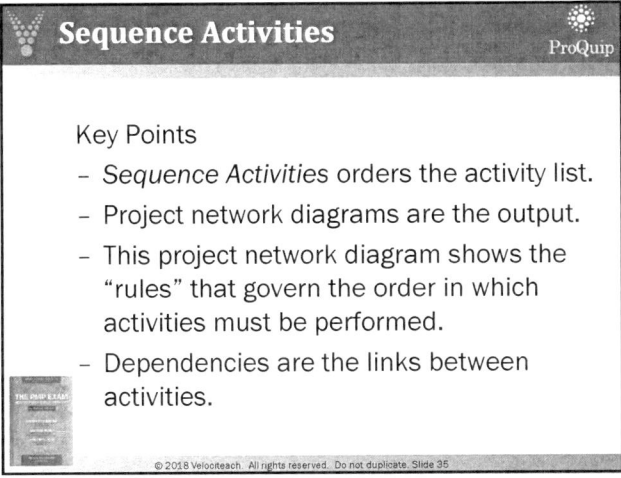

Key Points
- *Sequence Activities* orders the activity list.
- Project network diagrams are the output.
- This project network diagram shows the "rules" that govern the order in which activities must be performed.
- Dependencies are the links between activities.

© 2018 Velociteach. All rights reserved. Do not duplicate. Slide 35

Sequence Activities

The key inputs to this process are:

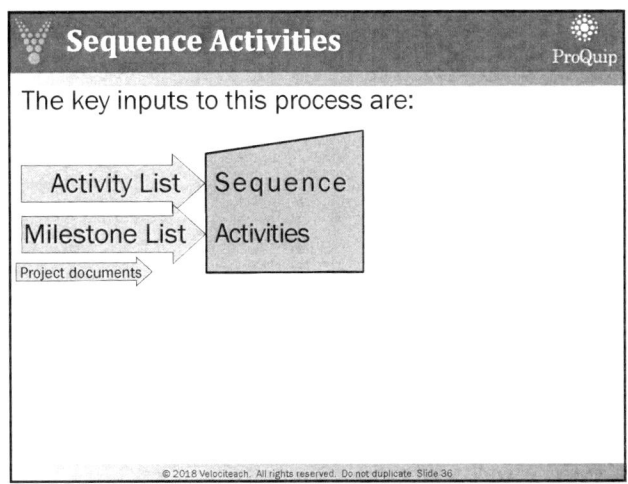

© 2018 Velociteach. All rights reserved. Do not duplicate. Slide 36

Sequence Activities

The tools in this process are:

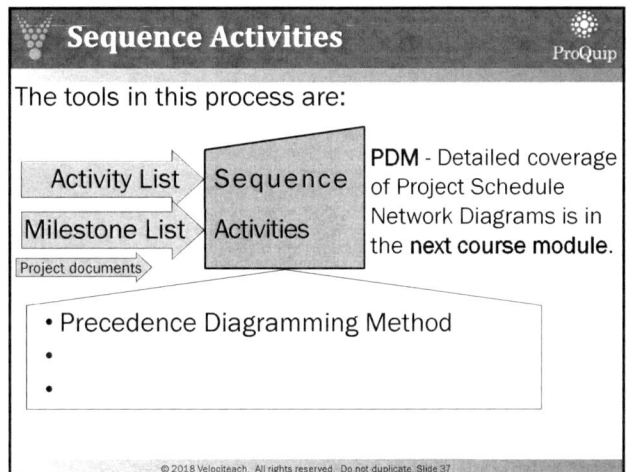

PDM - Detailed coverage of Project Schedule Network Diagrams is in the **next course module**.

- Precedence Diagramming Method
-
-

© 2018 Velociteach. All rights reserved. Do not duplicate. Slide 37

Sequence Activities

The tools in this process are:

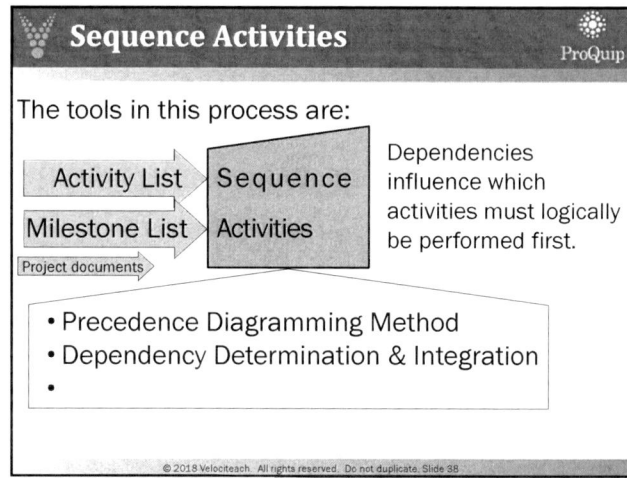

Dependencies influence which activities must logically be performed first.

- Precedence Diagramming Method
- Dependency Determination & Integration
-

© 2018 Velociteach. All rights reserved. Do not duplicate. Slide 38

Dependency

DEFINITION A relationship between two or more activities where one activity must be started or completed before another related activity can be started or completed

Types of Dependencies
Mandatory: hard logic; cannot be broken

OR

Discretionary: soft logic; preference

AND

Internal: within project team's design/control

OR

External: outside of project's control or scope

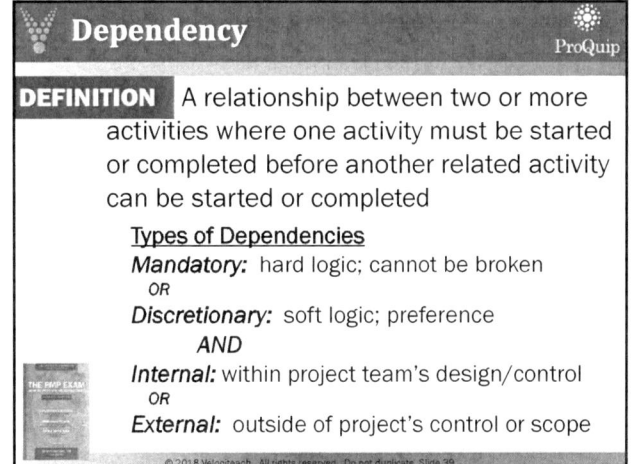

© 2018 Velociteach. All rights reserved. Do not duplicate. Slide 39

Logical Relationship

DEFINITION activity dependency

Types of Logical Relationships
Finish-Start
C must finish before D can start

Finish-Finish
F must finish before G can finish

Start-Start
K must start before L can start

Start-Finish
X must start before Y can finish

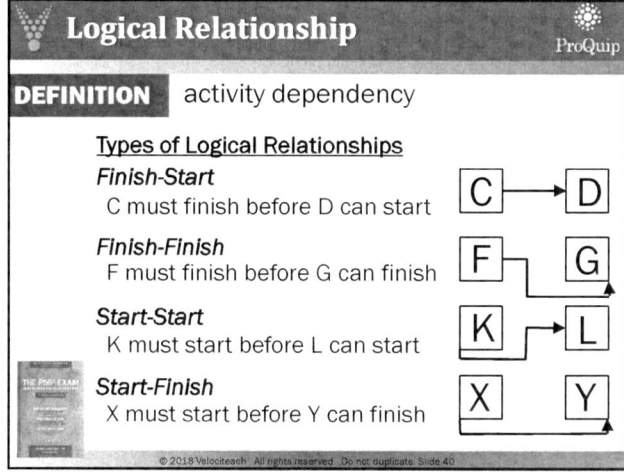

© 2018 Velociteach. All rights reserved. Do not duplicate. Slide 40

©2018 Velociteach. All rights reserved.

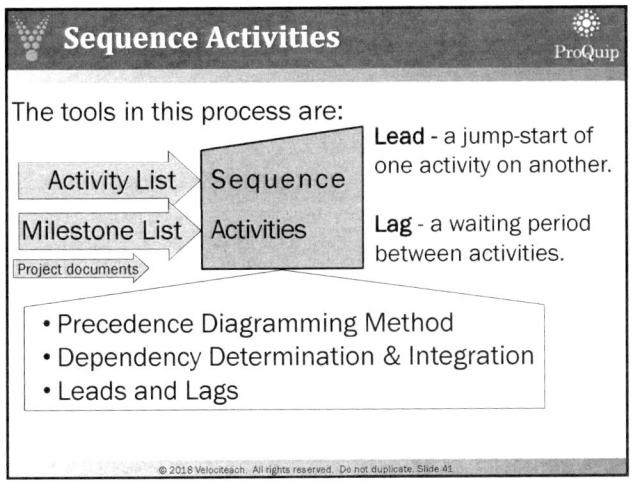

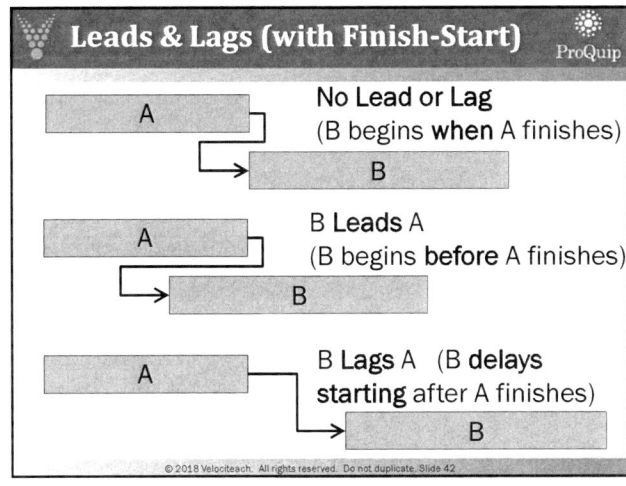

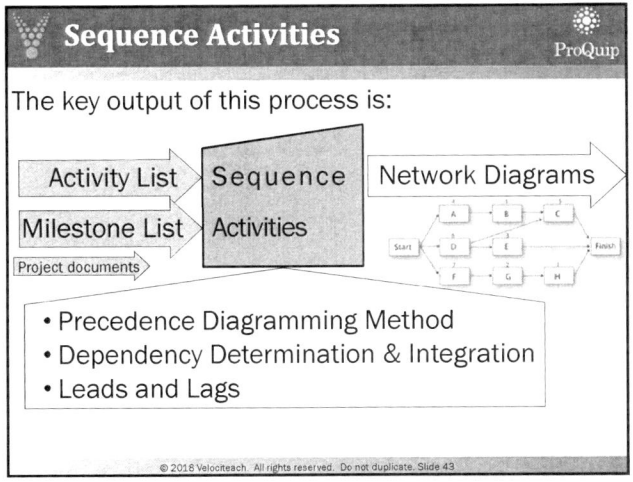

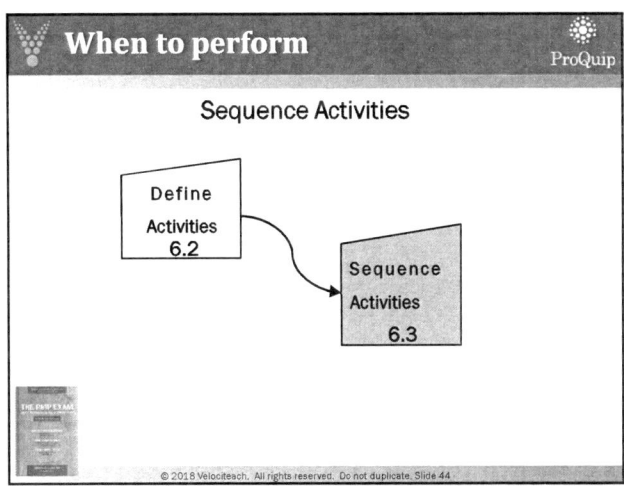

©2018 Velociteach. All rights reserved.   Page 119

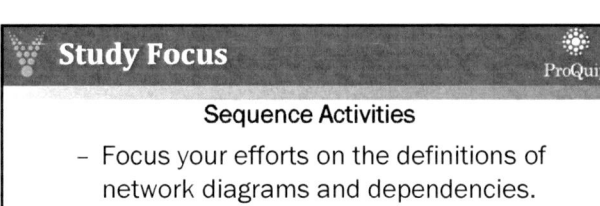

Study Focus

ProQuip

Sequence Activities

- Focus your efforts on the definitions of network diagrams and dependencies.
- Know that network diagrams show the order in which activities must be performed.
- Understand the concept of leads and lags.
- Know the types of dependencies and logical relationships.

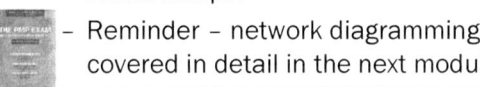

- Reminder – network diagramming is covered in detail in the next module.

© 2018 Velociteach. All rights reserved. Do not duplicate. Slide 45

Sequence Activities

© 2018 Velociteach. All rights reserved.

The 6 Schedule Mgmt Processes

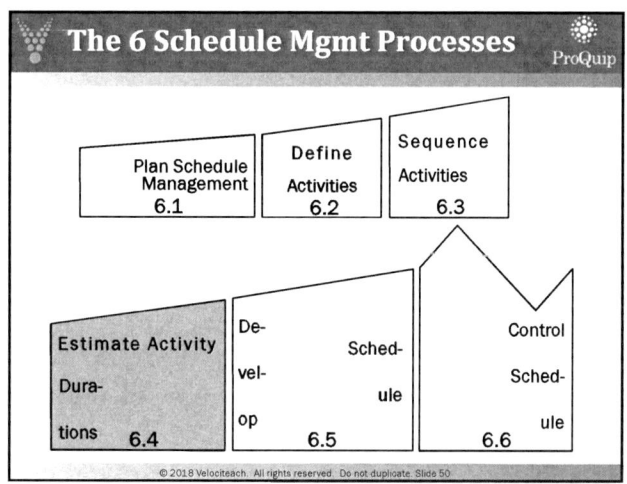

Plan Schedule Management 6.1 | Define Activities 6.2 | Sequence Activities 6.3

Estimate Activity Durations 6.4 | Develop 6.5 | Control Schedule 6.6

© 2018 Velociteach. All rights reserved. Do not duplicate. Slide 50

Estimate Activity Durations

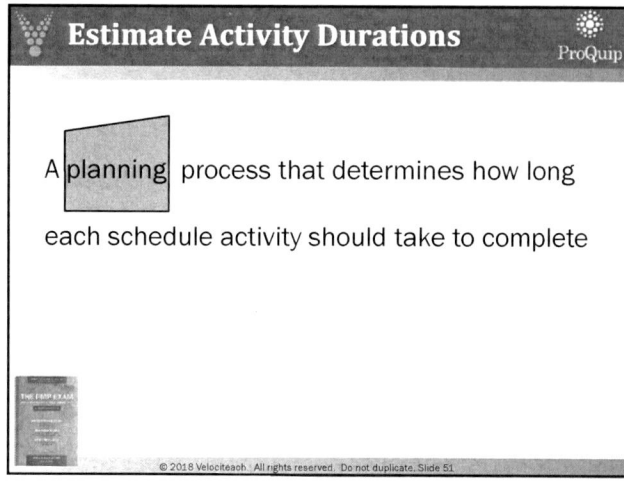

A planning process that determines how long each schedule activity should take to complete

© 2018 Velociteach. All rights reserved. Do not duplicate. Slide 51

Estimate Activity Durations

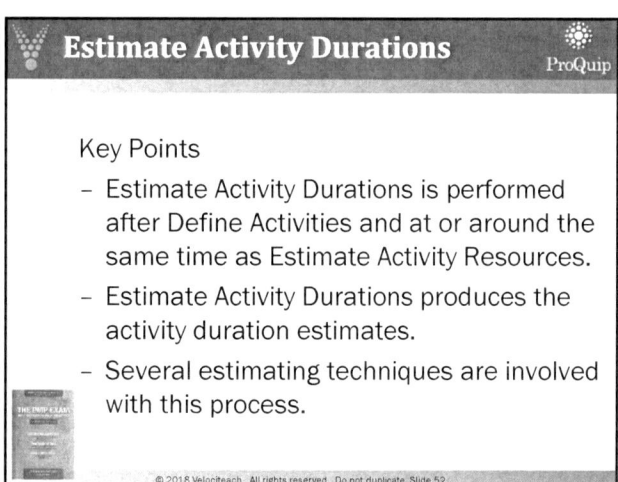

Key Points
- Estimate Activity Durations is performed after Define Activities and at or around the same time as Estimate Activity Resources.
- Estimate Activity Durations produces the activity duration estimates.
- Several estimating techniques are involved with this process.

© 2018 Velociteach. All rights reserved. Do not duplicate. Slide 52

Estimate Activity Durations

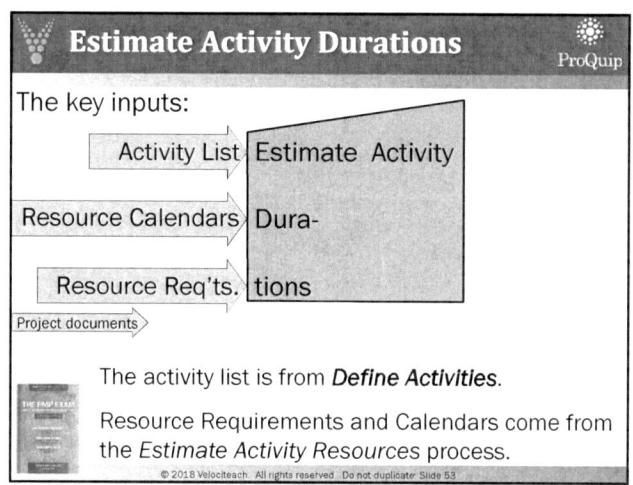

The key inputs:

Activity List · Resource Calendars · Resource Req'ts. · Project documents → Estimate Activity Durations

The activity list is from *Define Activities*.

Resource Requirements and Calendars come from the *Estimate Activity Resources* process.

© 2018 Velociteach. All rights reserved. Do not duplicate. Slide 53

Estimate Activity Durations

The focal tools:

A tool that generates estimates by using actual duration information from a *similar* activity previously performed on this or another project

Estimate Activity Durations

- Analogous Estimating
-
-
-

© 2018 Velociteach. All rights reserved. Do not duplicate. Slide 54

Estimate Activity Durations

The focal tools:

A tool that generates estimates by using historical information on linear or scalable activities;

No. of Units ÷ Unit duration

Estimate Activity Durations

Example:
   1000 feet of pipe
÷   100 feet of pipe / day
=   10 days duration

- Analogous Estimating
- Parametric Estimating
-
-

© 2018 Velociteach. All rights reserved. Do not duplicate. Slide 55

Estimate Activity Durations

The focal tools:

- Pessimistic
- Most-likely
- Optimistic

Average these three estimates

Estimate Activity Durations

- Analogous Estimating
- Parametric Estimating
- Three-Point Estimating
-

© 2018 Velociteach. All rights reserved. Do not duplicate. Slide 56

Three-Point Estimate

DEFINITION Average of worst-case (Pessimistic), best-case (Optimistic), and Most-likely estimates

Simple Average (Triangular)

$$\frac{P + M + O}{3}$$

Weighted Average (Beta)

$$\frac{P + 4M + O}{6}$$

aka PERT estimate

The standard deviation of a **PERT** estimate is:
(Pessimistic – Optimistic) ÷ 6

© 2018 Velociteach. All rights reserved. Do not duplicate. Slide 57

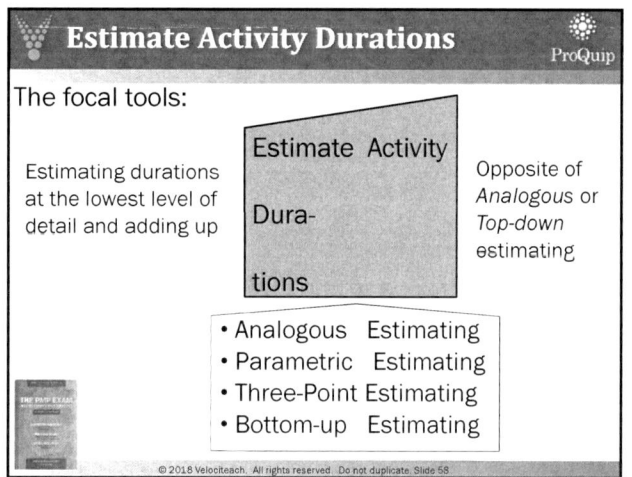

Estimate Activity Durations

The focal tools:

Estimating durations at the lowest level of detail and adding up

Estimate Activity Dura-tions

Opposite of *Analogous* or *Top-down* estimating

- Analogous Estimating
- Parametric Estimating
- Three-Point Estimating
- Bottom-up Estimating

© 2018 Velociteach. All rights reserved. Do not duplicate. Slide 58

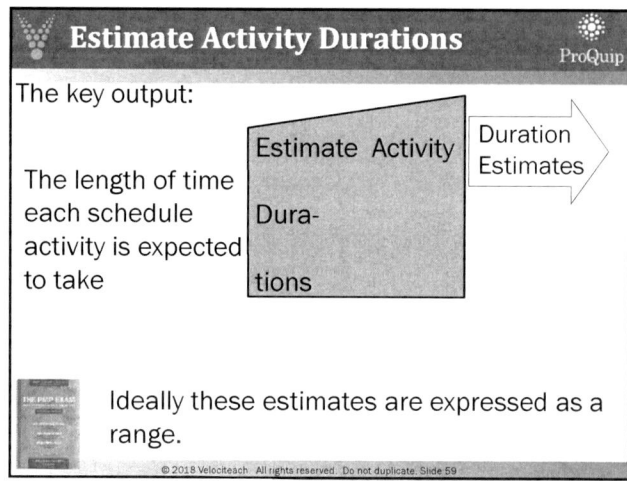

Estimate Activity Durations

The key output:

The length of time each schedule activity is expected to take

Estimate Activity Dura-tions

Duration Estimates

Ideally these estimates are expressed as a range.

© 2018 Velociteach. All rights reserved. Do not duplicate. Slide 59

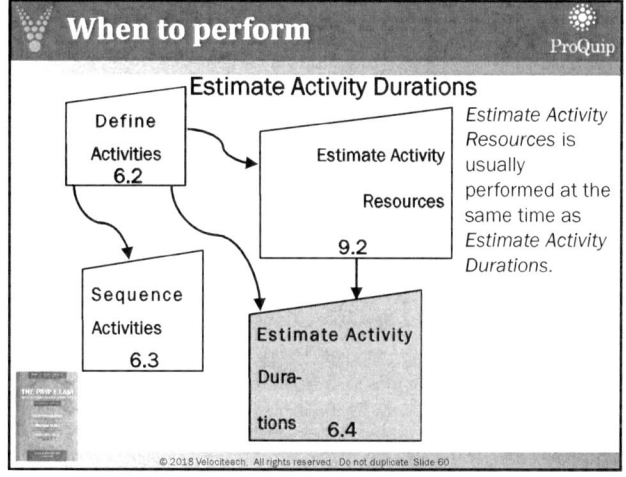

When to perform

Estimate Activity Durations

Define Activities 6.2

Estimate Activity Resources 9.2

Sequence Activities 6.3

Estimate Activity Dura-tions 6.4

Estimate Activity Resources is usually performed at the same time as *Estimate Activity Durations.*

© 2018 Velociteach. All rights reserved. Do not duplicate. Slide 60

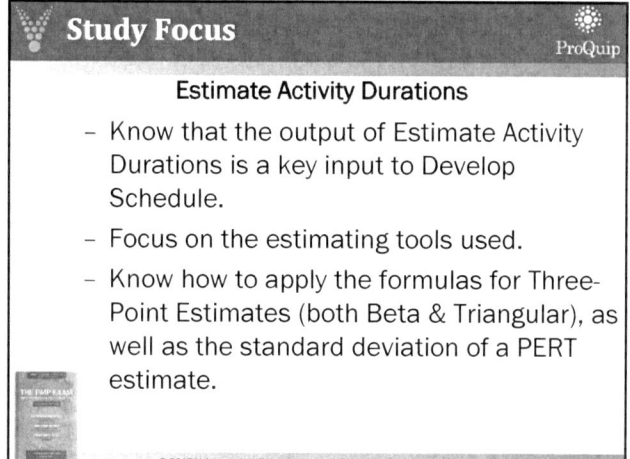

Study Focus

Estimate Activity Durations

- Know that the output of Estimate Activity Durations is a key input to Develop Schedule.
- Focus on the estimating tools used.
- Know how to apply the formulas for Three-Point Estimates (both Beta & Triangular), as well as the standard deviation of a PERT estimate.

© 2018 Velociteach. All rights reserved. Do not duplicate. Slide 61

Review the ITTOs

Estimate Activity Durations

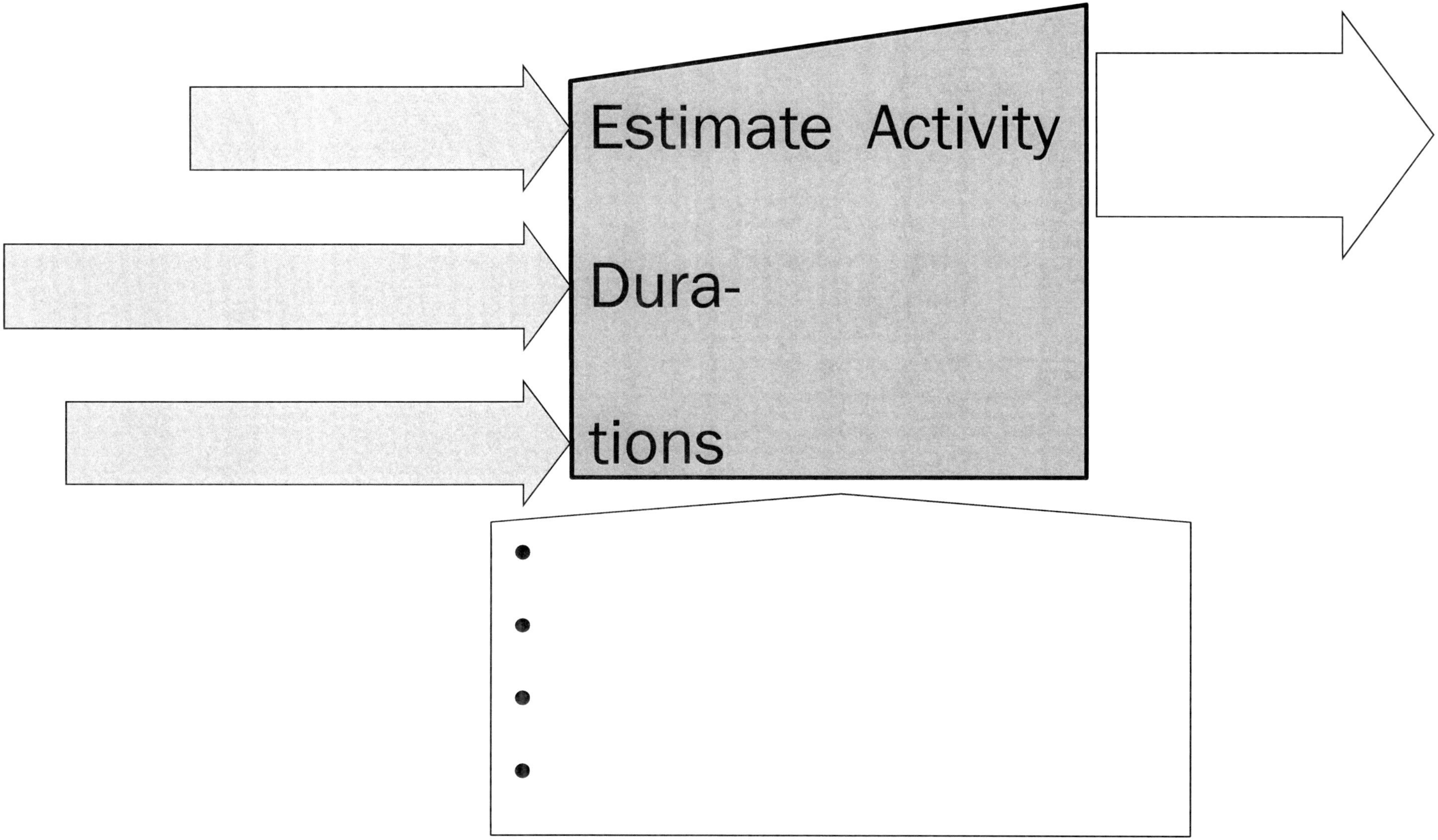

©2018 Velociteach. All rights reserved.

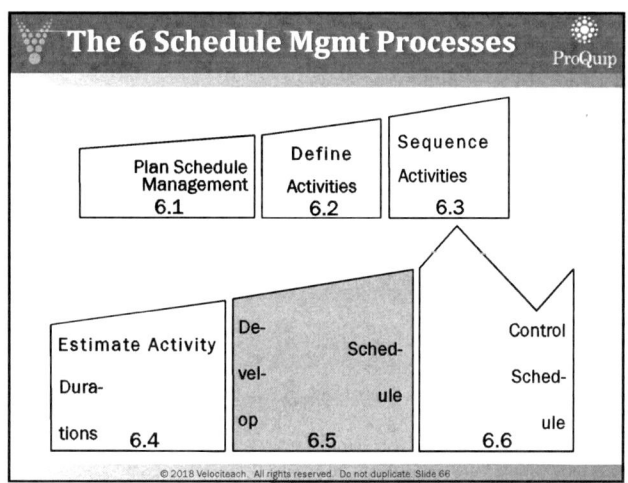

The 6 Schedule Mgmt Processes

ProQuip

- Plan Schedule Management 6.1
- Define Activities 6.2
- Sequence Activities 6.3
- Estimate Activity Durations 6.4
- Develop Schedule 6.5
- Control Schedule 6.6

© 2018 Velociteach. All rights reserved. Do not duplicate. Slide 66

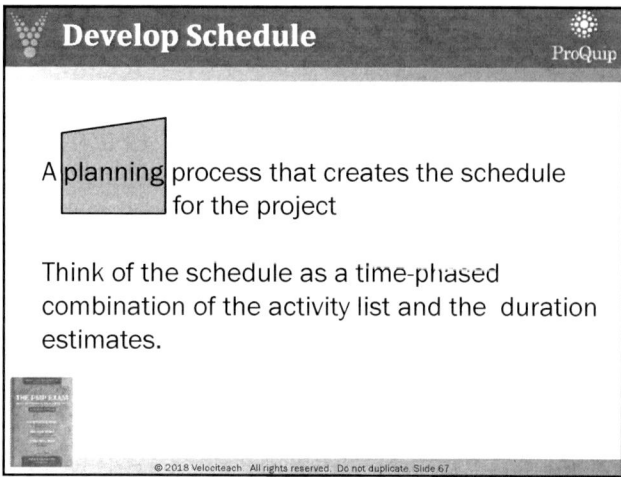

Develop Schedule

ProQuip

A planning process that creates the schedule for the project

Think of the schedule as a time-phased combination of the activity list and the duration estimates.

© 2018 Velociteach. All rights reserved. Do not duplicate. Slide 67

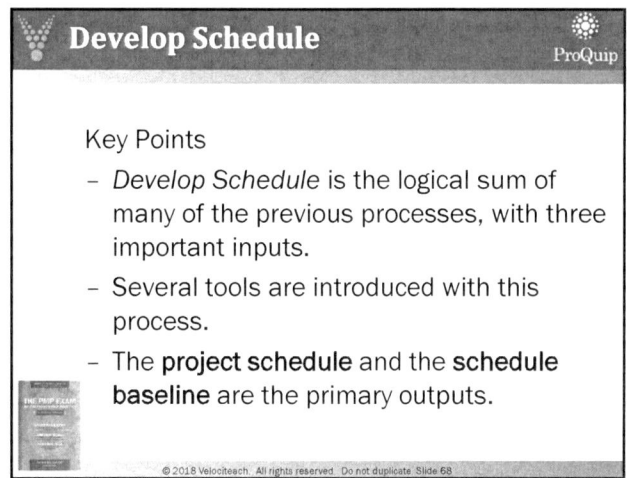

Develop Schedule

ProQuip

Key Points

- *Develop Schedule* is the logical sum of many of the previous processes, with three important inputs.
- Several tools are introduced with this process.
- The **project schedule** and the **schedule baseline** are the primary outputs.

© 2018 Velociteach. All rights reserved. Do not duplicate. Slide 68

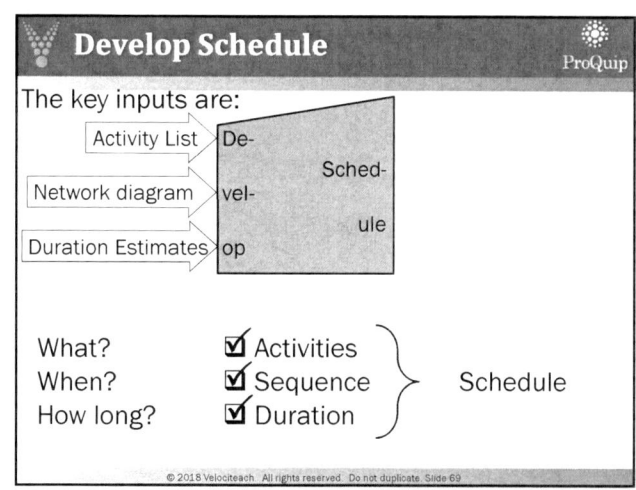

Develop Schedule

ProQuip

The key inputs are:

- Activity List
- Network diagram
- Duration Estimates

→ Develop → Schedule

What?	☑ Activities	
When?	☑ Sequence	Schedule
How long?	☑ Duration	

© 2018 Velociteach. All rights reserved. Do not duplicate. Slide 69

©2018 Velociteach. All rights reserved.   Page 126

Develop Schedule

The focal tools are:

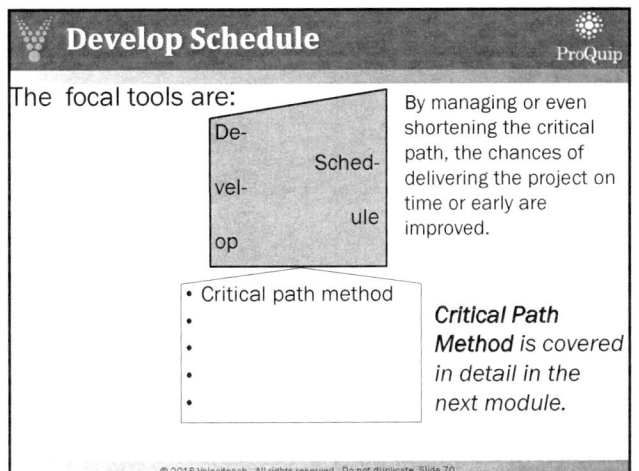

By managing or even shortening the critical path, the chances of delivering the project on time or early are improved.

- Critical path method
- •
- •
- •
- •

Critical Path Method is covered in detail in the next module.

© 2018 Velociteach. All rights reserved. Do not duplicate. Slide 70

Develop Schedule

The focal tools are:

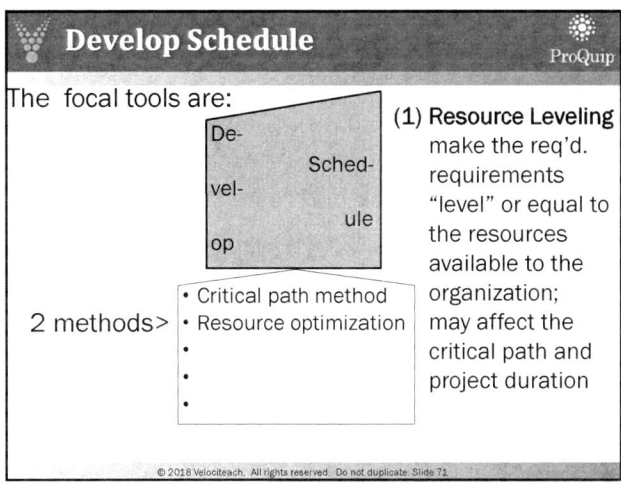

2 methods>

- Critical path method
- Resource optimization
- •
- •
- •

(1) Resource Leveling make the req'd. requirements "level" or equal to the resources available to the organization; may affect the critical path and project duration

© 2018 Velociteach. All rights reserved. Do not duplicate. Slide 71

Develop Schedule

The focal tools are:

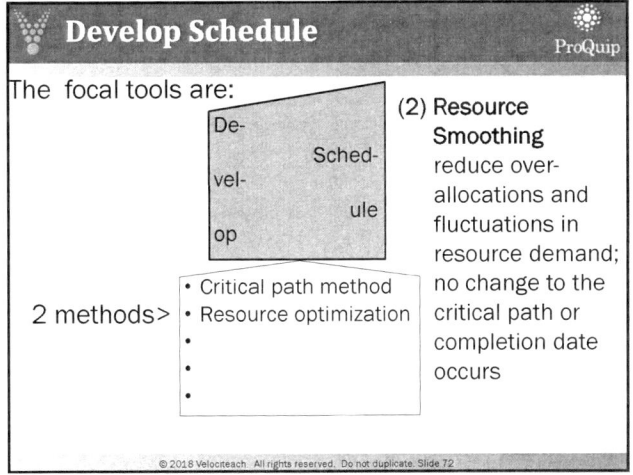

2 methods>

- Critical path method
- Resource optimization
- •
- •
- •

(2) Resource Smoothing reduce over-allocations and fluctuations in resource demand; no change to the critical path or completion date occurs

© 2018 Velociteach. All rights reserved. Do not duplicate. Slide 72

Develop Schedule

The focal tools are:

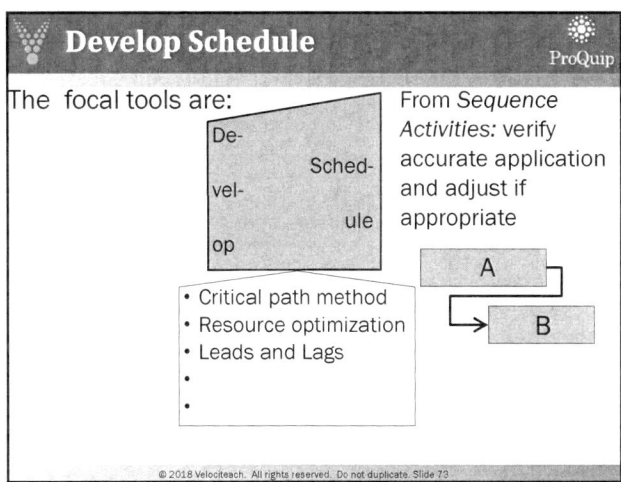

From *Sequence Activities:* verify accurate application and adjust if appropriate

- Critical path method
- Resource optimization
- Leads and Lags
- •
- •

© 2018 Velociteach. All rights reserved. Do not duplicate. Slide 73

©2018 Velociteach. All rights reserved.

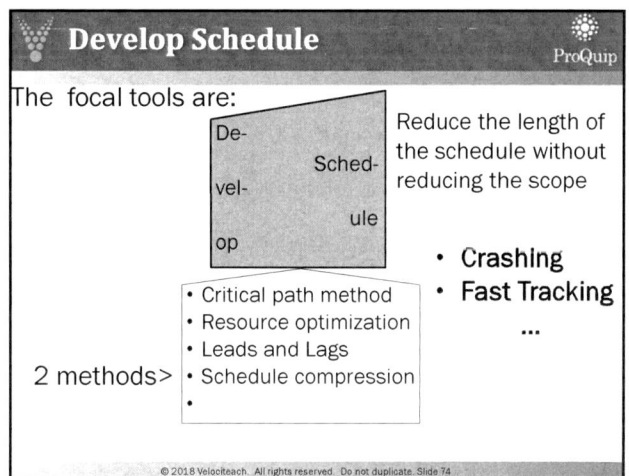

Develop Schedule — ProQuip

The focal tools are:

Develop Schedule

Reduce the length of the schedule without reducing the scope

- Crashing
- Fast Tracking
  ...

2 methods>
- Critical path method
- Resource optimization
- Leads and Lags
- Schedule compression
-

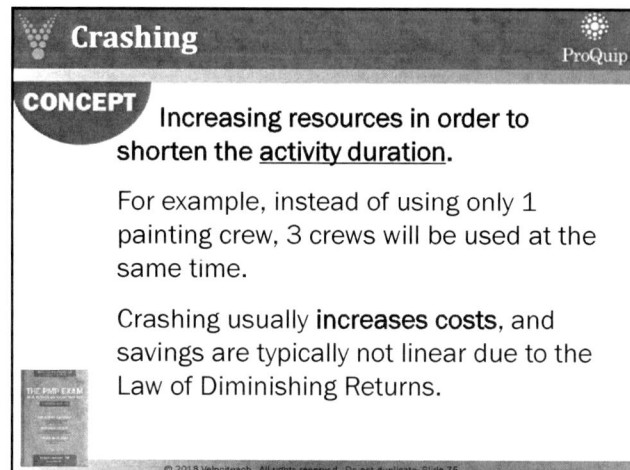

Crashing — ProQuip

CONCEPT Increasing resources in order to shorten the <u>activity duration</u>.

For example, instead of using only 1 painting crew, 3 crews will be used at the same time.

Crashing usually **increases costs**, and savings are typically not linear due to the Law of Diminishing Returns.

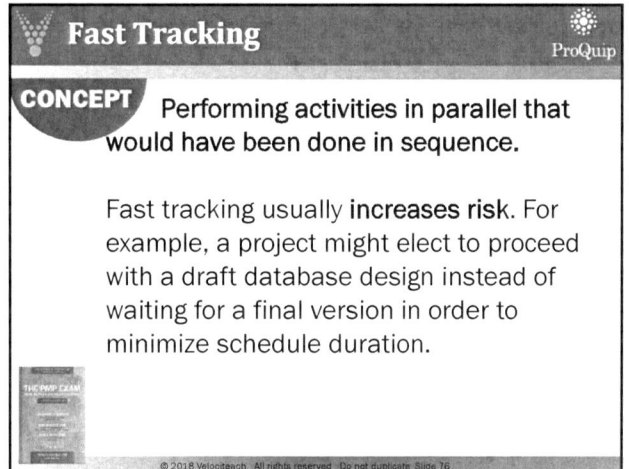

Fast Tracking — ProQuip

CONCEPT Performing activities in parallel that would have been done in sequence.

Fast tracking usually **increases risk**. For example, a project might elect to proceed with a draft database design instead of waiting for a final version in order to minimize schedule duration.

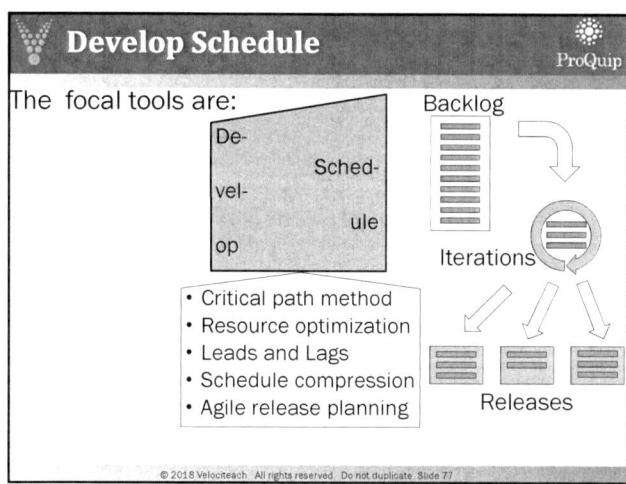

Develop Schedule — ProQuip

The focal tools are:

Develop Schedule

Backlog

Iterations

Releases

- Critical path method
- Resource optimization
- Leads and Lags
- Schedule compression
- Agile release planning

©2018 Velociteach. All rights reserved.

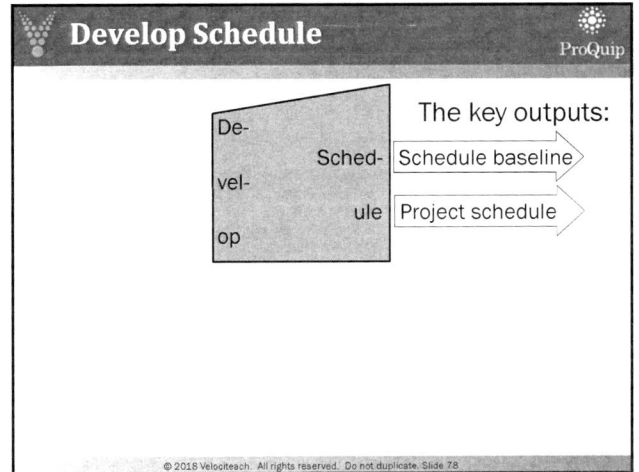

Develop Schedule

De-vel-op Sched-ule

The key outputs:

Schedule baseline

Project schedule

© 2018 Velociteach. All rights reserved. Do not duplicate. Slide 78

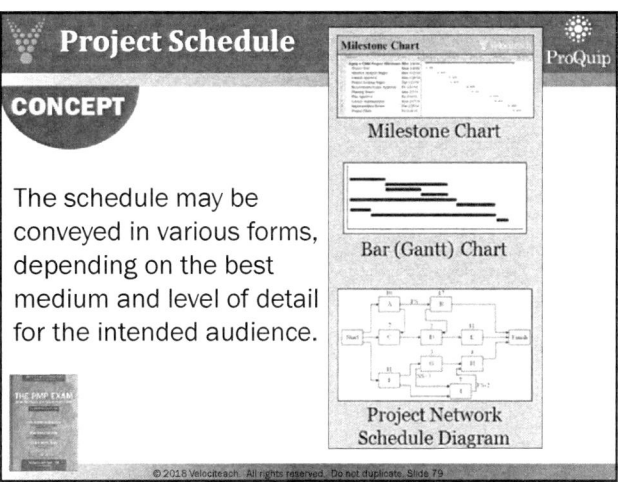

Project Schedule

CONCEPT

The schedule may be conveyed in various forms, depending on the best medium and level of detail for the intended audience.

Milestone Chart

Bar (Gantt) Chart

Project Network Schedule Diagram

© 2018 Velociteach. All rights reserved. Do not duplicate. Slide 79

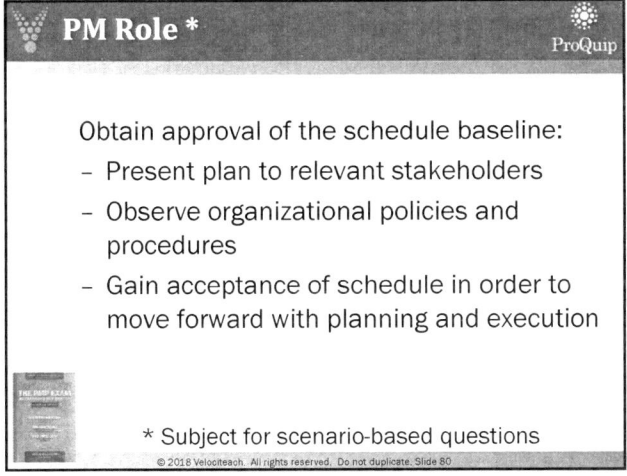

PM Role *

Obtain approval of the schedule baseline:

- Present plan to relevant stakeholders
- Observe organizational policies and procedures
- Gain acceptance of schedule in order to move forward with planning and execution

* Subject for scenario-based questions

© 2018 Velociteach. All rights reserved. Do not duplicate. Slide 80

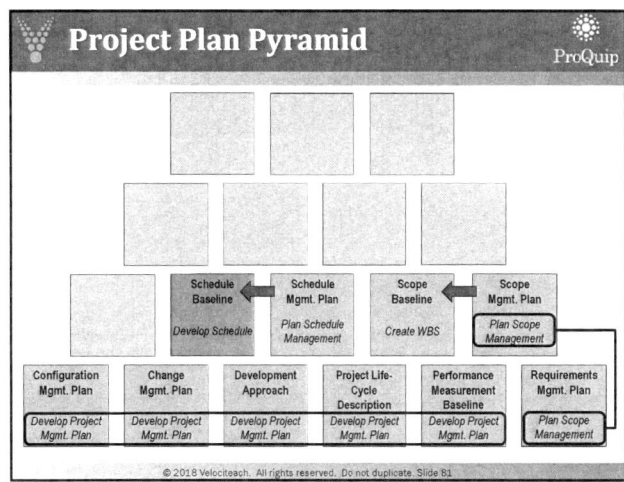

Project Plan Pyramid

| Schedule Baseline | Schedule Mgmt. Plan | Scope Baseline | Scope Mgmt. Plan |
| Develop Schedule | Plan Schedule Management | Create WBS | Plan Scope Management |

| Configuration Mgmt. Plan | Change Mgmt. Plan | Development Approach | Project Life-Cycle Description | Performance Measurement Baseline | Requirements Mgmt. Plan |
| Develop Project Mgmt. Plan | Develop Project Mgmt. Plan | Develop Project Mgmt. Plan | Develop Project Mgmt. Plan | Develop Project Mgmt. Plan | Plan Scope Management |

© 2018 Velociteach. All rights reserved. Do not duplicate. Slide 81

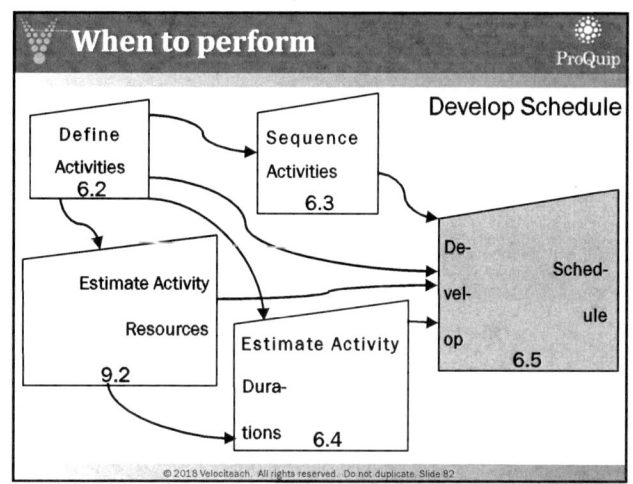

When to perform

Develop Schedule

- Define Activities 6.2
- Sequence Activities 6.3
- Estimate Activity Resources 9.2
- Estimate Activity Durations 6.4
- Develop Schedule 6.5

© 2018 Velociteach. All rights reserved. Do not duplicate. Slide 82

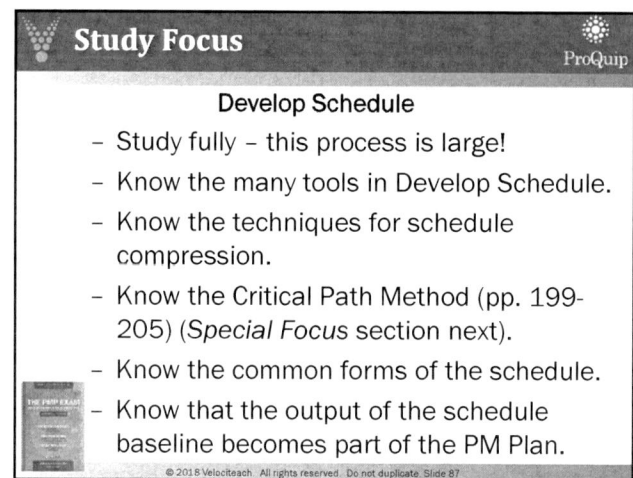

Study Focus

Develop Schedule
- Study fully – this process is large!
- Know the many tools in Develop Schedule.
- Know the techniques for schedule compression.
- Know the Critical Path Method (pp. 199-205) (*Special Focus* section next).
- Know the common forms of the schedule.
- Know that the output of the schedule baseline becomes part of the PM Plan.

© 2018 Velociteach. All rights reserved. Do not duplicate. Slide 87

Review the ITTOs

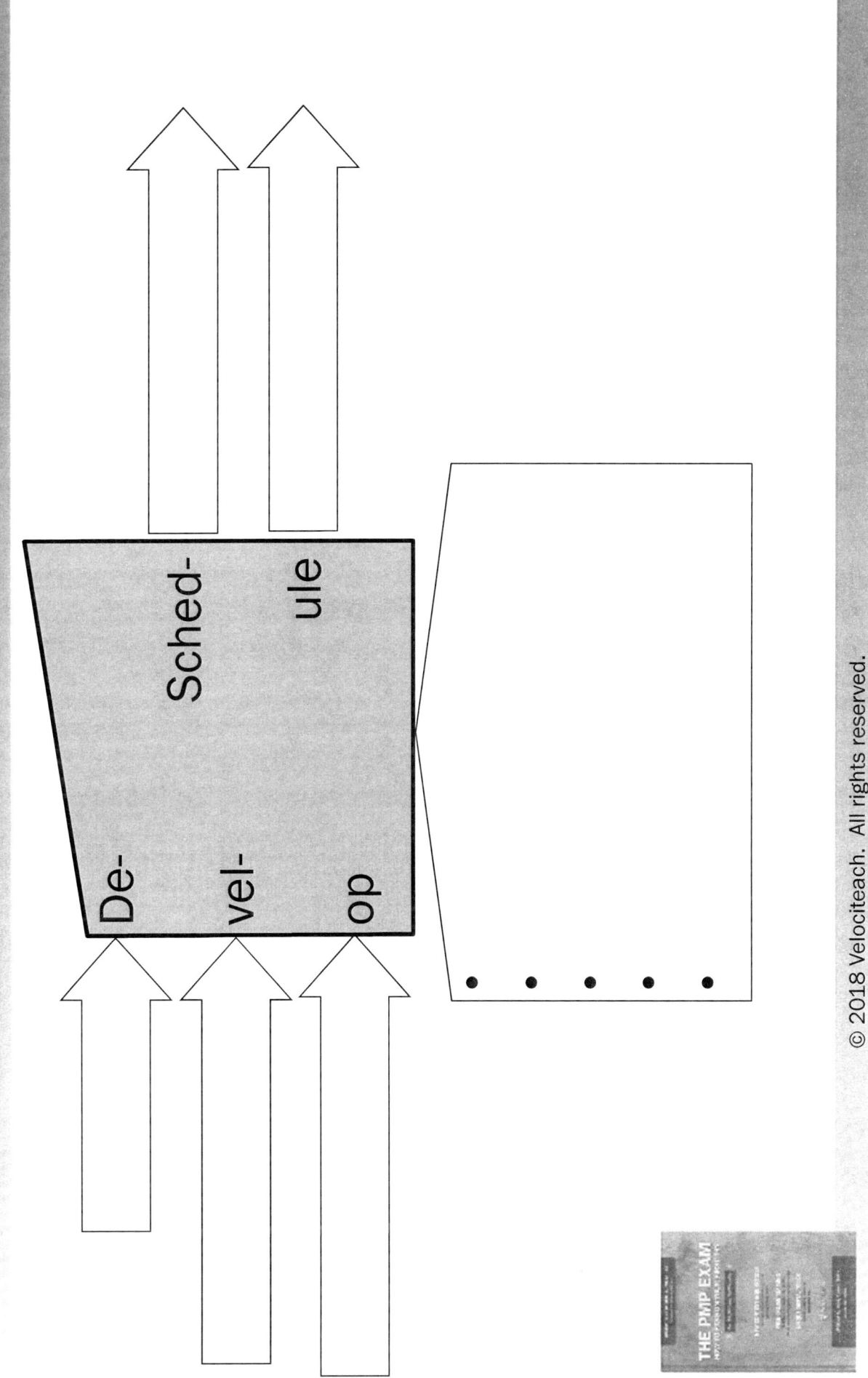

Develop Schedule

© 2018 Velociteach. All rights reserved.

This page left intentionally blank.

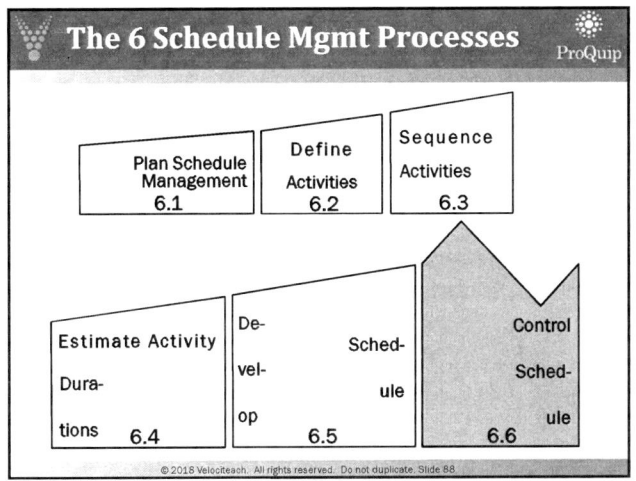

The 6 Schedule Mgmt Processes

Plan Schedule Management 6.1 | Define Activities 6.2 | Sequence Activities 6.3

Estimate Activity Durations 6.4 | Develop Schedule 6.5 | Control Schedule 6.6

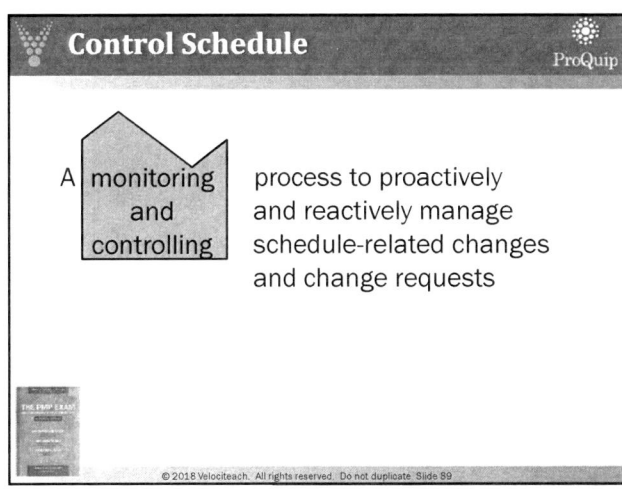

Control Schedule

A monitoring and controlling process to proactively and reactively manage schedule-related changes and change requests

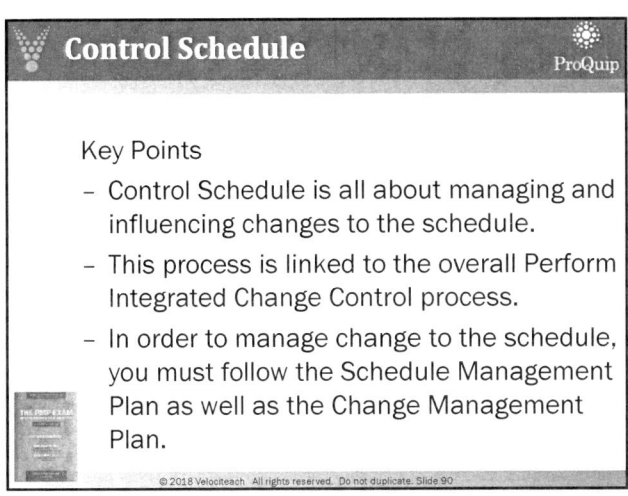

Control Schedule

Key Points
- Control Schedule is all about managing and influencing changes to the schedule.
- This process is linked to the overall Perform Integrated Change Control process.
- In order to manage change to the schedule, you must follow the Schedule Management Plan as well as the Change Management Plan.

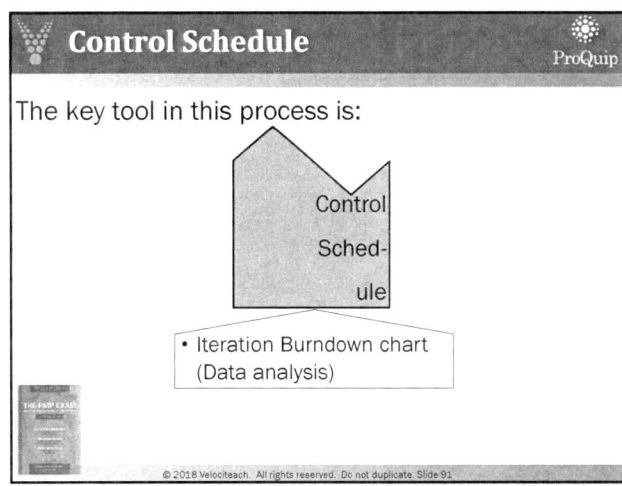

Control Schedule

The key tool in this process is:

Control Schedule

- Iteration Burndown chart (Data analysis)

©2018 Velociteach. All rights reserved. Do not duplicate. Slide 88

©2018 Velociteach. All rights reserved. Do not duplicate. Slide 89

©2018 Velociteach. All rights reserved. Do not duplicate. Slide 90

©2018 Velociteach. All rights reserved. Do not duplicate. Slide 91

Iteration Burndown Chart

CONCEPT

Page 195

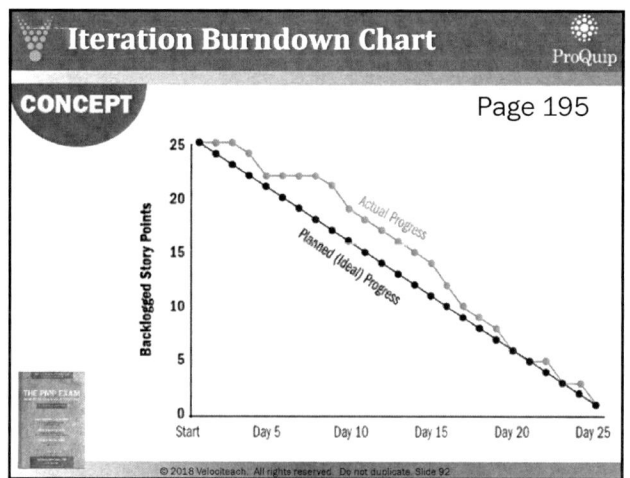

Control Schedule

The key outputs of this process are:

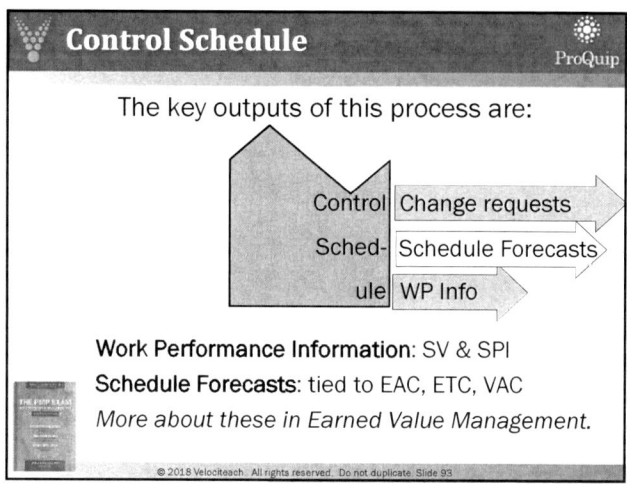

Control Sched-ule → Change requests

Schedule Forecasts

WP Info

Work Performance Information: SV & SPI
Schedule Forecasts: tied to EAC, ETC, VAC
More about these in Earned Value Management.

When to perform

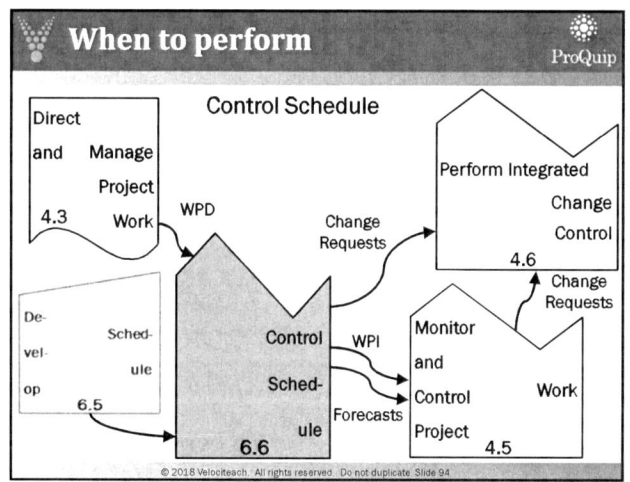

Study Focus

Control Schedule

- Know that this process is defined by the Schedule Management Plan.
- Know the Schedule and Baseline are being controlled.
- Know that this process starts as soon as the Schedule Baseline is created, approved, and placed under control.
- Know that Tools are similar to Develop Schedule.

Review the ITTOs

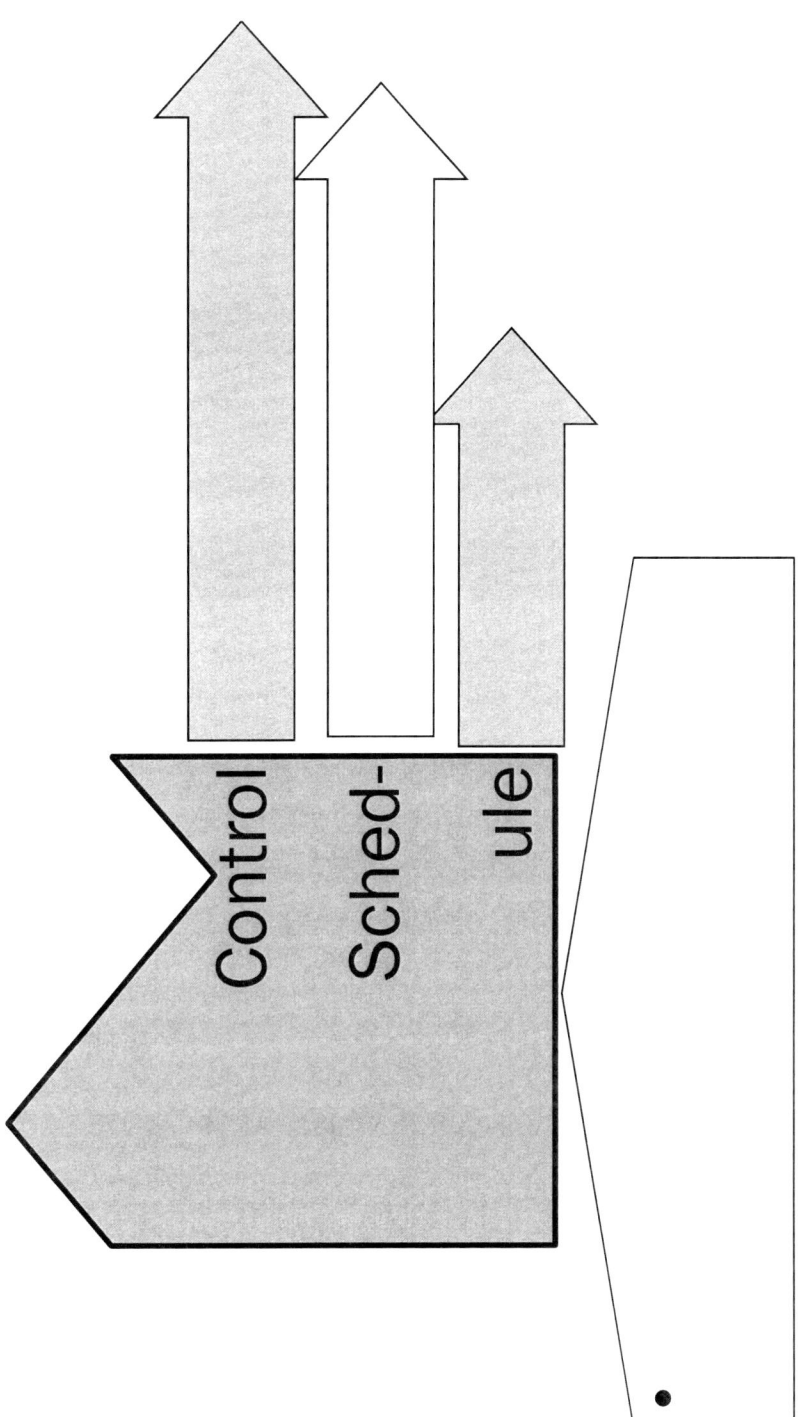

Control Schedule

-

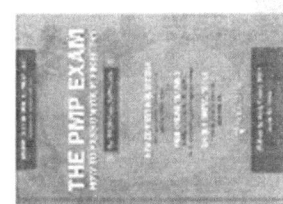

© 2018 Velociteach. All rights reserved.

ProQuip

©2018 Velociteach. All rights reserved. Page 135

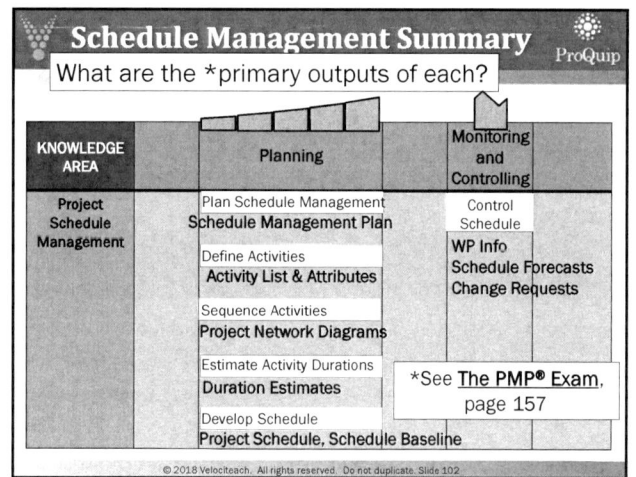

Schedule Management Summary
ProQuip

What are the *primary outputs of each?

KNOWLEDGE AREA	Planning	Monitoring and Controlling
Project Schedule Management	Plan Schedule Management **Schedule Management Plan**	Control Schedule **WP Info** **Schedule Forecasts** **Change Requests**
	Define Activities **Activity List & Attributes**	
	Sequence Activities **Project Network Diagrams**	
	Estimate Activity Durations **Duration Estimates**	*See The PMP® Exam, page 157
	Develop Schedule **Project Schedule, Schedule Baseline**	

© 2018 Velociteach. All rights reserved. Do not duplicate. Slide 102

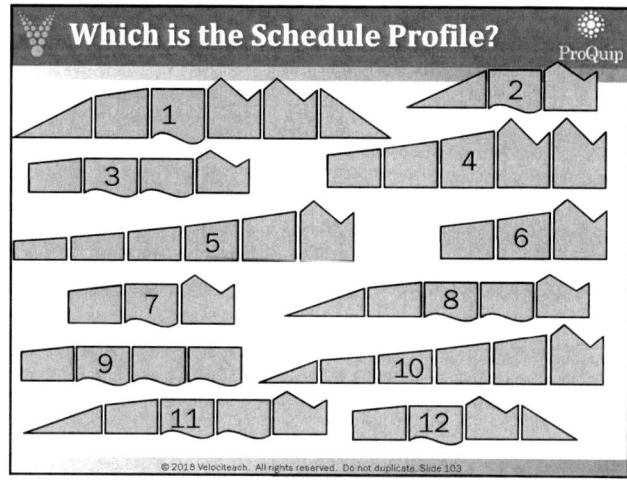

Which is the Schedule Profile?
ProQuip

1 2 3 4 5 6 7 8 9 10 11 12

© 2018 Velociteach. All rights reserved. Do not duplicate. Slide 103

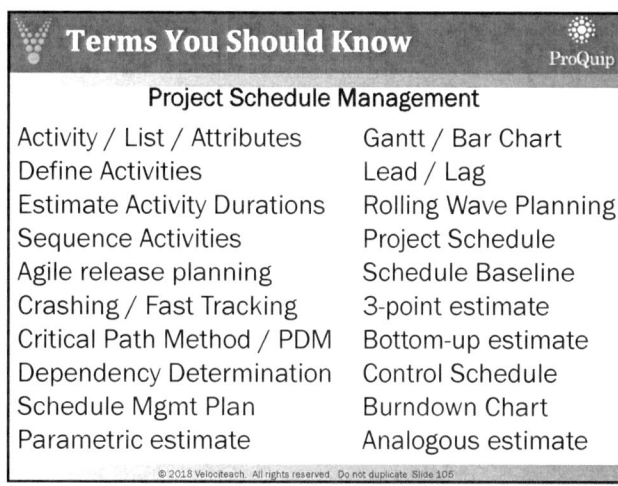

Terms You Should Know
ProQuip

Project Schedule Management

Activity / List / Attributes	Gantt / Bar Chart
Define Activities	Lead / Lag
Estimate Activity Durations	Rolling Wave Planning
Sequence Activities	Project Schedule
Agile release planning	Schedule Baseline
Crashing / Fast Tracking	3-point estimate
Critical Path Method / PDM	Bottom-up estimate
Dependency Determination	Control Schedule
Schedule Mgmt Plan	Burndown Chart
Parametric estimate	Analogous estimate

© 2018 Velociteach. All rights reserved. Do not duplicate. Slide 105

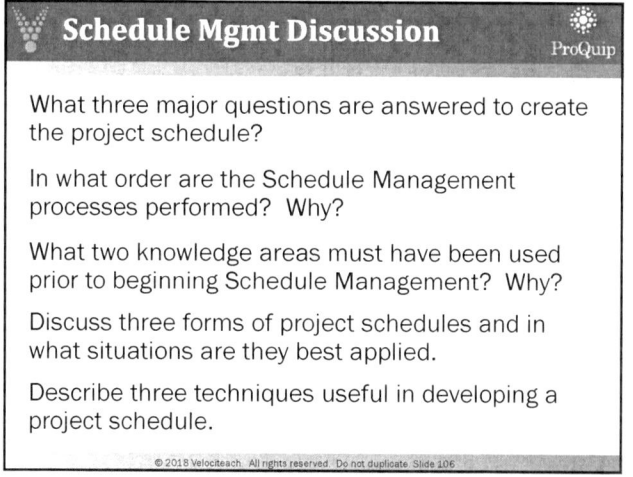

Schedule Mgmt Discussion
ProQuip

What three major questions are answered to create the project schedule?

In what order are the Schedule Management processes performed? Why?

What two knowledge areas must have been used prior to beginning Schedule Management? Why?

Discuss three forms of project schedules and in what situations are they best applied.

Describe three techniques useful in developing a project schedule.

© 2018 Velociteach. All rights reserved. Do not duplicate. Slide 106

Summary

Knowledge Area

KNOWLEDGE AREA	Initiating	Planning	Executing	Monitoring and Controlling	Closing
Project Management					

©2018 Velociteach. All rights reserved. Page 137

ProQuip

Special Focus:
Critical Path Method

Course Module 7

PMBOK® Guide Chapter 6

PMP® Exam Textbook Chapter 6

© 2018 Velociteach. All rights reserved. Do not duplicate. Slide 1

Activity on Node Method

ProQuip

This method of project network diagramming is named:

– **Activity on Node,** where the schedule activities are represented by rectangular nodes

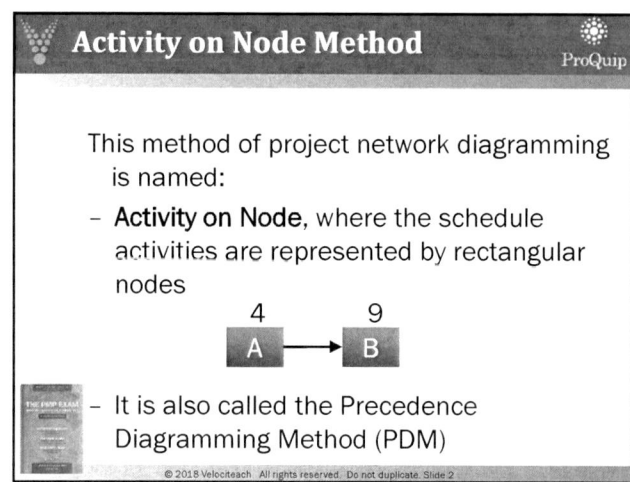

– It is also called the Precedence Diagramming Method (PDM)

© 2018 Velociteach. All rights reserved. Do not duplicate. Slide 2

Relationships

ProQuip

Each arrow represents a *dependency* between two activities:

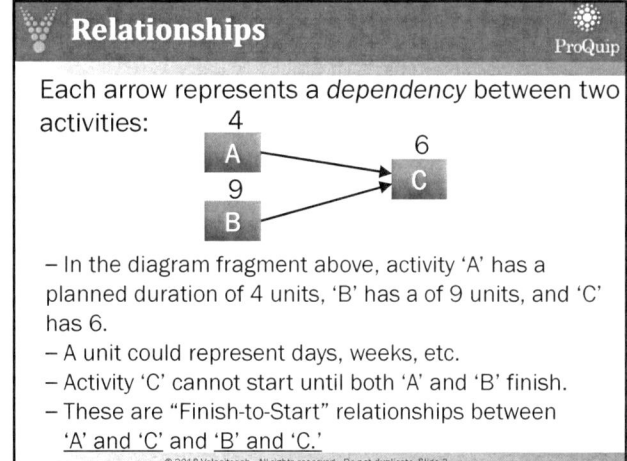

– In the diagram fragment above, activity 'A' has a planned duration of 4 units, 'B' has a of 9 units, and 'C' has 6.

– A unit could represent days, weeks, etc.

– Activity 'C' cannot start until both 'A' and 'B' finish.

– These are "Finish-to-Start" relationships between 'A' and 'C' and 'B' and 'C.'

© 2018 Velociteach. All rights reserved. Do not duplicate. Slide 3

Paths

ProQuip

Network paths are formed by combinations of boxes and arrows.

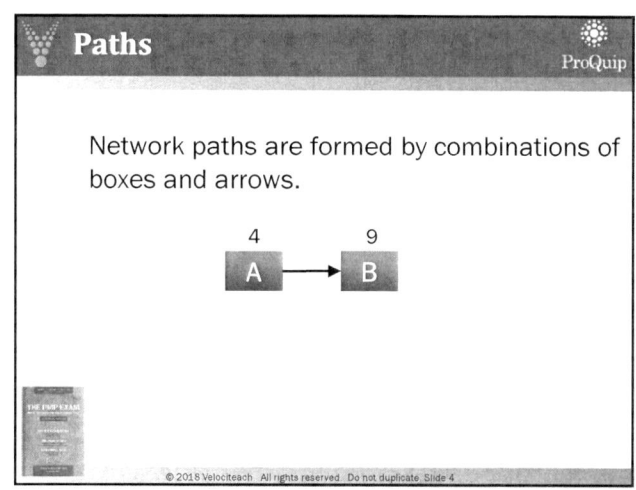

© 2018 Velociteach. All rights reserved. Do not duplicate. Slide 4

Paths

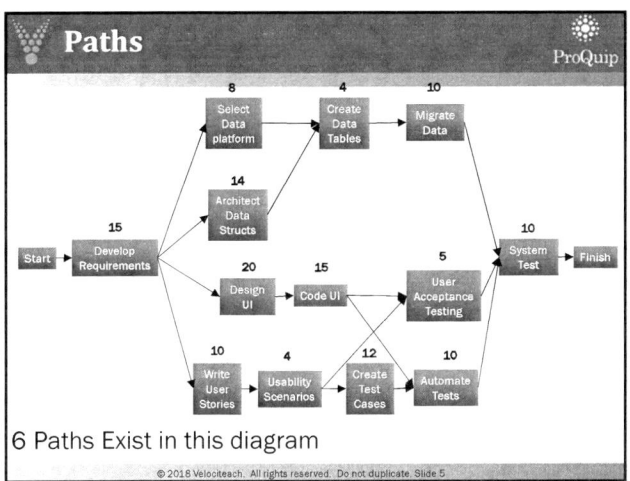

6 Paths Exist in this diagram

© 2018 Velociteach. All rights reserved. Do not duplicate. Slide 5

For ease of notation, assign a "Short Name" to each activity.

Short Name	Activity Name
Start	Start
A	Develop Requirements
B	Select Data Platform
C	Create Data Tables
D	Migrate Data
E	Architect Data Structs
F	Design UI
G	Code UI
H	User Acceptance Testing
I	Write User Stories
J	Usability Scenarios
K	Create Test Cases
L	Automate Tests
M	System Tests
Finish	Finish

© 2018 Velociteach. All rights reserved.

Path Notation

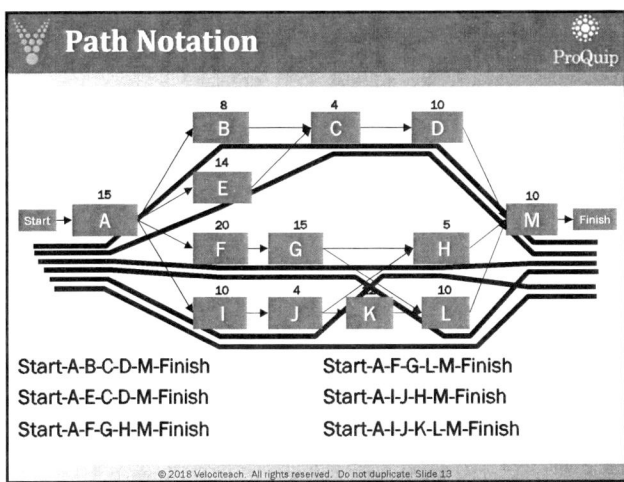

Start-A-B-C-D-M-Finish   Start-A-F-G-L-M-Finish

Start-A-E-C-D-M-Finish   Start-A-I-J-H-M-Finish

Start-A-F-G-H-M-Finish   Start-A-I-J-K-L-M-Finish

© 2018 Velociteach. All rights reserved. Do not duplicate. Slide 13

Critical Path

DEFINITION a. The combination of activities from project start to finish in which if any activity is delayed, it will delay the project;

b. the longest duration path

– The critical path is important because if any one activity slips, the project finish will be delayed.

– It is common for there to be more than one critical path.

© 2018 Velociteach. All rights reserved. Do not duplicate. Slide 14

©2018 Velociteach. All rights reserved.   Page 139

Which is the Critical Path?

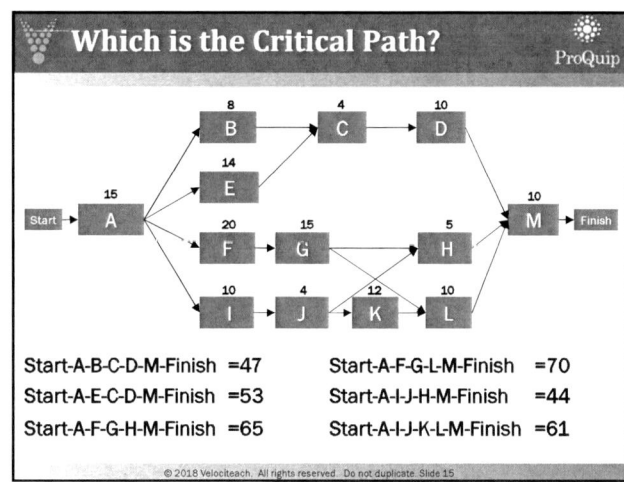

Start-A-B-C-D-M-Finish =47   Start-A-F-G-L-M-Finish =70
Start-A-E-C-D-M-Finish =53   Start-A-I-J-H-M-Finish =44
Start-A-F-G-H-M-Finish =65   Start-A-I-J-K-L-M-Finish =61

© 2018 Velociteach. All rights reserved. Do not duplicate. Slide 15

Creating a Network Diagram (AON)

In-Class Exercise

You need to be able to create a project network diagram from a chart (table) format.

All of the information you need is in the table.

What is the Critical Path of this project?

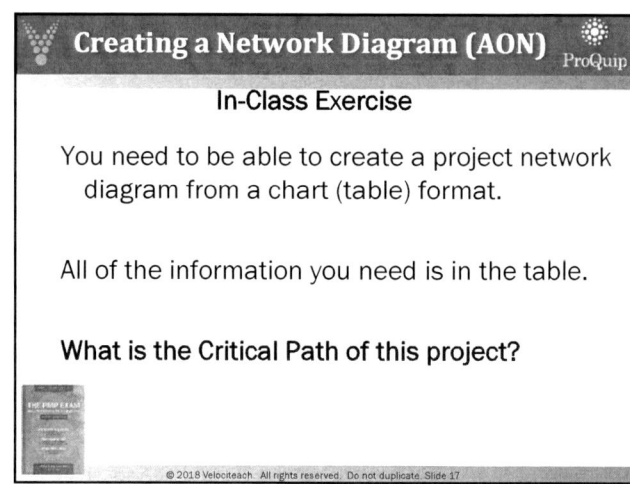

© 2018 Velociteach. All rights reserved. Do not duplicate. Slide 17

What is the Critical Path?

In-Class Exercise

Activity	Preceding Activity	Duration (days)
Start		0
A	Start	7
B	A	10
C	B	4
D	Start	10
E	D,G	11
F	E	8
G	Start	5
H	E	12
Finish	C,F,H	0

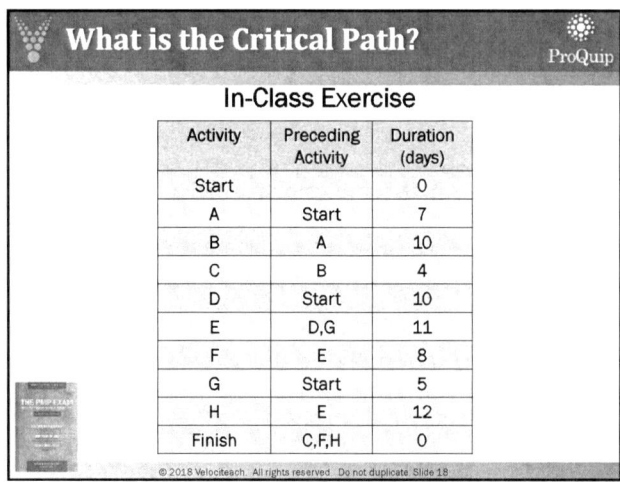

© 2018 Velociteach. All rights reserved. Do not duplicate. Slide 18

In-Class Exercise Review (AON)

ProQuip

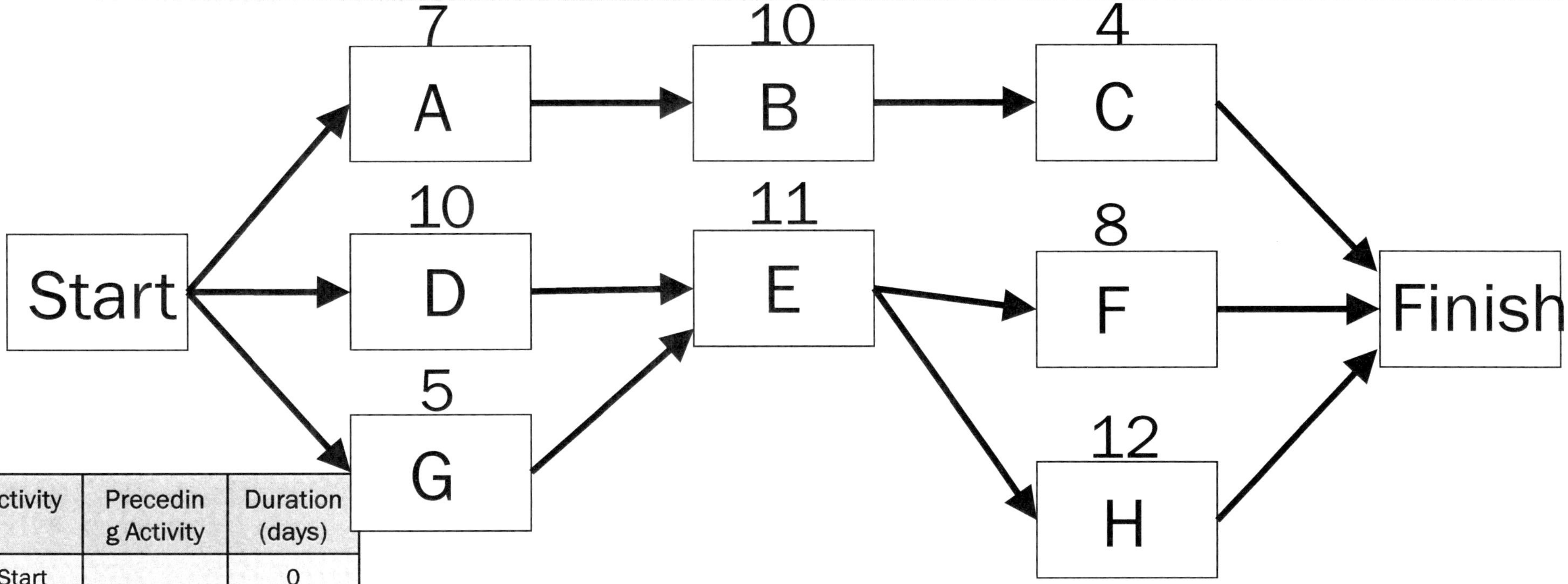

Finish

4 C

8 F

12 H

10 B

11 E

7 A

10 D

5 G

Start

Start-A-B-C-Finish = 21
Start-D-E-F-Finish = 29
Start-D-E-H-Finish = 33 Critical Path
Start-G-E-F-Finish = 24
Start-G-E-H-Finish = 28

Activity	Preceding Activity	Duration (days)
Start		0
A	Start	7
B	A	10
C	B	4
D	Start	10
E	D,G	11
F	E	8
G	Start	5
H	E	12
Finish	C,F,H	0

© 2018 Velociteach. All rights reserved. Do not duplicate. Slide 19

©2018 Velociteach. All rights reserved.

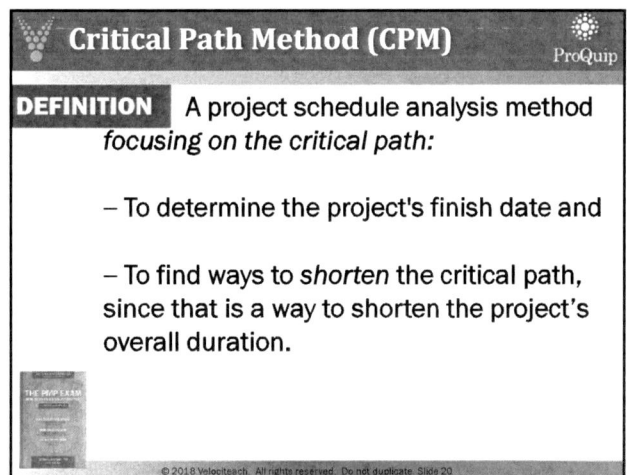

Critical Path Method (CPM)

ProQuip

DEFINITION A project schedule analysis method *focusing on the critical path:*

– To determine the project's finish date and

– To find ways to *shorten* the critical path, since that is a way to shorten the project's overall duration.

© 2018 Velociteach. All rights reserved. Do not duplicate. Slide 20

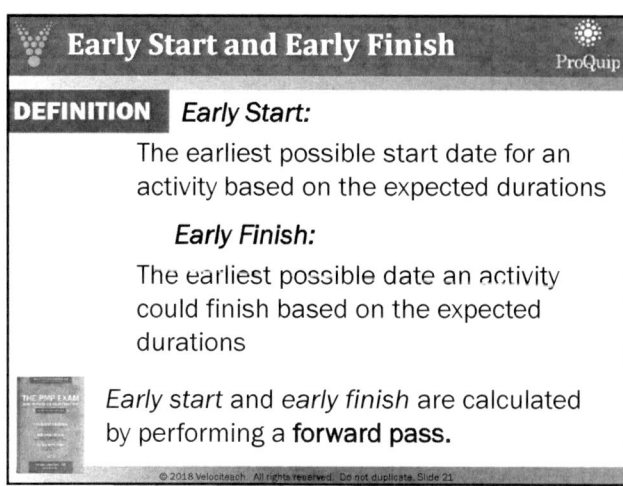

Early Start and Early Finish

ProQuip

DEFINITION *Early Start:*

The earliest possible start date for an activity based on the expected durations

Early Finish:

The earliest possible date an activity could finish based on the expected durations

Early start and *early finish* are calculated by performing a **forward pass.**

© 2018 Velociteach. All rights reserved. Do not duplicate. Slide 21

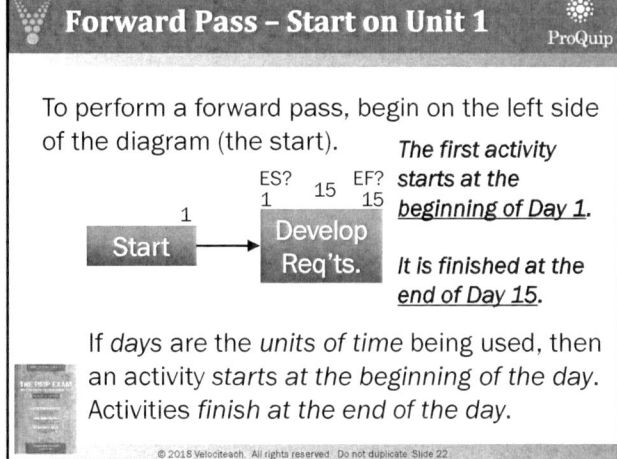

Forward Pass – Start on Unit 1

ProQuip

To perform a forward pass, begin on the left side of the diagram (the start).

The first activity starts at the beginning of Day 1.

ES? 15 EF?
1   15
Start → Develop Req'ts.

It is finished at the end of Day 15.

If *days* are the *units of time* being used, then an activity *starts at the beginning of the day.* Activities *finish at the end of the day.*

© 2018 Velociteach. All rights reserved. Do not duplicate. Slide 22

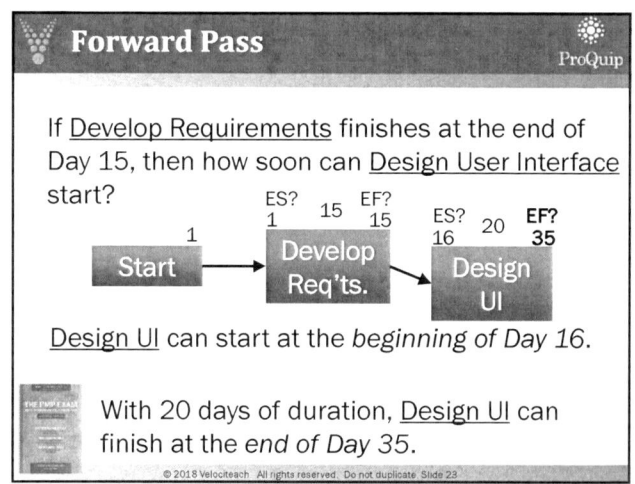

Forward Pass

ProQuip

If <u>Develop Requirements</u> finishes at the end of Day 15, then how soon can <u>Design User Interface</u> start?

ES? 15 EF?   ES? 20 EF?
1   15   16   35
Start → Develop Req'ts. → Design UI

<u>Design UI</u> can start at the *beginning of Day 16.*

With 20 days of duration, <u>Design UI</u> can finish at the *end of Day 35.*

© 2018 Velociteach. All rights reserved. Do not duplicate. Slide 23

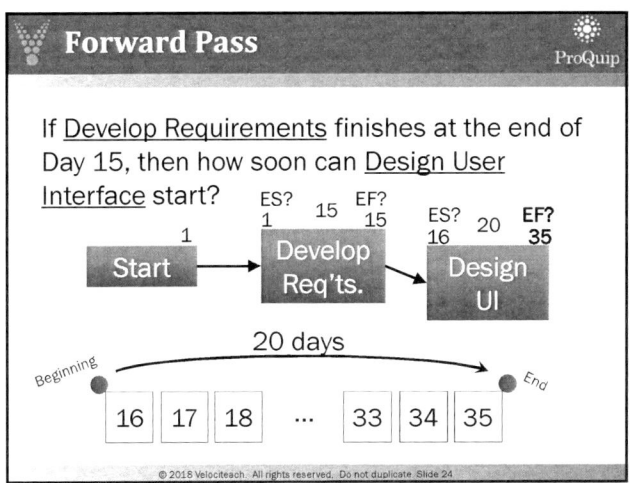

Forward Pass

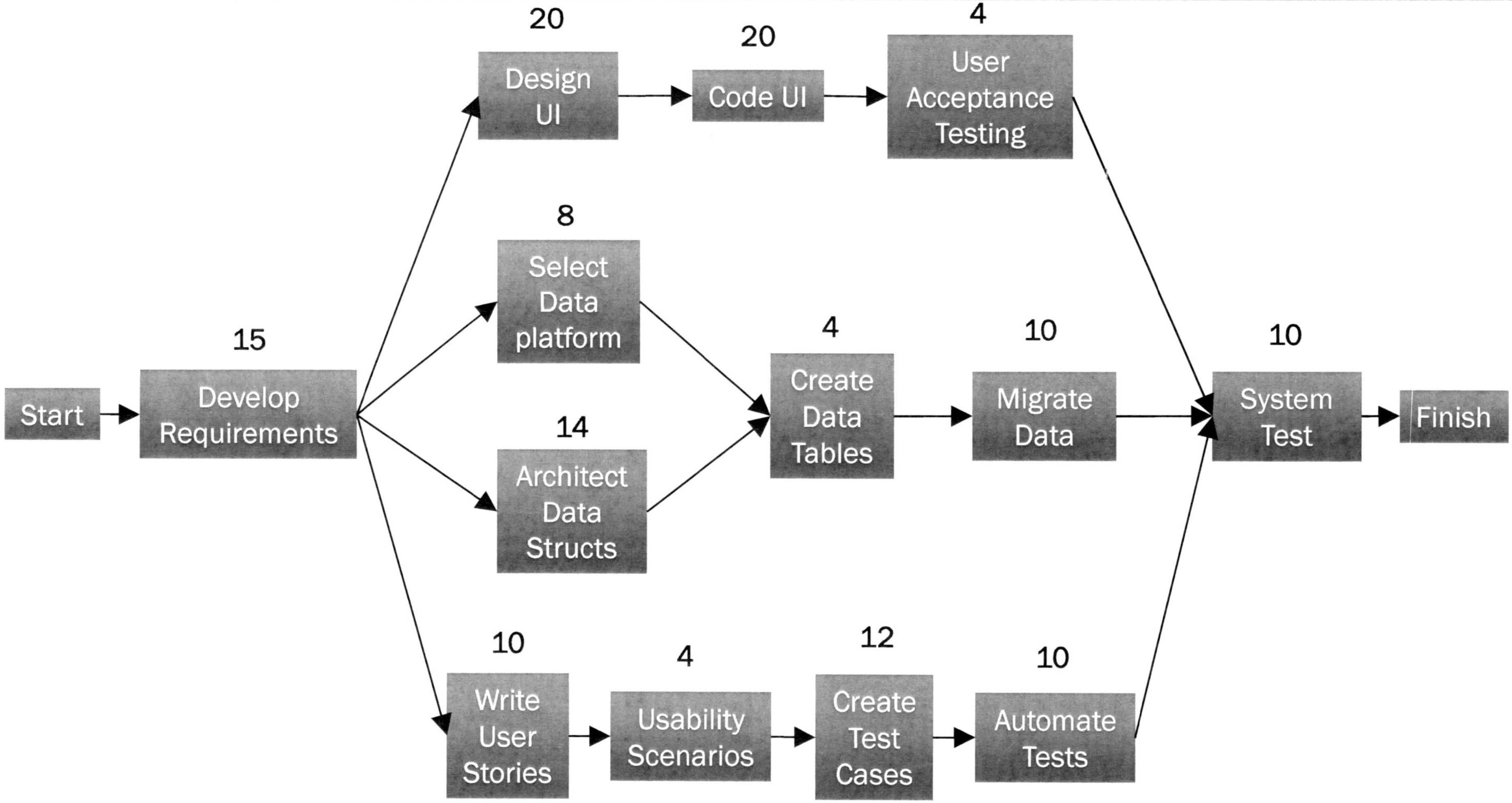

Early start and finish are calculated by working left to right
(i.e., starting at "Start")

© 2018 Velociteach. All rights reserved. Do not duplicate. Slide 25

Late Finish and Late Start

DEFINITION   *Late Finish:*

The latest possible date an activity could finish without delaying the Late Start of subsequent activities or the project finish date

Late Start:

The latest possible start date for an activity based on its Late Finish and expected duration

The traditional way to calculate these is to perform a **backward pass,** delaying each activity as much as possible **without changing the project finish date.**

© 2018 Velociteach. All rights reserved. Do not duplicate. Slide 27

Backward Pass

To perform a backward pass, begin on the right side of the diagram (the finish).

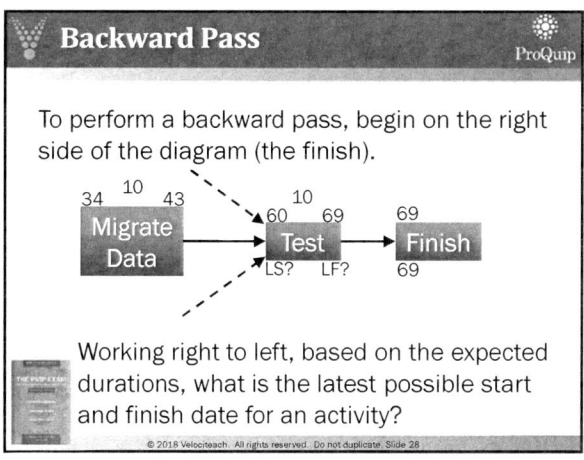

Working right to left, based on the expected durations, what is the latest possible start and finish date for an activity?

© 2018 Velociteach. All rights reserved. Do not duplicate. Slide 28

Backward Pass

If the project finishes at the end of Day 69, then how late can <u>Test</u> finish?   *At the end of Day 69*

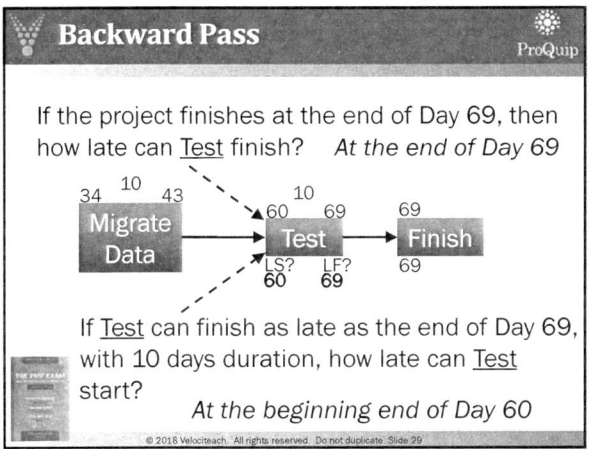

If <u>Test</u> can finish as late as the end of Day 69, with 10 days duration, how late can <u>Test</u> start?

At the beginning end of Day 60

© 2018 Velociteach. All rights reserved. Do not duplicate. Slide 29

Backward Pass

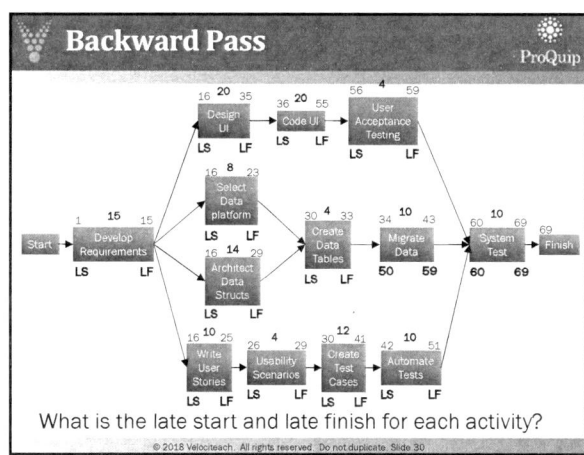

What is the late start and late finish for each activity?

© 2018 Velociteach. All rights reserved. Do not duplicate. Slide 30

Backward Pass

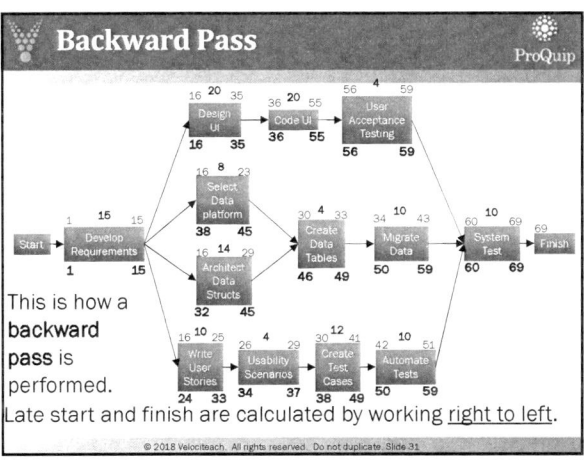

This is how a **backward pass** is performed.

Late start and finish are calculated by working <u>right to left</u>.

© 2018 Velociteach. All rights reserved. Do not duplicate. Slide 31

Note the Critical Path

The early start and late start <u>for each activity on the critical path</u> are the same.

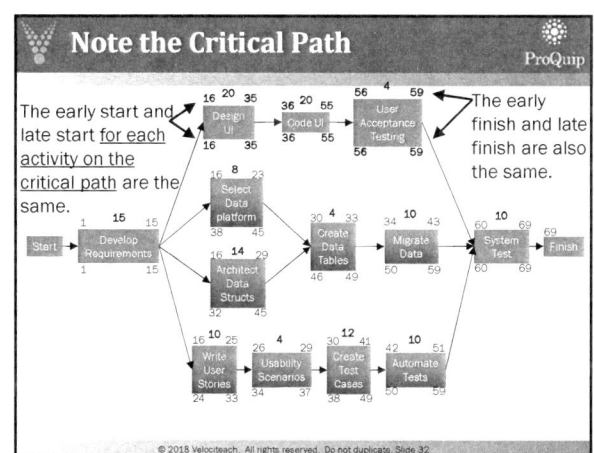

The early finish and late finish are also the same.

© 2018 Velociteach. All rights reserved. Do not duplicate. Slide 32

Float / Total Float / Total Slack

DEFINITION The amount of time a particular activity may be delayed without affecting (changing) the critical path

After you have performed a backward pass, you can easily calculate float for each activity:

Simply take the difference between the early start and late start for each activity.

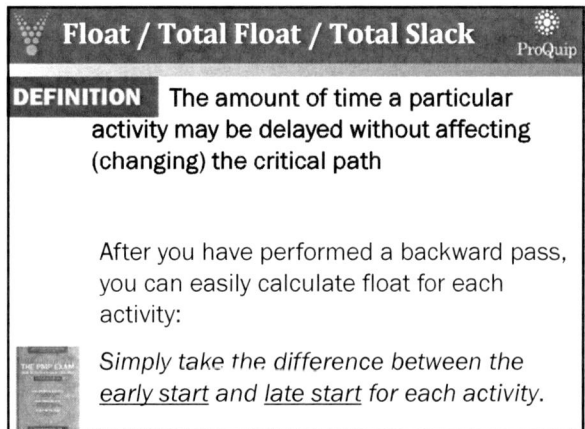

© 2018 Velociteach. All rights reserved. Do not duplicate. Slide 33

Critical Path Total Float is Zero

Note that the float for each activity on the critical path is 0.

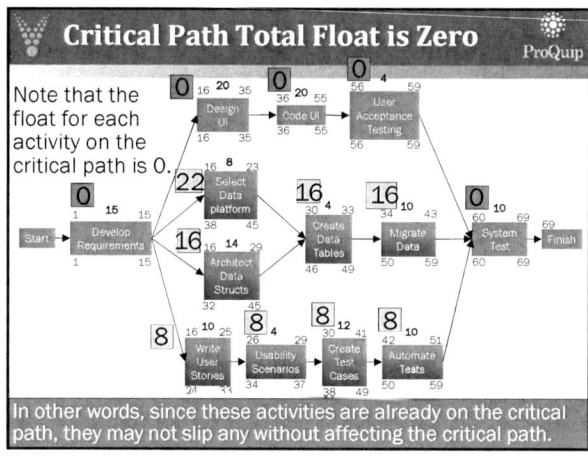

In other words, since these activities are already on the critical path, they may not slip any without affecting the critical path.

Another Way: What is C's Float?

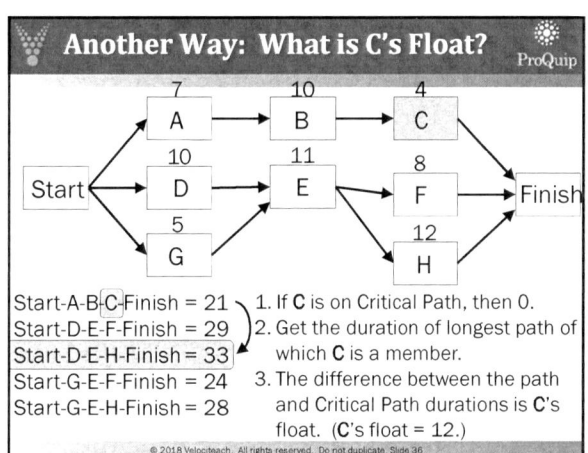

Start-A-B-C-Finish = 21
Start-D-E-F-Finish = 29
Start-D-E-H-Finish = 33
Start-G-E-F-Finish = 24
Start-G-E-H-Finish = 28

1. If **C** is on Critical Path, then 0.
2. Get the duration of longest path of which **C** is a member.
3. The difference between the path and Critical Path durations is **C**'s float. (**C**'s float = 12.)

© 2018 Velociteach. All rights reserved. Do not duplicate. Slide 36

Alternate Notation – Activity K

Another way to represent an activity is shown here. Pay attention to the location of ES, EF, LS, LF.

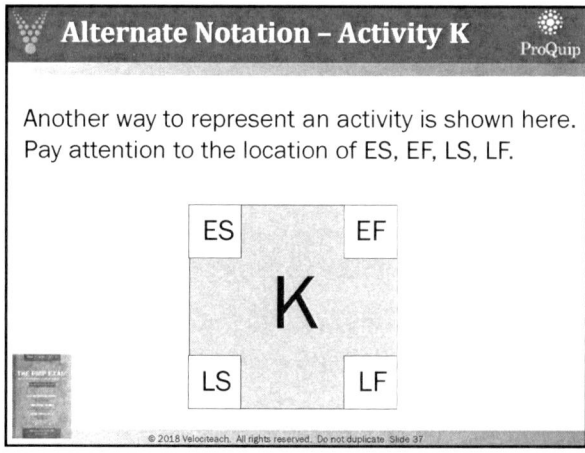

© 2018 Velociteach. All rights reserved. Do not duplicate. Slide 37

Alternate Notation

What is the duration of activity 'K'?

What is its float?

What is its late start?

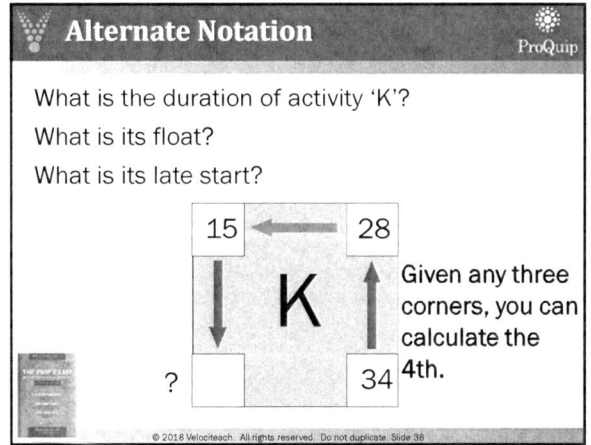

Given any three corners, you can calculate the 4th.

© 2018 Velociteach. All rights reserved. Do not duplicate. Slide 38

Free Float

DEFINITION The amount of time a schedule activity may be delayed without impacting the early start date of any subsequent schedule activities

- Free float will always be less than or equal to float.

- Float focuses on the finish and critical path, but <u>free float</u> looks at <u>subsequent activities</u>.

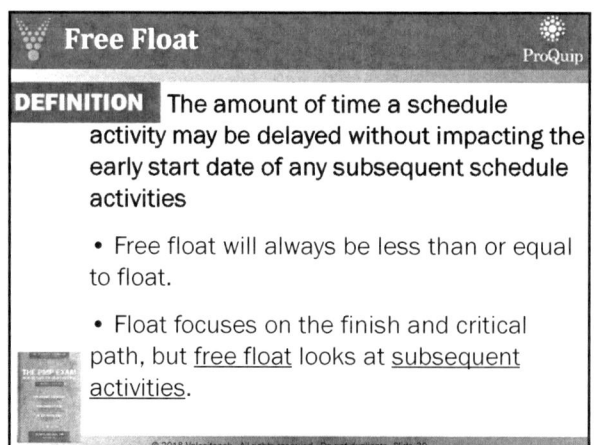

© 2018 Velociteach. All rights reserved. Do not duplicate. Slide 39

What is the Free Float of Activity E?

First, perform a forward pass:

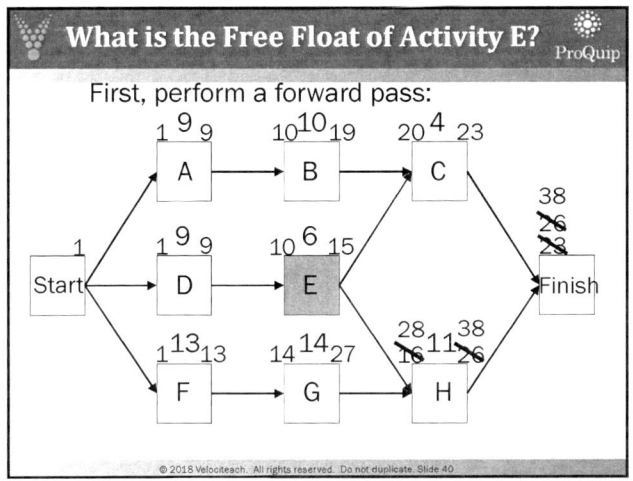

What is the Free Float of Activity E?

Second, Analyze the Early Start Dates of C & H:

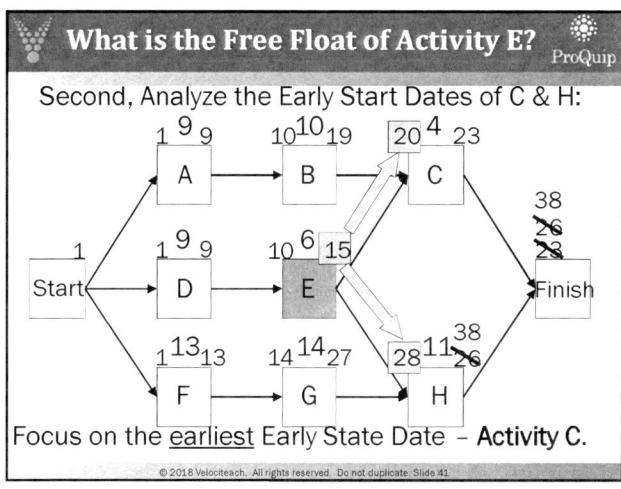

Focus on the <u>earliest</u> Early State Date – **Activity C.**

What is the Free Float of Activity E?

How long can Activity E be delayed before it impacts the Early Start of Activity

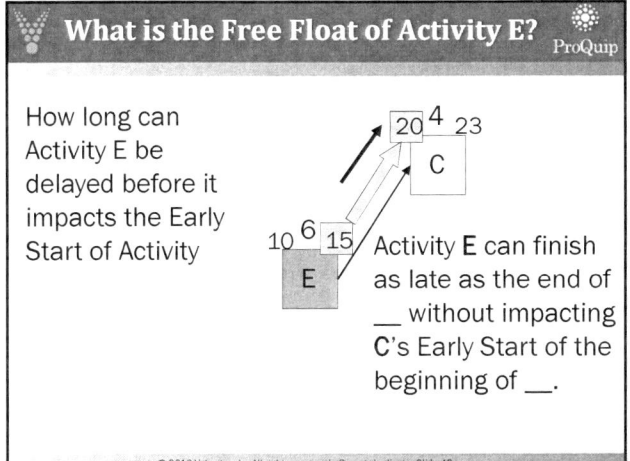

Activity **E** can finish as late as the end of __ without impacting C's Early Start of the beginning of __.

Negative Float

DEFINITION A situation where an activity's late start occurs before a predecessor's early finish.

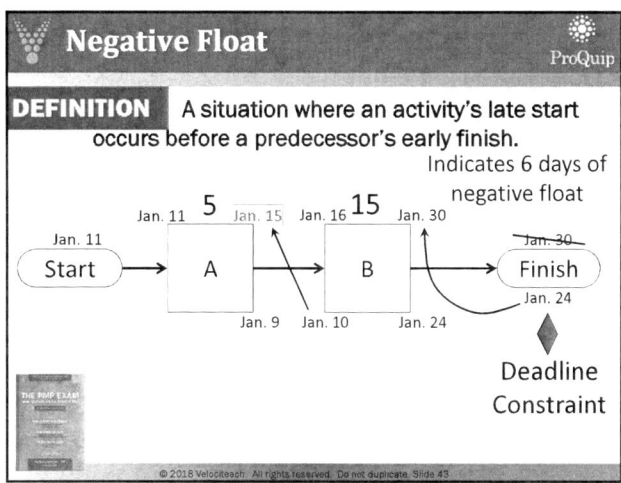

©2018 Velociteach. All rights reserved. Page 147

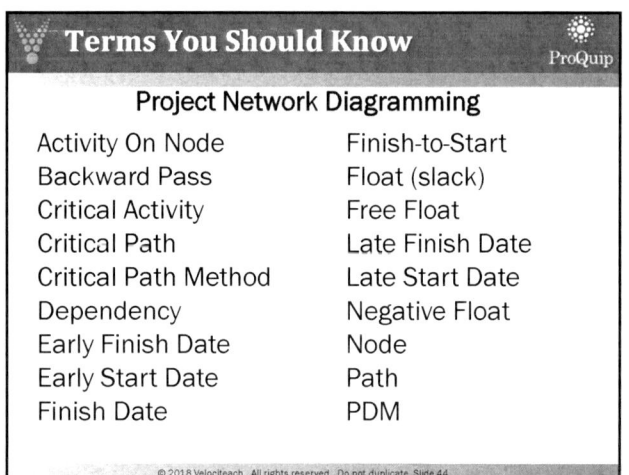

Terms You Should Know

ProQuip

Project Network Diagramming

Activity On Node	Finish-to-Start
Backward Pass	Float (slack)
Critical Activity	Free Float
Critical Path	Late Finish Date
Critical Path Method	Late Start Date
Dependency	Negative Float
Early Finish Date	Node
Early Start Date	Path
Finish Date	PDM

© 2018 Velociteach. All rights reserved. Do not duplicate. Slide 44

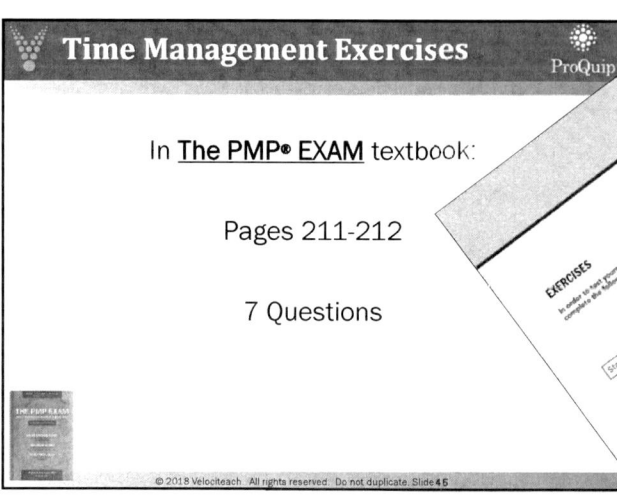

Time Management Exercises

ProQuip

In **The PMP® EXAM** textbook:

Pages 211-212

7 Questions

EXERCISES

© 2018 Velociteach. All rights reserved. Do not duplicate. Slide 45

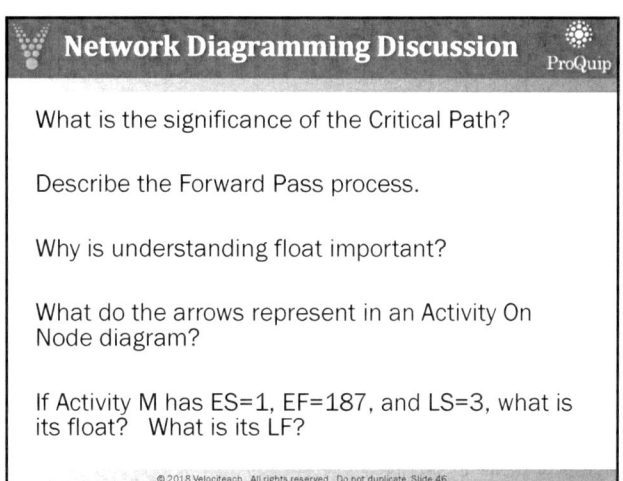

Network Diagramming Discussion

ProQuip

What is the significance of the Critical Path?

Describe the Forward Pass process.

Why is understanding float important?

What do the arrows represent in an Activity On Node diagram?

If Activity M has ES=1, EF=187, and LS=3, what is its float? What is its LF?

© 2018 Velociteach. All rights reserved. Do not duplicate. Slide 46

Score Sheet	**Schedule Management Exam**	 Velociteach

- **Mark one answer: A, B, C, or D.**
- **Circle the '?' symbol if you are guessing at the answer.**
- **Circle the Δ symbol if you change your answer.**

Total Correct: _____

% Correct: _____%

1.	A○	B○	C○	D○	? Δ
2.	A○	B○	C○	D○	? Δ
3.	A○	B○	C○	D○	? Δ
4.	A○	B○	C○	D○	? Δ
5.	A○	B○	C○	D○	? Δ
6.	A○	B○	C○	D○	? Δ
7.	A○	B○	C○	D○	? Δ
8.	A○	B○	C○	D○	? Δ
9.	A○	B○	C○	D○	? Δ
10.	A○	B○	C○	D○	? Δ
11.	A○	B○	C○	D○	? Δ
12.	A○	B○	C○	D○	? Δ
13.	A○	B○	C○	D○	? Δ
14.	A○	B○	C○	D○	? Δ
15.	A○	B○	C○	D○	? Δ
16.	A○	B○	C○	D○	? Δ
17.	A○	B○	C○	D○	? Δ
18.	A○	B○	C○	D○	? Δ
19.	A○	B○	C○	D○	? Δ
20.	A○	B○	C○	D○	? Δ
21.	A○	B○	C○	D○	? Δ
22.	A○	B○	C○	D○	? Δ
23.	A○	B○	C○	D○	? Δ
24.	A○	B○	C○	D○	? Δ
25.	A○	B○	C○	D○	? Δ

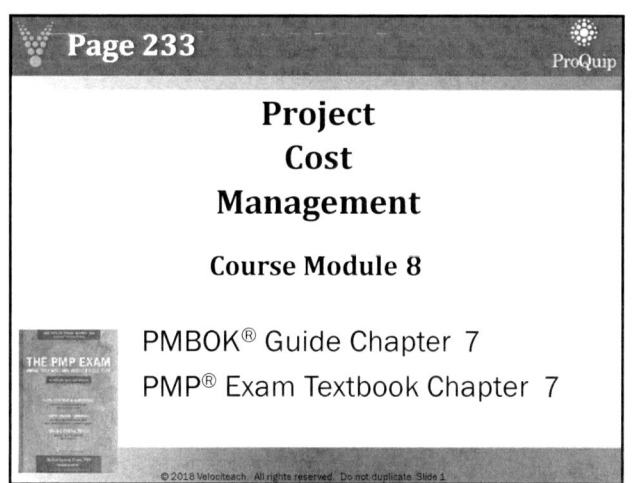

Page 233

ProQuip

Project Cost Management

Course Module 8

PMBOK® Guide Chapter 7

PMP® Exam Textbook Chapter 7

© 2018 Velociteach. All rights reserved. Do not duplicate. Slide 1

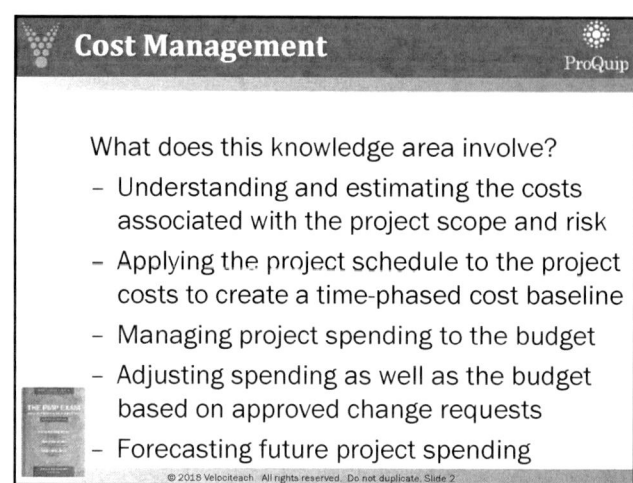

Cost Management

ProQuip

What does this knowledge area involve?

- Understanding and estimating the costs associated with the project scope and risk
- Applying the project schedule to the project costs to create a time-phased cost baseline
- Managing project spending to the budget
- Adjusting spending as well as the budget based on approved change requests
- Forecasting future project spending

© 2018 Velociteach. All rights reserved. Do not duplicate. Slide 2

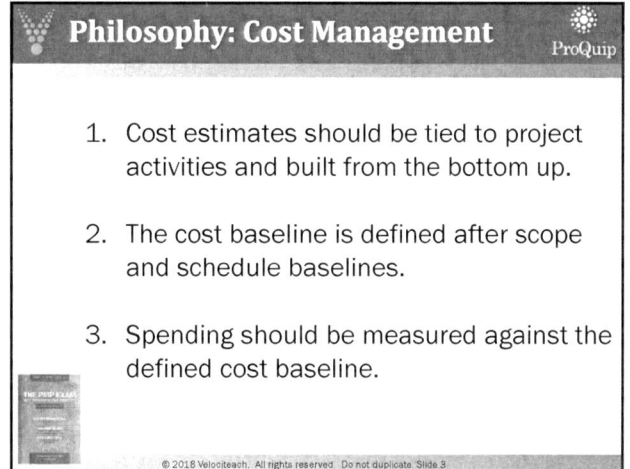

Philosophy: Cost Management

ProQuip

1. Cost estimates should be tied to project activities and built from the bottom up.

2. The cost baseline is defined after scope and schedule baselines.

3. Spending should be measured against the defined cost baseline.

© 2018 Velociteach. All rights reserved. Do not duplicate. Slide 3

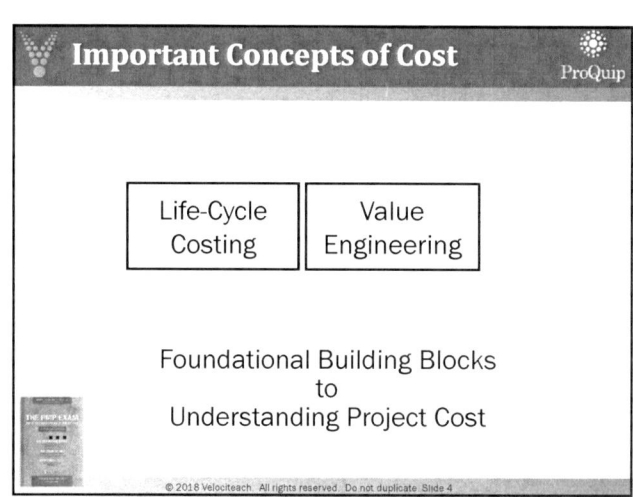

Important Concepts of Cost

ProQuip

Life-Cycle Costing	Value Engineering

Foundational Building Blocks
to
Understanding Project Cost

© 2018 Velociteach. All rights reserved. Do not duplicate. Slide 4

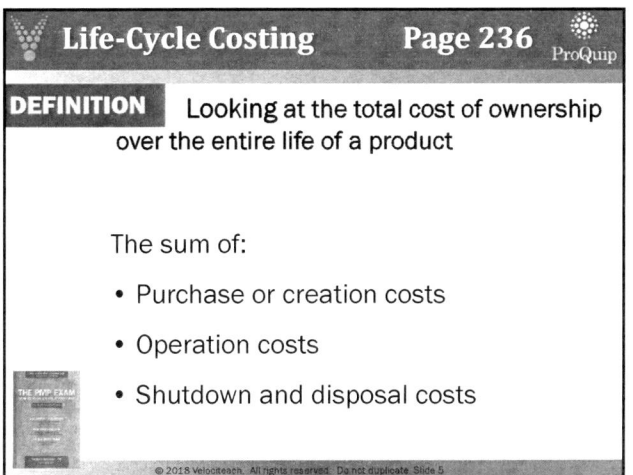

Life-Cycle Costing **Page 236** ProQuip

DEFINITION Looking at the total cost of ownership over the entire life of a product

The sum of:

- Purchase or creation costs
- Operation costs
- Shutdown and disposal costs

© 2018 Velociteach. All rights reserved. Do not duplicate. Slide 5

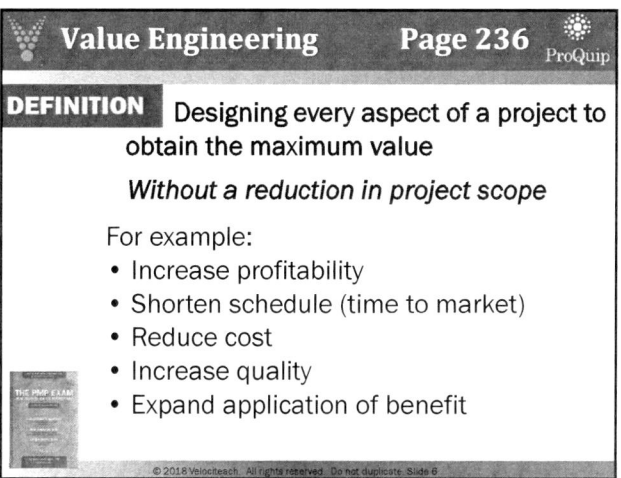

Value Engineering **Page 236** ProQuip

DEFINITION Designing every aspect of a project to obtain the maximum value

Without a reduction in project scope

For example:
- Increase profitability
- Shorten schedule (time to market)
- Reduce cost
- Increase quality
- Expand application of benefit

© 2018 Velociteach. All rights reserved. Do not duplicate. Slide 6

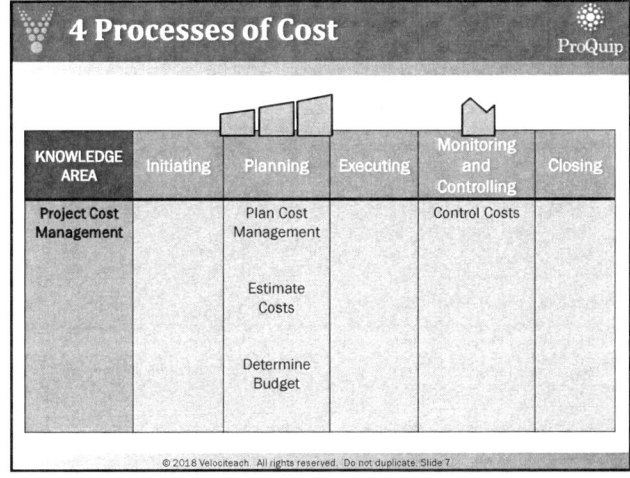

4 Processes of Cost ProQuip

KNOWLEDGE AREA	Initiating	Planning	Executing	Monitoring and Controlling	Closing
Project Cost Management		Plan Cost Management Estimate Costs Determine Budget		Control Costs	

© 2018 Velociteach. All rights reserved. Do not duplicate. Slide 7

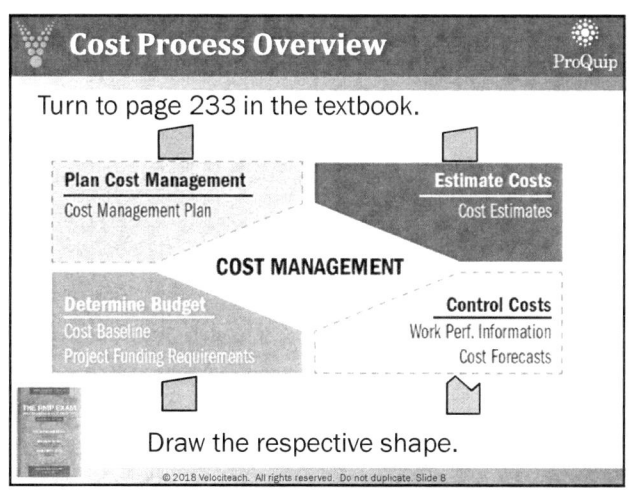

Cost Process Overview ProQuip

Turn to page 233 in the textbook.

Plan Cost Management
Cost Management Plan

Estimate Costs
Cost Estimates

COST MANAGEMENT

Determine Budget
Cost Baseline
Project Funding Requirements

Control Costs
Work Perf. Information
Cost Forecasts

Draw the respective shape.

© 2018 Velociteach. All rights reserved. Do not duplicate. Slide 8

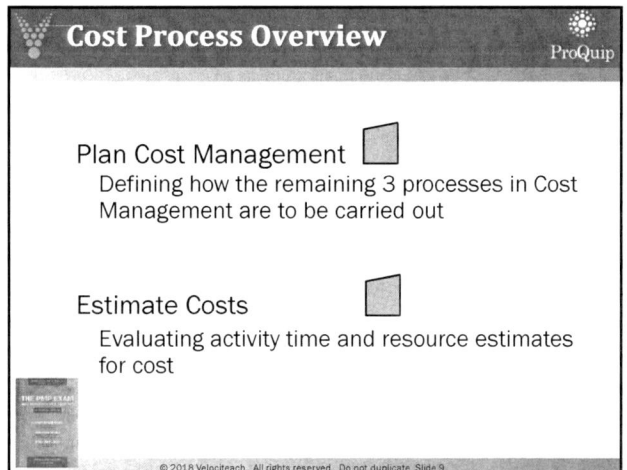

Cost Process Overview

Plan Cost Management
  Defining how the remaining 3 processes in Cost Management are to be carried out

Estimate Costs
  Evaluating activity time and resource estimates for cost

© 2018 Velociteach. All rights reserved. Do not duplicate. Slide 9

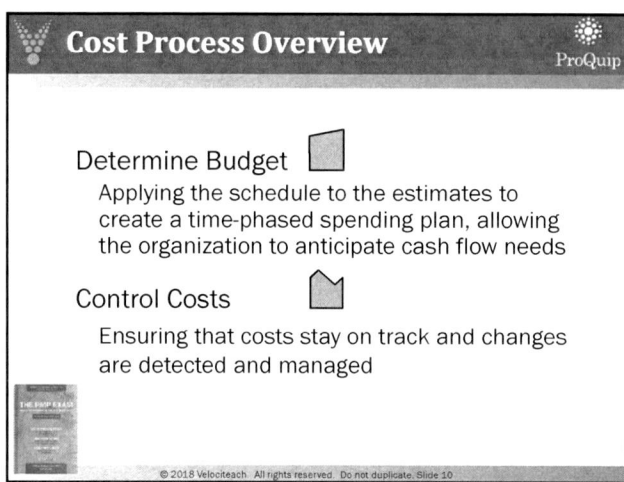

Cost Process Overview

Determine Budget
  Applying the schedule to the estimates to create a time-phased spending plan, allowing the organization to anticipate cash flow needs

Control Costs
  Ensuring that costs stay on track and changes are detected and managed

© 2018 Velociteach. All rights reserved. Do not duplicate. Slide 10

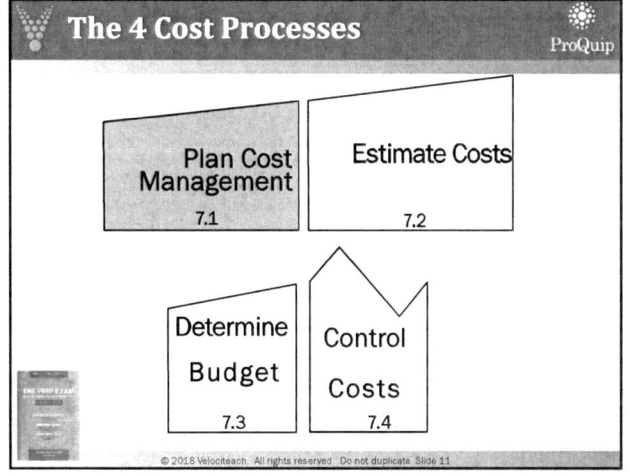

The 4 Cost Processes

Plan Cost Management
7.1

Estimate Costs
7.2

Determine Budget
7.3

Control Costs
7.4

© 2018 Velociteach. All rights reserved. Do not duplicate. Slide 11

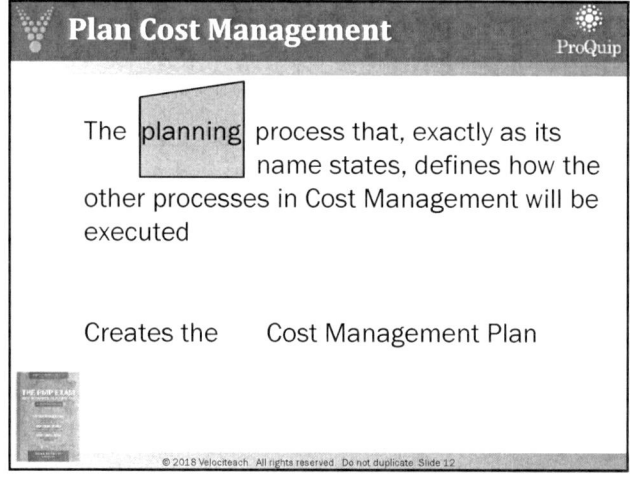

Plan Cost Management

The planning process that, exactly as its name states, defines how the other processes in Cost Management will be executed

Creates the   Cost Management Plan

© 2018 Velociteach. All rights reserved. Do not duplicate. Slide 12

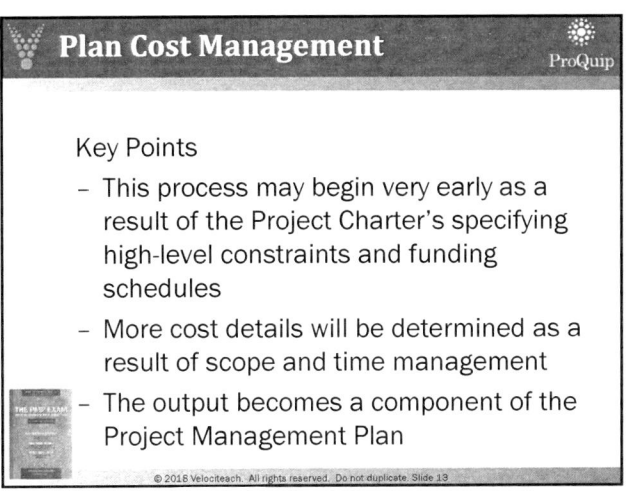

Plan Cost Management

Key Points

- This process may begin very early as a result of the Project Charter's specifying high-level constraints and funding schedules
- More cost details will be determined as a result of scope and time management
- The output becomes a component of the Project Management Plan

© 2018 Velociteach. All rights reserved. Do not duplicate. Slide 13

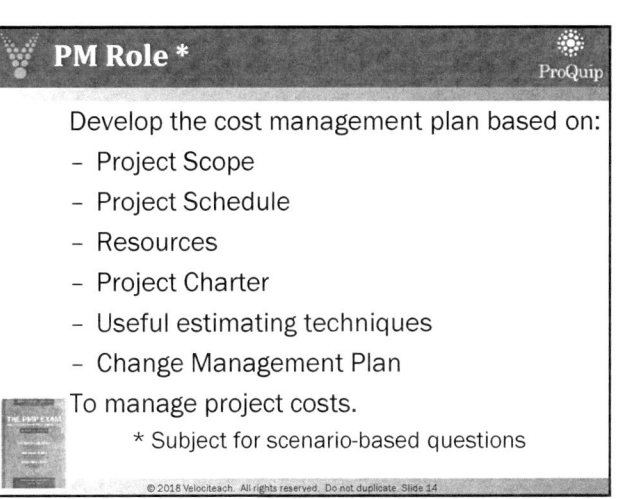

PM Role *

Develop the cost management plan based on:

- Project Scope
- Project Schedule
- Resources
- Project Charter
- Useful estimating techniques
- Change Management Plan

To manage project costs.

* Subject for scenario-based questions

© 2018 Velociteach. All rights reserved. Do not duplicate. Slide 14

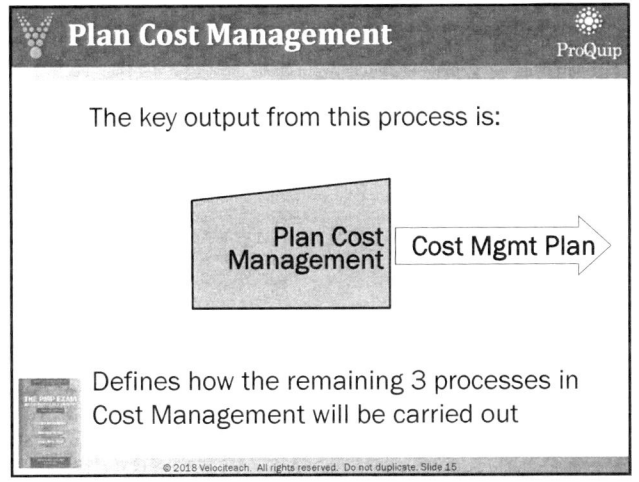

Plan Cost Management

The key output from this process is:

Plan Cost Management → Cost Mgmt Plan

Defines how the remaining 3 processes in Cost Management will be carried out

© 2018 Velociteach. All rights reserved. Do not duplicate. Slide 15

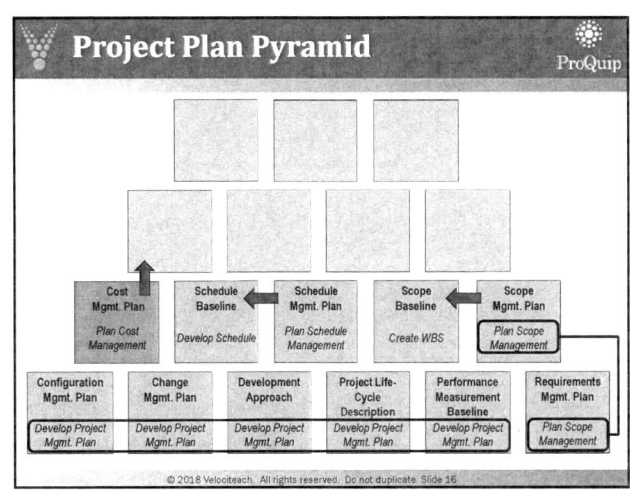

Project Plan Pyramid

© 2018 Velociteach. All rights reserved. Do not duplicate. Slide 16

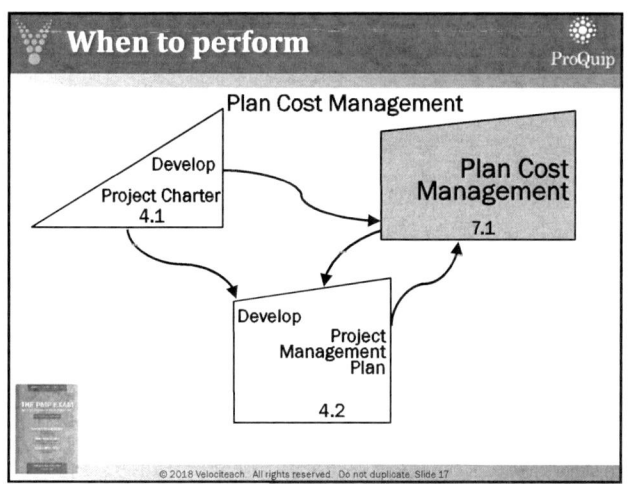

Plan Cost Management

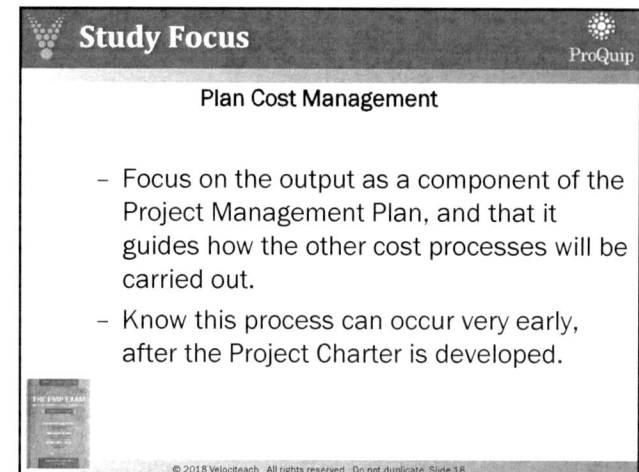

– Focus on the output as a component of the Project Management Plan, and that it guides how the other cost processes will be carried out.

– Know this process can occur very early, after the Project Charter is developed.

© 2018 Velociteach. All rights reserved. Do not duplicate. Slide 17

© 2018 Velociteach. All rights reserved. Do not duplicate. Slide 18

Review the ITTOs

Plan Cost Management

© 2018 Velociteach. All rights reserved.

The 4 Cost Processes

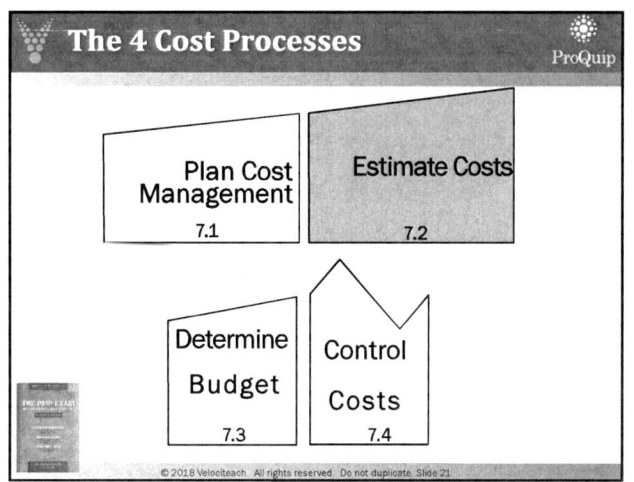

Plan Cost Management
7.1

Estimate Costs
7.2

Determine Budget
7.3

Control Costs
7.4

© 2018 Velociteach. All rights reserved. Do not duplicate. Slide 21

Estimate Costs

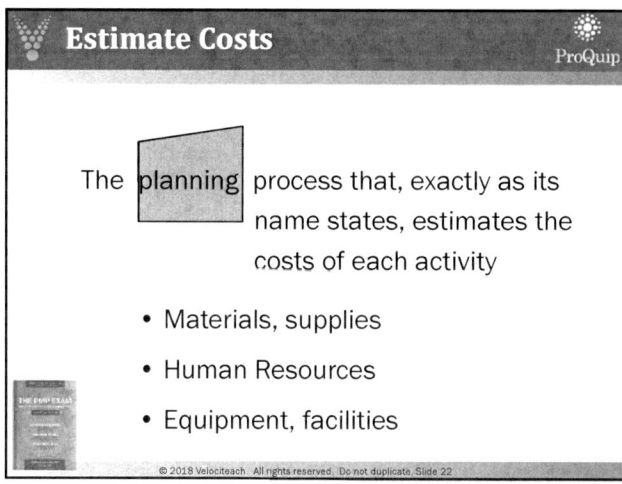

The planning process that, exactly as its name states, estimates the costs of each activity

- Materials, supplies
- Human Resources
- Equipment, facilities

© 2018 Velociteach. All rights reserved. Do not duplicate. Slide 22

Estimate Costs – "How much?"

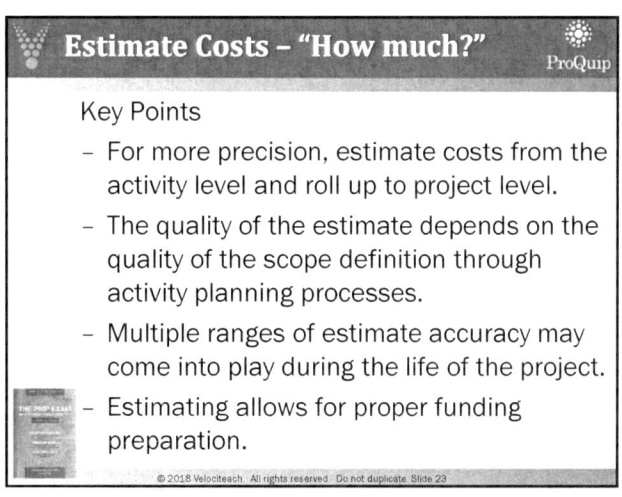

Key Points
- For more precision, estimate costs from the activity level and roll up to project level.
- The quality of the estimate depends on the quality of the scope definition through activity planning processes.
- Multiple ranges of estimate accuracy may come into play during the life of the project.
- Estimating allows for proper funding preparation.

© 2018 Velociteach. All rights reserved. Do not duplicate. Slide 23

PM Role *

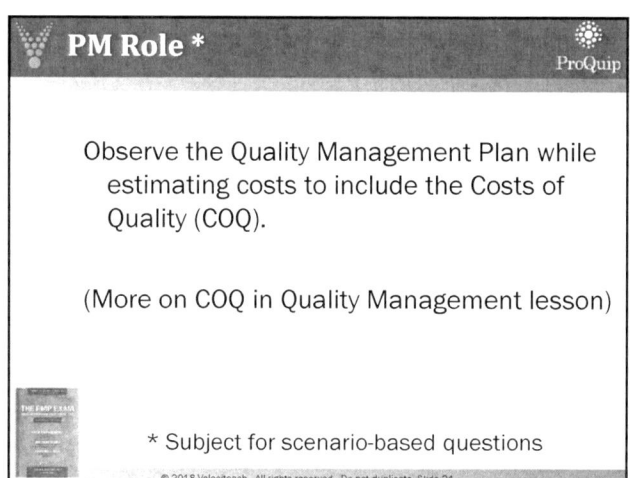

Observe the Quality Management Plan while estimating costs to include the Costs of Quality (COQ).

(More on COQ in Quality Management lesson)

* Subject for scenario-based questions

© 2018 Velociteach. All rights reserved. Do not duplicate. Slide 24

©2018 Velociteach. All rights reserved. Page 156

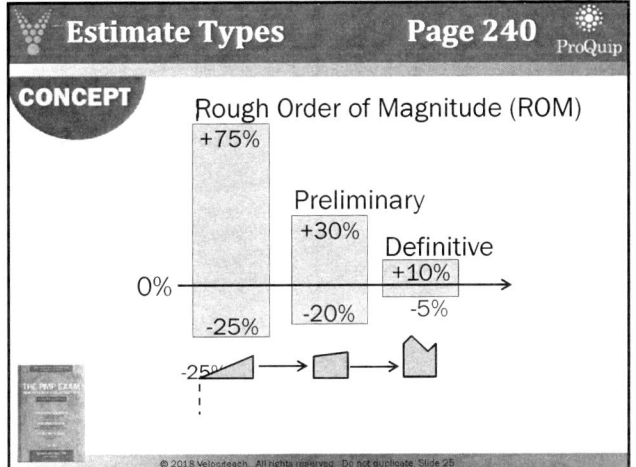

Estimate Types   Page 240

CONCEPT

Rough Order of Magnitude (ROM)
+75%

Preliminary
+30%

Definitive
+10%

0%

-25%   -20%   -5%

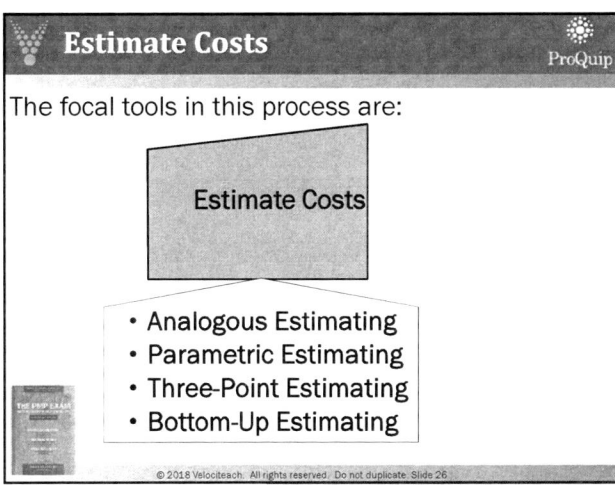

Estimate Costs

The focal tools in this process are:

Estimate Costs

- Analogous Estimating
- Parametric Estimating
- Three-Point Estimating
- Bottom-Up Estimating

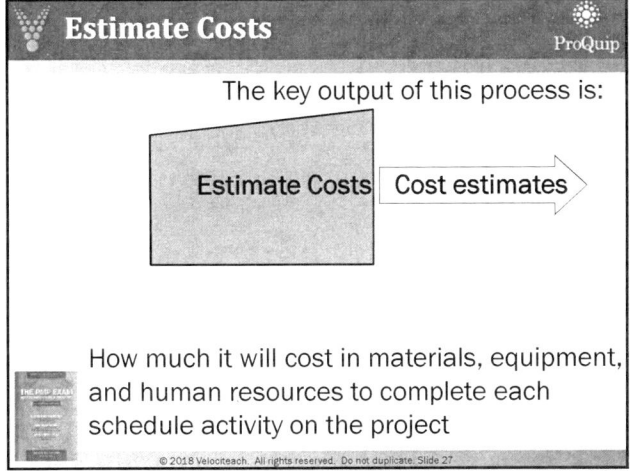

Estimate Costs

The key output of this process is:

Estimate Costs → Cost estimates

How much it will cost in materials, equipment, and human resources to complete each schedule activity on the project

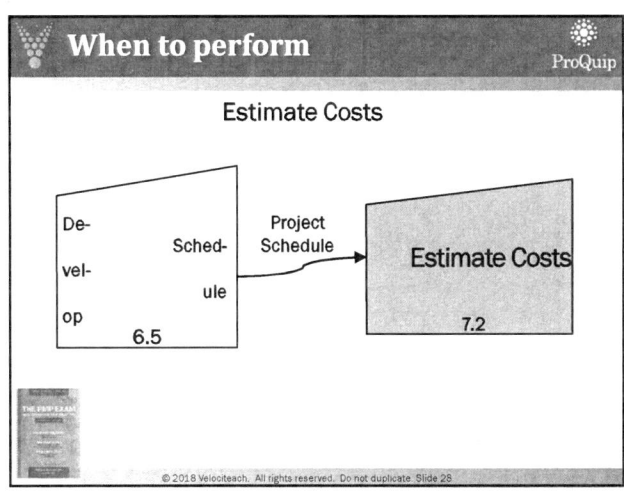

When to perform

Estimate Costs

Develop   Schedule   Project Schedule   Estimate Costs
6.5   7.2

©2018 Velociteach. All rights reserved. Page 157

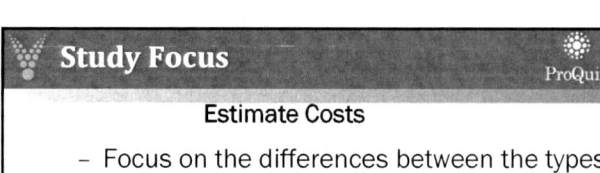

Study Focus

ProQuip

Estimate Costs

- Focus on the differences between the types of estimating techniques.
- Know that lower level details from the Schedule (Activity List and Attributes) are required to perform detailed estimating.
- Be familiar with the different estimate types and the relative ranges of "accuracy."
- Know that Estimate Costs may be iterative.

© 2018 Velociteach. All rights reserved. Do not duplicate. Slide 29

Review the ITTOs

Estimate Costs

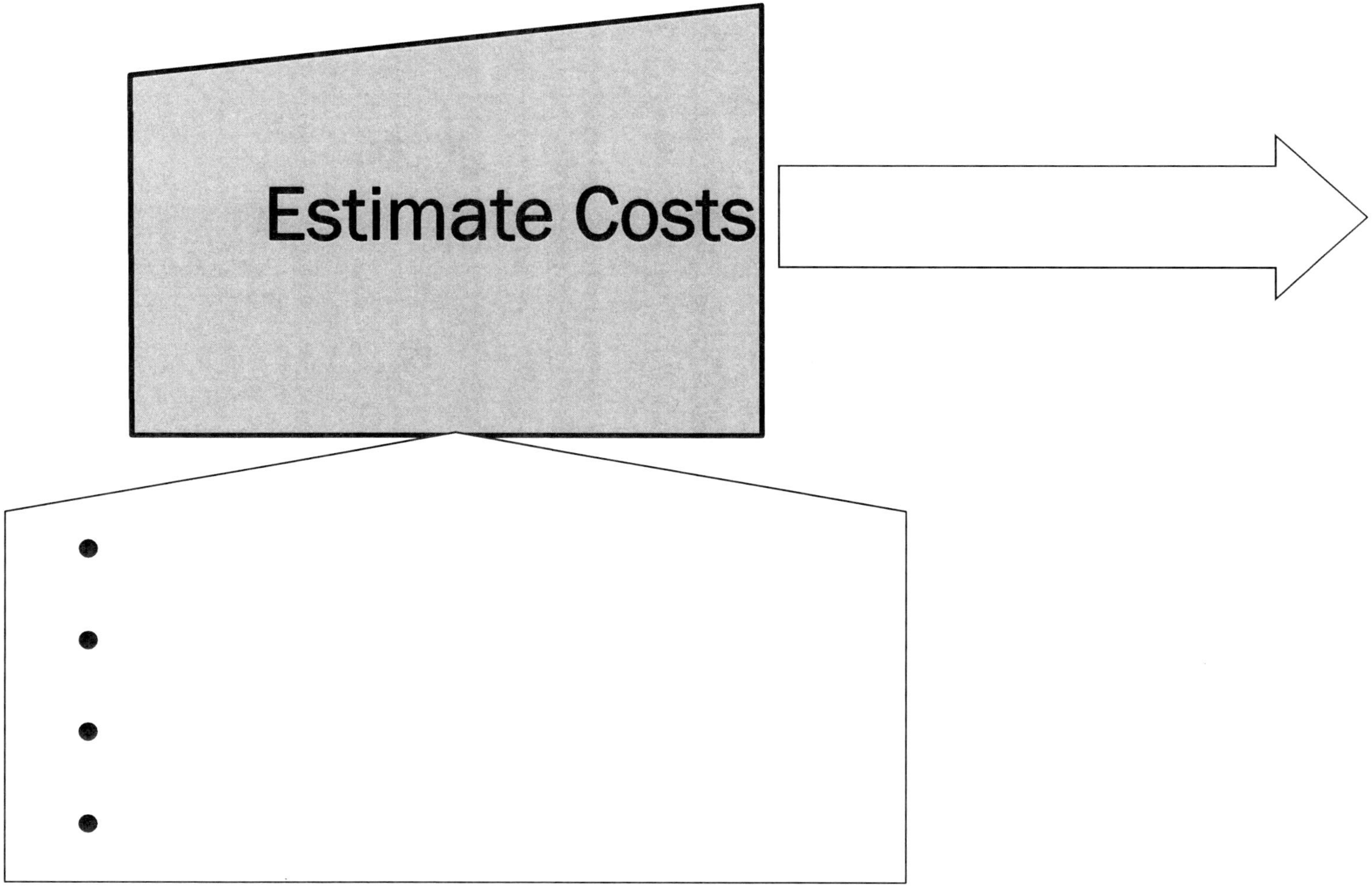

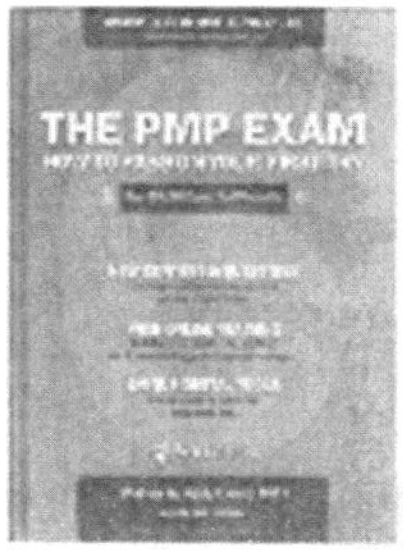

© 2018 Velociteach. All rights reserved.

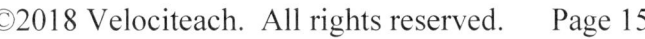

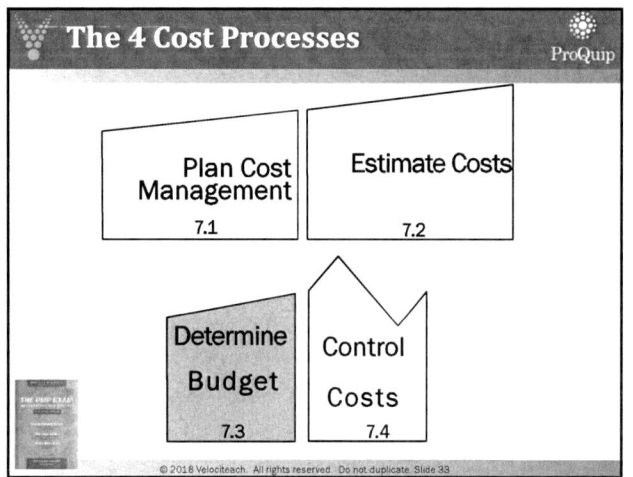

The 4 Cost Processes

Plan Cost Management 7.1

Estimate Costs 7.2

Determine Budget 7.3

Control Costs 7.4

© 2018 Velociteach. All rights reserved. Do not duplicate. Slide 33

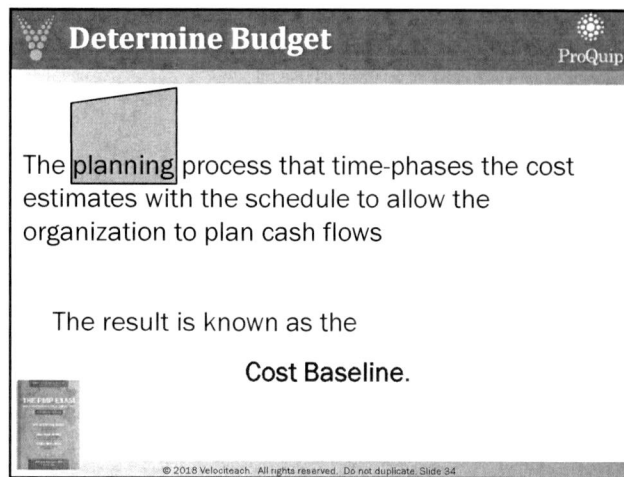

Determine Budget

The planning process that time-phases the cost estimates with the schedule to allow the organization to plan cash flows

The result is known as the

Cost Baseline.

© 2018 Velociteach. All rights reserved. Do not duplicate. Slide 34

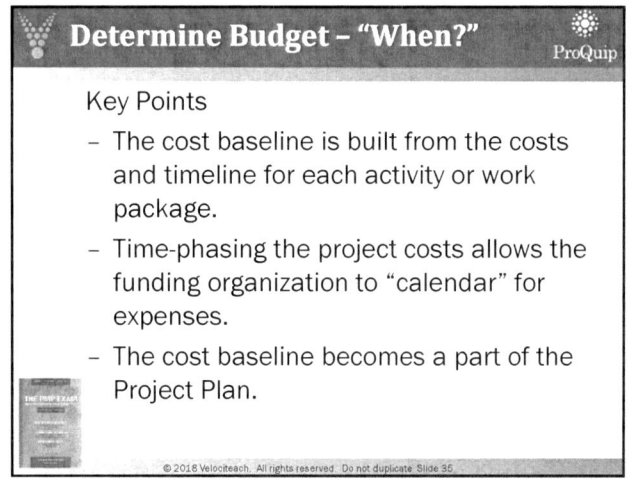

Determine Budget – "When?"

Key Points

– The cost baseline is built from the costs and timeline for each activity or work package.

– Time-phasing the project costs allows the funding organization to "calendar" for expenses.

– The cost baseline becomes a part of the Project Plan.

© 2018 Velociteach. All rights reserved. Do not duplicate. Slide 35

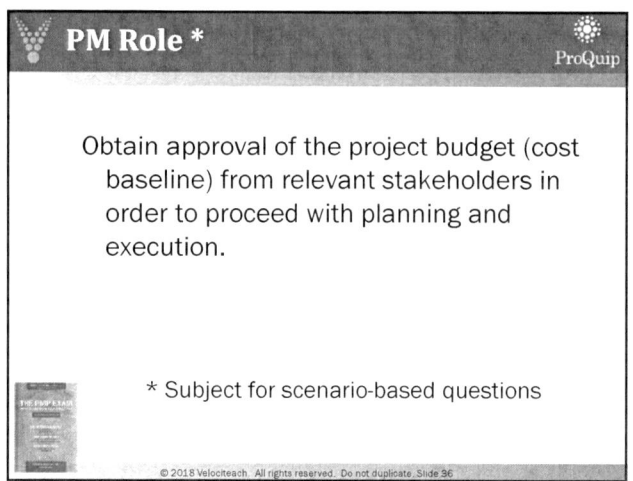

PM Role *

Obtain approval of the project budget (cost baseline) from relevant stakeholders in order to proceed with planning and execution.

* Subject for scenario-based questions

© 2018 Velociteach. All rights reserved. Do not duplicate. Slide 36

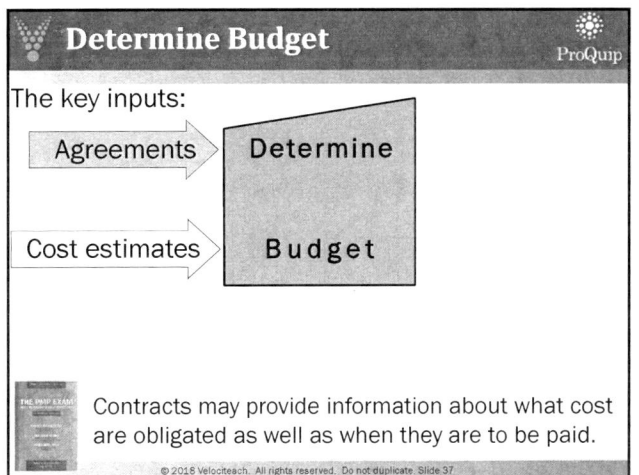

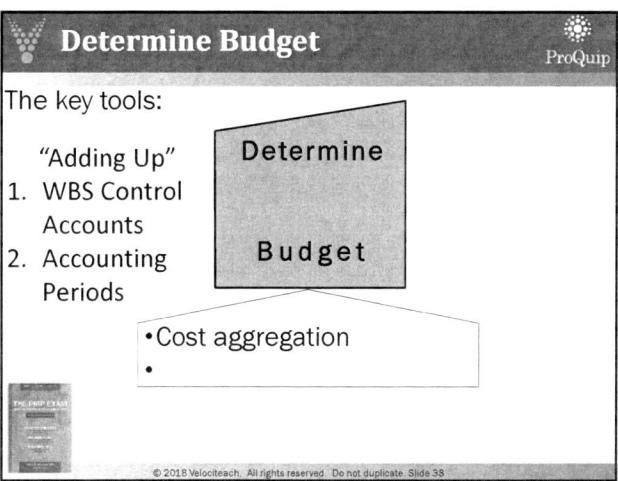

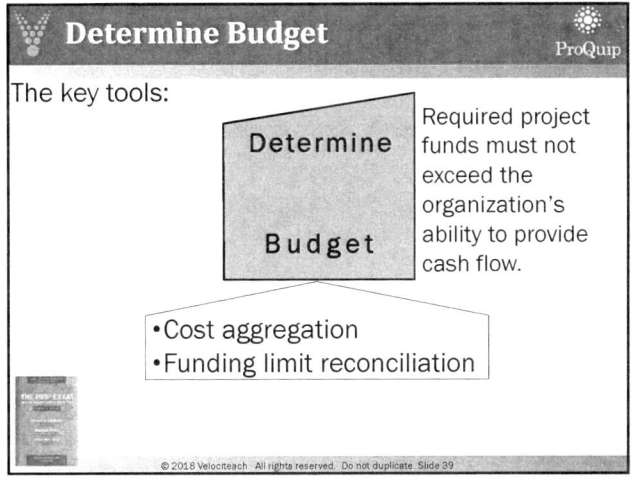

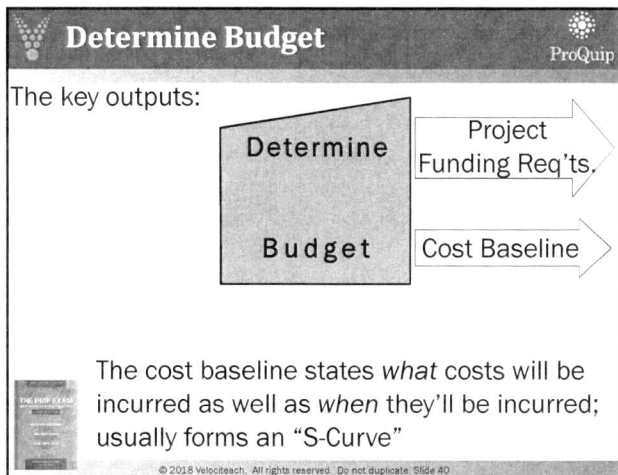

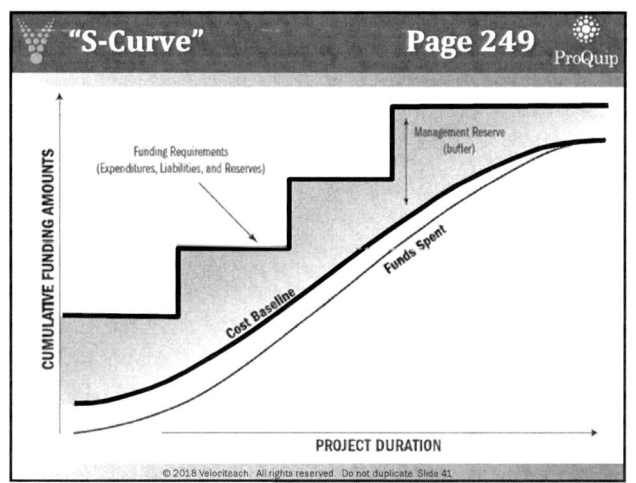

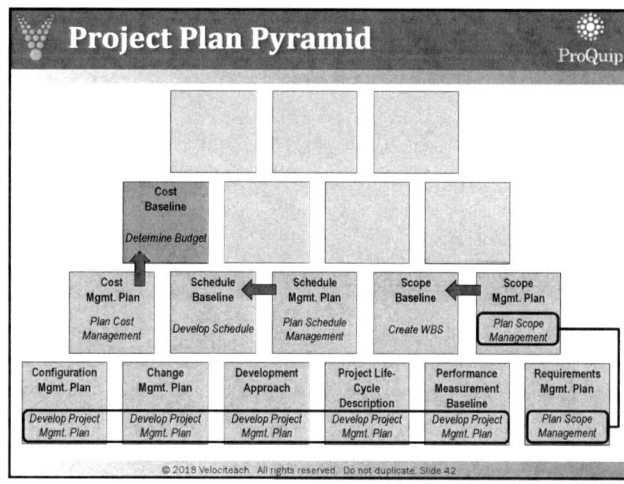

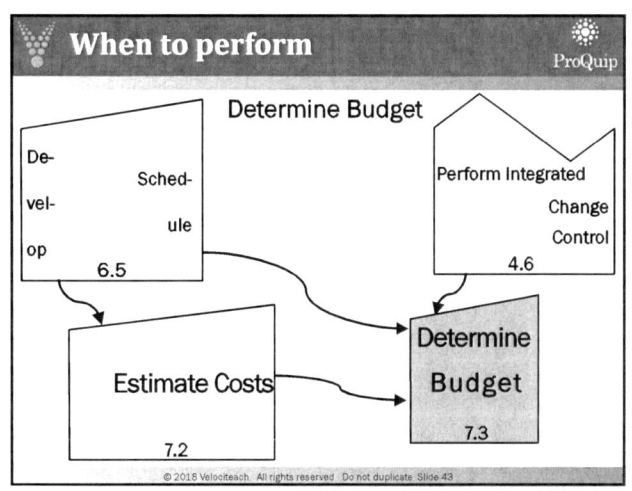

Study Focus

Determine Budget

- Know that the Cost Baseline is the approved spending plan, and becomes part of the Project Plan.
- Know that the Baseline is the Cost Estimates time-phased by the Schedule.
- Know that the required funds must be adjusted to fit within the organization's ability to fund the project.

© 2018 Velociteach. All rights reserved. Do not duplicate. Slide 44

ProQuip

Determine Budget

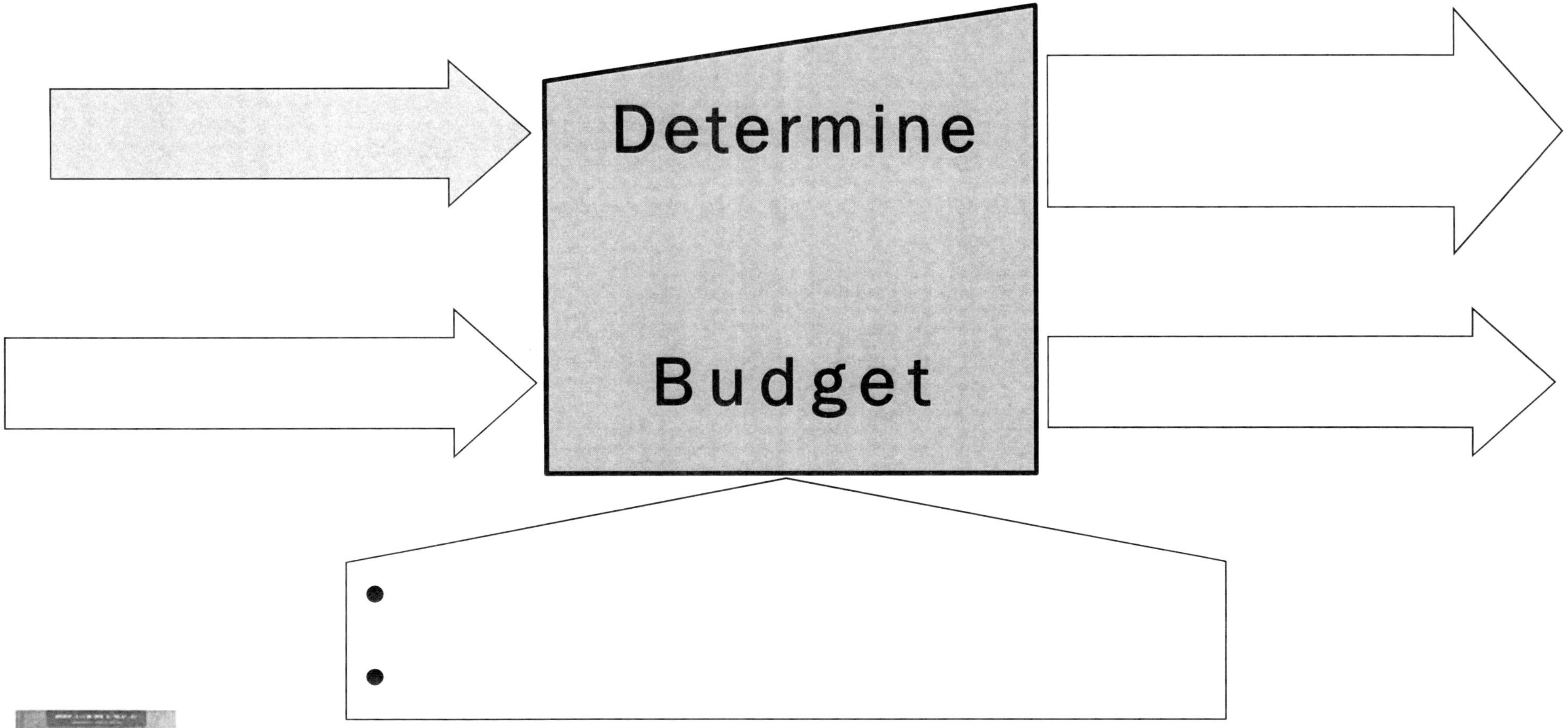

© 2018 Velociteach. All rights reserved.

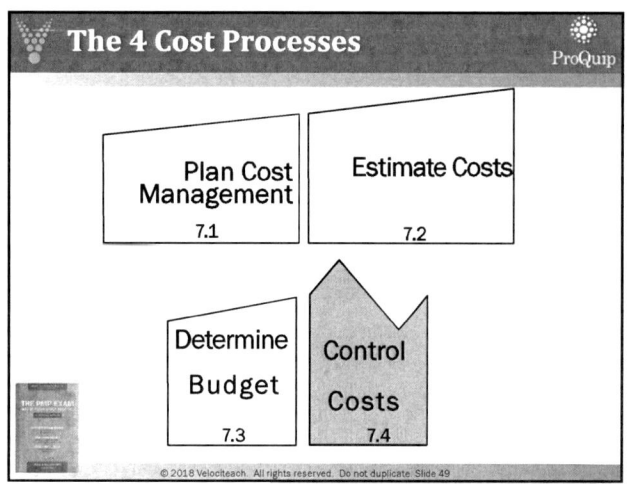

The 4 Cost Processes

Plan Cost Management 7.1

Estimate Costs 7.2

Determine Budget 7.3

Control Costs 7.4

© 2018 Velociteach. All rights reserved. Do not duplicate. Slide 49

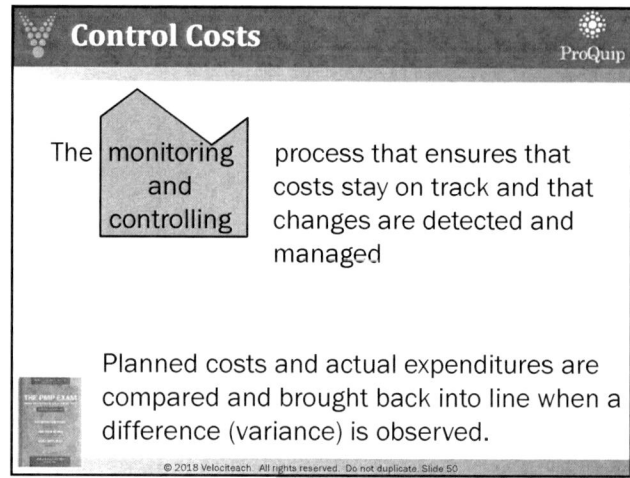

Control Costs

The monitoring and controlling process that ensures that costs stay on track and that changes are detected and managed

Planned costs and actual expenditures are compared and brought back into line when a difference (variance) is observed.

© 2018 Velociteach. All rights reserved. Do not duplicate. Slide 50

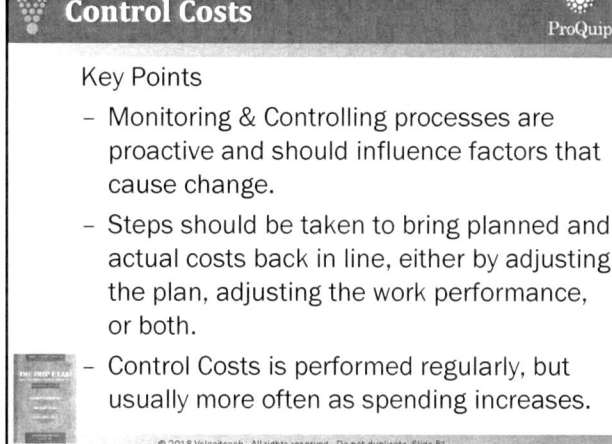

Control Costs

Key Points
- Monitoring & Controlling processes are proactive and should influence factors that cause change.
- Steps should be taken to bring planned and actual costs back in line, either by adjusting the plan, adjusting the work performance, or both.
- Control Costs is performed regularly, but usually more often as spending increases.

© 2018 Velociteach. All rights reserved. Do not duplicate. Slide 51

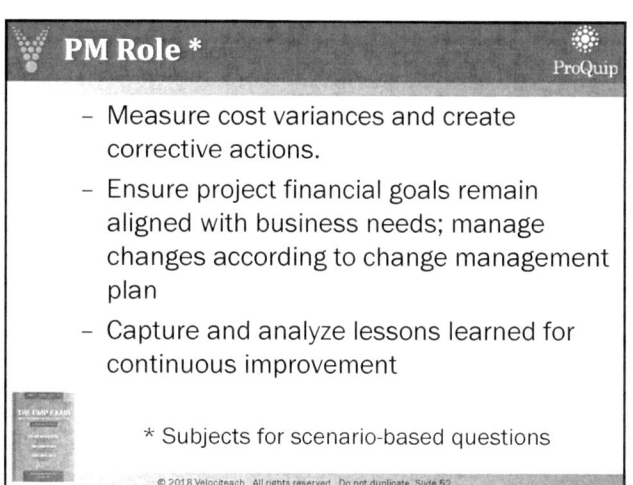

PM Role *

- Measure cost variances and create corrective actions.
- Ensure project financial goals remain aligned with business needs; manage changes according to change management plan
- Capture and analyze lessons learned for continuous improvement

* Subjects for scenario-based questions

© 2018 Velociteach. All rights reserved. Do not duplicate. Slide 52

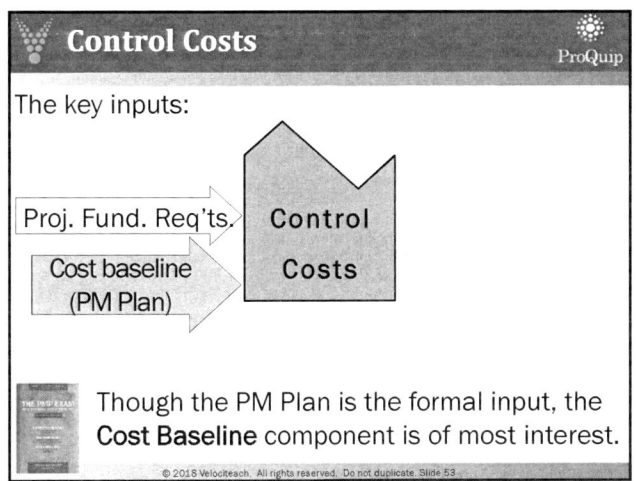

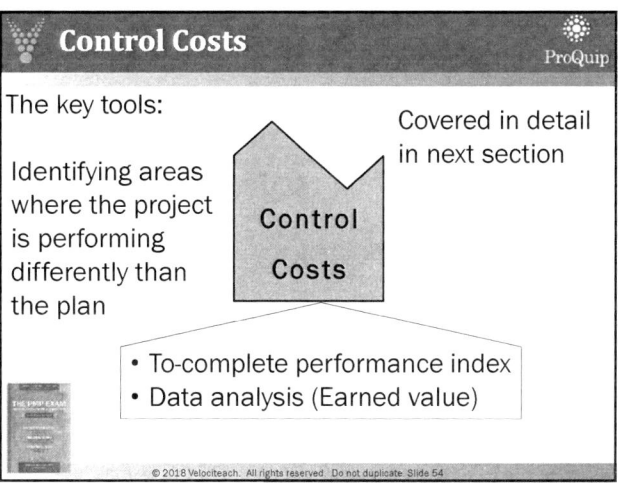

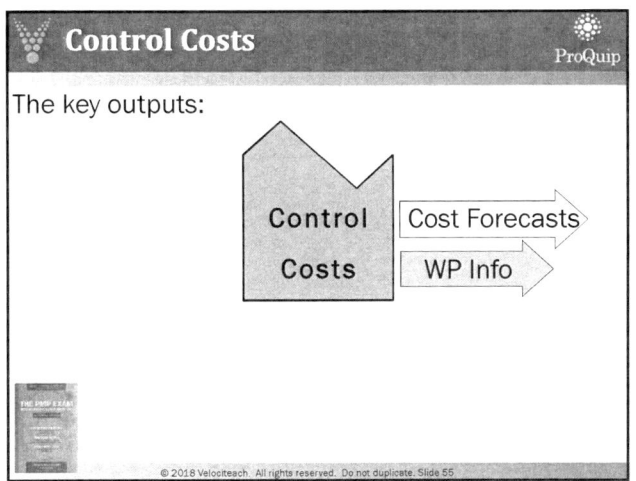

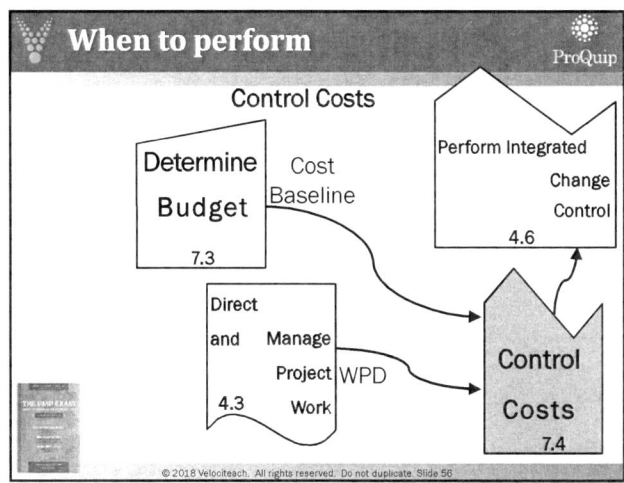

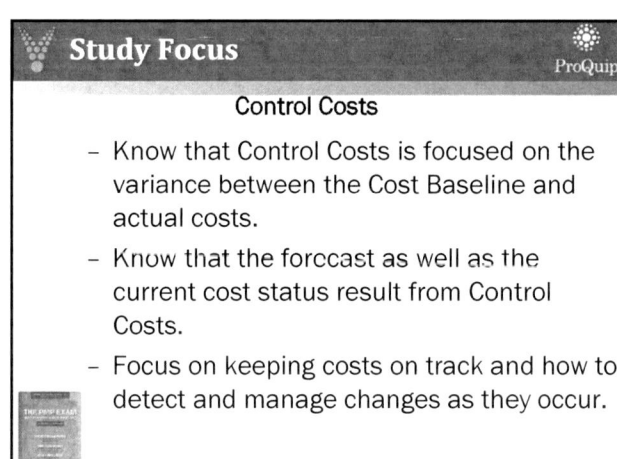

Study Focus

ProQuip

Control Costs

- Know that Control Costs is focused on the variance between the Cost Baseline and actual costs.

- Know that the forccast as well as the current cost status result from Control Costs.

- Focus on keeping costs on track and how to detect and manage changes as they occur.

© 2018 Velociteach. All rights reserved. Do not duplicate Slide 57

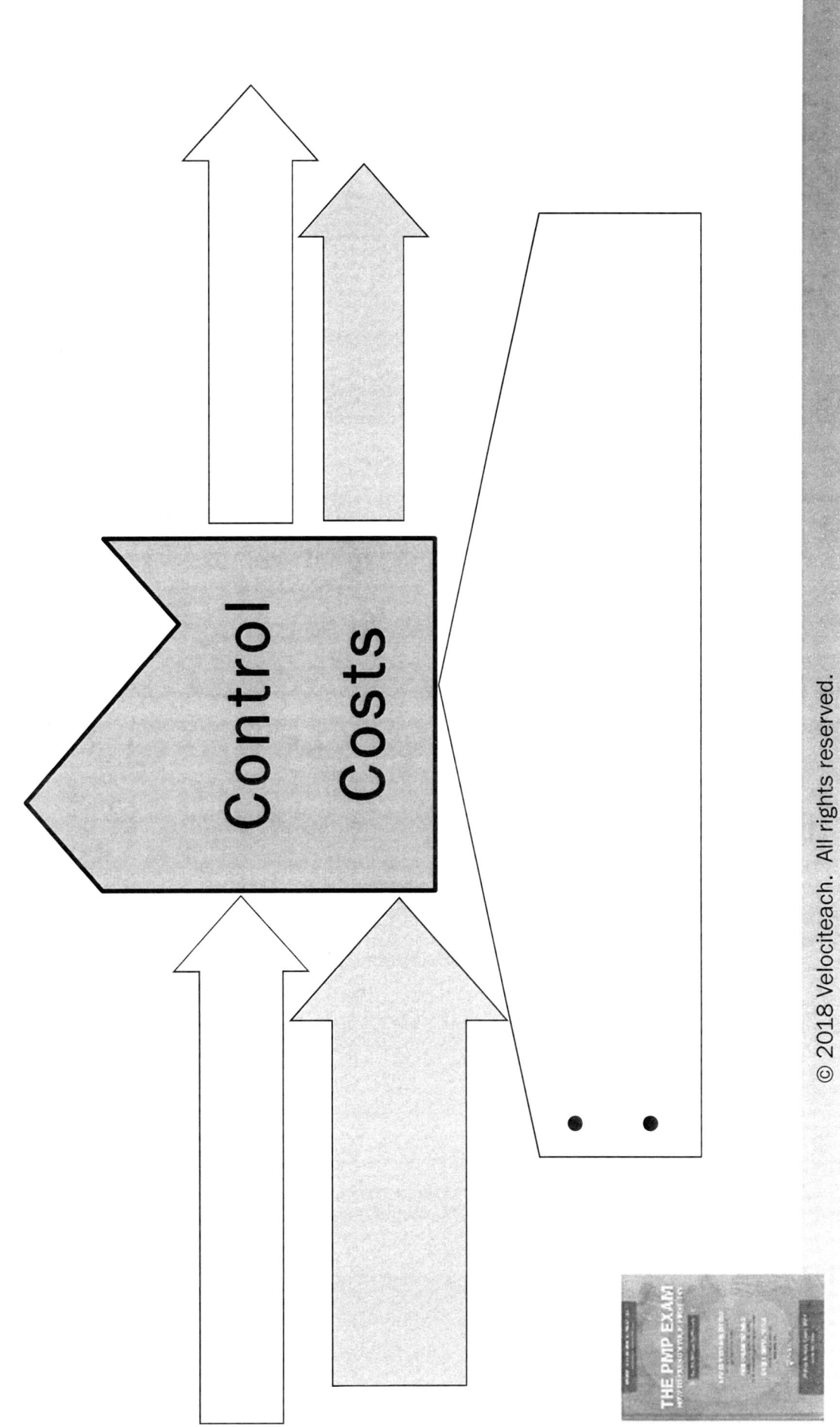

Review the ITTOs

Control Costs

© 2018 Velociteach. All rights reserved.

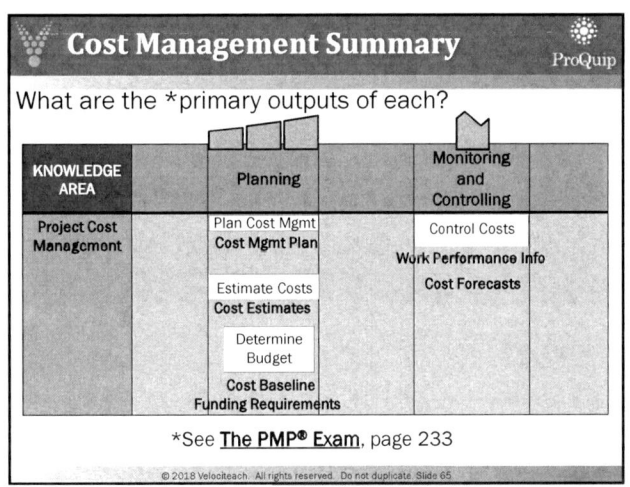

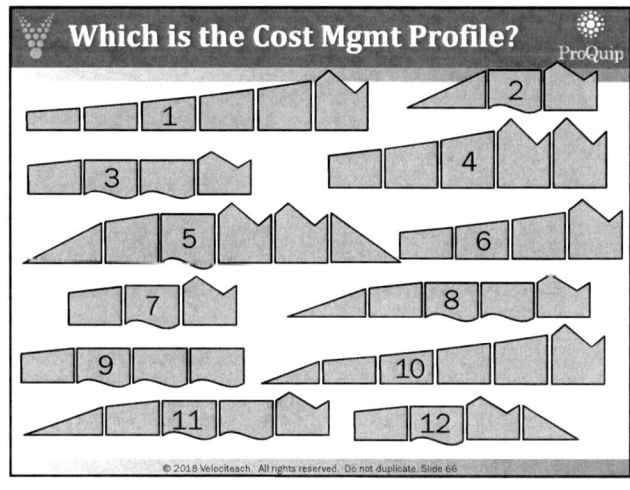

Terms You Should Know

Project Cost Management

Analogous Estimating	Life-cycle costing
Bottom-Up Estimating	Funding Requirements
Control Account	Cost Baseline
Control Account Manager	S-Curve
Value Engineering	Three-Point Estimate
Control Costs	Variance
Cost Management Plan	Management Reserve
Determine Budget	Cost estimates
Parametric Estimating	Earned Value
Funding Limit Reconciliation	

© 2018 Velociteach. All rights reserved. Do not duplicate. Slide 68

Cost Discussion

Why is the process of *Develop Schedule* performed before *Determine Budget*?

What is the basis for analogous estimating?

When are the processes of Cost Management performed?

What is a *variance* and why is it important?

Describe the *Control Costs* process.

© 2018 Velociteach. All rights reserved. Do not duplicate. Slide 69

Summary

ProQuip

Knowledge Area

KNOWLEDGE AREA	Initiating	Planning	Executing	Monitoring and Controlling	Closing
Project ___ Management					

©2018 Velociteach. All rights reserved.   Page 169

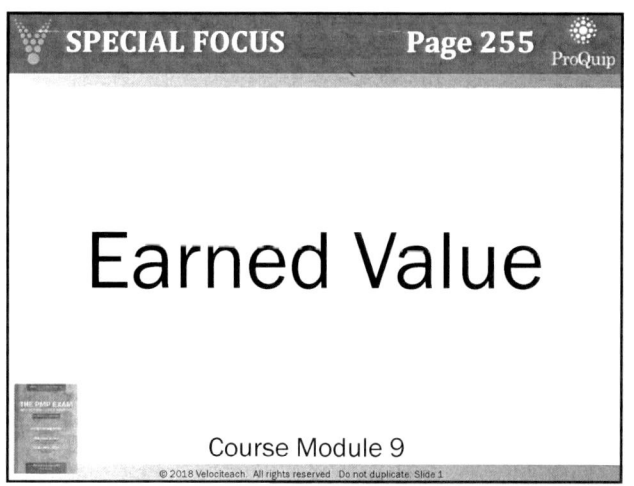

SPECIAL FOCUS   Page 255

Earned Value

Course Module 9

© 2018 Velociteach. All rights reserved. Do not duplicate. Slide 1

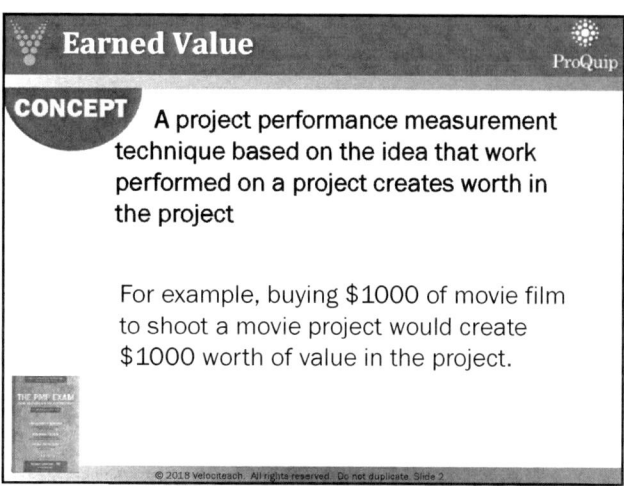

Earned Value

CONCEPT A project performance measurement technique based on the idea that work performed on a project creates worth in the project

For example, buying $1000 of movie film to shoot a movie project would create $1000 worth of value in the project.

© 2018 Velociteach. All rights reserved. Do not duplicate. Slide 2

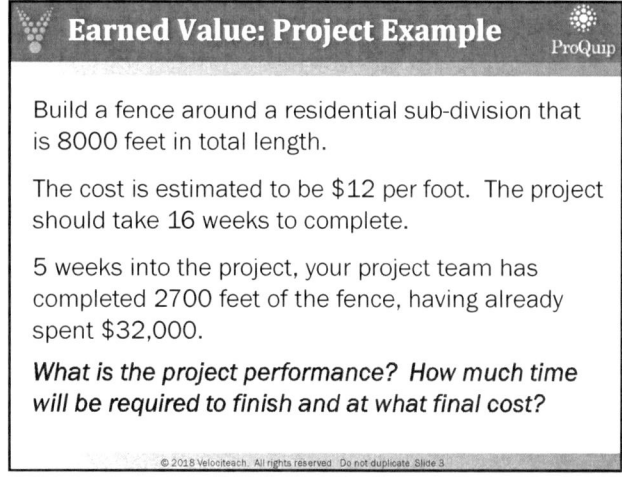

Earned Value: Project Example

Build a fence around a residential sub-division that is 8000 feet in total length.

The cost is estimated to be $12 per foot. The project should take 16 weeks to complete.

5 weeks into the project, your project team has completed 2700 feet of the fence, having already spent $32,000.

What is the project performance? How much time will be required to finish and at what final cost?

© 2018 Velociteach. All rights reserved. Do not duplicate. Slide 3

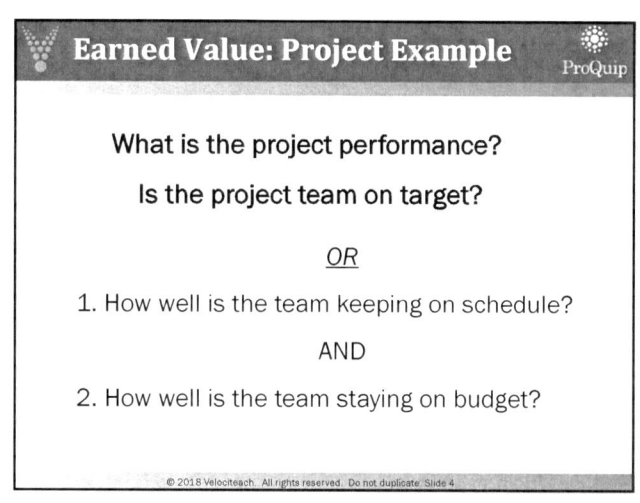

Earned Value: Project Example

What is the project performance?

Is the project team on target?

OR

1. How well is the team keeping on schedule?

AND

2. How well is the team staying on budget?

© 2018 Velociteach. All rights reserved. Do not duplicate. Slide 4

Earned Value: Project Example — ProQuip

1. How well is the team keeping on schedule?

First, state the project target in terms of original estimated value:

The project will be completed once the full value of the fence has been earned into the project. The full value is called the **Budgeted At Completion (BAC)**.

BAC = 8000 feet of fence X $12 per foot

BAC = $96,000

© 2018 Velociteach. All rights reserved. Do not duplicate. Slide 5

Earned Value: Project Example — ProQuip

1. How well is the team keeping on schedule?

Second, determine how much work was <u>planned</u> to have been done at this point in time, in terms of money. This is called the **Planned Value (PV)**.

PV = Planned % complete X BAC

5 weeks / 16 weeks = 31.25%

PV = 31.25% X $96,000

PV = $30,000

(AKA **BCWS** – <u>B</u>udgeted <u>C</u>ost of <u>W</u>ork <u>S</u>cheduled)

© 2018 Velociteach. All rights reserved. Do not duplicate. Slide 6

Earned Value: Project Example — ProQuip

1. How well is the team keeping on schedule?

Third, determine how much work was <u>actually</u> completed at this point in time, in terms of money.

This is called the **Earned Value (EV)**.

EV = Actual % complete X BAC

2700 feet / 8000 feet = 33.75%

EV = 33.75% X $96,000

EV = $32,400

(AKA **BCWP** – <u>B</u>udgeted <u>C</u>ost of <u>W</u>ork <u>P</u>erformed)

© 2018 Velociteach. All rights reserved. Do not duplicate. Slide 7

Earned Value: Project Example — ProQuip

1. How well is the team keeping on schedule?

EV = $32,400	Actually accomplished
— PV = $30,000	— Planned to accomplish
SV = $ 2,400	**Schedule Variance**

SV = EV - PV

0 Zero is good;   On schedule
+ Positive is good; Ahead of schedule
-   Negative is bad; Behind schedule

© 2018 Velociteach. All rights reserved. Do not duplicate. Slide 8

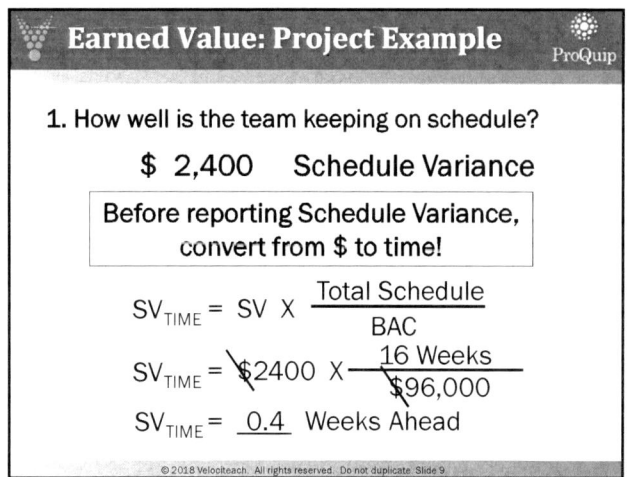

Earned Value: Project Example — ProQuip

1. How well is the team keeping on schedule?

$ 2,400   Schedule Variance

Before reporting Schedule Variance, convert from $ to time!

$$SV_{TIME} = SV \times \frac{Total\ Schedule}{BAC}$$

$$SV_{TIME} = \$2400 \times \frac{16\ Weeks}{\$96,000}$$

$$SV_{TIME} = \underline{0.4}\ Weeks\ Ahead$$

© 2018 Velociteach. All rights reserved. Do not duplicate. Slide 9

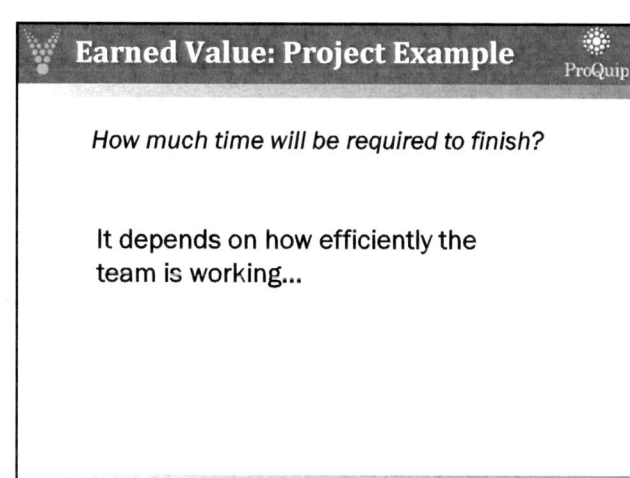

Earned Value: Project Example — ProQuip

How much time will be required to finish?

It depends on how efficiently the team is working...

© 2018 Velociteach. All rights reserved. Do not duplicate. Slide 10

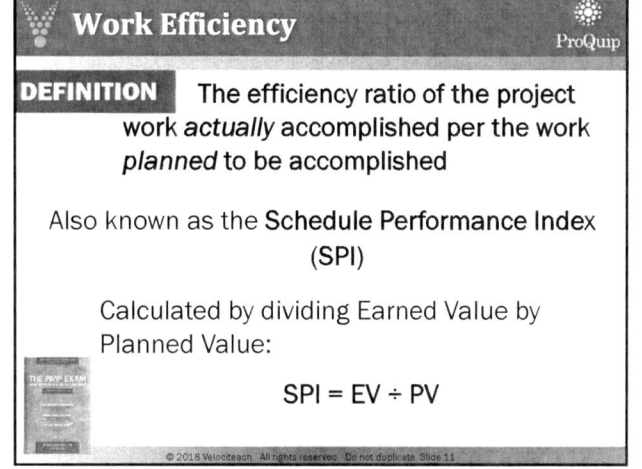

Work Efficiency — ProQuip

DEFINITION   The efficiency ratio of the project work *actually* accomplished per the work *planned* to be accomplished

Also known as the **Schedule Performance Index (SPI)**

Calculated by dividing Earned Value by Planned Value:

$$SPI = EV \div PV$$

© 2018 Velociteach. All rights reserved. Do not duplicate. Slide 11

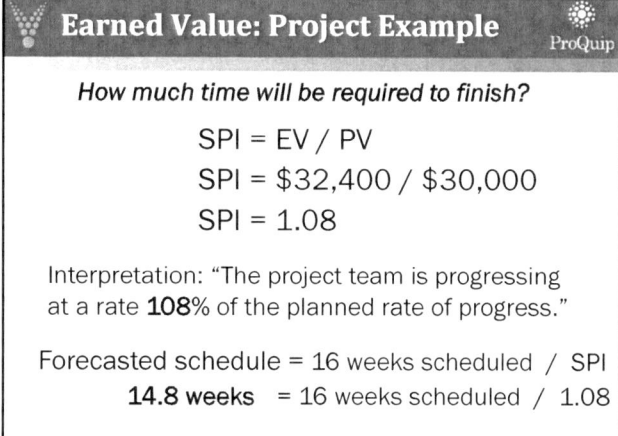

Earned Value: Project Example — ProQuip

How much time will be required to finish?

$$SPI = EV / PV$$
$$SPI = \$32,400 / \$30,000$$
$$SPI = 1.08$$

Interpretation: "The project team is progressing at a rate **108**% of the planned rate of progress."

Forecasted schedule = 16 weeks scheduled / SPI
14.8 weeks = 16 weeks scheduled / 1.08

© 2018 Velociteach. All rights reserved. Do not duplicate. Slide 12

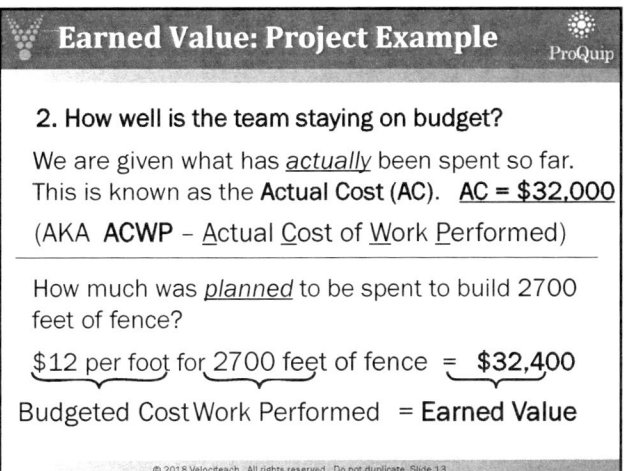

Earned Value: Project Example ProQuip

2. How well is the team staying on budget?

We are given what has _actually_ been spent so far. This is known as the **Actual Cost (AC)**. AC = $32,000

(AKA **ACWP** – Actual Cost of Work Performed)

How much was _planned_ to be spent to build 2700 feet of fence?

$12 per foot for 2700 feet of fence = $32,400

Budgeted Cost Work Performed = **Earned Value**

© 2018 Velociteach. All rights reserved. Do not duplicate. Slide 13

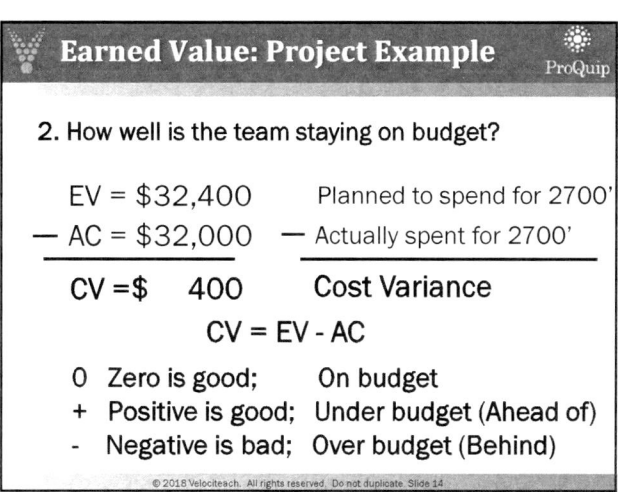

Earned Value: Project Example ProQuip

2. How well is the team staying on budget?

$$EV = \$32,400 \quad \text{Planned to spend for 2700'}$$
$$-\ AC = \$32,000 \quad -\ \text{Actually spent for 2700'}$$

$$CV = \$\quad 400 \quad \text{Cost Variance}$$

$$CV = EV - AC$$

0 Zero is good;   On budget
+ Positive is good; Under budget (Ahead of)
- Negative is bad;   Over budget (Behind)

© 2018 Velociteach. All rights reserved. Do not duplicate. Slide 14

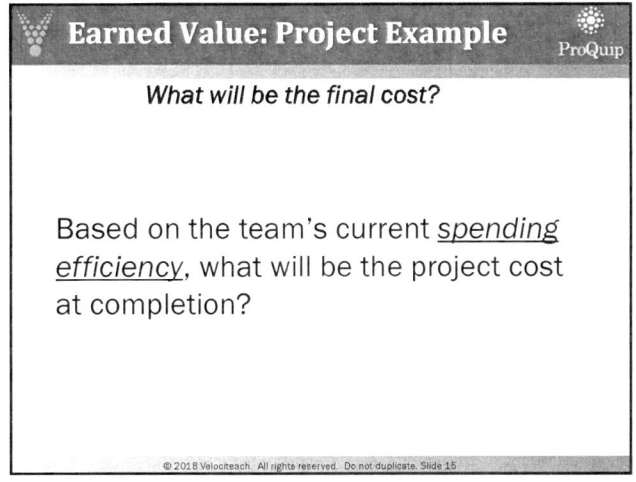

Earned Value: Project Example ProQuip

What will be the final cost?

Based on the team's current _spending efficiency_, what will be the project cost at completion?

© 2018 Velociteach. All rights reserved. Do not duplicate. Slide 15

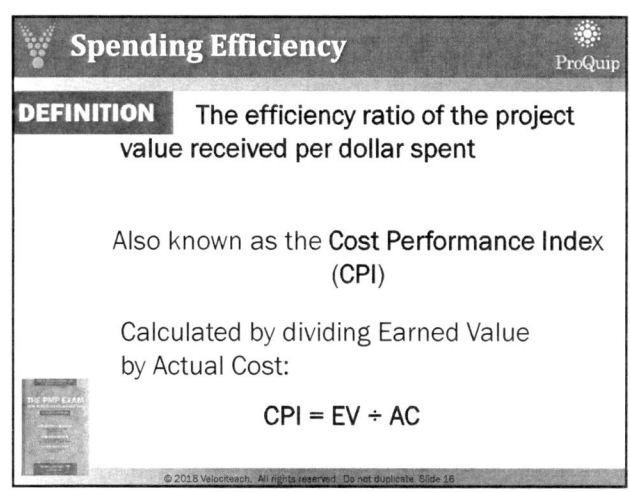

Spending Efficiency ProQuip

DEFINITION   The efficiency ratio of the project value received per dollar spent

Also known as the **Cost Performance Index (CPI)**

Calculated by dividing Earned Value by Actual Cost:

$$CPI = EV \div AC$$

© 2018 Velociteach. All rights reserved. Do not duplicate. Slide 16

Earned Value: Project Example

What will be the final cost?

First, calculate the Cost Performance Index (Spending Efficiency):

$$CPI = EV / AC$$
$$CPI = \$32,400 / \$32,000$$
$$CPI = 1.0125$$

Interpretation: "For every dollar the project team is spending, they receive a value of \$1.0125."

© 2018 Velociteach. All rights reserved. Do not duplicate Slide 17

Earned Value: Project Example

What will be the final cost?

Then, calculate the forecasted final cost, called the **Estimate At Complete (EAC).**

$$EAC = BAC / CPI^C$$
$$EAC = \$96,000 / 1.0125$$
$$EAC = \$94,814.81$$

Based on the team's spending efficiency, the completed fence should cost **\$94,814.81**.

© 2018 Velociteach. All rights reserved. Do not duplicate Slide 18

Estimate At Complete

There are many ways to forecast the EAC - more than 25 documented ways to calculate EAC!

For the PMP® Exam, *primarily remember:*

$$EAC = BAC / CPI^C$$
(in textbook table on page 256)

NOTE: The Forecasting method used primarily depends on the scenario

© 2018 Velociteach. All rights reserved. Do not duplicate Slide 19

Forecasts – EAC – Default

EAC "forecast for ETC work performed at present CPI"

Assumes past performance results will continue for the remainder of the project

$$EAC = BAC \div CPI^C$$

© 2018 Velociteach. All rights reserved. Do not duplicate Slide 20

Estimate At Complete

DEFINITION

The forecasted total cost of the project when it is complete.

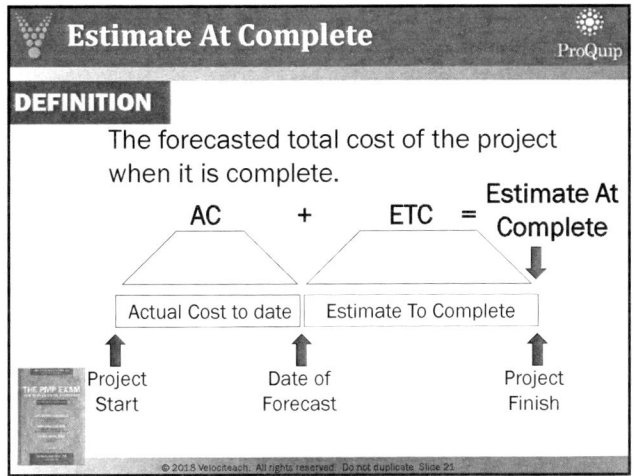

AC + ETC = Estimate At Complete

Actual Cost to date | Estimate To Complete

Project Start — Date of Forecast — Project Finish

© 2018 Velociteach. All rights reserved. Do not duplicate. Slide 21

Forecasts – EAC (2nd of 4)

Scenario: The forecast cannot be made based on the original estimates. The remainder of the project needs to be estimated again.

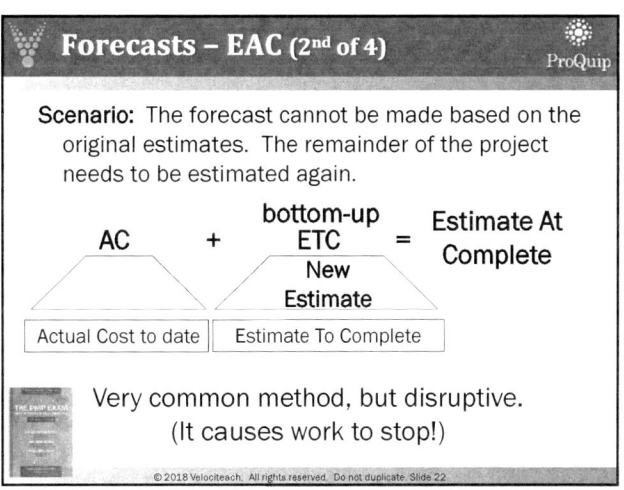

$$AC + \frac{\text{bottom-up}}{\text{ETC}} = \text{Estimate At Complete}$$

New Estimate

Actual Cost to date | Estimate To Complete

Very common method, but disruptive. (It causes work to stop!)

© 2018 Velociteach. All rights reserved. Do not duplicate. Slide 22

Forecasts – EAC (3rd of 4)

Scenario: The remaining work will be done at the originally budgeted rate.

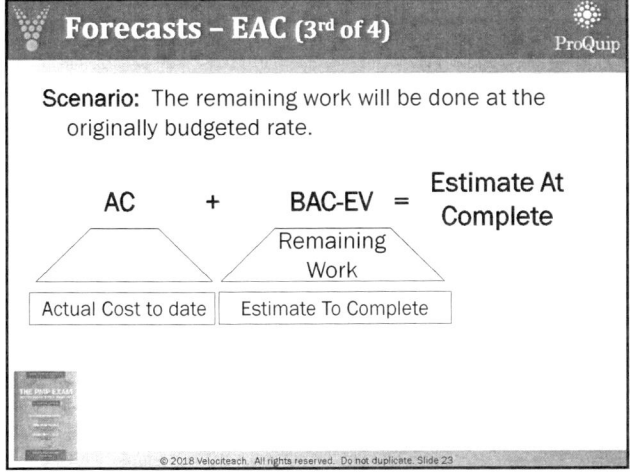

AC + BAC-EV = Estimate At Complete

Remaining Work

Actual Cost to date | Estimate To Complete

© 2018 Velociteach. All rights reserved. Do not duplicate. Slide 23

Forecasts – EAC (4th of 4)

Scenario: The remaining work will be done considering the current spending and working inefficiencies (CPI and SPI are both less than 1).

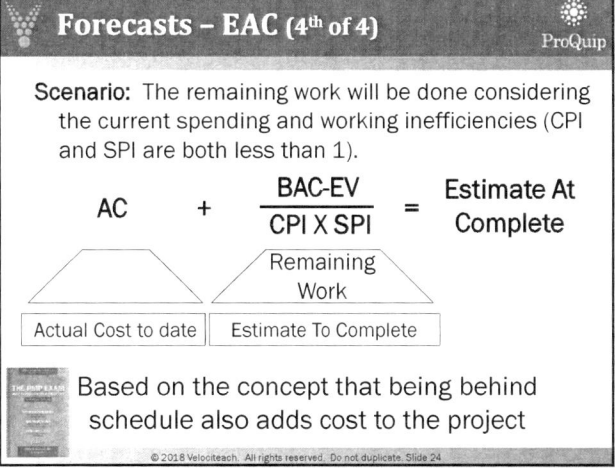

$$AC + \frac{\text{BAC-EV}}{\text{CPI X SPI}} = \text{Estimate At Complete}$$

Remaining Work

Actual Cost to date | Estimate To Complete

Based on the concept that being behind schedule also adds cost to the project

© 2018 Velociteach. All rights reserved. Do not duplicate. Slide 24

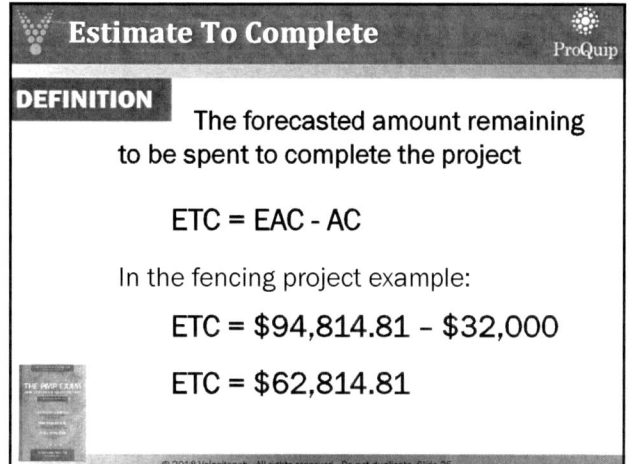

Estimate To Complete

ProQuip

DEFINITION

The forecasted amount remaining to be spent to complete the project

$$ETC = EAC - AC$$

In the fencing project example:

$$ETC = \$94,814.81 - \$32,000$$

$$ETC = \$62,814.81$$

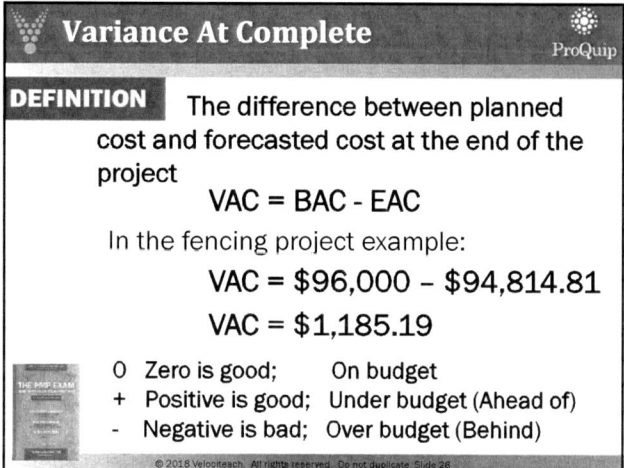

Variance At Complete

ProQuip

DEFINITION

The difference between planned cost and forecasted cost at the end of the project

$$VAC = BAC - EAC$$

In the fencing project example:

$$VAC = \$96,000 - \$94,814.81$$

$$VAC = \$1,185.19$$

0   Zero is good;   On budget
+   Positive is good;   Under budget (Ahead of)
-   Negative is bad;   Over budget (Behind)

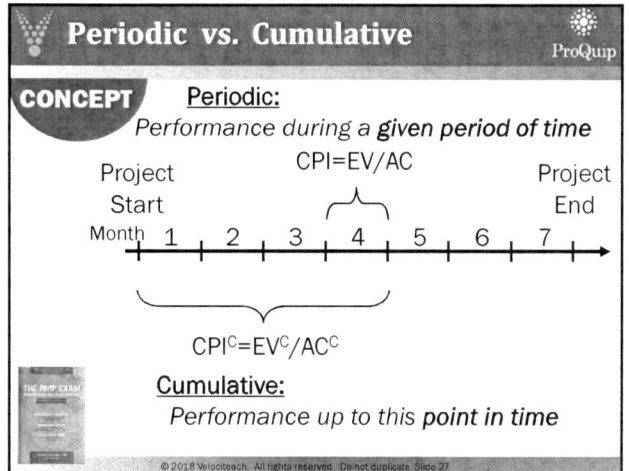

Periodic vs. Cumulative

ProQuip

CONCEPT

Periodic:
*Performance during a **given period of time***

Project Start $CPI = EV/AC$ Project End

Month 1   2   3   4   5   6   7

$$CPI^C = EV^C/AC^C$$

Cumulative:
*Performance up to this **point in time***

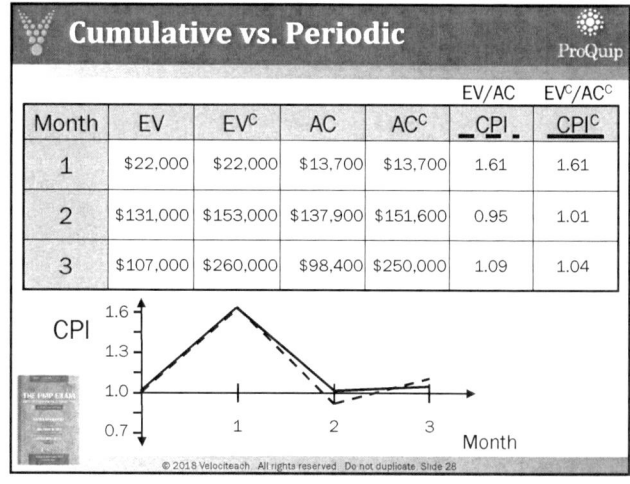

Cumulative vs. Periodic

ProQuip

Month	EV	EV^C	AC	AC^C	EV/AC CPI	EV^C/AC^C CPI^C
1	$22,000	$22,000	$13,700	$13,700	1.61	1.61
2	$131,000	$153,000	$137,900	$151,600	0.95	1.01
3	$107,000	$260,000	$98,400	$250,000	1.09	1.04

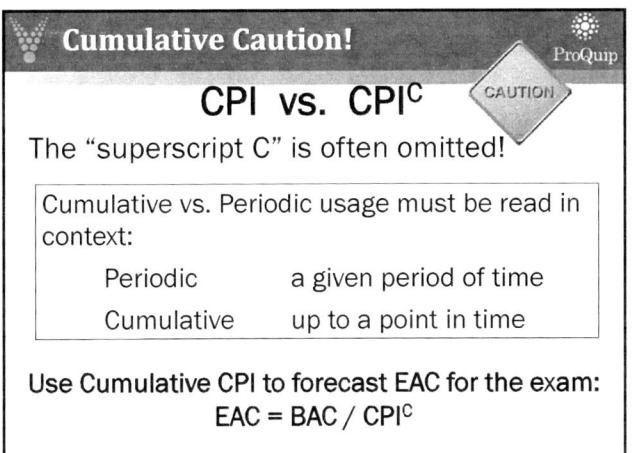

Cumulative Caution!
ProQuip

CPI vs. CPI^C
CAUTION

The "superscript C" is often omitted!

Cumulative vs. Periodic usage must be read in context:

| Periodic | a given period of time |
| Cumulative | up to a point in time |

Use Cumulative CPI to forecast EAC for the exam:
$$EAC = BAC / CPI^C$$

© 2018 Velociteach. All rights reserved. Do not duplicate. Slide 29

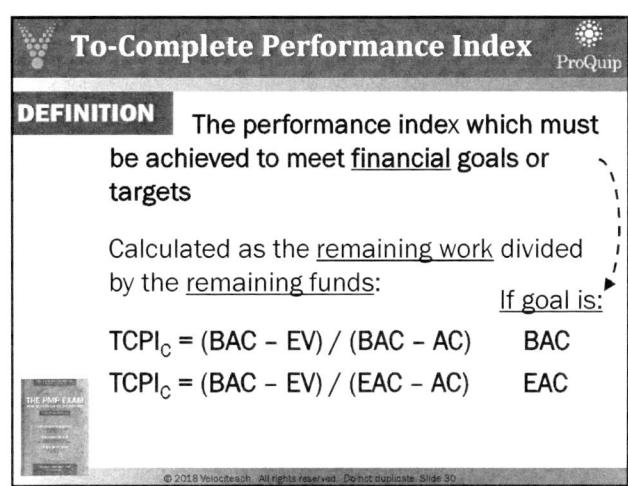

To-Complete Performance Index
ProQuip

DEFINITION The performance index which must be achieved to meet <u>financial</u> goals or targets

Calculated as the <u>remaining work</u> divided by the <u>remaining funds</u>:

If goal is:

$$TCPI_C = (BAC - EV) / (BAC - AC) \quad BAC$$
$$TCPI_C = (BAC - EV) / (EAC - AC) \quad EAC$$

© 2018 Velociteach. All rights reserved. Do not duplicate. Slide 30

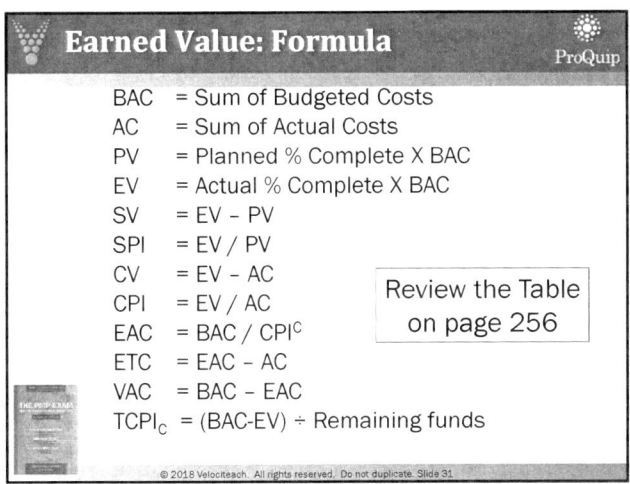

Earned Value: Formula
ProQuip

BAC	= Sum of Budgeted Costs
AC	= Sum of Actual Costs
PV	= Planned % Complete X BAC
EV	= Actual % Complete X BAC
SV	= EV – PV
SPI	= EV / PV
CV	= EV – AC
CPI	= EV / AC
EAC	= BAC / CPI^C
ETC	= EAC – AC
VAC	= BAC – EAC
TCPI$_C$	= (BAC-EV) ÷ Remaining funds

Review the Table on page 256

© 2018 Velociteach. All rights reserved. Do not duplicate. Slide 31

This page left intentionally blank.

Earned Value: Formula Map

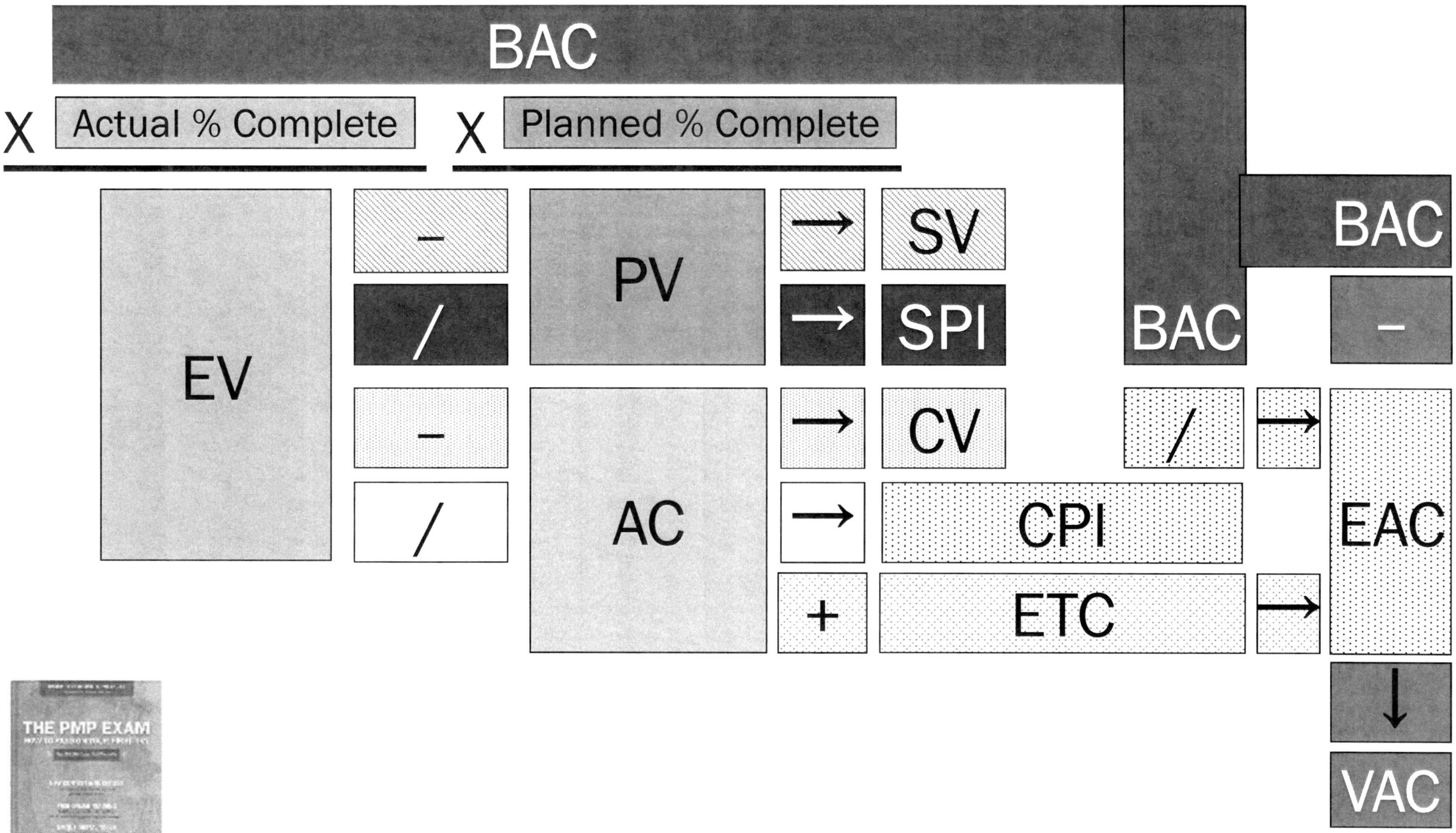

ProQuip

EV × Actual % Complete   X   Planned % Complete × BAC

BAC

						BAC
EV	−	PV	→	SV		−
	/		→	SPI		/
	−	AC	→	CV		BAC
	/		→	CPI	→	EAC
			+	ETC	→	
					→	VAC

© 2018 Velociteach. All rights reserved. Do not duplicate. Slide 32

THE PMP EXAM

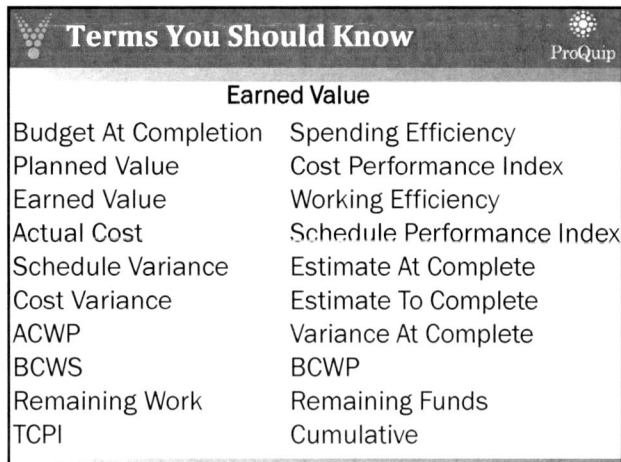

Terms You Should Know — ProQuip

Earned Value

Budget At Completion	Spending Efficiency
Planned Value	Cost Performance Index
Earned Value	Working Efficiency
Actual Cost	Schedule Performance Index
Schedule Variance	Estimate At Complete
Cost Variance	Estimate To Complete
ACWP	Variance At Complete
BCWS	BCWP
Remaining Work	Remaining Funds
TCPI	Cumulative

© 2018 Velociteach. All rights reserved. Do not duplicate. Slide 34

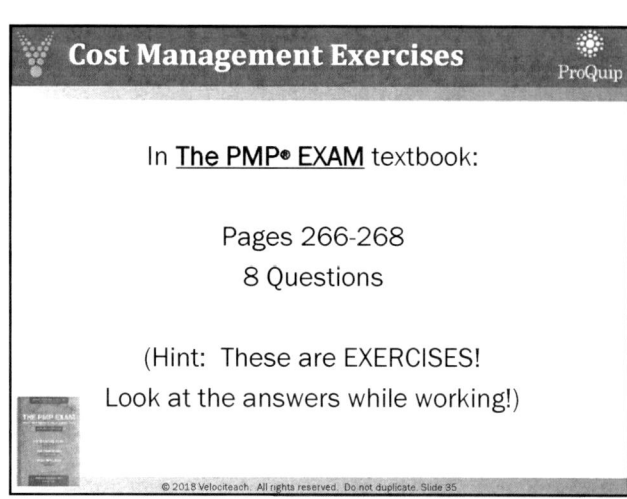

Cost Management Exercises — ProQuip

In **The PMP® EXAM** textbook:

Pages 266-268
8 Questions

(Hint: These are EXERCISES!
Look at the answers while working!)

© 2018 Velociteach. All rights reserved. Do not duplicate. Slide 35

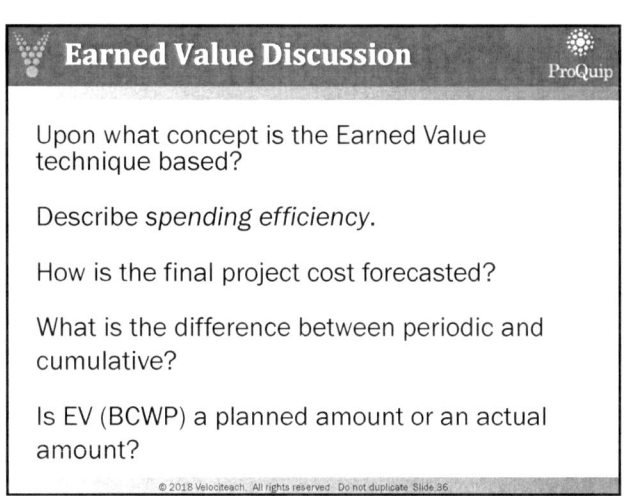

Earned Value Discussion — ProQuip

Upon what concept is the Earned Value technique based?

Describe *spending efficiency*.

How is the final project cost forecasted?

What is the difference between periodic and cumulative?

Is EV (BCWP) a planned amount or an actual amount?

© 2018 Velociteach. All rights reserved. Do not duplicate. Slide 36

- **Mark one answer: A, B, C, or D.**
- **Circle the '?' symbol if you are guessing at the answer.**
- **Circle the Δ symbol if you change your answer.**

Total Correct: _____

% Correct: _____%

1.	A O	B O	C O	D O	?	Δ
2.	A O	B O	C O	D O	?	Δ
3.	A O	B O	C O	D O	?	Δ
4.	A O	B O	C O	D O	?	Δ
5.	A O	B O	C O	D O	?	Δ
6.	A O	B O	C O	D O	?	Δ
7.	A O	B O	C O	D O	?	Δ
8.	A O	B O	C O	D O	?	Δ
9.	A O	B O	C O	D O	?	Δ
10.	A O	B O	C O	D O	?	Δ
11.	A O	B O	C O	D O	?	Δ
12.	A O	B O	C O	D O	?	Δ
13.	A O	B O	C O	D O	?	Δ
14.	A O	B O	C O	D O	?	Δ
15.	A O	B O	C O	D O	?	Δ
16.	A O	B O	C O	D O	?	Δ
17.	A O	B O	C O	D O	?	Δ
18.	A O	B O	C O	D O	?	Δ
19.	A O	B O	C O	D O	?	Δ
20.	A O	B O	C O	D O	?	Δ
21.	A O	B O	C O	D O	?	Δ
22.	A O	B O	C O	D O	?	Δ
23.	A O	B O	C O	D O	?	Δ
24.	A O	B O	C O	D O	?	Δ
25.	A O	B O	C O	D O	?	Δ

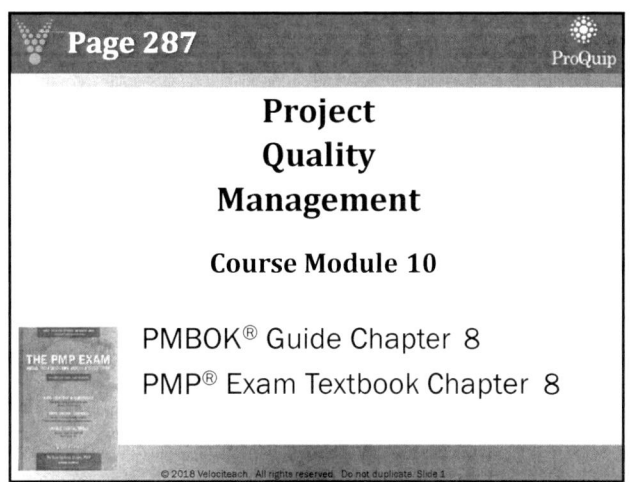

Page 287
ProQuip

Project Quality Management

Course Module 10

PMBOK® Guide Chapter 8
PMP® Exam Textbook Chapter 8

© 2018 Velociteach. All rights reserved. Do not duplicate. Slide 1

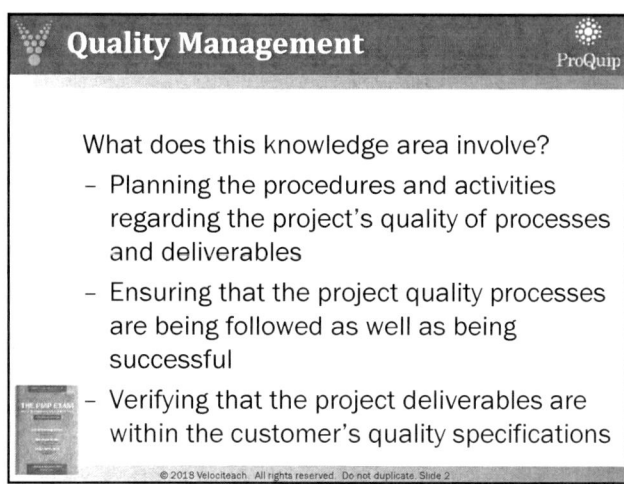

Quality Management
ProQuip

What does this knowledge area involve?
- Planning the procedures and activities regarding the project's quality of processes and deliverables
- Ensuring that the project quality processes are being followed as well as being successful
- Verifying that the project deliverables are within the customer's quality specifications

© 2018 Velociteach. All rights reserved. Do not duplicate. Slide 2

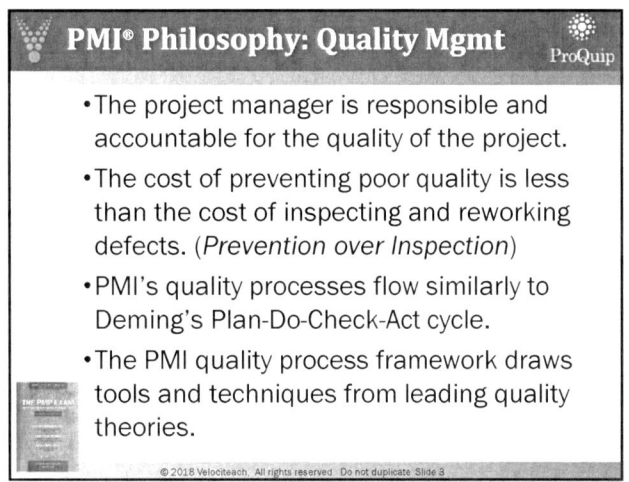

PMI® Philosophy: Quality Mgmt
ProQuip

- The project manager is responsible and accountable for the quality of the project.
- The cost of preventing poor quality is less than the cost of inspecting and reworking defects. (*Prevention over Inspection*)
- PMI's quality processes flow similarly to Deming's Plan-Do-Check-Act cycle.
- The PMI quality process framework draws tools and techniques from leading quality theories.

© 2018 Velociteach. All rights reserved. Do not duplicate. Slide 3

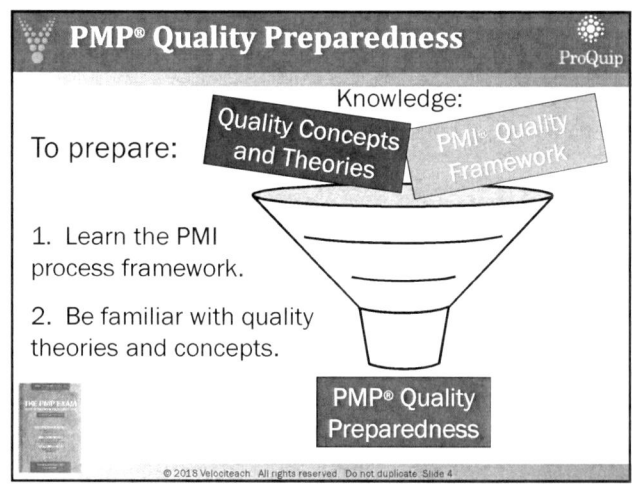

PMP® Quality Preparedness
ProQuip

Knowledge:
Quality Concepts and Theories
PMI® Quality Framework

To prepare:

1. Learn the PMI process framework.

2. Be familiar with quality theories and concepts.

PMP® Quality Preparedness

© 2018 Velociteach. All rights reserved. Do not duplicate. Slide 4

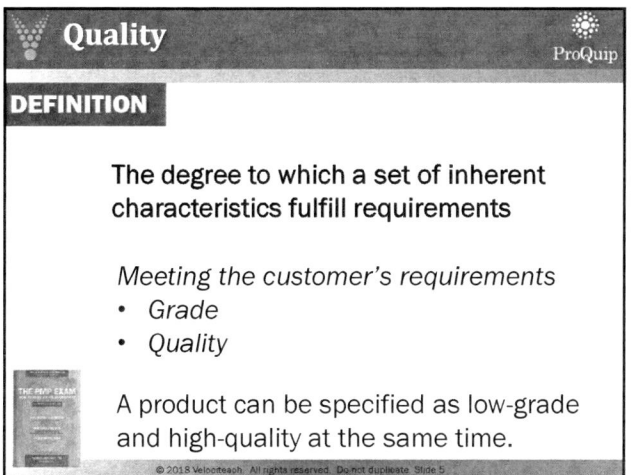

Quality

DEFINITION

The degree to which a set of inherent characteristics fulfill requirements

Meeting the customer's requirements
- *Grade*
- *Quality*

A product can be specified as low-grade and high-quality at the same time.

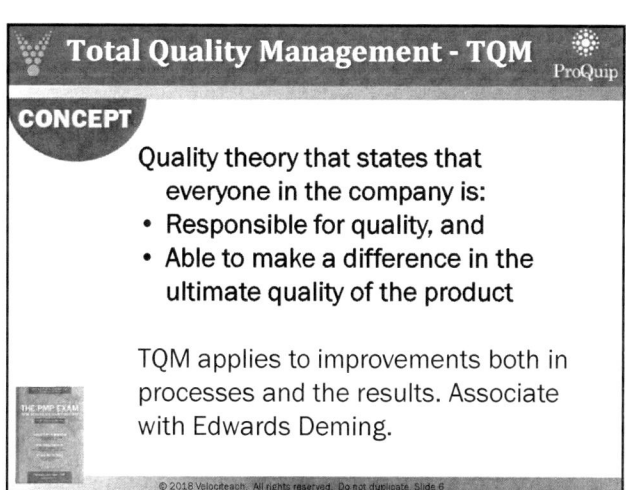

Total Quality Management - TQM

CONCEPT

Quality theory that states that everyone in the company is:
- Responsible for quality, and
- Able to make a difference in the ultimate quality of the product

TQM applies to improvements both in processes and the results. Associate with Edwards Deming.

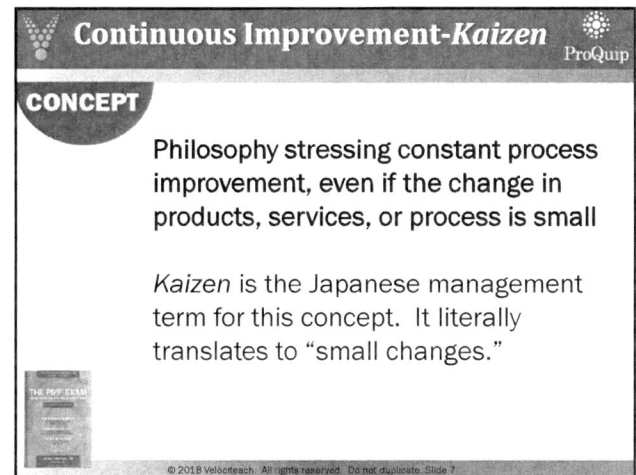

Continuous Improvement-*Kaizen*

CONCEPT

Philosophy stressing constant process improvement, even if the change in products, services, or process is small

Kaizen is the Japanese management term for this concept. It literally translates to "small changes."

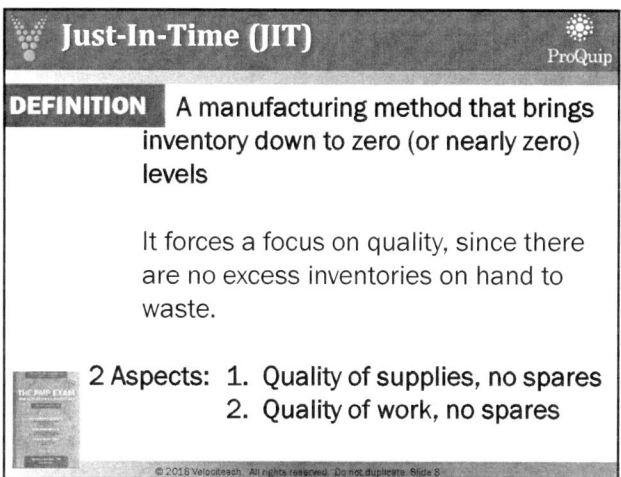

Just-In-Time (JIT)

DEFINITION A manufacturing method that brings inventory down to zero (or nearly zero) levels

It forces a focus on quality, since there are no excess inventories on hand to waste.

2 Aspects: 1. Quality of supplies, no spares
            2. Quality of work, no spares

Achieve Quality via Standards ProQuip

CONCEPT

- **BSI** – British Standards Institution (by Royal Charter, 1929) **BS 5750** gave way to **ISO 9000** series

- **ISO 9000** (International Organization for Standardization): Certification of processes, documentation, and adherence

© 2018 Velociteach. All rights reserved. Do not duplicate. Slide 9

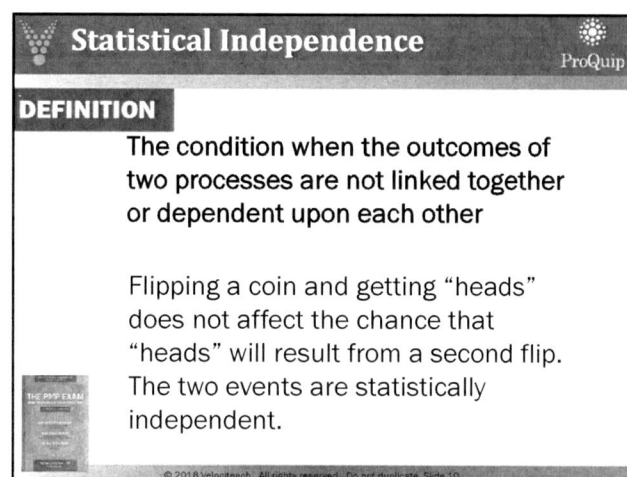

Statistical Independence ProQuip

DEFINITION

The condition when the outcomes of two processes are not linked together or dependent upon each other

Flipping a coin and getting "heads" does not affect the chance that "heads" will result from a second flip. The two events are statistically independent.

© 2018 Velociteach. All rights reserved. Do not duplicate. Slide 10

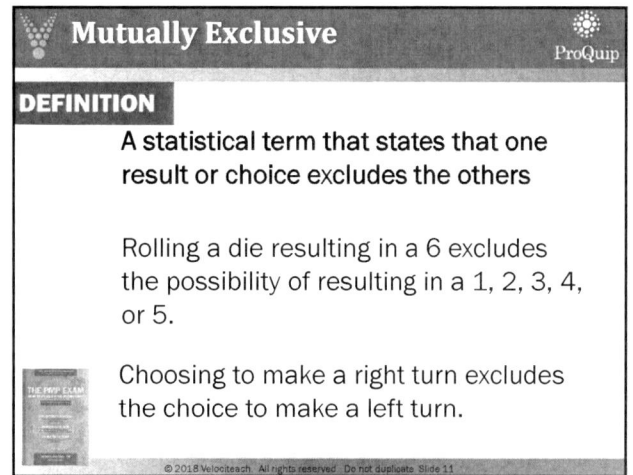

Mutually Exclusive ProQuip

DEFINITION

A statistical term that states that one result or choice excludes the others

Rolling a die resulting in a 6 excludes the possibility of resulting in a 1, 2, 3, 4, or 5.

Choosing to make a right turn excludes the choice to make a left turn.

© 2018 Velociteach. All rights reserved. Do not duplicate. Slide 11

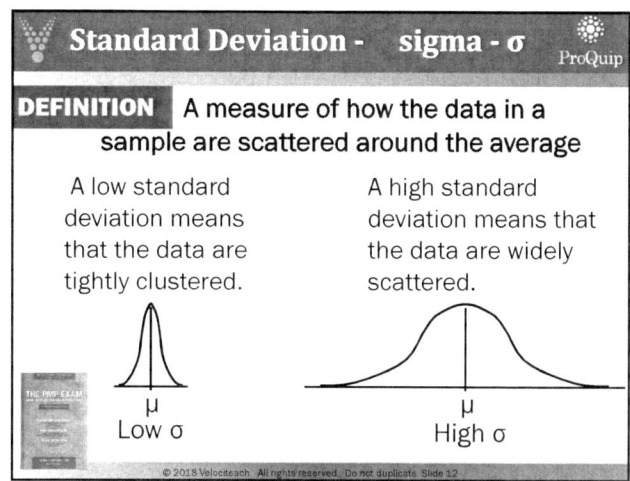

Standard Deviation - sigma - σ ProQuip

DEFINITION A measure of how the data in a sample are scattered around the average

A low standard deviation means that the data are tightly clustered.

A high standard deviation means that the data are widely scattered.

μ
Low σ

μ
High σ

© 2018 Velociteach. All rights reserved. Do not duplicate. Slide 12

Bell Curve (Normal Distribution)

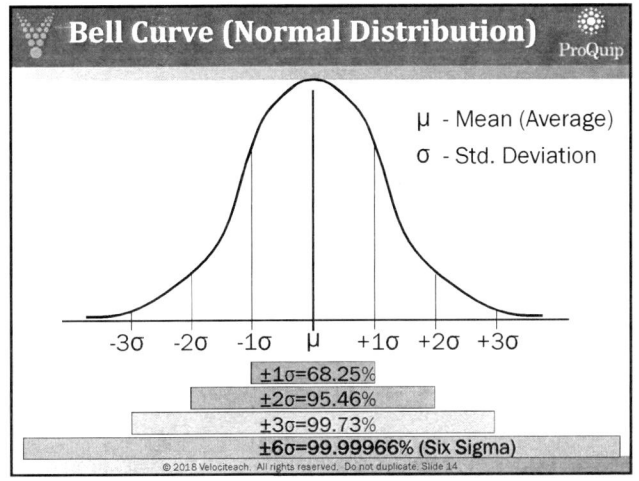

μ - Mean (Average)
σ - Std. Deviation

-3σ -2σ -1σ μ +1σ +2σ +3σ

±1σ=68.25%
±2σ=95.46%
±3σ=99.73%
±6σ=99.99966% (Six Sigma)

© 2018 Velociteach. All rights reserved. Do not duplicate. Slide 14

Six Sigma Quality

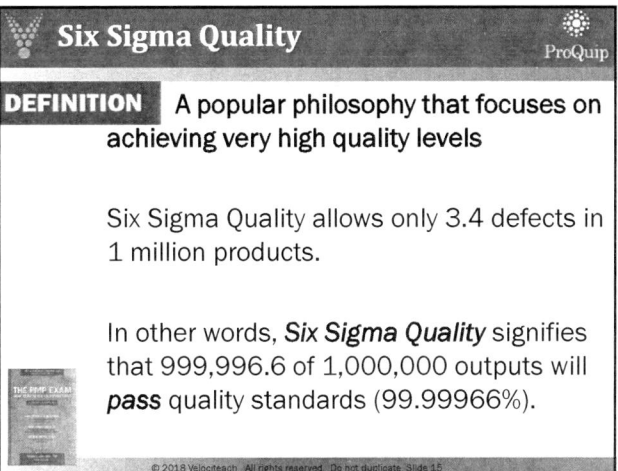

DEFINITION A popular philosophy that focuses on achieving very high quality levels

Six Sigma Quality allows only 3.4 defects in 1 million products.

In other words, *Six Sigma Quality* signifies that 999,996.6 of 1,000,000 outputs will *pass* quality standards (99.99966%).

© 2018 Velociteach. All rights reserved. Do not duplicate. Slide 15

Three Sigma Quality

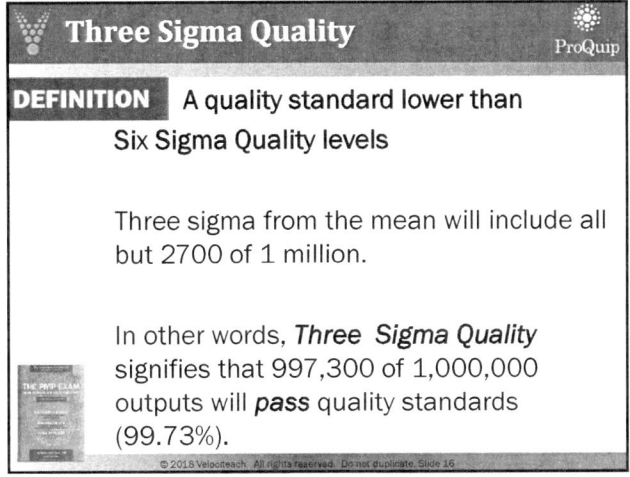

DEFINITION A quality standard lower than Six Sigma Quality levels

Three sigma from the mean will include all but 2700 of 1 million.

In other words, *Three Sigma Quality* signifies that 997,300 of 1,000,000 outputs will *pass* quality standards (99.73%).

© 2018 Velociteach. All rights reserved. Do not duplicate. Slide 16

Sampling: Attribute vs. Variable

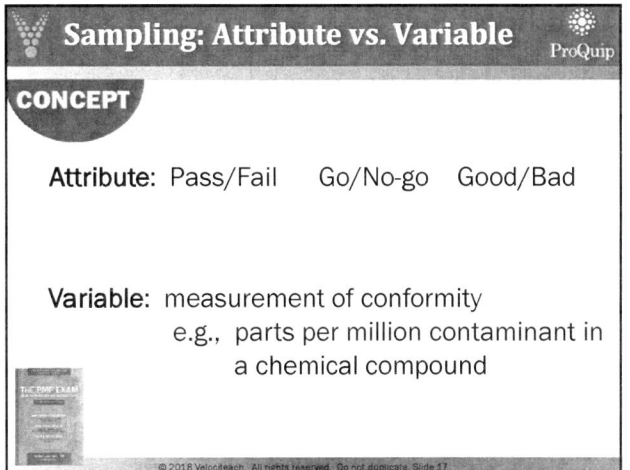

CONCEPT

Attribute: Pass/Fail   Go/No-go   Good/Bad

Variable: measurement of conformity
e.g., parts per million contaminant in a chemical compound

© 2018 Velociteach. All rights reserved. Do not duplicate. Slide 17

Causes: Special vs. Common

CONCEPT

Special Causes: unusual and preventable

e.g., Error in manufacturing process; preventable by process improvement; adjustment issues, faulty equipment

Common Causes: normal; generally accepted

e.g., defect due to normal fluctuation, predictable variation, natural pattern

© 2018 Velociteach. All rights reserved. Do not duplicate. Slide 18

Tolerances vs. Control Limits

CONCEPT

Tolerances: customer's specifications for acceptance of product

e.g., 1-foot +/- .12-inches; +/- 1% of spec

Control Limits: variation limits for process

e.g., +/- 3 sigma (std. dev.) from the mean

© 2018 Velociteach. All rights reserved. Do not duplicate. Slide 19

3 Processes of Quality

KNOWLEDGE AREA	Initiating	Planning	Executing	Monitoring and Controlling	Closing
Project Quality Management		Plan Quality Management	Manage Quality	Control Quality	

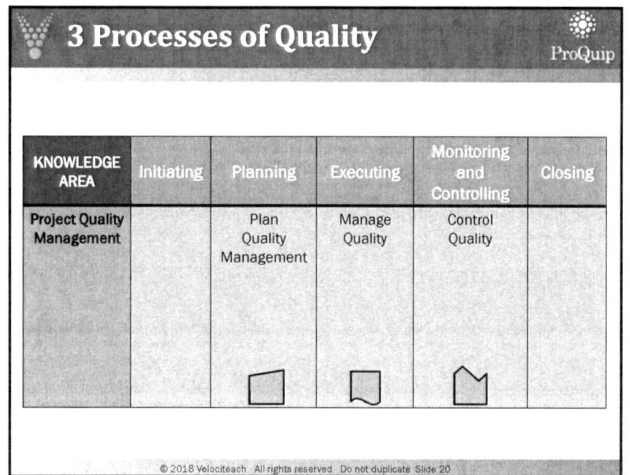

© 2018 Velociteach. All rights reserved. Do not duplicate. Slide 20

Quality Process Overview

Turn to page 287 in the textbook.

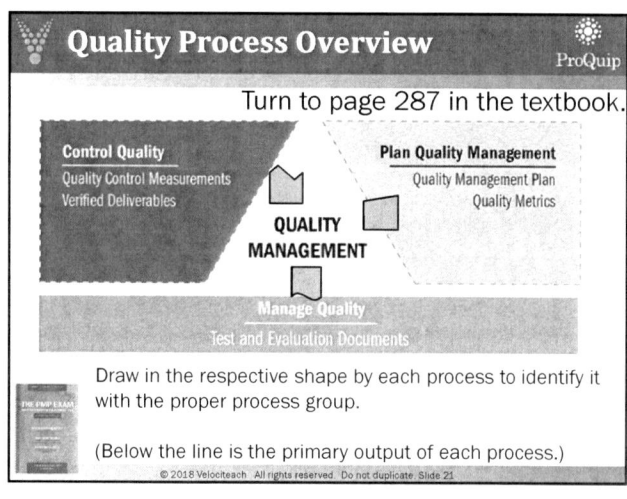

Control Quality
Quality Control Measurements
Verified Deliverables

Plan Quality Management
Quality Management Plan
Quality Metrics

QUALITY MANAGEMENT

Manage Quality
Test and Evaluation Documents

Draw in the respective shape by each process to identify it with the proper process group.

(Below the line is the primary output of each process.)

© 2018 Velociteach. All rights reserved. Do not duplicate. Slide 21

©2018 Velociteach. All rights reserved. Page 186

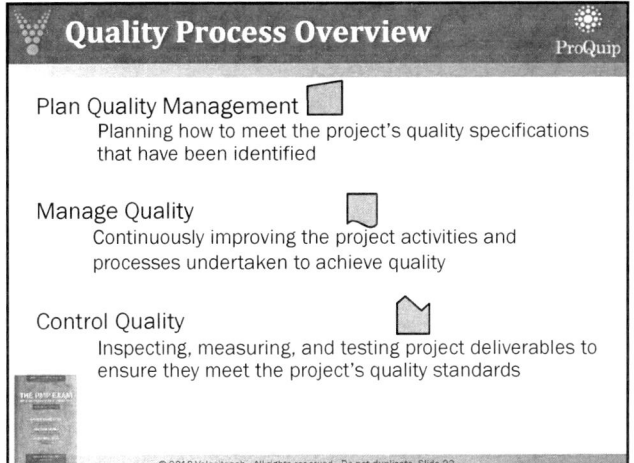

Quality Process Overview

Plan Quality Management
   Planning how to meet the project's quality specifications that have been identified

Manage Quality
   Continuously improving the project activities and processes undertaken to achieve quality

Control Quality
   Inspecting, measuring, and testing project deliverables to ensure they meet the project's quality standards

© 2018 Velociteach. All rights reserved. Do not duplicate. Slide 22

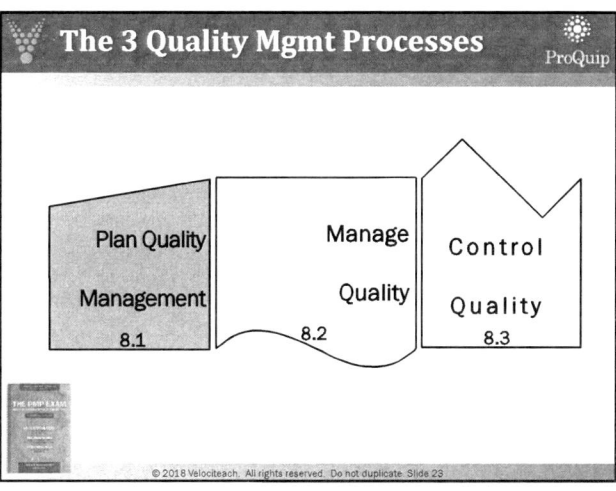

The 3 Quality Mgmt Processes

Plan Quality Management 8.1 | Manage Quality 8.2 | Control Quality 8.3

© 2018 Velociteach. All rights reserved. Do not duplicate. Slide 23

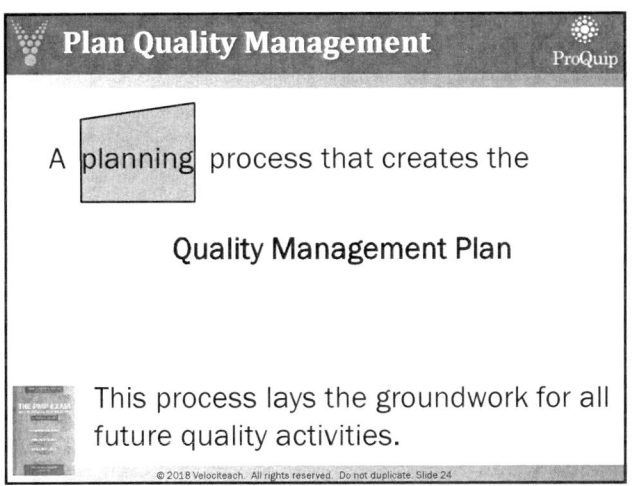

Plan Quality Management

A planning process that creates the

Quality Management Plan

This process lays the groundwork for all future quality activities.

© 2018 Velociteach. All rights reserved. Do not duplicate. Slide 24

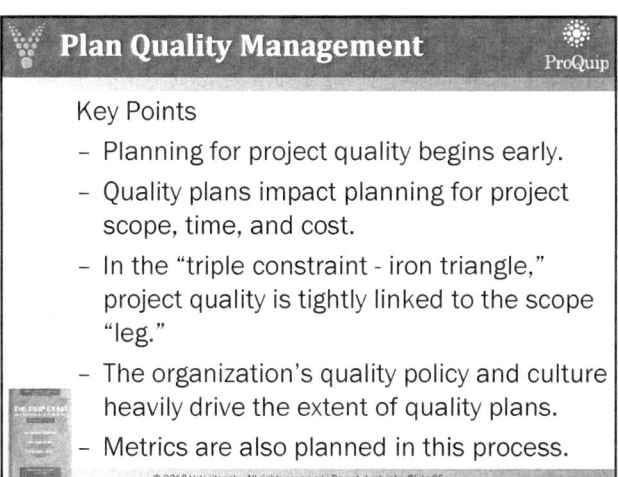

Plan Quality Management

Key Points
- Planning for project quality begins early.
- Quality plans impact planning for project scope, time, and cost.
- In the "triple constraint - iron triangle," project quality is tightly linked to the scope "leg."
- The organization's quality policy and culture heavily drive the extent of quality plans.
- Metrics are also planned in this process.

© 2018 Velociteach. All rights reserved. Do not duplicate. Slide 25

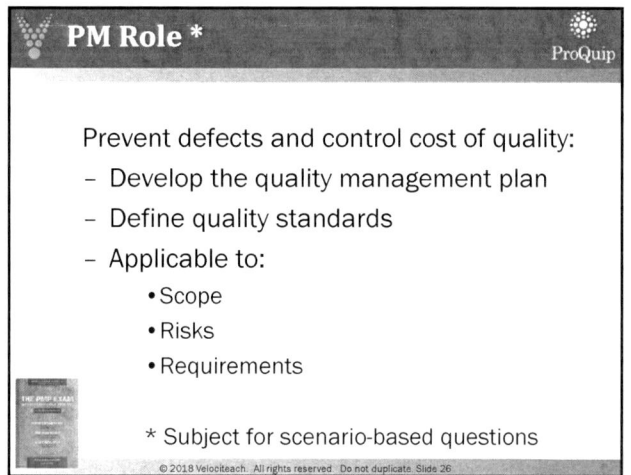

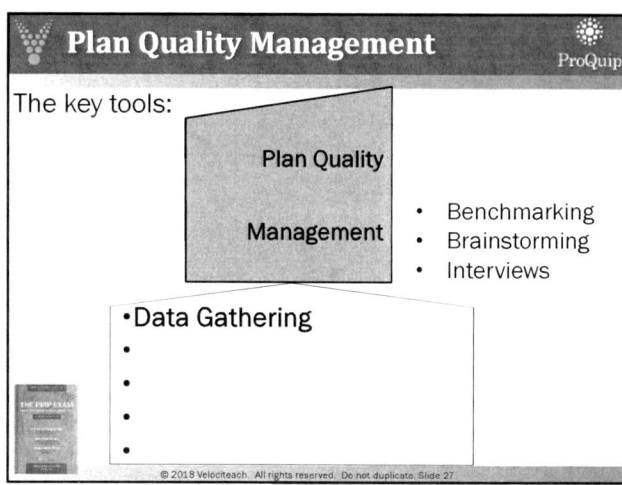

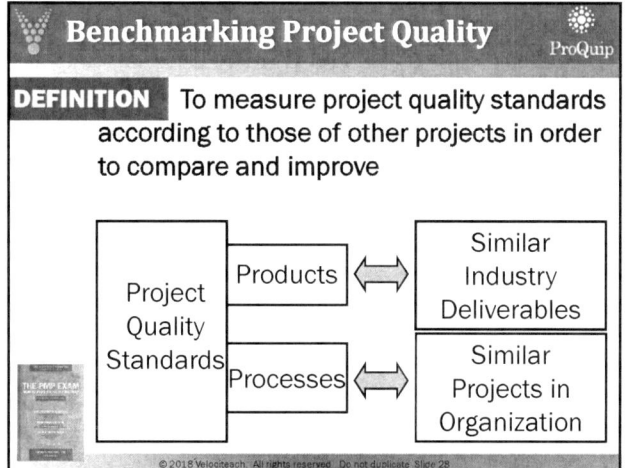

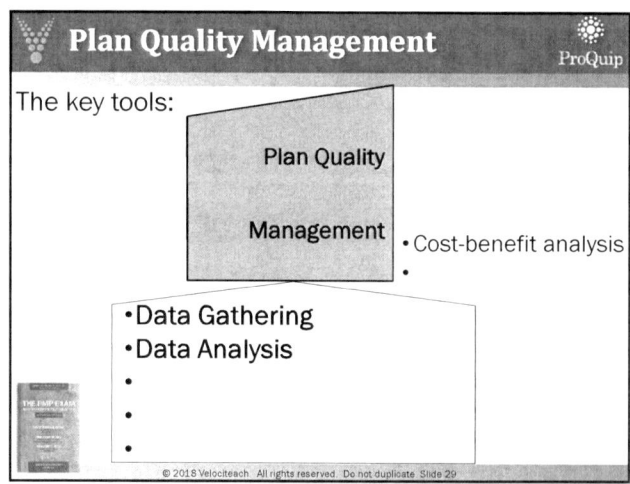

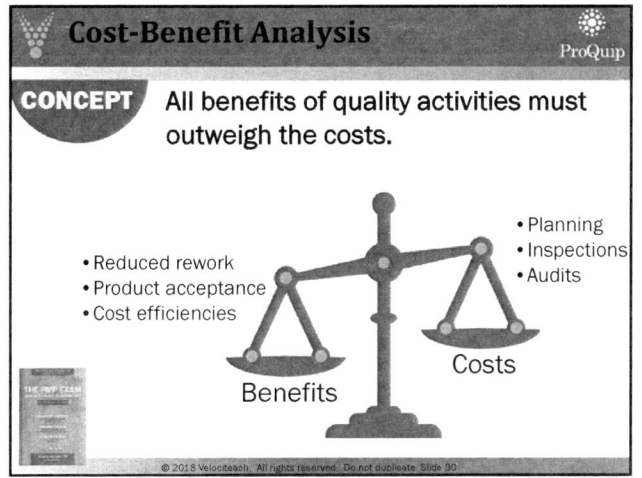

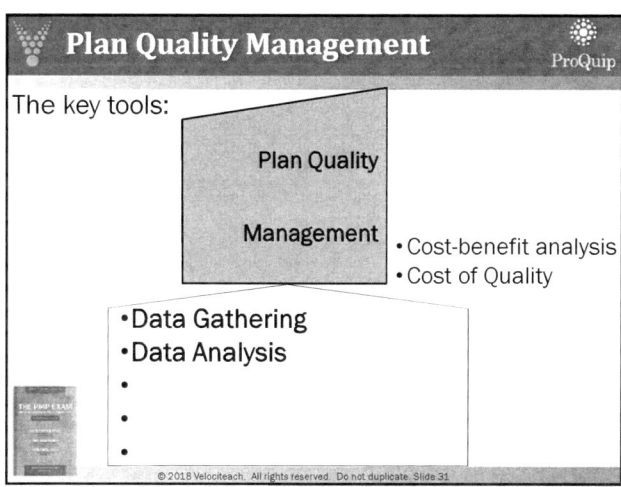

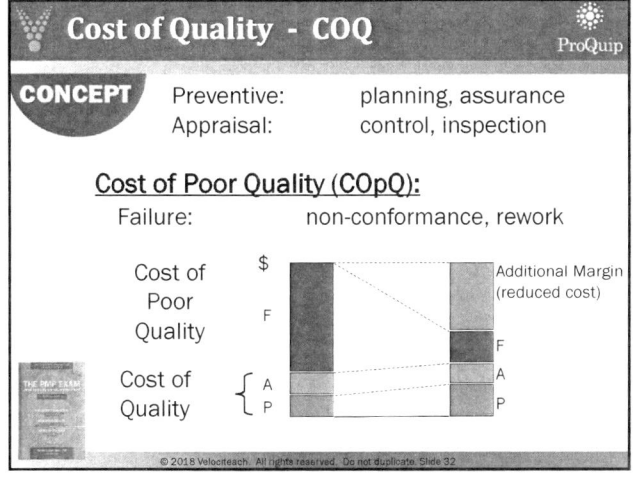

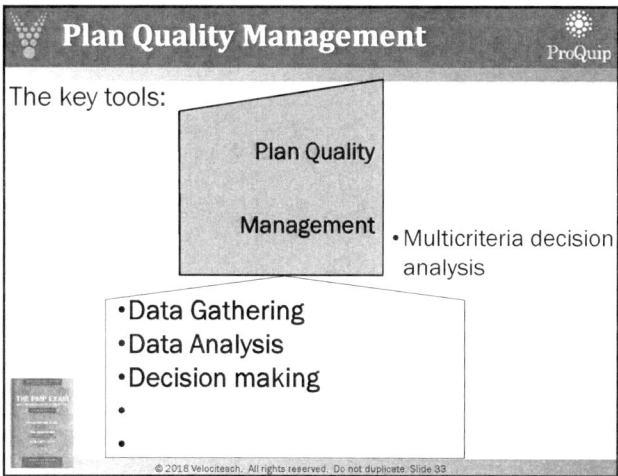

©2018 Velociteach. All rights reserved.   Page 189

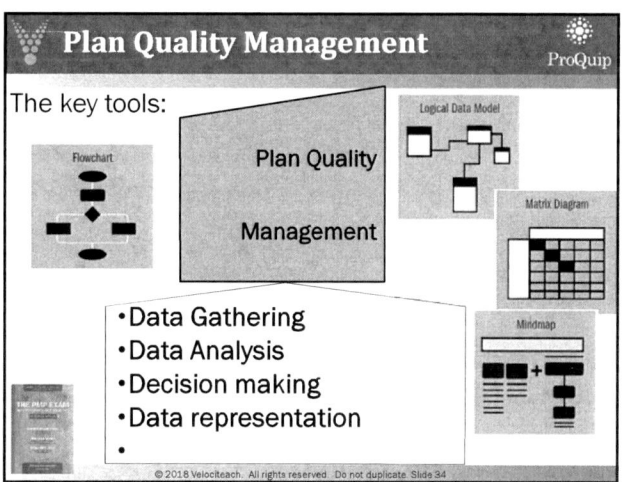

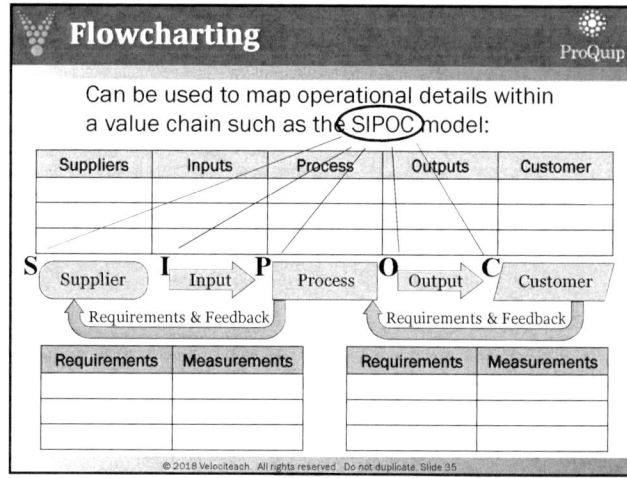

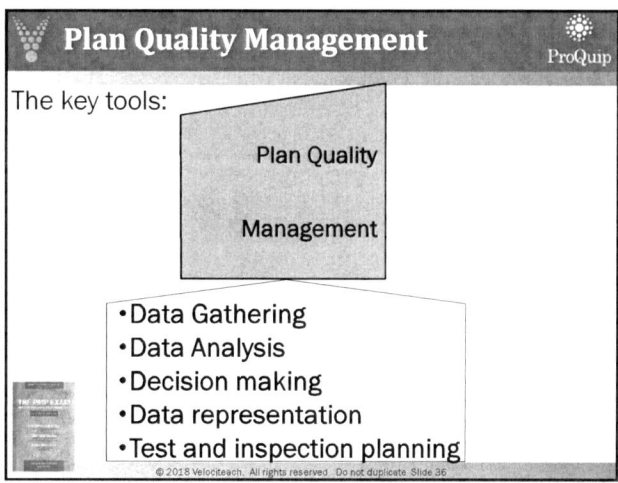

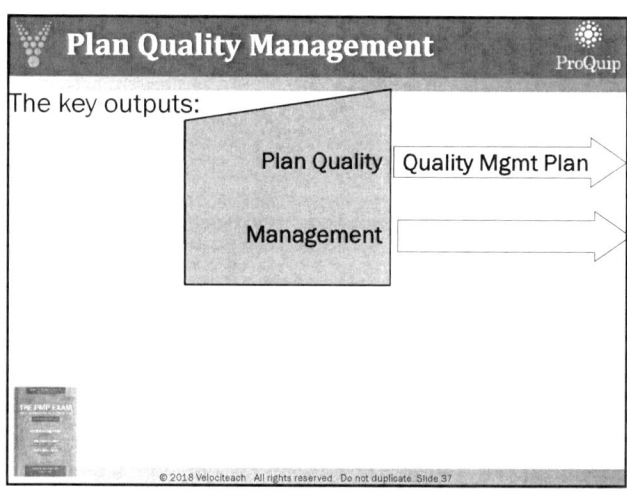

Quality Management Plan

DEFINITION A component of the Project Management Plan that states how the quality policy will be met

The plan contains descriptions of how *Manage Quality, Control Quality*, and **continuous process improvement** will be performed.

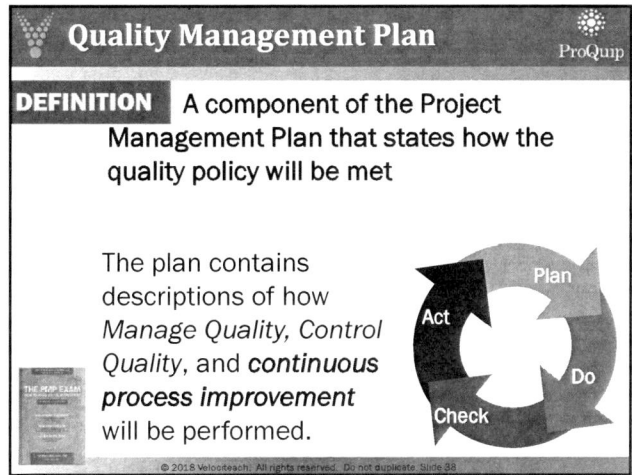

© 2018 Velociteach. All rights reserved. Do not duplicate. Slide 38

Project Plan Pyramid

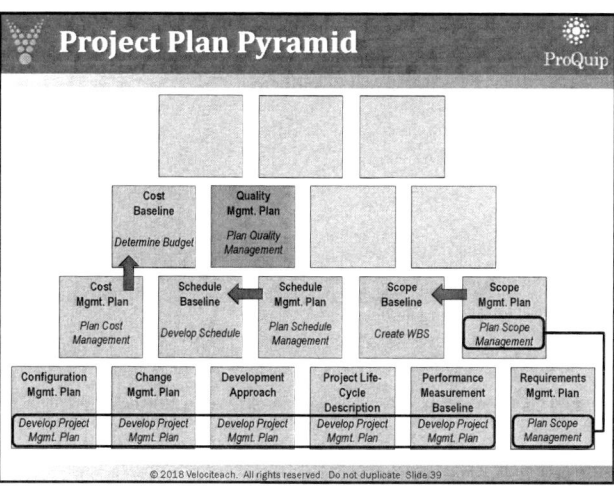

© 2018 Velociteach. All rights reserved. Do not duplicate. Slide 39

Plan Quality Management

The key outputs:

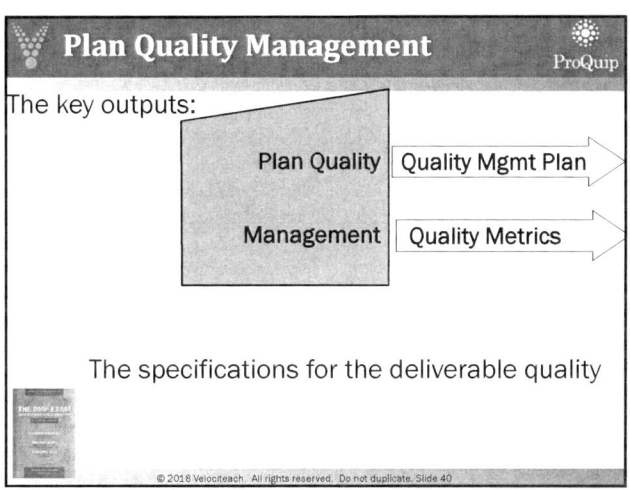

Plan Quality Management → Quality Mgmt Plan

→ Quality Metrics

The specifications for the deliverable quality

© 2018 Velociteach. All rights reserved. Do not duplicate. Slide 40

Quality Metrics

DEFINITION The targeted measures that define when the specified quality is achieved

"Rapid response time" does not define a metric; it is not measureable.

Metric: System response within 2 seconds, 99% of all requests of 1000 simultaneous users

© 2018 Velociteach. All rights reserved. Do not duplicate. Slide 41

©2018 Velociteach. All rights reserved. Page 191

ProQuip

Plan Quality Management

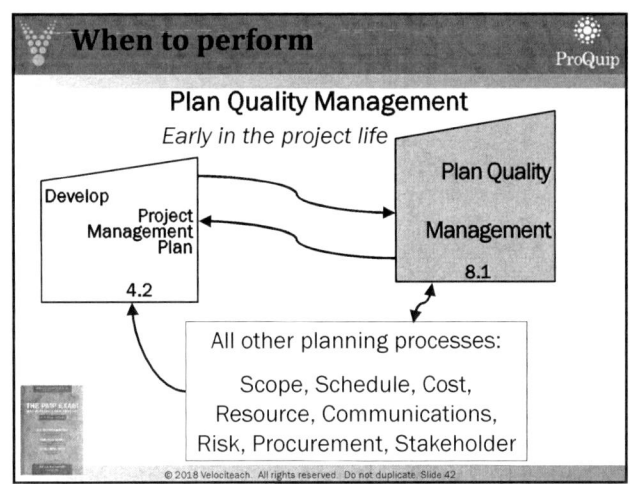

© 2018 Velociteach. All rights reserved. Do not duplicate. Slide 42

ProQuip

Plan Quality Management

- Focus your efforts on understanding the primary outputs, the Quality Management Plan and the Quality Metrics.
- Know the focal tools.
- Know that this process begins early.
- Know that the quality of both the deliverables and processes are goals.

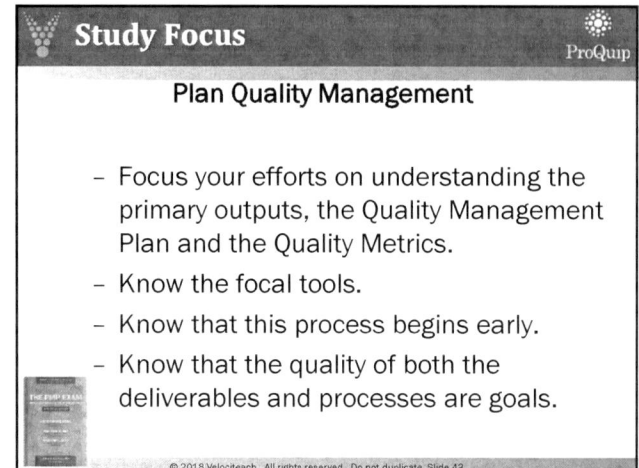

© 2018 Velociteach. All rights reserved. Do not duplicate. Slide 43

ProQuip

Review the ITTOs

Plan Quality Management

© 2018 Velociteach. All rights reserved.

This page left intentionally blank.

The 3 Quality Mgmt Processes

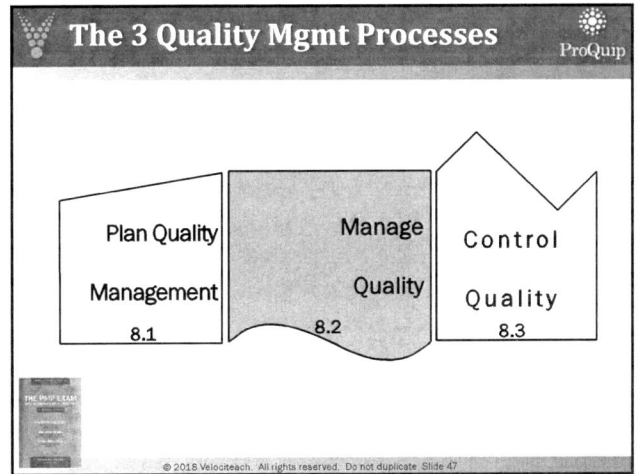

Plan Quality Management 8.1

Manage Quality 8.2

Control Quality 8.3

© 2018 Velociteach. All rights reserved. Do not duplicate. Slide 47

Manage Quality

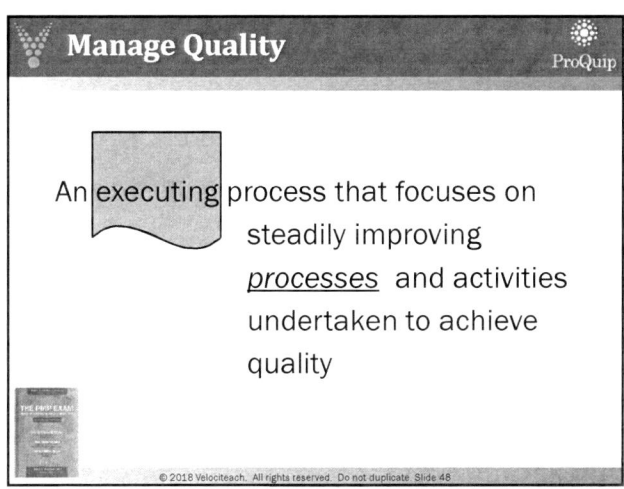

An executing process that focuses on steadily improving *processes* and activities undertaken to achieve quality

© 2018 Velociteach. All rights reserved. Do not duplicate. Slide 48

Manage Quality

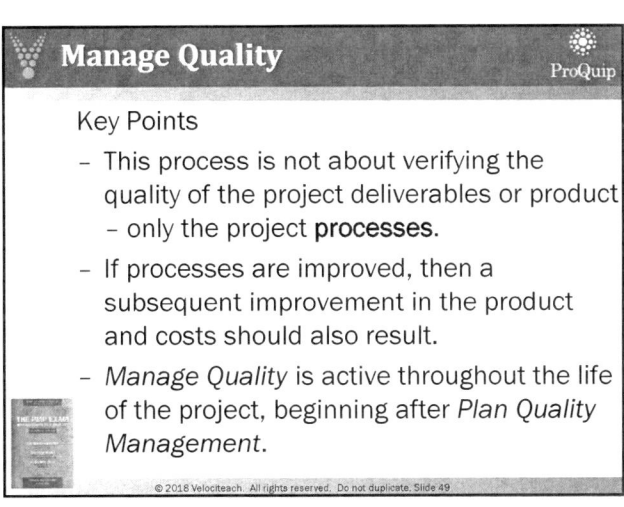

Key Points

- This process is not about verifying the quality of the project deliverables or product – only the project **processes**.

- If processes are improved, then a subsequent improvement in the product and costs should also result.

- *Manage Quality* is active throughout the life of the project, beginning after *Plan Quality Management*.

© 2018 Velociteach. All rights reserved. Do not duplicate. Slide 49

PM Role *

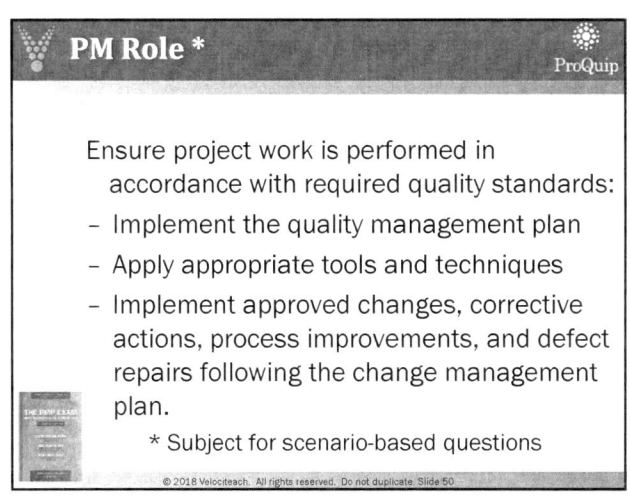

Ensure project work is performed in accordance with required quality standards:

- Implement the quality management plan

- Apply appropriate tools and techniques

- Implement approved changes, corrective actions, process improvements, and defect repairs following the change management plan.

* Subject for scenario-based questions

© 2018 Velociteach. All rights reserved. Do not duplicate. Slide 50

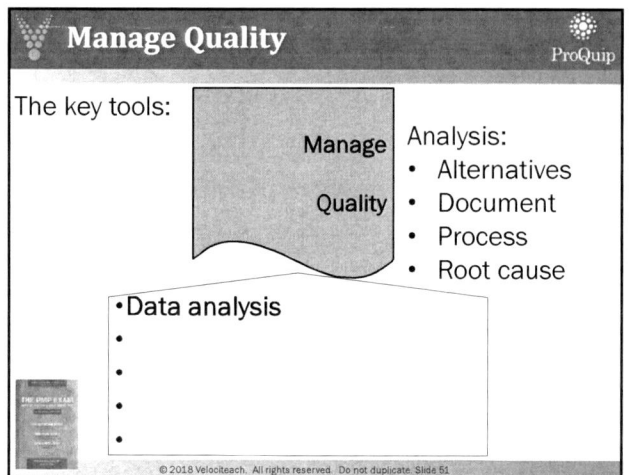

Manage Quality

The key tools:

Manage Quality

Analysis:
- Alternatives
- Document
- Process
- Root cause

- Data analysis
-
-
-
-

© 2018 Velociteach. All rights reserved. Do not duplicate. Slide 51

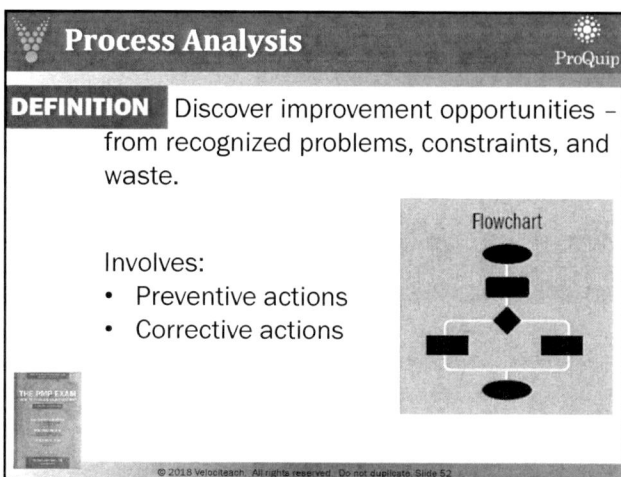

Process Analysis

DEFINITION Discover improvement opportunities – from recognized problems, constraints, and waste.

Involves:
- Preventive actions
- Corrective actions

Flowchart

© 2018 Velociteach. All rights reserved. Do not duplicate. Slide 52

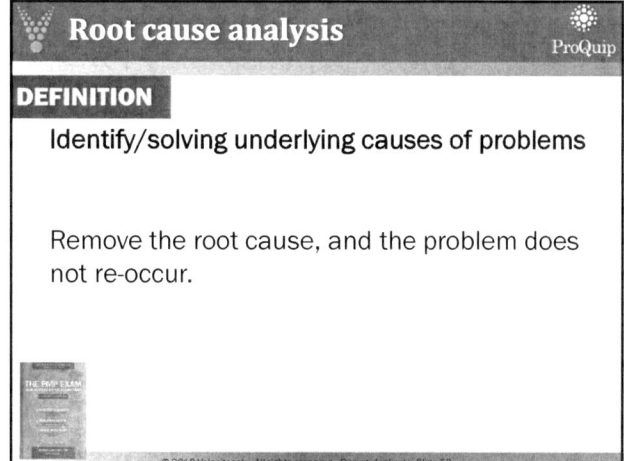

Root cause analysis

DEFINITION

Identify/solving underlying causes of problems

Remove the root cause, and the problem does not re-occur.

© 2018 Velociteach. All rights reserved. Do not duplicate. Slide 53

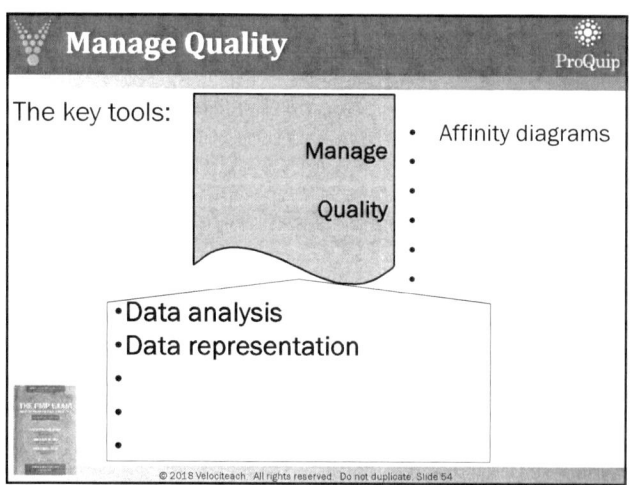

Manage Quality

The key tools:

Manage Quality

- Affinity diagrams
-
-
-
-

- Data analysis
- Data representation
-
-
-

© 2018 Velociteach. All rights reserved. Do not duplicate. Slide 54

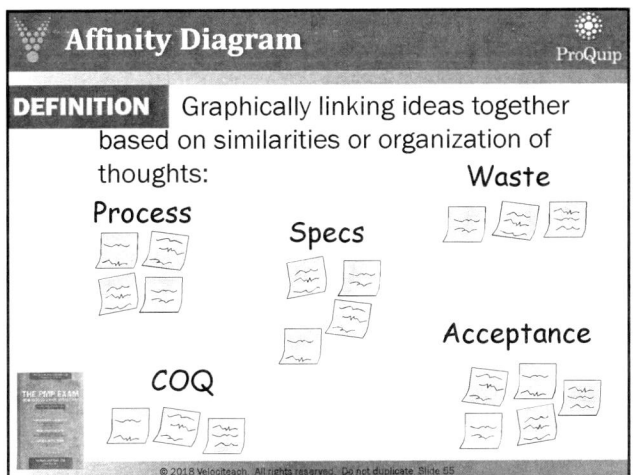

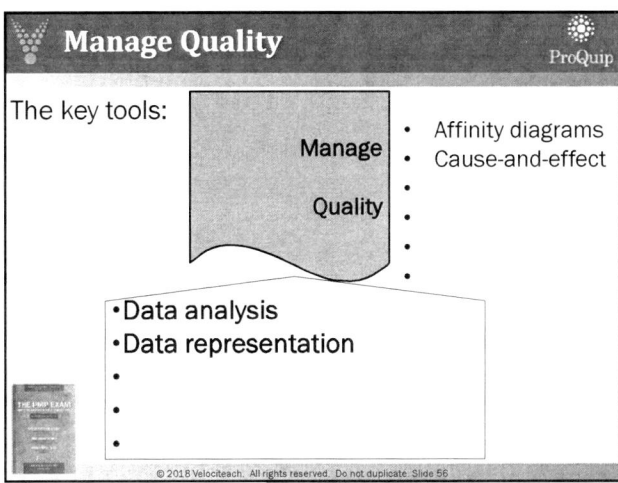

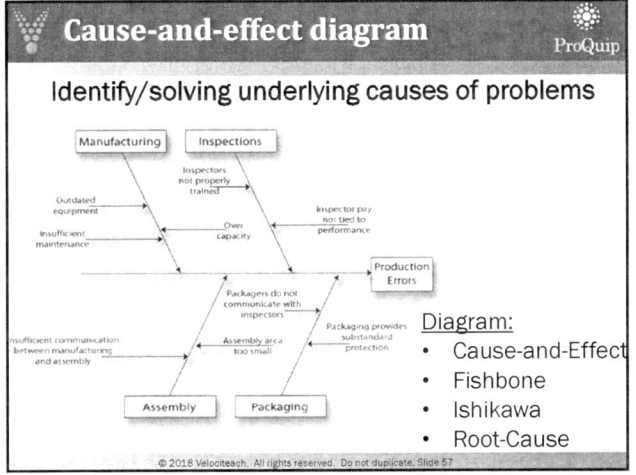

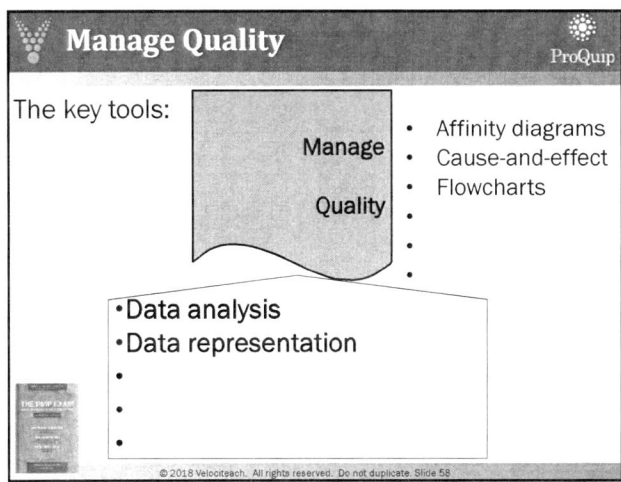

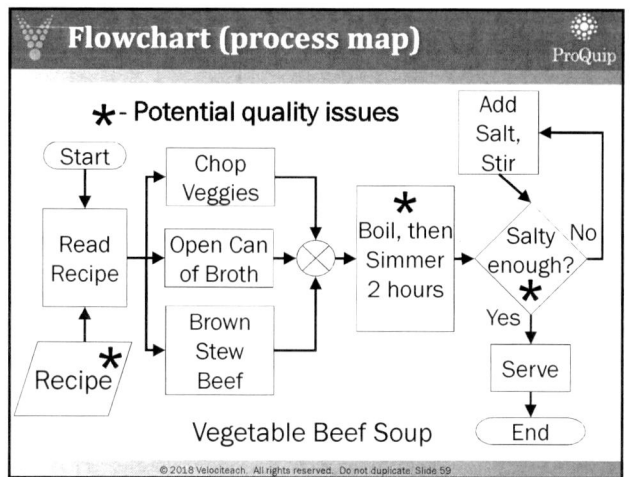

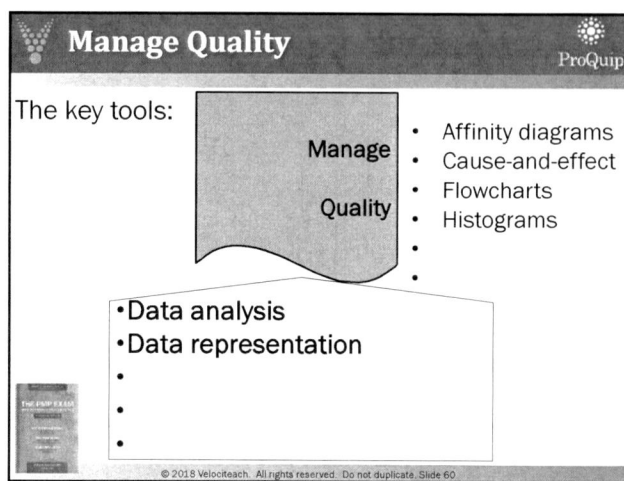

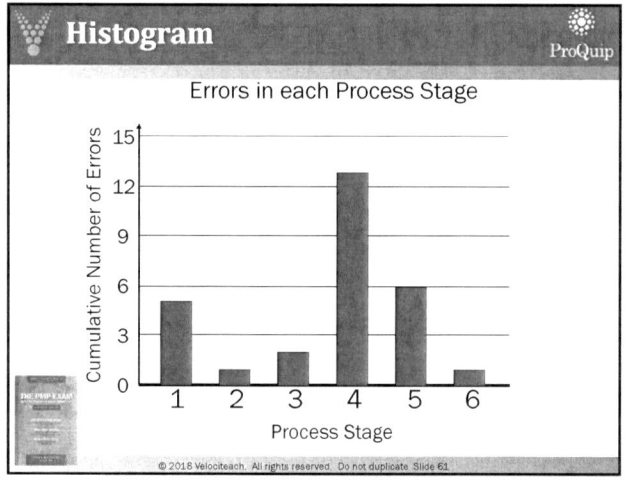

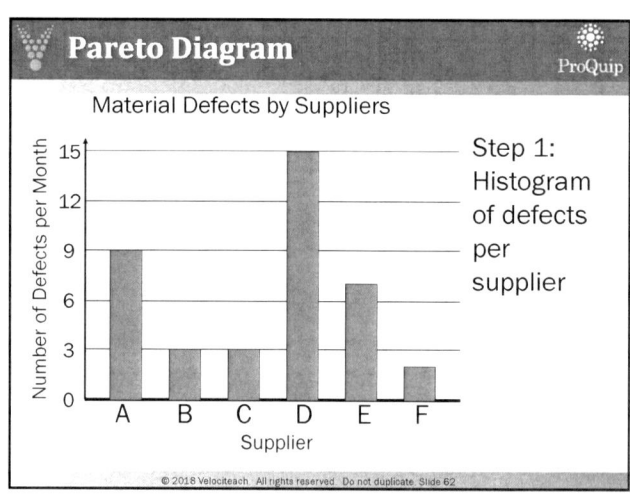

©2018 Velociteach. All rights reserved. Page 198

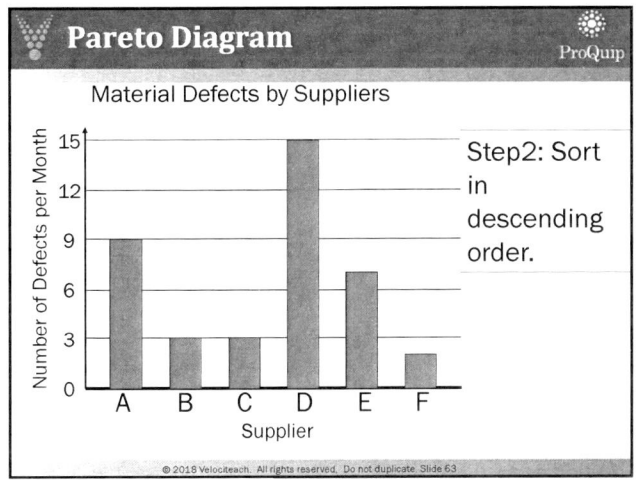

Pareto Diagram

Material Defects by Suppliers

Step2: Sort in descending order.

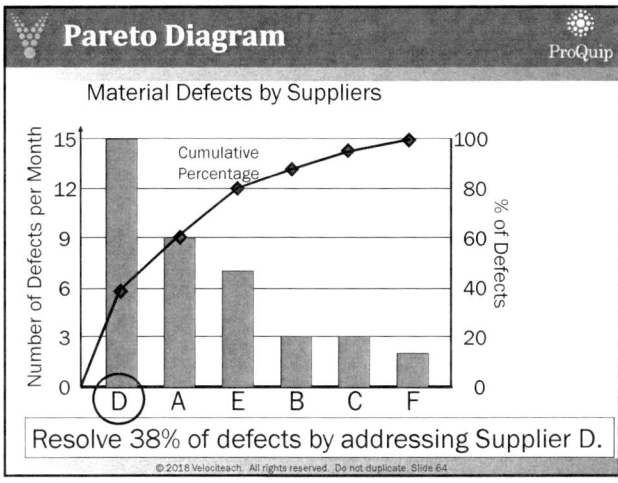

Pareto Diagram

Material Defects by Suppliers

Resolve 38% of defects by addressing Supplier D.

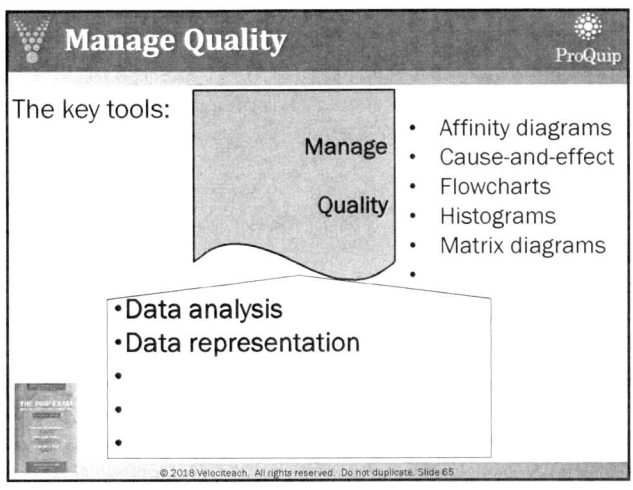

Manage Quality

The key tools:

Manage Quality

- Affinity diagrams
- Cause-and-effect
- Flowcharts
- Histograms
- Matrix diagrams
-

- Data analysis
- Data representation

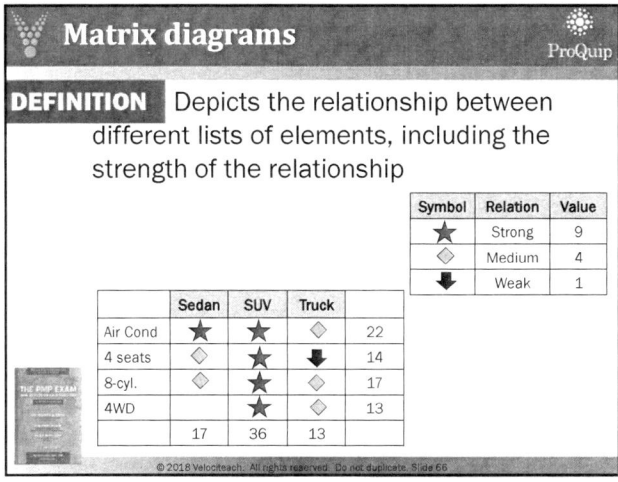

Matrix diagrams

DEFINITION Depicts the relationship between different lists of elements, including the strength of the relationship

Symbol	Relation	Value
★	Strong	9
◇	Medium	4
⬇	Weak	1

	Sedan	SUV	Truck	
Air Cond	★	★	◇	22
4 seats	◇	★	⬇	14
8-cyl.	◇	★	◇	17
4WD		★	◇	13
	17	36	13	

©2018 Velociteach. All rights reserved. Page 199

Manage Quality

The key tools:

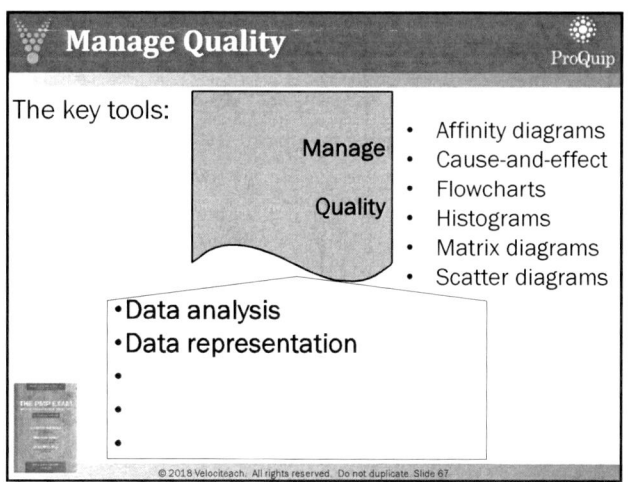

- Affinity diagrams
- Cause-and-effect
- Flowcharts
- Histograms
- Matrix diagrams
- Scatter diagrams

- Data analysis
- Data representation
-
-
-

© 2018 Velociteach. All rights reserved. Do not duplicate. Slide 67

Scatter Diagram

Statistical Correlation of Two Variables

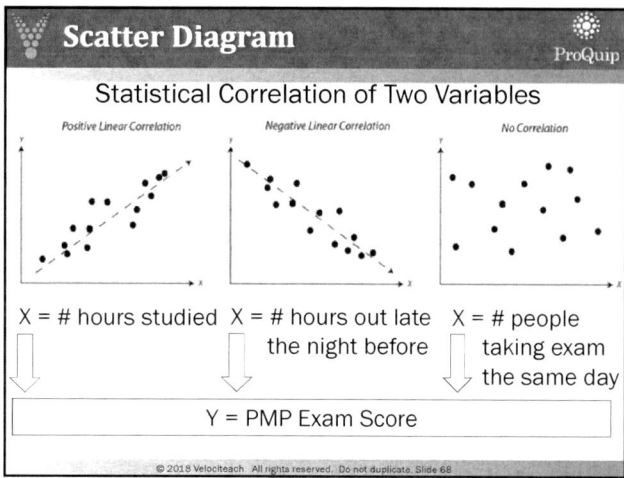

X = # hours studied   X = # hours out late the night before   X = # people taking exam the same day

Y = PMP Exam Score

© 2018 Velociteach. All rights reserved. Do not duplicate. Slide 68

Manage Quality

The key tools:

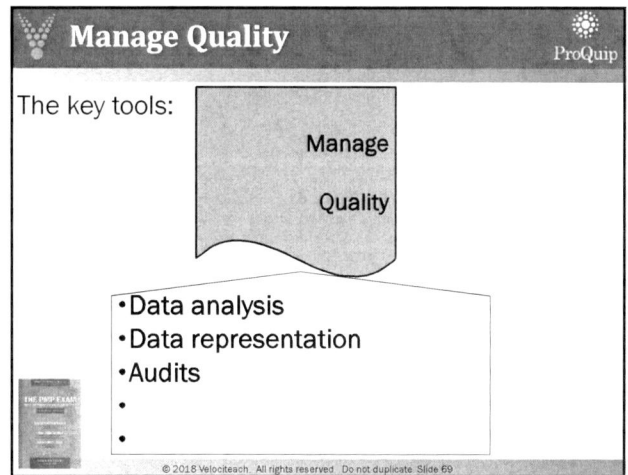

- Data analysis
- Data representation
- Audits
-
-

© 2018 Velociteach. All rights reserved. Do not duplicate. Slide 69

Quality Audit

DEFINITION   An activity to understand if project processes are compliant with policy and procedures

Discover:
- Areas for productivity improvement
- Incorrect or non-proper processes
- Lessons learned & Best practices
- Potential reductions in COQ
- Improvements in deliverables acceptance

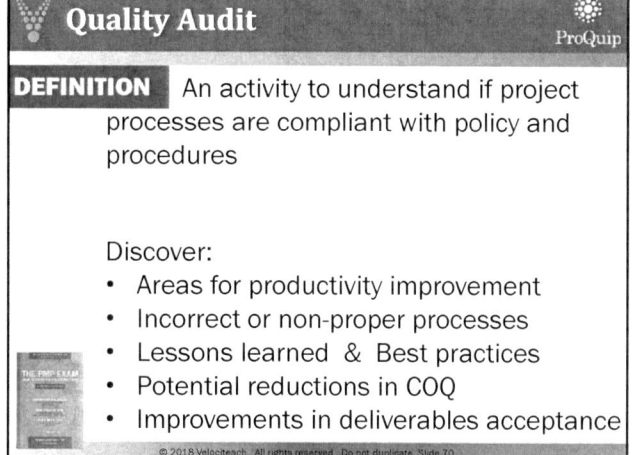

© 2018 Velociteach. All rights reserved. Do not duplicate. Slide 70

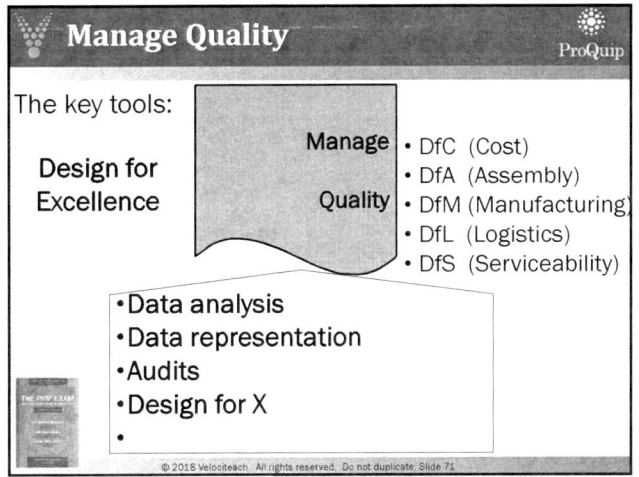

Manage Quality — ProQuip

The key tools:

Design for Excellence

Manage Quality

- DfC (Cost)
- DfA (Assembly)
- DfM (Manufacturing)
- DfL (Logistics)
- DfS (Serviceability)

- Data analysis
- Data representation
- Audits
- Design for X
-

© 2018 Velociteach. All rights reserved. Do not duplicate. Slide 71

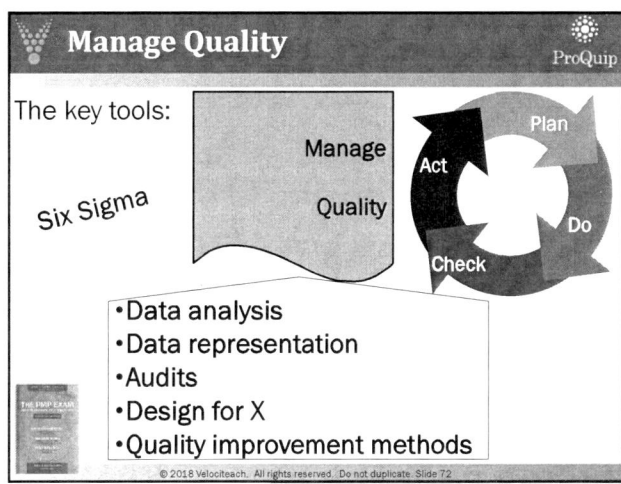

Manage Quality — ProQuip

The key tools:

Six Sigma

Manage Quality

Plan · Do · Check · Act

- Data analysis
- Data representation
- Audits
- Design for X
- Quality improvement methods

© 2018 Velociteach. All rights reserved. Do not duplicate. Slide 72

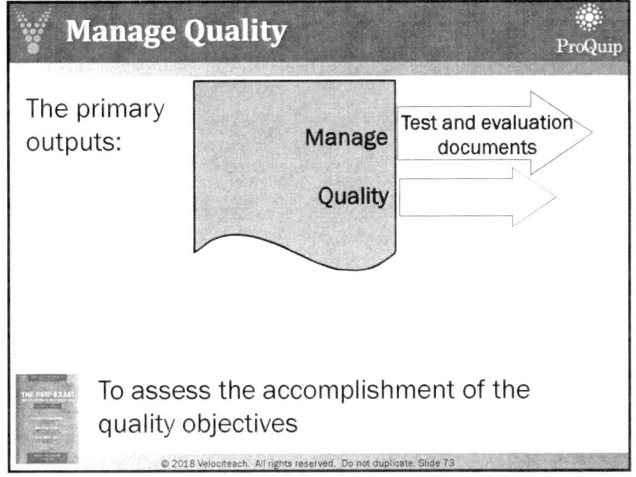

Manage Quality — ProQuip

The primary outputs:

Manage Quality

→ Test and evaluation documents

→

To assess the accomplishment of the quality objectives

© 2018 Velociteach. All rights reserved. Do not duplicate. Slide 73

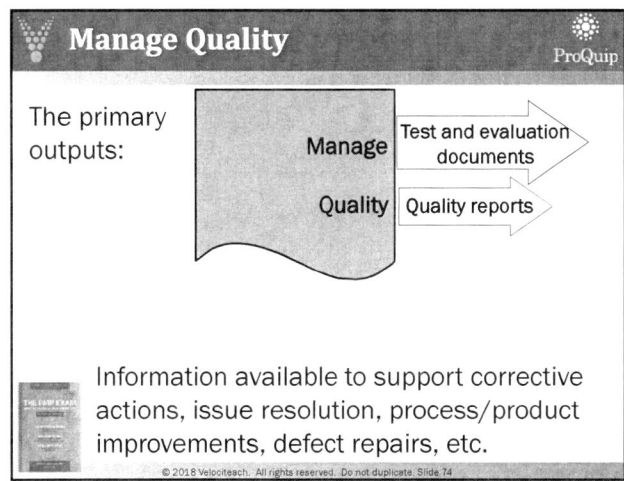

Manage Quality — ProQuip

The primary outputs:

Manage Quality

→ Test and evaluation documents

→ Quality reports

Information available to support corrective actions, issue resolution, process/product improvements, defect repairs, etc.

© 2018 Velociteach. All rights reserved. Do not duplicate. Slide 74

When to

Manage Quality

Begins early in the project life

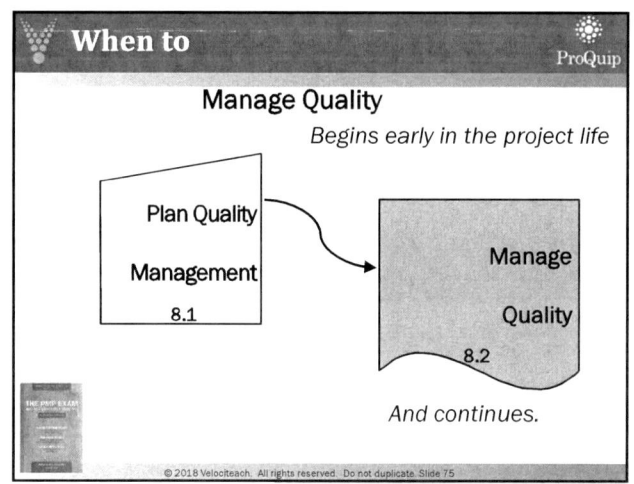

And continues.

© 2018 Velociteach. All rights reserved. Do not duplicate. Slide 75

Study Focus

Manage Quality

- Know that Manage Quality is an executing process focusing on the project processes, not the product quality.
- Know the primary tools.
- Know that Plan Quality Management happens prior to Manage Quality.
- Know that continuous process improvement is a key attitude and goal.

© 2018 Velociteach. All rights reserved. Do not duplicate. Slide 76

Review the ITTOs

ProQuip

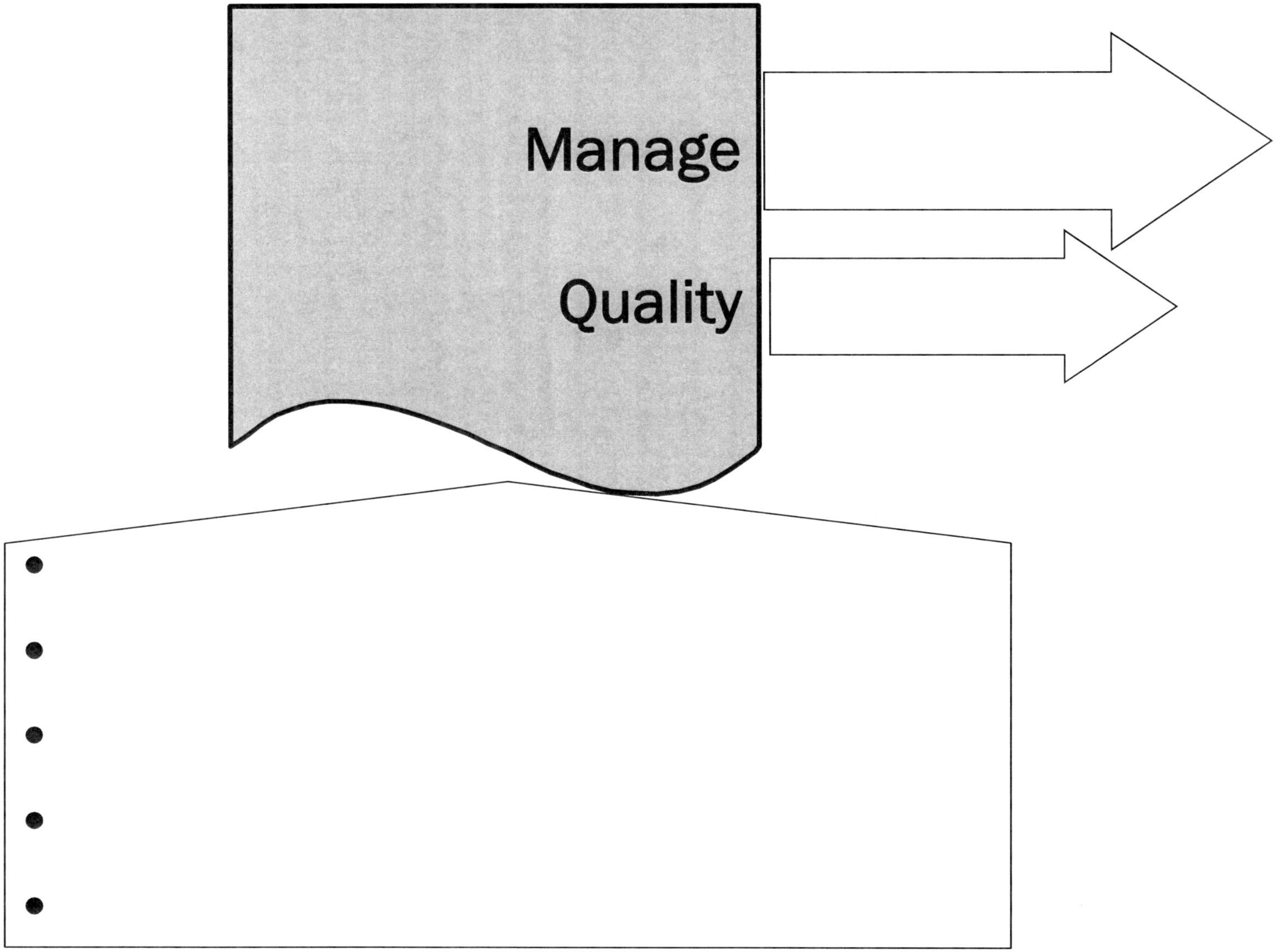

Manage Quality

© 2018 Velociteach. All rights reserved.

The 3 Quality Mgmt Processes

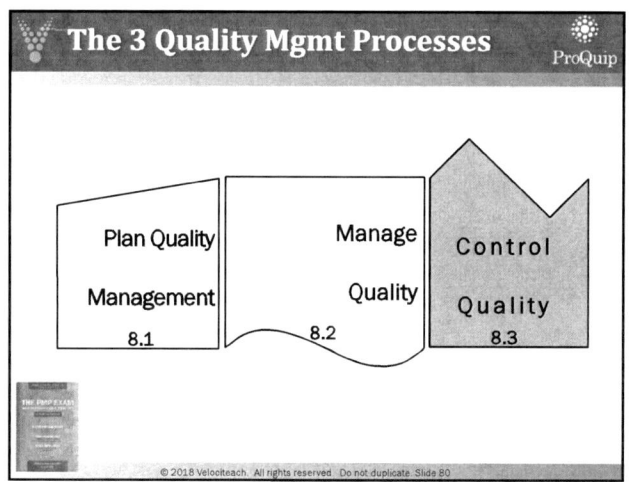

Plan Quality Management 8.1

Manage Quality 8.2

Control Quality 8.3

© 2018 Velociteach. All rights reserved. Do not duplicate. Slide 80

Control Quality

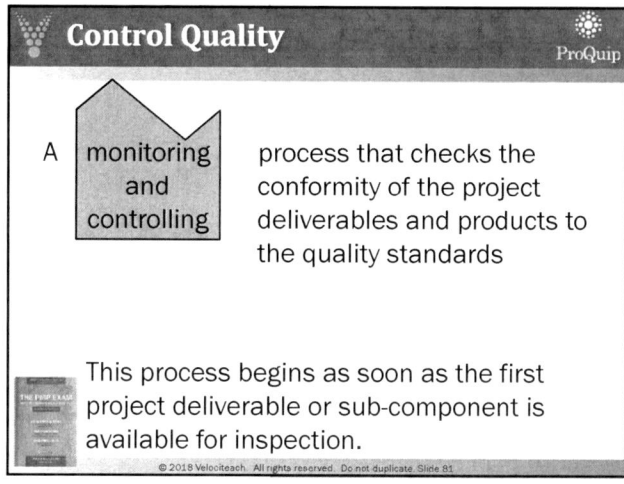

A monitoring and controlling process that checks the conformity of the project deliverables and products to the quality standards

This process begins as soon as the first project deliverable or sub-component is available for inspection.

© 2018 Velociteach. All rights reserved. Do not duplicate. Slide 81

Control Quality

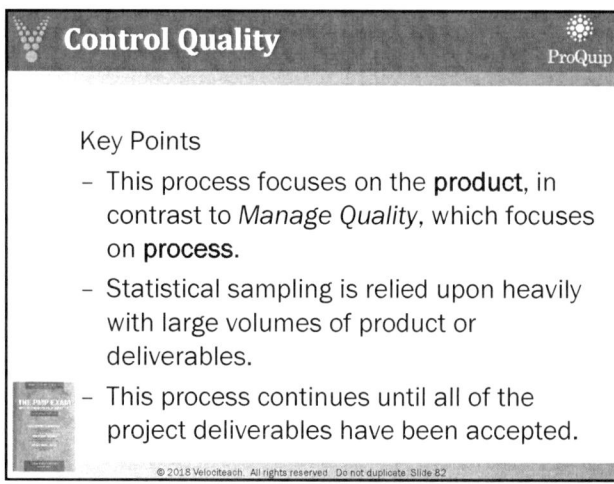

Key Points
- This process focuses on the **product**, in contrast to *Manage Quality*, which focuses on **process.**
- Statistical sampling is relied upon heavily with large volumes of product or deliverables.
- This process continues until all of the project deliverables have been accepted.

© 2018 Velociteach. All rights reserved. Do not duplicate. Slide 82

Control Quality vs Validate Scope

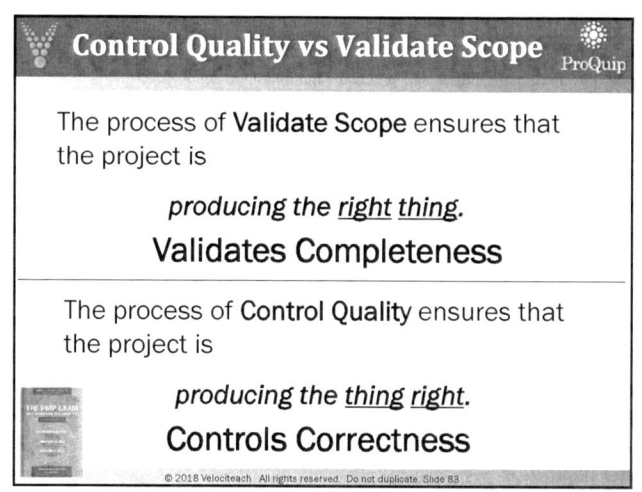

The process of **Validate Scope** ensures that the project is

producing the right thing.
Validates Completeness

The process of **Control Quality** ensures that the project is

producing the thing right.
Controls Correctness

© 2018 Velociteach. All rights reserved. Do not duplicate. Slide 83

PM Role *

Verify that deliverables conform to the quality standards

- According to the quality management plan
- Applying appropriate tools and techniques
- Ensuring changes maintain alignment of project goals with business needs
- Identify and quantify variances and corrective actions
- Capture lessons learned for continuous improvement

    * Subjects for scenario-based questions

© 2018 Velociteach. All rights reserved. Do not duplicate. Slide 84

Control Quality

The key inputs:

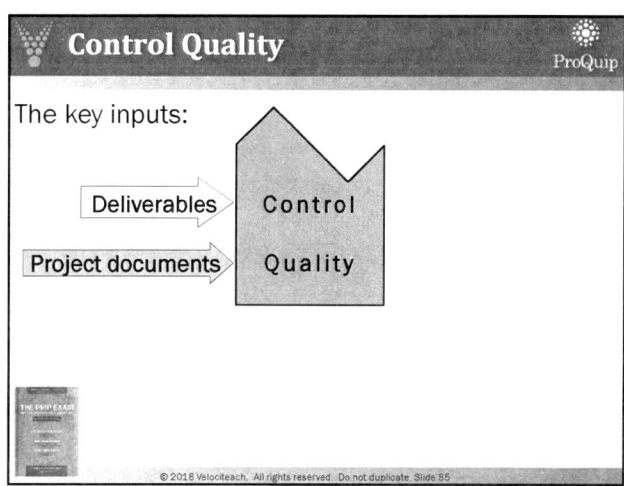

© 2018 Velociteach. All rights reserved. Do not duplicate. Slide 85

Control Quality

The key tools:

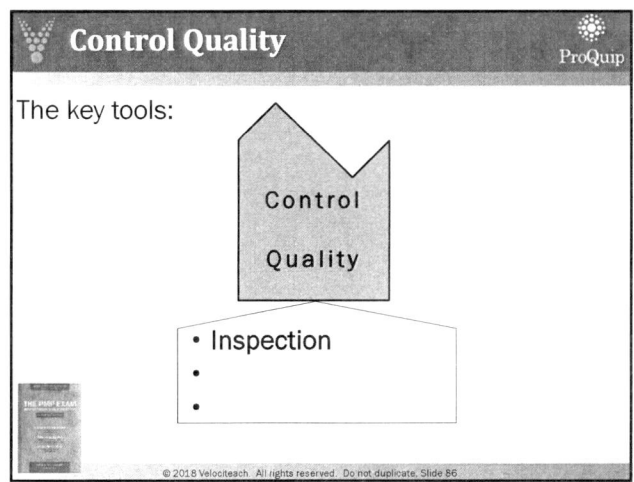

- Inspection
-
-

© 2018 Velociteach. All rights reserved. Do not duplicate. Slide 86

Inspection – for Correctness

Examining
Comparing
Testing
Reviewing
Measuring
Auditing

Products

Deliverables

Relative to Quality Metrics

© 2018 Velociteach. All rights reserved. Do not duplicate. Slide 87

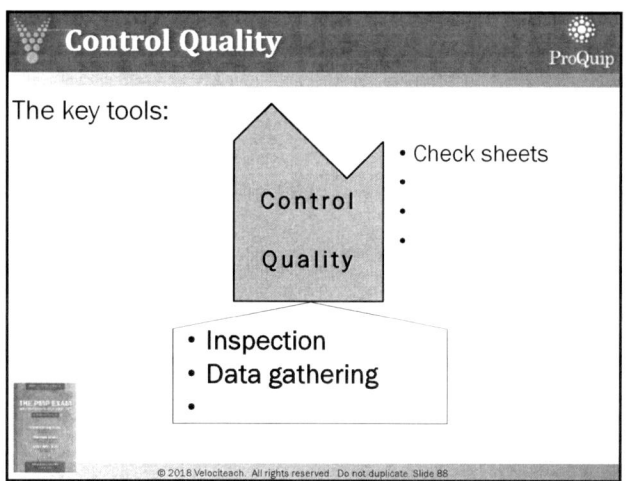

Control Quality

The key tools:

Control Quality
- Check sheets
- •
- •
- •

- Inspection
- Data gathering
- •

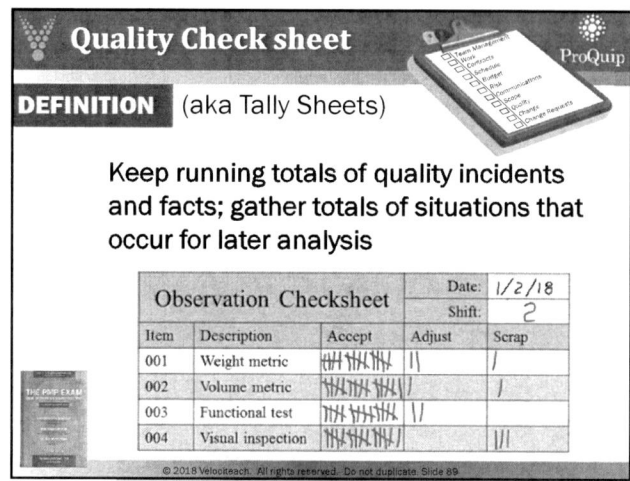

Quality Check sheet

DEFINITION (aka Tally Sheets)

Keep running totals of quality incidents and facts; gather totals of situations that occur for later analysis

| Observation Checksheet | | | Date: 1/2/18 | |
| | | | Shift: 2 | |
Item	Description	Accept	Adjust	Scrap
001	Weight metric	₩ ₩ ₩	II	I
002	Volume metric	₩ ₩ ₩ I		I
003	Functional test	₩ ₩ ₩	II	
004	Visual inspection	₩ ₩ ₩ I		III

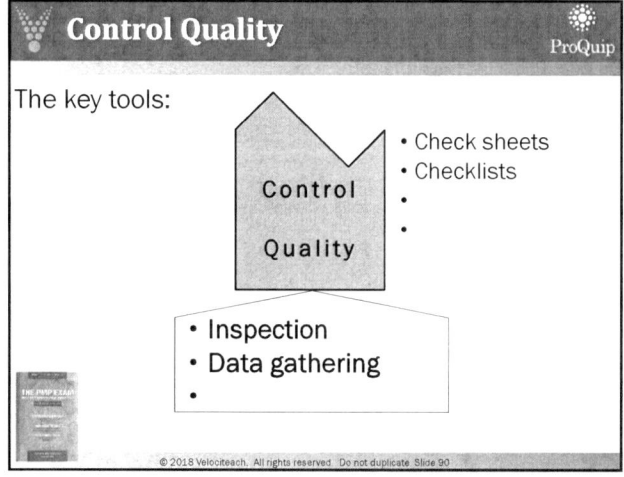

Control Quality

The key tools:

Control Quality
- Check sheets
- Checklists
- •
- •

- Inspection
- Data gathering
- •

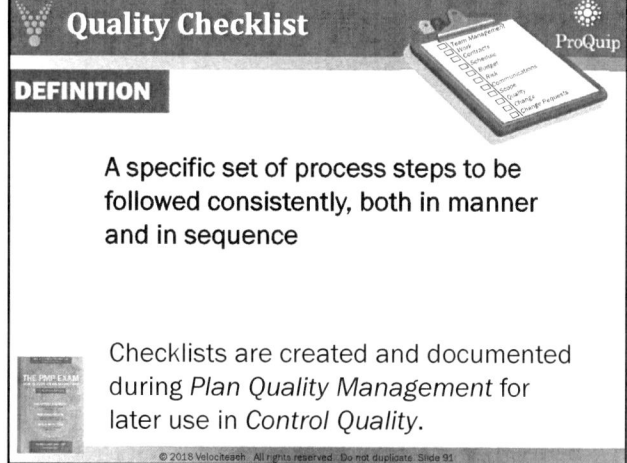

Quality Checklist

DEFINITION

A specific set of process steps to be followed consistently, both in manner and in sequence

Checklists are created and documented during *Plan Quality Management* for later use in *Control Quality*.

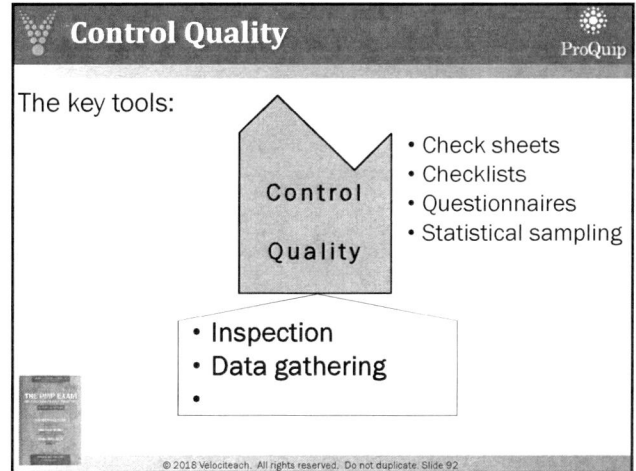

Control Quality

ProQuip

The key tools:

Control Quality

- Check sheets
- Checklists
- Questionnaires
- Statistical sampling

- Inspection
- Data gathering
-

© 2018 Velociteach. All rights reserved. Do not duplicate. Slide 92

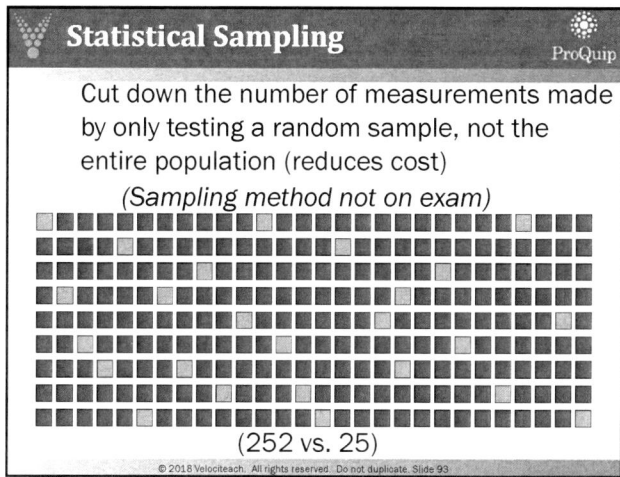

Statistical Sampling

ProQuip

Cut down the number of measurements made by only testing a random sample, not the entire population (reduces cost)

(Sampling method not on exam)

(252 vs. 25)

© 2018 Velociteach. All rights reserved. Do not duplicate. Slide 93

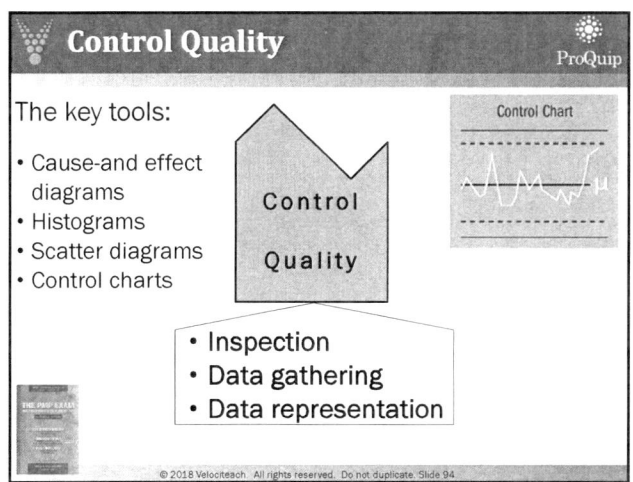

Control Quality

ProQuip

The key tools:

- Cause-and effect diagrams
- Histograms
- Scatter diagrams
- Control charts

Control Quality

Control Chart

- Inspection
- Data gathering
- Data representation

© 2018 Velociteach. All rights reserved. Do not duplicate. Slide 94

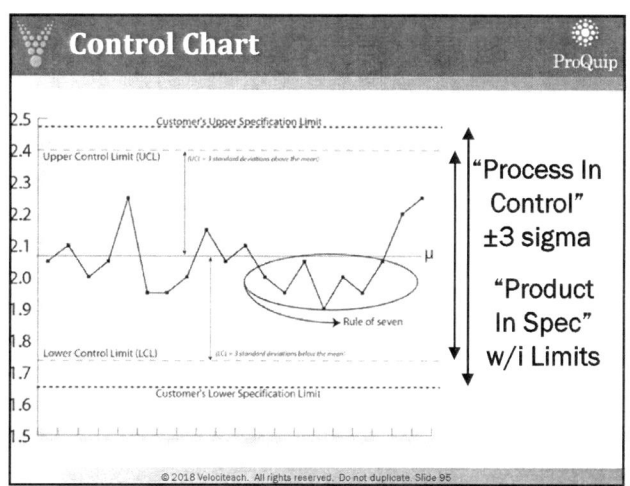

Control Chart

ProQuip

"Process In Control" ±3 sigma

"Product In Spec" w/i Limits

© 2018 Velociteach. All rights reserved. Do not duplicate. Slide 95

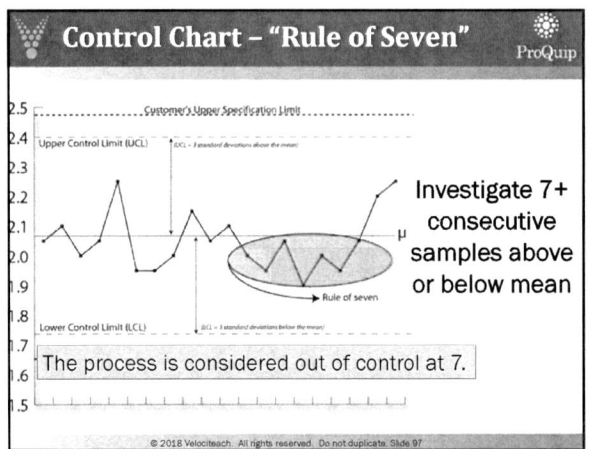

Control Chart – "Rule of Seven"

Investigate 7+ consecutive samples above or below mean

The process is considered out of control at 7.

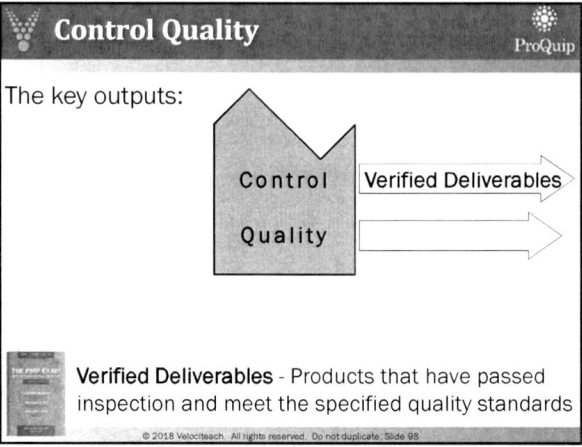

Control Quality

The key outputs:

Control Quality → Verified Deliverables

Verified Deliverables - Products that have passed inspection and meet the specified quality standards

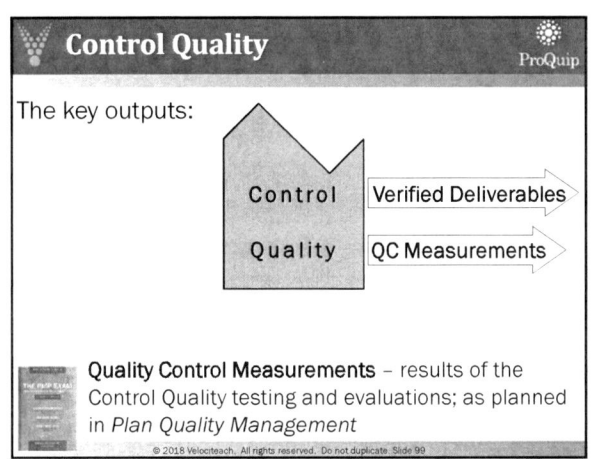

Control Quality

The key outputs:

Control Quality → Verified Deliverables
→ QC Measurements

Quality Control Measurements – results of the Control Quality testing and evaluations; as planned in *Plan Quality Management*

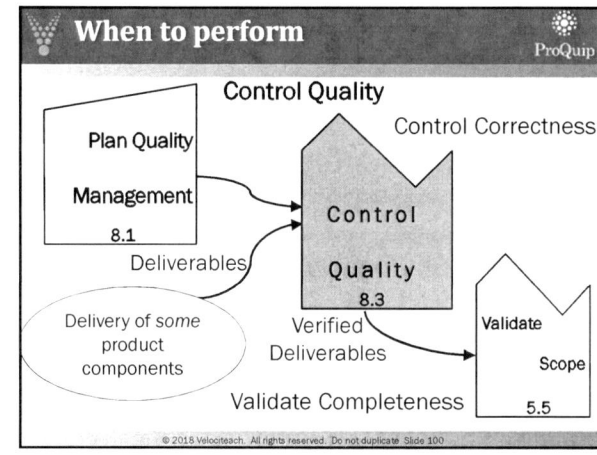

When to perform

Control Quality

Plan Quality Management 8.1 → Deliverables → Control Quality 8.3 → Verified Deliverables → Validate Scope 5.5

Control Correctness

Delivery of *some* product components

Validate Completeness

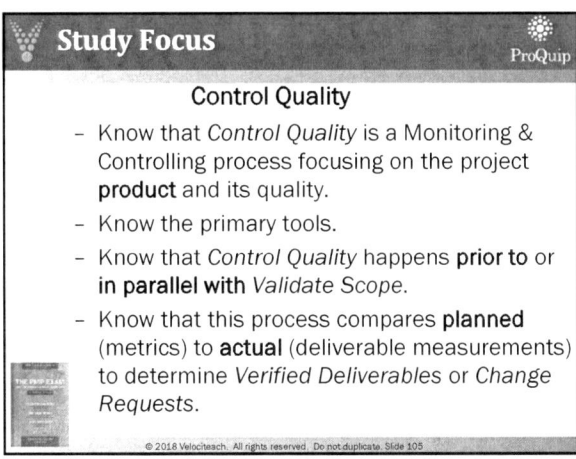

Study Focus

Control Quality

- Know that *Control Quality* is a Monitoring & Controlling process focusing on the project **product** and its quality.
- Know the primary tools.
- Know that *Control Quality* happens **prior to** or **in parallel with** *Validate Scope*.
- Know that this process compares **planned** (metrics) to **actual** (deliverable measurements) to determine *Verified Deliverables* or *Change Requests*.

©2018 Velociteach. All rights reserved.

Review the ITTOs

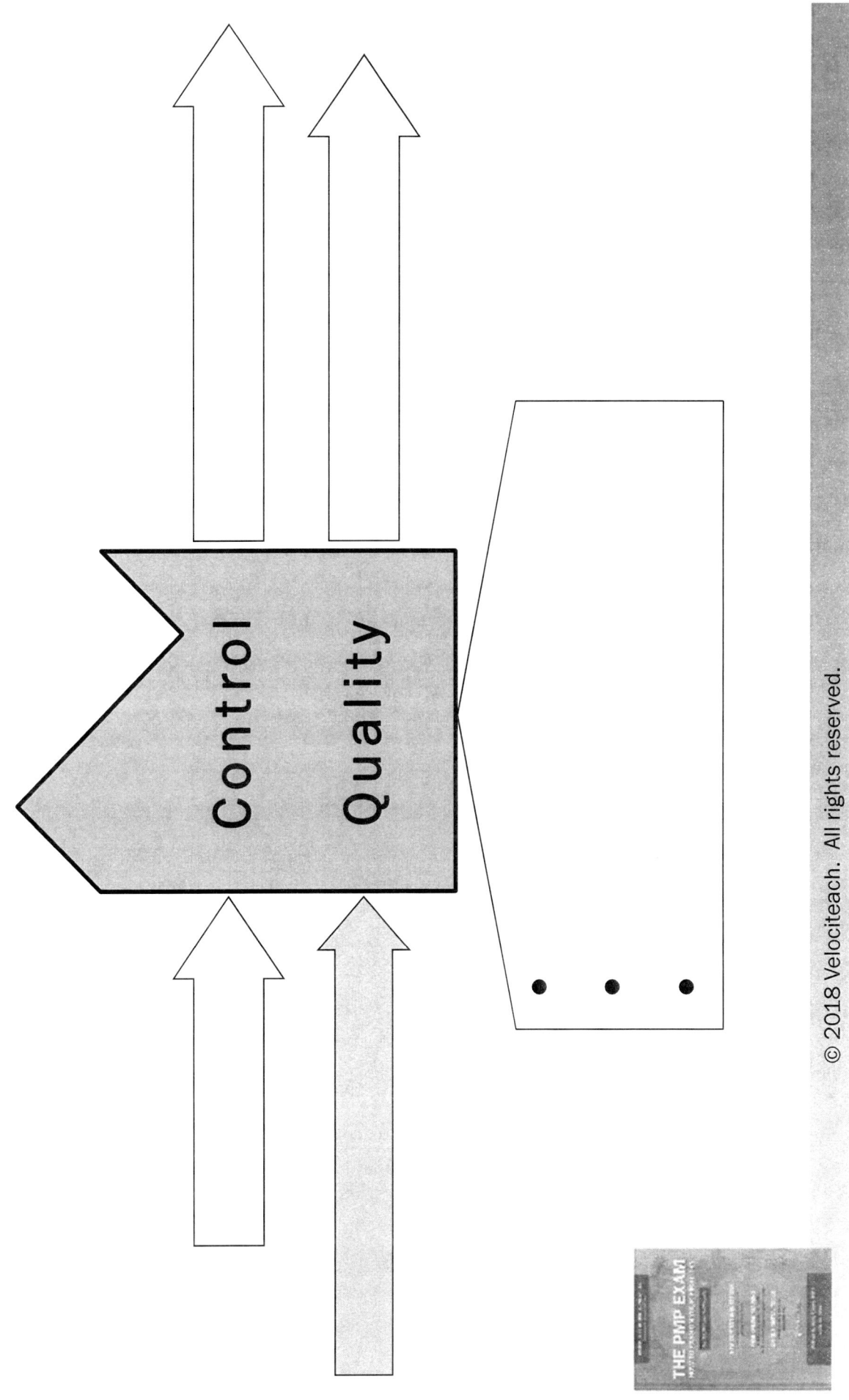

Control Quality

© 2018 Velociteach. All rights reserved.

ProQuip

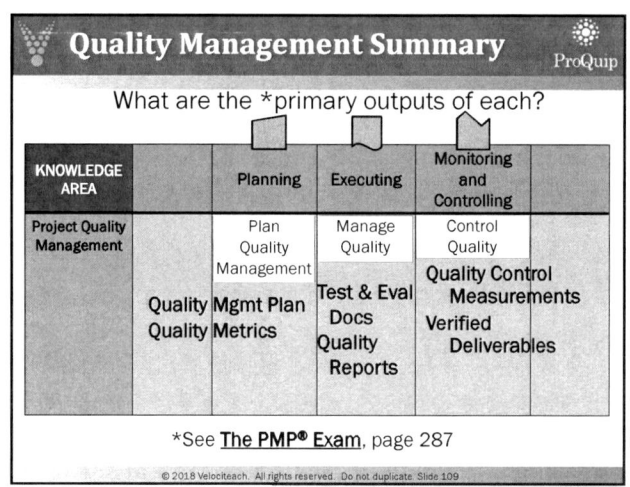

Quality Management Summary

What are the *primary outputs of each?

KNOWLEDGE AREA		Planning	Executing	Monitoring and Controlling
Project Quality Management		Plan Quality Management	Manage Quality	Control Quality
	Quality Mgmt Plan Quality Metrics		Test & Eval Docs Quality Reports	Quality Control Measurements Verified Deliverables

*See The PMP® Exam, page 287

© 2018 Velociteach. All rights reserved. Do not duplicate. Slide 109

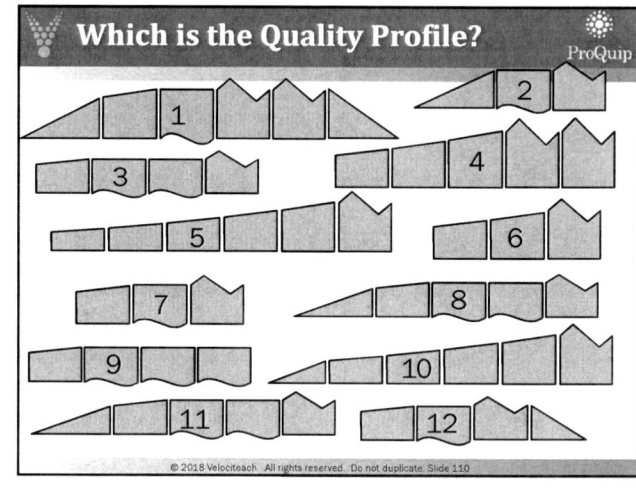

Which is the Quality Profile?

© 2018 Velociteach. All rights reserved. Do not duplicate. Slide 110

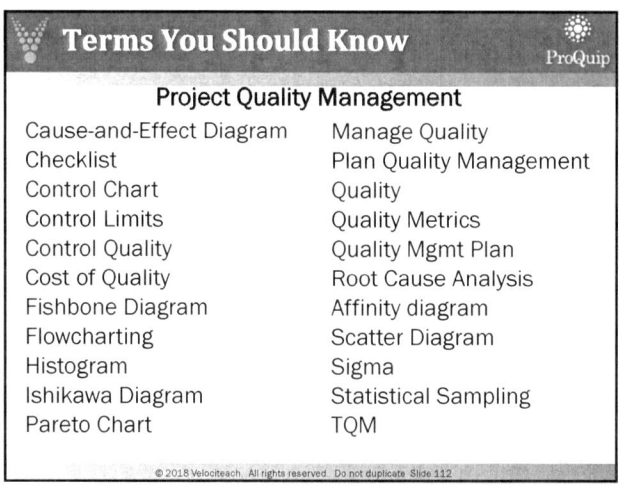

Terms You Should Know

Project Quality Management

Cause-and-Effect Diagram	Manage Quality
Checklist	Plan Quality Management
Control Chart	Quality
Control Limits	Quality Metrics
Control Quality	Quality Mgmt Plan
Cost of Quality	Root Cause Analysis
Fishbone Diagram	Affinity diagram
Flowcharting	Scatter Diagram
Histogram	Sigma
Ishikawa Diagram	Statistical Sampling
Pareto Chart	TQM

© 2018 Velociteach. All rights reserved. Do not duplicate. Slide 112

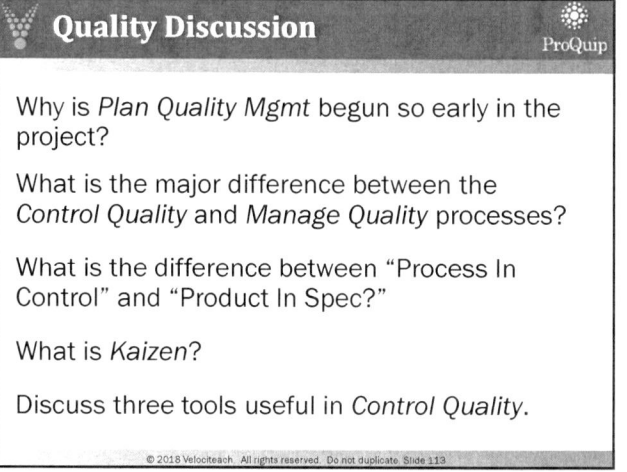

Quality Discussion

Why is *Plan Quality Mgmt* begun so early in the project?

What is the major difference between the *Control Quality* and *Manage Quality* processes?

What is the difference between "Process In Control" and "Product In Spec?"

What is *Kaizen*?

Discuss three tools useful in *Control Quality*.

© 2018 Velociteach. All rights reserved. Do not duplicate. Slide 113

Summary

ProQuip

Knowledge Area

KNOWLEDGE AREA	Initiating	Planning	Executing	Monitoring and Controlling	Closing
Project Management					

©2018 Velociteach. All rights reserved.   Page 211

Score Sheet	**Quality Management Exam**	 Velociteach

- **Mark one answer: A, B, C, or D.**
- **Circle the '?' symbol if you are guessing at the answer.**
- **Circle the Δ symbol if you change your answer.**

Total Correct: _____

% Correct: _____%

1.	A O	B O	C O	D O	? Δ
2.	A O	B O	C O	D O	? Δ
3.	A O	B O	C O	D O	? Δ
4.	A O	B O	C O	D O	? Δ
5.	A O	B O	C O	D O	? Δ
6.	A O	B O	C O	D O	? Δ
7.	A O	B O	C O	D O	? Δ
8.	A O	B O	C O	D O	? Δ
9.	A O	B O	C O	D O	? Δ
10.	A O	B O	C O	D O	? Δ
11.	A O	B O	C O	D O	? Δ
12.	A O	B O	C O	D O	? Δ
13.	A O	B O	C O	D O	? Δ
14.	A O	B O	C O	D O	? Δ
15.	A O	B O	C O	D O	? Δ
16.	A O	B O	C O	D O	? Δ
17.	A O	B O	C O	D O	? Δ
18.	A O	B O	C O	D O	? Δ
19.	A O	B O	C O	D O	? Δ
20.	A O	B O	C O	D O	? Δ
21.	A O	B O	C O	D O	? Δ
22.	A O	B O	C O	D O	? Δ
23.	A O	B O	C O	D O	? Δ
24.	A O	B O	C O	D O	? Δ
25.	A O	B O	C O	D O	? Δ

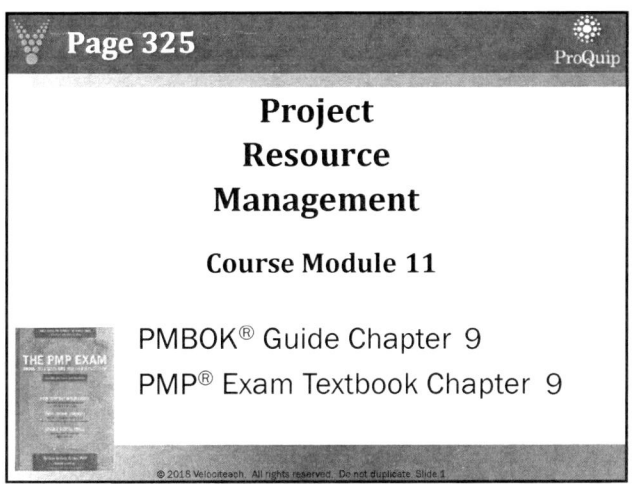

Page 325   ProQuip

Project Resource Management

Course Module 11

PMBOK® Guide Chapter 9

PMP® Exam Textbook Chapter 9

© 2018 Velociteach. All rights reserved. Do not duplicate. Slide 1

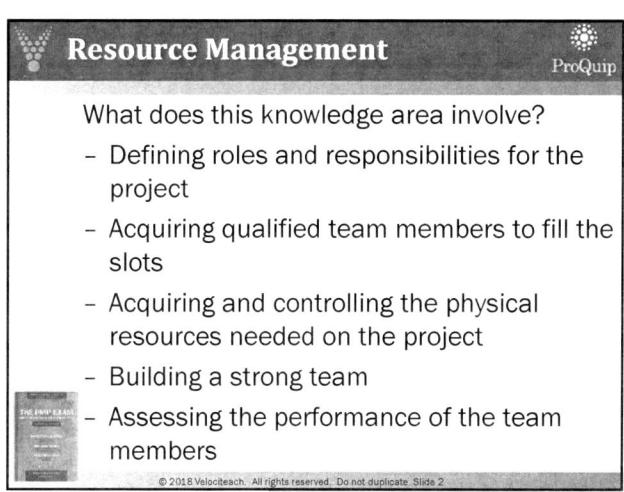

Resource Management   ProQuip

What does this knowledge area involve?

- Defining roles and responsibilities for the project
- Acquiring qualified team members to fill the slots
- Acquiring and controlling the physical resources needed on the project
- Building a strong team
- Assessing the performance of the team members

© 2018 Velociteach. All rights reserved. Do not duplicate. Slide 2

PMI Philosophy: Resource Mgmt   ProQuip

- Everyone's role should be clearly defined.

- Physical resources are included, e.g., materials, supplies, equipment, facilities

- The project manager is in charge of the project.

- Project managers lead, motivate, inspire, and delegate to team members, and they influence other project stakeholders.

© 2018 Velociteach. All rights reserved. Do not duplicate. Slide 3

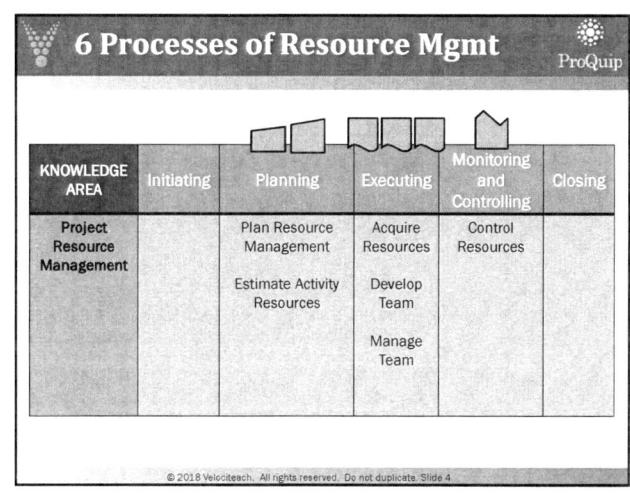

6 Processes of Resource Mgmt   ProQuip

KNOWLEDGE AREA	Initiating	Planning	Executing	Monitoring and Controlling	Closing
Project Resource Management		Plan Resource Management Estimate Activity Resources	Acquire Resources Develop Team Manage Team	Control Resources	

© 2018 Velociteach. All rights reserved. Do not duplicate. Slide 4

Resource Process Overview

Turn to page 325 in the textbook.

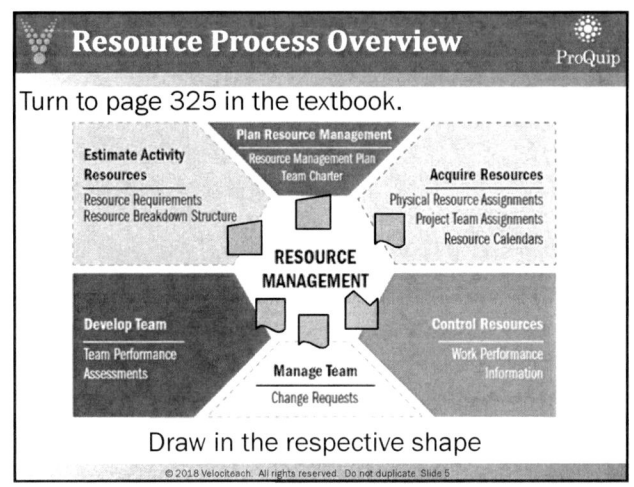

Draw in the respective shape

© 2018 Velociteach. All rights reserved. Do not duplicate. Slide 5

Resource Process Overview

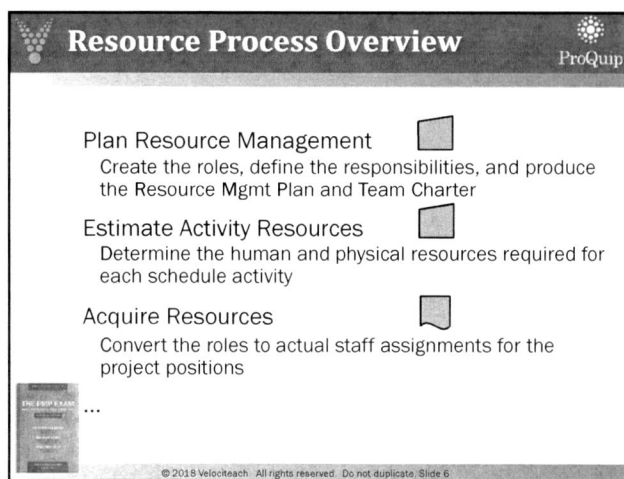

Plan Resource Management

Create the roles, define the responsibilities, and produce the Resource Mgmt Plan and Team Charter

Estimate Activity Resources

Determine the human and physical resources required for each schedule activity

Acquire Resources

Convert the roles to actual staff assignments for the project positions

...

© 2018 Velociteach. All rights reserved. Do not duplicate. Slide 6

Resource Process Overview

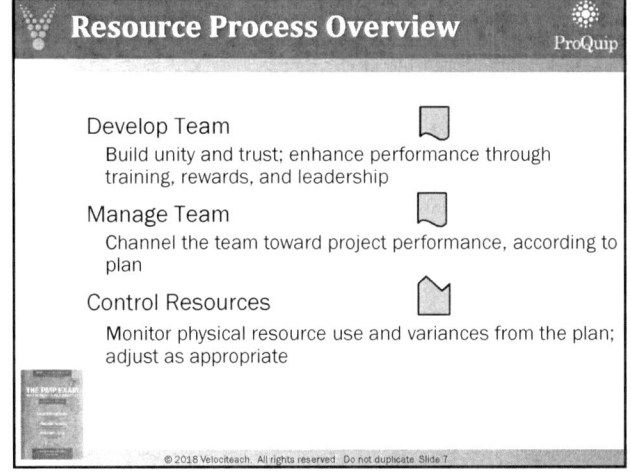

Develop Team

Build unity and trust; enhance performance through training, rewards, and leadership

Manage Team

Channel the team toward project performance, according to plan

Control Resources

Monitor physical resource use and variances from the plan; adjust as appropriate

© 2018 Velociteach. All rights reserved. Do not duplicate. Slide 7

The 6 Resource Processes

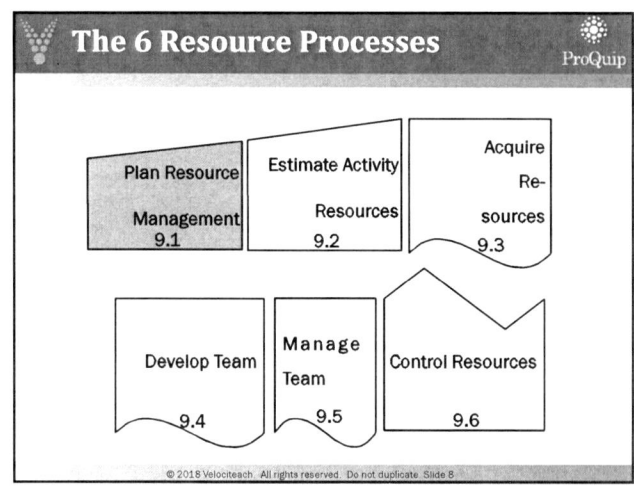

© 2018 Velociteach. All rights reserved. Do not duplicate. Slide 8

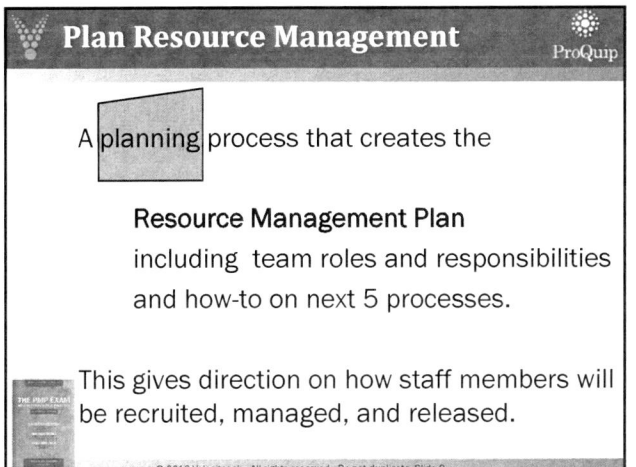

Plan Resource Management — ProQuip

A planning process that creates the

Resource Management Plan
including team roles and responsibilities
and how-to on next 5 processes.

This gives direction on how staff members will be recruited, managed, and released.

© 2018 Velociteach. All rights reserved. Do not duplicate. Slide 9

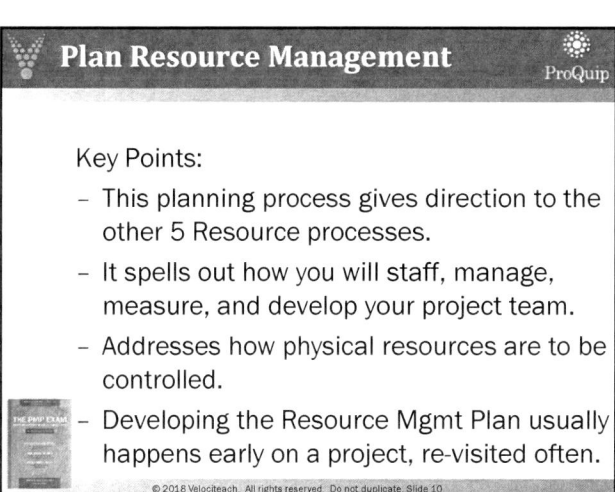

Plan Resource Management — ProQuip

Key Points:
- This planning process gives direction to the other 5 Resource processes.
- It spells out how you will staff, manage, measure, and develop your project team.
- Addresses how physical resources are to be controlled.
- Developing the Resource Mgmt Plan usually happens early on a project, re-visited often.

© 2018 Velociteach. All rights reserved. Do not duplicate. Slide 10

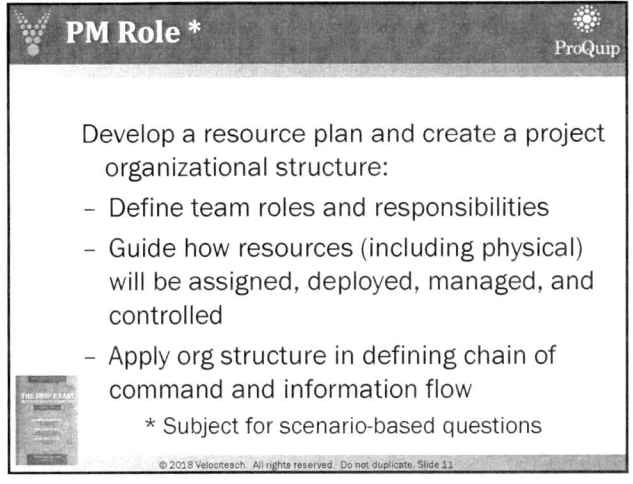

PM Role * — ProQuip

Develop a resource plan and create a project organizational structure:
- Define team roles and responsibilities
- Guide how resources (including physical) will be assigned, deployed, managed, and controlled
- Apply org structure in defining chain of command and information flow
  * Subject for scenario-based questions

© 2018 Velociteach. All rights reserved. Do not duplicate. Slide 11

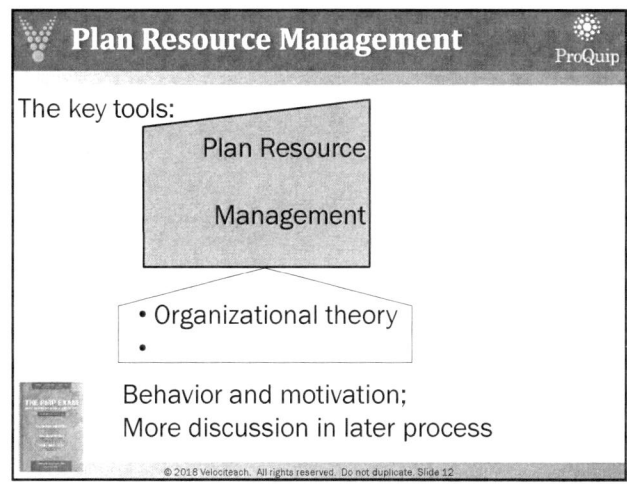

Plan Resource Management — ProQuip

The key tools:

Plan Resource Management

• Organizational theory
•

Behavior and motivation;
More discussion in later process

© 2018 Velociteach. All rights reserved. Do not duplicate. Slide 12

©2018 Velociteach. All rights reserved.   Page 215

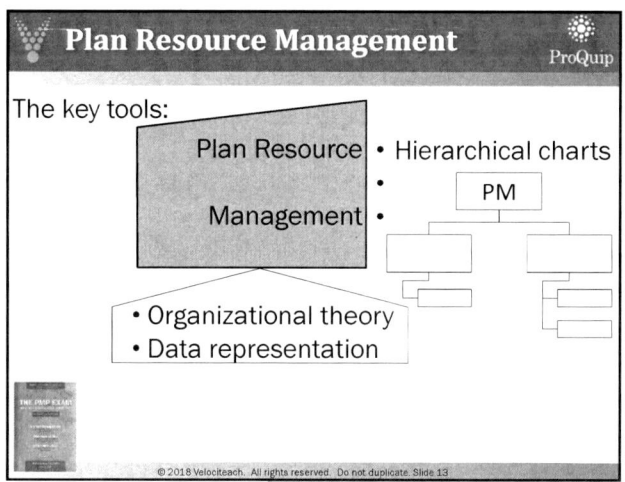

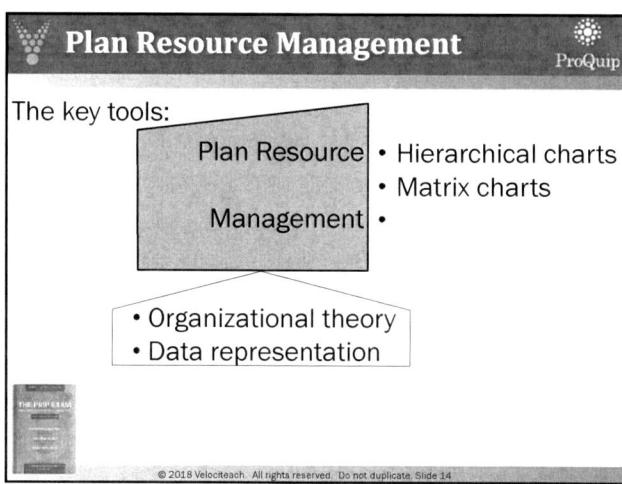

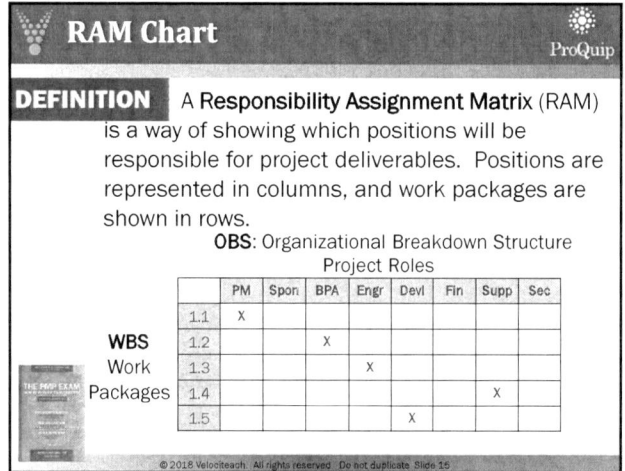

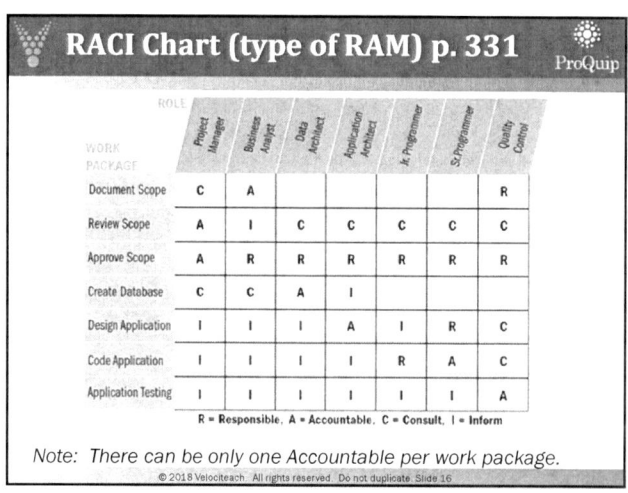

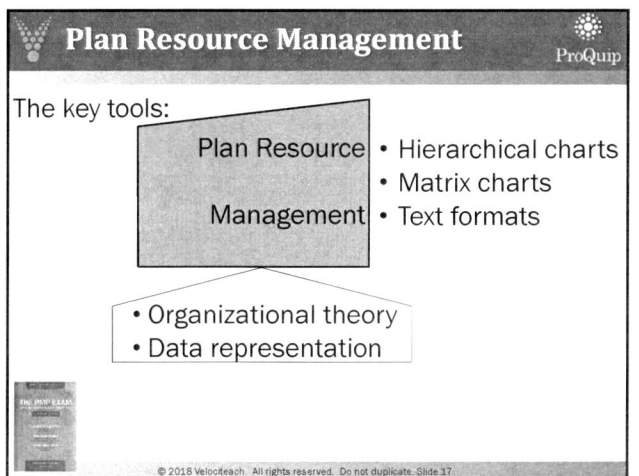

Plan Resource Management   ProQuip

The key tools:

Plan Resource Management
- Hierarchical charts
- Matrix charts
- Text formats

- Organizational theory
- Data representation

© 2018 Velociteach. All rights reserved. Do not duplicate. Slide 17

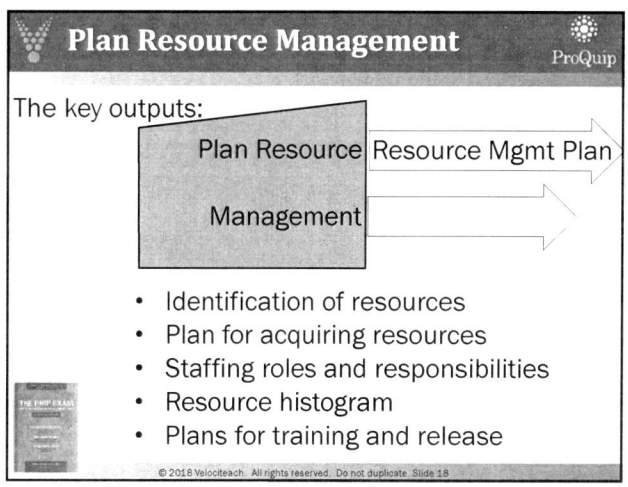

Plan Resource Management   ProQuip

The key outputs:

Plan Resource Management → Resource Mgmt Plan

- Identification of resources
- Plan for acquiring resources
- Staffing roles and responsibilities
- Resource histogram
- Plans for training and release

© 2018 Velociteach. All rights reserved. Do not duplicate. Slide 18

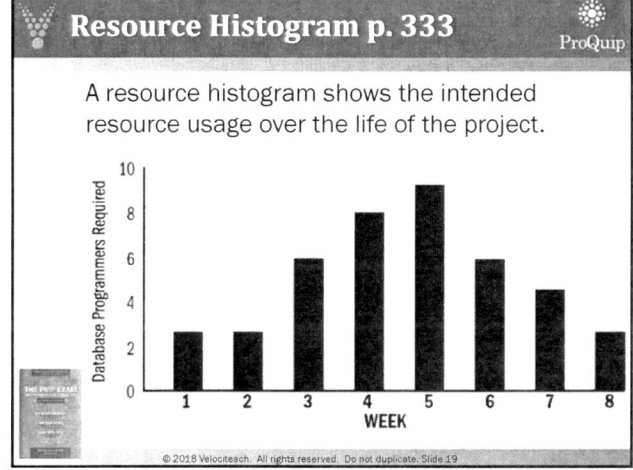

Resource Histogram p. 333   ProQuip

A resource histogram shows the intended resource usage over the life of the project.

© 2018 Velociteach. All rights reserved. Do not duplicate. Slide 19

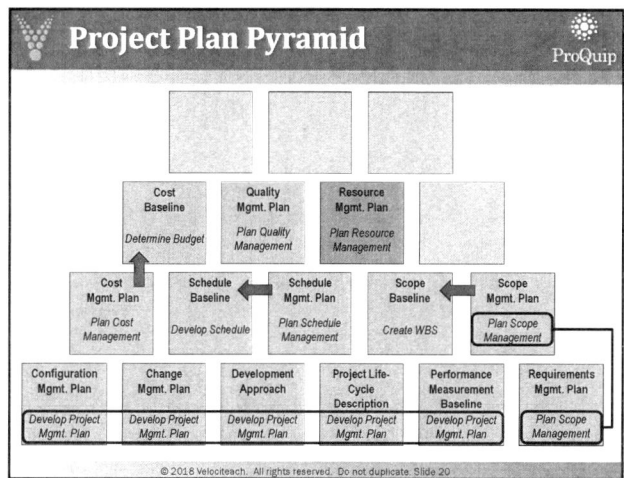

Project Plan Pyramid   ProQuip

© 2018 Velociteach. All rights reserved. Do not duplicate. Slide 20

©2018 Velociteach. All rights reserved. Page 217

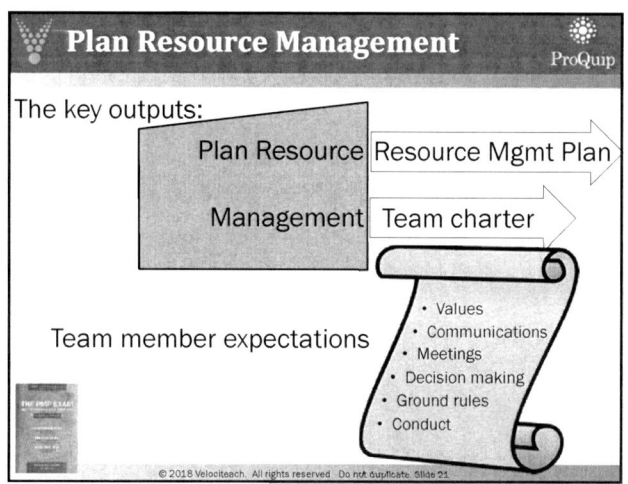

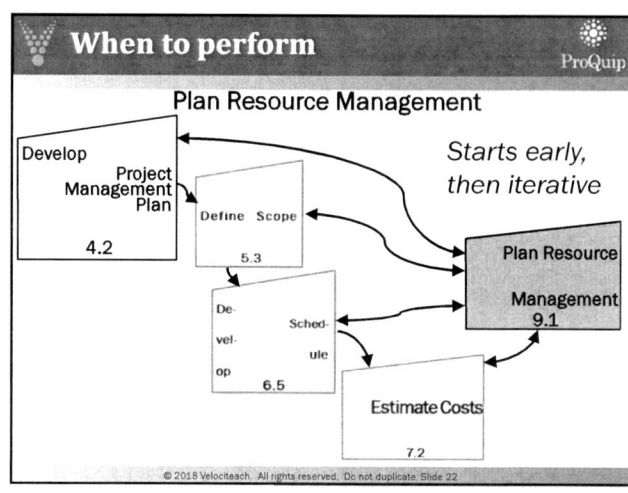

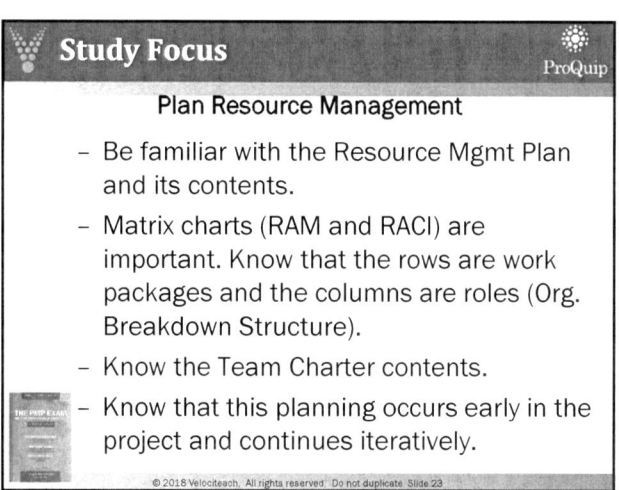

©2018 Velociteach. All rights reserved. Page 218

Review the ITTOs

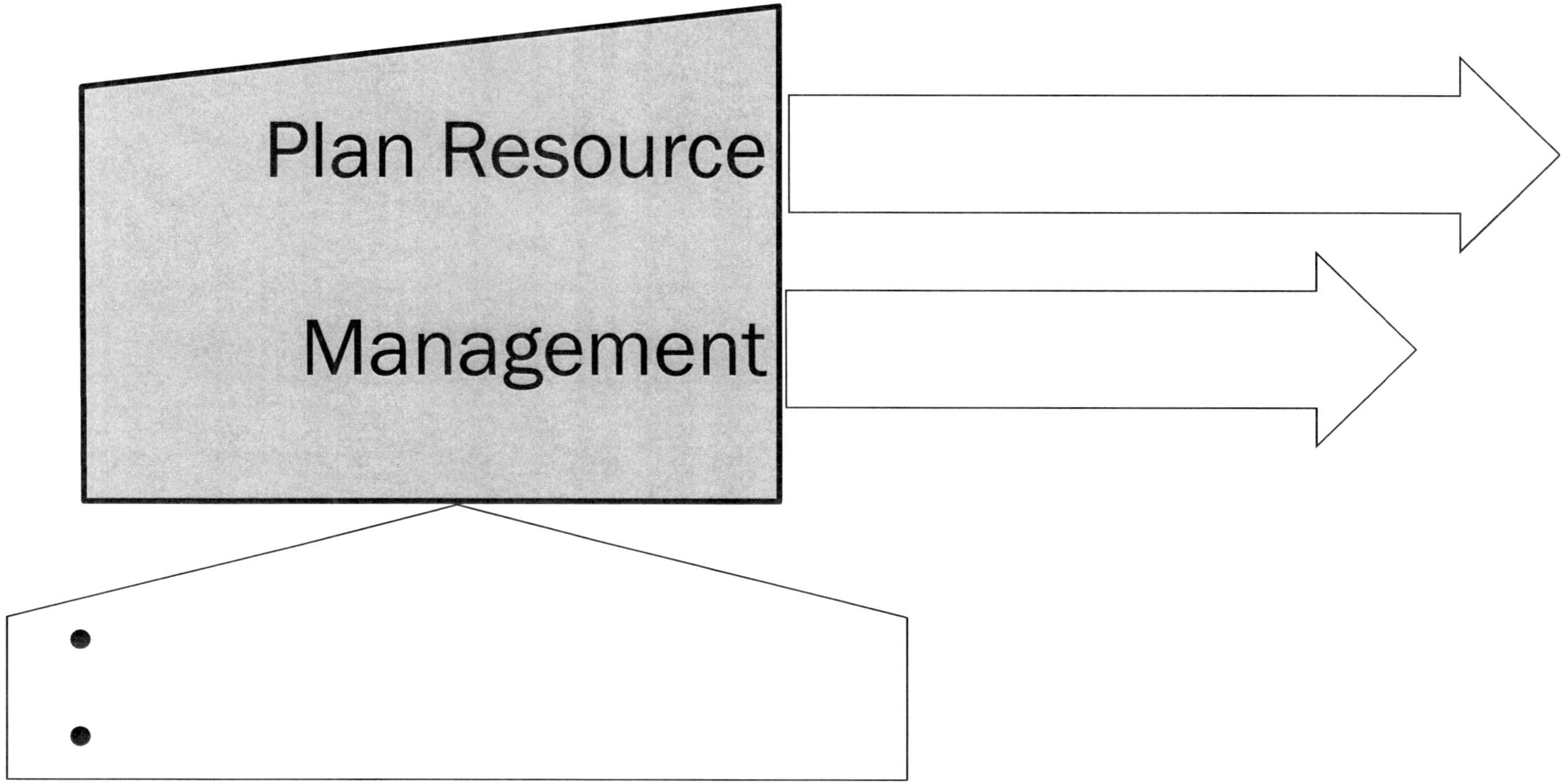

Plan Resource Management

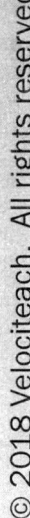

© 2018 Velociteach. All rights reserved.

ProQuip

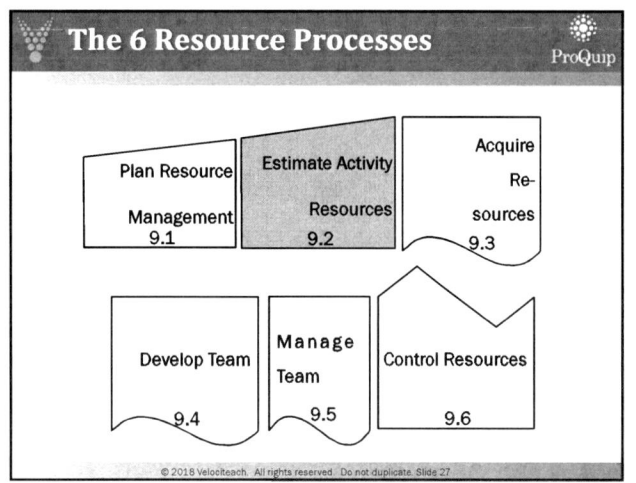

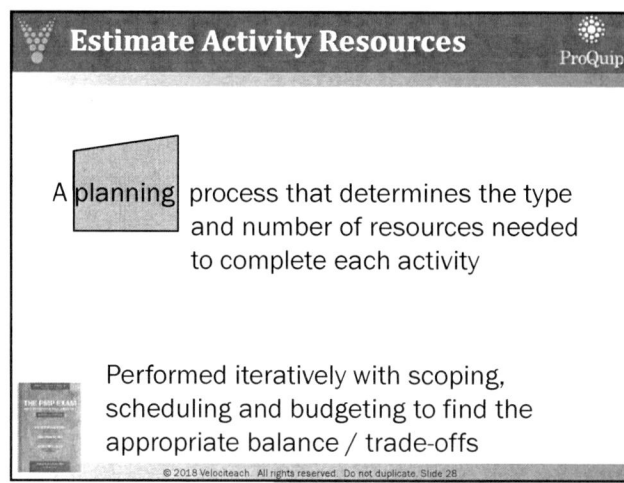

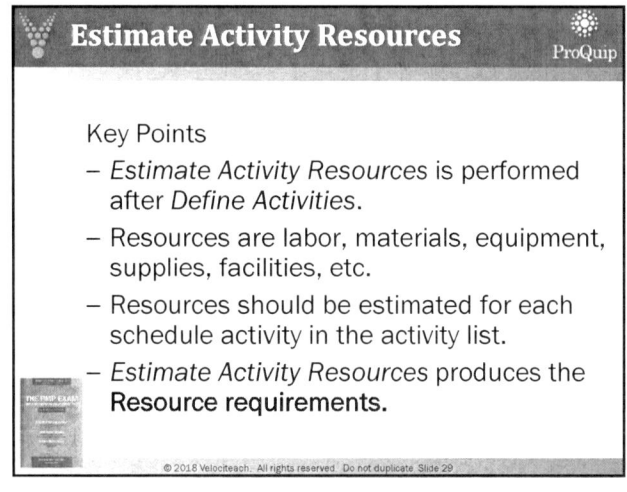

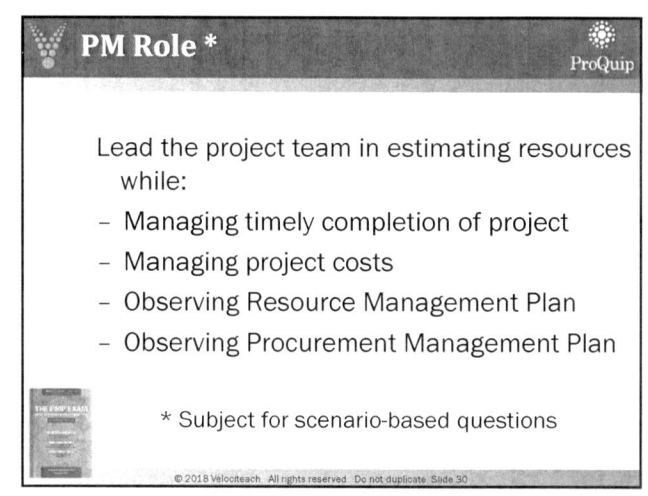

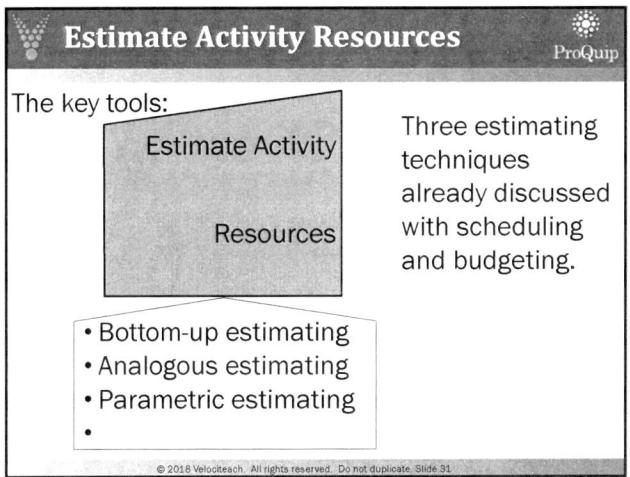

Estimate Activity Resources

The key tools:

Estimate Activity Resources

Three estimating techniques already discussed with scheduling and budgeting.

- Bottom-up estimating
- Analogous estimating
- Parametric estimating
-

© 2018 Velociteach. All rights reserved. Do not duplicate. Slide 31

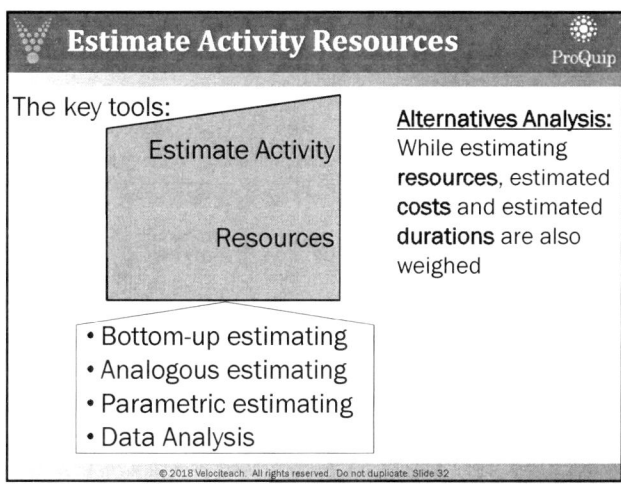

Estimate Activity Resources

The key tools:

Estimate Activity Resources

Alternatives Analysis: While estimating **resources**, estimated **costs** and estimated **durations** are also weighed

- Bottom-up estimating
- Analogous estimating
- Parametric estimating
- Data Analysis

© 2018 Velociteach. All rights reserved. Do not duplicate. Slide 32

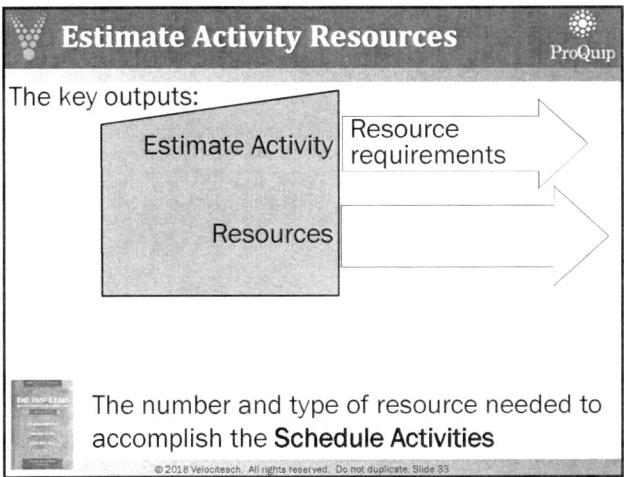

Estimate Activity Resources

The key outputs:

Estimate Activity Resources → Resource requirements →

The number and type of resource needed to accomplish the **Schedule Activities**

© 2018 Velociteach. All rights reserved. Do not duplicate. Slide 33

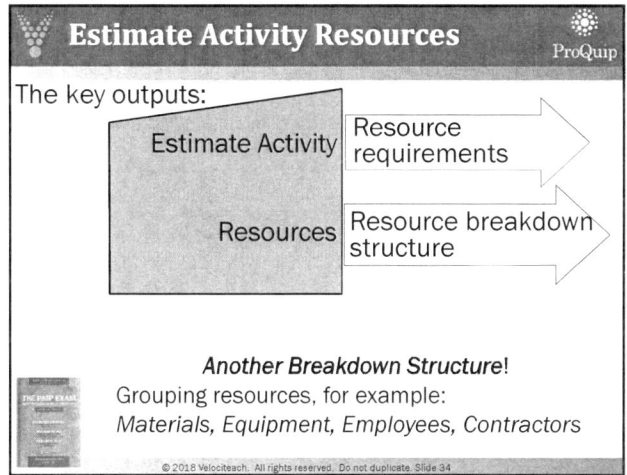

Estimate Activity Resources

The key outputs:

Estimate Activity Resources → Resource requirements →

Resource breakdown structure →

Another Breakdown Structure!
Grouping resources, for example:
Materials, Equipment, Employees, Contractors

© 2018 Velociteach. All rights reserved. Do not duplicate. Slide 34

When to perform

Estimate Activity Resources

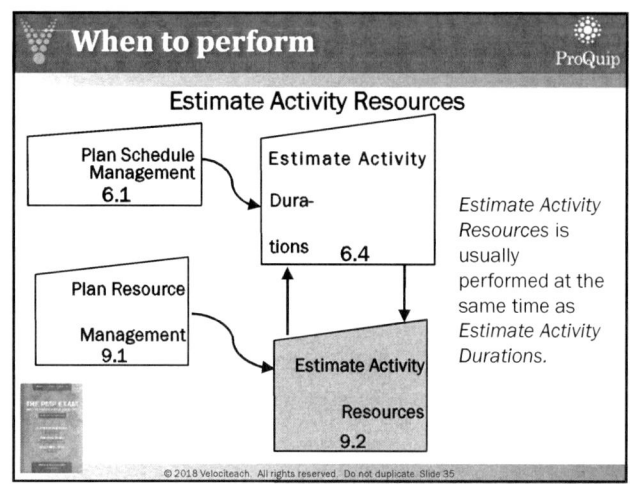

Estimate Activity Resources is usually performed at the same time as *Estimate Activity Durations.*

© 2018 Velociteach. All rights reserved. Do not duplicate. Slide 35

Study Focus

Estimate Activity Resources

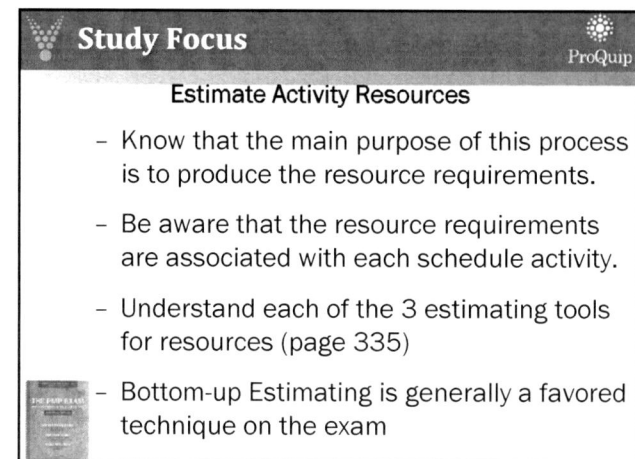

- Know that the main purpose of this process is to produce the resource requirements.

- Be aware that the resource requirements are associated with each schedule activity.

- Understand each of the 3 estimating tools for resources (page 335)

- Bottom-up Estimating is generally a favored technique on the exam

© 2018 Velociteach. All rights reserved. Do not duplicate. Slide 36

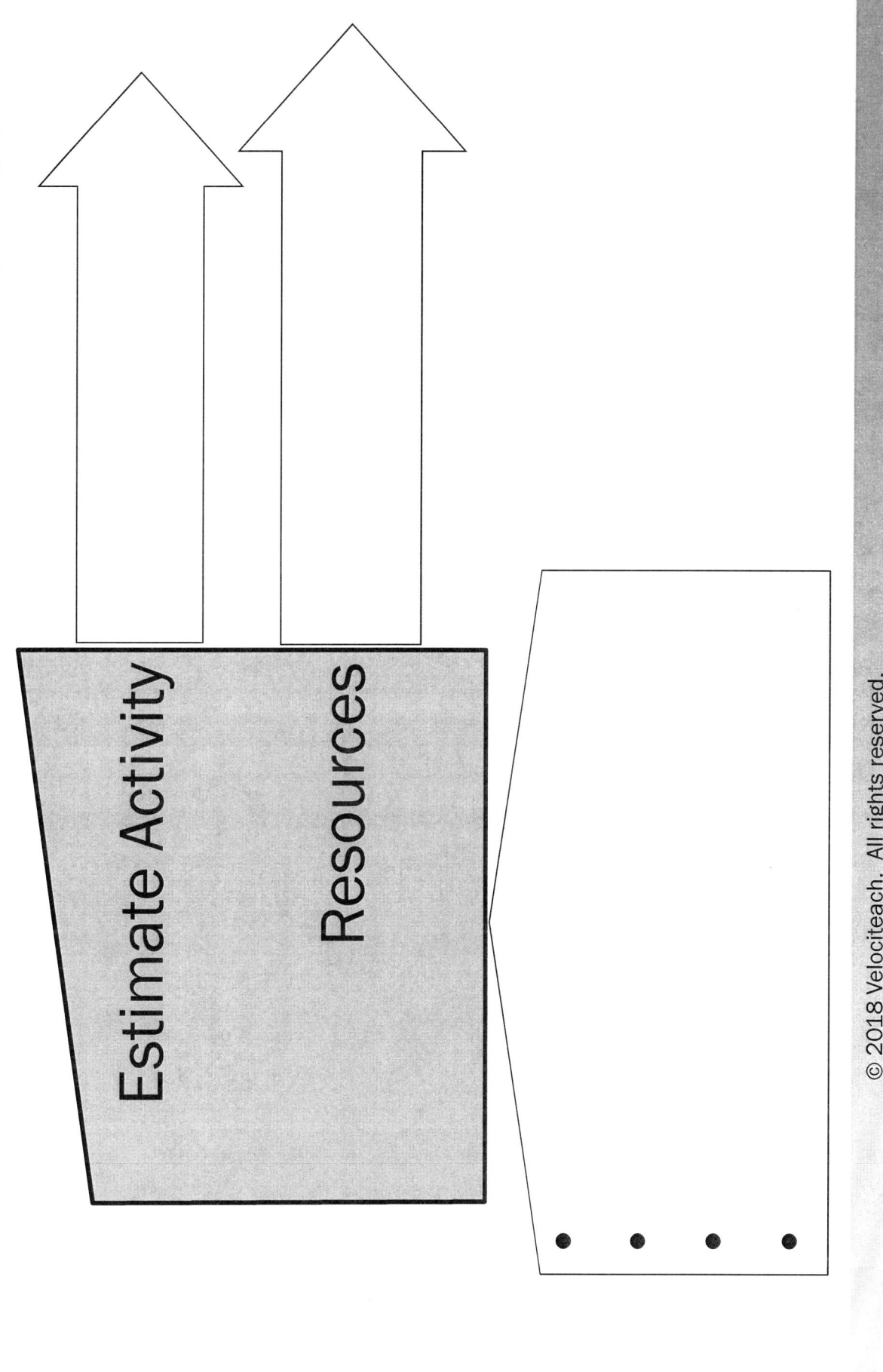

Review the ITTOs

Estimate Activity Resources

© 2018 Velociteach. All rights reserved.

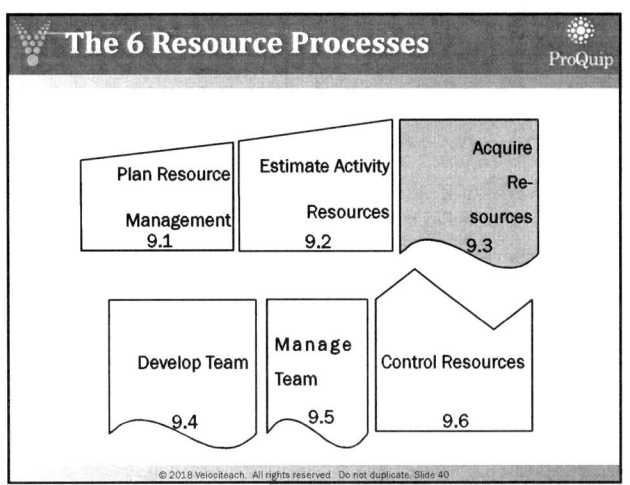

The 6 Resource Processes

ProQuip

- Plan Resource Management 9.1
- Estimate Activity Resources 9.2
- Acquire Resources 9.3
- Develop Team 9.4
- Manage Team 9.5
- Control Resources 9.6

© 2018 Velociteach. All rights reserved. Do not duplicate. Slide 40

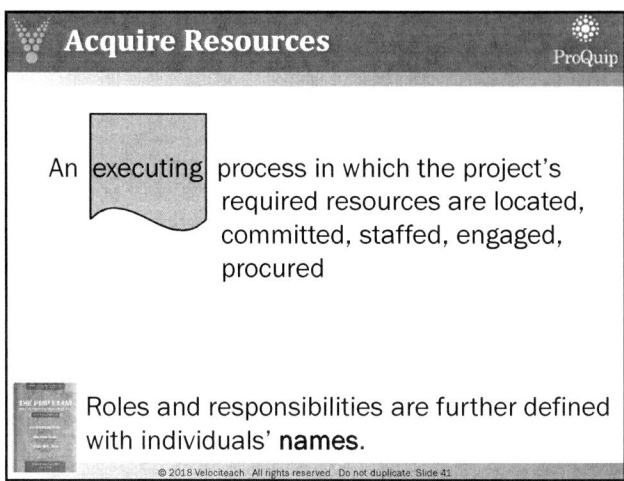

Acquire Resources

ProQuip

An executing process in which the project's required resources are located, committed, staffed, engaged, procured

Roles and responsibilities are further defined with individuals' **names**.

© 2018 Velociteach. All rights reserved. Do not duplicate. Slide 41

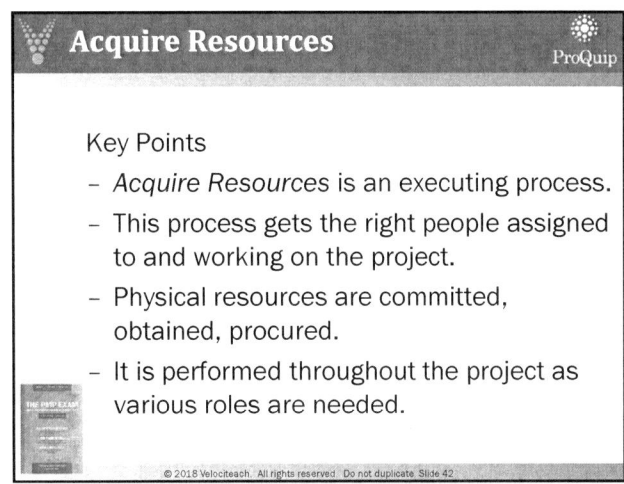

Acquire Resources

ProQuip

Key Points
- *Acquire Resources* is an executing process.
- This process gets the right people assigned to and working on the project.
- Physical resources are committed, obtained, procured.
- It is performed throughout the project as various roles are needed.

© 2018 Velociteach. All rights reserved. Do not duplicate. Slide 42

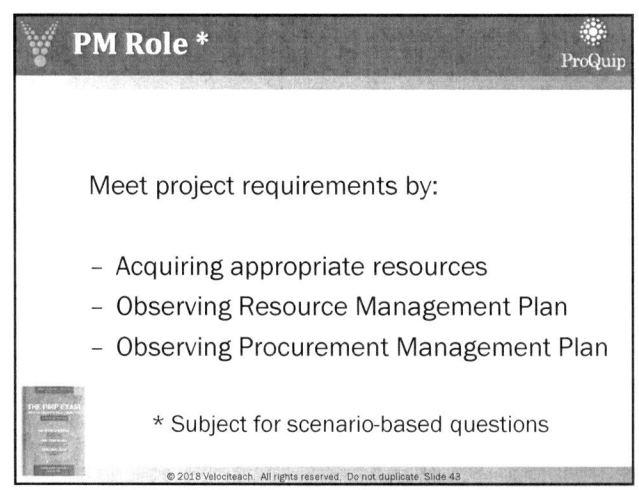

PM Role *

ProQuip

Meet project requirements by:

- Acquiring appropriate resources
- Observing Resource Management Plan
- Observing Procurement Management Plan

* Subject for scenario-based questions

© 2018 Velociteach. All rights reserved. Do not duplicate. Slide 43

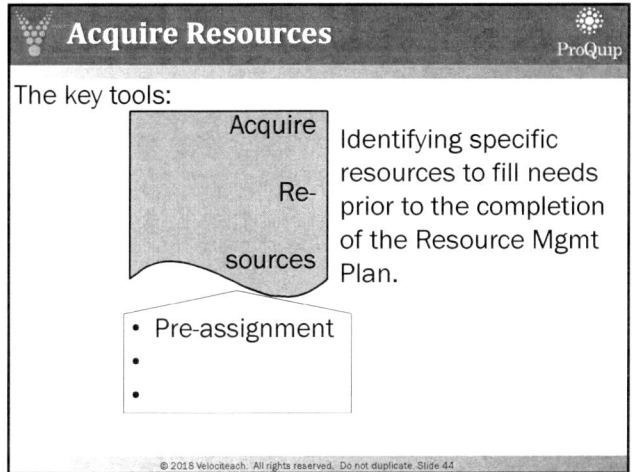

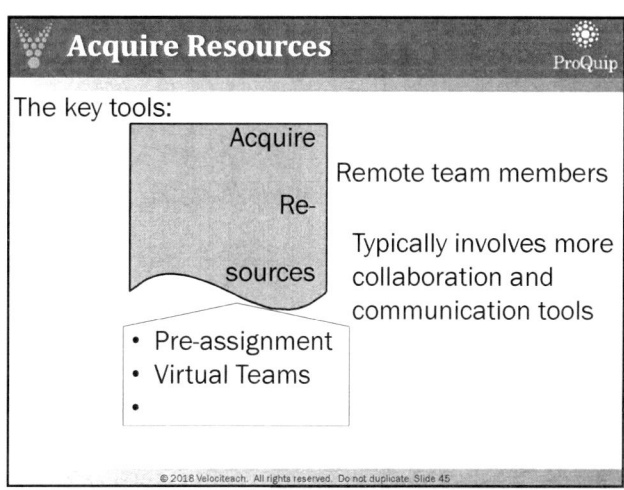

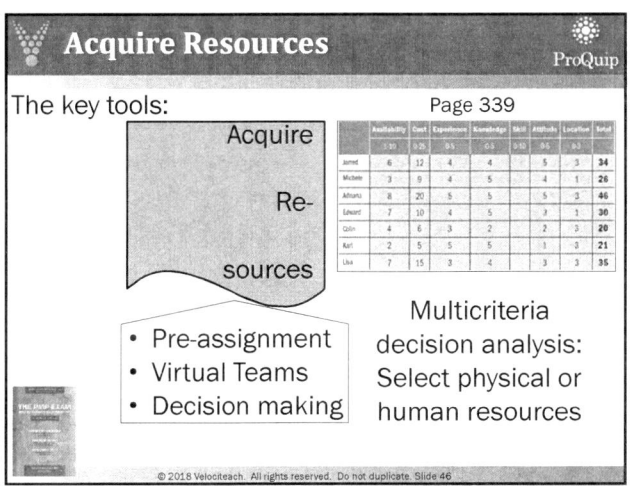

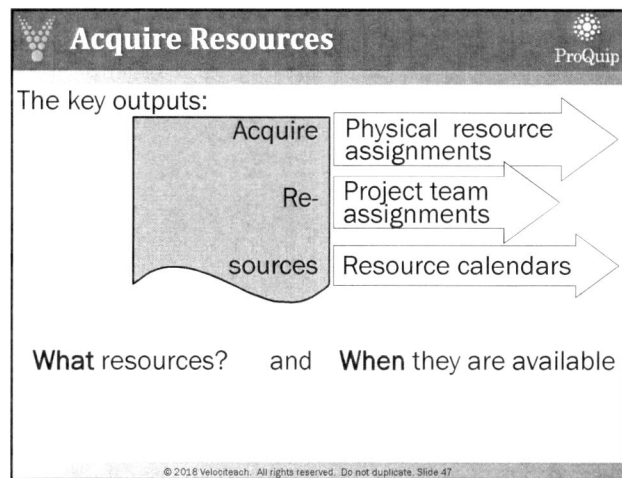

Acquire Resources

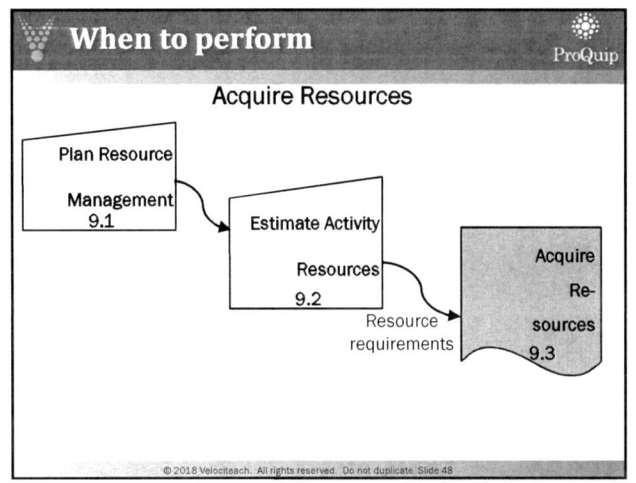

© 2018 Velociteach. All rights reserved. Do not duplicate. Slide 48

Acquire Resources

– Remember that this is a relatively simple executing process that produces staff assignments (Names) and physical resource assignments.

– Understand the importance of the tools: Pre-Assignment, Virtual Teams, and Decision making.

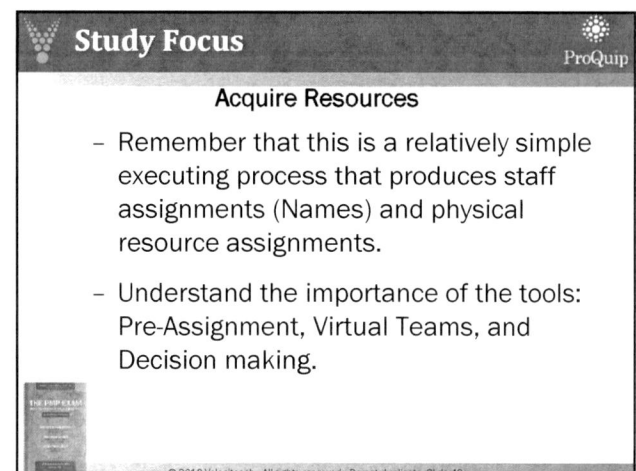

© 2018 Velociteach. All rights reserved. Do not duplicate. Slide 49

Review the ITTOs

ProQuip

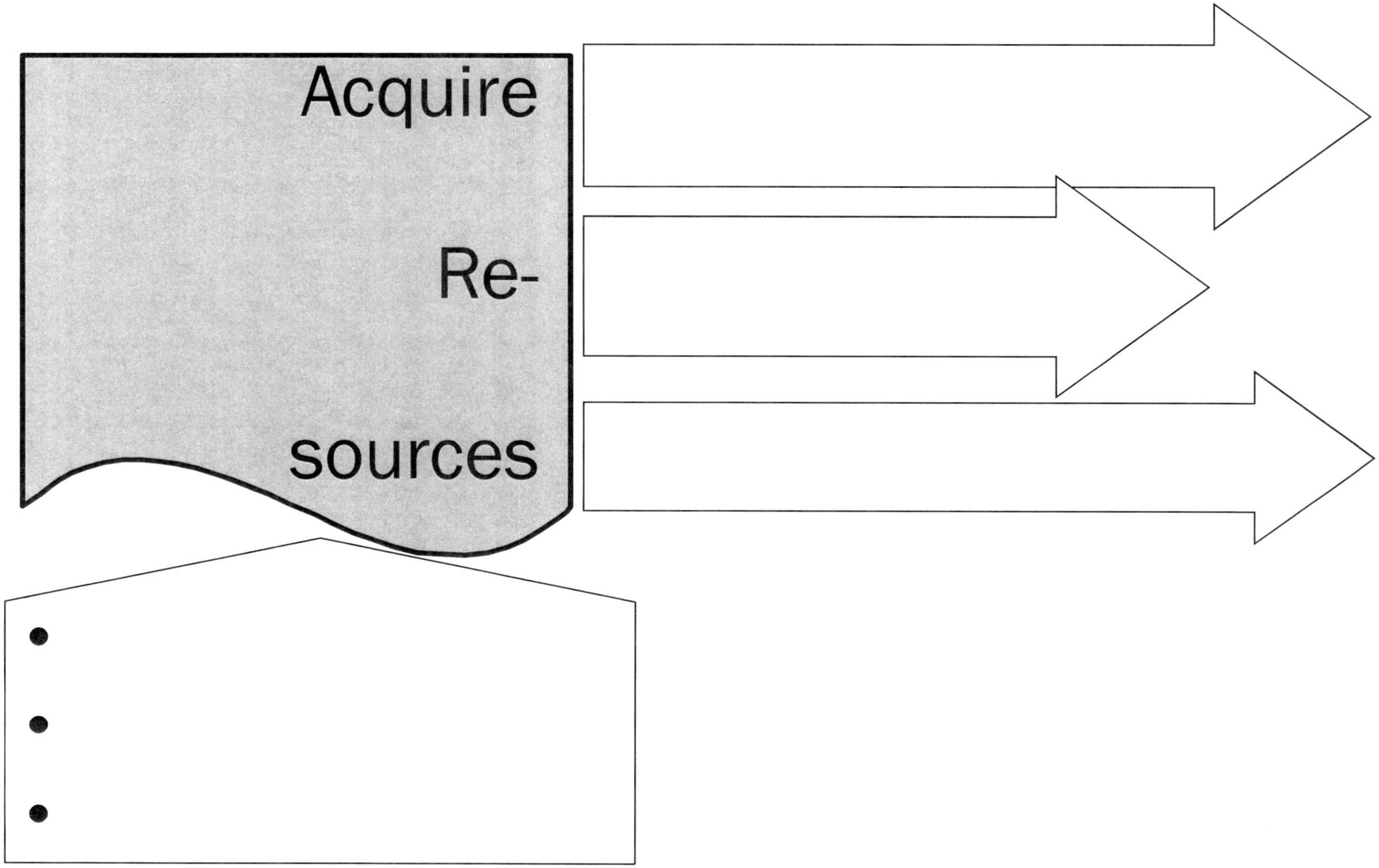
Acquire
Re-
sources

© 2018 Velociteach. All rights reserved.

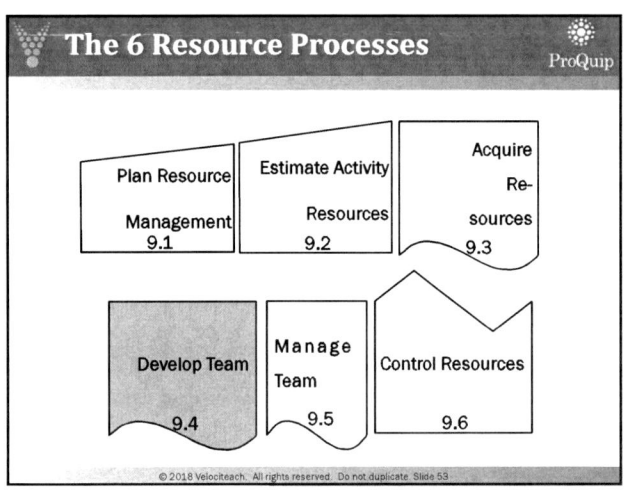

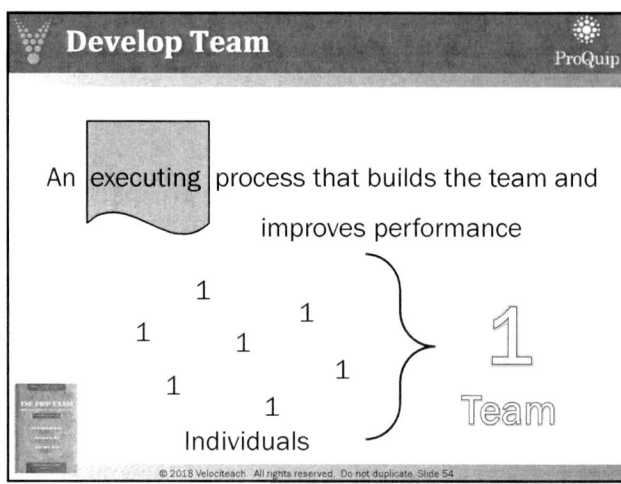

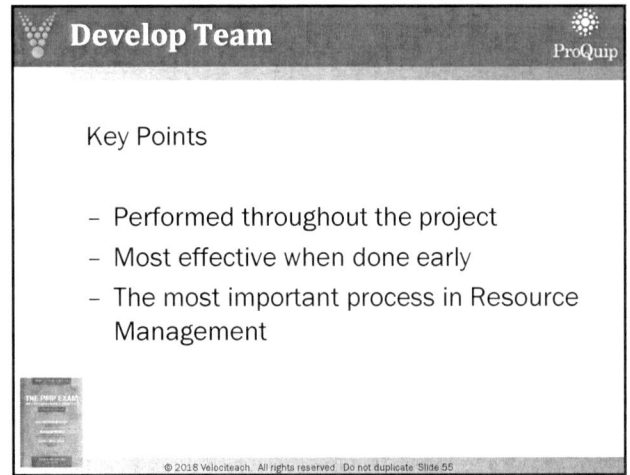

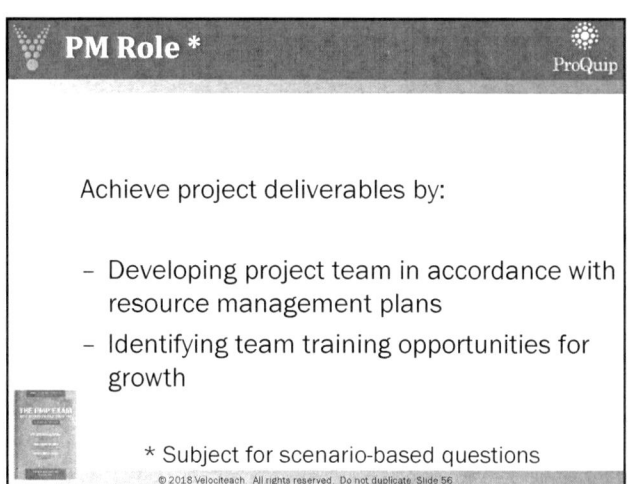

©2018 Velociteach. All rights reserved.   Page 228

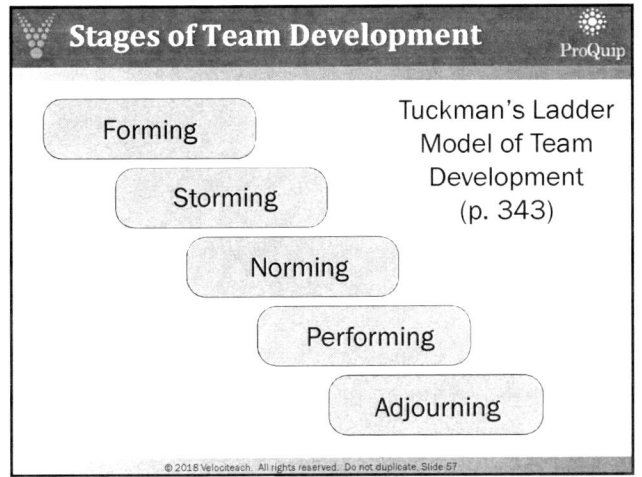

Stages of Team Development

Forming
Storming
Norming
Performing
Adjourning

Tuckman's Ladder Model of Team Development (p. 343)

© 2018 Velociteach. All rights reserved. Do not duplicate. Slide 57

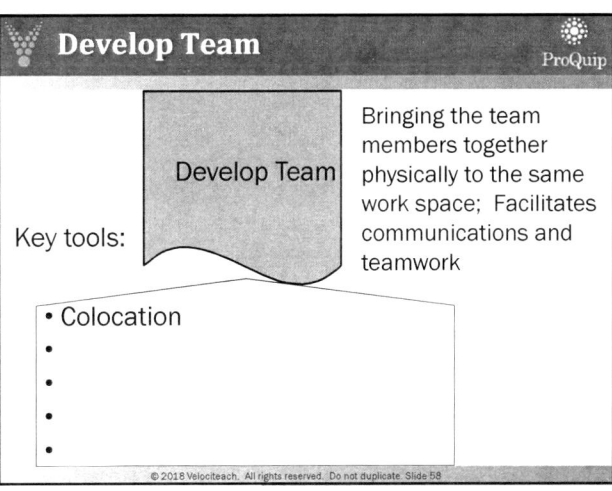

Develop Team

Develop Team

Key tools:

Bringing the team members together physically to the same work space; Facilitates communications and teamwork

• Colocation
•
•
•
•

© 2018 Velociteach. All rights reserved. Do not duplicate. Slide 58

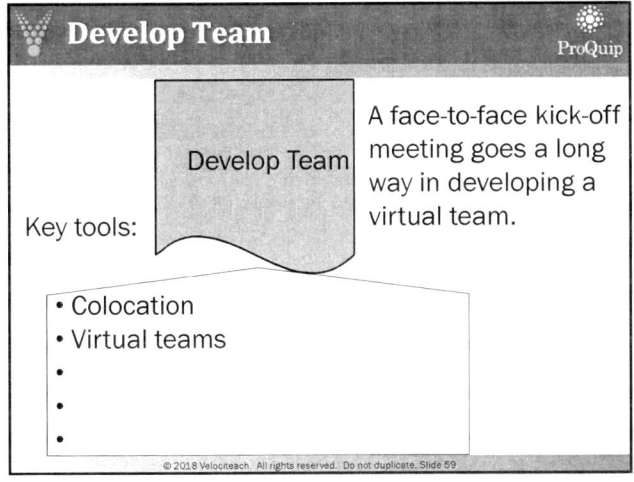

Develop Team

Develop Team

Key tools:

A face-to-face kick-off meeting goes a long way in developing a virtual team.

• Colocation
• Virtual teams
•
•
•

© 2018 Velociteach. All rights reserved. Do not duplicate. Slide 59

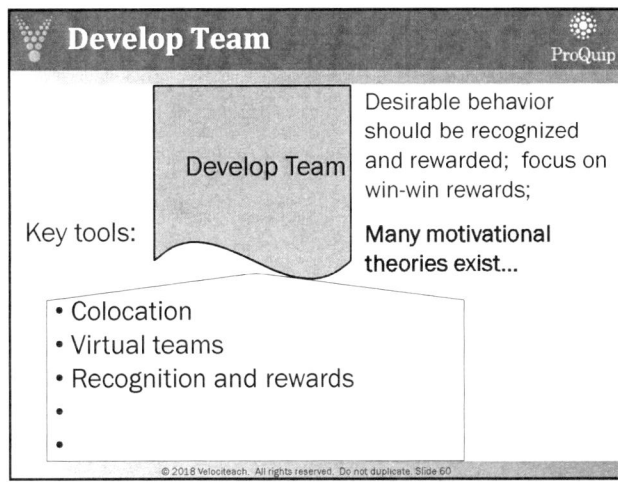

Develop Team

Develop Team

Key tools:

Desirable behavior should be recognized and rewarded; focus on win-win rewards;

Many motivational theories exist...

• Colocation
• Virtual teams
• Recognition and rewards
•
•

© 2018 Velociteach. All rights reserved. Do not duplicate. Slide 60

©2018 Velociteach. All rights reserved.

Maslow's Hierarchy of Needs

The theory that someone cannot live or work at his full potential until his lower and more basic needs are met

Maslow's Hierarchy is a perennial exam favorite.

Page 344

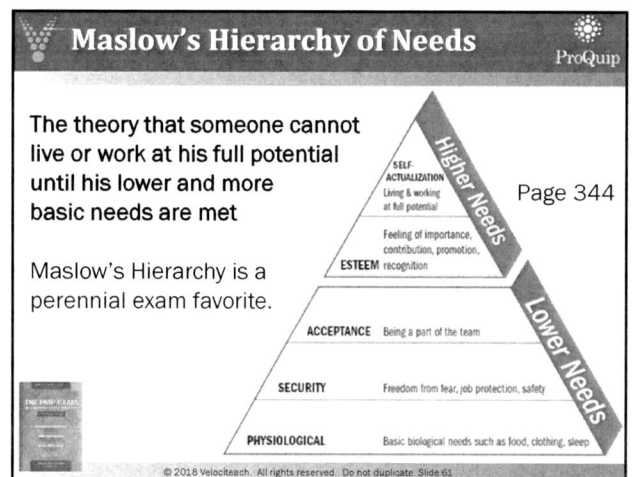

© 2018 Velociteach. All rights reserved. Do not duplicate. Slide 61

Expectancy Theory

A theory of motivation that states that a promise of a reward (or positive outcome) motivates performance;

It is only effective if it is believed that the outcome is achievable.

(Victor Vroom's theory)

© 2018 Velociteach. All rights reserved. Do not duplicate. Slide 62

McGregor's Theory X & Theory Y

There are two kinds of managers:

• **Theory X managers** assume workers are lazy and unmotivated. They believe in close supervision and micromanagement.

• **Theory Y managers** assume workers are intrinsically motivated and may be trusted to get the job done.

PMI does not advocate Theory Y over Theory X. Instead, different environments and individuals may call for one style or another.

© 2018 Velociteach. All rights reserved. Do not duplicate. Slide 63

Contingency Theory

A theory which states that the effectiveness of a leader's style is **contingent** upon the situation

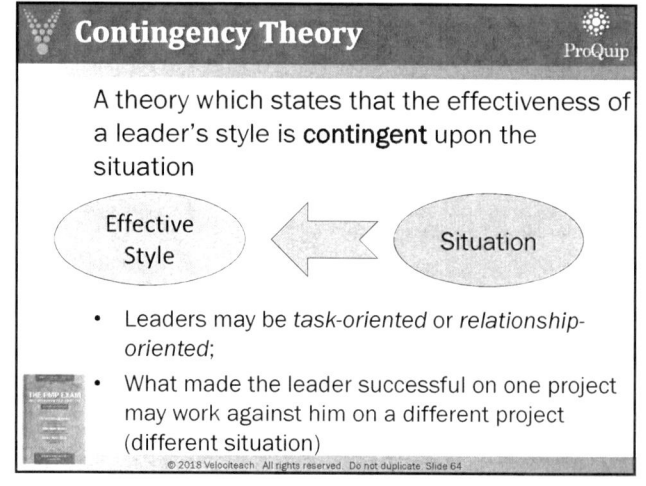

• Leaders may be *task-oriented* or *relationship-oriented*;
• What made the leader successful on one project may work against him on a different project (different situation)

© 2018 Velociteach. All rights reserved. Do not duplicate. Slide 64

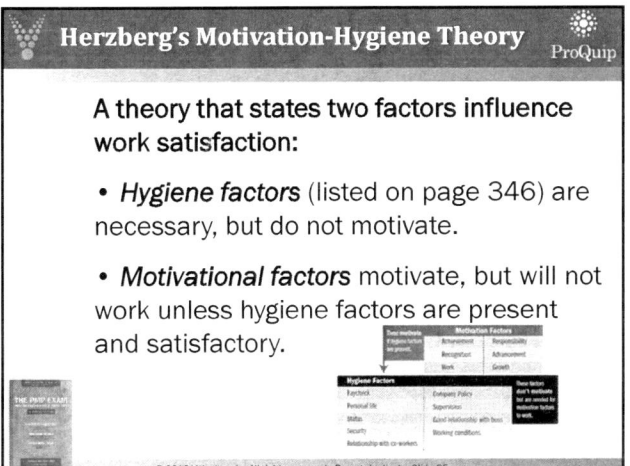

Herzberg's Motivation-Hygiene Theory — ProQuip

A theory that states two factors influence work satisfaction:

• *Hygiene factors* (listed on page 346) are necessary, but do not motivate.

• *Motivational factors* motivate, but will not work unless hygiene factors are present and satisfactory.

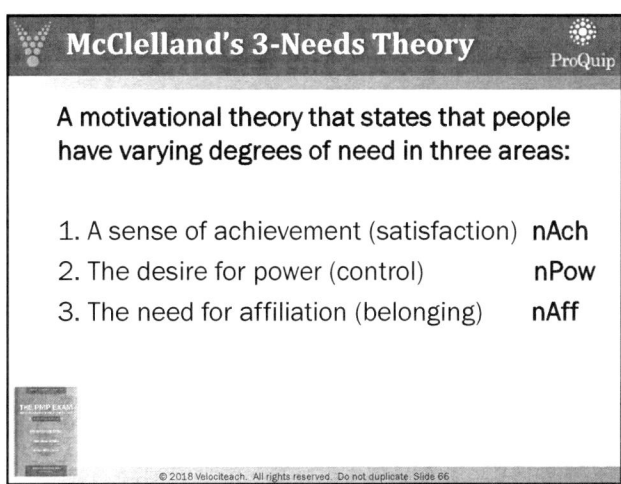

McClelland's 3-Needs Theory — ProQuip

A motivational theory that states that people have varying degrees of need in three areas:

1. A sense of achievement (satisfaction) nAch
2. The desire for power (control) nPow
3. The need for affiliation (belonging) nAff

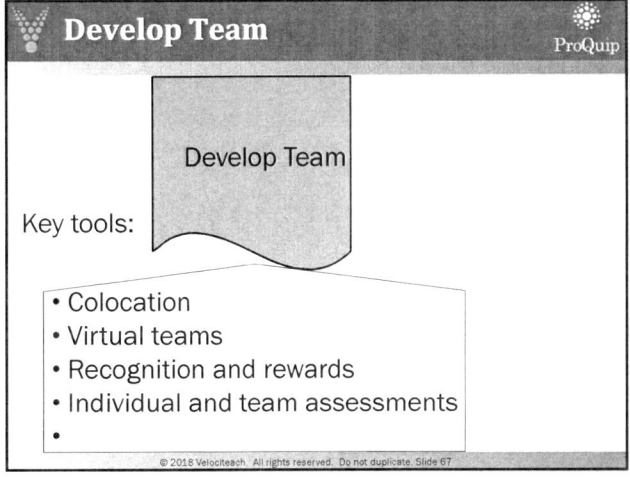

Develop Team — ProQuip

Develop Team

Key tools:

• Colocation
• Virtual teams
• Recognition and rewards
• Individual and team assessments
•

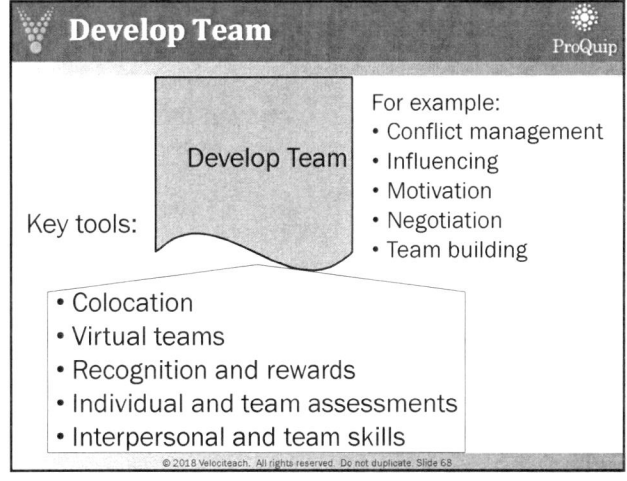

Develop Team — ProQuip

Develop Team

For example:
• Conflict management
• Influencing
• Motivation
• Negotiation
• Team building

Key tools:

• Colocation
• Virtual teams
• Recognition and rewards
• Individual and team assessments
• Interpersonal and team skills

©2018 Velociteach. All rights reserved.   Page 231

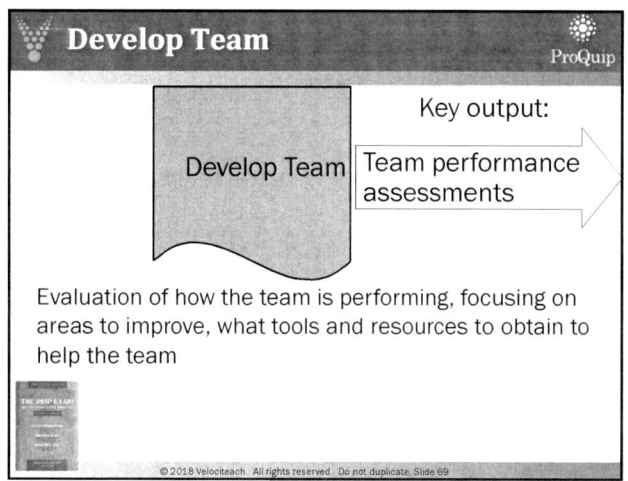

Develop Team

Develop Team

Key output:

Team performance assessments

Evaluation of how the team is performing, focusing on areas to improve, what tools and resources to obtain to help the team

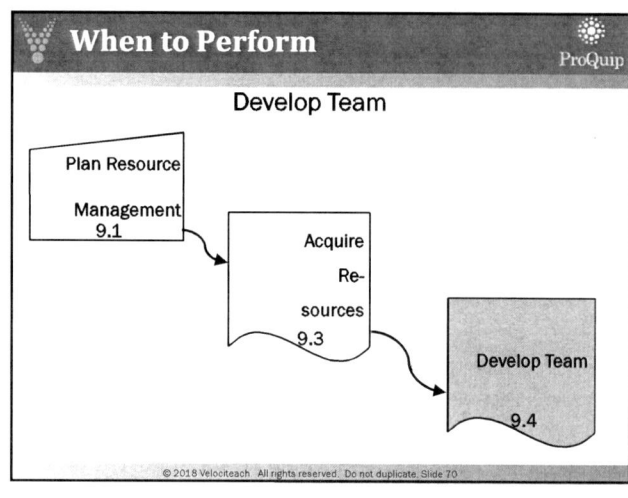

When to Perform

Develop Team

Plan Resource Management 9.1

Acquire Re-sources 9.3

Develop Team 9.4

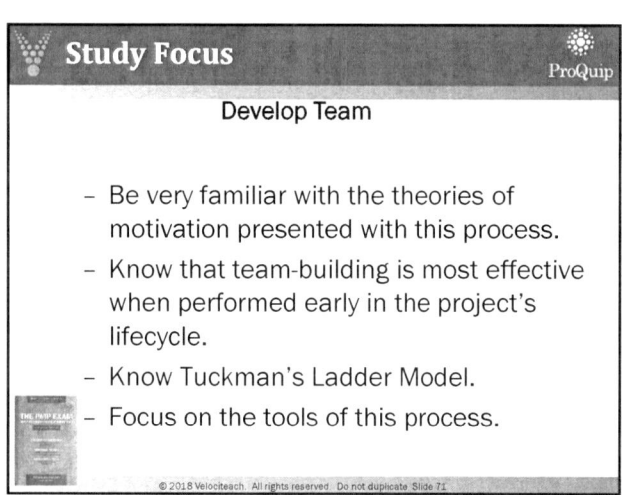

Study Focus

Develop Team

- Be very familiar with the theories of motivation presented with this process.
- Know that team-building is most effective when performed early in the project's lifecycle.
- Know Tuckman's Ladder Model.
- Focus on the tools of this process.

ProQuip

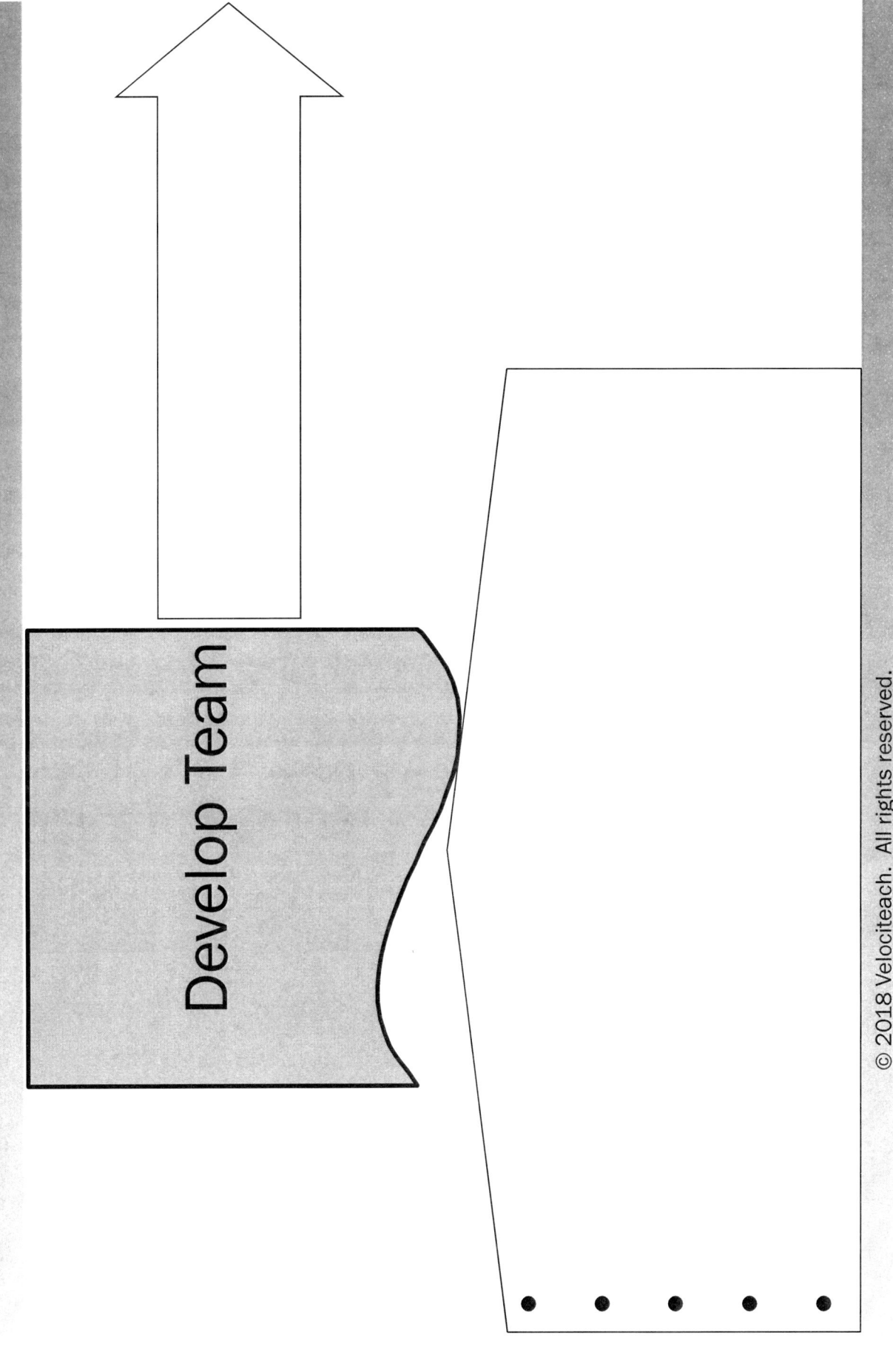

Develop Team

© 2018 Velociteach. All rights reserved.

This page left intentionally blank.

©2018 Velociteach. All rights reserved.

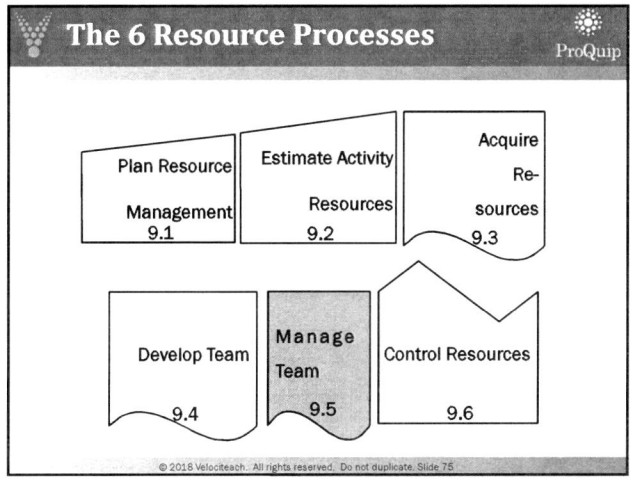

An executing process that makes sure the team is performing according to the plan.

Focuses on project performance by team

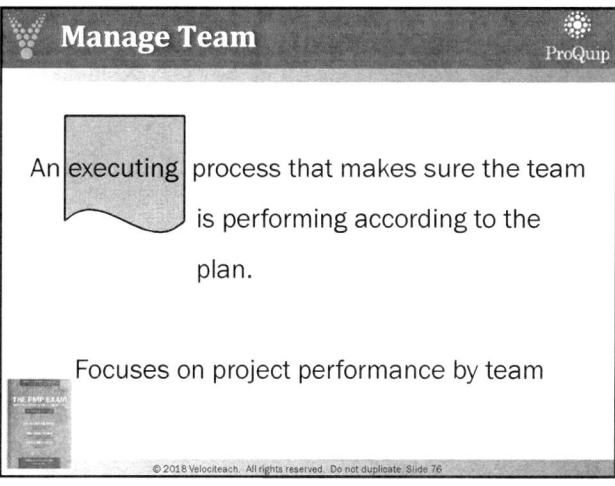

Key Points
- This process is all about comparing the team's results with the planned assignments.
- It is performed throughout the life of the project.
- The goal is to optimize team performance toward project goals by managing according to the plan.

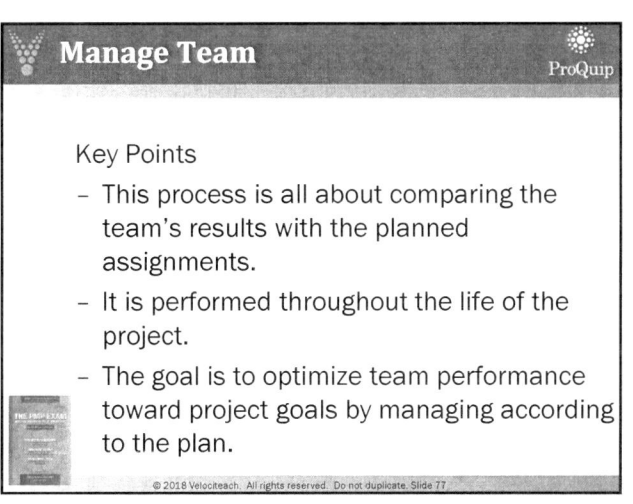

Achieve project deliverables by:
- Leading and managing resources in task execution
- Ensuring quality
- Leading implementation of approved changes and corrective actions
- Responding to risks
- Managing the information flow
  * Subject for scenario-based questions

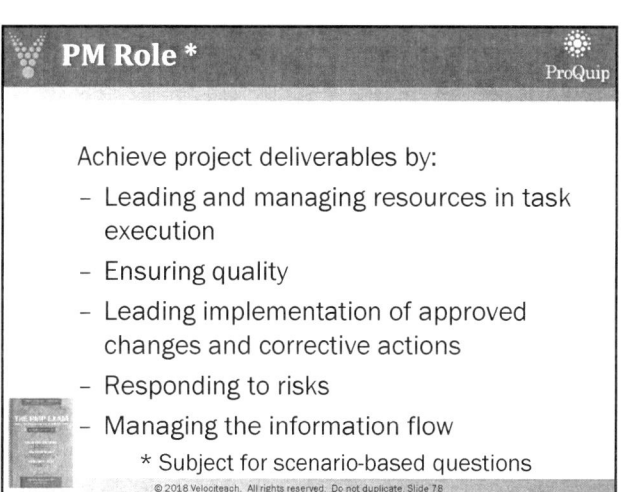

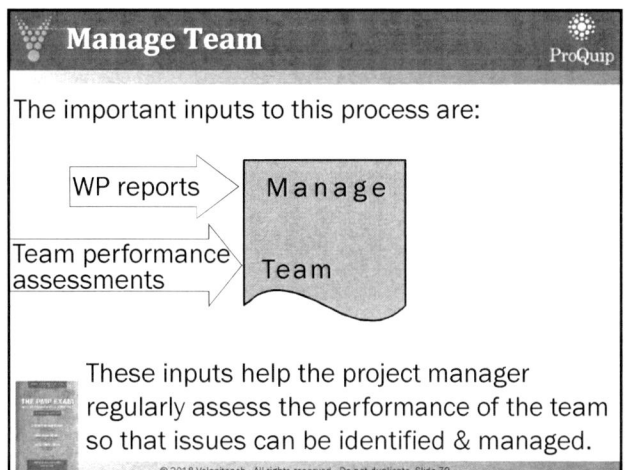

Manage Team

The important inputs to this process are:

WP reports → **Manage Team**

Team performance assessments →

These inputs help the project manager regularly assess the performance of the team so that issues can be identified & managed.

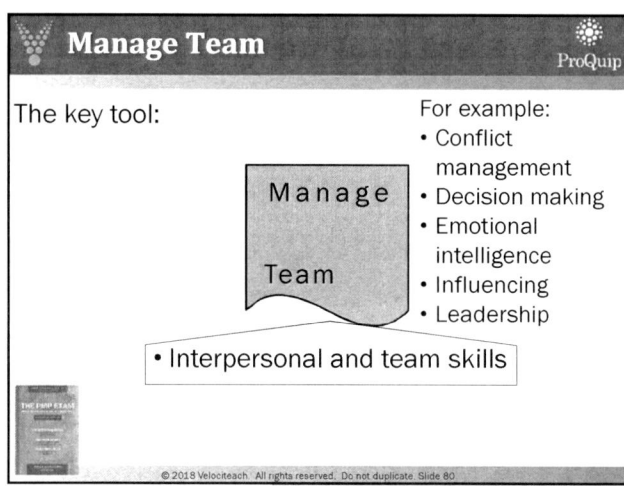

Manage Team

The key tool:

Manage Team

• Interpersonal and team skills

For example:
• Conflict management
• Decision making
• Emotional intelligence
• Influencing
• Leadership

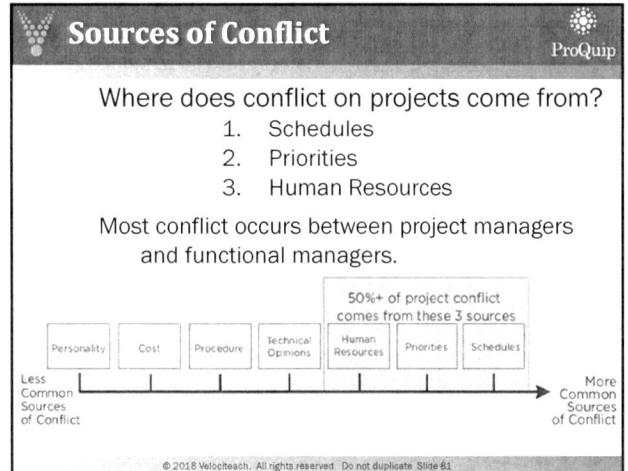

Sources of Conflict

Where does conflict on projects come from?
1. Schedules
2. Priorities
3. Human Resources

Most conflict occurs between project managers and functional managers.

50%+ of project conflict comes from these 3 sources

| Personality | Cost | Procedure | Technical Opinions | Human Resources | Priorities | Schedules |

Less Common Sources of Conflict → More Common Sources of Conflict

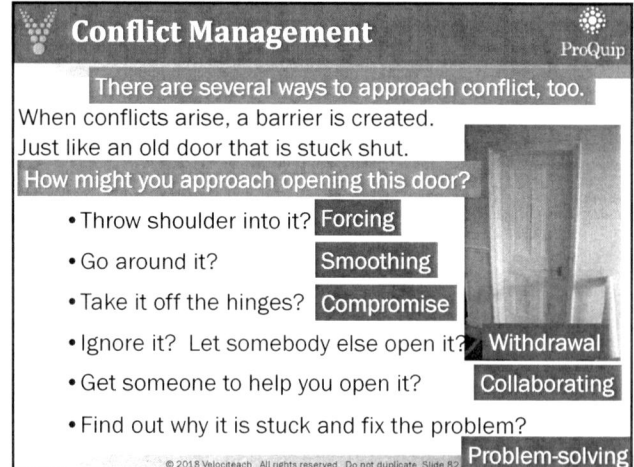

Conflict Management

There are several ways to approach conflict, too.
When conflicts arise, a barrier is created.
Just like an old door that is stuck shut.
How might you approach opening this door?

• Throw shoulder into it? **Forcing**
• Go around it? **Smoothing**
• Take it off the hinges? **Compromise**
• Ignore it? Let somebody else open it? **Withdrawal**
• Get someone to help you open it? **Collaborating**
• Find out why it is stuck and fix the problem?
Problem-solving

©2018 Velociteach. All rights reserved. Page 236

Conflict Management

ProQuip

Problem-solving	Confront problem head-on, resolve root cause
Compromise	Mutual sacrifice to achieve result
Forcing	Bring to bear whatever power necessary
Smoothing	Downplay problem; focus on what's going well
Withdrawal	Avoid or remove yourself from the situation
Collaborating	Seek viewpoints, consensus, and commitment

© 2018 Velociteach. All rights reserved. Do not duplicate. Slide 84

Team Roles   Page 353

ProQuip

The PM should recognize and deal with roles on the team related to conflict management:

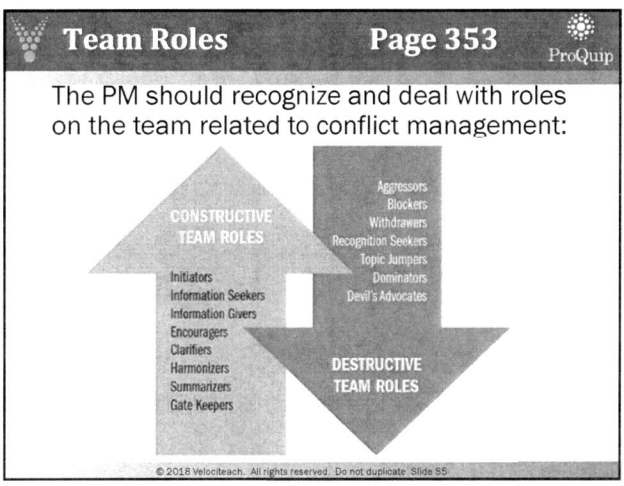

© 2018 Velociteach. All rights reserved. Do not duplicate. Slide 85

Emotional Intelligence

ProQuip

The PM needs a strong ability to relate and to negotiate.   ("EI" or "EQ"- Emotional Quotient)

Combination of:
- Self-awareness
    - o Knowing own strengths and weaknesses
- Social-awareness
    - o Aware of how one is perceived by others;
    - o Tailoring behavior as needed
- Gauging the mood and emotions of others

© 2018 Velociteach. All rights reserved. Do not duplicate. Slide 86

Influencing – Forms of Power

ProQuip

Reward
- Ability to provide money, time off, promotions   **Most effective**

Expert
- You know more about this than anyone else

Legitimate (formal authority)
- You are the boss   **Pages 347-348**

Referent   (2 perspectives)
- Based on who you are associated with
- OR... Respect, personal magnetism, or charisma – based on how liked you are

Punishment   (coercive)   **Least effective**
- Ability to fire, demote, or generally punish

© 2018 Velociteach. All rights reserved. Do not duplicate. Slide 87

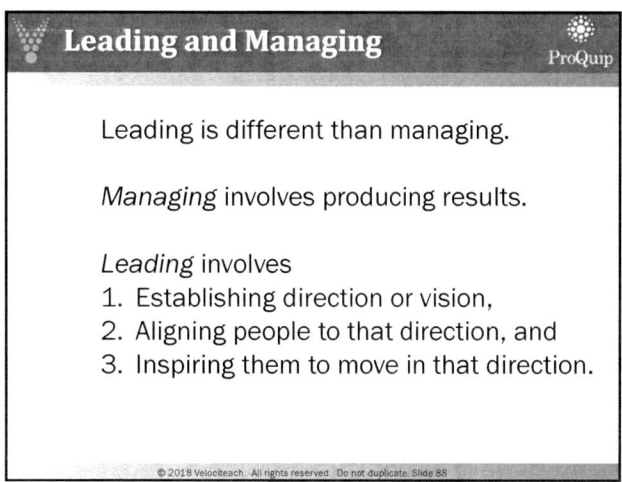

Leading and Managing

Leading is different than managing.

Managing involves producing results.

Leading involves
1. Establishing direction or vision,
2. Aligning people to that direction, and
3. Inspiring them to move in that direction.

© 2018 Velociteach. All rights reserved. Do not duplicate. Slide 88

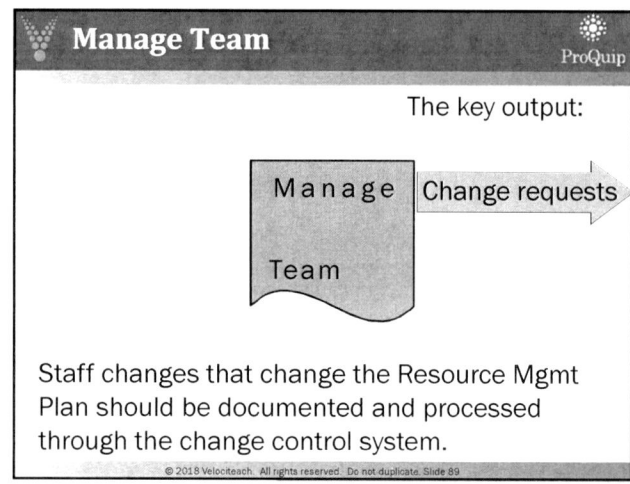

Manage Team

The key output:

Manage Team → Change requests

Staff changes that change the Resource Mgmt Plan should be documented and processed through the change control system.

© 2018 Velociteach. All rights reserved. Do not duplicate. Slide 89

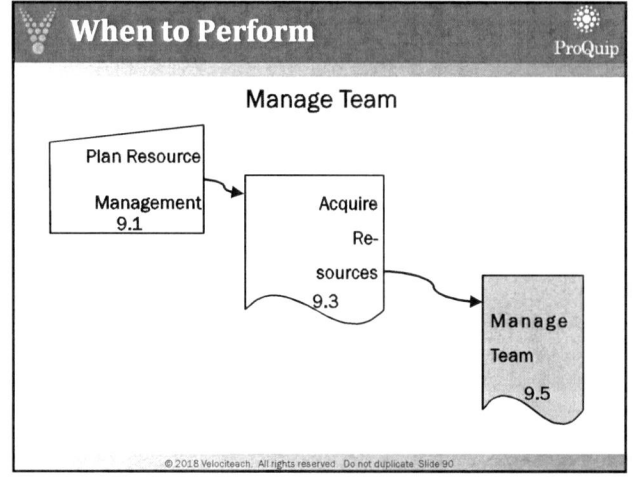

When to Perform

Manage Team

Plan Resource Management 9.1 → Acquire Resources 9.3 → Manage Team 9.5

© 2018 Velociteach. All rights reserved. Do not duplicate. Slide 90

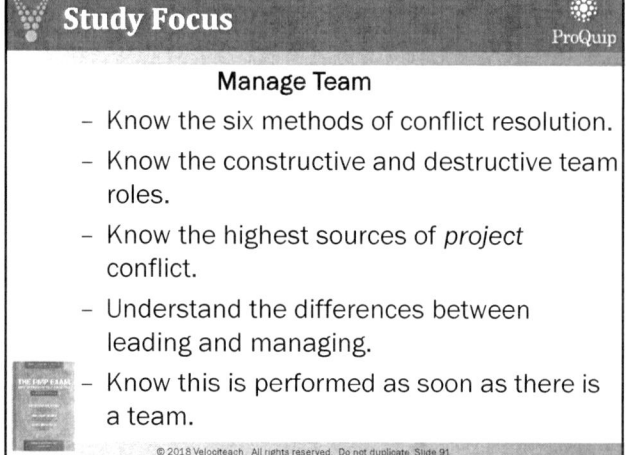

Study Focus

Manage Team
- Know the six methods of conflict resolution.
- Know the constructive and destructive team roles.
- Know the highest sources of *project* conflict.
- Understand the differences between leading and managing.
- Know this is performed as soon as there is a team.

© 2018 Velociteach. All rights reserved. Do not duplicate. Slide 91

ProQuip

Manage Team

© 2018 Velociteach. All rights reserved.

The 6 Resource Processes

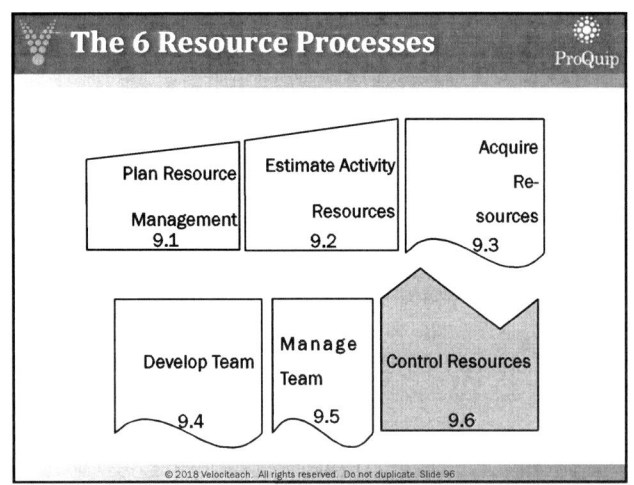

Plan Resource Management 9.1

Estimate Activity Resources 9.2

Acquire Resources 9.3

Develop Team 9.4

Manage Team 9.5

Control Resources 9.6

© 2018 Velociteach. All rights reserved. Do not duplicate. Slide 96

Control Resources

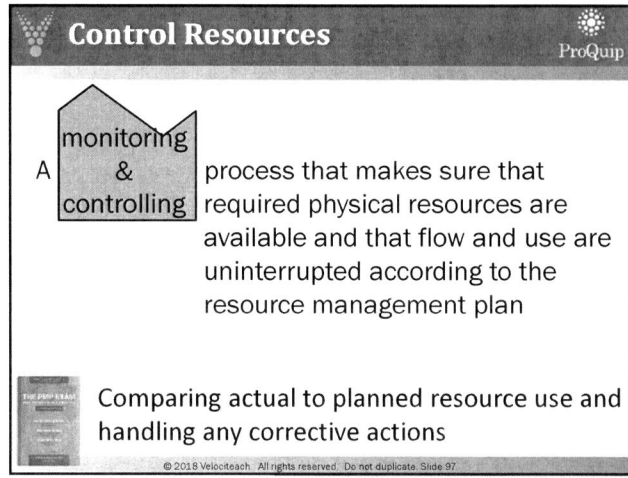

A [monitoring & controlling] process that makes sure that required physical resources are available and that flow and use are uninterrupted according to the resource management plan

Comparing actual to planned resource use and handling any corrective actions

© 2018 Velociteach. All rights reserved. Do not duplicate. Slide 97

Control Resources

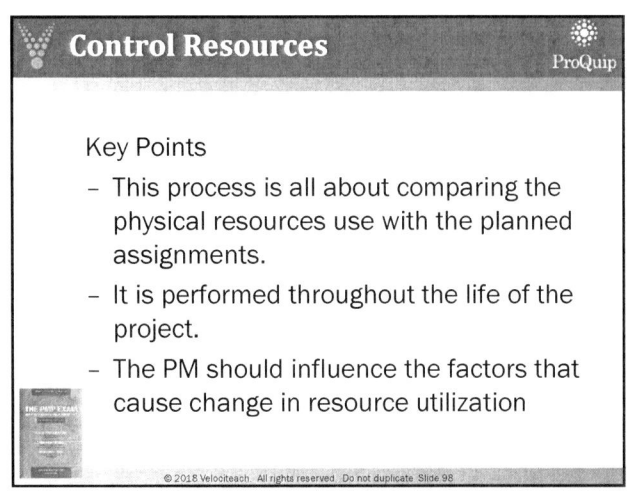

Key Points
- This process is all about comparing the physical resources use with the planned assignments.
- It is performed throughout the life of the project.
- The PM should influence the factors that cause change in resource utilization

© 2018 Velociteach. All rights reserved. Do not duplicate. Slide 98

PM Role *

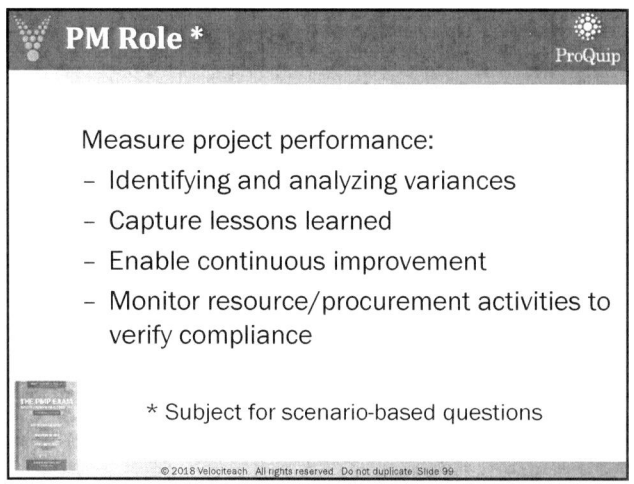

Measure project performance:
- Identifying and analyzing variances
- Capture lessons learned
- Enable continuous improvement
- Monitor resource/procurement activities to verify compliance

* Subject for scenario-based questions

© 2018 Velociteach. All rights reserved. Do not duplicate. Slide 99

©2018 Velociteach. All rights reserved.   Page 240

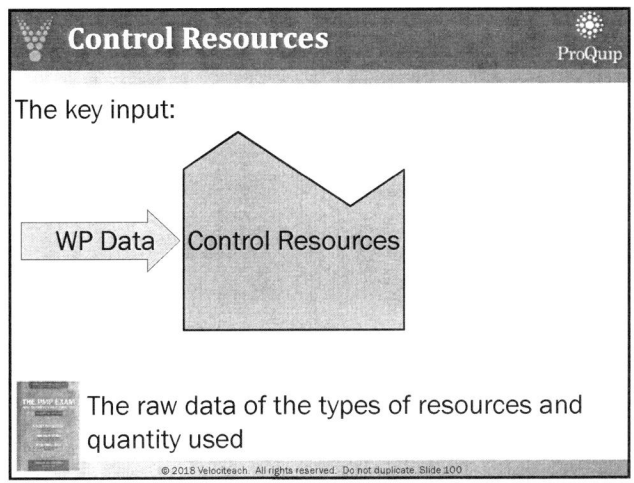

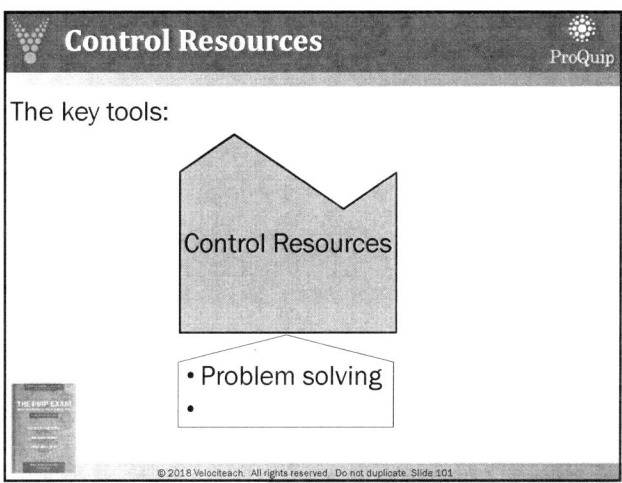

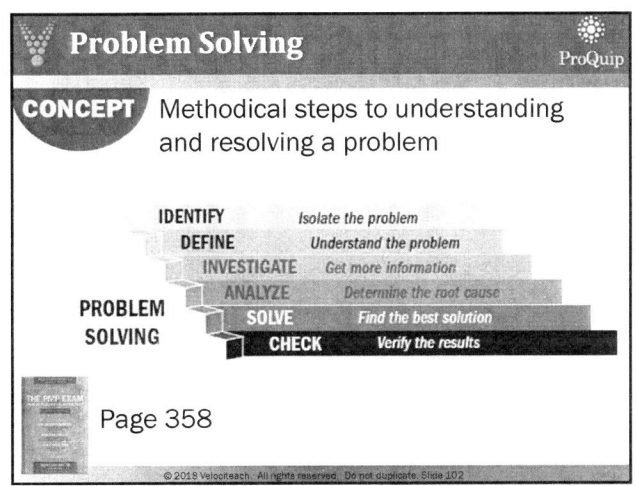

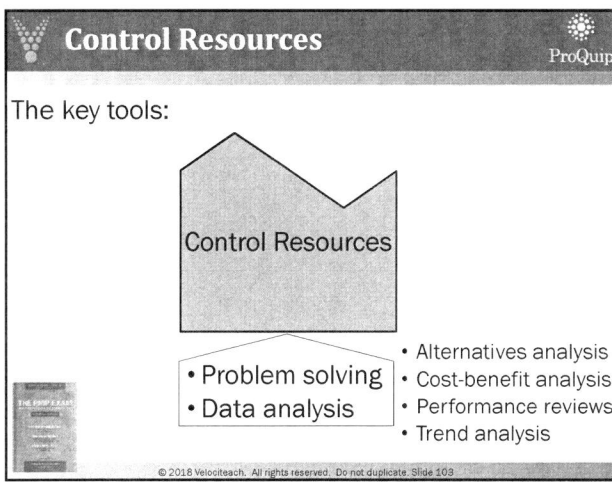

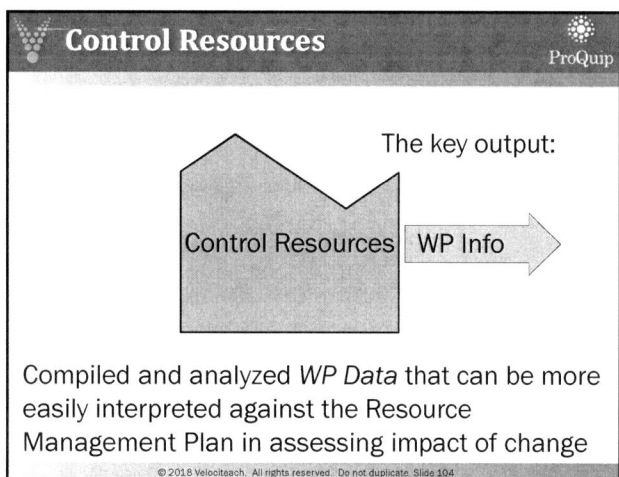

Control Resources

The key output:

Control Resources → WP Info

Compiled and analyzed *WP Data* that can be more easily interpreted against the Resource Management Plan in assessing impact of change

© 2018 Velociteach. All rights reserved. Do not duplicate Slide 104

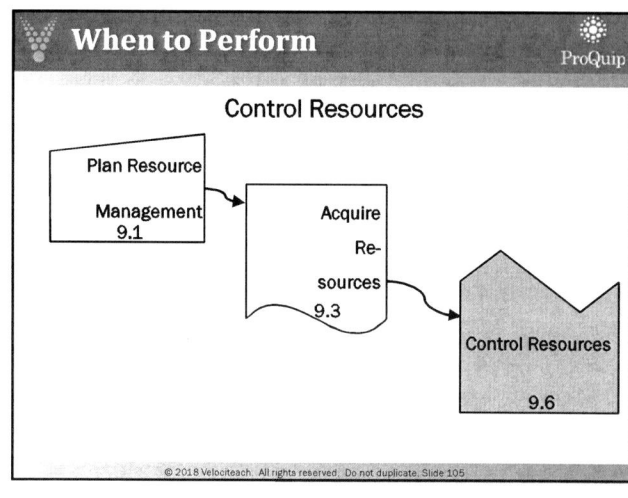

When to Perform

Control Resources

Plan Resource Management 9.1 → Acquire Re-sources 9.3 → Control Resources 9.6

© 2018 Velociteach. All rights reserved. Do not duplicate Slide 105

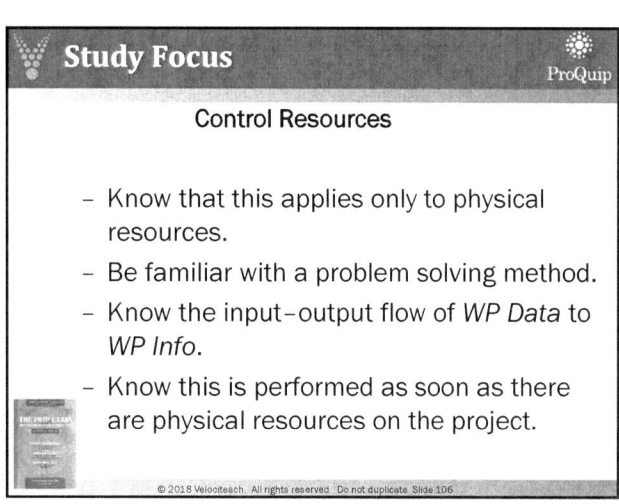

Study Focus

Control Resources

- Know that this applies only to physical resources.
- Be familiar with a problem solving method.
- Know the input–output flow of *WP Data* to *WP Info*.
- Know this is performed as soon as there are physical resources on the project.

© 2018 Velociteach. All rights reserved. Do not duplicate Slide 106

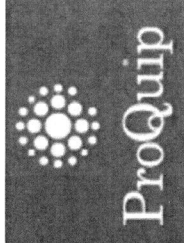

Review the ITTOs

ProQuip

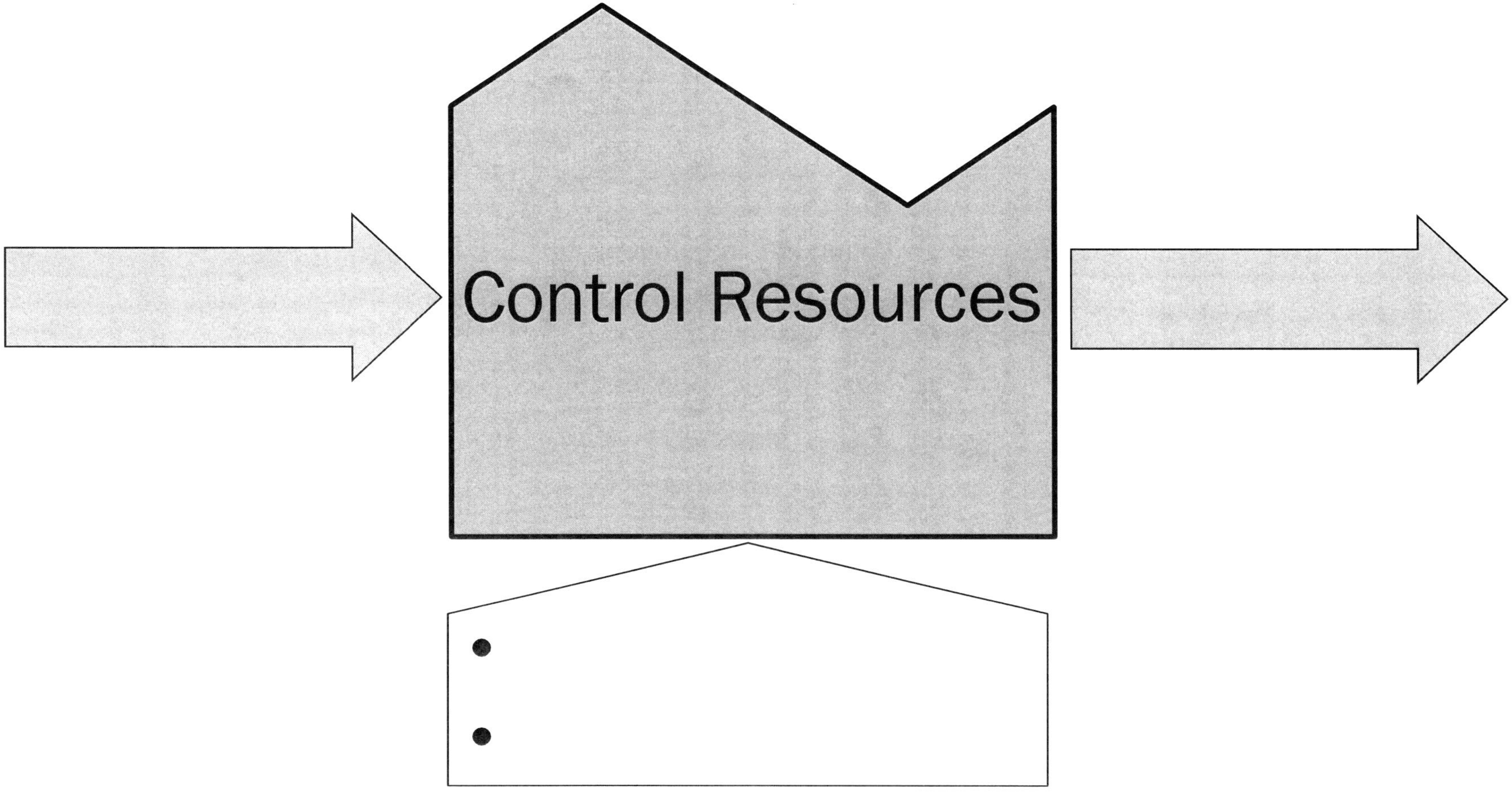
Control Resources

© 2018 Velociteach. All rights reserved.

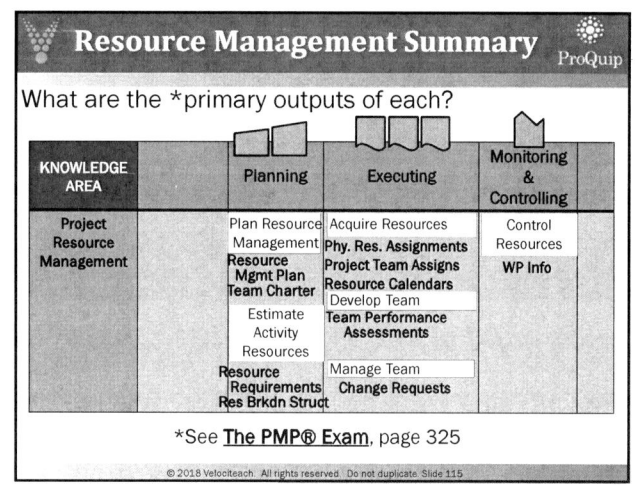

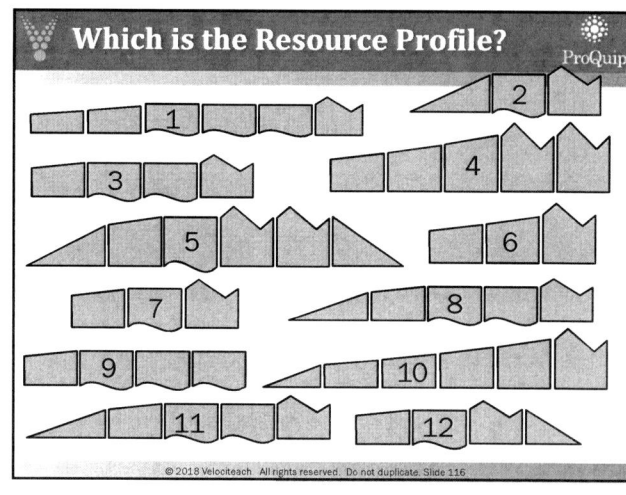

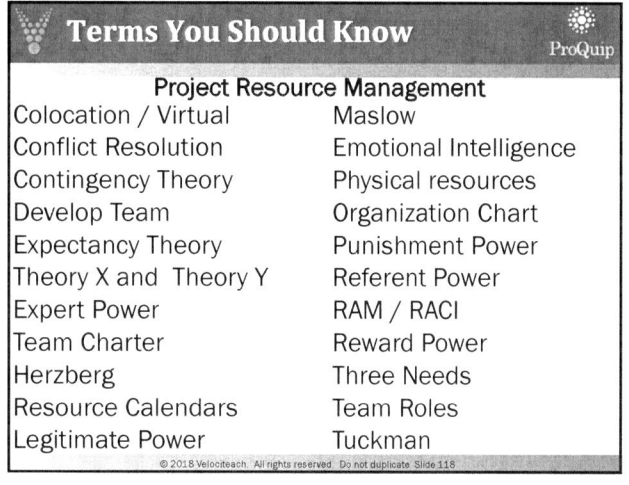

Terms You Should Know

Project Resource Management

Colocation / Virtual	Maslow
Conflict Resolution	Emotional Intelligence
Contingency Theory	Physical resources
Develop Team	Organization Chart
Expectancy Theory	Punishment Power
Theory X and Theory Y	Referent Power
Expert Power	RAM / RACI
Team Charter	Reward Power
Herzberg	Three Needs
Resource Calendars	Team Roles
Legitimate Power	Tuckman

© 2018 Velociteach. All rights reserved. Do not duplicate. Slide 118

Resource Mgmt Discussion

Explain the differences between the Resource Mgmt Plan and Team Charter.

What are two important considerations when using virtual teams and why are they important?

What differences exist between Maslow's and Herzberg's motivational theories?

Discuss the basic three-step leadership formula and how leading differs from managing.

Describe an approach to problem solving.

© 2018 Velociteach. All rights reserved. Do not duplicate. Slide 119

©2018 Velociteach. All rights reserved. Page 244

Summary

ProQuip

Knowledge Area

KNOWLEDGE AREA	Initiating	Planning	Executing	Monitoring and Controlling	Closing
Project Management					

©2018 Velociteach. All rights reserved. Page 245

This page left intentionally blank.

©2018 Velociteach. All rights reserved.

- **Mark one answer: A, B, C, or D.**
- **Circle the '?' symbol if you are guessing at the answer.**
- **Circle the Δ symbol if you change your answer.**

Total Correct: _____

% Correct: _____%

1.	A O	B O	C O	D O	? Δ
2.	A O	B O	C O	D O	? Δ
3.	A O	B O	C O	D O	? Δ
4.	A O	B O	C O	D O	? Δ
5.	A O	B O	C O	D O	? Δ
6.	A O	B O	C O	D O	? Δ
7.	A O	B O	C O	D O	? Δ
8.	A O	B O	C O	D O	? Δ
9.	A O	B O	C O	D O	? Δ
10.	A O	B O	C O	D O	? Δ
11.	A O	B O	C O	D O	? Δ
12.	A O	B O	C O	D O	? Δ
13.	A O	B O	C O	D O	? Δ
14.	A O	B O	C O	D O	? Δ
15.	A O	B O	C O	D O	? Δ
16.	A O	B O	C O	D O	? Δ
17.	A O	B O	C O	D O	? Δ
18.	A O	B O	C O	D O	? Δ
19.	A O	B O	C O	D O	? Δ
20.	A O	B O	C O	D O	? Δ
21.	A O	B O	C O	D O	? Δ
22.	A O	B O	C O	D O	? Δ
23.	A O	B O	C O	D O	? Δ
24.	A O	B O	C O	D O	? Δ
25.	A O	B O	C O	D O	? Δ

**Project
Communications
Management**

Course Module 12

PMBOK® Guide Chapter 10
PMP® Exam Textbook Chapter 10

© 2018 Velociteach. All rights reserved. Do not duplicate. Slide 1

Communications Management

What does this knowledge area involve?
- Analyzing the communication requirements
- Planning project communications
- Distributing the information to the stakeholders
- Informing stakeholders of the project's performance
- 90% of an effective project manager's time (50% spent communicating with the team)

© 2018 Velociteach. All rights reserved. Do not duplicate. Slide 2

Philosophy: Communications

- Distribute information proactively.

- Information should be thorough, accurate, and timely.

- Stakeholders should be kept informed throughout the life of the project.

© 2018 Velociteach. All rights reserved. Do not duplicate. Slide 3

---

3 Processes of Communications

KNOWLEDGE AREA	Initiating	Planning	Executing	Monitoring and Controlling	Closing
Project Communications Management		Plan Communications Management	Manage Communications	Monitor Communications	

© 2018 Velociteach. All rights reserved. Do not duplicate. Slide 4

©2018 Velociteach. All rights reserved.   Page 248

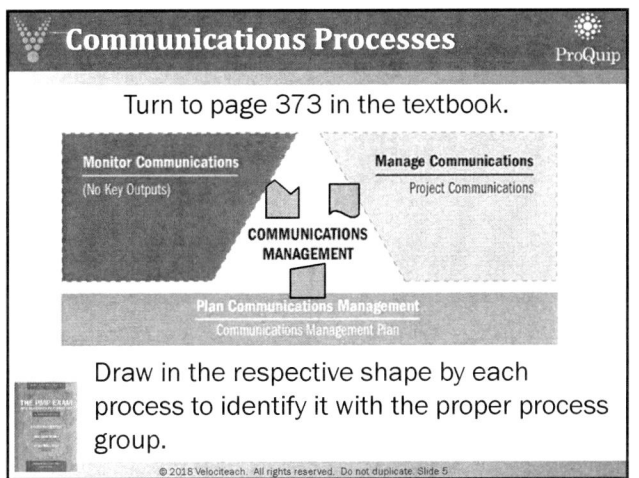

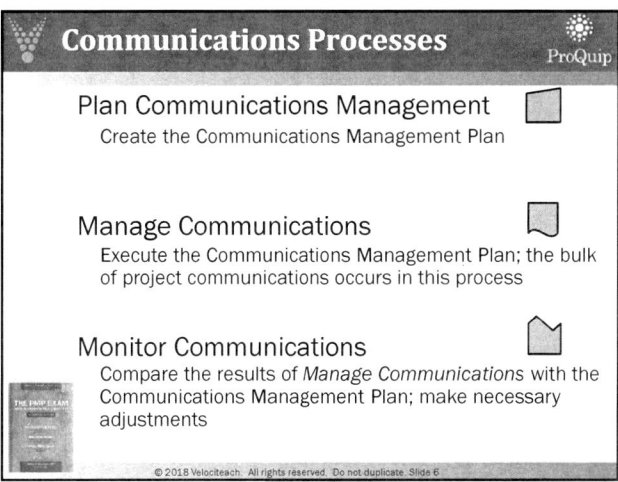

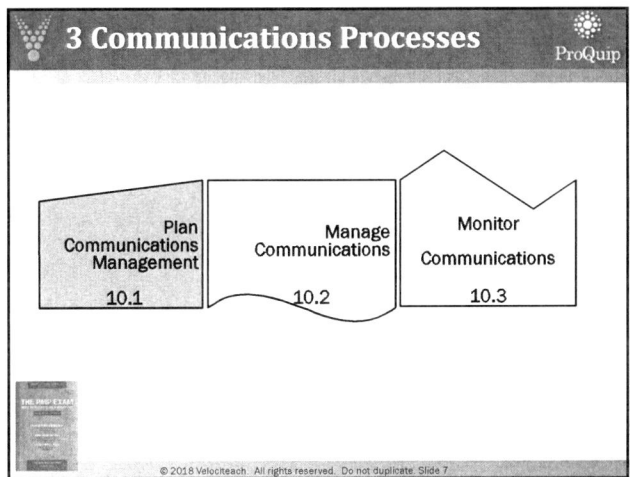

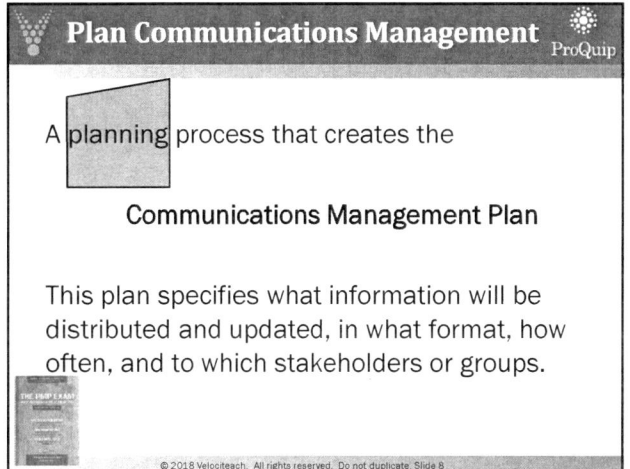

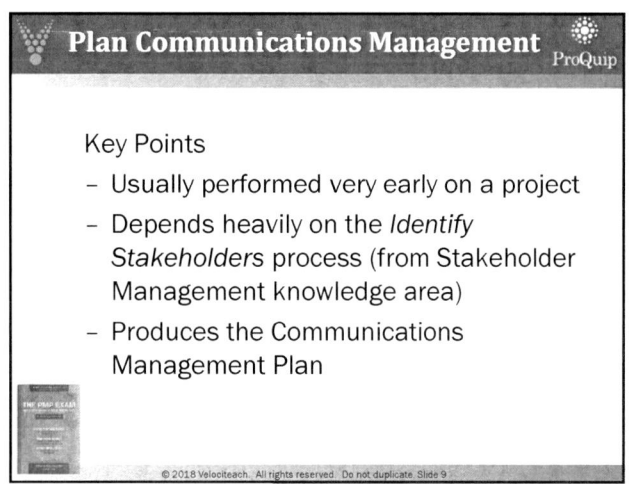

Plan Communications Management

Key Points

- Usually performed very early on a project
- Depends heavily on the *Identify Stakeholders* process (from Stakeholder Management knowledge area)
- Produces the Communications Management Plan

© 2018 Velociteach. All rights reserved. Do not duplicate. Slide 9

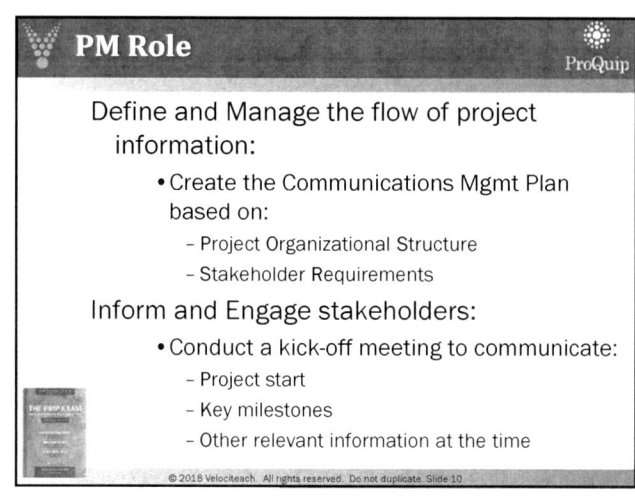

PM Role

Define and Manage the flow of project information:

- Create the Communications Mgmt Plan based on:
  - Project Organizational Structure
  - Stakeholder Requirements

Inform and Engage stakeholders:

- Conduct a kick-off meeting to communicate:
  - Project start
  - Key milestones
  - Other relevant information at the time

© 2018 Velociteach. All rights reserved. Do not duplicate. Slide 10

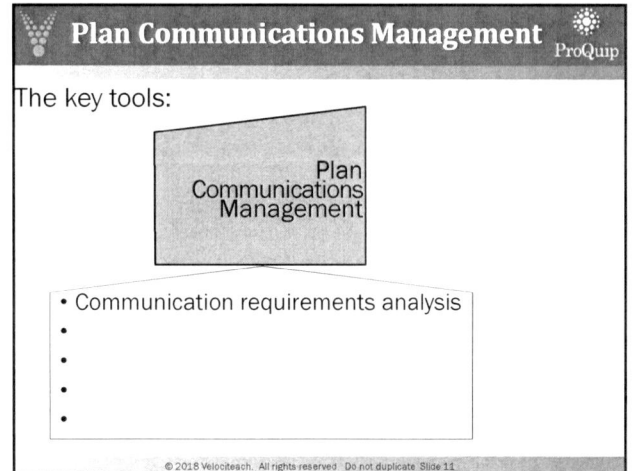

Plan Communications Management

The key tools:

Plan Communications Management

- Communication requirements analysis
-
-
-
-

© 2018 Velociteach. All rights reserved. Do not duplicate. Slide 11

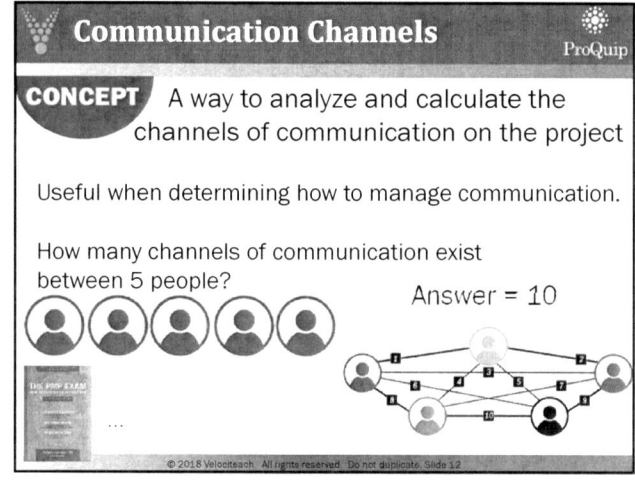

Communication Channels

CONCEPT A way to analyze and calculate the channels of communication on the project

Useful when determining how to manage communication.

How many channels of communication exist between 5 people?

Answer = 10

...

© 2018 Velociteach. All rights reserved. Do not duplicate. Slide 12

Communication Channels

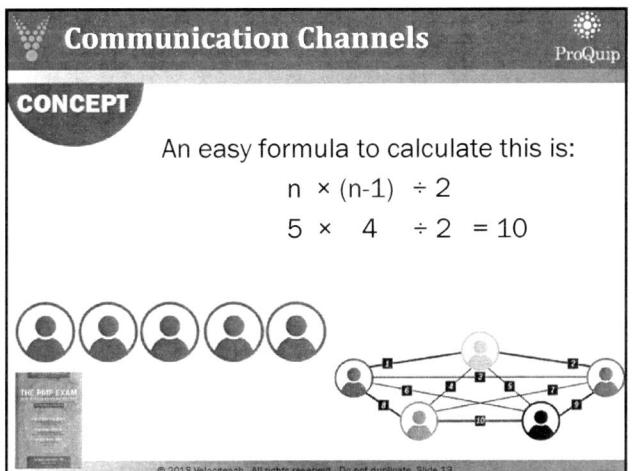

CONCEPT

An easy formula to calculate this is:

n × (n-1) ÷ 2

5 × 4 ÷ 2 = 10

© 2018 Velociteach. All rights reserved. Do not duplicate. Slide 13

Plan Communications Management

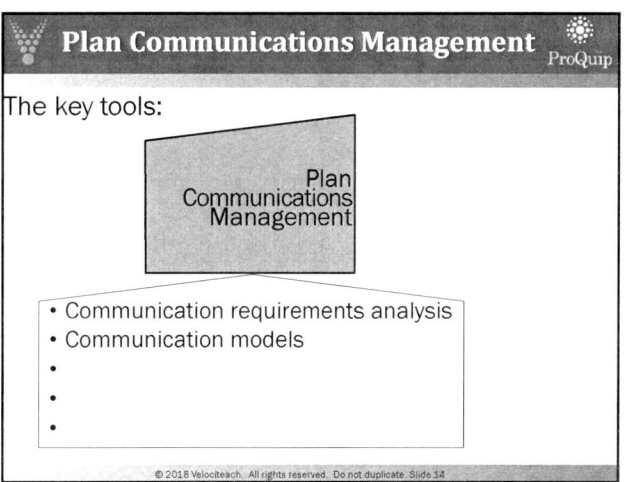

The key tools:

Plan Communications Management

- Communication requirements analysis
- Communication models
-
-
-

© 2018 Velociteach. All rights reserved. Do not duplicate. Slide 14

Communication Models (p. 380)

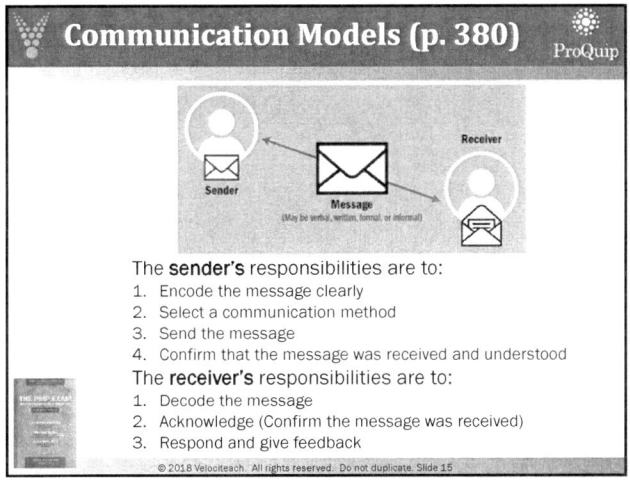

The **sender's** responsibilities are to:
1. Encode the message clearly
2. Select a communication method
3. Send the message
4. Confirm that the message was received and understood

The **receiver's** responsibilities are to:
1. Decode the message
2. Acknowledge (Confirm the message was received)
3. Respond and give feedback

© 2018 Velociteach. All rights reserved. Do not duplicate. Slide 15

Other Terms of Communicating

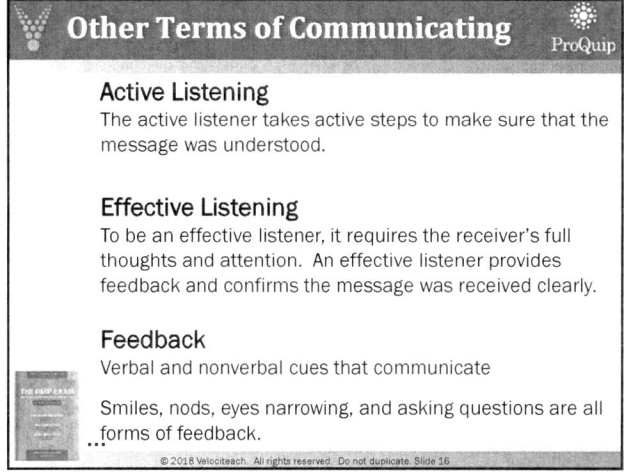

Active Listening
The active listener takes active steps to make sure that the message was understood.

Effective Listening
To be an effective listener, it requires the receiver's full thoughts and attention. An effective listener provides feedback and confirms the message was received clearly.

Feedback
Verbal and nonverbal cues that communicate

Smiles, nods, eyes narrowing, and asking questions are all forms of feedback.

© 2018 Velociteach. All rights reserved. Do not duplicate. Slide 16

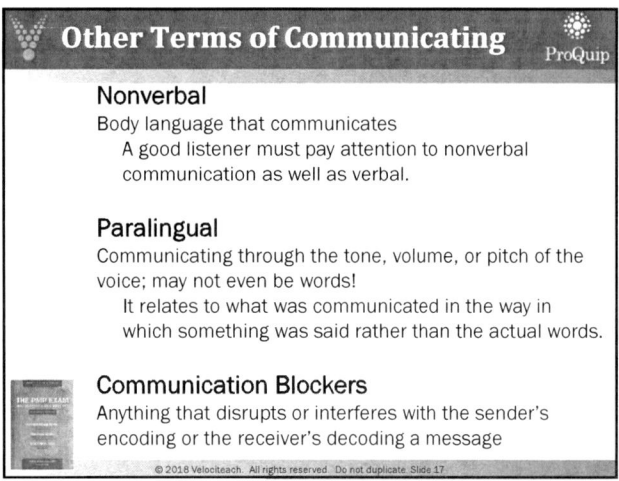

Other Terms of Communicating

Nonverbal
Body language that communicates
  A good listener must pay attention to nonverbal communication as well as verbal.

Paralingual
Communicating through the tone, volume, or pitch of the voice; may not even be words!
  It relates to what was communicated in the way in which something was said rather than the actual words.

Communication Blockers
Anything that disrupts or interferes with the sender's encoding or the receiver's decoding a message

© 2018 Velociteach. All rights reserved. Do not duplicate Slide 17

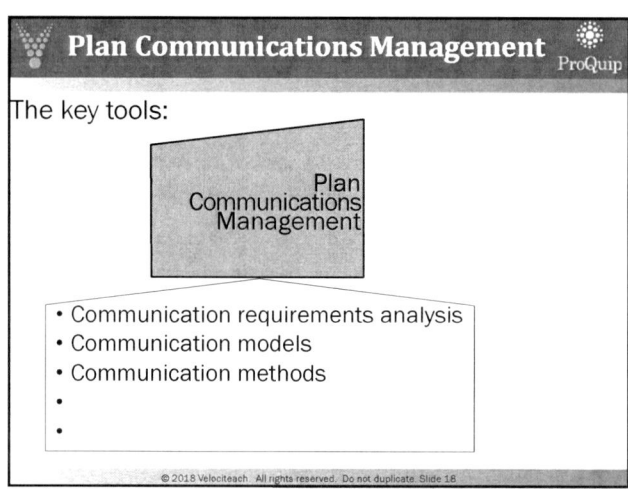

Plan Communications Management

The key tools:

Plan Communications Management

• Communication requirements analysis
• Communication models
• Communication methods
•
•

© 2018 Velociteach. All rights reserved. Do not duplicate Slide 18

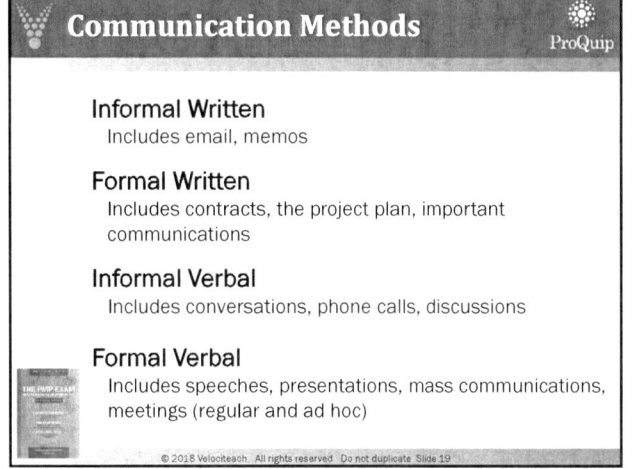

Communication Methods

Informal Written
  Includes email, memos

Formal Written
  Includes contracts, the project plan, important communications

Informal Verbal
  Includes conversations, phone calls, discussions

Formal Verbal
  Includes speeches, presentations, mass communications, meetings (regular and ad hoc)

© 2018 Velociteach. All rights reserved. Do not duplicate Slide 19

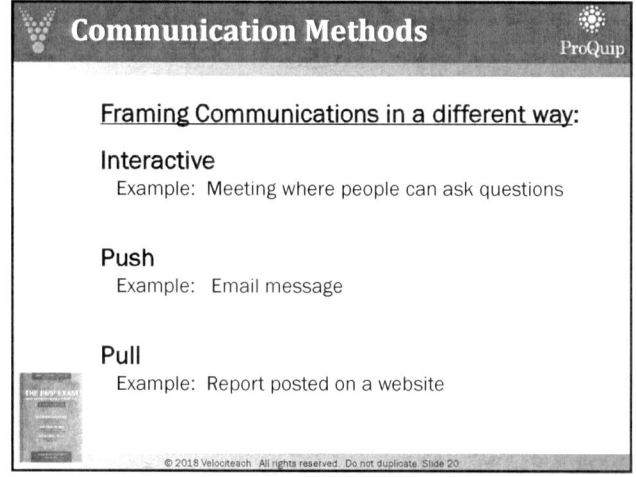

Communication Methods

<u>Framing Communications in a different way:</u>

Interactive
  Example: Meeting where people can ask questions

Push
  Example: Email message

Pull
  Example: Report posted on a website

© 2018 Velociteach. All rights reserved. Do not duplicate Slide 20

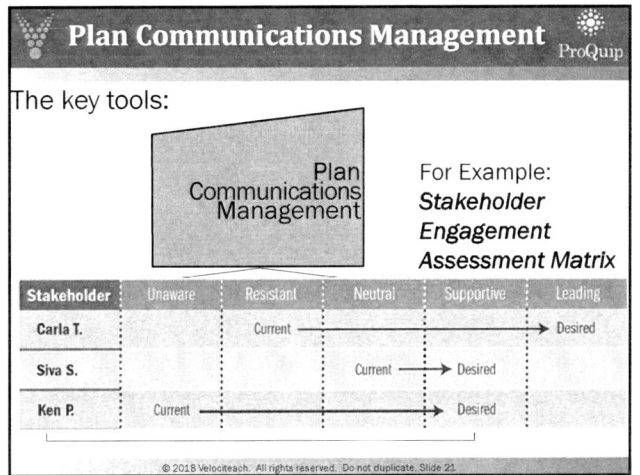

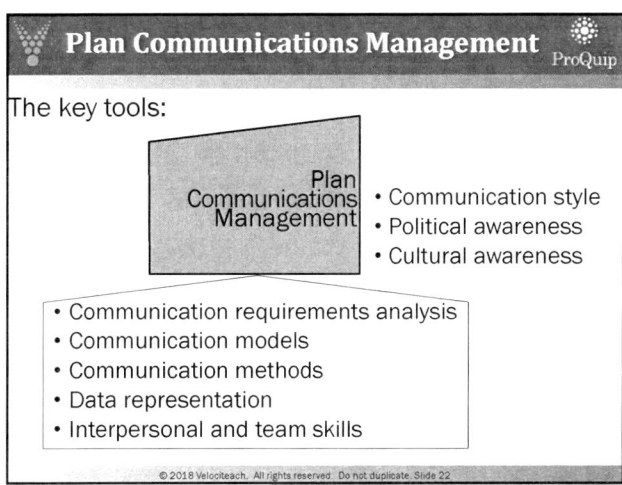

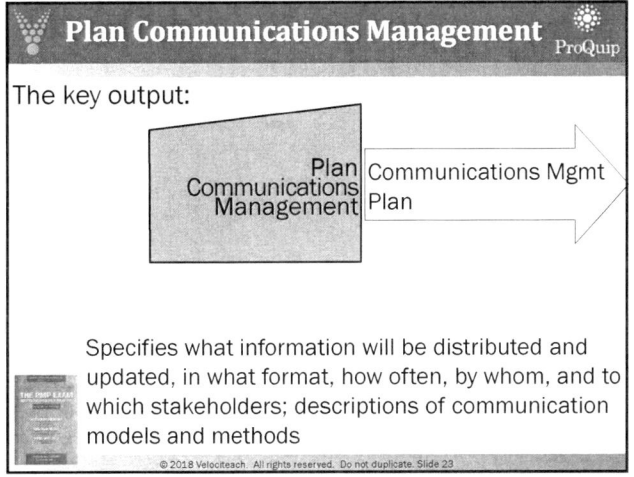

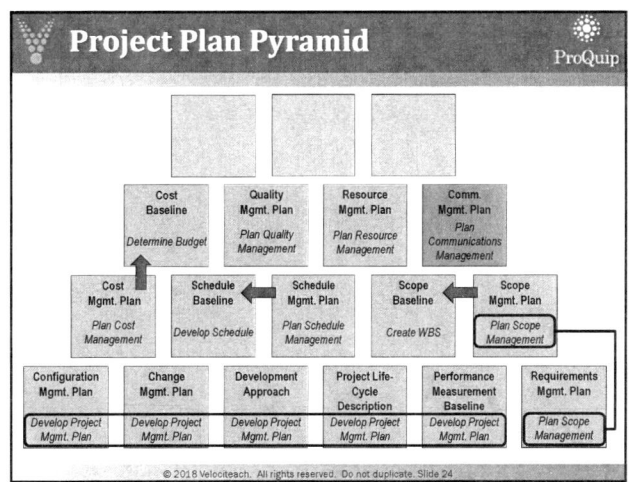

When to perform

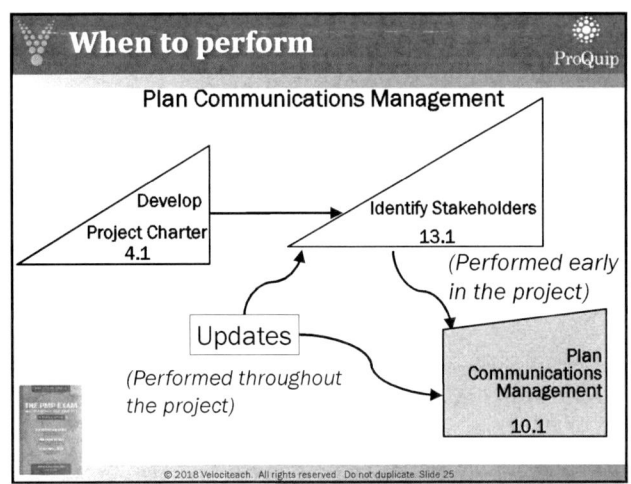

Plan Communications Management

Develop Project Charter 4.1 → Identify Stakeholders 13.1

(Performed early in the project)

Updates
(Performed throughout the project)

Plan Communications Management 10.1

© 2018 Velociteach. All rights reserved. Do not duplicate. Slide 25

Study Focus

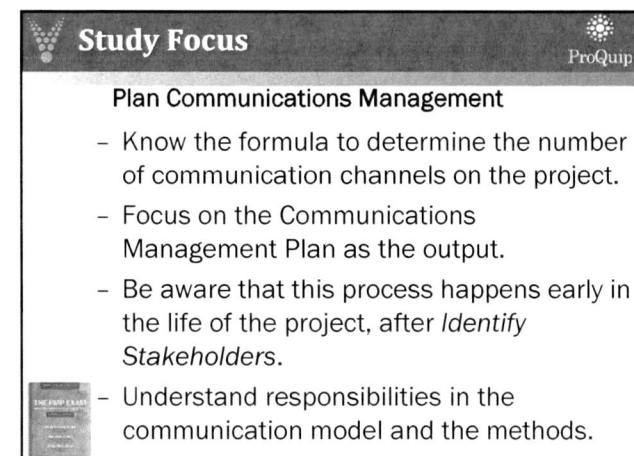

Plan Communications Management

– Know the formula to determine the number of communication channels on the project.

– Focus on the Communications Management Plan as the output.

– Be aware that this process happens early in the life of the project, after *Identify Stakeholders*.

– Understand responsibilities in the communication model and the methods.

© 2018 Velociteach. All rights reserved. Do not duplicate. Slide 26

©2018 Velociteach. All rights reserved. Page 254

Review the ITTOs

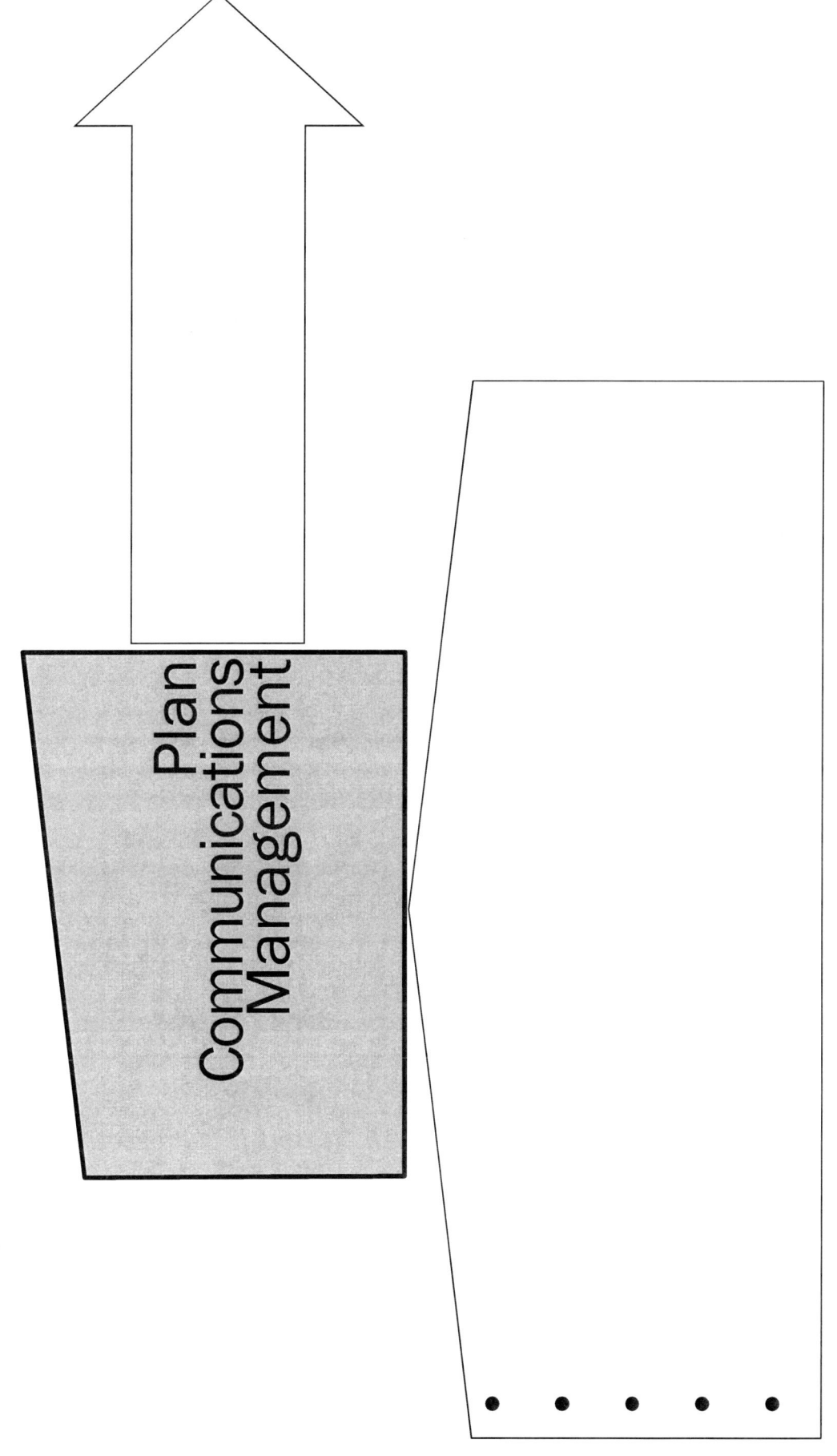

Plan Communications Management

© 2018 Velociteach. All rights reserved.

3 Communications Processes

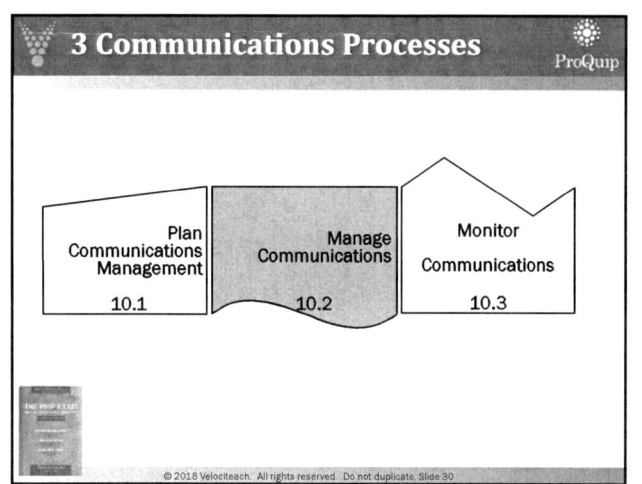

| Plan Communications Management 10.1 | Manage Communications 10.2 | Monitor Communications 10.3 |

© 2018 Velociteach. All rights reserved. Do not duplicate. Slide 30

Manage Communications

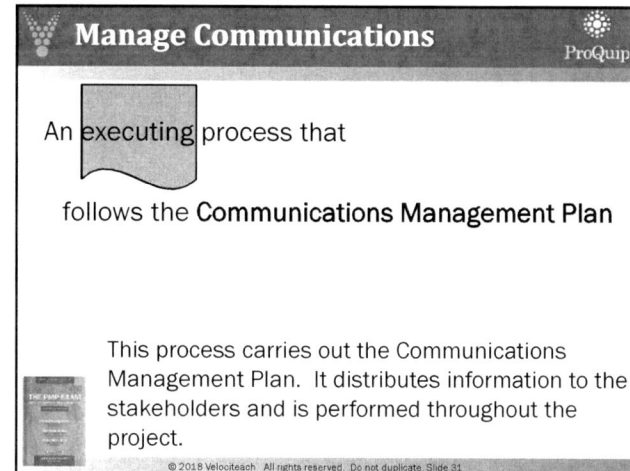

An executing process that

follows the **Communications Management Plan**

This process carries out the Communications Management Plan. It distributes information to the stakeholders and is performed throughout the project.

© 2018 Velociteach All rights reserved. Do not duplicate. Slide 31

Manage Communications

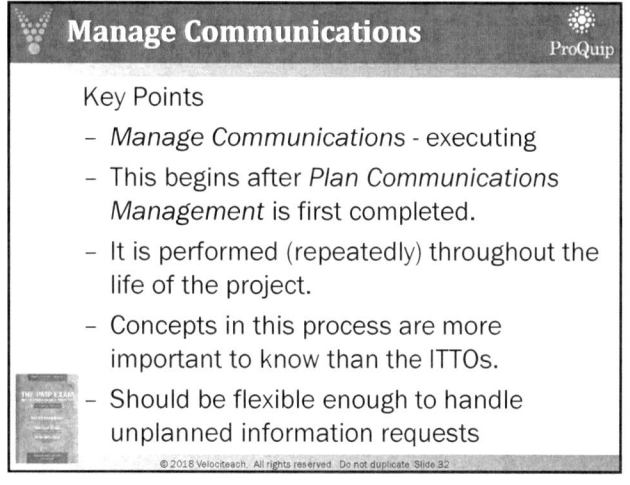

Key Points
- *Manage Communications* - executing
- This begins after *Plan Communications Management* is first completed.
- It is performed (repeatedly) throughout the life of the project.
- Concepts in this process are more important to know than the ITTOs.
- Should be flexible enough to handle unplanned information requests

© 2018 Velociteach. All rights reserved. Do not duplicate. Slide 32

PM Role *

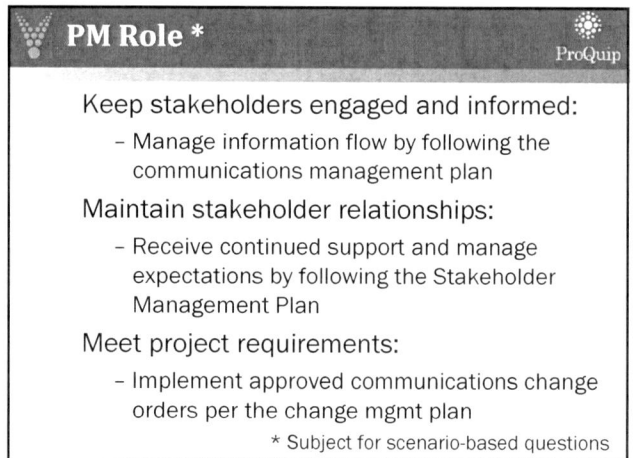

Keep stakeholders engaged and informed:
- Manage information flow by following the communications management plan

Maintain stakeholder relationships:
- Receive continued support and manage expectations by following the Stakeholder Management Plan

Meet project requirements:
- Implement approved communications change orders per the change mgmt plan
  * Subject for scenario-based questions

© 2018 Velociteach All rights reserved. Do not duplicate. Slide 33

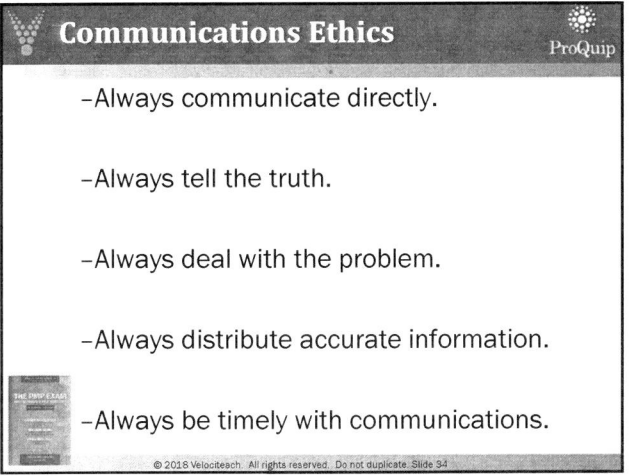

Communications Ethics

–Always communicate directly.

–Always tell the truth.

–Always deal with the problem.

–Always distribute accurate information.

–Always be timely with communications.

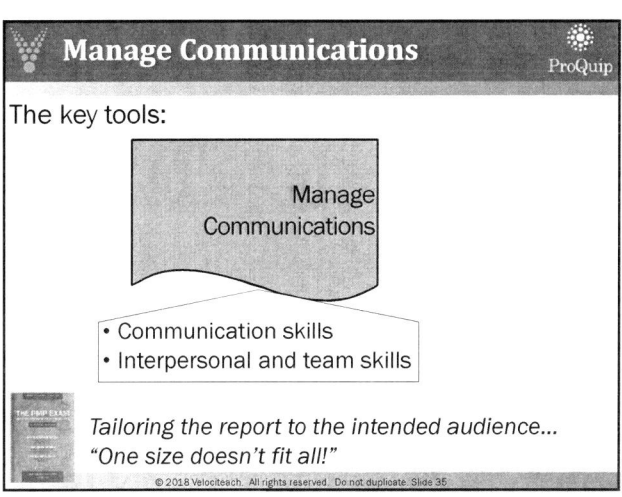

Manage Communications

The key tools:

Manage Communications

- Communication skills
- Interpersonal and team skills

Tailoring the report to the intended audience...
"One size doesn't fit all!"

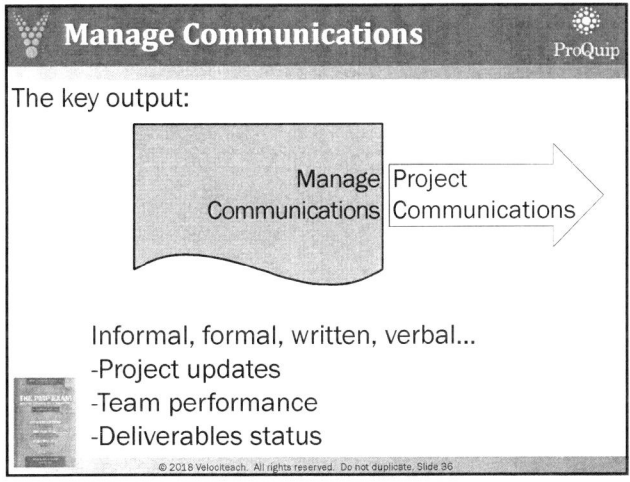

Manage Communications

The key output:

Manage Communications → Project Communications

Informal, formal, written, verbal...
-Project updates
-Team performance
-Deliverables status

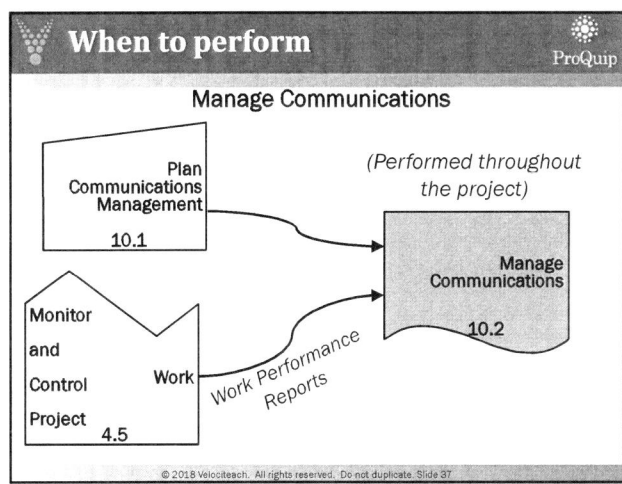

When to perform

Manage Communications

Plan Communications Management 10.1

(Performed throughout the project)

Monitor and Control Project 4.5

Work

Work Performance Reports

Manage Communications 10.2

©2018 Velociteach. All rights reserved.

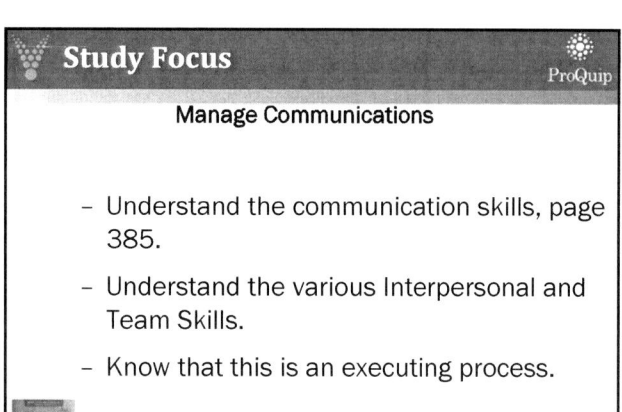

Study Focus

ProQuip

Manage Communications

- Understand the communication skills, page 385.

- Understand the various Interpersonal and Team Skills.

- Know that this is an executing process.

© 2018 Velociteach. All rights reserved. Do not duplicate. Slide 38

Review the ITTOs

ProQuip

Manage
Communications

THE PMP EXAM

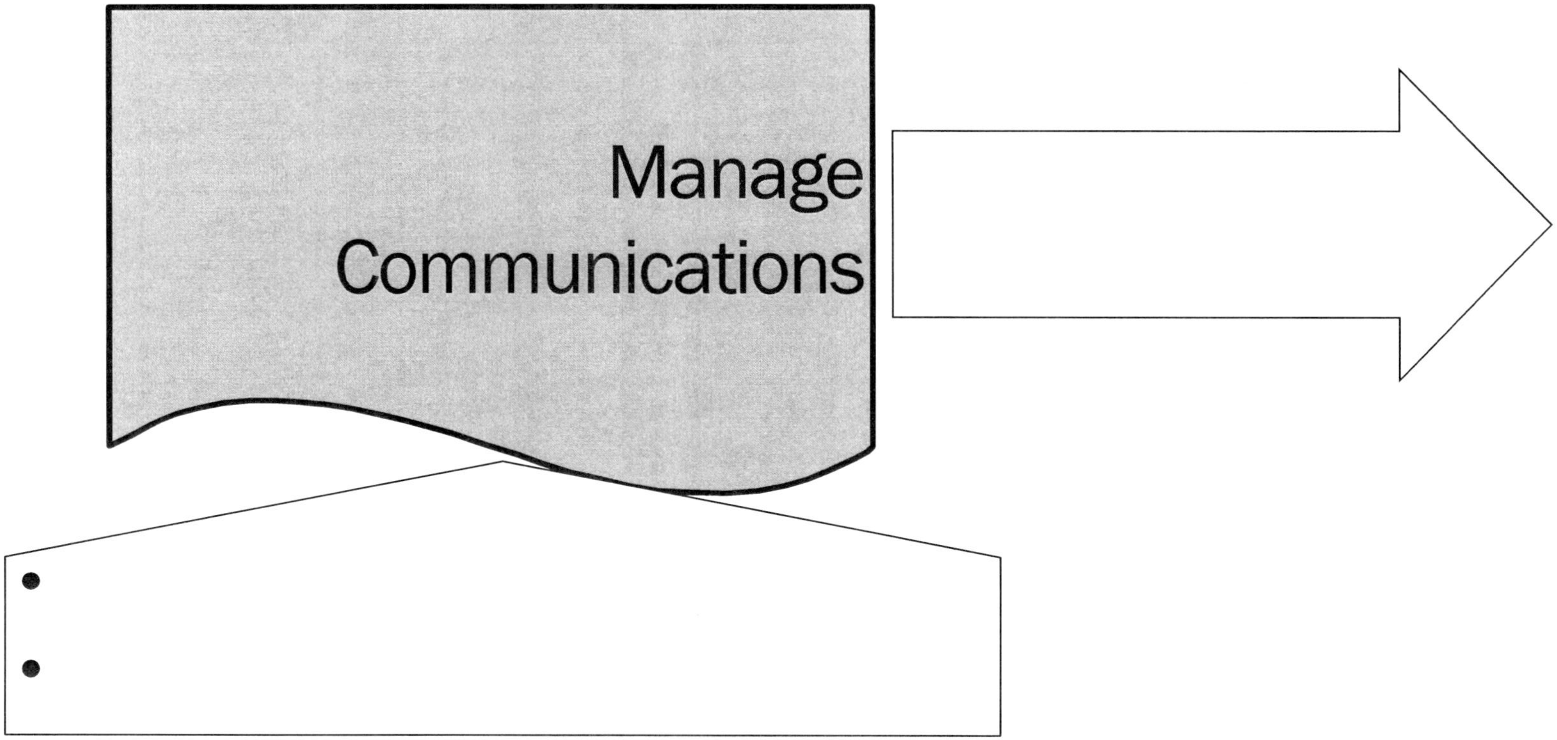

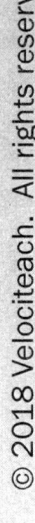

© 2018 Velociteach. All rights reserved.

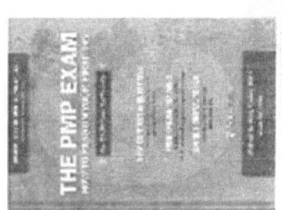

This page left intentionally blank.

©2018 Velociteach. All rights reserved.

3 Communications Processes

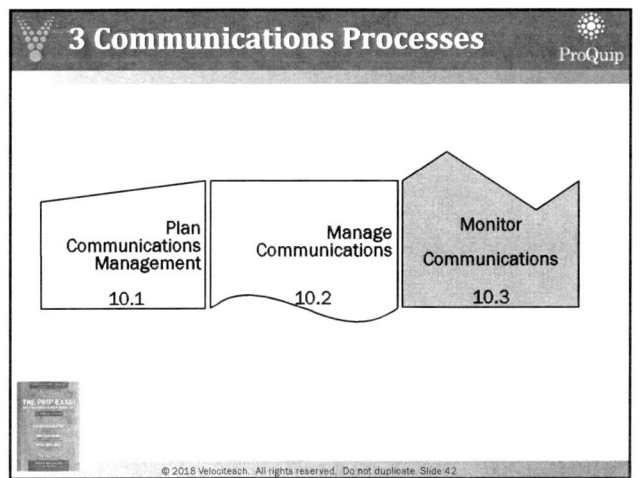

ProQuip

Plan Communications Management 10.1 → Manage Communications 10.2 → Monitor Communications 10.3

Monitor Communications

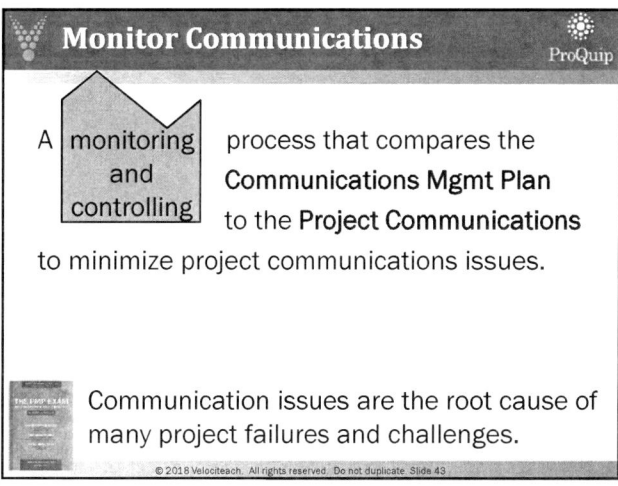

ProQuip

A **monitoring and controlling** process that compares the **Communications Mgmt Plan** to the **Project Communications** to minimize project communications issues.

Communication issues are the root cause of many project failures and challenges.

Monitor Communications

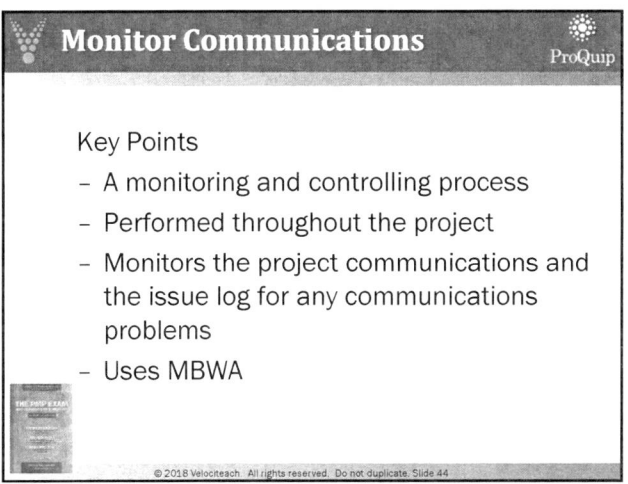

ProQuip

Key Points
- A monitoring and controlling process
- Performed throughout the project
- Monitors the project communications and the issue log for any communications problems
- Uses MBWA

PM Role *

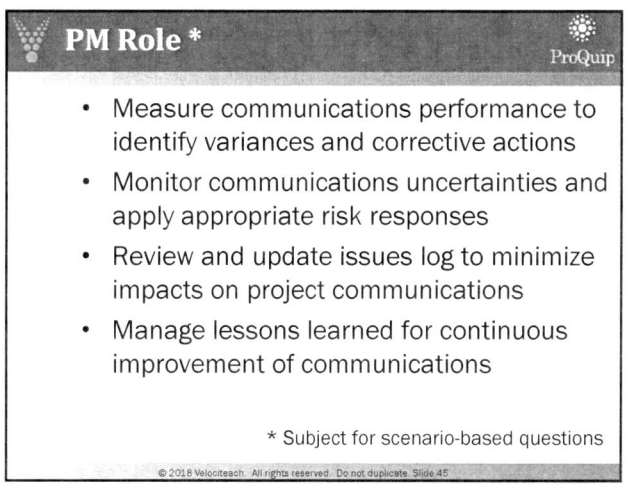

ProQuip

- Measure communications performance to identify variances and corrective actions
- Monitor communications uncertainties and apply appropriate risk responses
- Review and update issues log to minimize impacts on project communications
- Manage lessons learned for continuous improvement of communications

* Subject for scenario-based questions

©2018 Velociteach. All rights reserved. Page 261

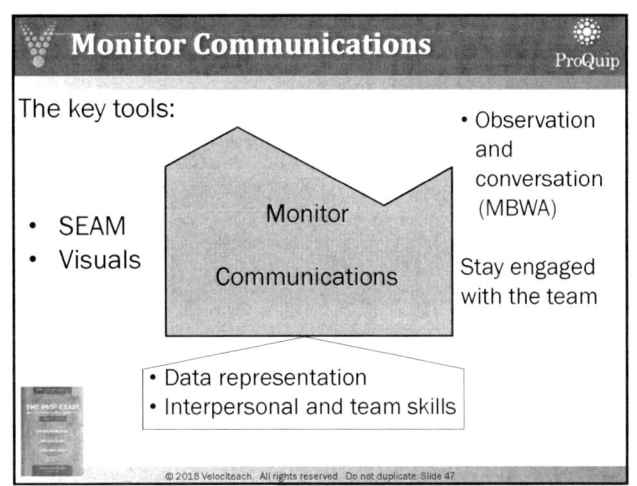

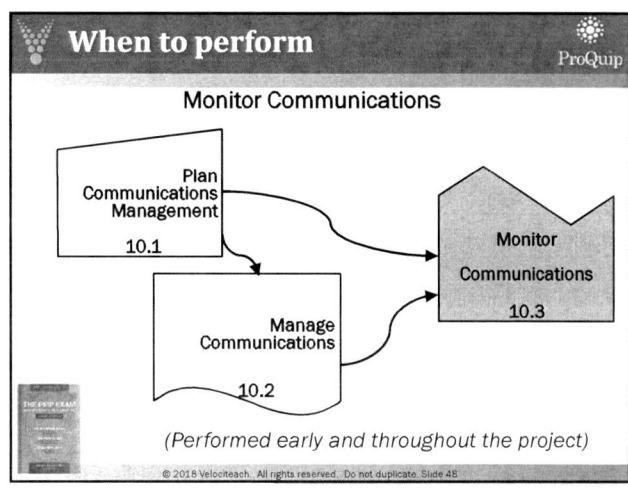

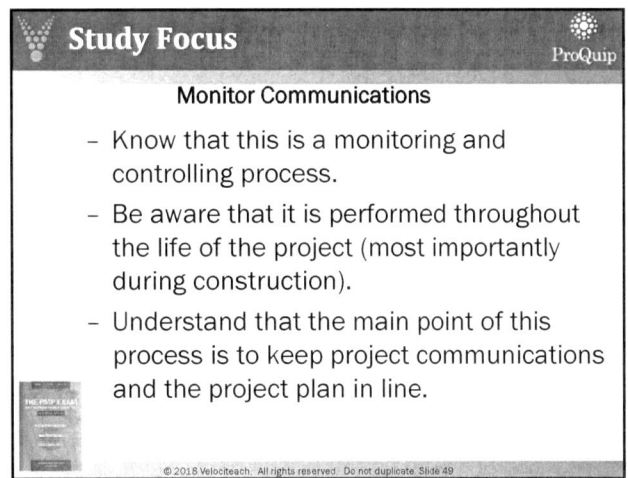

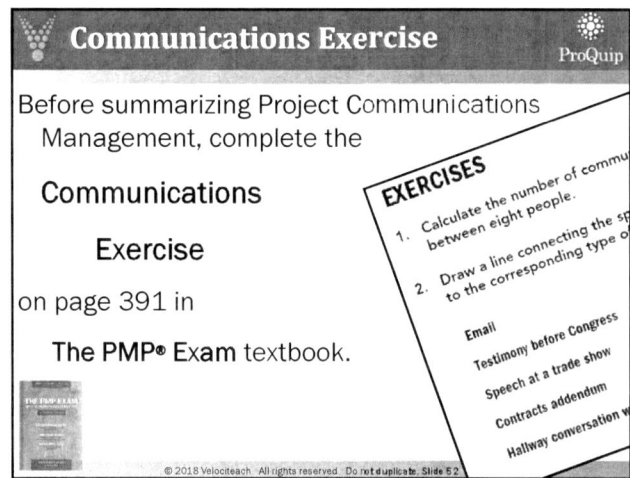

ProQuip

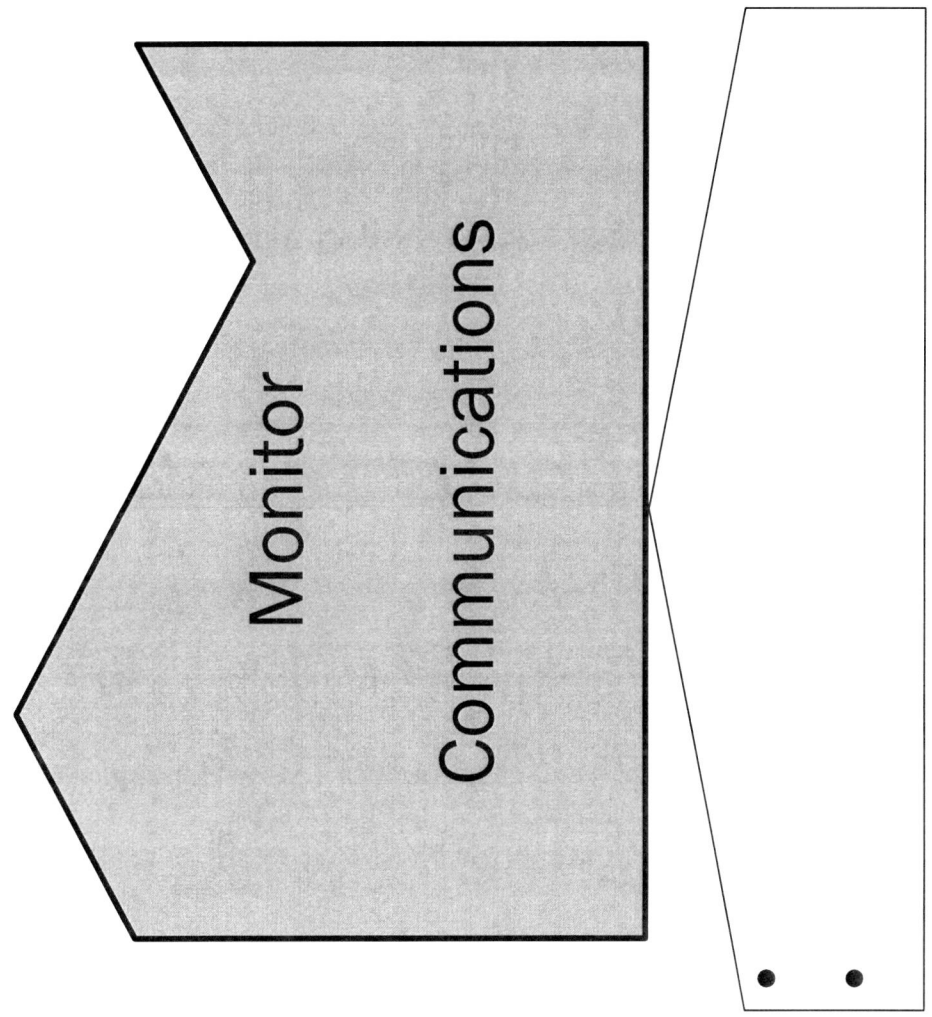

Monitor
Communications

© 2018 Velociteach. All rights reserved.

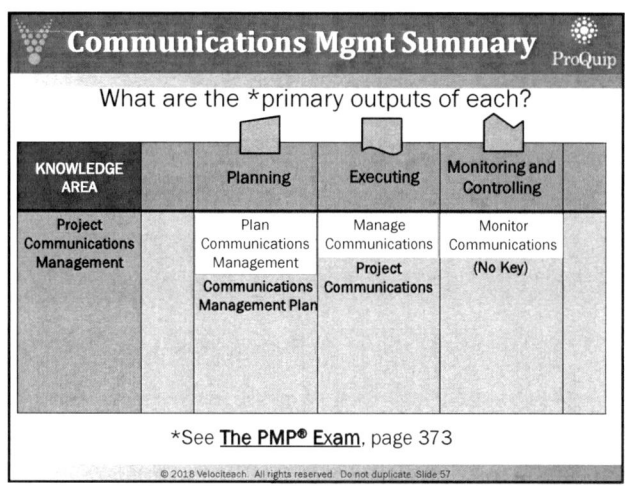

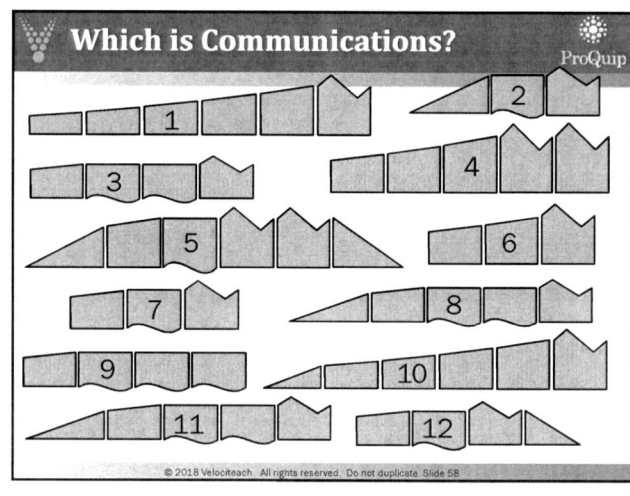

Communications Discussion

Defend the statement that 90% of an effective project manager's time is spent communicating.

What should be included in a good Communications Management Plan?

How is *Manage Communications* different from *Monitor Communications*?

Demonstrate one example each of a *paralingual* and a *nonverbal* communication. Explain.

Describe the seven responsibilities in the Communication Model and to whom they belong.

© 2018 Velociteach. All rights reserved. Do not duplicate. Slide 61

Summary

ProQuip

Knowledge Area

KNOWLEDGE AREA	Initiating	Planning	Executing	Monitoring and Controlling	Closing
Project Management					

©2018 Velociteach. All rights reserved.   Page 265

This page left intentionally blank.

©2018 Velociteach. All rights reserved.

| Score Sheet | Communications Management Exam |  |

Velociteach

- Mark one answer: A, B, C, or D.
- Circle the '?' symbol if you are guessing at the answer.
- Circle the Δ symbol if you change your answer.

Total Correct: _____

% Correct: _____%

1.	A O	B O	C O	D O	?	Δ
2.	A O	B O	C O	D O	?	Δ
3.	A O	B O	C O	D O	?	Δ
4.	A O	B O	C O	D O	?	Δ
5.	A O	B O	C O	D O	?	Δ
6.	A O	B O	C O	D O	?	Δ
7.	A O	B O	C O	D O	?	Δ
8.	A O	B O	C O	D O	?	Δ
9.	A O	B O	C O	D O	?	Δ
10.	A O	B O	C O	D O	?	Δ
11.	A O	B O	C O	D O	?	Δ
12.	A O	B O	C O	D O	?	Δ
13.	A O	B O	C O	D O	?	Δ
14.	A O	B O	C O	D O	?	Δ
15.	A O	B O	C O	D O	?	Δ
16.	A O	B O	C O	D O	?	Δ
17.	A O	B O	C O	D O	?	Δ
18.	A O	B O	C O	D O	?	Δ
19.	A O	B O	C O	D O	?	Δ
20.	A O	B O	C O	D O	?	Δ
21.	A O	B O	C O	D O	?	Δ
22.	A O	B O	C O	D O	?	Δ
23.	A O	B O	C O	D O	?	Δ
24.	A O	B O	C O	D O	?	Δ
25.	A O	B O	C O	D O	?	Δ

Page 405

ProQuip

Project Risk Management

Course Module 13

PMBOK® Guide Chapter 11

PMP® Exam Textbook Chapter 11

© 2018 Velociteach. All rights reserved. Do not duplicate. Slide 1

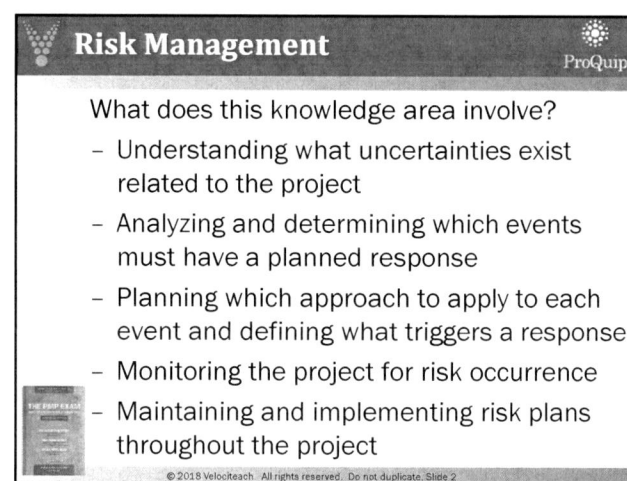

Risk Management

ProQuip

What does this knowledge area involve?

- Understanding what uncertainties exist related to the project
- Analyzing and determining which events must have a planned response
- Planning which approach to apply to each event and defining what triggers a response
- Monitoring the project for risk occurrence
- Maintaining and implementing risk plans throughout the project

© 2018 Velociteach. All rights reserved. Do not duplicate. Slide 2

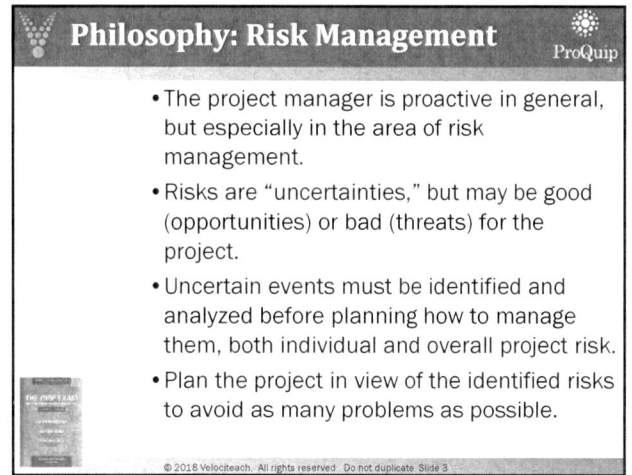

Philosophy: Risk Management

ProQuip

- The project manager is proactive in general, but especially in the area of risk management.
- Risks are "uncertainties," but may be good (opportunities) or bad (threats) for the project.
- Uncertain events must be identified and analyzed before planning how to manage them, both individual and overall project risk.
- Plan the project in view of the identified risks to avoid as many problems as possible.

© 2018 Velociteach. All rights reserved. Do not duplicate. Slide 3

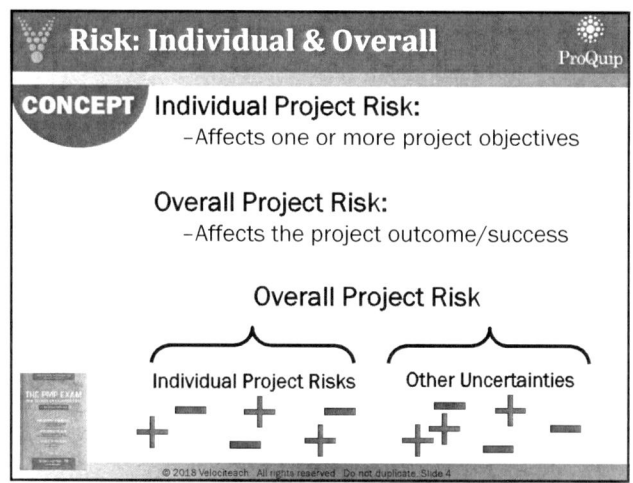

Risk: Individual & Overall

ProQuip

CONCEPT Individual Project Risk:
- Affects one or more project objectives

Overall Project Risk:
- Affects the project outcome/success

Overall Project Risk

Individual Project Risks   Other Uncertainties

© 2018 Velociteach. All rights reserved. Do not duplicate. Slide 4

©2018 Velociteach. All rights reserved.

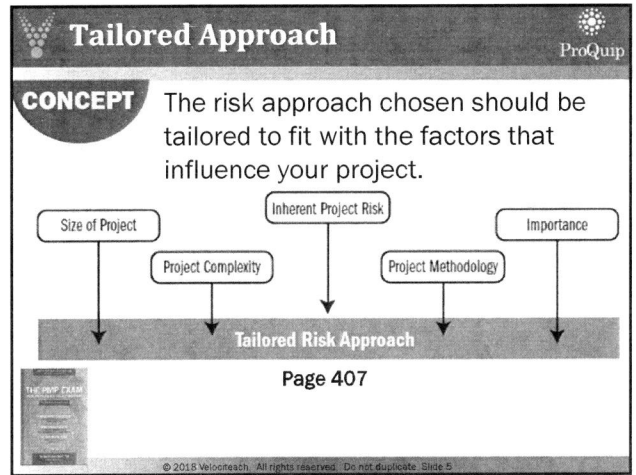

Tailored Approach

ProQuip

CONCEPT The risk approach chosen should be tailored to fit with the factors that influence your project.

Size of Project · Project Complexity · Inherent Project Risk · Project Methodology · Importance

Tailored Risk Approach

Page 407

© 2018 Velociteach. All rights reserved. Do not duplicate. Slide 5

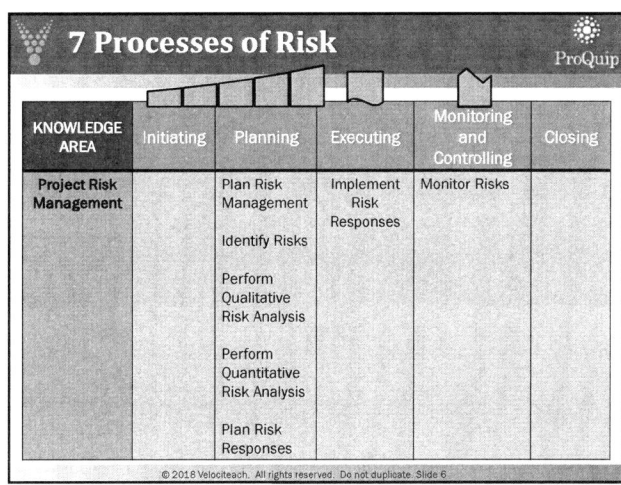

7 Processes of Risk

ProQuip

KNOWLEDGE AREA	Initiating	Planning	Executing	Monitoring and Controlling	Closing
Project Risk Management		Plan Risk Management	Implement Risk Responses	Monitor Risks	
		Identify Risks			
		Perform Qualitative Risk Analysis			
		Perform Quantitative Risk Analysis			
		Plan Risk Responses			

© 2018 Velociteach. All rights reserved. Do not duplicate. Slide 6

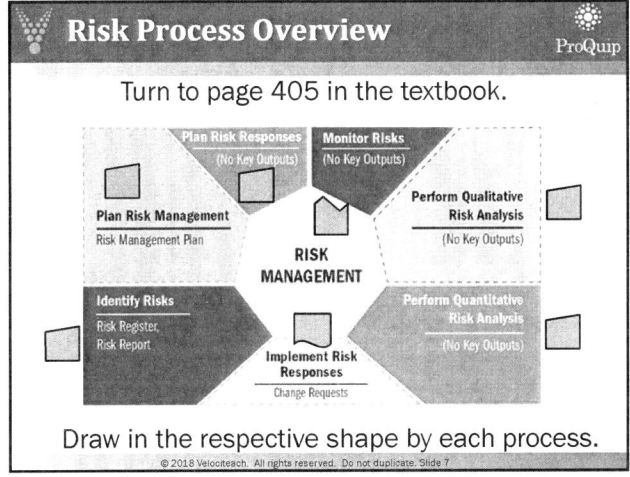

Risk Process Overview

ProQuip

Turn to page 405 in the textbook.

Plan Risk Responses (No Key Outputs) · Monitor Risks (No Key Outputs)

Plan Risk Management — Risk Management Plan

Perform Qualitative Risk Analysis (No Key Outputs)

RISK MANAGEMENT

Identify Risks — Risk Register, Risk Report

Implement Risk Responses — Change Requests

Perform Quantitative Risk Analysis (No Key Outputs)

Draw in the respective shape by each process.

© 2018 Velociteach. All rights reserved. Do not duplicate. Slide 7

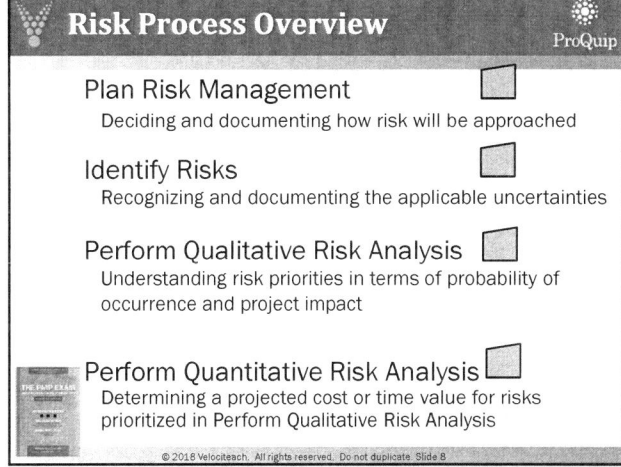

Risk Process Overview

ProQuip

Plan Risk Management
Deciding and documenting how risk will be approached

Identify Risks
Recognizing and documenting the applicable uncertainties

Perform Qualitative Risk Analysis
Understanding risk priorities in terms of probability of occurrence and project impact

Perform Quantitative Risk Analysis
Determining a projected cost or time value for risks prioritized in Perform Qualitative Risk Analysis

© 2018 Velociteach. All rights reserved. Do not duplicate. Slide 8

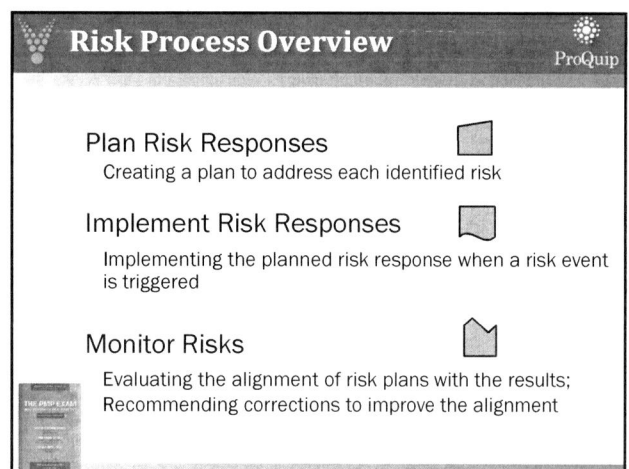

Risk Process Overview

Plan Risk Responses
Creating a plan to address each identified risk

Implement Risk Responses
Implementing the planned risk response when a risk event is triggered

Monitor Risks
Evaluating the alignment of risk plans with the results; Recommending corrections to improve the alignment

© 2018 Velociteach. All rights reserved. Do not duplicate. Slide 9

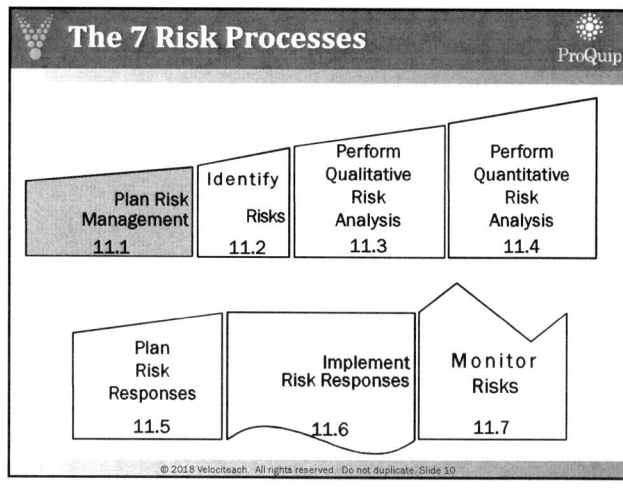

The 7 Risk Processes

| Plan Risk Management 11.1 | Identify Risks 11.2 | Perform Qualitative Risk Analysis 11.3 | Perform Quantitative Risk Analysis 11.4 |

| Plan Risk Responses 11.5 | Implement Risk Responses 11.6 | Monitor Risks 11.7 |

© 2018 Velociteach. All rights reserved. Do not duplicate. Slide 10

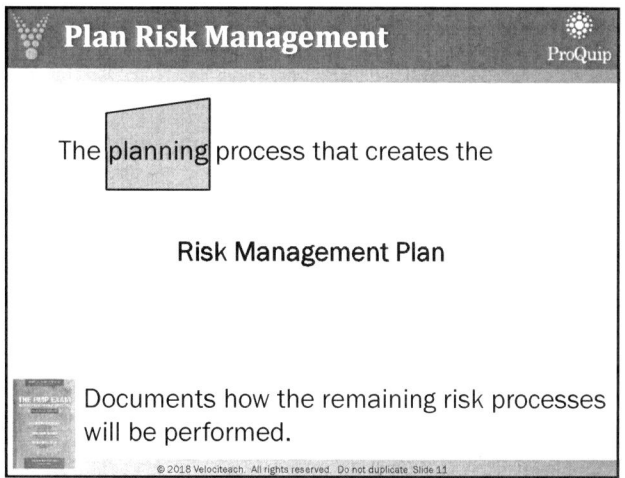

Plan Risk Management

The planning process that creates the

Risk Management Plan

Documents how the remaining risk processes will be performed.

© 2018 Velociteach. All rights reserved. Do not duplicate. Slide 11

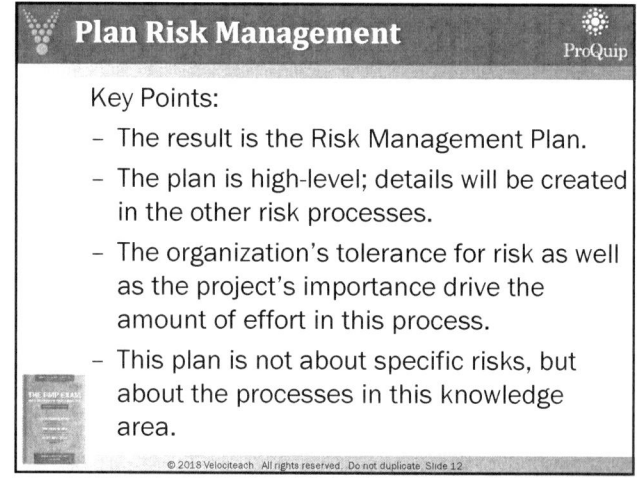

Plan Risk Management

Key Points:
- The result is the Risk Management Plan.
- The plan is high-level; details will be created in the other risk processes.
- The organization's tolerance for risk as well as the project's importance drive the amount of effort in this process.
- This plan is not about specific risks, but about the processes in this knowledge area.

© 2018 Velociteach. All rights reserved. Do not duplicate. Slide 12

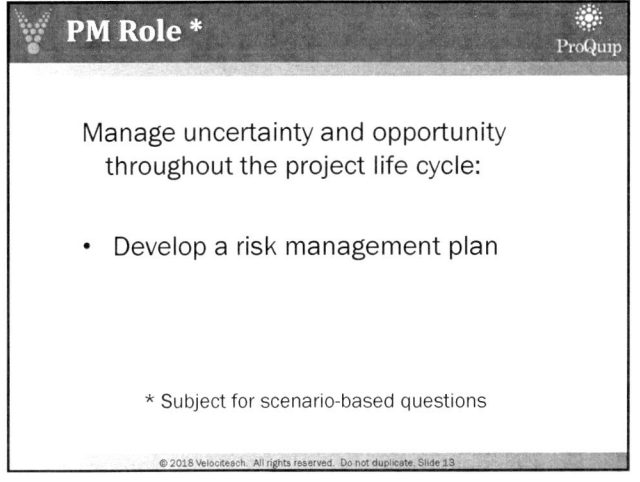

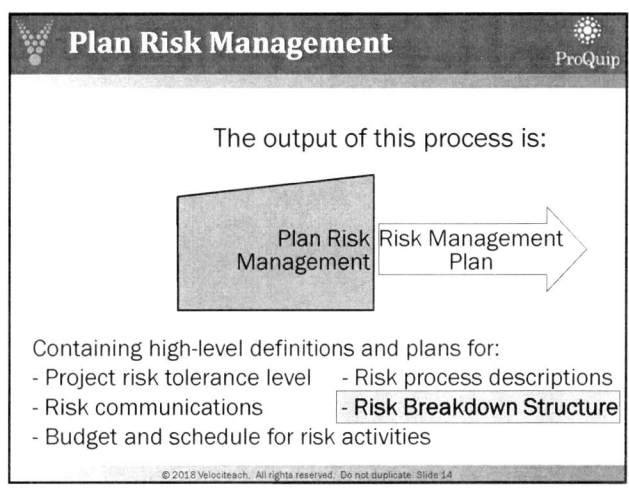

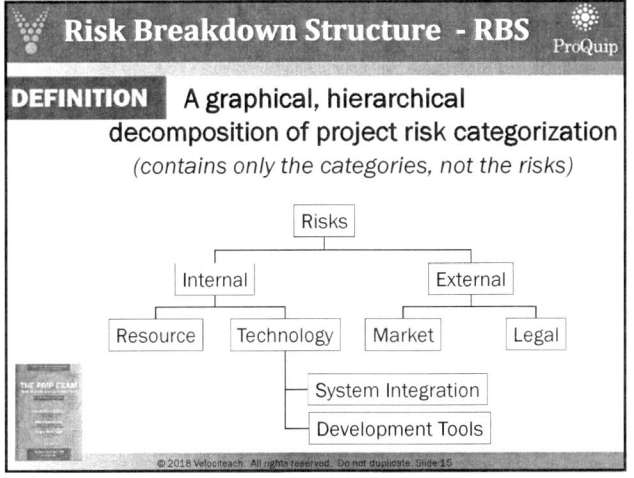

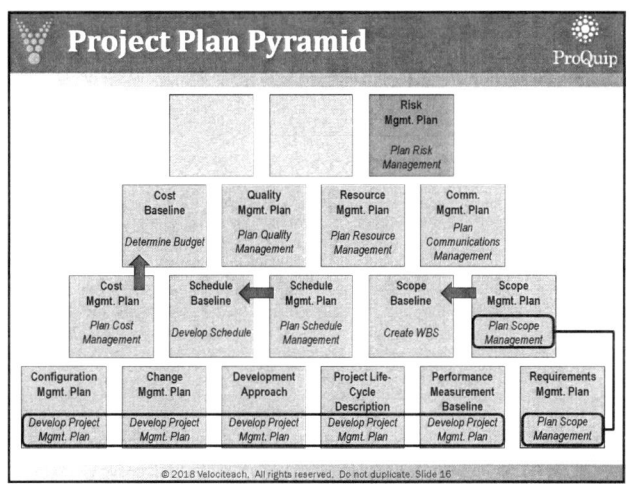

When to perform

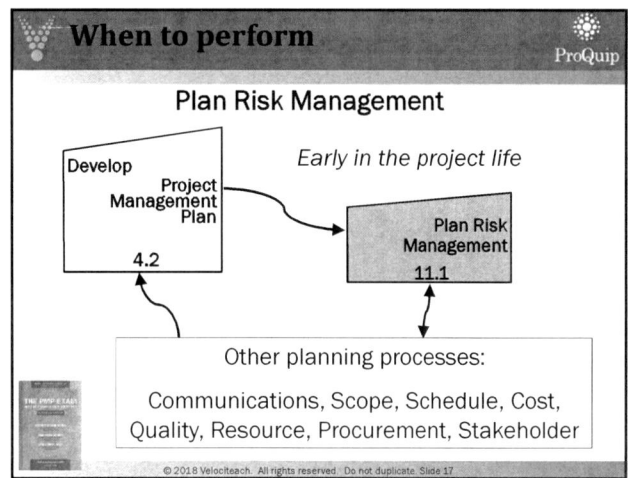

Plan Risk Management

Early in the project life

Develop Project Management Plan 4.2

Plan Risk Management 11.1

Other planning processes:

Communications, Scope, Schedule, Cost, Quality, Resource, Procurement, Stakeholder

Study Focus

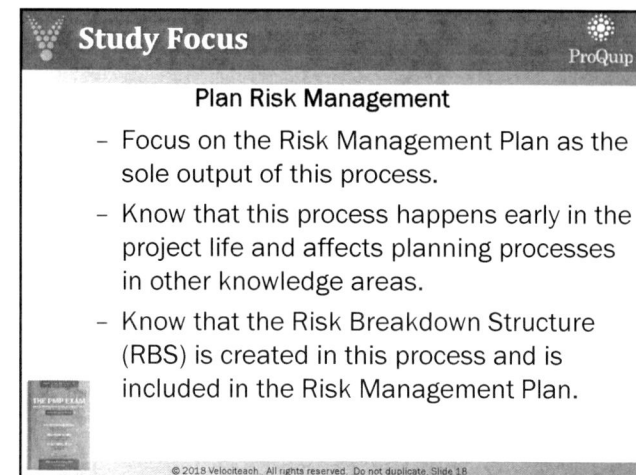

Plan Risk Management

- Focus on the Risk Management Plan as the sole output of this process.
- Know that this process happens early in the project life and affects planning processes in other knowledge areas.
- Know that the Risk Breakdown Structure (RBS) is created in this process and is included in the Risk Management Plan.

© 2018 Velociteach. All rights reserved. Do not duplicate. Slide 17

© 2018 Velociteach. All rights reserved. Do not duplicate. Slide 18

Review the ITTOs

Plan Risk Management

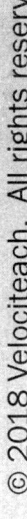

© 2018 Velociteach. All rights reserved.

This page left intentionally blank.

©2018 Velociteach. All rights reserved.   Page 274

The 7 Risk Processes

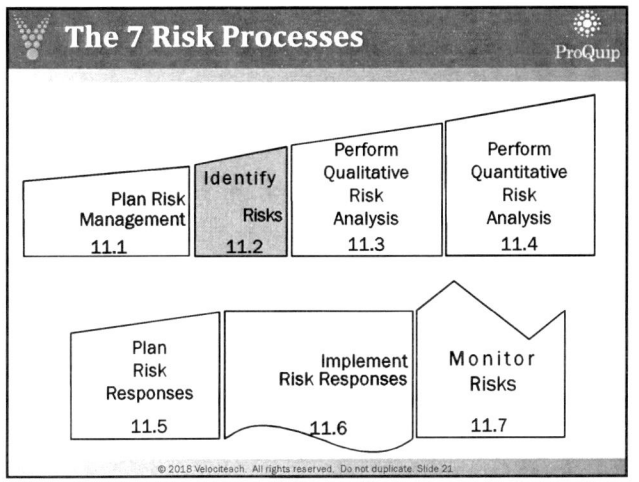

ProQuip

Plan Risk Management 11.1	Identify Risks 11.2	Perform Qualitative Risk Analysis 11.3	Perform Quantitative Risk Analysis 11.4
Plan Risk Responses 11.5	Implement Risk Responses 11.6	Monitor Risks 11.7	

© 2018 Velociteach. All rights reserved. Do not duplicate. Slide 21

Identify Risks

ProQuip

The planning process that creates the

Risk Register,

the heart of Risk Management

The Risk Register is a list of each recognized risk and provides a location to document the results of the remaining risk processes.

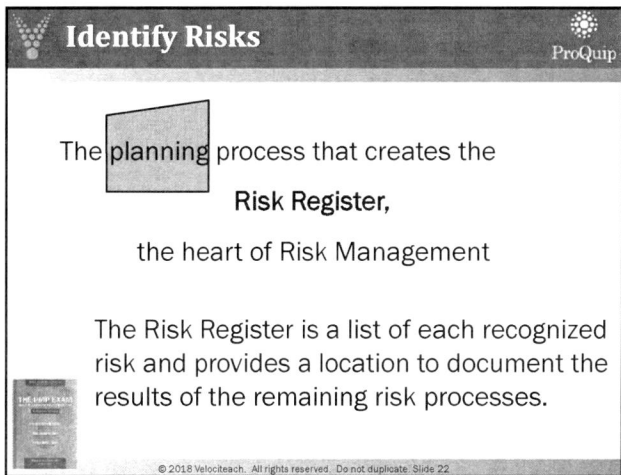

© 2018 Velociteach. All rights reserved. Do not duplicate. Slide 22

Identify Risks

ProQuip

Key Points:

- The Risk Register is an important output; it is used by the remaining five risk processes.
- The Risk Register is a "living document" that is updated throughout the project.
- *Identify Risks* begins early in the project, but is performed multiple times.

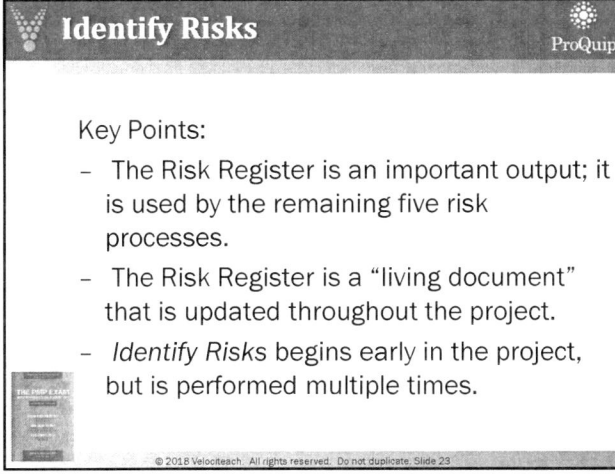

© 2018 Velociteach. All rights reserved. Do not duplicate. Slide 23

PM Role *

ProQuip

Manage uncertainty and opportunity throughout the project life cycle:

- Identify Risks
- Create a Risk Register

* Subject for scenario-based questions

© 2018 Velociteach. All rights reserved. Do not duplicate. Slide 24

©2018 Velociteach. All rights reserved.

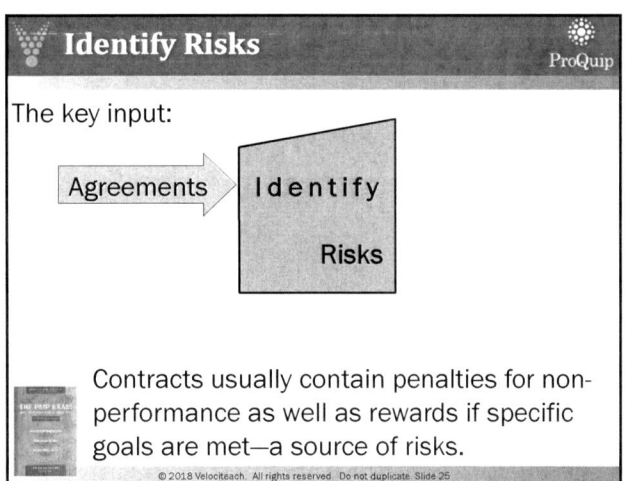

Identify Risks

The key input:

Agreements → Identify Risks

Contracts usually contain penalties for non-performance as well as rewards if specific goals are met—a source of risks.

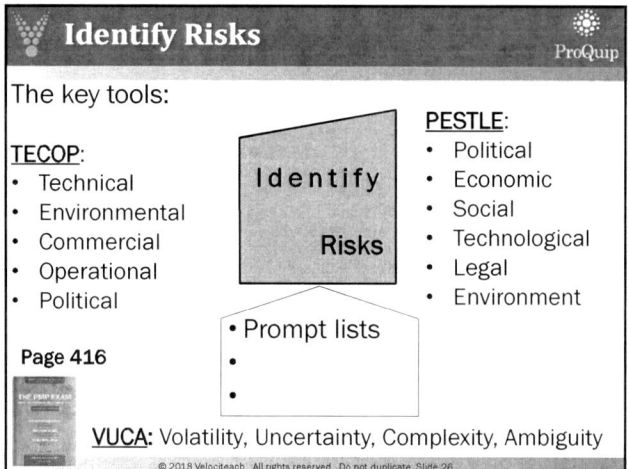

Identify Risks

The key tools:

TECOP:
• Technical
• Environmental
• Commercial
• Operational
• Political

Page 416

PESTLE:
• Political
• Economic
• Social
• Technological
• Legal
• Environment

Identify Risks

• Prompt lists
•
•

VUCA: Volatility, Uncertainty, Complexity, Ambiguity

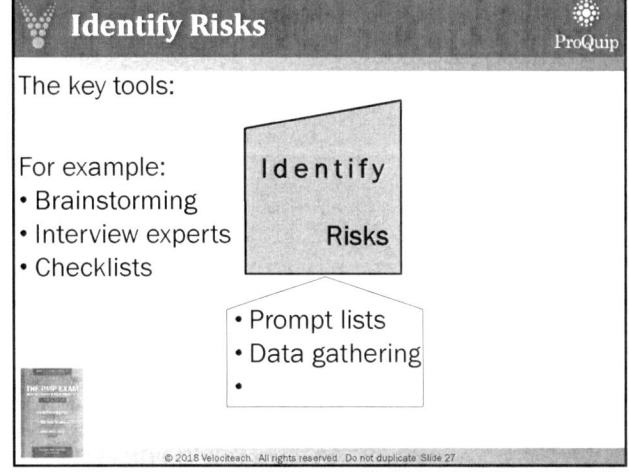

Identify Risks

The key tools:

For example:
• Brainstorming
• Interview experts
• Checklists

Identify Risks

• Prompt lists
• Data gathering
•

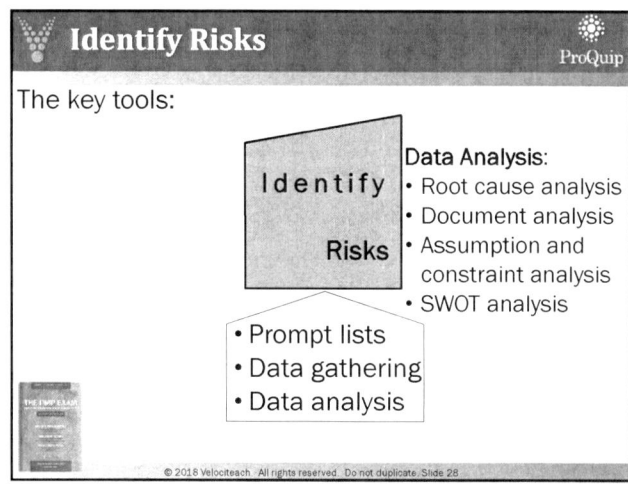

Identify Risks

The key tools:

Identify Risks

Data Analysis:
• Root cause analysis
• Document analysis
• Assumption and constraint analysis
• SWOT analysis

• Prompt lists
• Data gathering
• Data analysis

©2018 Velociteach. All rights reserved.   Page 276

SWOT Analysis

ProQuip

DEFINITION Measure internal Strengths and Weakness, observe external Threats and Opportunities; Plot to find highest negative and positive risks

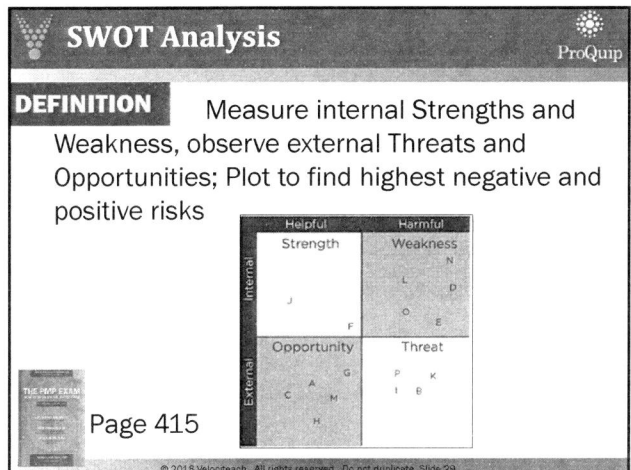

Page 415

© 2018 Velociteach. All rights reserved. Do not duplicate. Slide 29

Identify Risks

ProQuip

The key outputs:

A list of all identified risks with specific, updated information about each

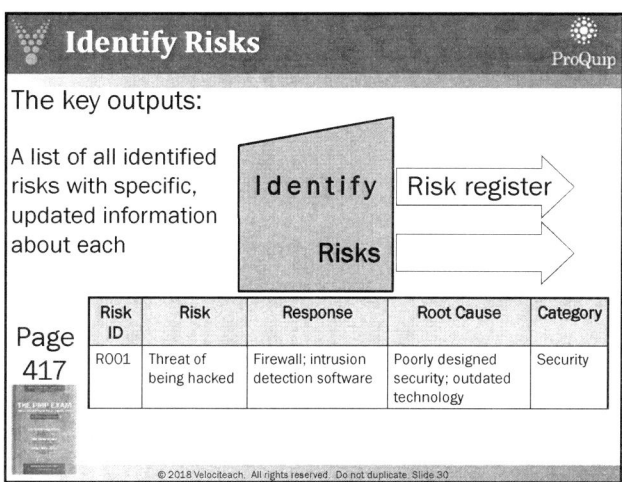

	Risk ID	Risk	Response	Root Cause	Category
Page 417	R001	Threat of being hacked	Firewall; intrusion detection software	Poorly designed security; outdated technology	Security

© 2018 Velociteach. All rights reserved. Do not duplicate. Slide 30

Identify Risks

ProQuip

The key outputs:

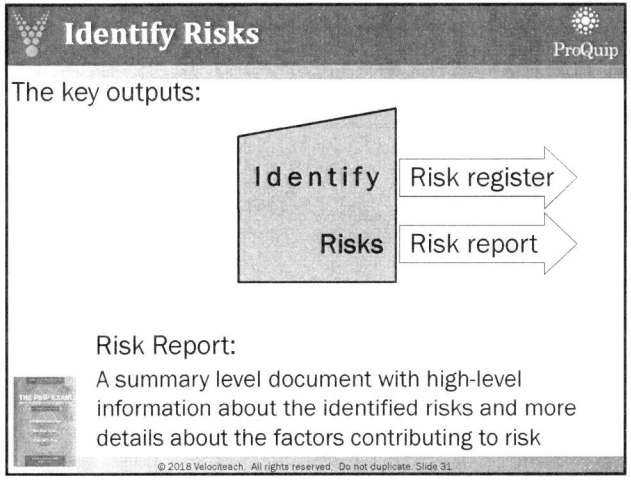

Risk Report:

A summary level document with high-level information about the identified risks and more details about the factors contributing to risk

© 2018 Velociteach. All rights reserved. Do not duplicate. Slide 31

When to perform

ProQuip

Identify Risks
Begins early in project

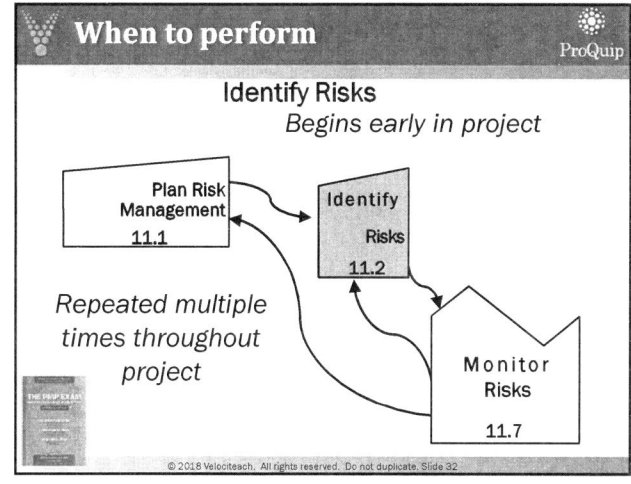

Repeated multiple times throughout project

© 2018 Velociteach. All rights reserved. Do not duplicate. Slide 32

Identify Risks

- Know that the Risk Register, the output of this process, should contain all data related to each identified risk.

- Know that the Risk Register serves as an input to all of the remaining risk processes.

- Know that this process begins early and is performed multiple times in the project.

 - Know the tools to identify risks.

- Know the Risk Report is a summary.

© 2018 Velociteach. All rights reserved. Do not duplicate. Slide 33

ProQuip

Review the ITTOs

Identify Risks

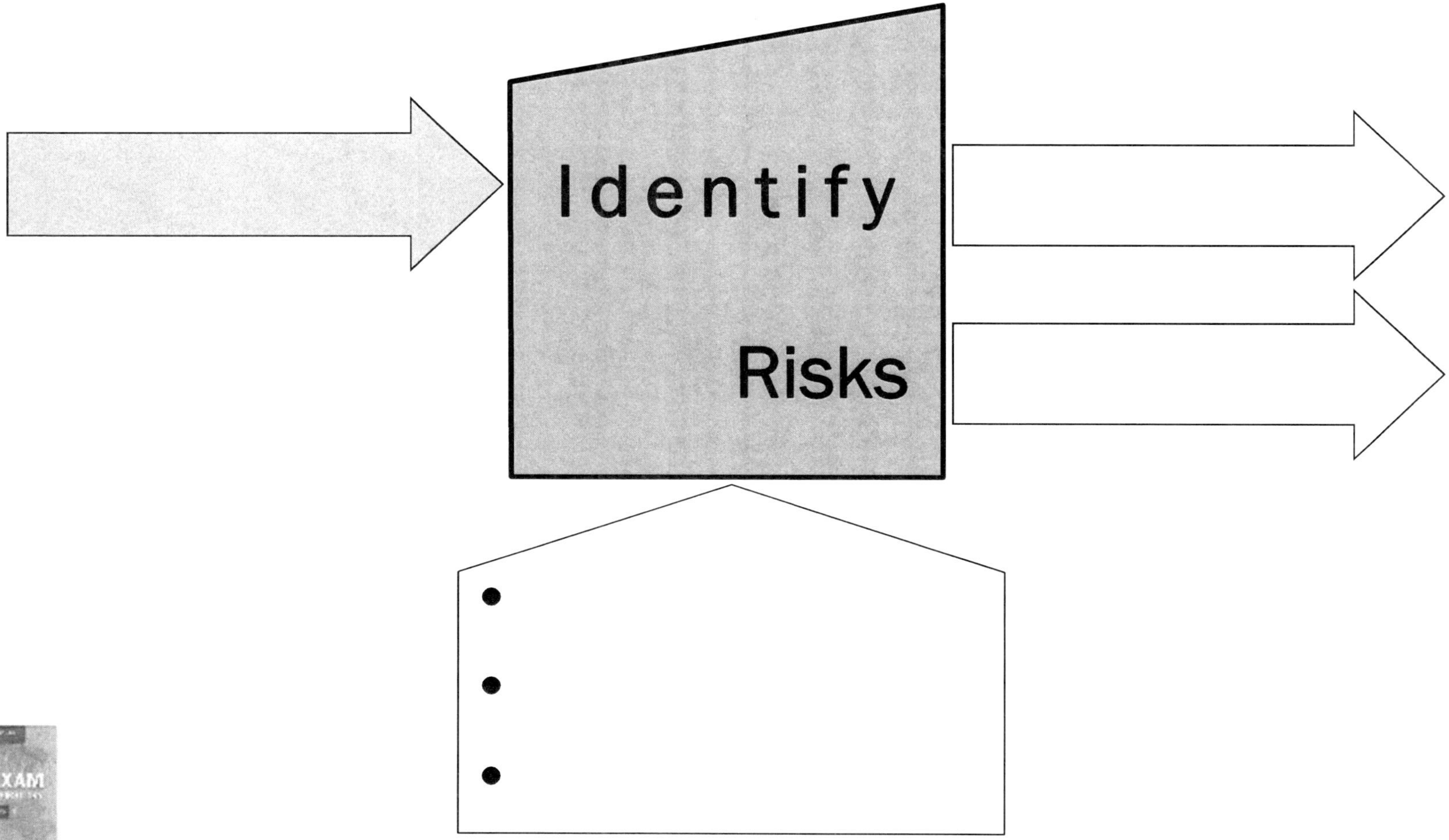

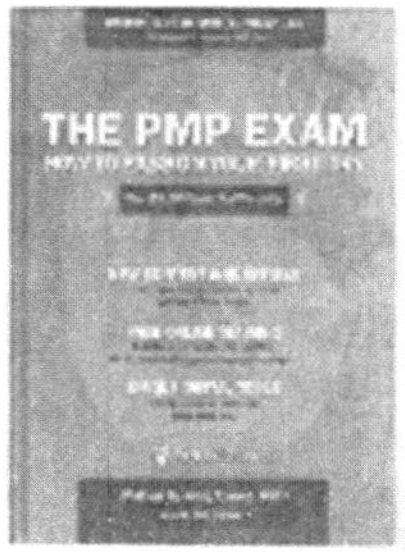

© 2018 Velociteach. All rights reserved.

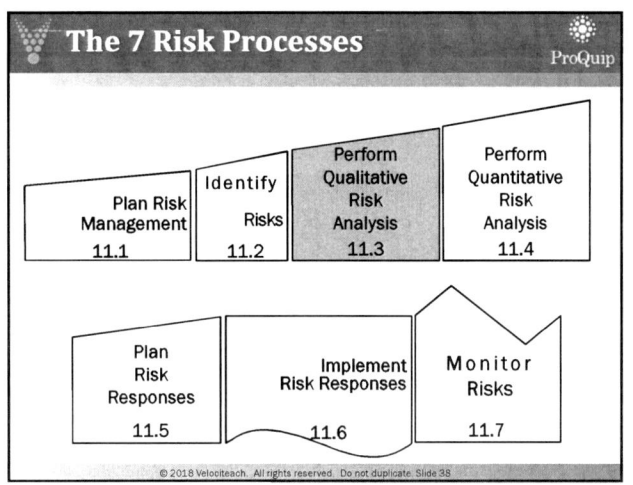

The 7 Risk Processes

- Plan Risk Management 11.1
- Identify Risks 11.2
- Perform Qualitative Risk Analysis 11.3
- Perform Quantitative Risk Analysis 11.4
- Plan Risk Responses 11.5
- Implement Risk Responses 11.6
- Monitor Risks 11.7

© 2018 Velociteach. All rights reserved. Do not duplicate. Slide 38

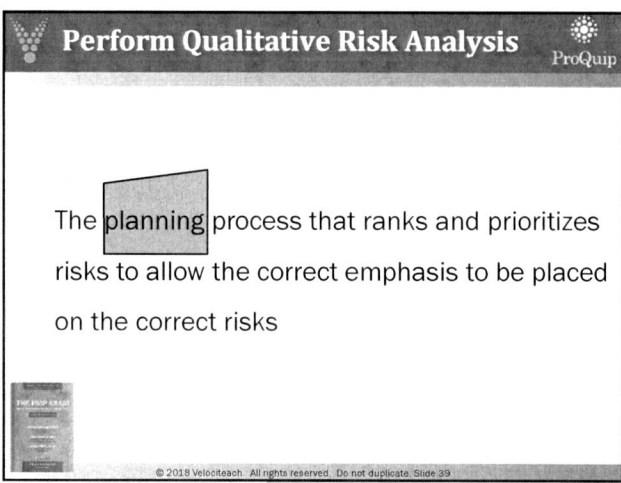

Perform Qualitative Risk Analysis

The planning process that ranks and prioritizes risks to allow the correct emphasis to be placed on the correct risks

© 2018 Velociteach. All rights reserved. Do not duplicate. Slide 39

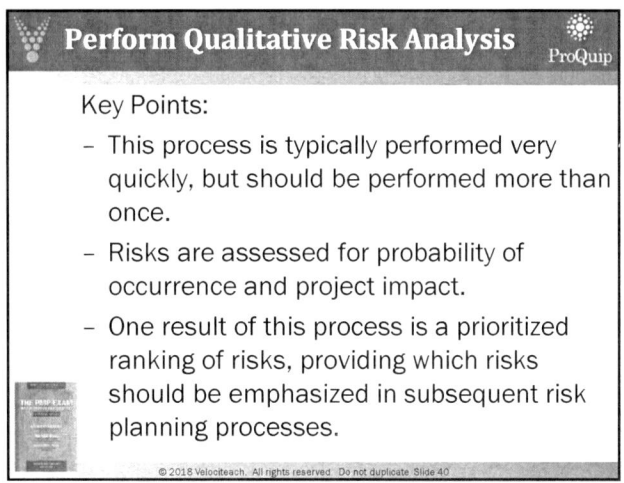

Perform Qualitative Risk Analysis

Key Points:
- This process is typically performed very quickly, but should be performed more than once.
- Risks are assessed for probability of occurrence and project impact.
- One result of this process is a prioritized ranking of risks, providing which risks should be emphasized in subsequent risk planning processes.

© 2018 Velociteach. All rights reserved. Do not duplicate. Slide 40

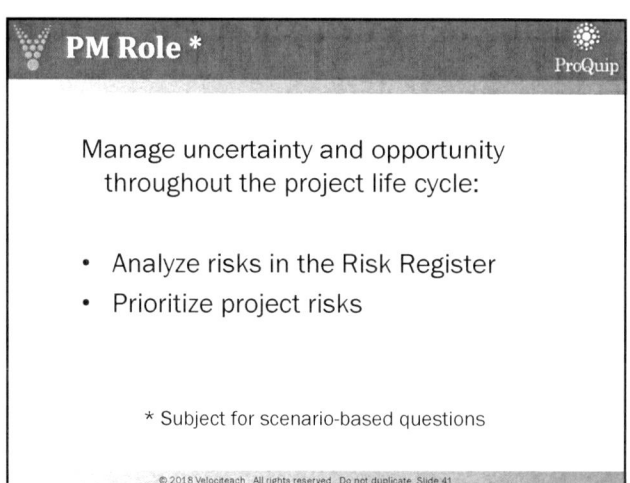

PM Role *

Manage uncertainty and opportunity throughout the project life cycle:

- Analyze risks in the Risk Register
- Prioritize project risks

* Subject for scenario-based questions

© 2018 Velociteach. All rights reserved. Do not duplicate. Slide 41

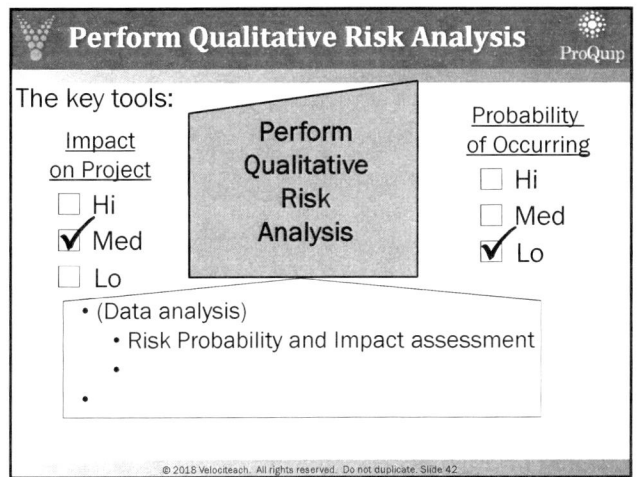

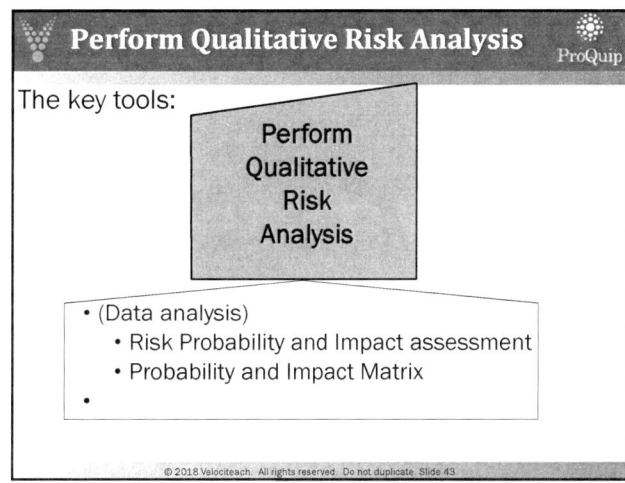

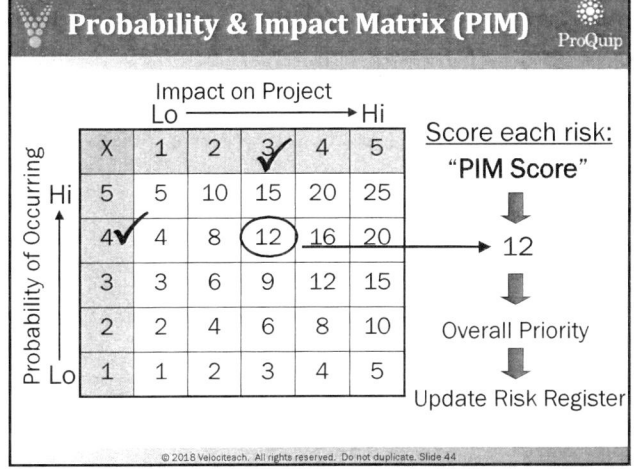

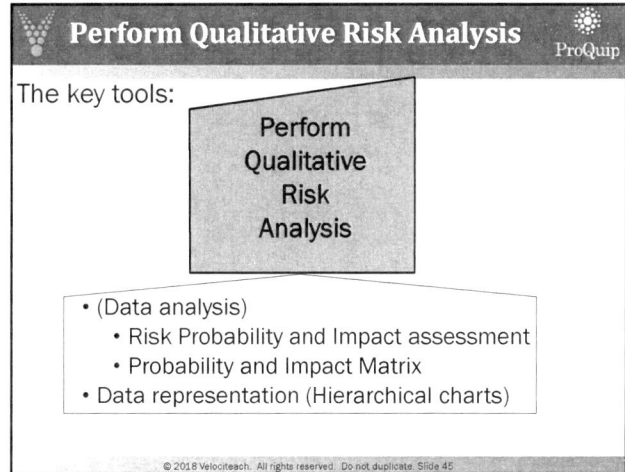

©2018 Velociteach. All rights reserved.   Page 281

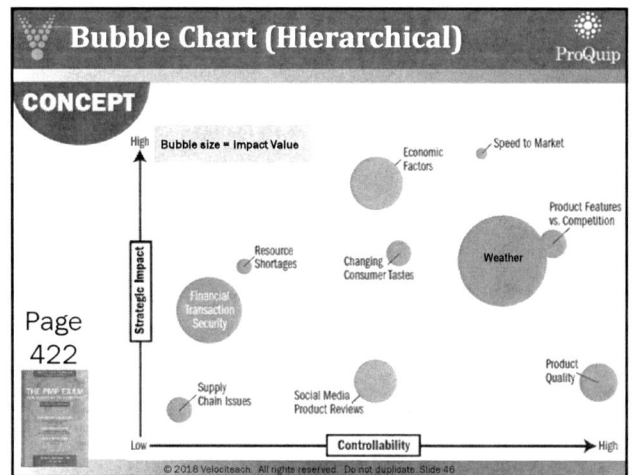

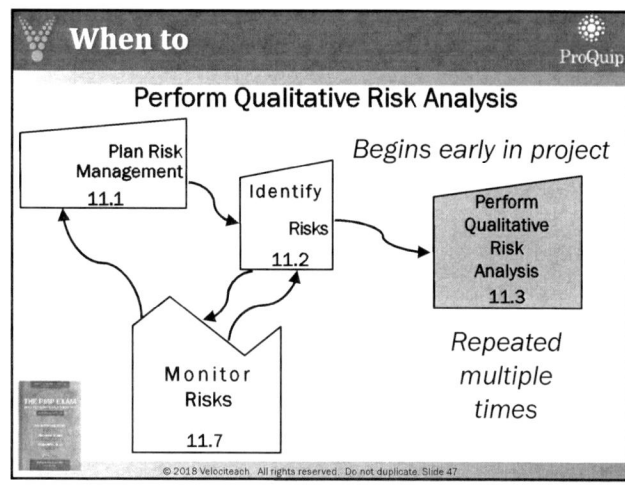

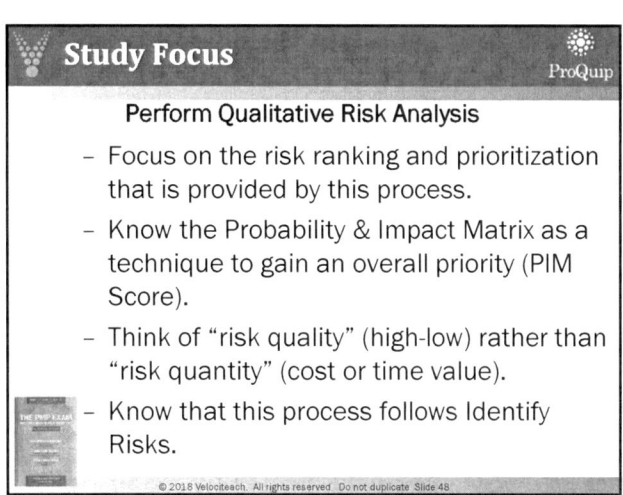

ProQuip

Perform Qualitative Risk Analysis

© 2018 Velociteach. All rights reserved.

This page left intentionally blank.

©2018 Velociteach. All rights reserved.

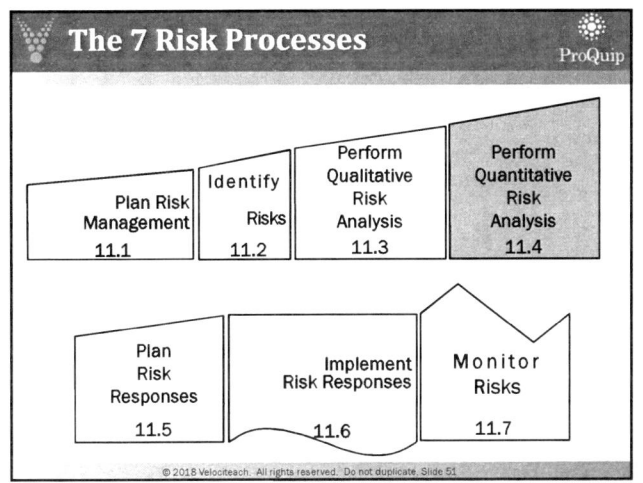

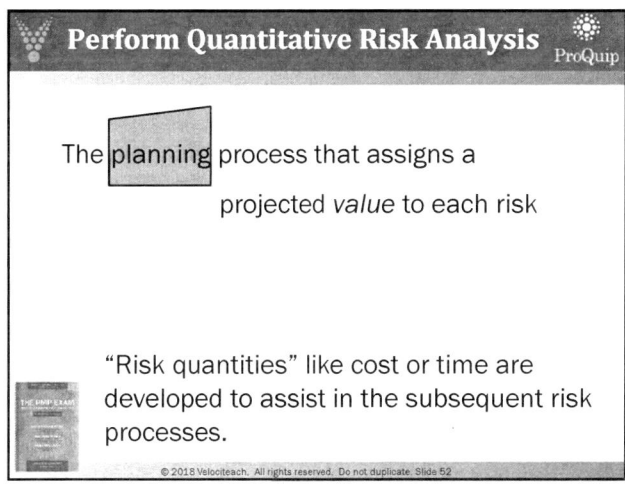

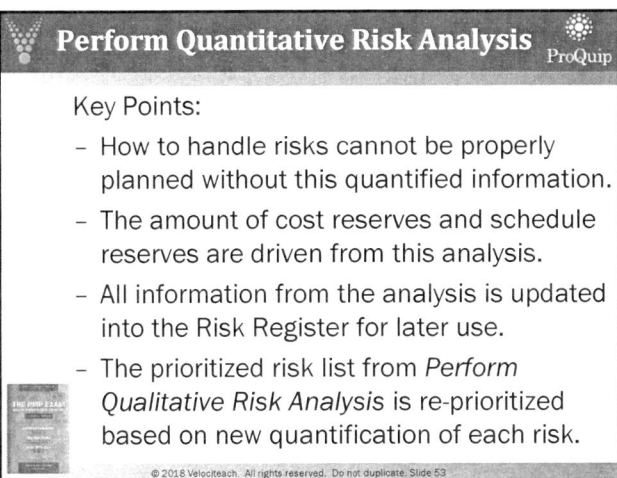

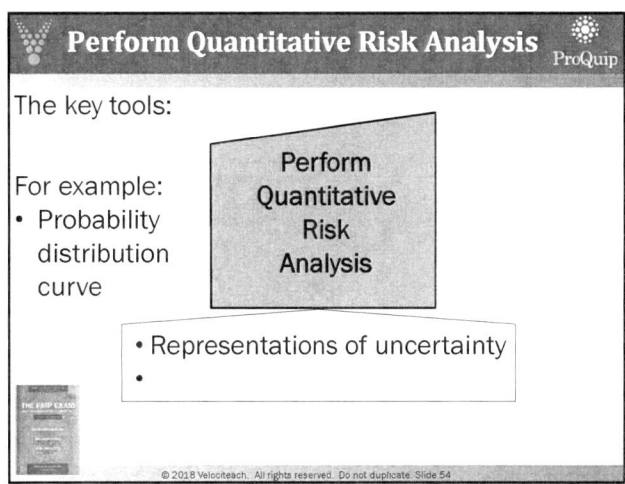

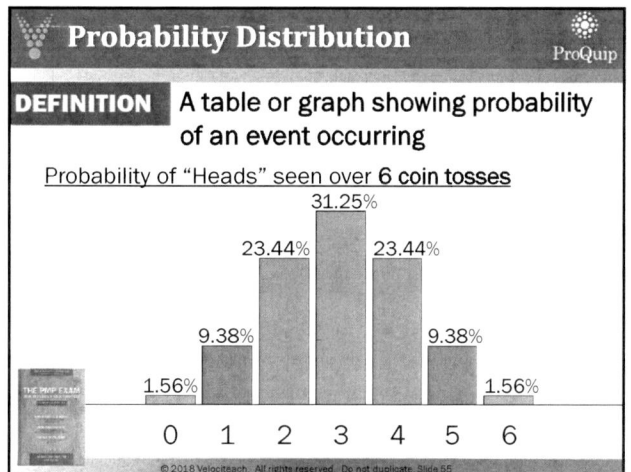

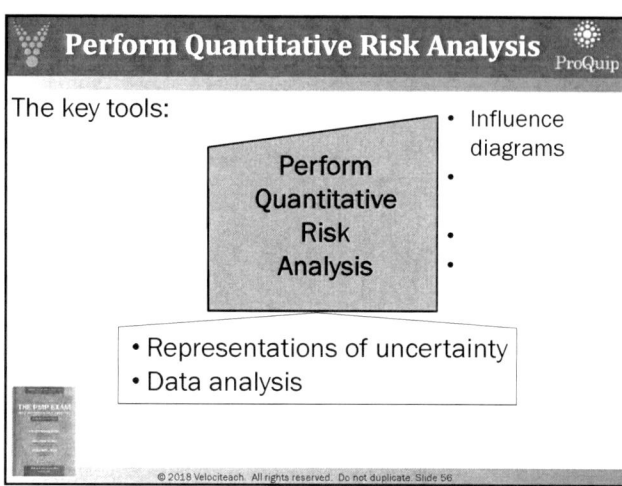

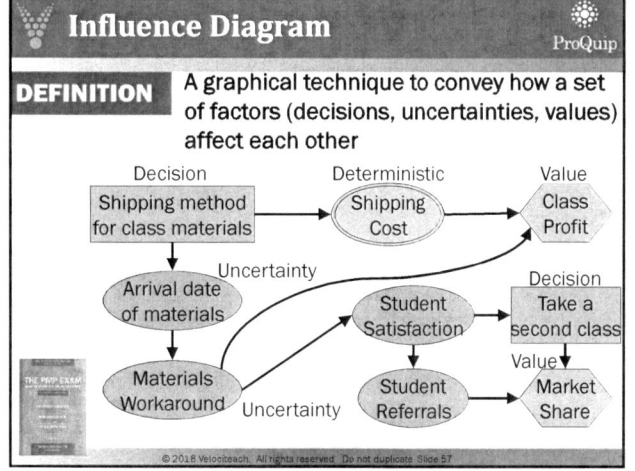

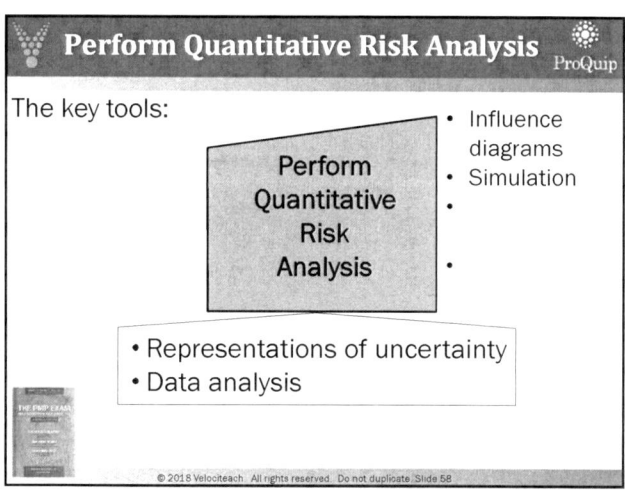

©2018 Velociteach. All rights reserved.   Page 286

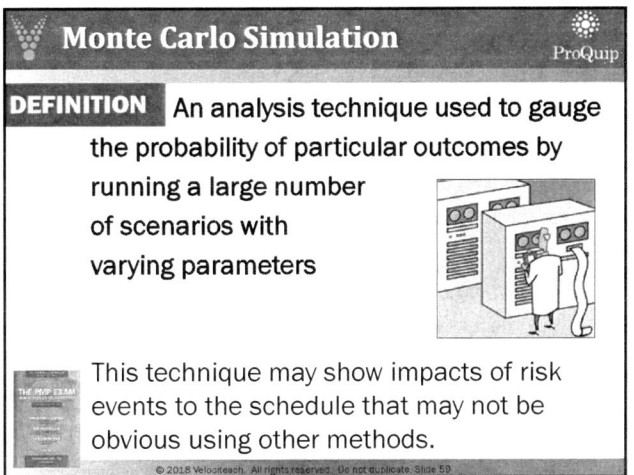

Monte Carlo Simulation

DEFINITION An analysis technique used to gauge the probability of particular outcomes by running a large number of scenarios with varying parameters

This technique may show impacts of risk events to the schedule that may not be obvious using other methods.

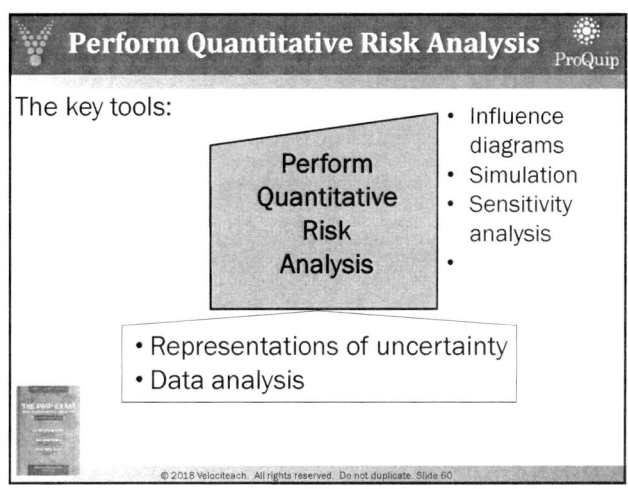

Perform Quantitative Risk Analysis

The key tools:

Perform Quantitative Risk Analysis

- Influence diagrams
- Simulation
- Sensitivity analysis
-

- Representations of uncertainty
- Data analysis

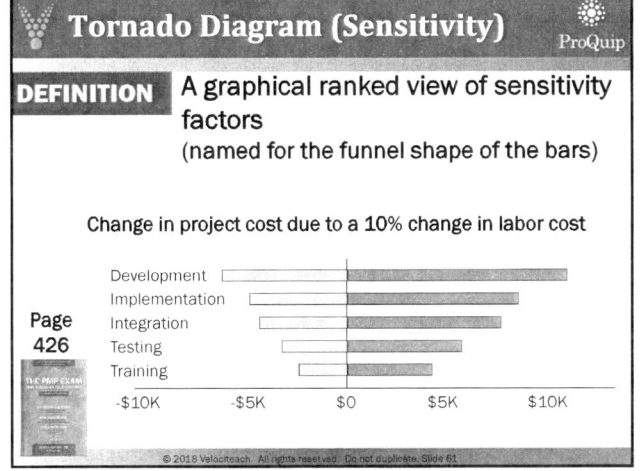

Tornado Diagram (Sensitivity)

DEFINITION A graphical ranked view of sensitivity factors
(named for the funnel shape of the bars)

Change in project cost due to a 10% change in labor cost

Page 426

Development
Implementation
Integration
Testing
Training

-$10K   -$5K $0 $5K $10K

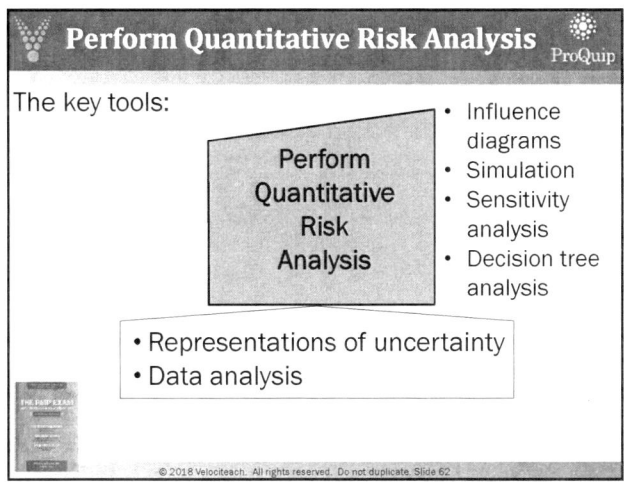

Perform Quantitative Risk Analysis

The key tools:

Perform Quantitative Risk Analysis

- Influence diagrams
- Simulation
- Sensitivity analysis
- Decision tree analysis

- Representations of uncertainty
- Data analysis

©2018 Velociteach. All rights reserved.   Page 287

Expected Monetary Value (EMV)

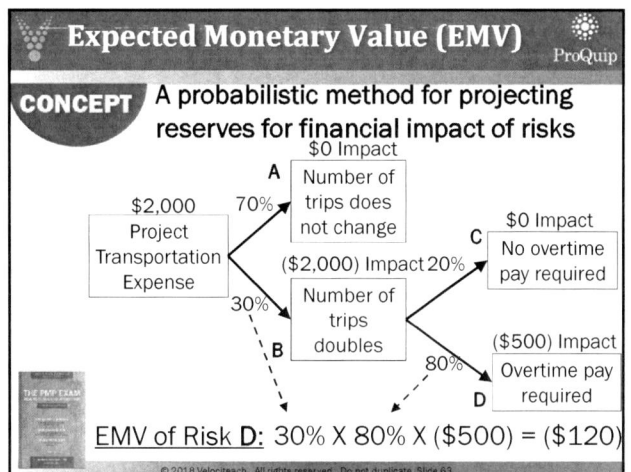

CONCEPT A probabilistic method for projecting reserves for financial impact of risks

EMV of Risk D: 30% X 80% X ($500) = ($120)

© 2018 Velociteach. All rights reserved. Do not duplicate Slide 63

Decision Tree (using EMV)

Technique used to combine probability and impact of the potential results of a decision

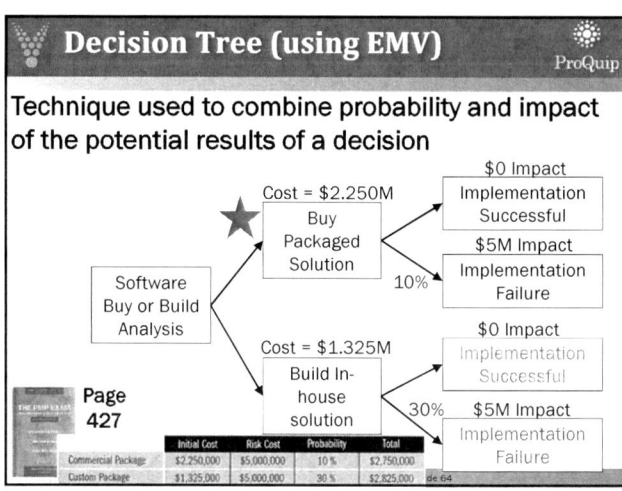

Page 427

	Initial Cost	Risk Cost	Probability	Total
Commercial Package	$2,250,000	$5,000,000	10 %	$2,750,000
Custom Package	$1,325,000	$5,000,000	30 %	$2,825,000

When to

Perform Quantitative Risk Analysis

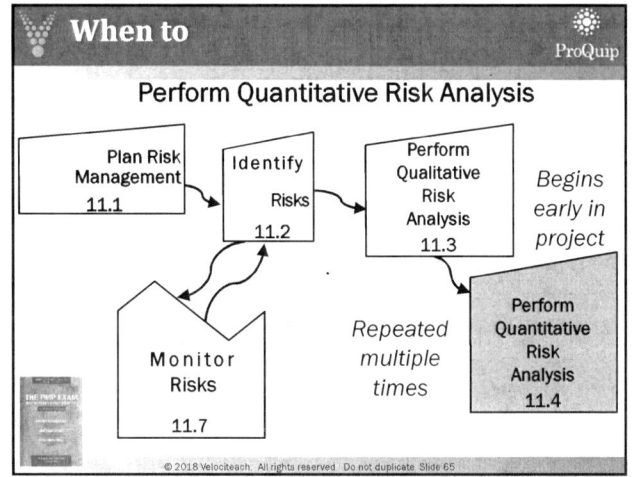

© 2018 Velociteach. All rights reserved. Do not duplicate Slide 65

Study Focus

Perform Quantitative Risk Analysis

– Focus on the word "quantity" for Quantitative analysis vs. "quality" for Qualitative analysis.

– Know that values for cost as well as time are developed during this process.

– Be familiar with Decision Trees as well as Expected Monetary Value analysis.

– Know that the Risk Register is updated with the values developed for each risk.

© 2018 Velociteach. All rights reserved. Do not duplicate Slide 68

Review the ITTOs

Perform Quantitative Risk Analysis

© 2018 Velociteach. All rights reserved.

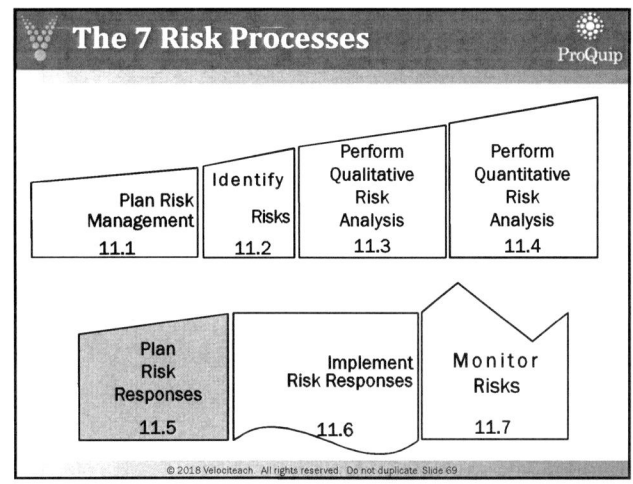

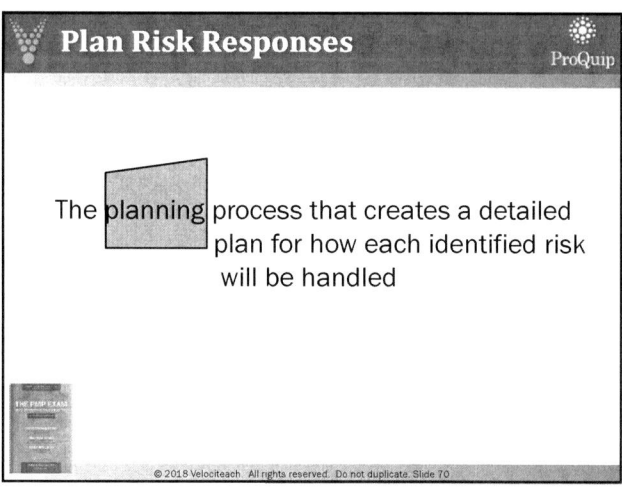

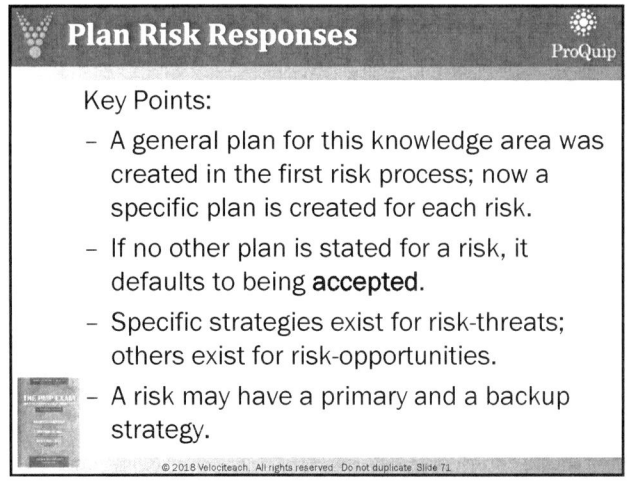

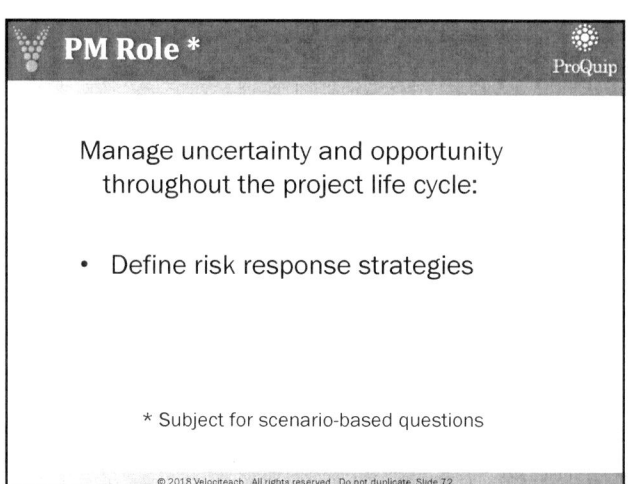

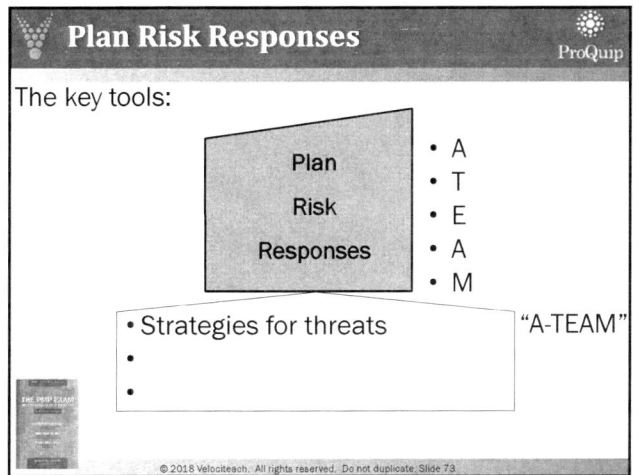

Plan Risk Responses   ProQuip

The key tools:

Plan Risk Responses

- A
- T
- E
- A
- M

"A-TEAM"

- Strategies for threats
-
-

© 2018 Velociteach. All rights reserved. Do not duplicate. Slide 73

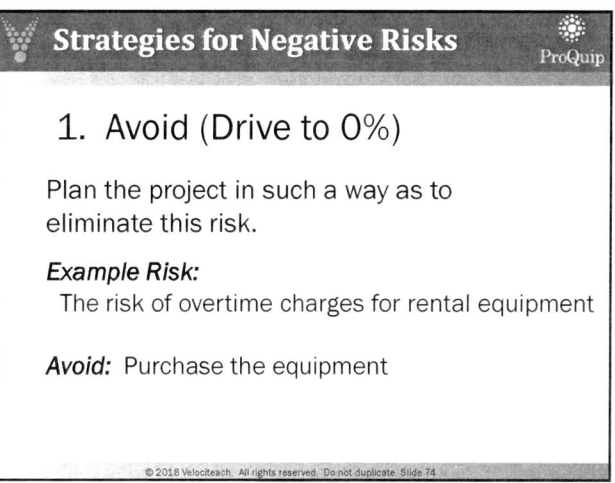

Strategies for Negative Risks   ProQuip

1. Avoid (Drive to 0%)

Plan the project in such a way as to eliminate this risk.

Example Risk:
The risk of overtime charges for rental equipment

Avoid: Purchase the equipment

© 2018 Velociteach. All rights reserved. Do not duplicate. Slide 74

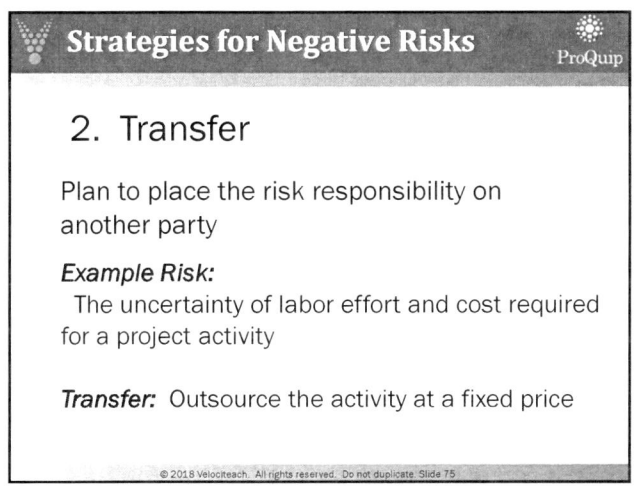

Strategies for Negative Risks   ProQuip

2. Transfer

Plan to place the risk responsibility on another party

Example Risk:
The uncertainty of labor effort and cost required for a project activity

Transfer: Outsource the activity at a fixed price

© 2018 Velociteach. All rights reserved. Do not duplicate. Slide 75

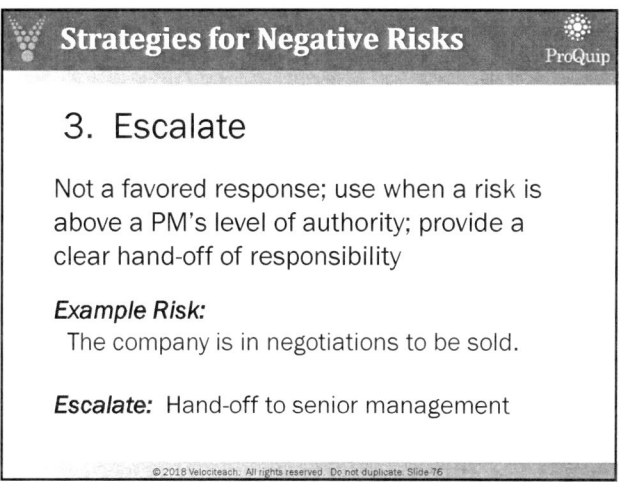

Strategies for Negative Risks   ProQuip

3. Escalate

Not a favored response; use when a risk is above a PM's level of authority; provide a clear hand-off of responsibility

Example Risk:
The company is in negotiations to be sold.

Escalate: Hand-off to senior management

© 2018 Velociteach. All rights reserved. Do not duplicate. Slide 76

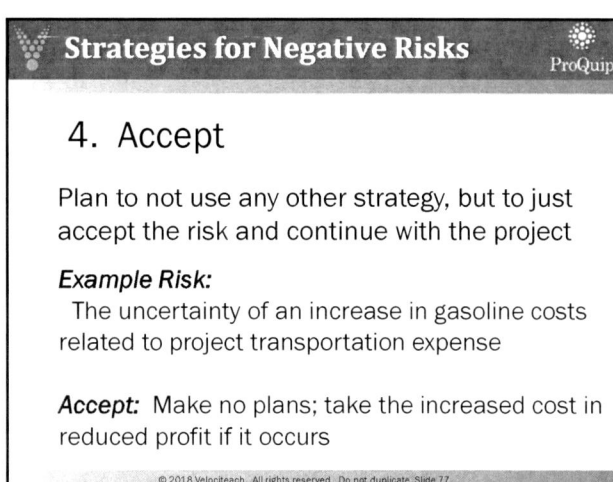

Strategies for Negative Risks

ProQuip

4. Accept

Plan to not use any other strategy, but to just accept the risk and continue with the project

Example Risk:
  The uncertainty of an increase in gasoline costs related to project transportation expense

Accept: Make no plans; take the increased cost in reduced profit if it occurs

© 2018 Velociteach. All rights reserved. Do not duplicate. Slide 77

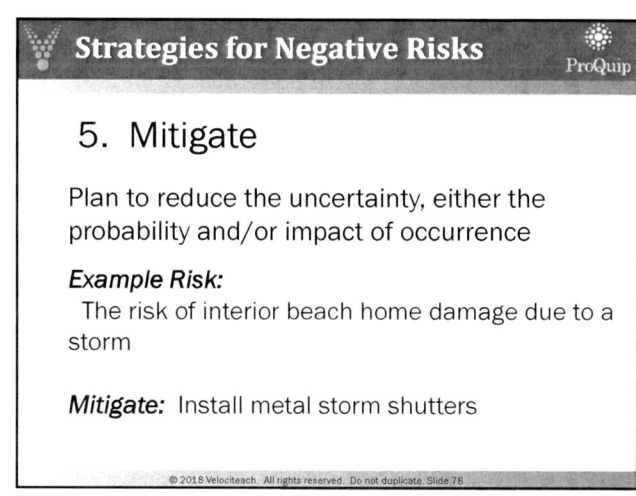

Strategies for Negative Risks

ProQuip

5. Mitigate

Plan to reduce the uncertainty, either the probability and/or impact of occurrence

Example Risk:
  The risk of interior beach home damage due to a storm

Mitigate: Install metal storm shutters

© 2018 Velociteach. All rights reserved. Do not duplicate. Slide 78

Plan Risk Responses

ProQuip

The key tools:

Plan Risk Responses

- Accept
- Transfer
- Escalate
- Avoid
- Mitigate

- Strategies for threats   "A-TEAM"
-
-

© 2018 Velociteach. All rights reserved. Do not duplicate. Slide 79

Plan Risk Responses

ProQuip

The key tools:

Plan Risk Responses

- E
- A
- S
- E
- E

- Strategies for threats
- Strategies for opportunities   "EASEE"
-

© 2018 Velociteach. All rights reserved. Do not duplicate. Slide 80

©2018 Velociteach. All rights reserved.

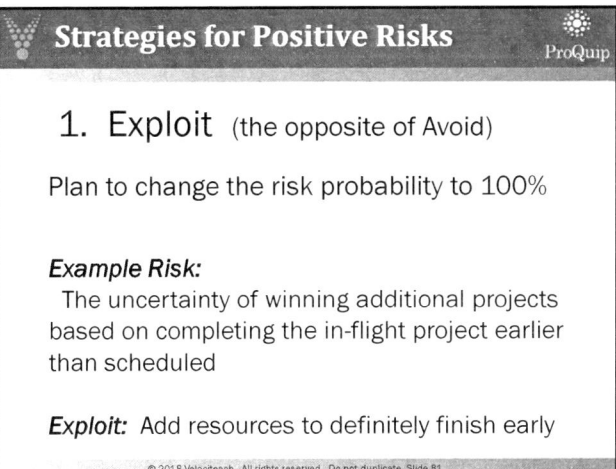

Strategies for Positive Risks   ProQuip

1. Exploit (the opposite of Avoid)

Plan to change the risk probability to 100%

Example Risk:
The uncertainty of winning additional projects based on completing the in-flight project earlier than scheduled

Exploit: Add resources to definitely finish early

© 2018 Velociteach. All rights reserved. Do not duplicate. Slide 81

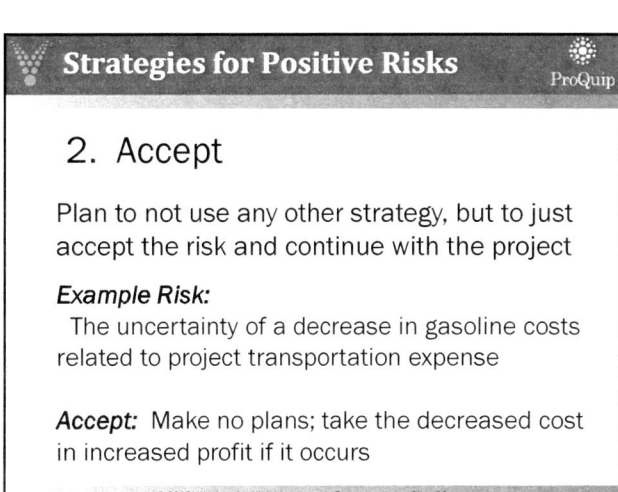

Strategies for Positive Risks   ProQuip

2. Accept

Plan to not use any other strategy, but to just accept the risk and continue with the project

Example Risk:
The uncertainty of a decrease in gasoline costs related to project transportation expense

Accept: Make no plans; take the decreased cost in increased profit if it occurs

© 2018 Velociteach. All rights reserved. Do not duplicate. Slide 82

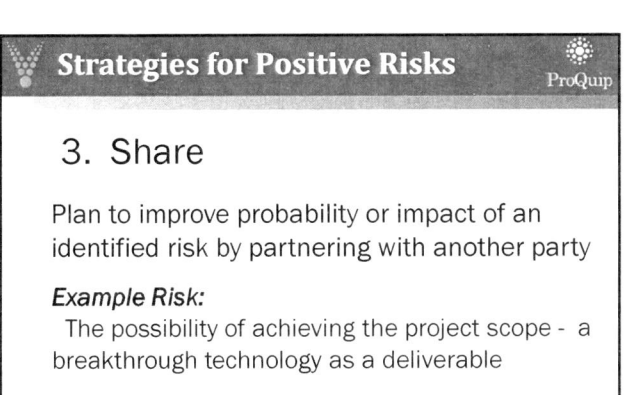

Strategies for Positive Risks   ProQuip

3. Share

Plan to improve probability or impact of an identified risk by partnering with another party

Example Risk:
The possibility of achieving the project scope - a breakthrough technology as a deliverable

Share: Structure the project as a joint venture with your team and a research & development firm

© 2018 Velociteach. All rights reserved. Do not duplicate. Slide 83

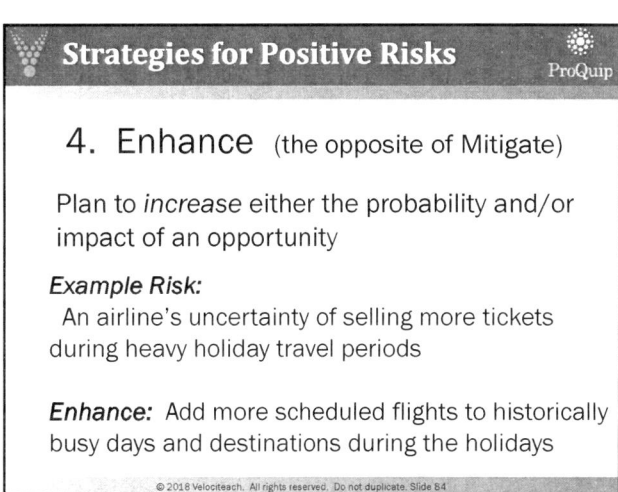

Strategies for Positive Risks   ProQuip

4. Enhance (the opposite of Mitigate)

Plan to *increase* either the probability and/or impact of an opportunity

Example Risk:
An airline's uncertainty of selling more tickets during heavy holiday travel periods

Enhance: Add more scheduled flights to historically busy days and destinations during the holidays

© 2018 Velociteach. All rights reserved. Do not duplicate. Slide 84

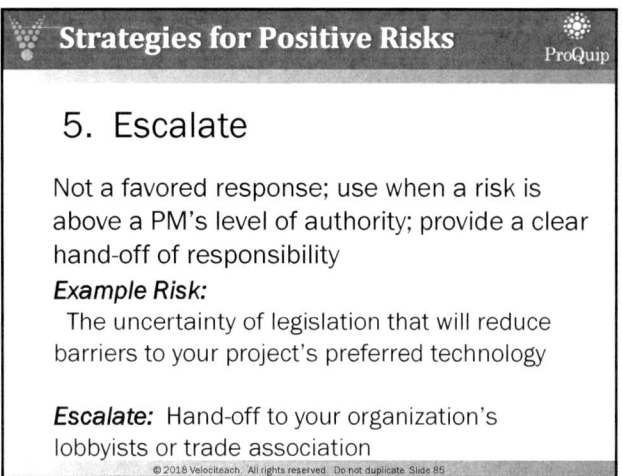

Strategies for Positive Risks

5. Escalate

Not a favored response; use when a risk is above a PM's level of authority; provide a clear hand-off of responsibility

Example Risk:
  The uncertainty of legislation that will reduce barriers to your project's preferred technology

Escalate: Hand-off to your organization's lobbyists or trade association

© 2018 Velociteach. All rights reserved. Do not duplicate. Slide 85

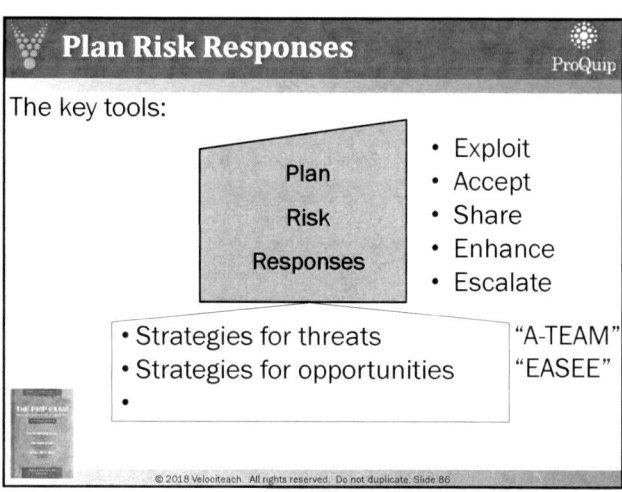

Plan Risk Responses

The key tools:

Plan Risk Responses

- Exploit
- Accept
- Share
- Enhance
- Escalate

- Strategies for threats
- Strategies for opportunities
-

"A-TEAM"
"EASEE"

© 2018 Velociteach. All rights reserved. Do not duplicate. Slide 86

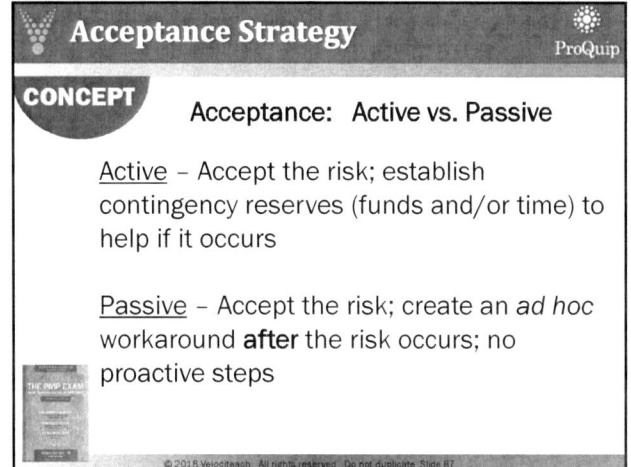

Acceptance Strategy

CONCEPT   Acceptance: Active vs. Passive

Active – Accept the risk; establish contingency reserves (funds and/or time) to help if it occurs

Passive – Accept the risk; create an *ad hoc* workaround **after** the risk occurs; no proactive steps

© 2018 Velociteach. All rights reserved. Do not duplicate. Slide 87

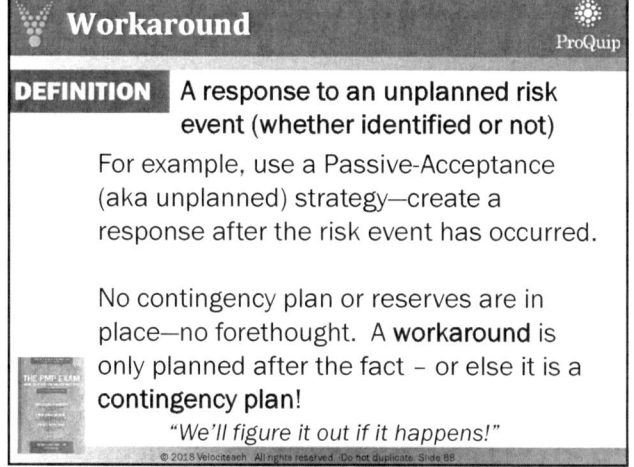

Workaround

DEFINITION A response to an unplanned risk event (whether identified or not)

For example, use a Passive-Acceptance (aka unplanned) strategy—create a response after the risk event has occurred.

No contingency plan or reserves are in place—no forethought. A **workaround** is only planned after the fact – or else it is a **contingency plan**!

"We'll figure it out if it happens!"

© 2018 Velociteach. All rights reserved. Do not duplicate. Slide 88

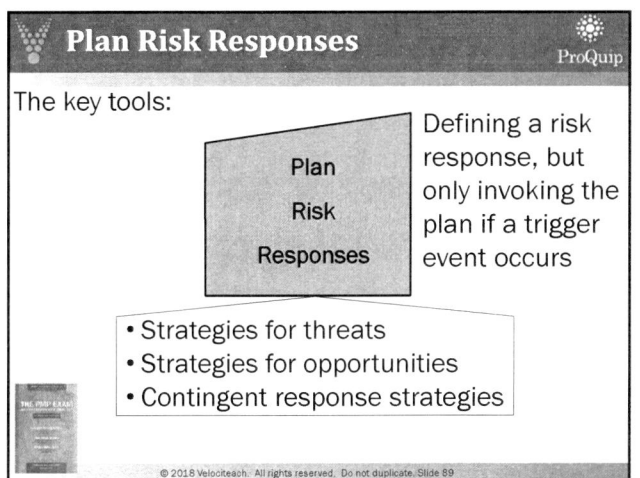

Plan Risk Responses

The key tools:

Plan Risk Responses

Defining a risk response, but only invoking the plan if a trigger event occurs

- Strategies for threats
- Strategies for opportunities
- Contingent response strategies

© 2018 Velociteach. All rights reserved. Do not duplicate. Slide 89

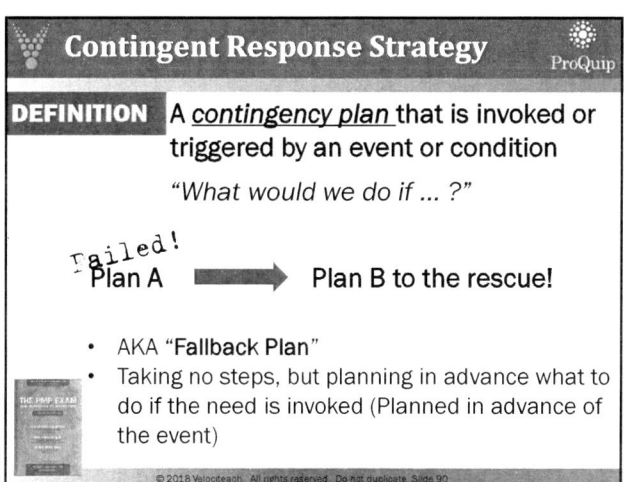

Contingent Response Strategy

DEFINITION A *contingency plan* that is invoked or triggered by an event or condition

"What would we do if … ?"

Failed!
Plan A ⟹ Plan B to the rescue!

- AKA "Fallback Plan"
- Taking no steps, but planning in advance what to do if the need is invoked (Planned in advance of the event)

© 2018 Velociteach. All rights reserved. Do not duplicate. Slide 90

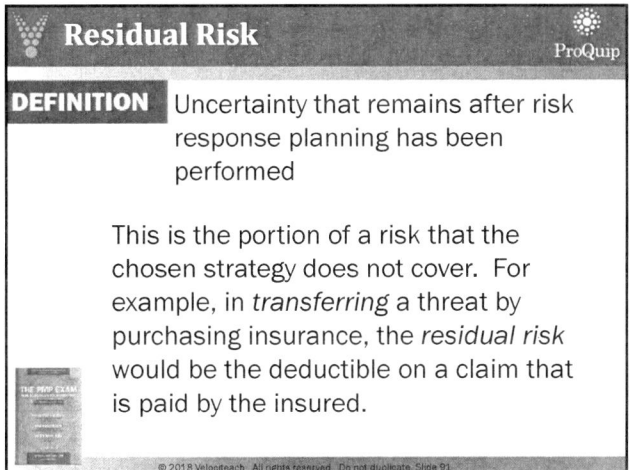

Residual Risk

DEFINITION Uncertainty that remains after risk response planning has been performed

This is the portion of a risk that the chosen strategy does not cover. For example, in *transferring* a threat by purchasing insurance, the *residual risk* would be the deductible on a claim that is paid by the insured.

© 2018 Velociteach. All rights reserved. Do not duplicate. Slide 91

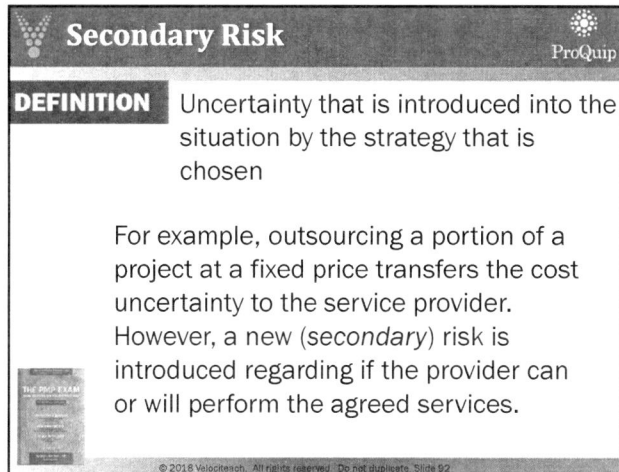

Secondary Risk

DEFINITION Uncertainty that is introduced into the situation by the strategy that is chosen

For example, outsourcing a portion of a project at a fixed price transfers the cost uncertainty to the service provider. However, a new (*secondary*) risk is introduced regarding if the provider can or will perform the agreed services.

© 2018 Velociteach. All rights reserved. Do not duplicate. Slide 92

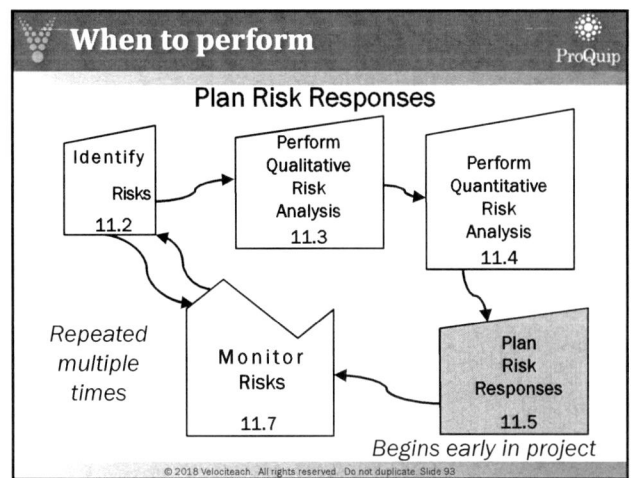

When to perform

Plan Risk Responses

Identify Risks 11.2 → Perform Qualitative Risk Analysis 11.3 → Perform Quantitative Risk Analysis 11.4

Repeated multiple times

Monitor Risks 11.7 ← Plan Risk Responses 11.5

Begins early in project

© 2018 Velociteach. All rights reserved. Do not duplicate. Slide 93

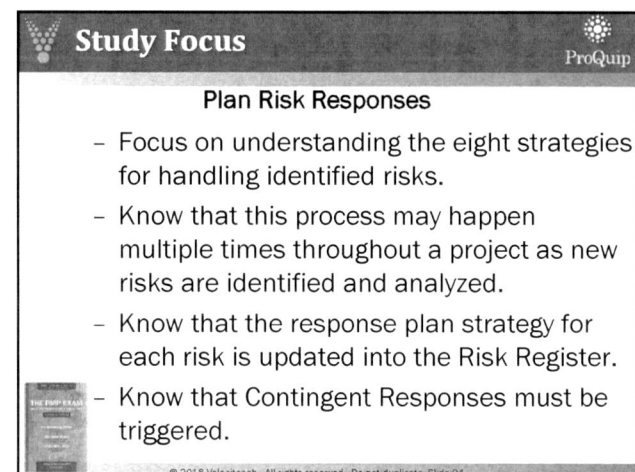

Study Focus

Plan Risk Responses

- Focus on understanding the eight strategies for handling identified risks.
- Know that this process may happen multiple times throughout a project as new risks are identified and analyzed.
- Know that the response plan strategy for each risk is updated into the Risk Register.
- Know that Contingent Responses must be triggered.

© 2018 Velociteach. All rights reserved. Do not duplicate. Slide 94

ProQuip

Review the ITTOs

Plan
Risk
Responses

● ● ●

© 2018 Velociteach. All rights reserved.

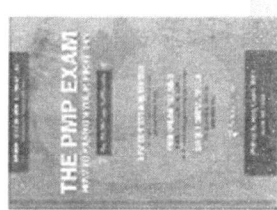

This page left intentionally blank.

©2018 Velociteach. All rights reserved.

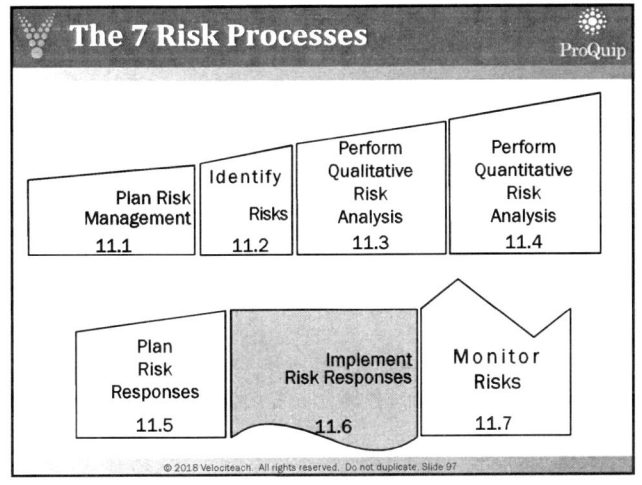

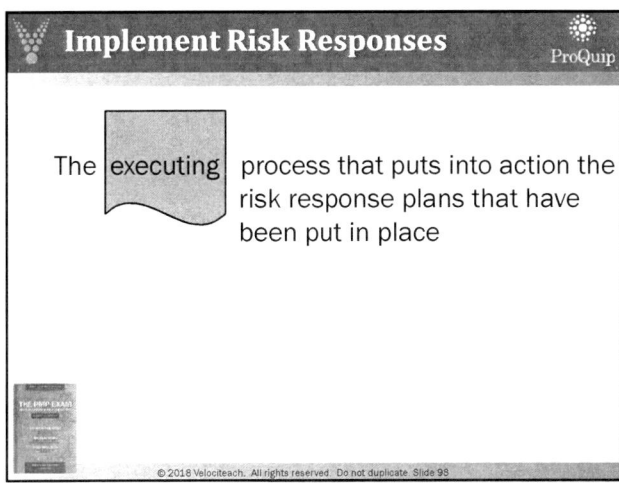

The executing process that puts into action the risk response plans that have been put in place

Key Points:

- This process is performed when the identified risks and responses appear.
- Risk owners must proactively manage performing the response plans for effective risk management.

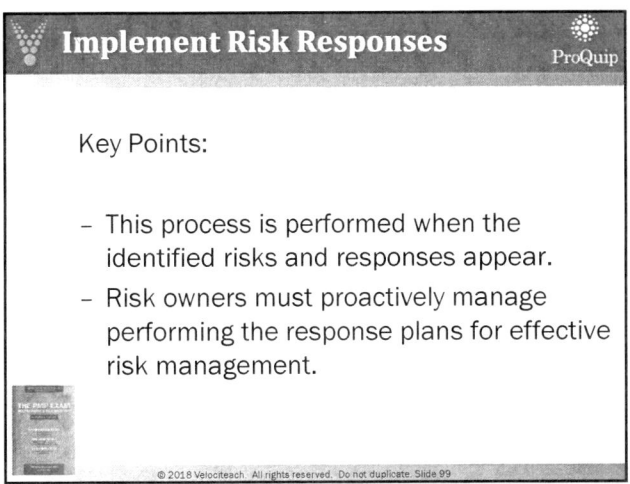

The key output:

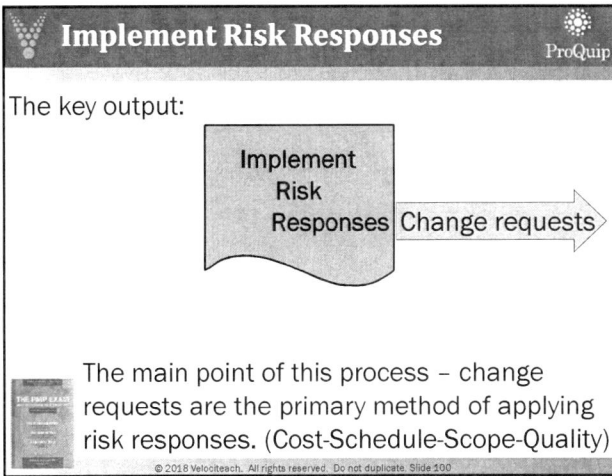

The main point of this process – change requests are the primary method of applying risk responses. (Cost-Schedule-Scope-Quality)

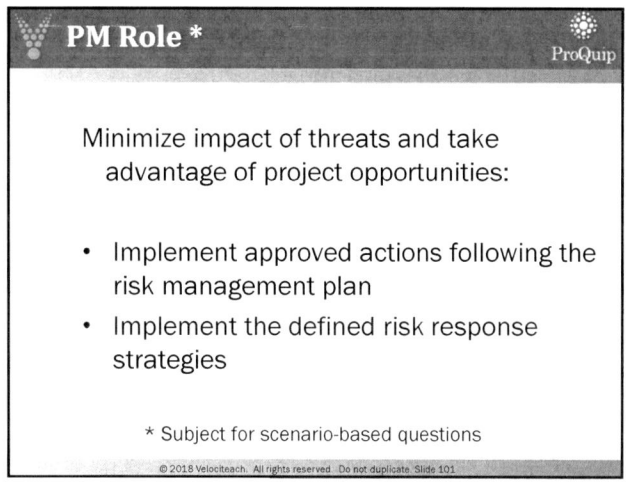

© 2018 Velociteach. All rights reserved. Do not duplicate. Slide 101

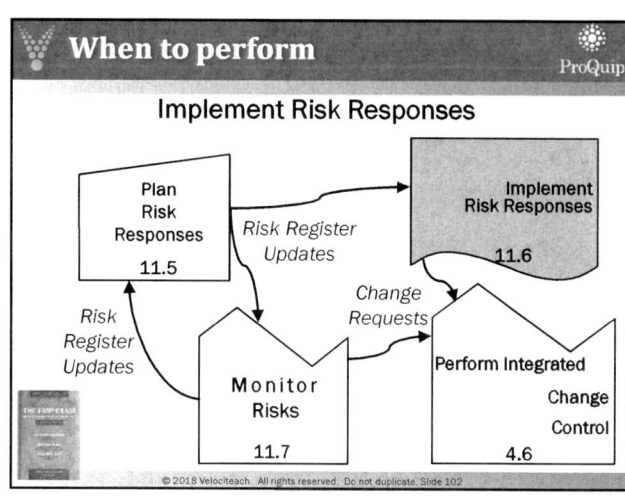

© 2018 Velociteach. All rights reserved. Do not duplicate. Slide 102

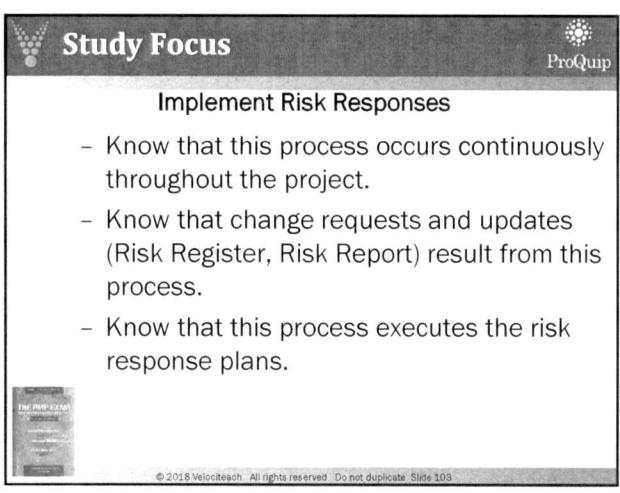

© 2018 Velociteach. All rights reserved. Do not duplicate. Slide 103

©2018 Velociteach. All rights reserved.

Review the ITTOs

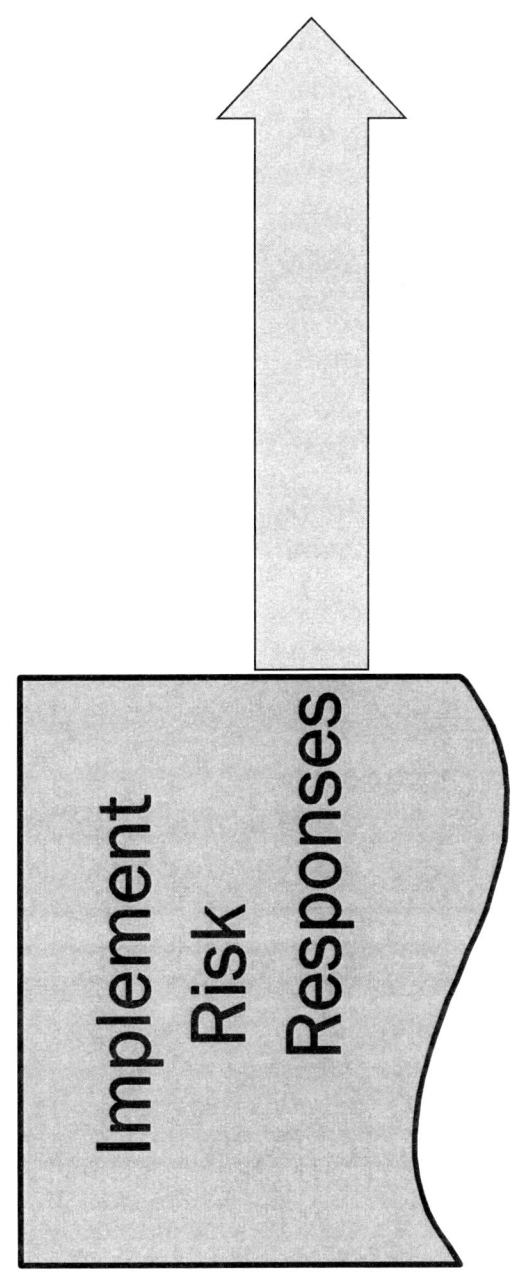

Implement Risk Responses

© 2018 Velociteach. All rights reserved.

This page left intentionally blank.

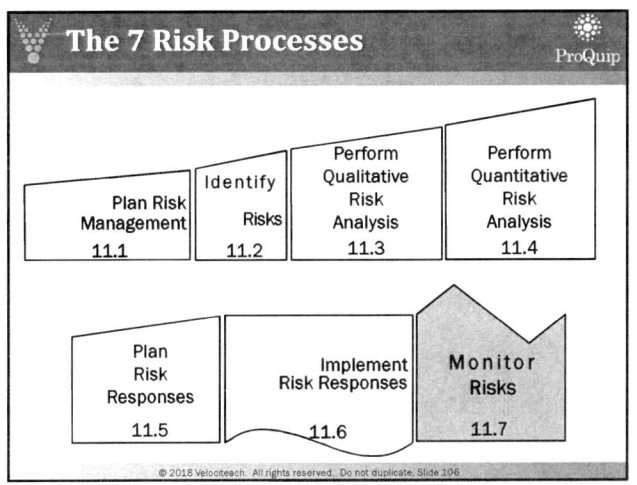

The 7 Risk Processes

Plan Risk Management 11.1 | Identify Risks 11.2 | Perform Qualitative Risk Analysis 11.3 | Perform Quantitative Risk Analysis 11.4

Plan Risk Responses 11.5 | Implement Risk Responses 11.6 | Monitor Risks 11.7

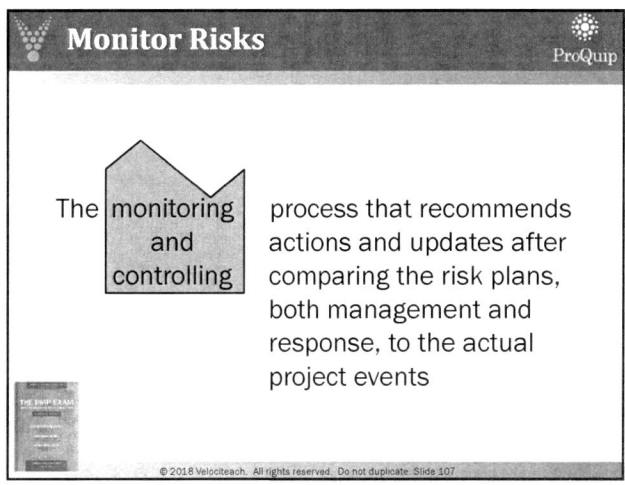

Monitor Risks

The monitoring and controlling process that recommends actions and updates after comparing the risk plans, both management and response, to the actual project events

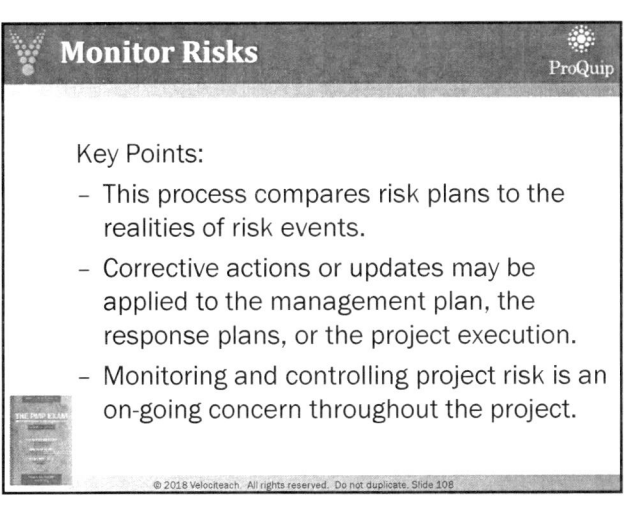

Monitor Risks

Key Points:

- This process compares risk plans to the realities of risk events.
- Corrective actions or updates may be applied to the management plan, the response plans, or the project execution.
- Monitoring and controlling project risk is an on-going concern throughout the project.

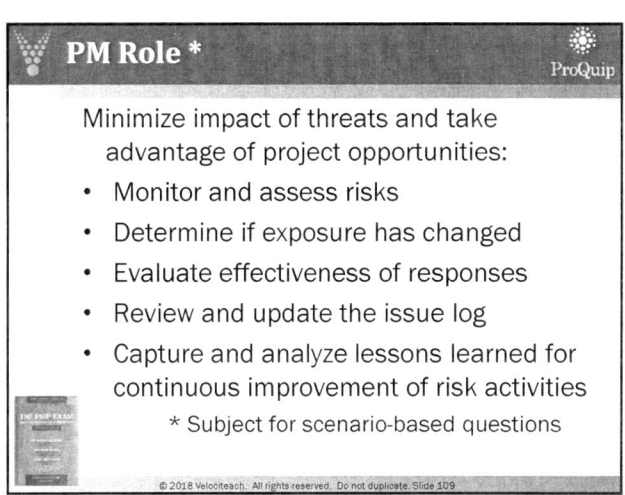

PM Role *

Minimize impact of threats and take advantage of project opportunities:

- Monitor and assess risks
- Determine if exposure has changed
- Evaluate effectiveness of responses
- Review and update the issue log
- Capture and analyze lessons learned for continuous improvement of risk activities

* Subject for scenario-based questions

©2018 Velociteach. All rights reserved. Page 303

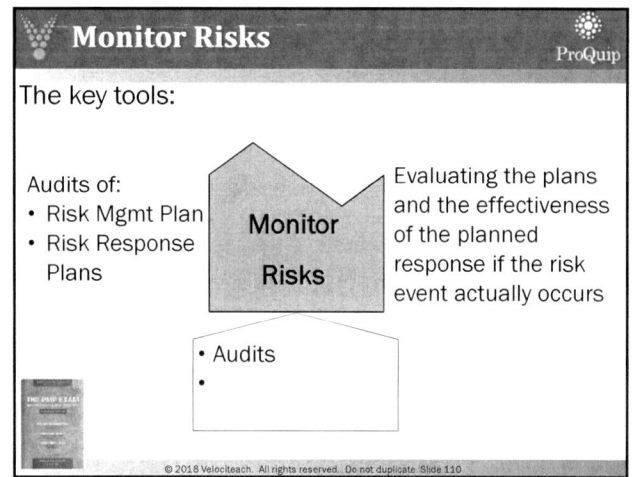

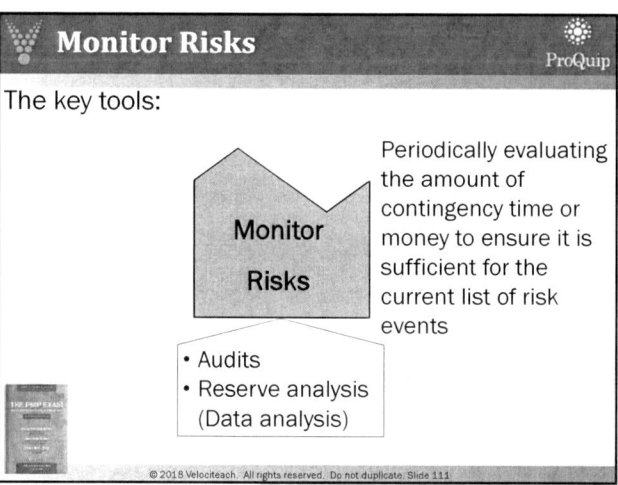

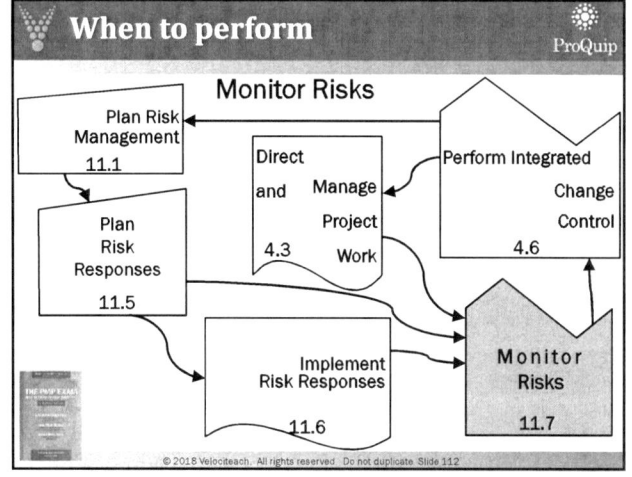

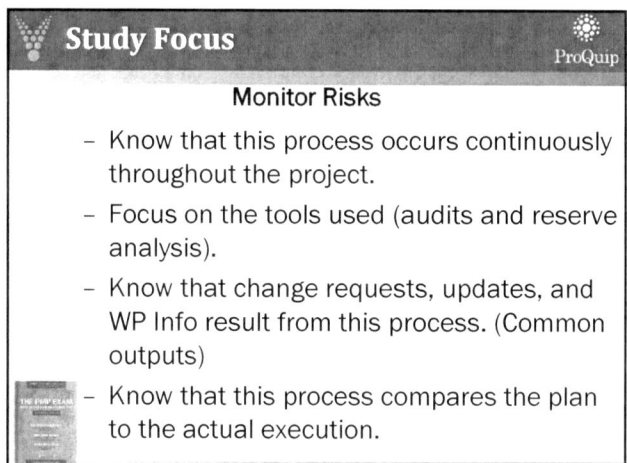

ProQuip

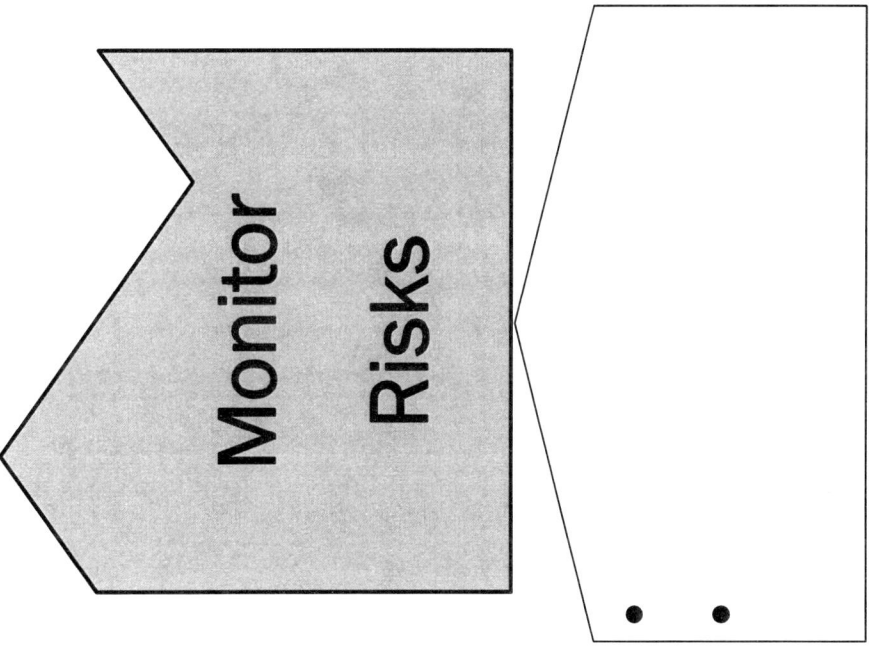

Monitor Risks

© 2018 Velociteach. All rights reserved.

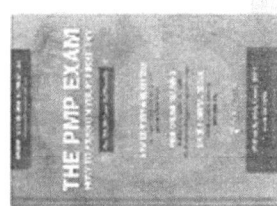

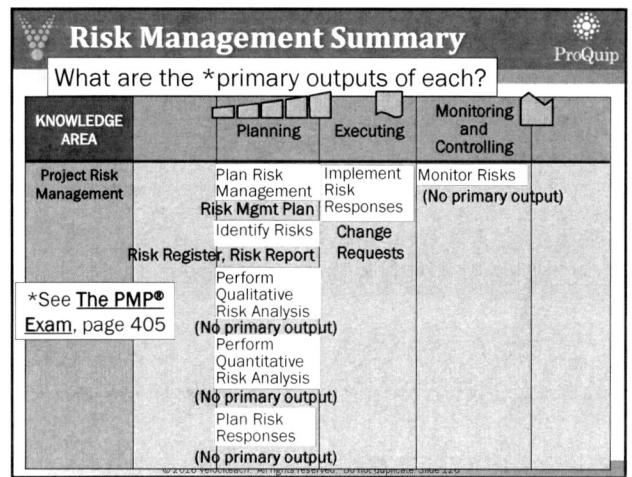

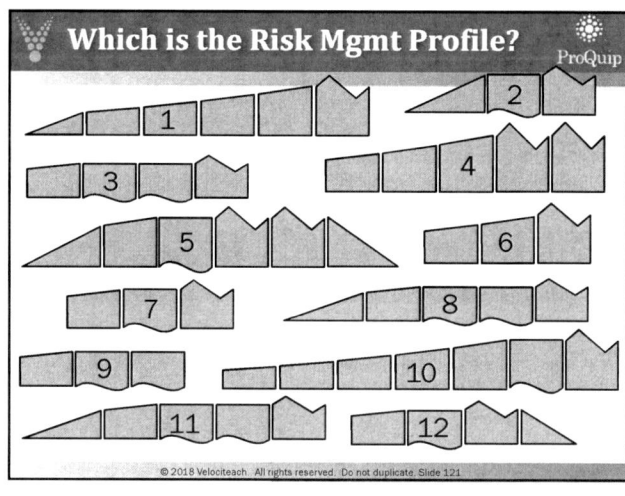

Terms You Should Know

Project Risk Management

Risk Management Plan	Identify Risks
Contingency / Reserve	Risk Breakdown Structure
Decision Tree / EMV	Risk Register / Risk Report
Reserve Analysis	Plan Risk Responses:
Influence Diagram	– Risk Acceptance
Monte Carlo Analysis	– Risk Avoidance
Opportunity / Threat	– Risk Enhancement
Probability & Impact Matrix	– Risk Escalation
Qualitative Risk Analysis	– Risk Exploitation
Quantitative Risk Analysis	– Risk Mitigation
Tornado Diagram	– Risk Transference
Residual / Secondary Risk	– Risk Sharing

© 2018 Velociteach. All rights reserved. Do not duplicate. Slide 123

Risk Discussion

Why can risks be considered positive or negative? What one word best describes risk?

When is a workaround created?

What is contained in the Risk Management Plan?

What does it mean to exploit an opportunity?

Describe three risk response strategies.

What happens with the values resulting from *Perform Quantitative Risk Analysis*?

© 2018 Velociteach. All rights reserved. Do not duplicate. Slide 124

Summary

ProQuip

Knowledge Area

KNOWLEDGE AREA	Initiating	Planning	Executing	Monitoring and Controlling	Closing
Project Management					

©2018 Velociteach. All rights reserved. Page 307

This page left intentionally blank.

©2018 Velociteach. All rights reserved.

Score Sheet	**Risk Management Exam**	 Velociteach			

- **Mark one answer: A, B, C, or D.**
- **Circle the '?' symbol if you are guessing at the answer.**
- **Circle the Δ symbol if you change your answer.**

Total Correct: _____

% Correct: _____%

1.	A ○	B ○	C ○	D ○	? Δ
2.	A ○	B ○	C ○	D ○	? Δ
3.	A ○	B ○	C ○	D ○	? Δ
4.	A ○	B ○	C ○	D ○	? Δ
5.	A ○	B ○	C ○	D ○	? Δ
6.	A ○	B ○	C ○	D ○	? Δ
7.	A ○	B ○	C ○	D ○	? Δ
8.	A ○	B ○	C ○	D ○	? Δ
9.	A ○	B ○	C ○	D ○	? Δ
10.	A ○	B ○	C ○	D ○	? Δ
11.	A ○	B ○	C ○	D ○	? Δ
12.	A ○	B ○	C ○	D ○	? Δ
13.	A ○	B ○	C ○	D ○	? Δ
14.	A ○	B ○	C ○	D ○	? Δ
15.	A ○	B ○	C ○	D ○	? Δ
16.	A ○	B ○	C ○	D ○	? Δ
17.	A ○	B ○	C ○	D ○	? Δ
18.	A ○	B ○	C ○	D ○	? Δ
19.	A ○	B ○	C ○	D ○	? Δ
20.	A ○	B ○	C ○	D ○	? Δ
21.	A ○	B ○	C ○	D ○	? Δ
22.	A ○	B ○	C ○	D ○	? Δ
23.	A ○	B ○	C ○	D ○	? Δ
24.	A ○	B ○	C ○	D ○	? Δ
25.	A ○	B ○	C ○	D ○	? Δ

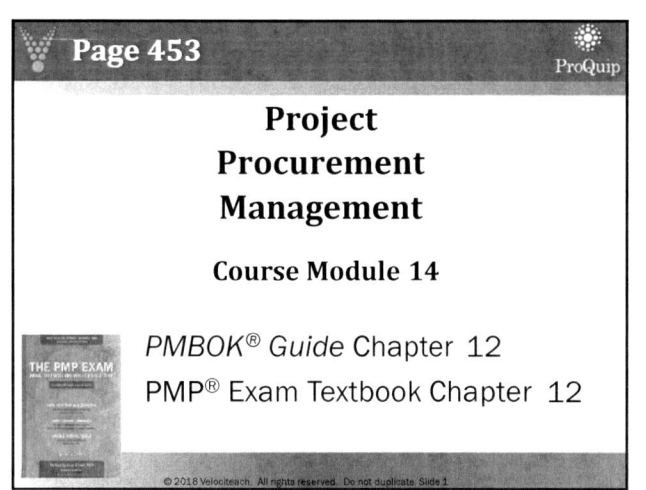

Page 453
ProQuip

Project Procurement Management

Course Module 14

PMBOK® Guide Chapter 12
PMP® Exam Textbook Chapter 12

© 2018 Velociteach. All rights reserved. Do not duplicate. Slide 1

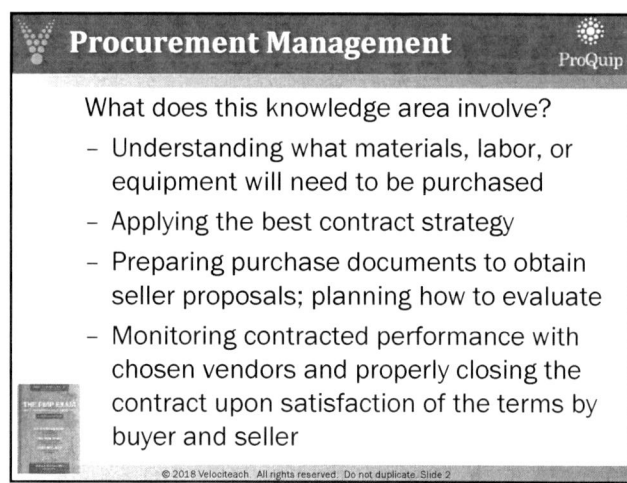

Procurement Management
ProQuip

What does this knowledge area involve?
- Understanding what materials, labor, or equipment will need to be purchased
- Applying the best contract strategy
- Preparing purchase documents to obtain seller proposals; planning how to evaluate
- Monitoring contracted performance with chosen vendors and properly closing the contract upon satisfaction of the terms by buyer and seller

© 2018 Velociteach. All rights reserved. Do not duplicate. Slide 2

Philosophy: Procurement Mgmt
ProQuip

- Procurement management should be formal; include your legal and purchasing departments.

- The approach is rigid, patterned after that of U.S. government and military practices.

- The Procurement process framework applies to a formal contractual relationship between a buyer and a seller. It may also be applied to agreements between internal units of an organization.

© 2018 Velociteach. All rights reserved. Do not duplicate. Slide 3

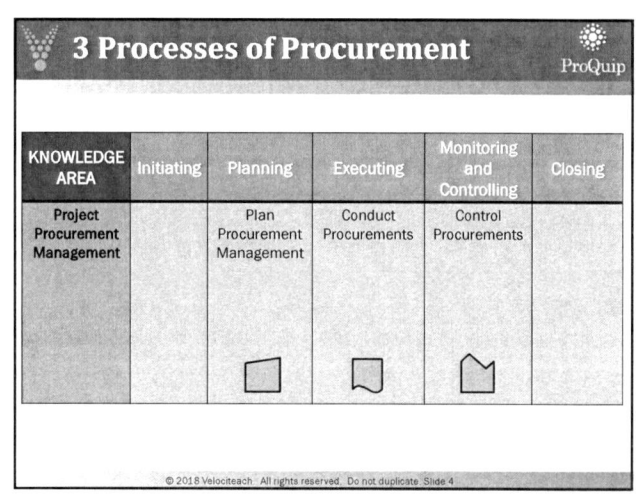

3 Processes of Procurement
ProQuip

KNOWLEDGE AREA	Initiating	Planning	Executing	Monitoring and Controlling	Closing
Project Procurement Management		Plan Procurement Management	Conduct Procurements	Control Procurements	

© 2018 Velociteach. All rights reserved. Do not duplicate. Slide 4

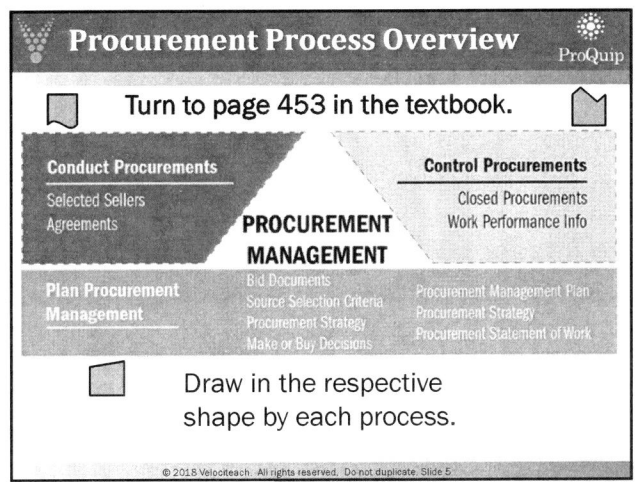

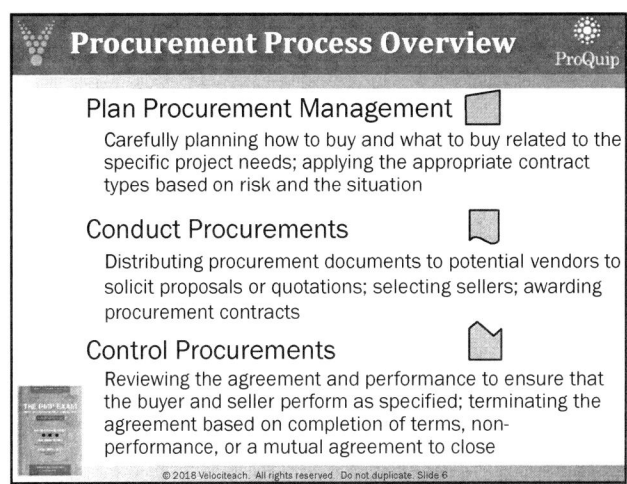

©2018 Velociteach. All rights reserved.　Page 311

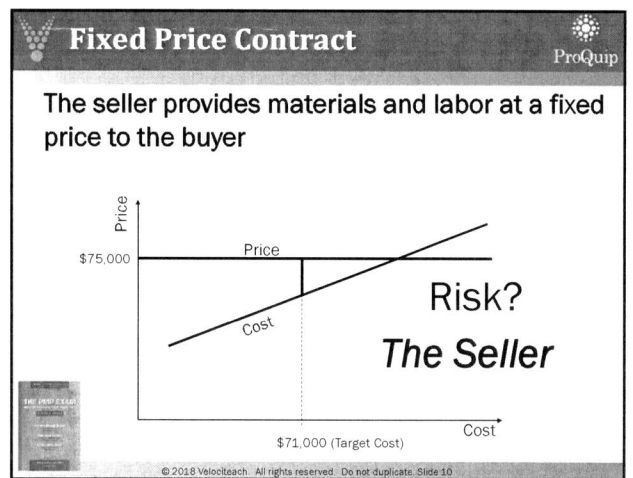

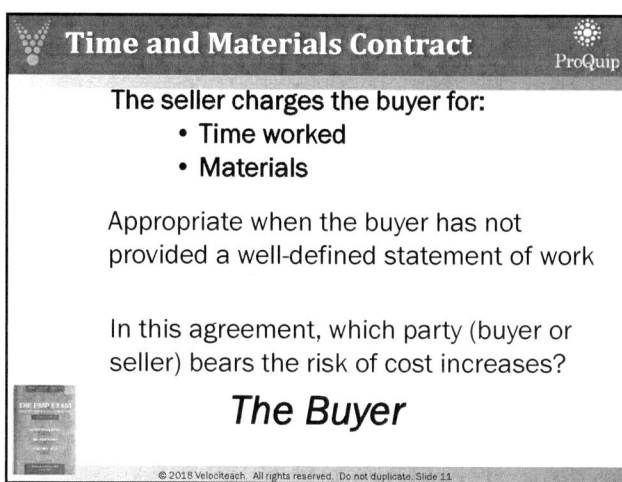

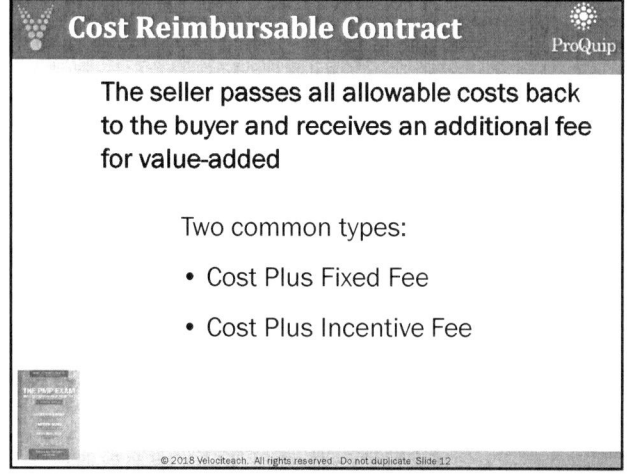

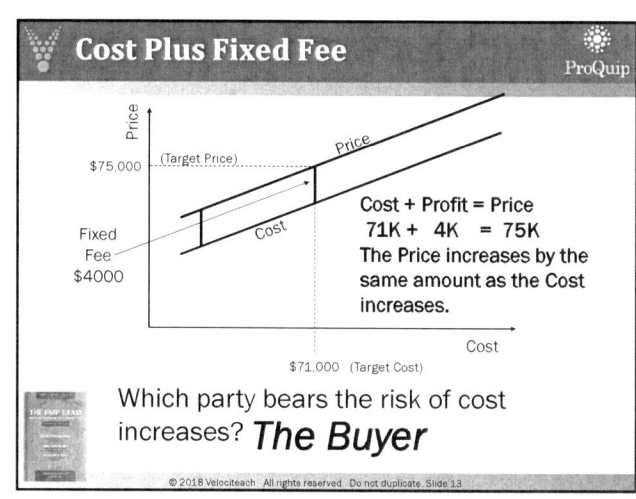

©2018 Velociteach. All rights reserved.   Page 312

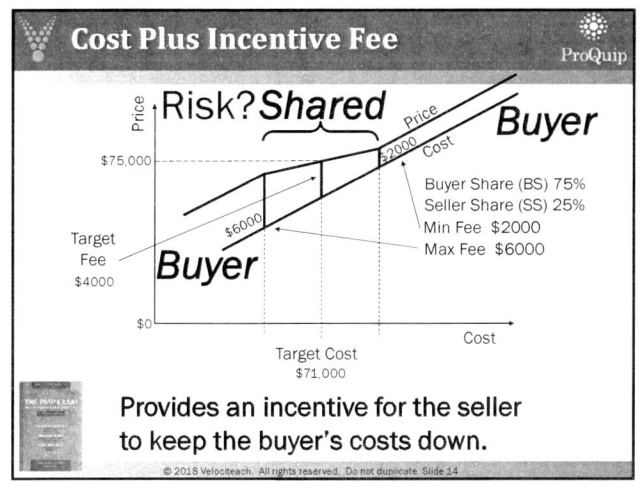

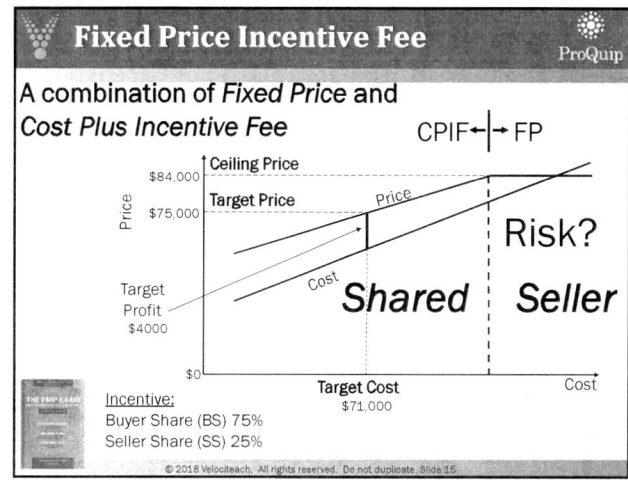

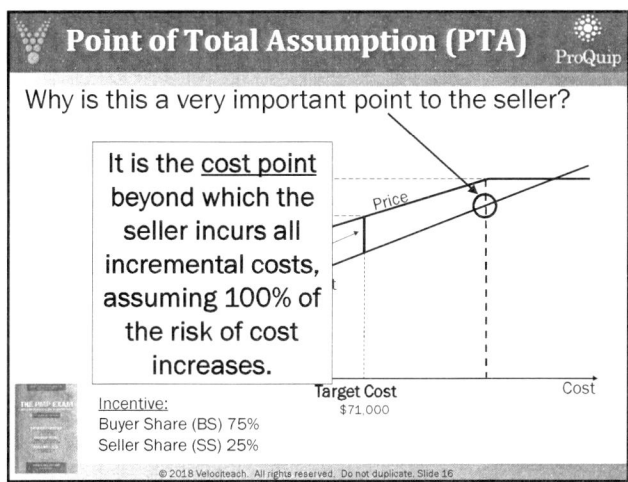

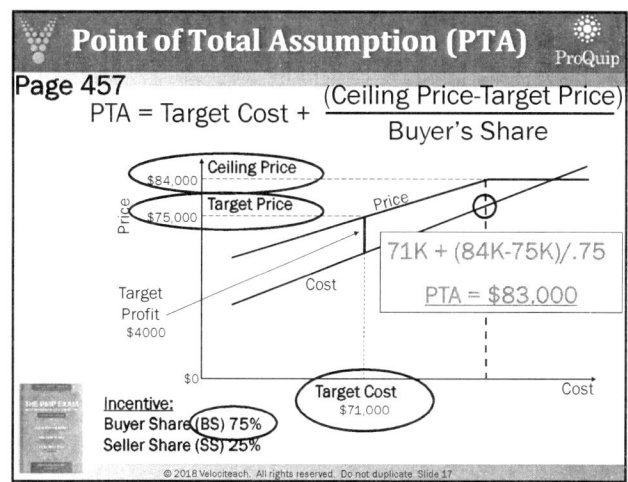

Fixed Price with EPA

Economic Price Adjustments (EPA)

Useful in a long-term (years) contract to adjust the contract price based on a financial index

Risk? It is still a fixed price contract with the seller bearing the performance risk; however, the EPA provides pre-defined protection for both the buyer and seller tied to interest rates, prices indices, or exchange rates, for example.

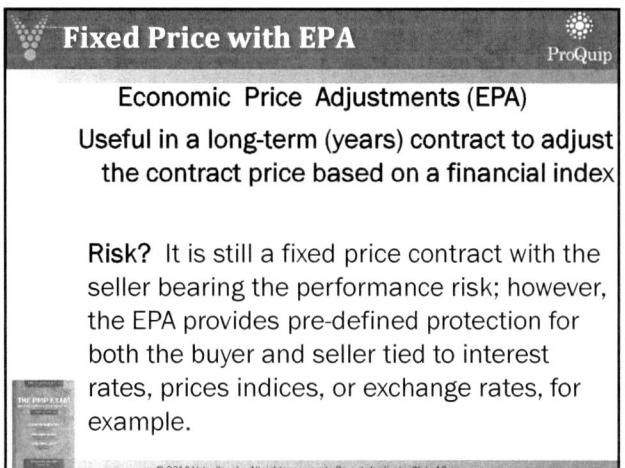

© 2018 Velociteach. All rights reserved. Do not duplicate. Slide 18

The 3 Procurement Processes

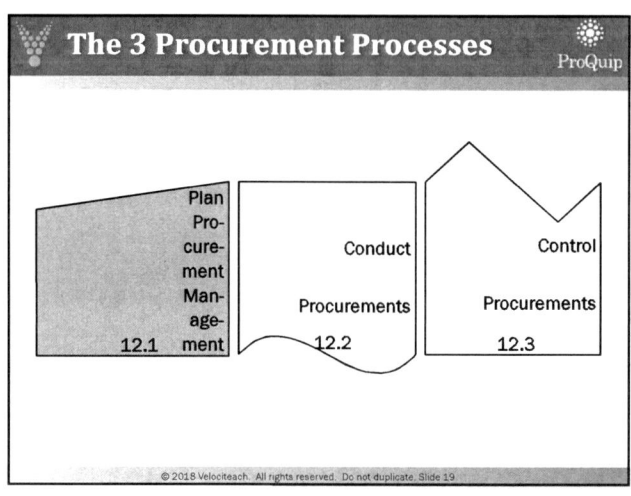

Plan Procurement Management 12.1

Conduct Procurements 12.2

Control Procurements 12.3

© 2018 Velociteach. All rights reserved. Do not duplicate. Slide 19

Plan Procurement Management

The planning process that ascertains which project services or products will be purchased from outside the organization and how

This results in creating the

Procurement Management Plan

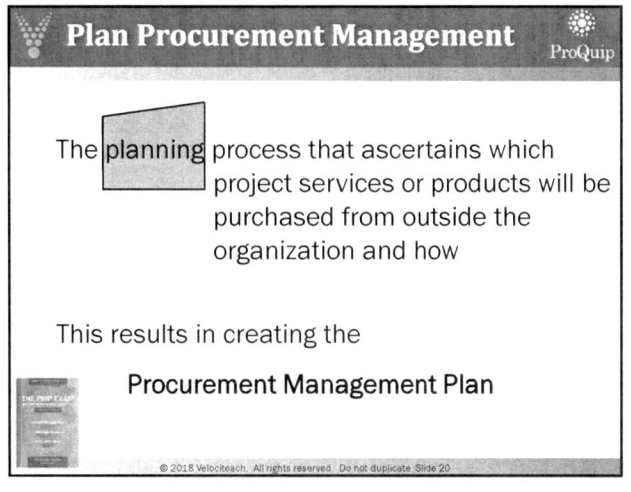

© 2018 Velociteach. All rights reserved. Do not duplicate. Slide 20

Plan Procurement Management

Key Points

- Planning helps ensure that the right products are purchased the right way.
- "Make vs. buy" decisions occur in this process.
- Not just what to buy is important, but also how to buy; what is the most appropriate contract type?
- Risk decisions affect contract selections.
- Plan how sellers' proposals will be evaluated; include pertinent data requests in the Request For Proposal (RFP) to receive back the data needed to make a selection.

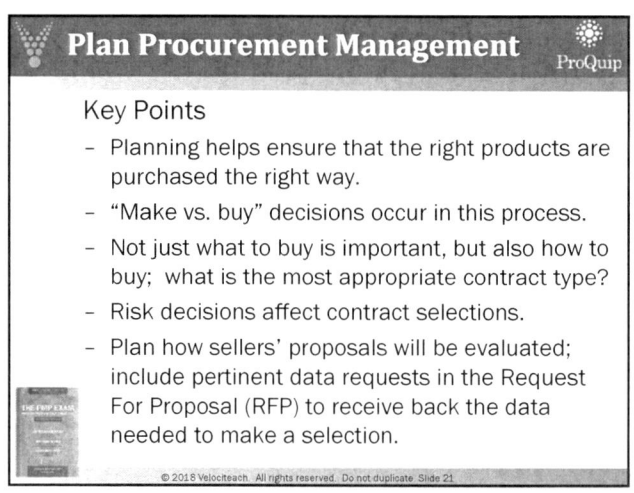

© 2018 Velociteach. All rights reserved. Do not duplicate. Slide 21

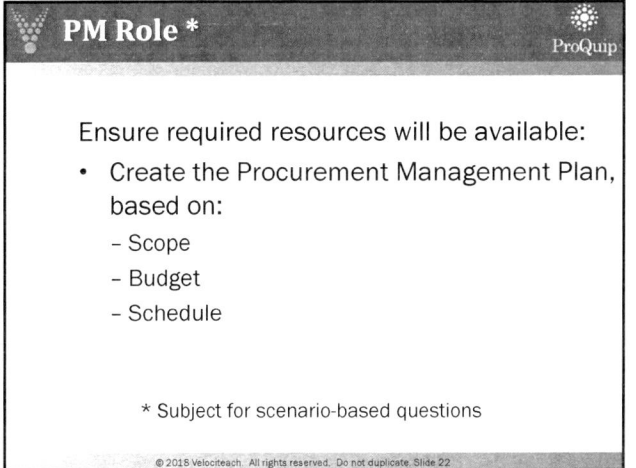

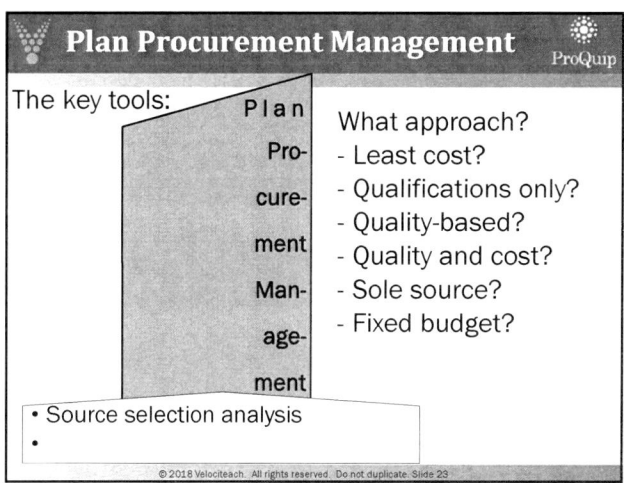

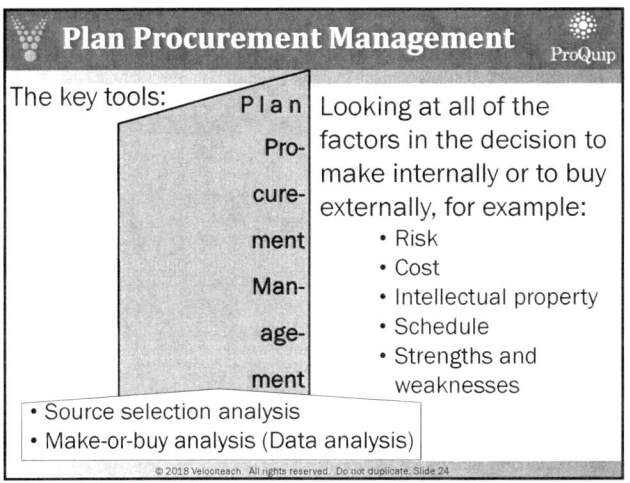

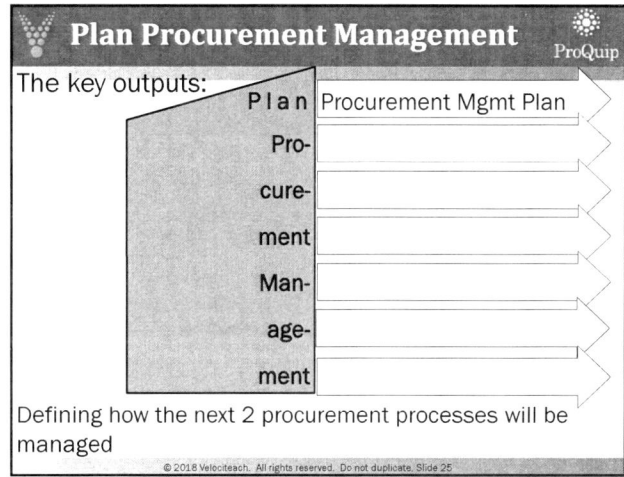

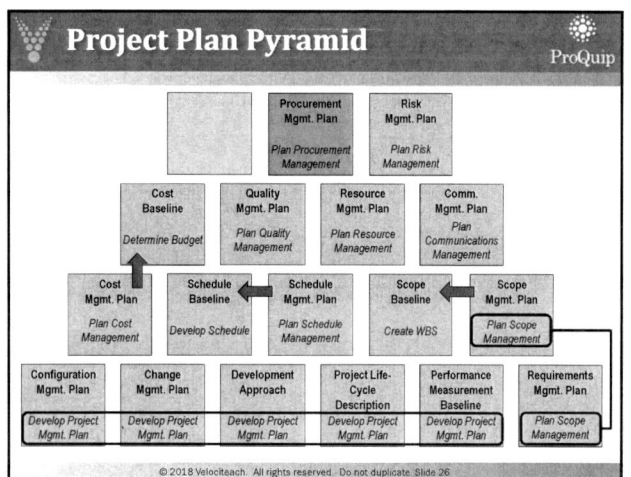

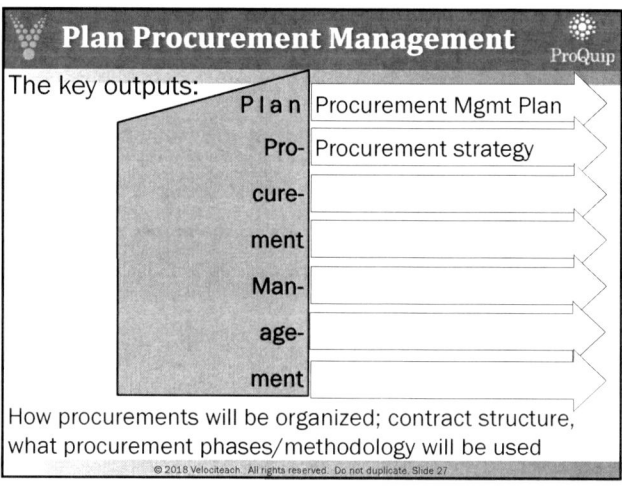

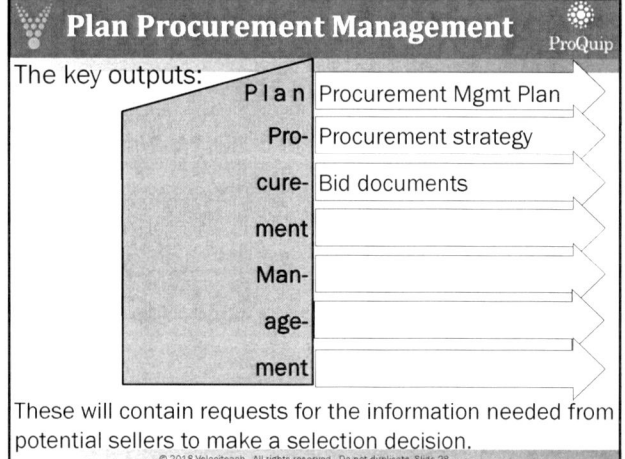

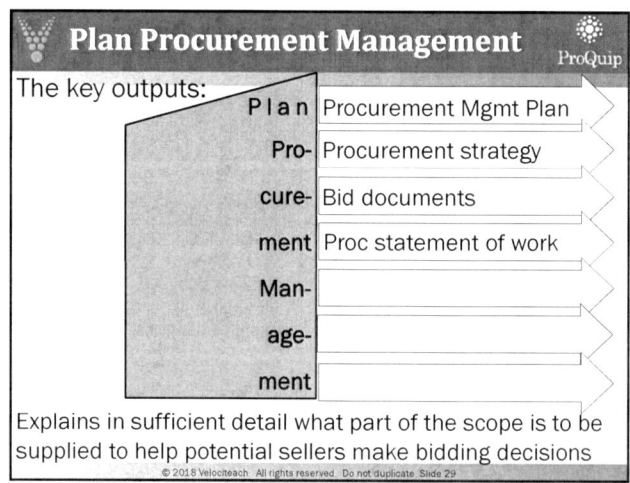

Plan Procurement Management

The key outputs:

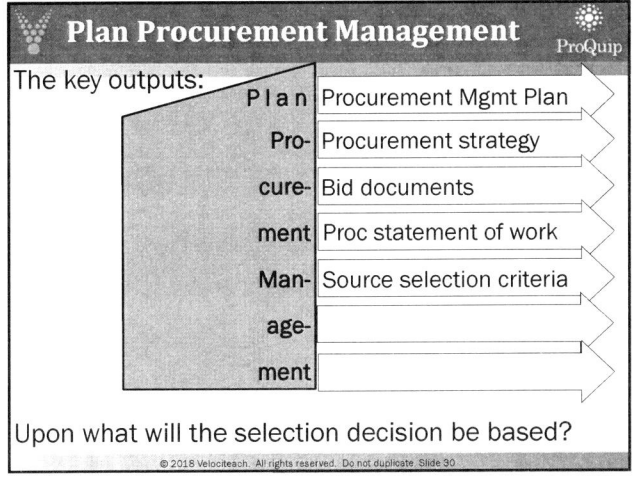

Plan	Procurement Mgmt Plan
Pro-	Procurement strategy
cure-	Bid documents
ment	Proc statement of work
Man-	Source selection criteria
age-	
ment	

Upon what will the selection decision be based?

© 2018 Velociteach. All rights reserved. Do not duplicate. Slide 30

Plan Procurement Management

The key outputs:

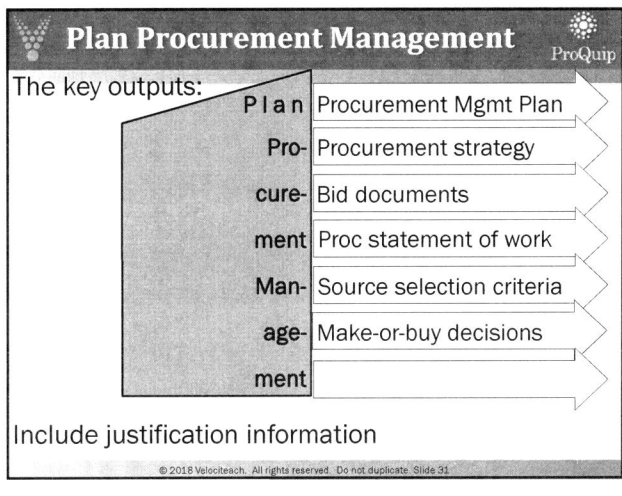

Plan	Procurement Mgmt Plan
Pro-	Procurement strategy
cure-	Bid documents
ment	Proc statement of work
Man-	Source selection criteria
age-	Make-or-buy decisions
ment	

Include justification information

© 2018 Velociteach. All rights reserved. Do not duplicate. Slide 31

Plan Procurement Management

The key outputs:

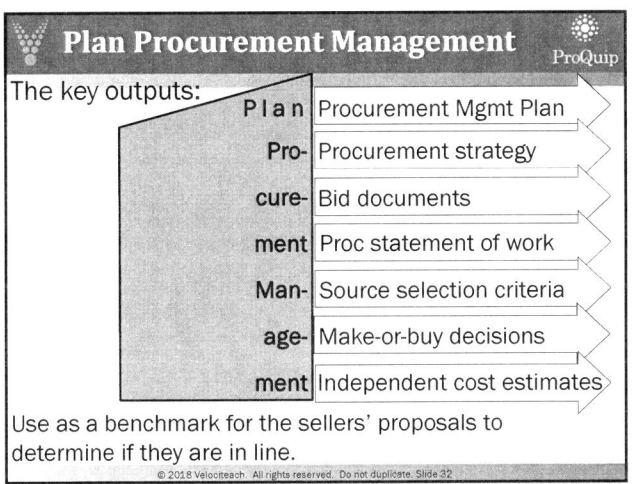

Plan	Procurement Mgmt Plan
Pro-	Procurement strategy
cure-	Bid documents
ment	Proc statement of work
Man-	Source selection criteria
age-	Make-or-buy decisions
ment	Independent cost estimates

Use as a benchmark for the sellers' proposals to determine if they are in line.

© 2018 Velociteach. All rights reserved. Do not duplicate. Slide 32

When to perform

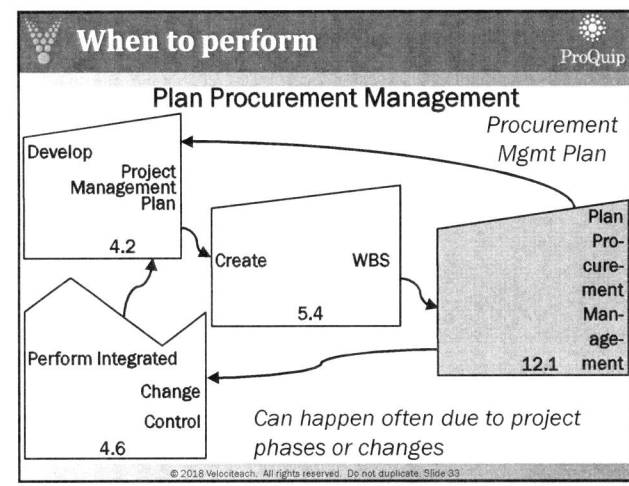

Plan Procurement Management

Can happen often due to project phases or changes

© 2018 Velociteach. All rights reserved. Do not duplicate. Slide 33

Study Focus
ProQuip

Plan Procurement Management

- Know that the Procurement Management Plan defines how the other procurement processes will be carried out.

- Focus on the different contract types, who bears the risk, and the Point of Total Assumption definition and formula.

- Know that Make-or-Buy Decisions separate the team's work from outsourced work and should be based on core competencies of the organization.

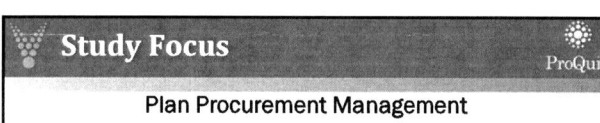

- Know that Source Selection Criteria are created at the same time as the procurement documents.

© 2018 Velociteach. All rights reserved Do not duplicate. Slide 34

Review the ITTOs

Plan Pro-cure-ment Man-age-ment

© 2018 Velociteach. All rights reserved.

The 3 Procurement Processes

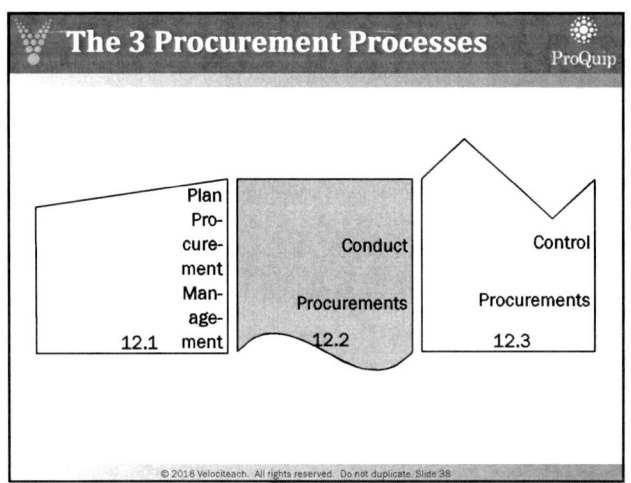

Plan Procurement Management 12.1

Conduct Procurements 12.2

Control Procurements 12.3

© 2018 Velociteach. All rights reserved. Do not duplicate. Slide 38

Conduct Procurements

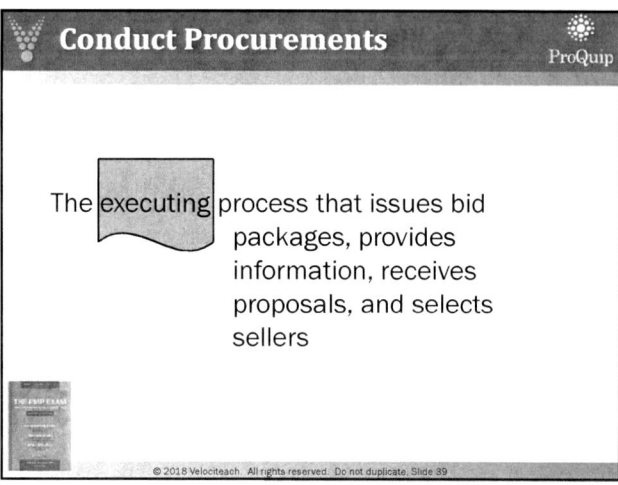

The executing process that issues bid packages, provides information, receives proposals, and selects sellers

© 2018 Velociteach. All rights reserved. Do not duplicate. Slide 39

Conduct Procurements

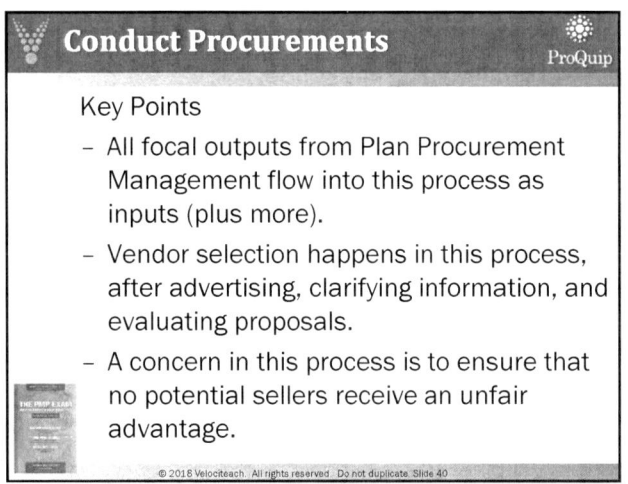

Key Points

- All focal outputs from Plan Procurement Management flow into this process as inputs (plus more).
- Vendor selection happens in this process, after advertising, clarifying information, and evaluating proposals.
- A concern in this process is to ensure that no potential sellers receive an unfair advantage.

© 2018 Velociteach. All rights reserved. Do not duplicate. Slide 40

PM Role *

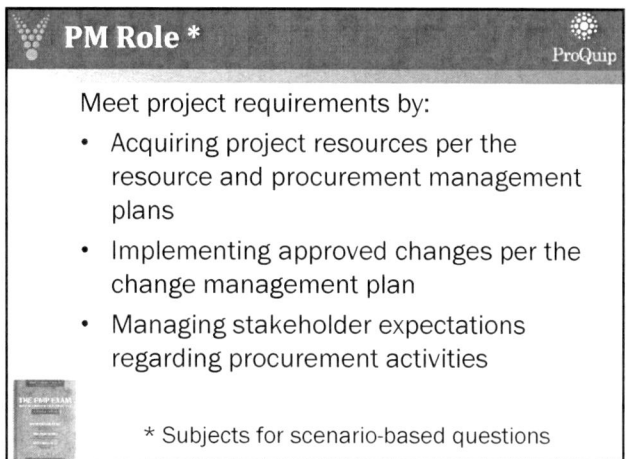

Meet project requirements by:

- Acquiring project resources per the resource and procurement management plans
- Implementing approved changes per the change management plan
- Managing stakeholder expectations regarding procurement activities

* Subjects for scenario-based questions

© 2018 Velociteach. All rights reserved. Do not duplicate. Slide 41

©2018 Velociteach. All rights reserved.

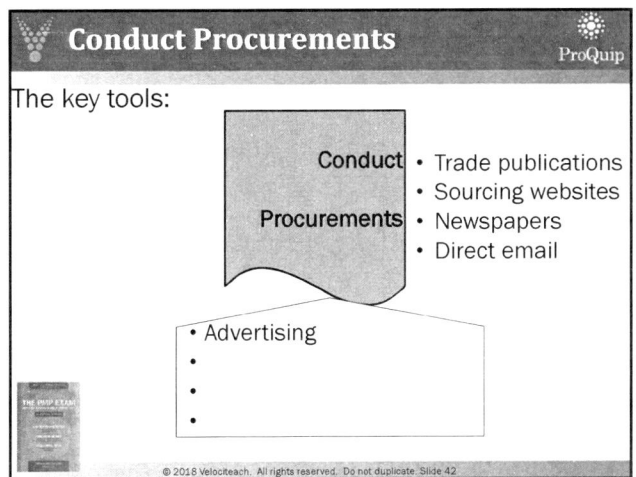

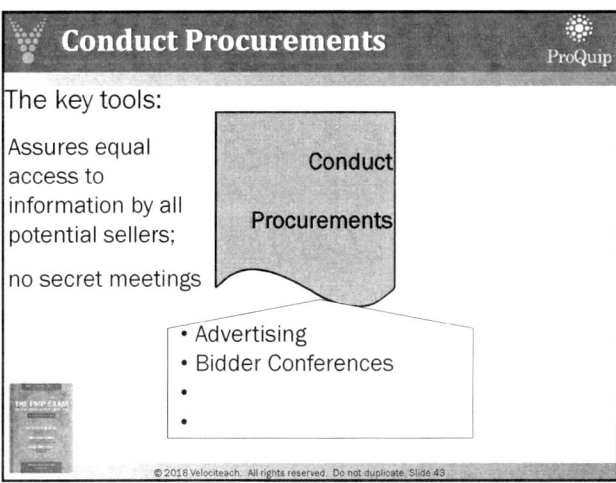

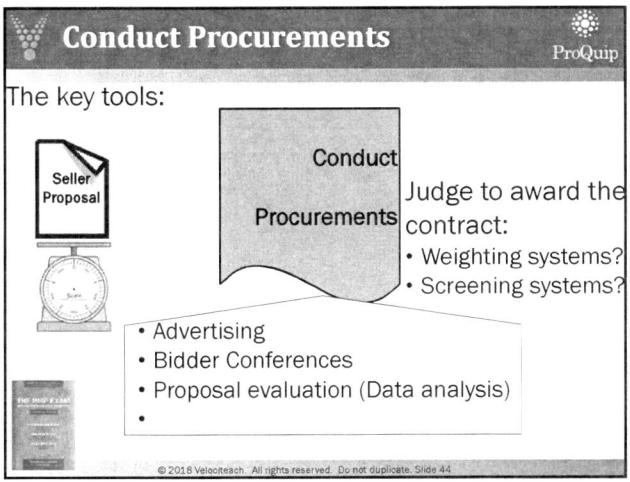

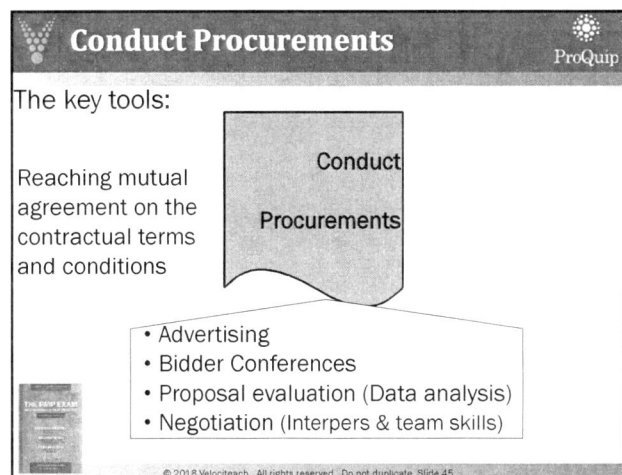

©2018 Velociteach. All rights reserved. Page 321

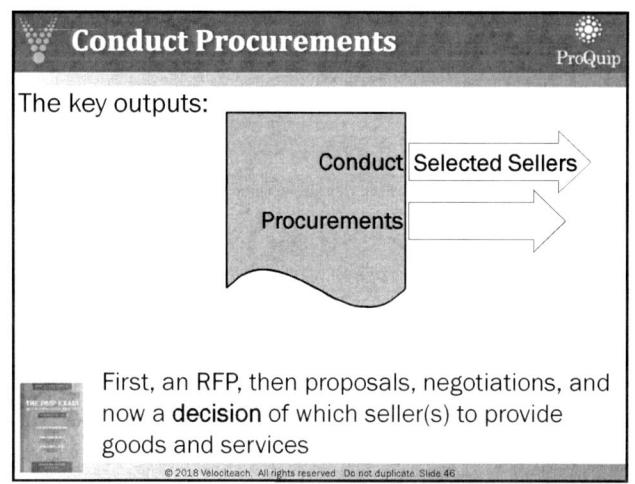

Conduct Procurements — ProQuip

The key outputs:

Conduct Procurements → Selected Sellers

First, an RFP, then proposals, negotiations, and now a **decision** of which seller(s) to provide goods and services

© 2018 Velociteach. All rights reserved. Do not duplicate. Slide 46

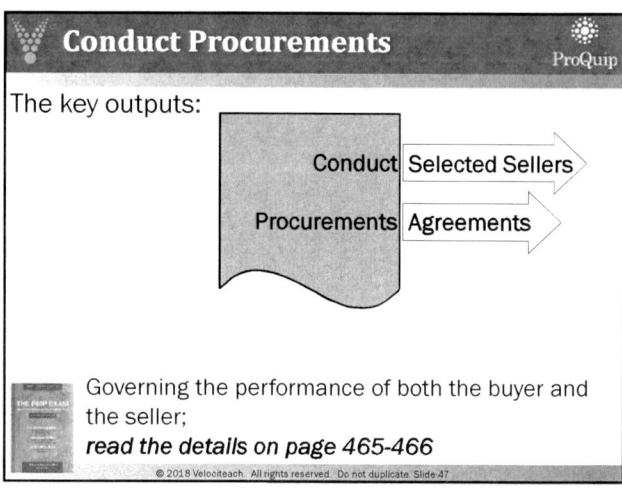

Conduct Procurements — ProQuip

The key outputs:

Conduct Procurements → Selected Sellers / Agreements

Governing the performance of both the buyer and the seller;
read the details on page 465-466

© 2018 Velociteach. All rights reserved. Do not duplicate. Slide 47

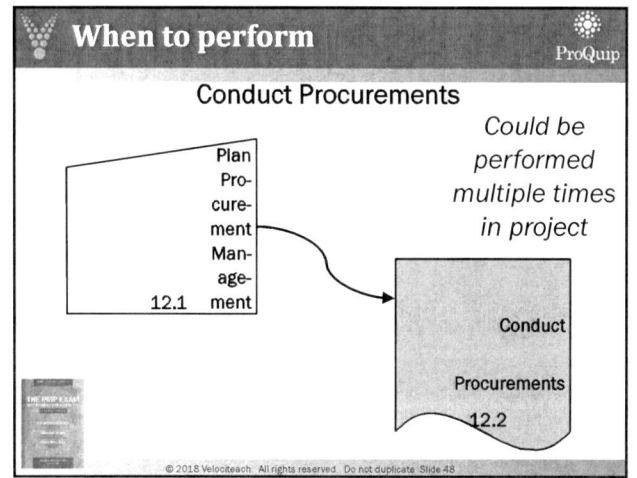

When to perform — ProQuip

Conduct Procurements

Plan Pro-cure-ment Man-age-ment 12.1

Could be performed multiple times in project

Conduct Procurements 12.2

© 2018 Velociteach. All rights reserved. Do not duplicate. Slide 48

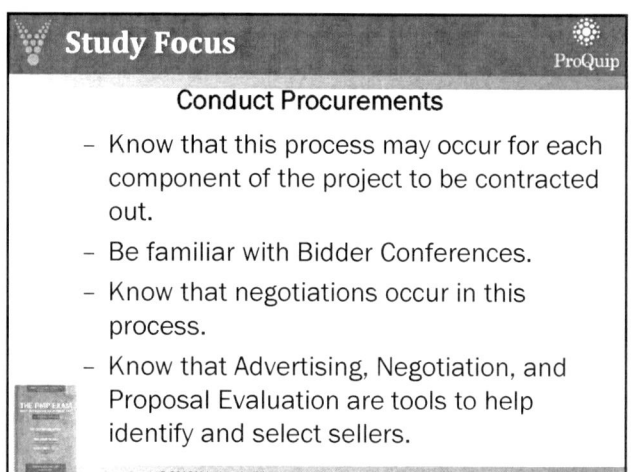

Study Focus — ProQuip

Conduct Procurements

– Know that this process may occur for each component of the project to be contracted out.
– Be familiar with Bidder Conferences.
– Know that negotiations occur in this process.
– Know that Advertising, Negotiation, and Proposal Evaluation are tools to help identify and select sellers.

© 2018 Velociteach. All rights reserved. Do not duplicate. Slide 49

©2018 Velociteach. All rights reserved. Page 322

Review the ITTOs

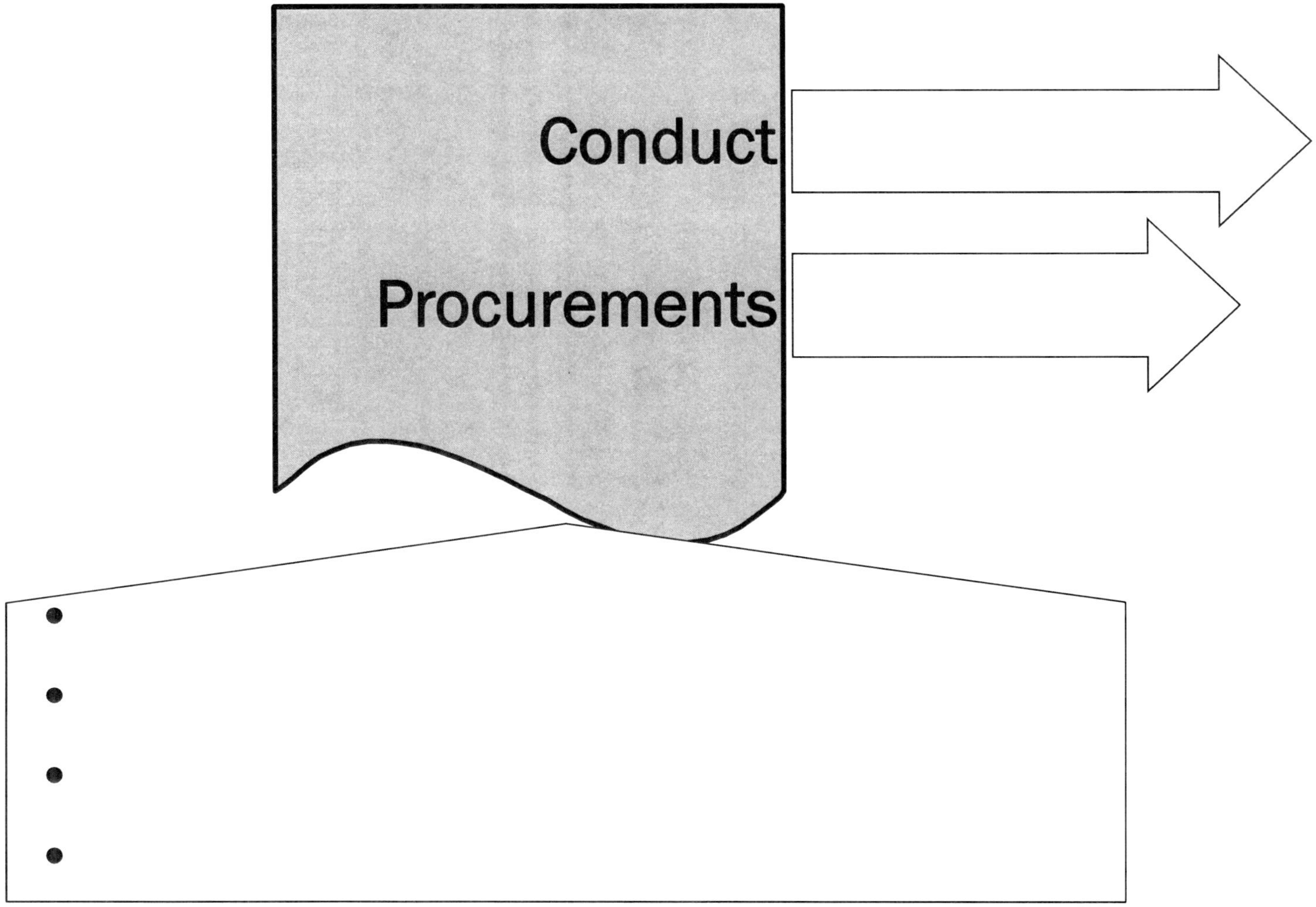

Conduct Procurements

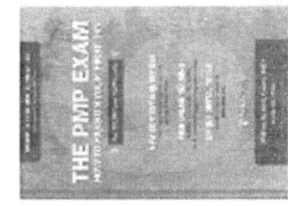

© 2018 Velociteach. All rights reserved.

This page left intentionally blank.

©2018 Velociteach. All rights reserved.

The 3 Procurement Processes

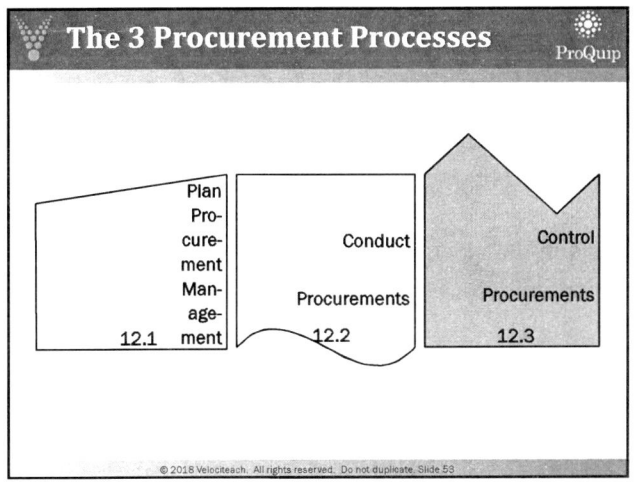

Plan Procurement Management 12.1

Conduct Procurements 12.2

Control Procurements 12.3

© 2018 Velociteach. All rights reserved. Do not duplicate. Slide 53

Control Procurements

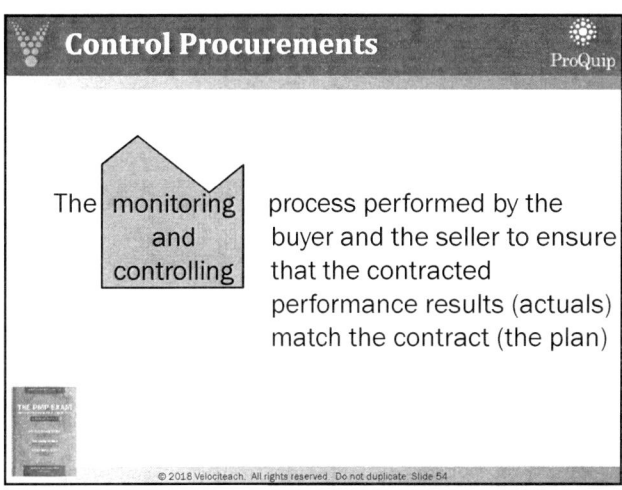

The monitoring and controlling process performed by the buyer and the seller to ensure that the contracted performance results (actuals) match the contract (the plan)

© 2018 Velociteach. All rights reserved. Do not duplicate. Slide 54

Control Procurements

Key Points
- Performance is reviewed against the contract in the areas of:
  - On-time delivery of goods or services
  - Correct and timely invoices and payments
  - Satisfaction of other terms & conditions
- This legalistic process involves a lot of paper and detail.
- The contract itself spells out how the contract will be controlled and closed.
- Performed by Buyer and Seller

© 2018 Velociteach. All rights reserved. Do not duplicate. Slide 55

Control Procurements

The key tools:

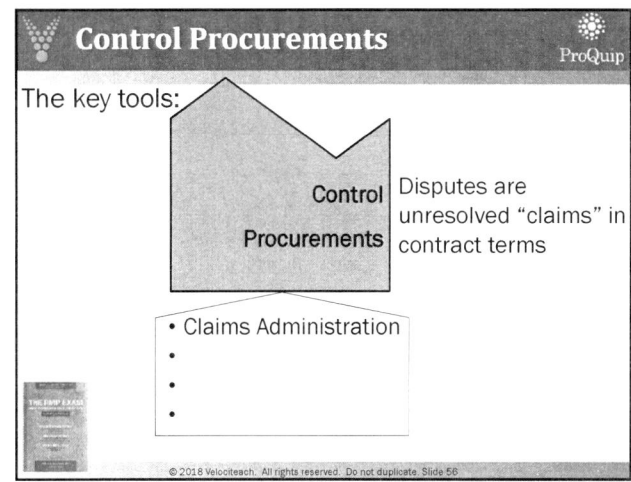

Control Procurements

Disputes are unresolved "claims" in contract terms

- Claims Administration
-
-
-

© 2018 Velociteach. All rights reserved. Do not duplicate. Slide 56

©2018 Velociteach. All rights reserved.   Page 325

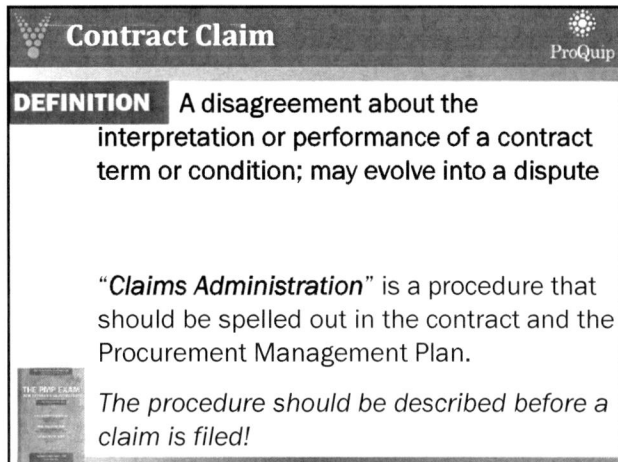

Contract Claim

DEFINITION A disagreement about the interpretation or performance of a contract term or condition; may evolve into a dispute

"*Claims Administration*" is a procedure that should be spelled out in the contract and the Procurement Management Plan.

The procedure should be described before a claim is filed!

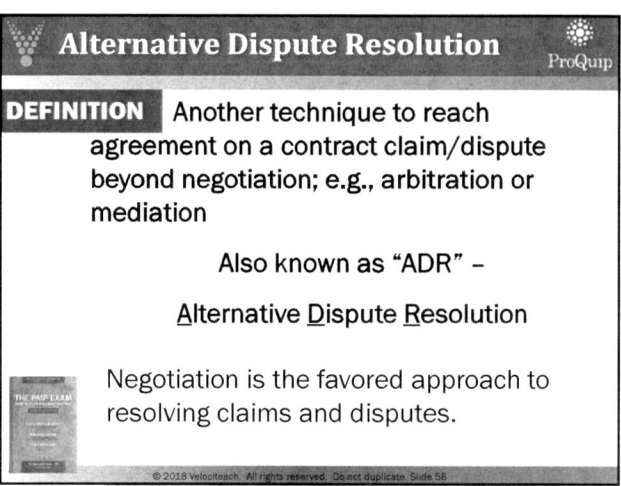

Alternative Dispute Resolution

DEFINITION Another technique to reach agreement on a contract claim/dispute beyond negotiation; e.g., arbitration or mediation

Also known as "ADR" –

Alternative Dispute Resolution

Negotiation is the favored approach to resolving claims and disputes.

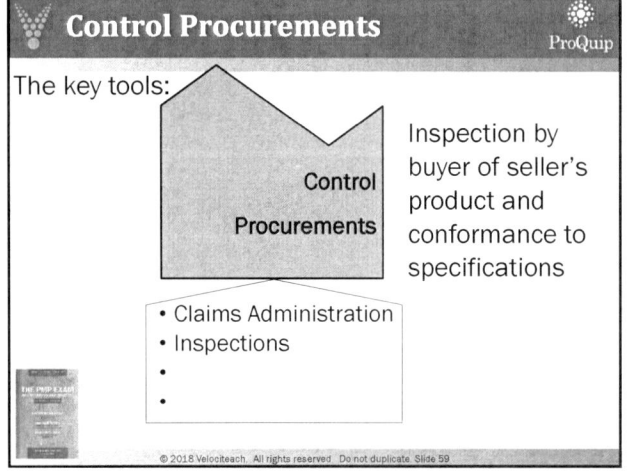

Control Procurements

The key tools:

Control Procurements

Inspection by buyer of seller's product and conformance to specifications

• Claims Administration
• Inspections
•
•

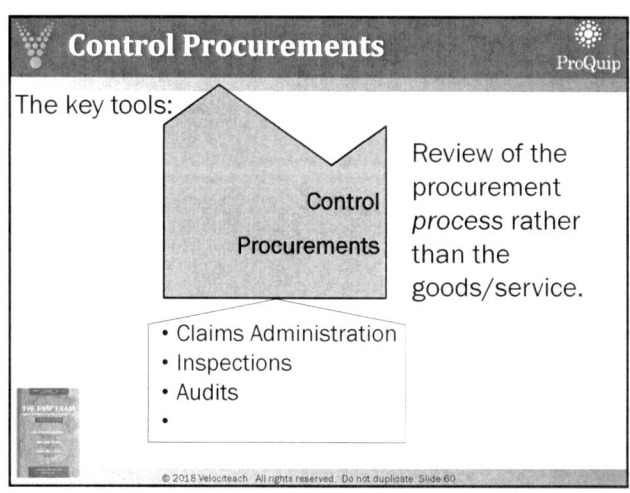

Control Procurements

The key tools:

Control Procurements

Review of the procurement *process* rather than the goods/service.

• Claims Administration
• Inspections
• Audits
•

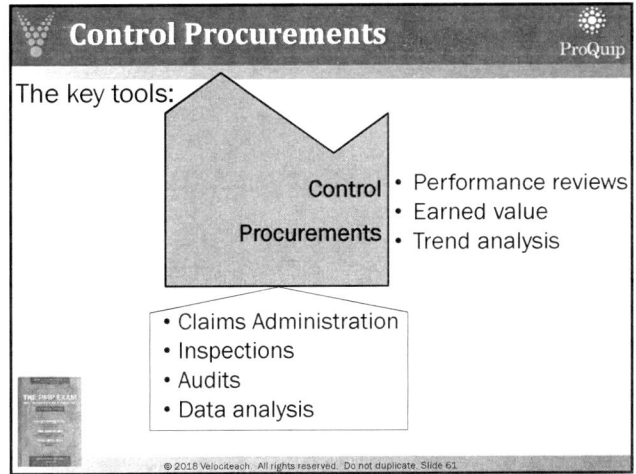

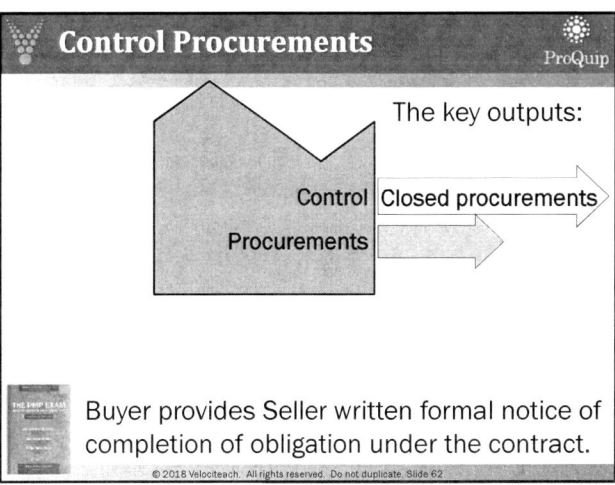

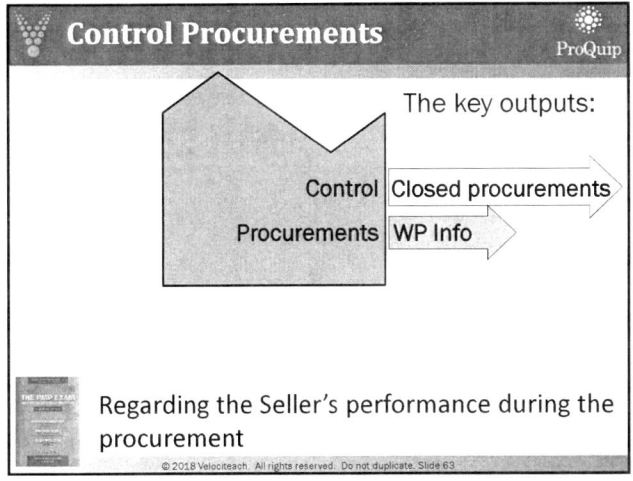

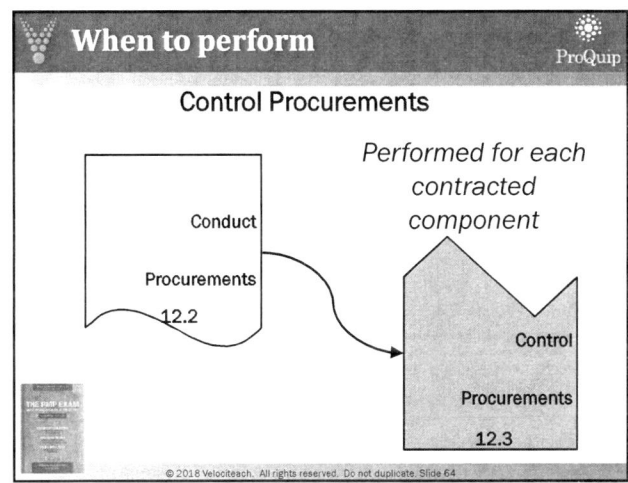

Study Focus

ProQuip

Control Procurements

- Know that this process is performed by the buyer and the seller.
- Know that this process is like other monitoring & controlling processes, comparing actuals (contract results) against the plan (the contract).
- Know the tools and outputs
- Understand claims, disputes, and ADRs

© 2018 Velociteach. All rights reserved. Do not duplicate. Slide 65

Review the ITTOs

ProQuip

Control
Procurements

THE PMP EXAM

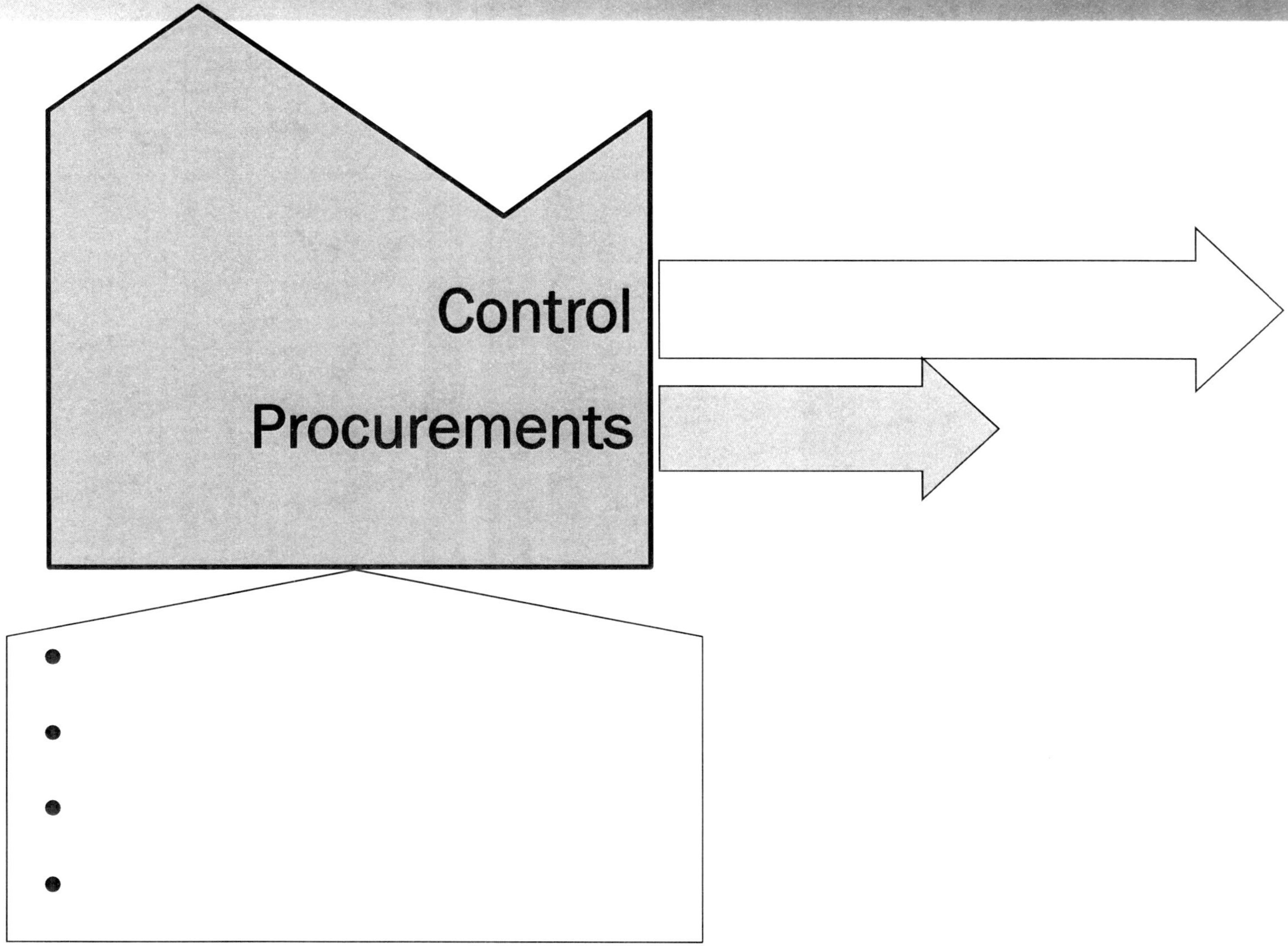

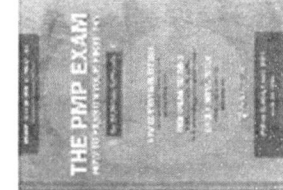

© 2018 Velociteach. All rights reserved.

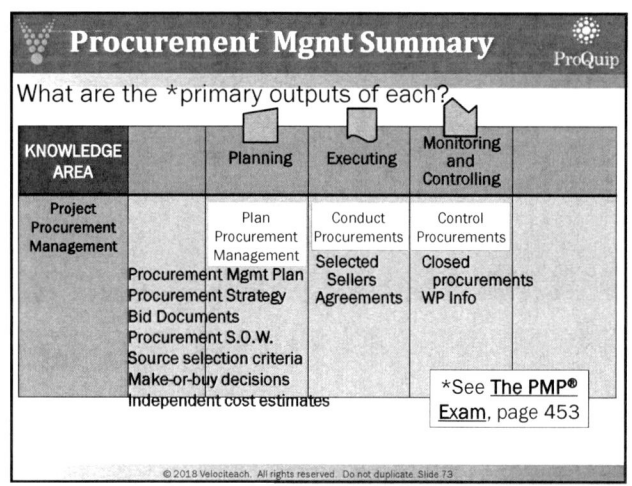

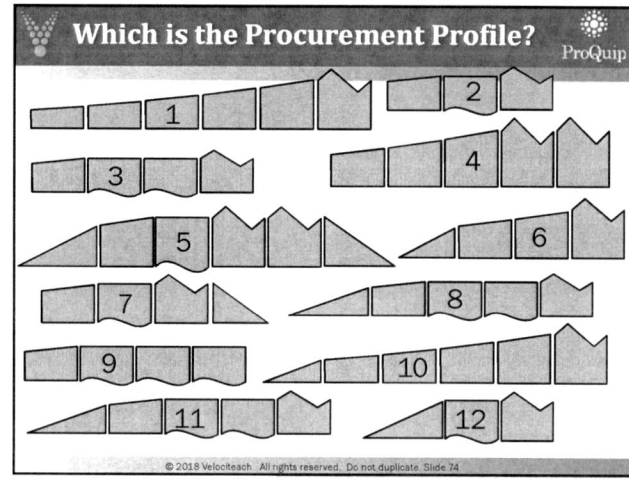

Terms You Should Know

Project Procurement Management

ADR	Make-or-Buy
Agreement	Audits
Bidder Conference	Negotiation
Claims Administration	Point of Total Assumption
Cost-Plus-Fixed-Fee	Procurement
Cost-Plus-Incentive-Fee	Request For Proposal
Cost Reimbursable	Statement of Work
Firm-Fixed-Price	Time & Materials
Fixed-Price w/EPA	Inspections
Fixed-Price-Incentive-Fee	Performance review

© 2018 Velociteach. All rights reserved. Do not duplicate. Slide 76

Procurement Discussion

From what process are Seller Proposals an output? Input?

What is the significance of a bidder conference?

Discuss how different contract types affect risk for buyers and sellers.

What methods might be utilized in selecting a vendor for contracting a project component?

As a project manager, what two departments in your organization should assist you with procurement aspects of your project?

© 2018 Velociteach. All rights reserved. Do not duplicate. Slide 77

Summary

Knowledge Area

ProQuip

KNOWLEDGE AREA	Initiating	Planning	Executing	Monitoring and Controlling	Closing
Project ___ Management					

©2018 Velociteach. All rights reserved.

Score Sheet	**Procurement Management Exam**				

- Mark one answer: A, B, C, or D.
- Circle the '?' symbol if you are guessing at the answer.
- Circle the Δ symbol if you change your answer.

Total Correct: _____

% Correct: _____ %

1.	A ○	B ○	C ○	D ○	? Δ
2.	A ○	B ○	C ○	D ○	? Δ
3.	A ○	B ○	C ○	D ○	? Δ
4.	A ○	B ○	C ○	D ○	? Δ
5.	A ○	B ○	C ○	D ○	? Δ
6.	A ○	B ○	C ○	D ○	? Δ
7.	A ○	B ○	C ○	D ○	? Δ
8.	A ○	B ○	C ○	D ○	? Δ
9.	A ○	B ○	C ○	D ○	? Δ
10.	A ○	B ○	C ○	D ○	? Δ
11.	A ○	B ○	C ○	D ○	? Δ
12.	A ○	B ○	C ○	D ○	? Δ
13.	A ○	B ○	C ○	D ○	? Δ
14.	A ○	B ○	C ○	D ○	? Δ
15.	A ○	B ○	C ○	D ○	? Δ
16.	A ○	B ○	C ○	D ○	? Δ
17.	A ○	B ○	C ○	D ○	? Δ
18.	A ○	B ○	C ○	D ○	? Δ
19.	A ○	B ○	C ○	D ○	? Δ
20.	A ○	B ○	C ○	D ○	? Δ
21.	A ○	B ○	C ○	D ○	? Δ
22.	A ○	B ○	C ○	D ○	? Δ
23.	A ○	B ○	C ○	D ○	? Δ
24.	A ○	B ○	C ○	D ○	? Δ
25.	A ○	B ○	C ○	D ○	? Δ

©2018 Velociteach. All rights reserved.

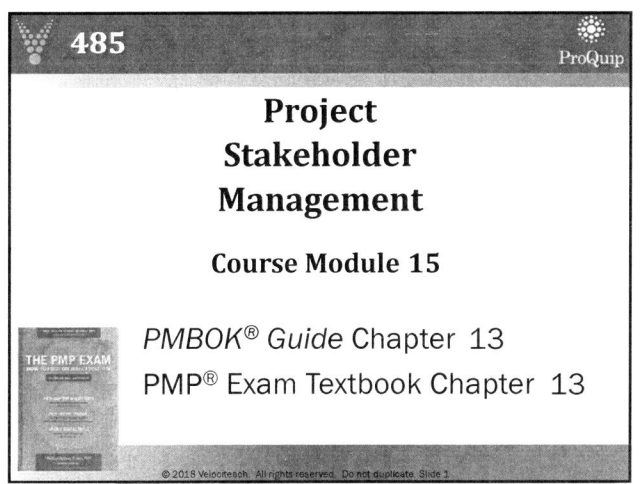

485

Project Stakeholder Management

Course Module 15

PMBOK® Guide Chapter 13

PMP® Exam Textbook Chapter 13

© 2018 Velociteach. All rights reserved. Do not duplicate. Slide 1

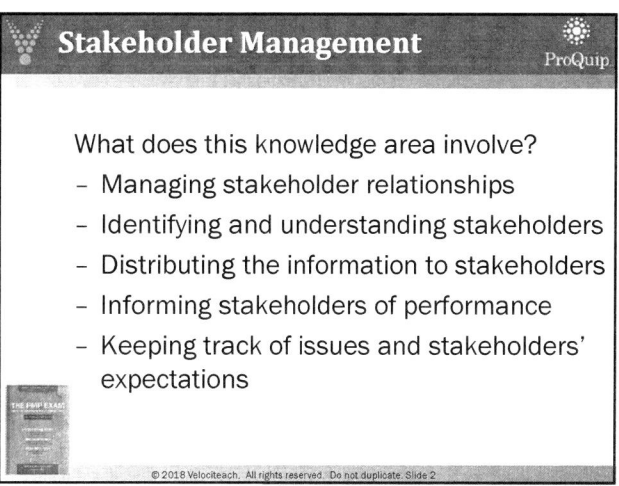

Stakeholder Management

What does this knowledge area involve?
- Managing stakeholder relationships
- Identifying and understanding stakeholders
- Distributing the information to stakeholders
- Informing stakeholders of performance
- Keeping track of issues and stakeholders' expectations

© 2018 Velociteach. All rights reserved. Do not duplicate. Slide 2

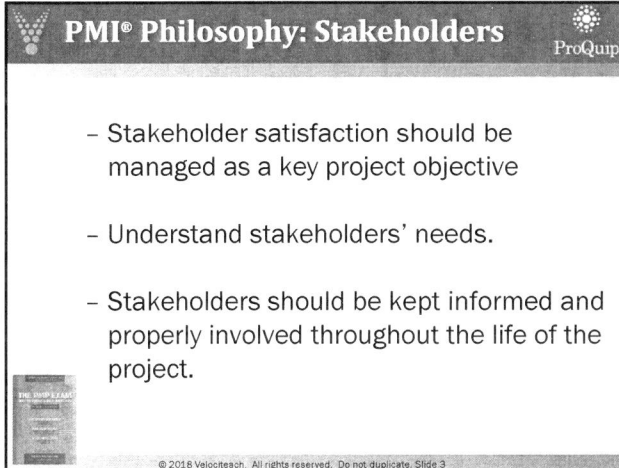

PMI® Philosophy: Stakeholders

- Stakeholder satisfaction should be managed as a key project objective

- Understand stakeholders' needs.

- Stakeholders should be kept informed and properly involved throughout the life of the project.

© 2018 Velociteach. All rights reserved. Do not duplicate. Slide 3

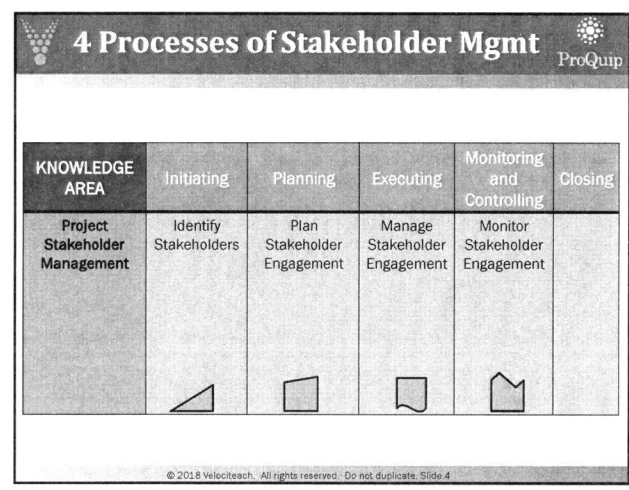

4 Processes of Stakeholder Mgmt

KNOWLEDGE AREA	Initiating	Planning	Executing	Monitoring and Controlling	Closing
Project Stakeholder Management	Identify Stakeholders	Plan Stakeholder Engagement	Manage Stakeholder Engagement	Monitor Stakeholder Engagement	

© 2018 Velociteach. All rights reserved. Do not duplicate. Slide 4

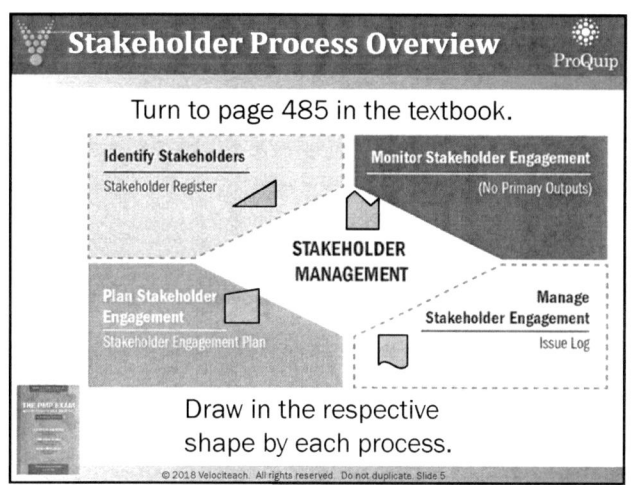

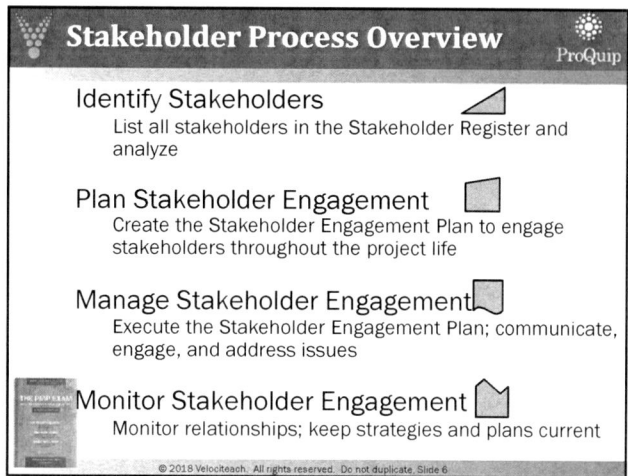

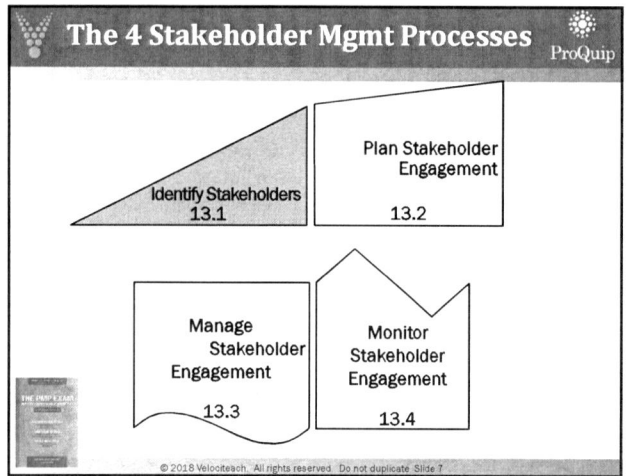

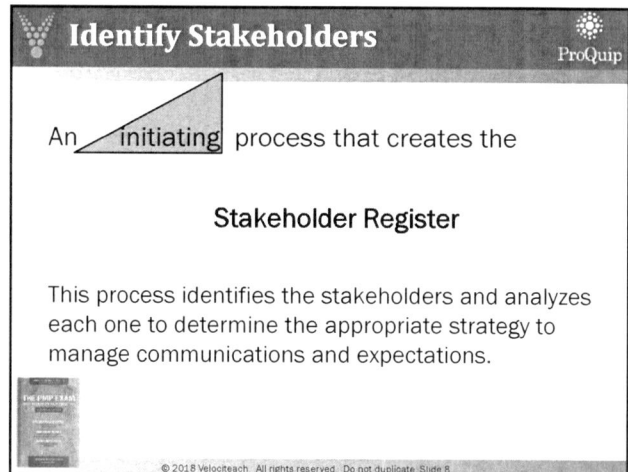

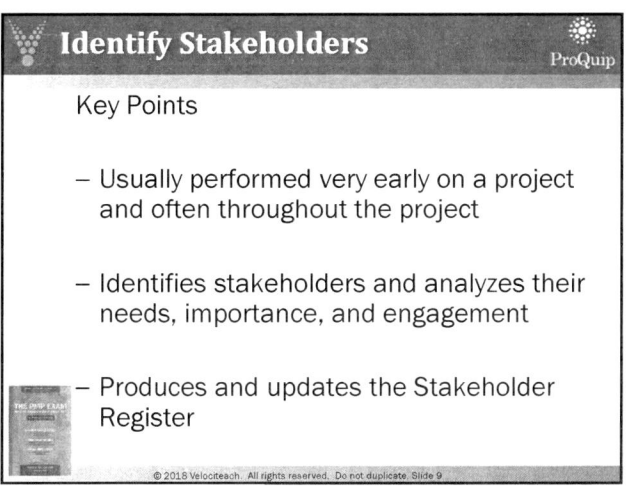

Identify Stakeholders

Key Points

- Usually performed very early on a project and often throughout the project

- Identifies stakeholders and analyzes their needs, importance, and engagement

- Produces and updates the Stakeholder Register

© 2018 Velociteach. All rights reserved. Do not duplicate. Slide 9

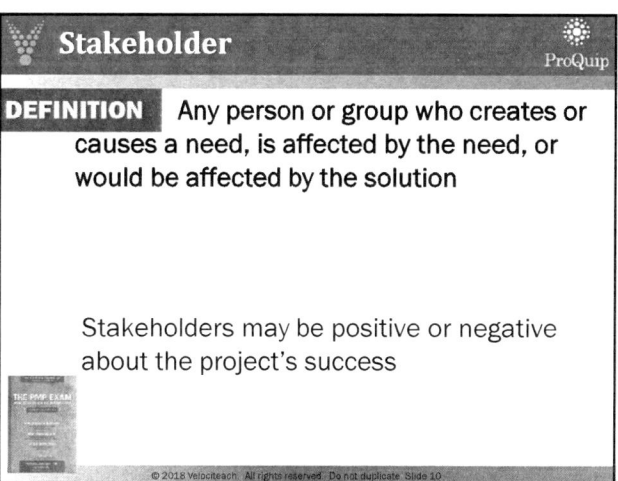

Stakeholder

DEFINITION Any person or group who creates or causes a need, is affected by the need, or would be affected by the solution

Stakeholders may be positive or negative about the project's success

© 2018 Velociteach. All rights reserved. Do not duplicate. Slide 10

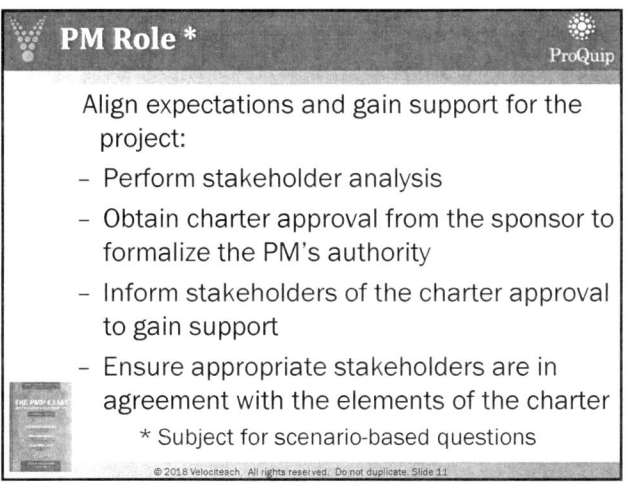

PM Role *

Align expectations and gain support for the project:

- Perform stakeholder analysis
- Obtain charter approval from the sponsor to formalize the PM's authority
- Inform stakeholders of the charter approval to gain support
- Ensure appropriate stakeholders are in agreement with the elements of the charter

* Subject for scenario-based questions

© 2018 Velociteach. All rights reserved. Do not duplicate. Slide 11

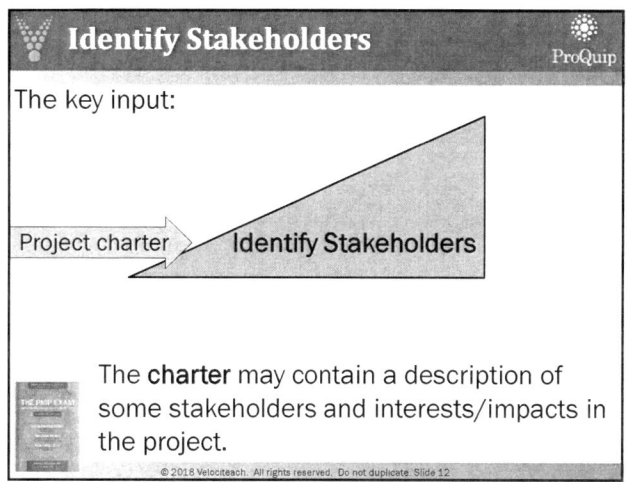

Identify Stakeholders

The key input:

Project charter → Identify Stakeholders

The **charter** may contain a description of some stakeholders and interests/impacts in the project.

© 2018 Velociteach. All rights reserved. Do not duplicate. Slide 12

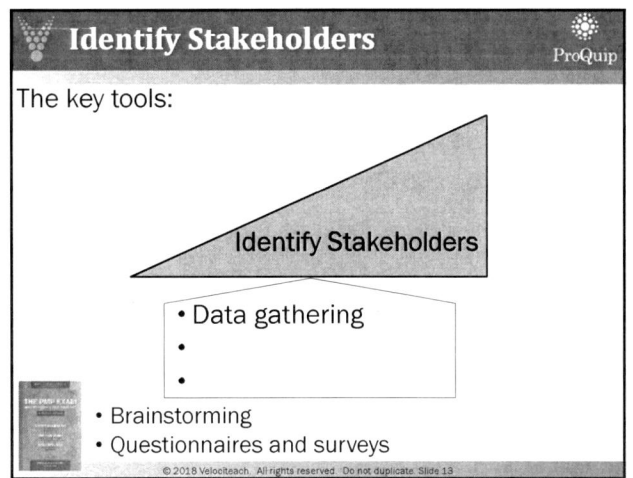

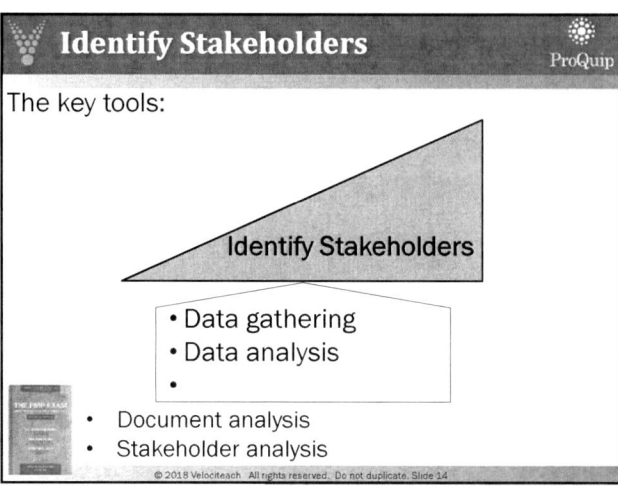

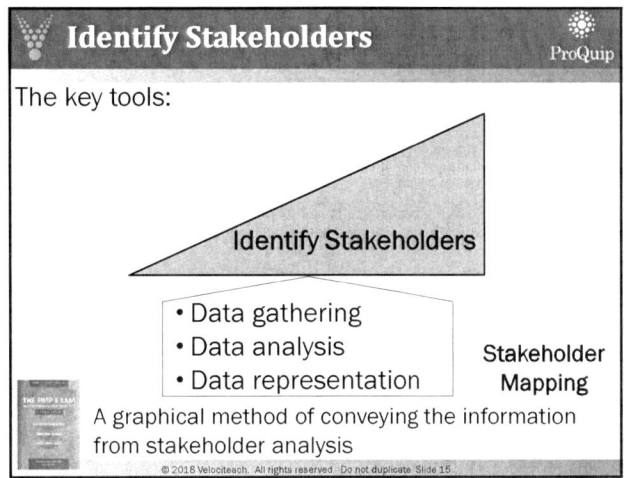

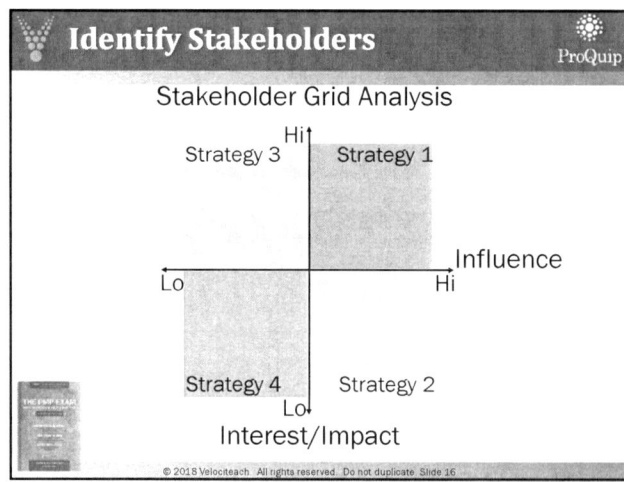

Identify Stakeholders' Salience

Salience: being prominent, important, noticeable

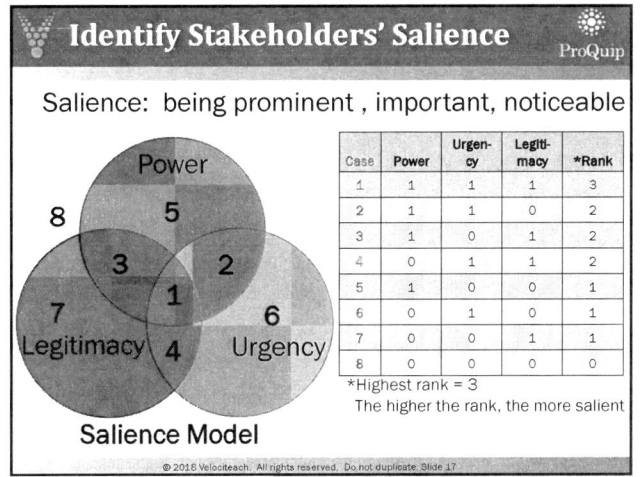

Salience Model

Case	Power	Urgen-cy	Legiti-macy	*Rank
1	1	1	1	3
2	1	1	0	2
3	1	0	1	2
4	0	1	1	2
5	1	0	0	1
6	0	1	0	1
7	0	0	1	1
8	0	0	0	0

*Highest rank = 3
The higher the rank, the more salient

© 2018 Velociteach. All rights reserved. Do not duplicate. Slide 17

Directions of Influence diagram

Classify according to influence on the project or the team

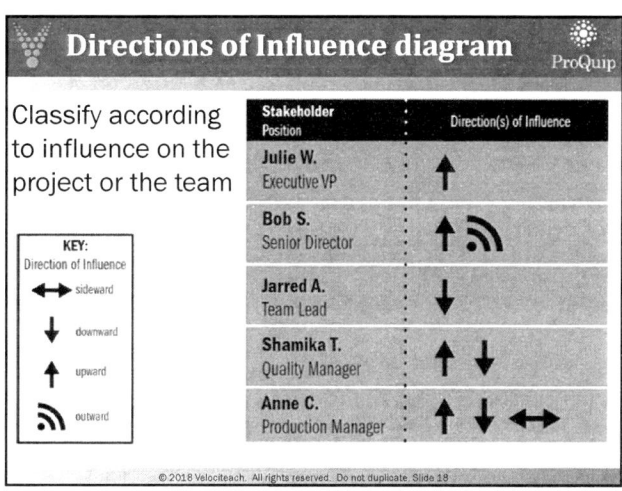

© 2018 Velociteach. All rights reserved. Do not duplicate. Slide 18

Identify Stakeholders

The key output:

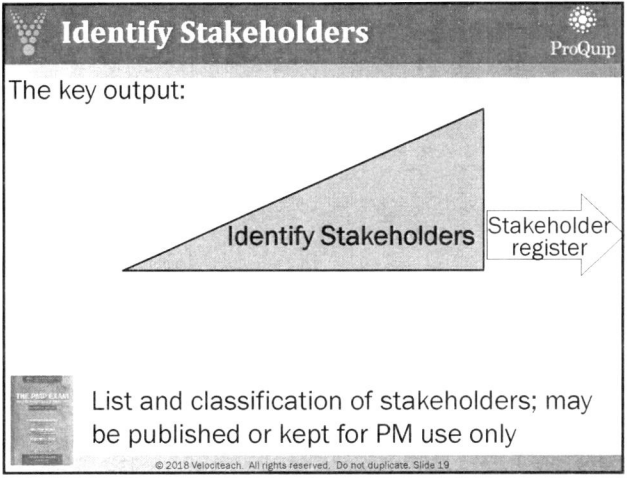

List and classification of stakeholders; may be published or kept for PM use only

© 2018 Velociteach. All rights reserved. Do not duplicate. Slide 19

When to perform

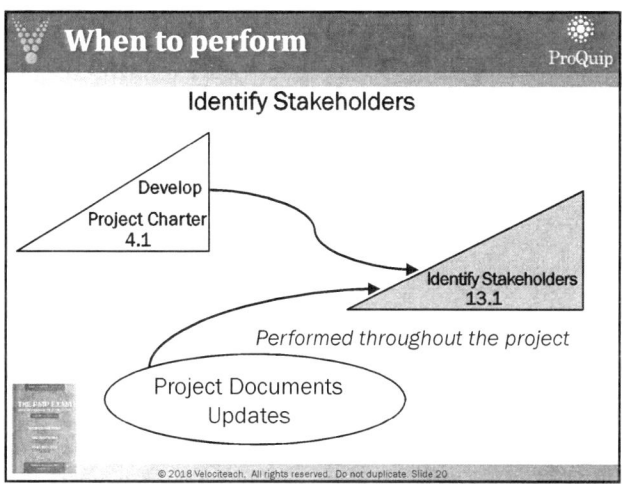

Performed throughout the project

© 2018 Velociteach. All rights reserved. Do not duplicate. Slide 20

©2018 Velociteach. All rights reserved. Page 337

Identify Stakeholders

- Know the tool of stakeholder analysis and the concept of grids or quadrant analysis.
- Focus on the Stakeholder Register as the output.
- Be aware that this process happens very early in the life of the project, immediately after *Develop Project Charter*.

- Know the three "Data" tool groups: Gathering, Analysis, Representation

© 2018 Velociteach. All rights reserved. Do not duplicate. Slide 21

ProQuip

Identify Stakeholders

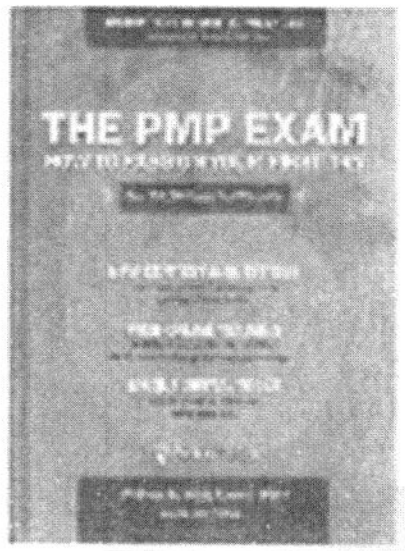

•   •   •

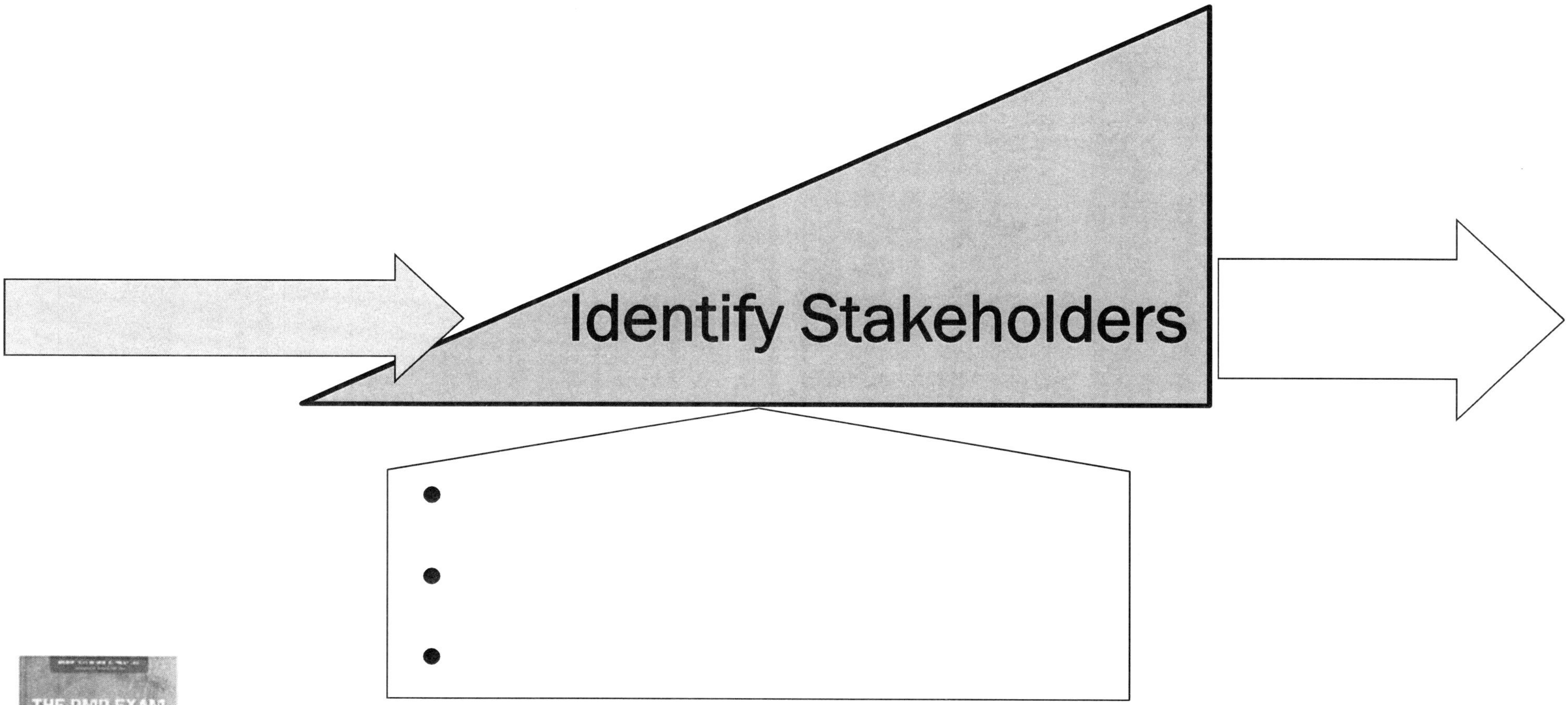

© 2018 Velociteach. All rights reserved.

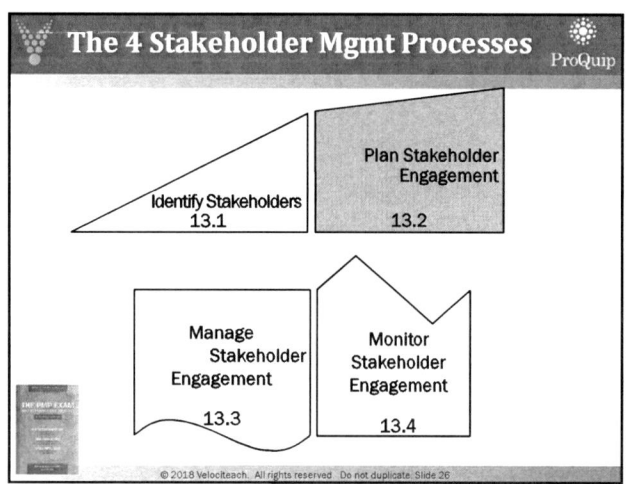

The 4 Stakeholder Mgmt Processes
ProQuip

Identify Stakeholders
13.1

Plan Stakeholder Engagement
13.2

Manage Stakeholder Engagement
13.3

Monitor Stakeholder Engagement
13.4

© 2018 Velociteach. All rights reserved. Do not duplicate. Slide 26

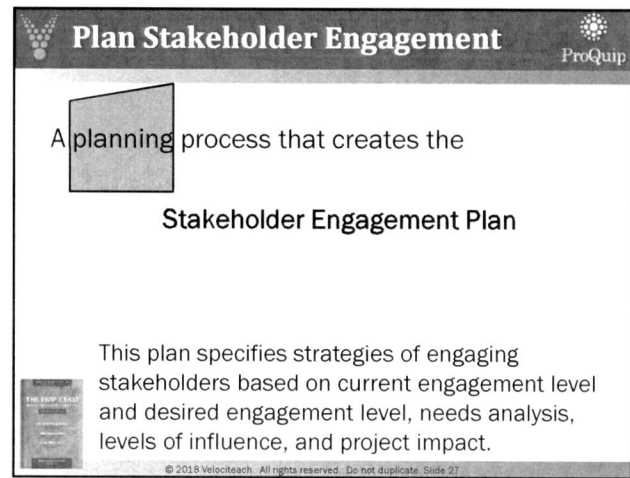

Plan Stakeholder Engagement
ProQuip

A planning process that creates the

Stakeholder Engagement Plan

This plan specifies strategies of engaging stakeholders based on current engagement level and desired engagement level, needs analysis, levels of influence, and project impact.

© 2018 Velociteach. All rights reserved. Do not duplicate. Slide 27

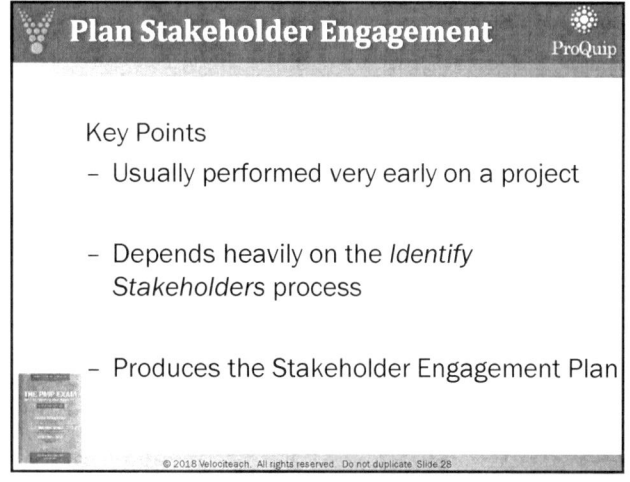

Plan Stakeholder Engagement
ProQuip

Key Points

– Usually performed very early on a project

– Depends heavily on the *Identify Stakeholders* process

– Produces the Stakeholder Engagement Plan

© 2018 Velociteach. All rights reserved. Do not duplicate. Slide 28

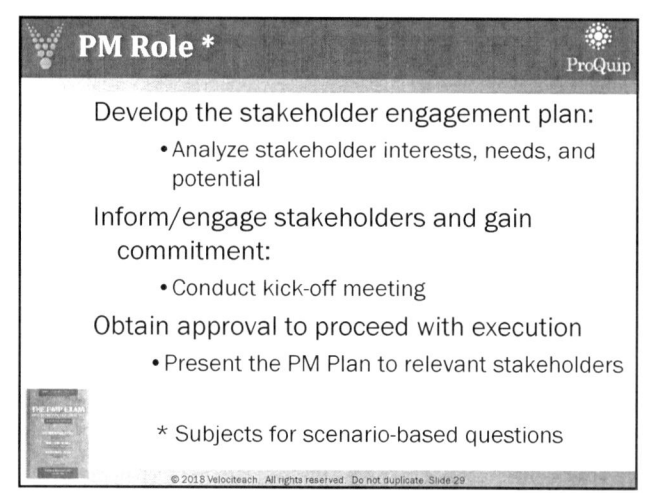

PM Role *
ProQuip

Develop the stakeholder engagement plan:
• Analyze stakeholder interests, needs, and potential

Inform/engage stakeholders and gain commitment:
• Conduct kick-off meeting

Obtain approval to proceed with execution
• Present the PM Plan to relevant stakeholders

* Subjects for scenario-based questions

© 2018 Velociteach. All rights reserved. Do not duplicate. Slide 29

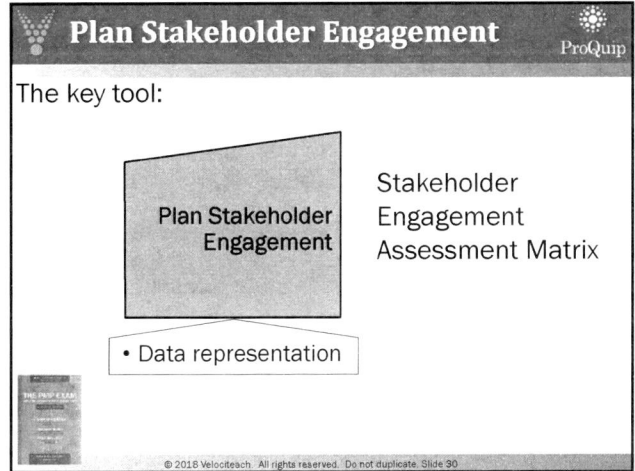

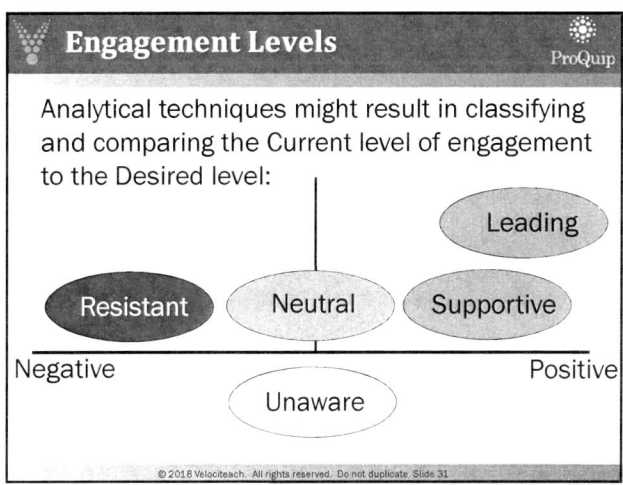

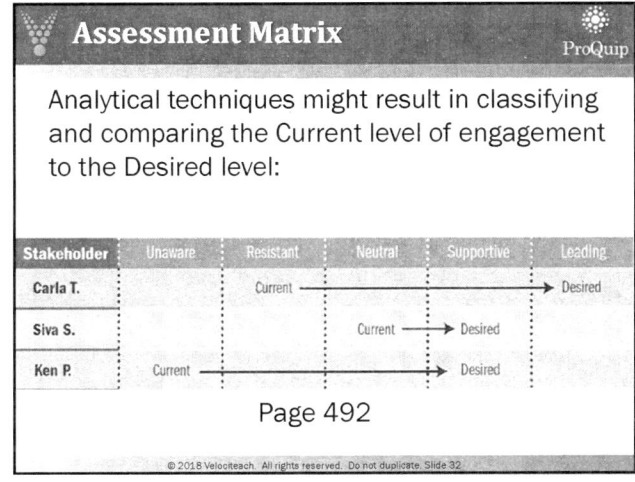

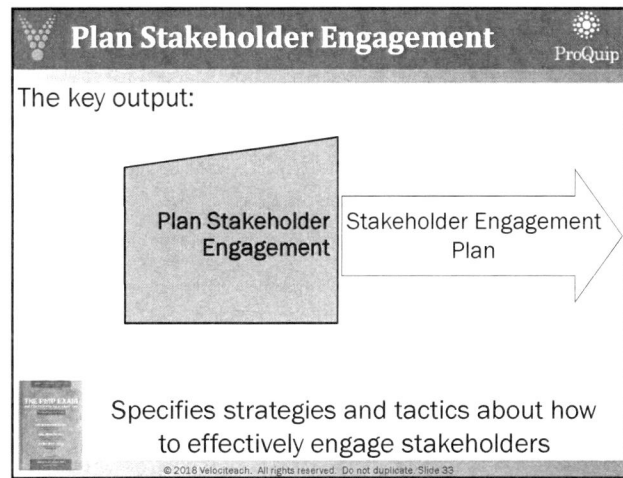

Stakeholder Engagement Plan

DEFINITION Describes how the team will engage stakeholders, manage expectations and the engagement level, and deal with issues, all toward the goal of satisfying stakeholders

It may provide:
- Engagement level and impact assessments
- Overlap and interrelationships of stakeholders
- Communication requirements of stakeholders
- Reporting methods, content, and frequency
- How to perform processes of Manage and Control Stakeholder Engagements

© 2018 Velociteach. All rights reserved. Do not duplicate. Slide 34

Project Plan Pyramid

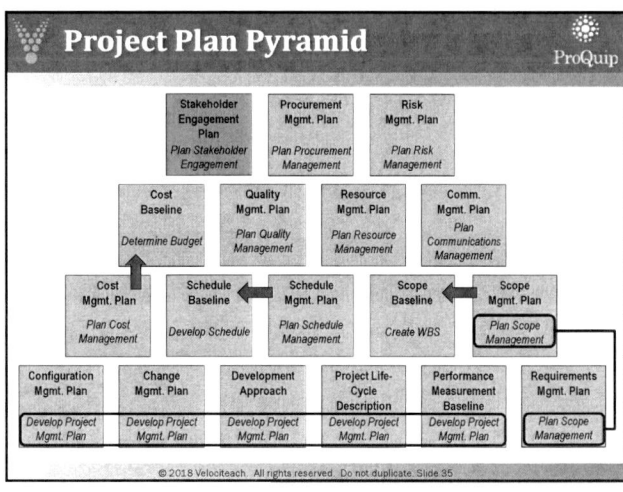

© 2018 Velociteach. All rights reserved. Do not duplicate. Slide 35

When to perform

Plan Stakeholder Engagement

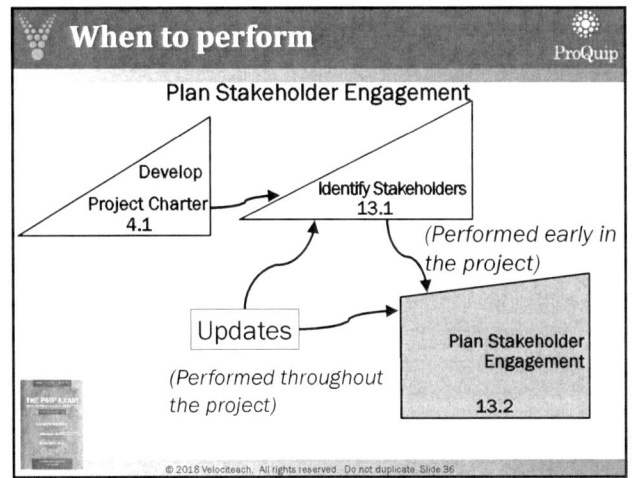

© 2018 Velociteach. All rights reserved. Do not duplicate. Slide 36

Study Focus

Plan Stakeholder Engagement

- Focus on the Stakeholder Engagement Plan as the output.
- Be aware that this process happens early in the life of the project, after *Identify Stakeholders*.
- Understand classifying and planning the engagement levels of stakeholders.
- Understand the SEAM: Stakeholder Engagement Assessment Matrix

© 2018 Velociteach. All rights reserved. Do not duplicate. Slide 37

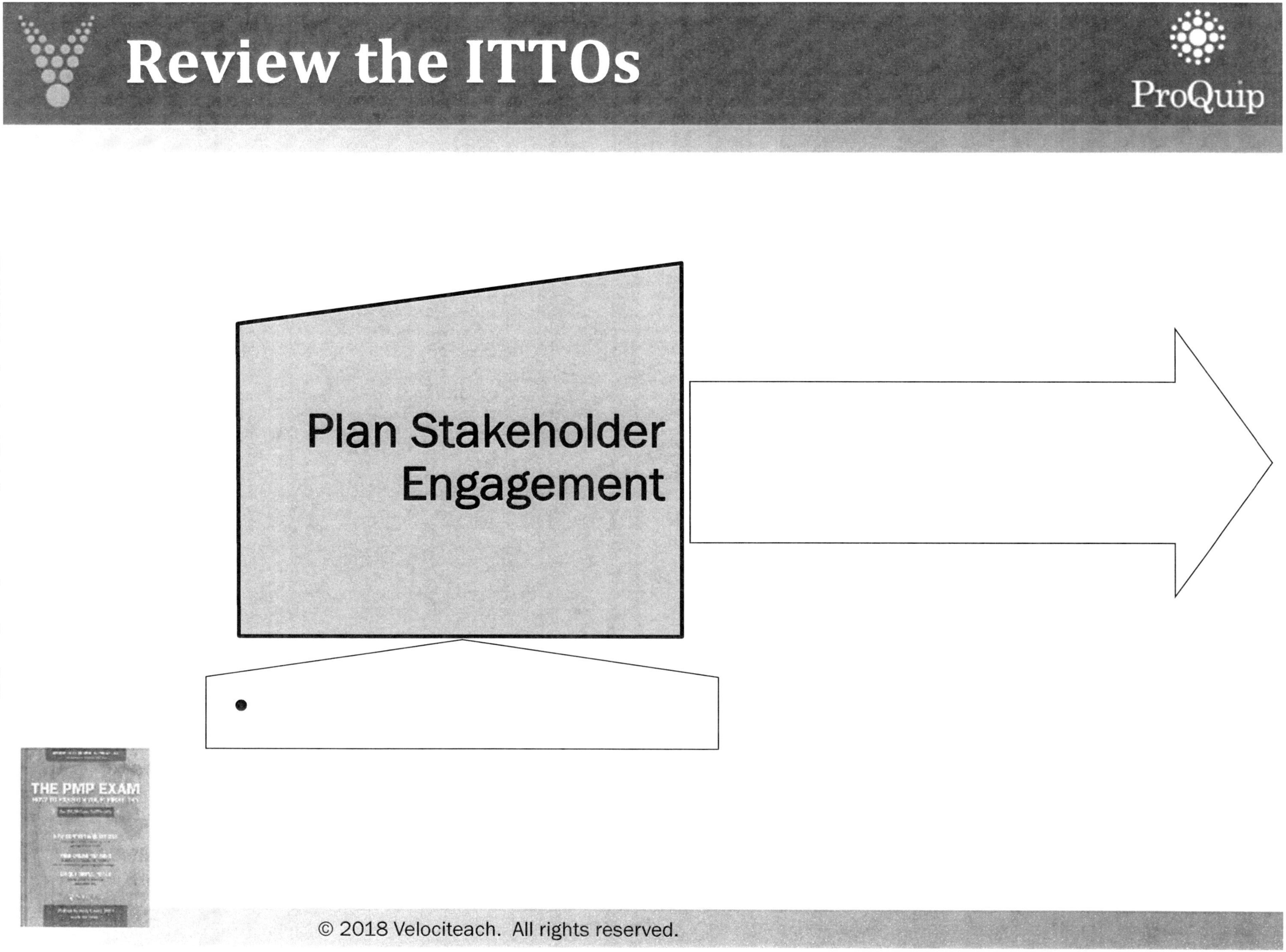

Plan Stakeholder Engagement

© 2018 Velociteach. All rights reserved.

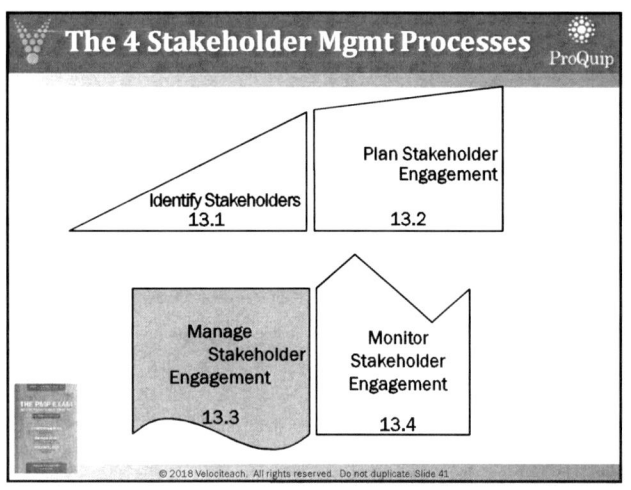

The 4 Stakeholder Mgmt Processes

Identify Stakeholders 13.1

Plan Stakeholder Engagement 13.2

Manage Stakeholder Engagement 13.3

Monitor Stakeholder Engagement 13.4

© 2018 Velociteach. All rights reserved. Do not duplicate. Slide 41

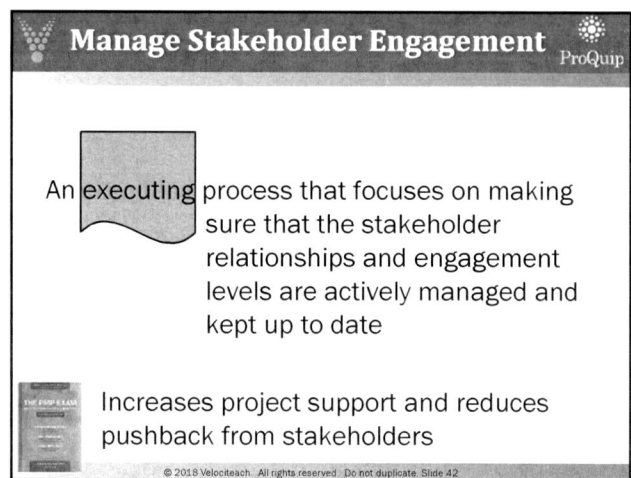

Manage Stakeholder Engagement

An executing process that focuses on making sure that the stakeholder relationships and engagement levels are actively managed and kept up to date

Increases project support and reduces pushback from stakeholders

© 2018 Velociteach. All rights reserved. Do not duplicate. Slide 42

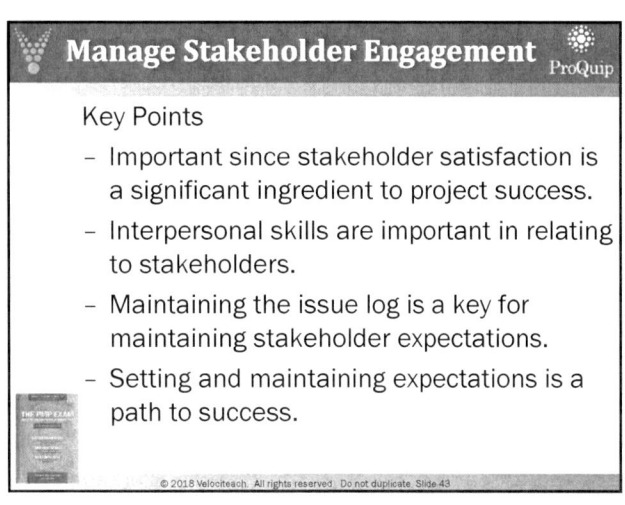

Manage Stakeholder Engagement

Key Points
- Important since stakeholder satisfaction is a significant ingredient to project success.
- Interpersonal skills are important in relating to stakeholders.
- Maintaining the issue log is a key for maintaining stakeholder expectations.
- Setting and maintaining expectations is a path to success.

© 2018 Velociteach. All rights reserved. Do not duplicate. Slide 43

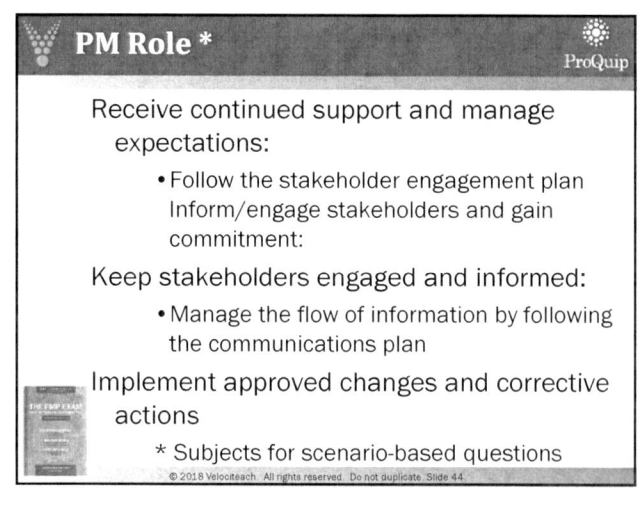

PM Role *

Receive continued support and manage expectations:
- Follow the stakeholder engagement plan Inform/engage stakeholders and gain commitment:

Keep stakeholders engaged and informed:
- Manage the flow of information by following the communications plan

Implement approved changes and corrective actions
 * Subjects for scenario-based questions

© 2018 Velociteach. All rights reserved. Do not duplicate. Slide 44

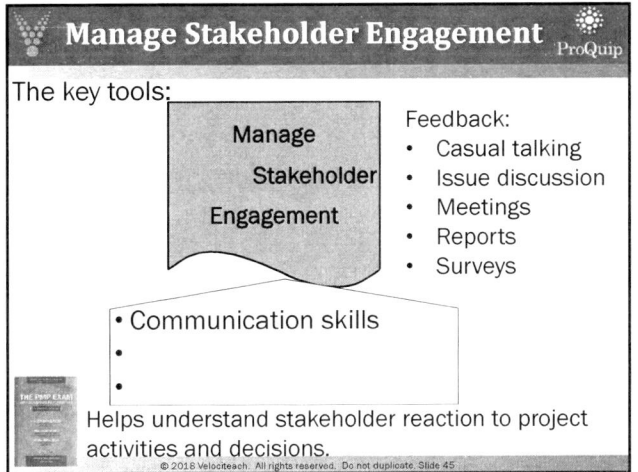

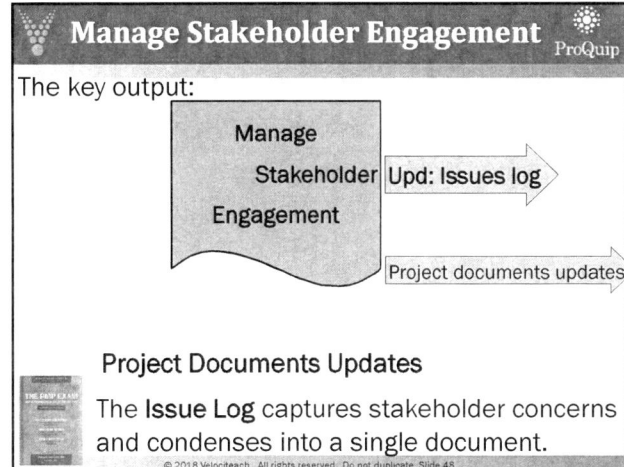

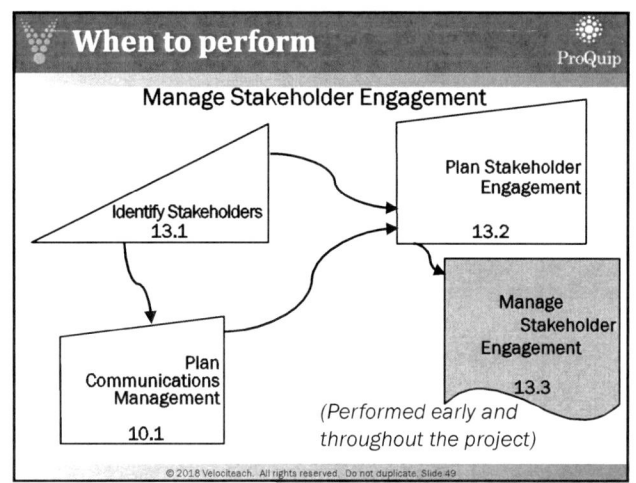

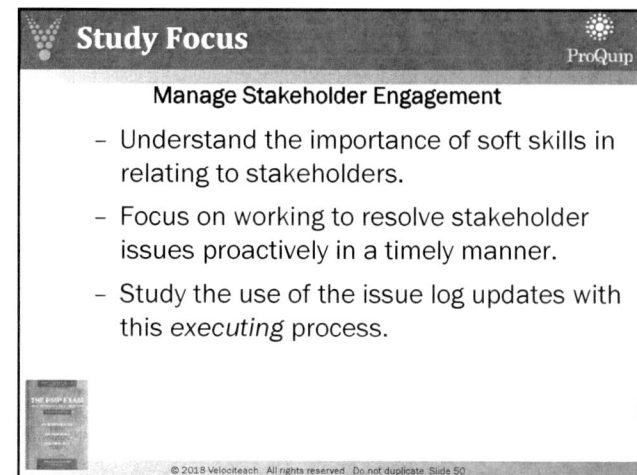

Study Focus

Manage Stakeholder Engagement

- Understand the importance of soft skills in relating to stakeholders.

- Focus on working to resolve stakeholder issues proactively in a timely manner.

- Study the use of the issue log updates with this *executing* process.

©2018 Velociteach. All rights reserved.   Page 346

Review the ITTOs

ProQuip

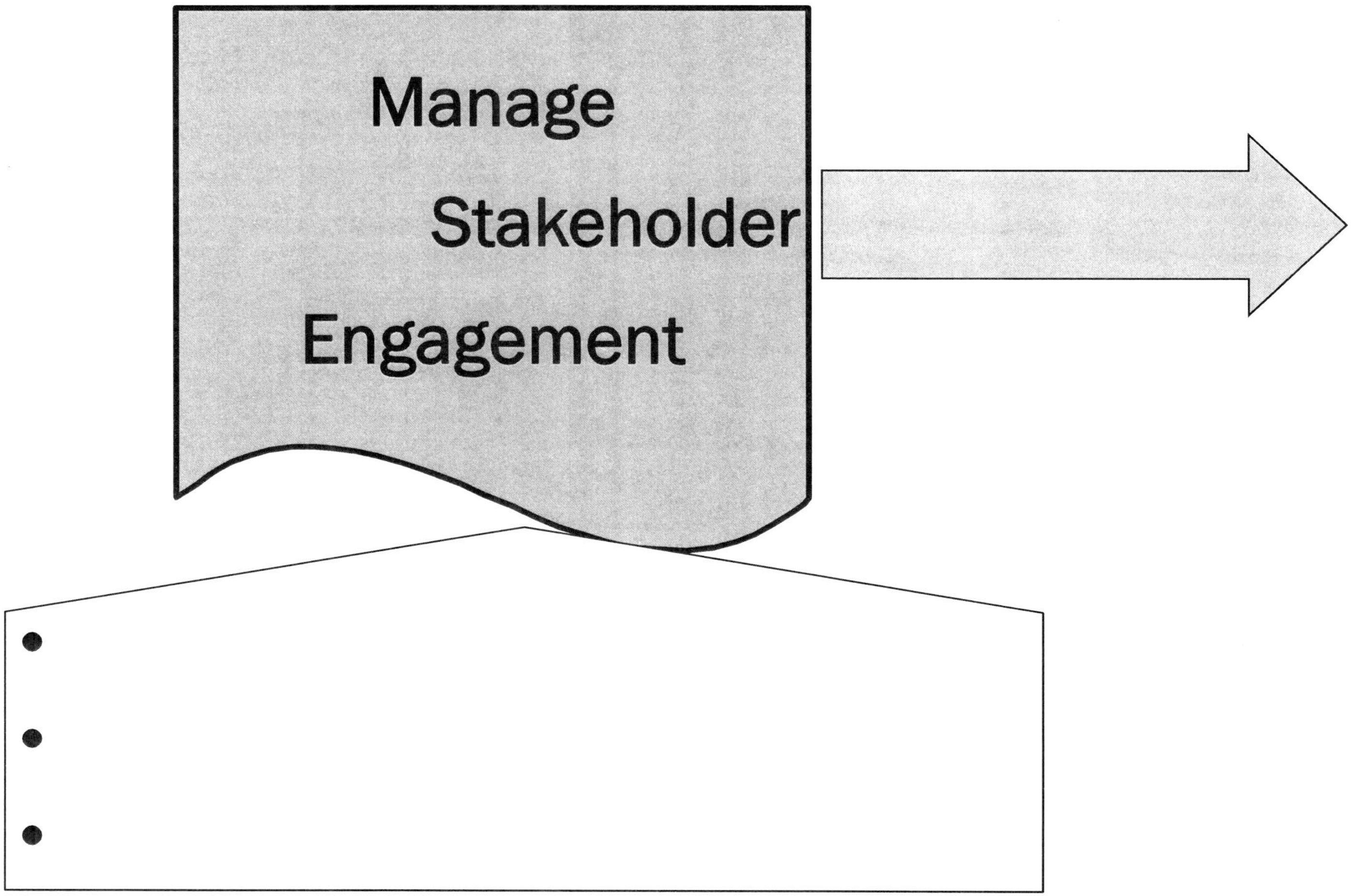

Manage Stakeholder Engagement

© 2018 Velociteach. All rights reserved.

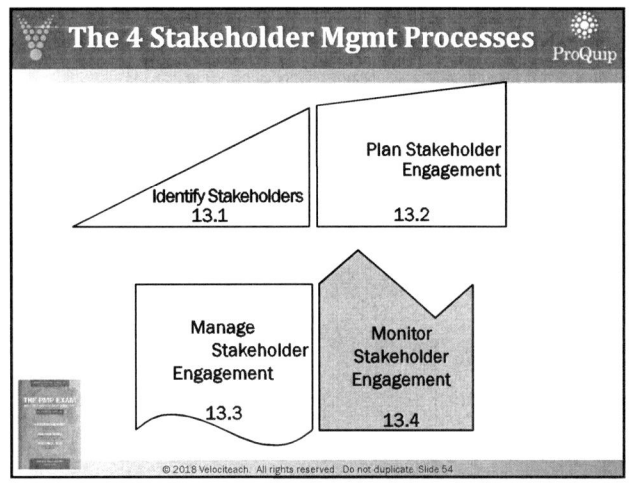

The 4 Stakeholder Mgmt Processes

Identify Stakeholders 13.1

Plan Stakeholder Engagement 13.2

Manage Stakeholder Engagement 13.3

Monitor Stakeholder Engagement 13.4

© 2018 Velociteach. All rights reserved. Do not duplicate. Slide 54

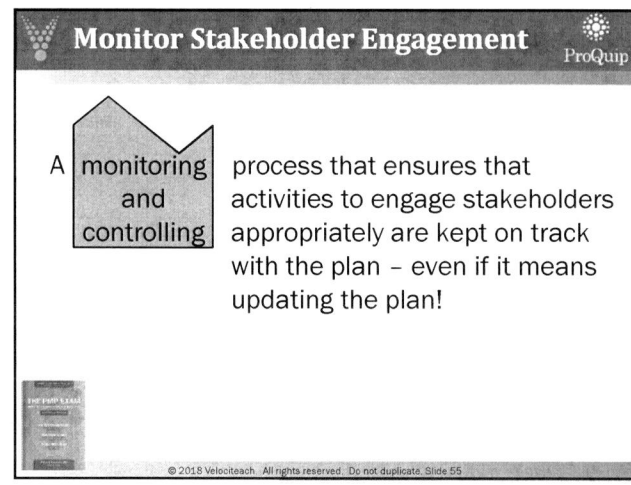

Monitor Stakeholder Engagement

A monitoring and controlling process that ensures that activities to engage stakeholders appropriately are kept on track with the plan – even if it means updating the plan!

© 2018 Velociteach. All rights reserved. Do not duplicate. Slide 55

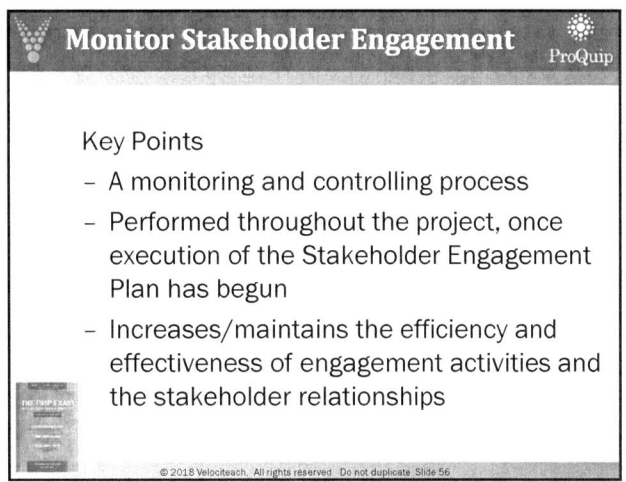

Monitor Stakeholder Engagement

Key Points

- A monitoring and controlling process
- Performed throughout the project, once execution of the Stakeholder Engagement Plan has begun
- Increases/maintains the efficiency and effectiveness of engagement activities and the stakeholder relationships

© 2018 Velociteach. All rights reserved. Do not duplicate. Slide 56

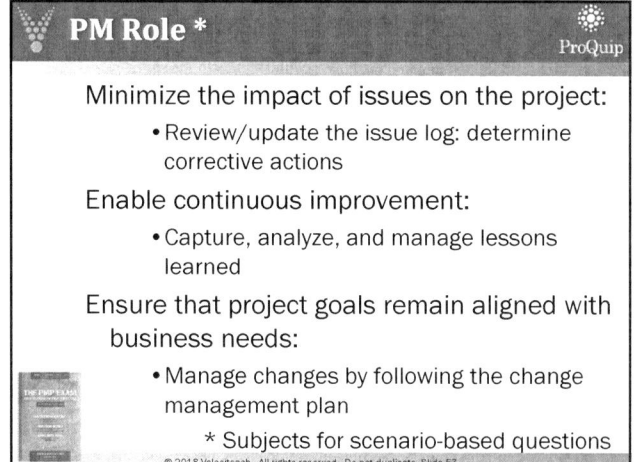

PM Role *

Minimize the impact of issues on the project:
- Review/update the issue log: determine corrective actions

Enable continuous improvement:
- Capture, analyze, and manage lessons learned

Ensure that project goals remain aligned with business needs:
- Manage changes by following the change management plan

  * Subjects for scenario-based questions

© 2018 Velociteach. All rights reserved. Do not duplicate. Slide 57

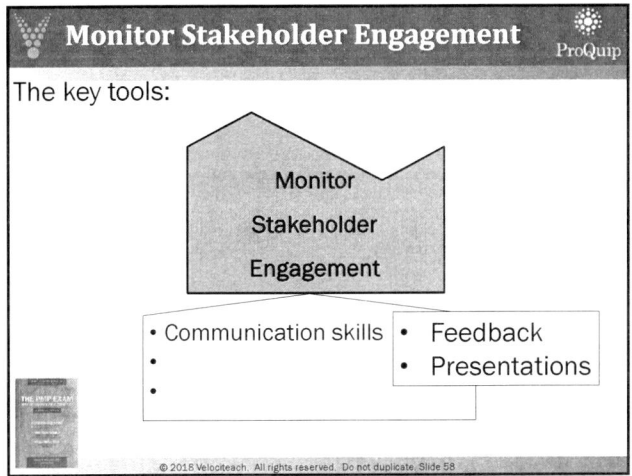

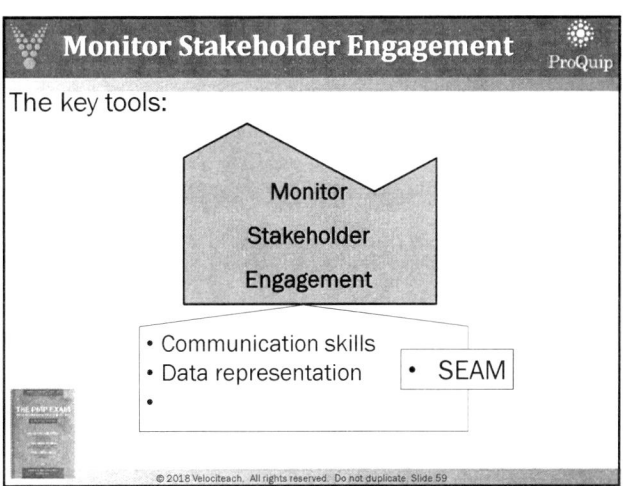

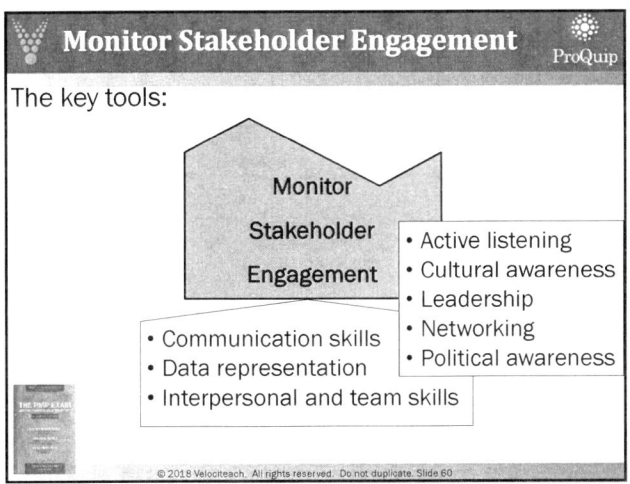

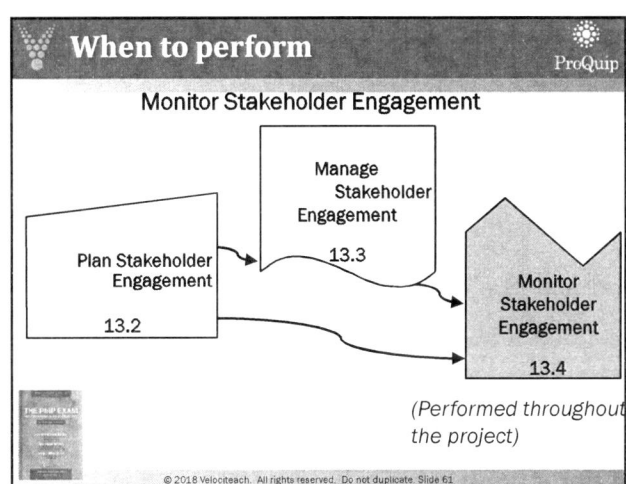

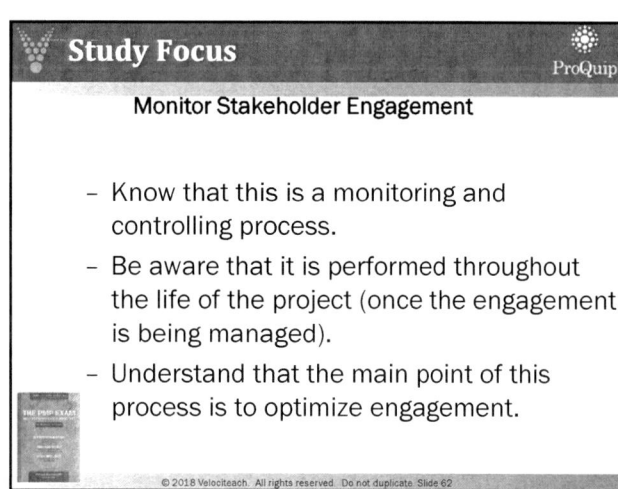

Review the ITTOs

ProQuip

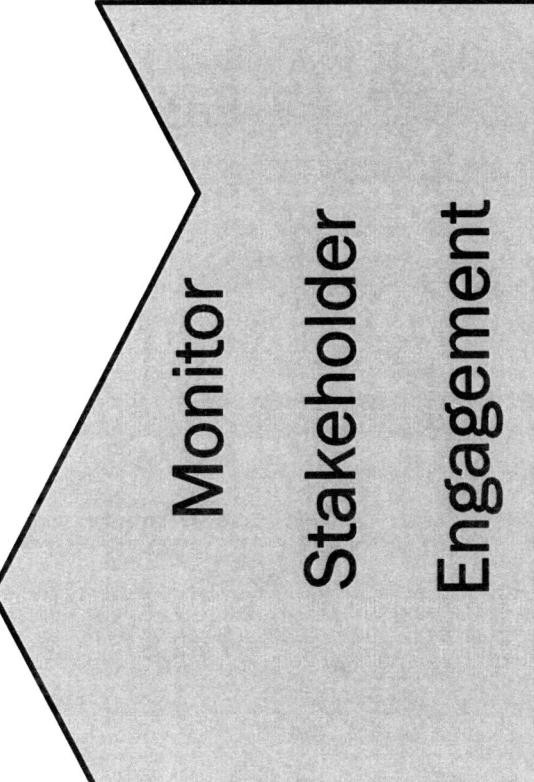

Monitor Stakeholder Engagement

- •
- •
- •

© 2018 Velociteach. All rights reserved.

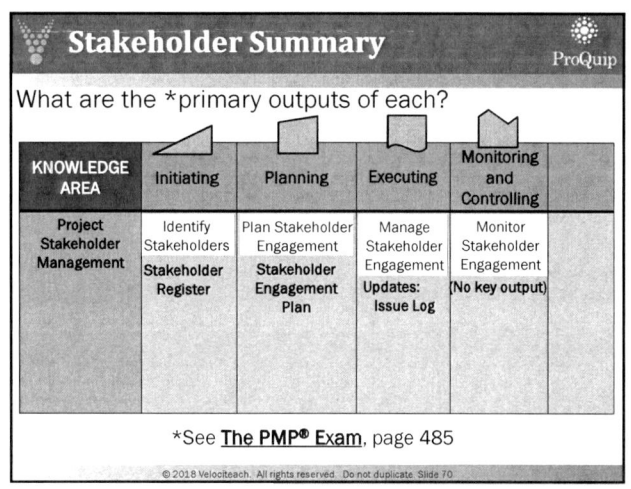

Stakeholder Summary

What are the *primary outputs of each?

KNOWLEDGE AREA	Initiating	Planning	Executing	Monitoring and Controlling
Project Stakeholder Management	Identify Stakeholders / Stakeholder Register	Plan Stakeholder Engagement / Stakeholder Engagement Plan	Manage Stakeholder Engagement / Updates: Issue Log	Monitor Stakeholder Engagement / (No key output)

*See **The PMP® Exam**, page 485

© 2018 Velociteach. All rights reserved. Do not duplicate. Slide 70

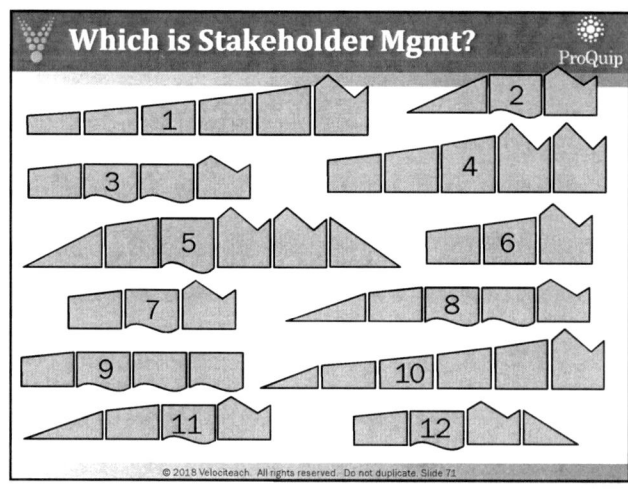

Which is Stakeholder Mgmt?

© 2018 Velociteach. All rights reserved. Do not duplicate. Slide 71

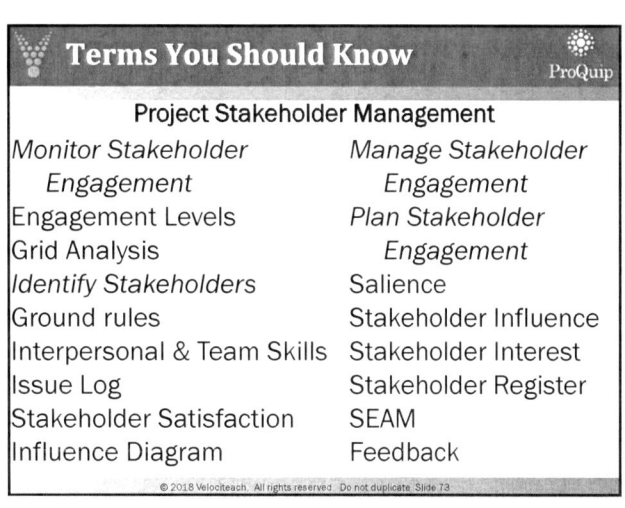

Terms You Should Know

Project Stakeholder Management

Monitor Stakeholder Engagement
Engagement Levels
Grid Analysis
Identify Stakeholders
Ground rules
Interpersonal & Team Skills
Issue Log
Stakeholder Satisfaction
Influence Diagram

Manage Stakeholder Engagement
Plan Stakeholder Engagement
Salience
Stakeholder Influence
Stakeholder Interest
Stakeholder Register
SEAM
Feedback

© 2018 Velociteach. All rights reserved. Do not duplicate. Slide 73

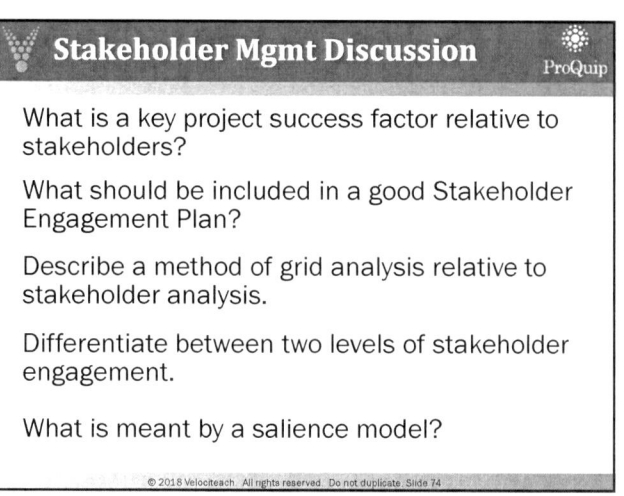

Stakeholder Mgmt Discussion

What is a key project success factor relative to stakeholders?

What should be included in a good Stakeholder Engagement Plan?

Describe a method of grid analysis relative to stakeholder analysis.

Differentiate between two levels of stakeholder engagement.

What is meant by a salience model?

© 2018 Velociteach. All rights reserved. Do not duplicate. Slide 74

Summary

ProQuip

Knowledge Area

KNOWLEDGE AREA	Initiating	Planning	Executing	Monitoring and Controlling	Closing
Project ____ Management					

©2018 Velociteach. All rights reserved.

Score Sheet	**Stakeholder Management Exam**	

- Mark one answer: A, B, C, or D.
- Circle the '?' symbol if you are guessing at the answer.
- Circle the Δ symbol if you change your answer.

Total Correct: _____

% Correct: _____%

1.	A ○	B ○	C ○	D ○	?	Δ
2.	A ○	B ○	C ○	D ○	?	Δ
3.	A ○	B ○	C ○	D ○	?	Δ
4.	A ○	B ○	C ○	D ○	?	Δ
5.	A ○	B ○	C ○	D ○	?	Δ
6.	A ○	B ○	C ○	D ○	?	Δ
7.	A ○	B ○	C ○	D ○	?	Δ
8.	A ○	B ○	C ○	D ○	?	Δ
9.	A ○	B ○	C ○	D ○	?	Δ
10.	A ○	B ○	C ○	D ○	?	Δ

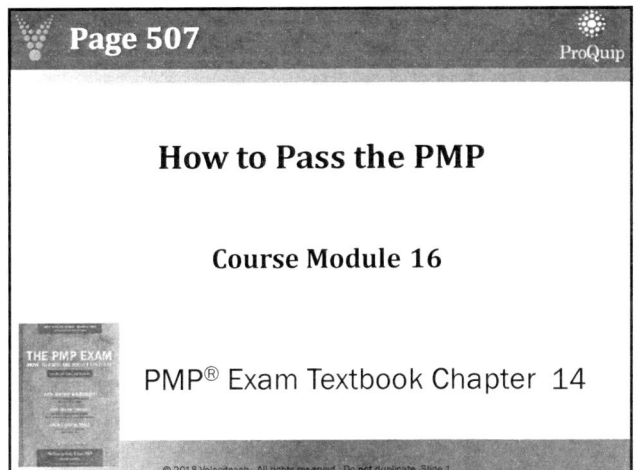

Page 507 ProQuip

How to Pass the PMP

Course Module 16

PMP® Exam Textbook Chapter 14

© 2018 Velociteach. All rights reserved. Do not duplicate. Slide 1

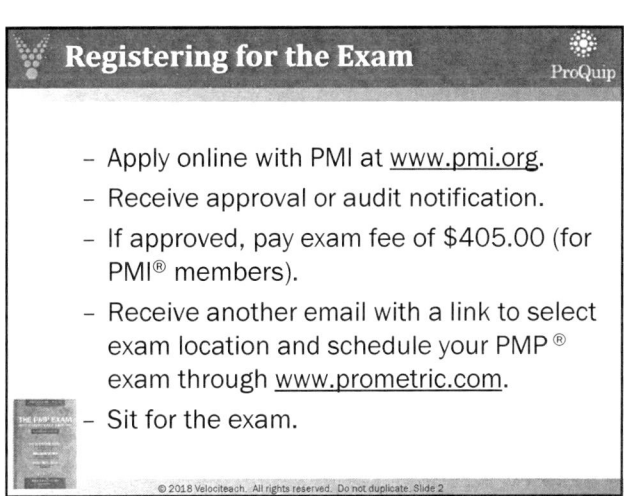

Registering for the Exam ProQuip

- Apply online with PMI at www.pmi.org.
- Receive approval or audit notification.
- If approved, pay exam fee of $405.00 (for PMI® members).
- Receive another email with a link to select exam location and schedule your PMP® exam through www.prometric.com.
- Sit for the exam.

© 2018 Velociteach. All rights reserved. Do not duplicate. Slide 2

Sitting for the Exam ProQuip

To reduce stress:

- Find the testing center in advance. Don't get lost the day of the exam.

- Plan to arrive 30 to 45 minutes early.

- Bring requested identification (2 forms of ID):

  * A government-issued photo ID, and

  * Another with a signature, like a credit card.

© 2018 Velociteach. All rights reserved. Do not duplicate. Slide 3

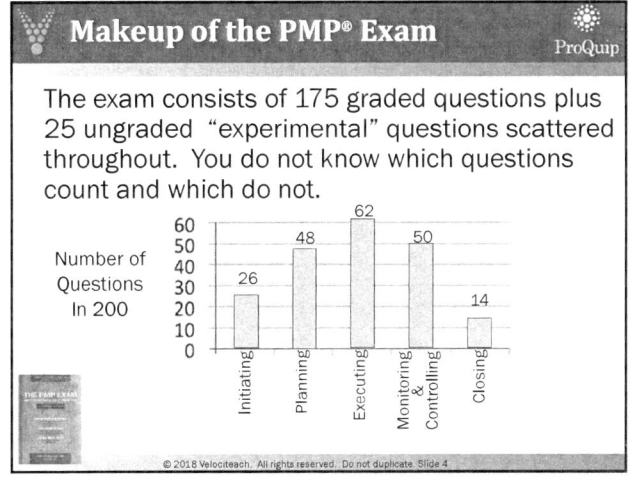

Makeup of the PMP® Exam ProQuip

The exam consists of 175 graded questions plus 25 ungraded "experimental" questions scattered throughout. You do not know which questions count and which do not.

© 2018 Velociteach. All rights reserved. Do not duplicate. Slide 4

©2018 Velociteach. All rights reserved.   Page 355

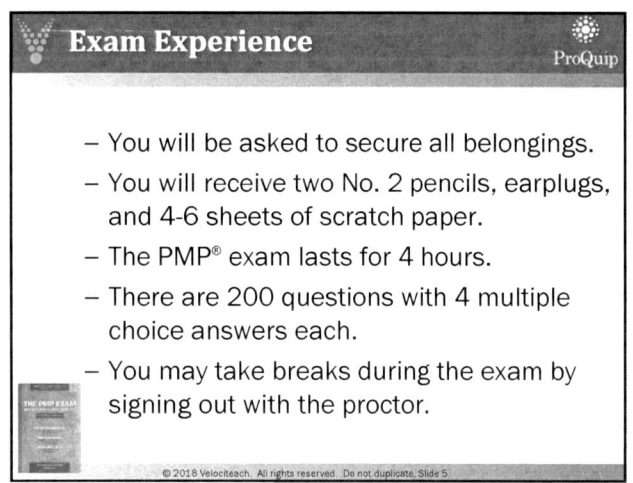

Exam Experience

- You will be asked to secure all belongings.
- You will receive two No. 2 pencils, earplugs, and 4-6 sheets of scratch paper.
- The PMP® exam lasts for 4 hours.
- There are 200 questions with 4 multiple choice answers each.
- You may take breaks during the exam by signing out with the proctor.

© 2018 Velociteach. All rights reserved. Do not duplicate. Slide 5

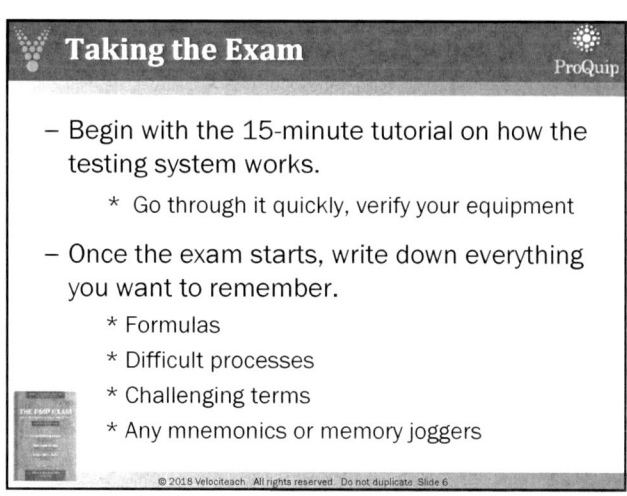

Taking the Exam

- Begin with the 15-minute tutorial on how the testing system works.
    * Go through it quickly, verify your equipment
- Once the exam starts, write down everything you want to remember.
    * Formulas
    * Difficult processes
    * Challenging terms
    * Any mnemonics or memory joggers

© 2018 Velociteach. All rights reserved. Do not duplicate. Slide 6

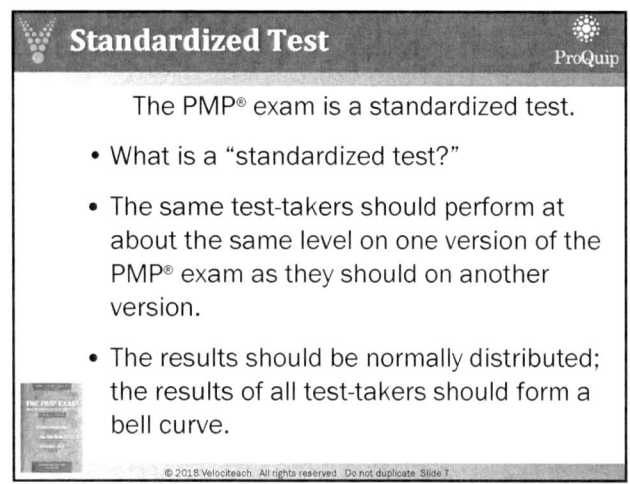

Standardized Test

The PMP® exam is a standardized test.

- What is a "standardized test?"

- The same test-takers should perform at about the same level on one version of the PMP® exam as they should on another version.

- The results should be normally distributed; the results of all test-takers should form a bell curve.

© 2018 Velociteach. All rights reserved. Do not duplicate. Slide 7

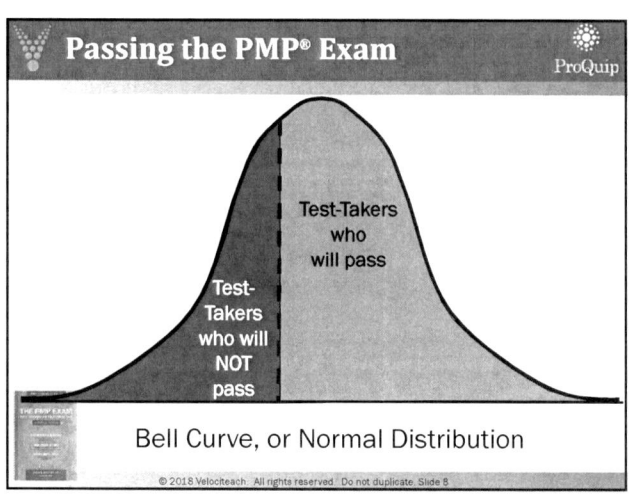

Passing the PMP® Exam

Test-Takers who will pass

Test-Takers who will NOT pass

Bell Curve, or Normal Distribution

© 2018 Velociteach. All rights reserved. Do not duplicate. Slide 8

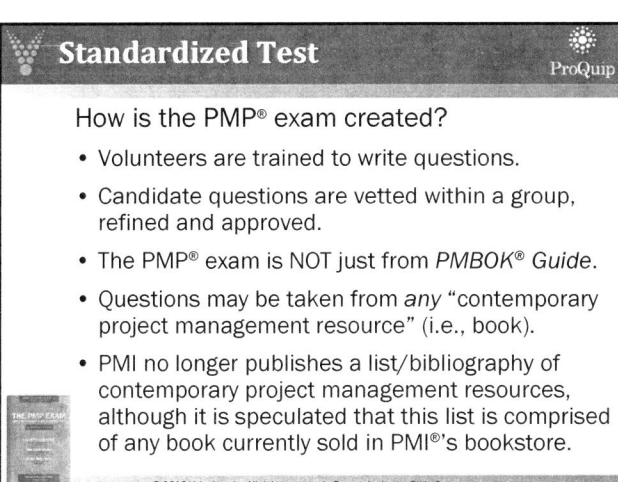

Standardized Test — ProQuip

How is the PMP® exam created?

- Volunteers are trained to write questions.
- Candidate questions are vetted within a group, refined and approved.
- The PMP® exam is NOT just from *PMBOK® Guide*.
- Questions may be taken from *any* "contemporary project management resource" (i.e., book).
- PMI no longer publishes a list/bibliography of contemporary project management resources, although it is speculated that this list is comprised of any book currently sold in PMI®'s bookstore.

© 2018 Velociteach. All rights reserved. Do not duplicate. Slide 9

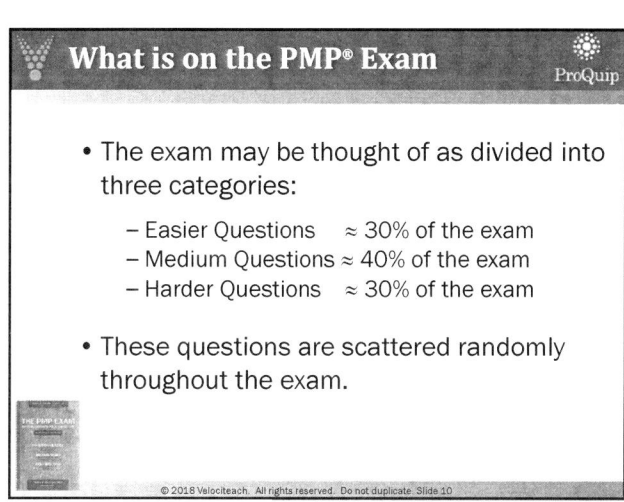

What is on the PMP® Exam — ProQuip

- The exam may be thought of as divided into three categories:
    - Easier Questions ≈ 30% of the exam
    - Medium Questions ≈ 40% of the exam
    - Harder Questions ≈ 30% of the exam

- These questions are scattered randomly throughout the exam.

© 2018 Velociteach. All rights reserved. Do not duplicate. Slide 10

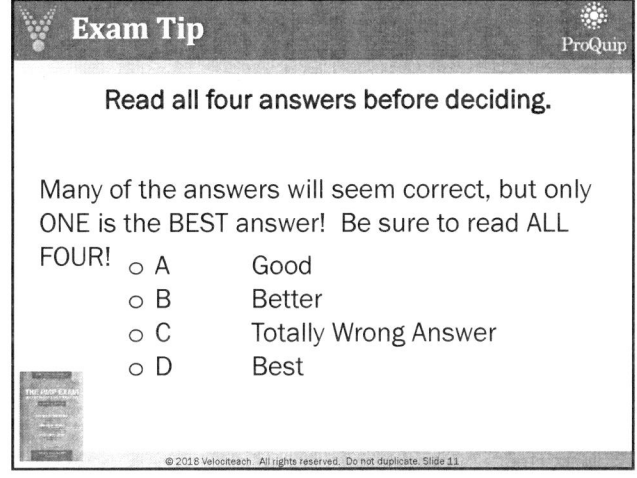

Exam Tip — ProQuip

Read all four answers before deciding.

Many of the answers will seem correct, but only ONE is the BEST answer! Be sure to read ALL FOUR!

- ○ A   Good
- ○ B   Better
- ○ C   Totally Wrong Answer
- ○ D   Best

© 2018 Velociteach. All rights reserved. Do not duplicate. Slide 11

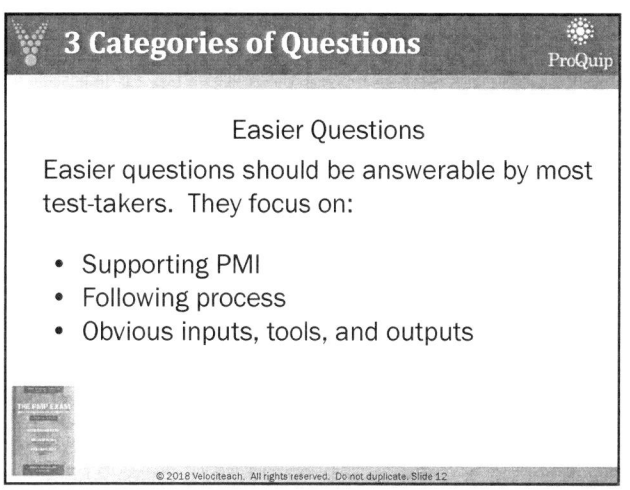

3 Categories of Questions — ProQuip

Easier Questions

Easier questions should be answerable by most test-takers. They focus on:

- Supporting PMI
- Following process
- Obvious inputs, tools, and outputs

© 2018 Velociteach. All rights reserved. Do not duplicate. Slide 12

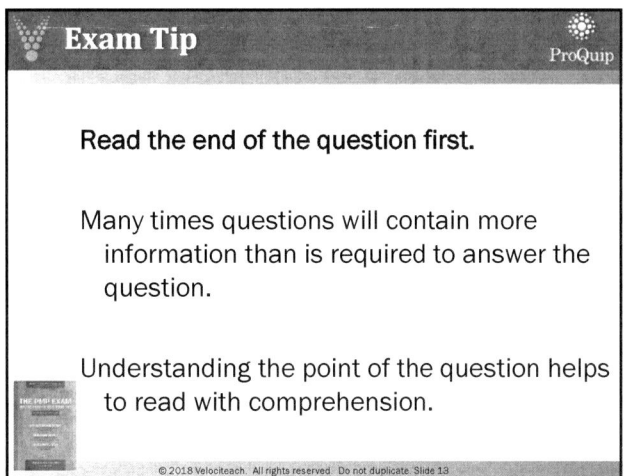

Exam Tip

Read the end of the question first.

Many times questions will contain more information than is required to answer the question.

Understanding the point of the question helps to read with comprehension.

© 2018 Velociteach. All rights reserved. Do not duplicate. Slide 13

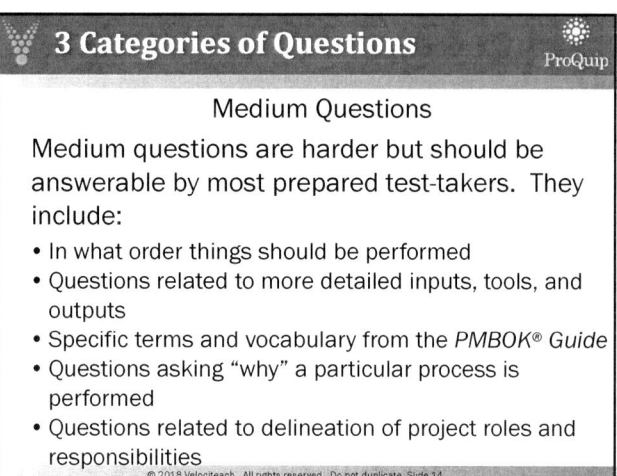

3 Categories of Questions

Medium Questions

Medium questions are harder but should be answerable by most prepared test-takers. They include:

- In what order things should be performed
- Questions related to more detailed inputs, tools, and outputs
- Specific terms and vocabulary from the *PMBOK® Guide*
- Questions asking "why" a particular process is performed
- Questions related to delineation of project roles and responsibilities

© 2018 Velociteach. All rights reserved. Do not duplicate. Slide 14

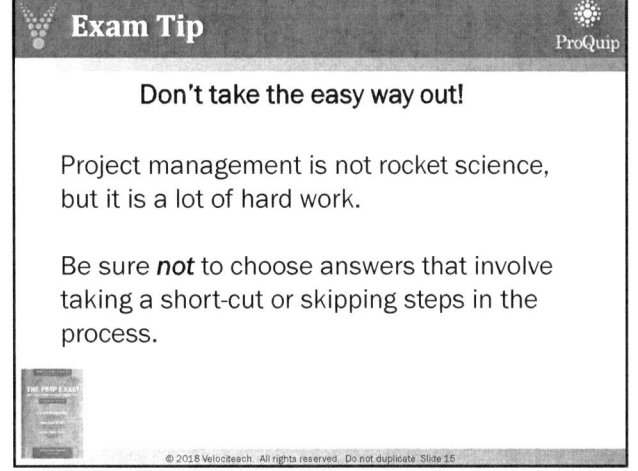

Exam Tip

Don't take the easy way out!

Project management is not rocket science, but it is a lot of hard work.

Be sure *not* to choose answers that involve taking a short-cut or skipping steps in the process.

© 2018 Velociteach. All rights reserved. Do not duplicate. Slide 15

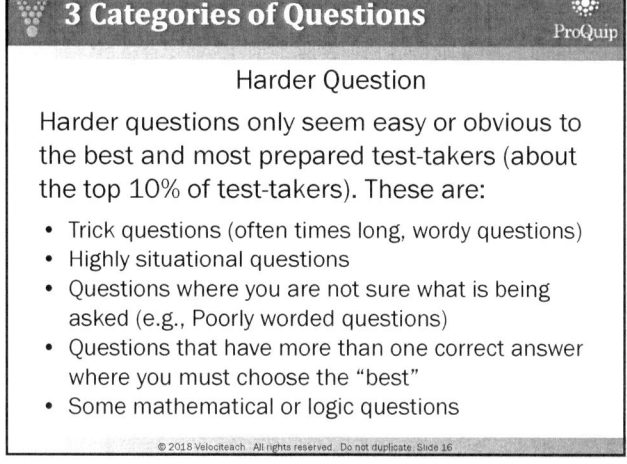

3 Categories of Questions

Harder Question

Harder questions only seem easy or obvious to the best and most prepared test-takers (about the top 10% of test-takers). These are:

- Trick questions (often times long, wordy questions)
- Highly situational questions
- Questions where you are not sure what is being asked (e.g., Poorly worded questions)
- Questions that have more than one correct answer where you must choose the "best"
- Some mathematical or logic questions

© 2018 Velociteach. All rights reserved. Do not duplicate. Slide 16

Expectations: Question Difficulty

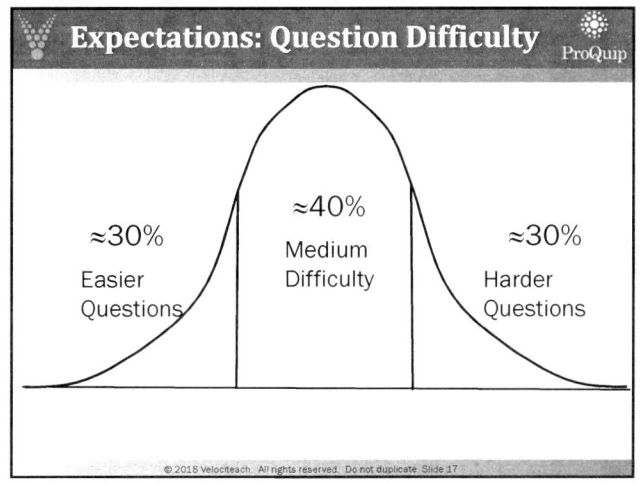

≈30%
Easier Questions

≈40%
Medium Difficulty

≈30%
Harder Questions

© 2018 Velociteach. All rights reserved. Do not duplicate. Slide 17

Exam Tip

Use your instincts; eliminate wrong answers.

After completing this course, your first instinct about the correct answer should be reliable. Gravitate toward answers that sound familiar from the course.

Eliminate answers that involve terms that are unfamiliar.

© 2018 Velociteach. All rights reserved. Do not duplicate. Slide 18

Test-Taker Interface

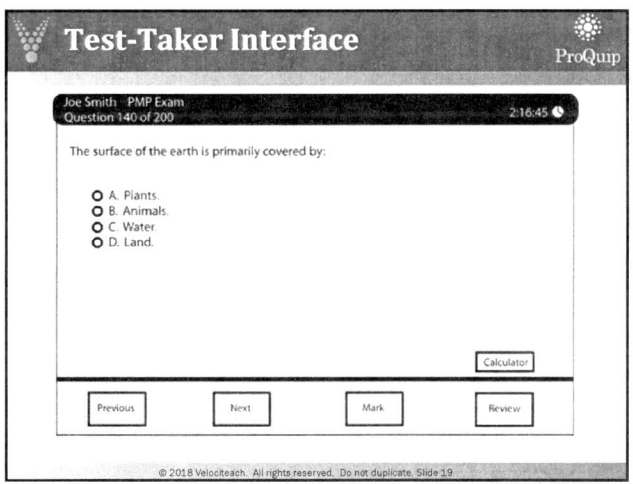

© 2018 Velociteach. All rights reserved. Do not duplicate. Slide 19

Exam Tip

Don't get stuck! Mark harder questions for review.

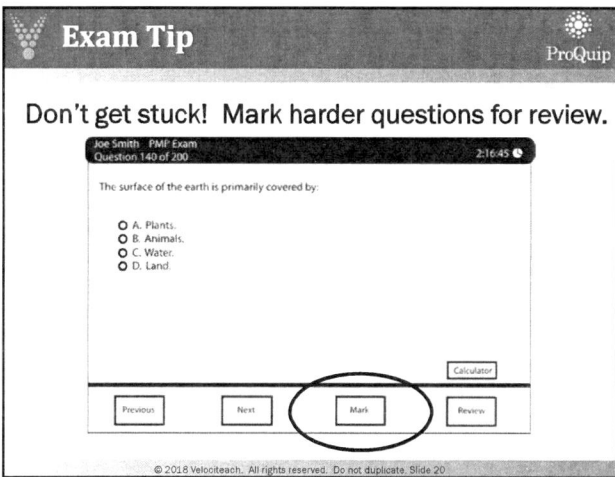

© 2018 Velociteach. All rights reserved. Do not duplicate. Slide 20

Exam Tip

ProQuip

Anxious? Take a deep breath and release slowly.

It's OK, and advisable, to take a *short* break, especially if you begin to feel anxious.

Take a deep breath and release.
Take another deep breath, hold it 6 seconds, and release slowly. You'll feel calmer.

© 2018 Velociteach. All rights reserved. Do not duplicate. Slide 21

Exam Strategy: Harder Questions

ProQuip

- For harder questions, most test-takers *will not* naturally gravitate toward the right answer.
- Look for the trap. Read the question and all four answers again.
- Make sure this is a harder question and that you aren't over-analyzing.
- Ask yourself what answer the novice would pick. Then eliminate that answer off the list.
- Unless you are a strong test-taker, this is not the time to trust your instincts.
- Practice this strategy on **InSite.**

© 2018 Velociteach. All rights reserved. Do not duplicate. Slide 22

Exam Tip

ProQuip

Make the decision, be proactive, be the Professional!

Remember the role of the Project Manager is to be in charge, proactive, and authorized to make decisions.

Don't pass the responsibility of decision-making to anyone else.

© 2018 Velociteach. All rights reserved. Do not duplicate. Slide 23

Final Preparation

ProQuip

- Review the glossary in your orange textbook (page 661). You cannot read this too many times!

- Know the formulas for earned value.

- *Memorizing* the processes and their major inputs, tools, and outputs is **good.** *Understanding* why they are there is **better.**

- Practice on **InSite.** The more questions you take, the more prepared you will be.

© 2018 Velociteach. All rights reserved. Do not duplicate. Slide 24

© 2018 Velociteach. All rights reserved. Do not duplicate. Slide 25

Process Explorer

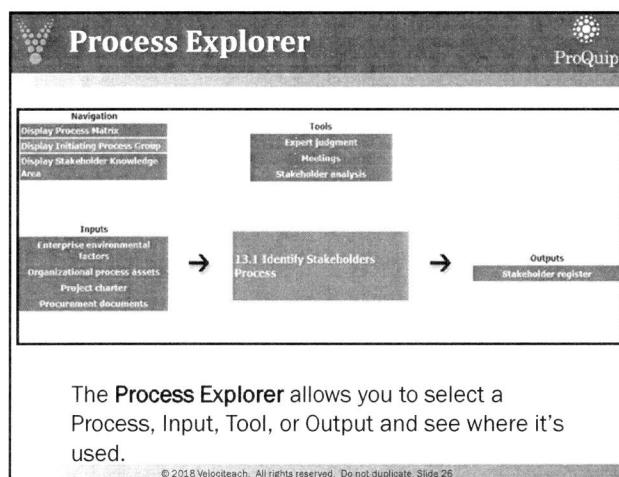

The **Process Explorer** allows you to select a Process, Input, Tool, or Output and see where it's used.

© 2018 Velociteach. All rights reserved. Do not duplicate. Slide 26

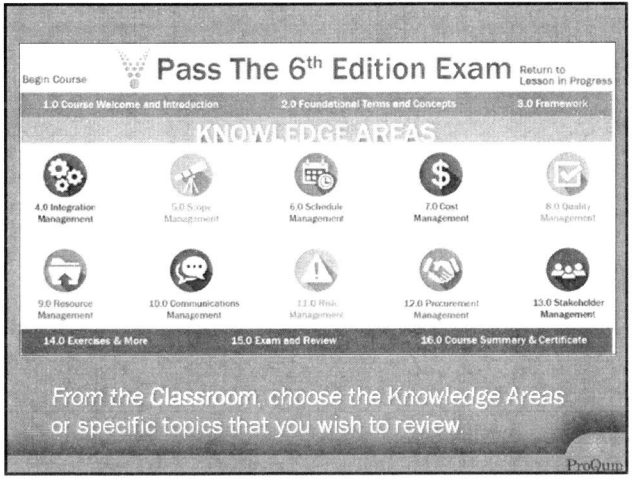

From the Classroom, choose the Knowledge Areas or specific topics that you wish to review.

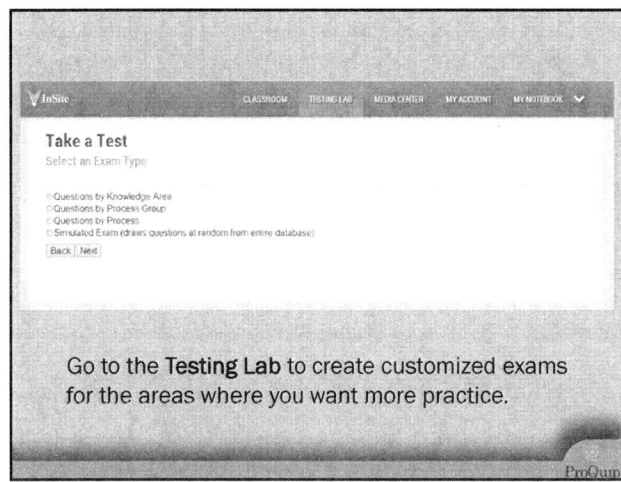

Go to the **Testing Lab** to create customized exams for the areas where you want more practice.

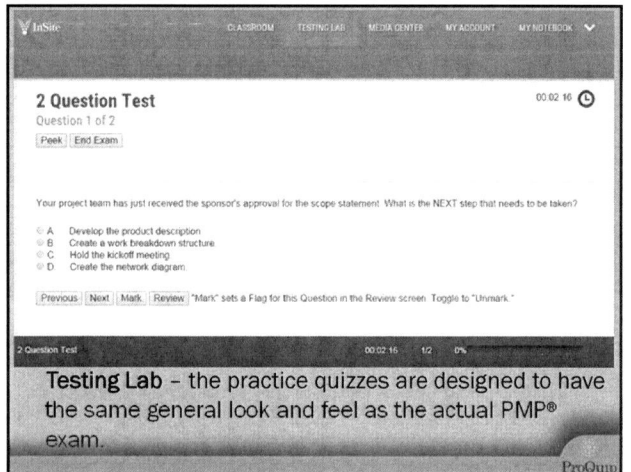

Testing Lab – the practice quizzes are designed to have the same general look and feel as the actual PMP® exam.

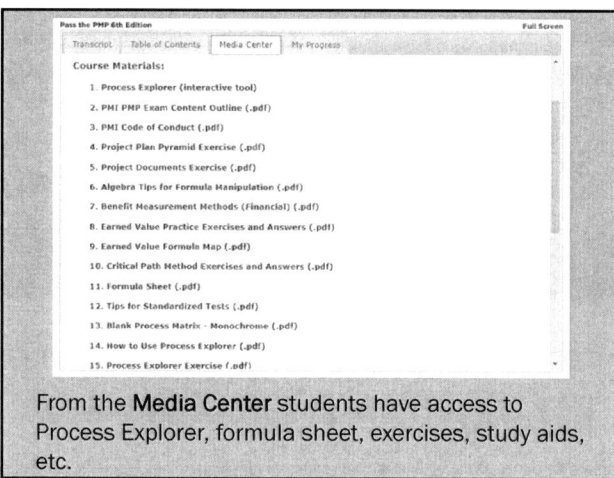

From the **Media Center** students have access to Process Explorer, formula sheet, exercises, study aids, etc.

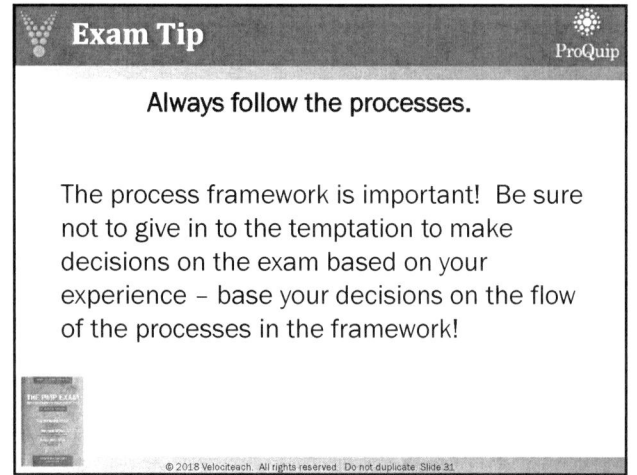

Exam Tip

ProQuip

Always follow the processes.

The process framework is important! Be sure not to give in to the temptation to make decisions on the exam based on your experience – base your decisions on the flow of the processes in the framework!

© 2018 Velociteach. All rights reserved. Do not duplicate. Slide 31

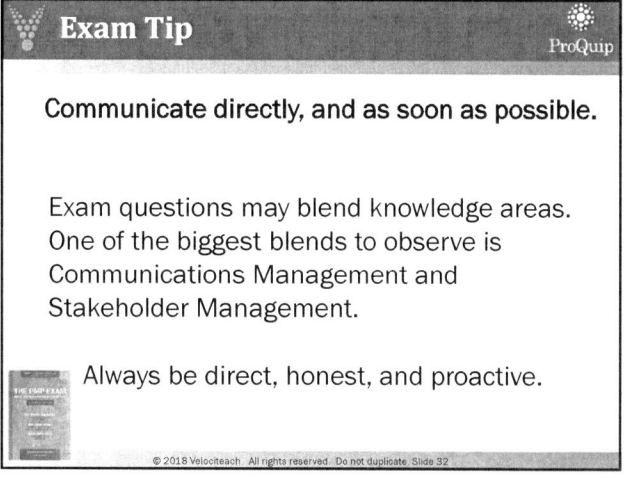

Exam Tip

ProQuip

Communicate directly, and as soon as possible.

Exam questions may blend knowledge areas. One of the biggest blends to observe is Communications Management and Stakeholder Management.

Always be direct, honest, and proactive.

© 2018 Velociteach. All rights reserved. Do not duplicate. Slide 32

Know the project roles and the organization types.

Make sure the project manager and functional manager roles and associated authority levels are in keeping with the organizational type alluded to in the question scenario.

Default to a Balanced Matrix unless otherwise specified.

© 2018 Velociteach. All rights reserved. Do not duplicate. Slide 33

Time Management for the Exam ProQuip

Once the exam has begun (p. 518 in textbook):

- Take the first 75 questions in about 45 minutes.
- Take a 5 minute break.
- Take the next 75 questions in 45 to 50 minutes.
- Take a 10 minute break.
- Answer the final 50 questions in the last 45 minutes. Include any questions marked for review.
- Take a 15 minute break.
- Review 100 questions in approximately 25 minutes.
- Review the last 100 questions in the remaining time.

© 2018 Velociteach. All rights reserved. Do not duplicate. Slide 34

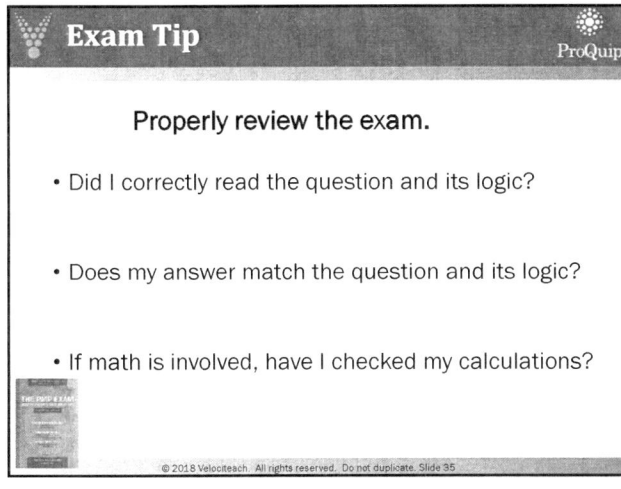

Exam Tip ProQuip

Properly review the exam.

- Did I correctly read the question and its logic?

- Does my answer match the question and its logic?

- If math is involved, have I checked my calculations?

© 2018 Velociteach. All rights reserved. Do not duplicate. Slide 35

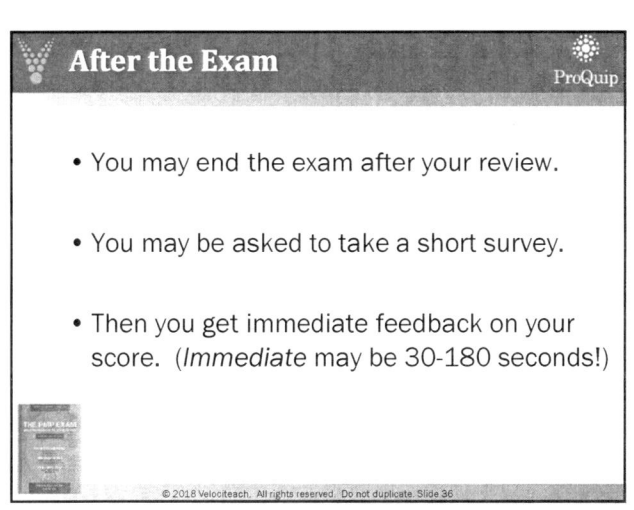

After the Exam ProQuip

- You may end the exam after your review.

- You may be asked to take a short survey.

- Then you get immediate feedback on your score. (*Immediate* may be 30-180 seconds!)

© 2018 Velociteach. All rights reserved. Do not duplicate. Slide 36

Score Sheet

When you finish, you get a score sheet similar to the one shown at right.

The score sheet provides a little guidance. BUT – a **deeper analysis** is available from PMI!

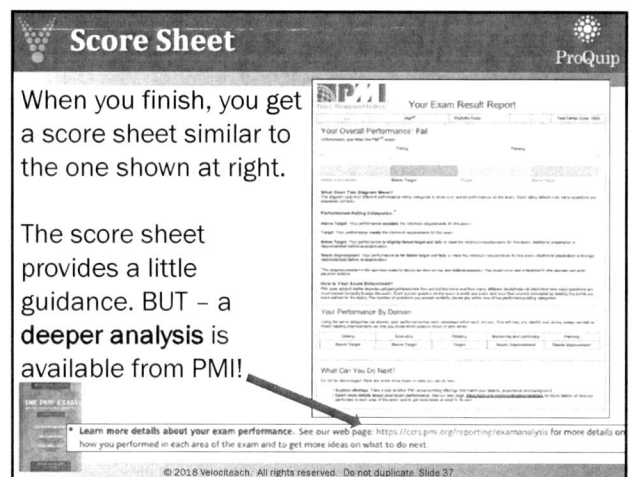

A New PMP® Among Us!

– The moment you pass the PMP® exam, you are a PMP®. You may start using the ", PMP" designation after your name.

– You will receive a certificate and a PMP® pin in the mail from PMI.

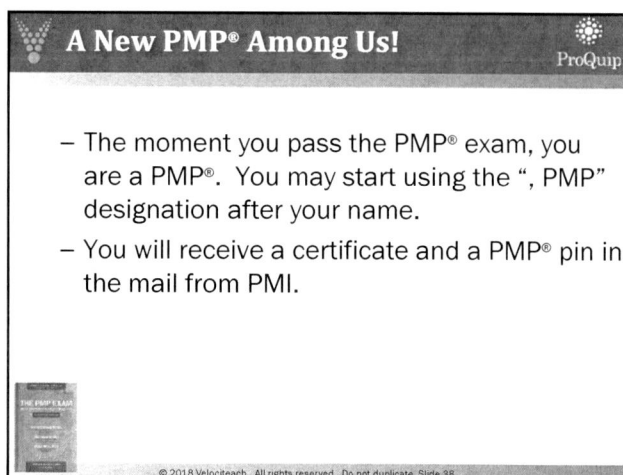

539

Course Conclusion

Course Module 17

Best wishes from Velociteach for your PMP® success!

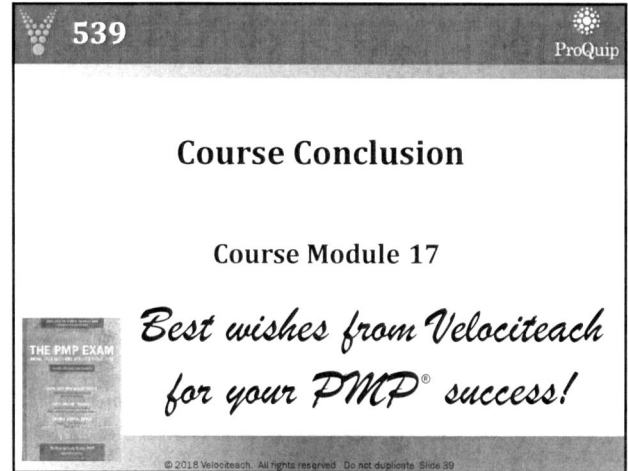

Final Exam

Final Exam

The PMP® Exam Textbook
(page 539)

Course Module 17

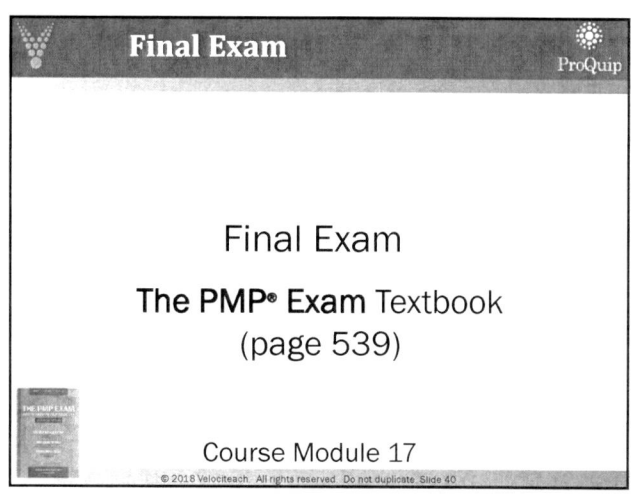

©2018 Velociteach. All rights reserved.

1.	A ○	B ●	C ○	D ○	? Δ		51.	A ○	B ●	C ○	D ○	? Δ
2.	A ○	B ○	C ○	D ○	? Δ		52.	A ○	B ●	C ○	D ○	? Δ
3.	A ○	B ●	C ○	D ○	? Δ		53.	A ○	B ●	C ○	D ○	? Δ
4.	A ○	B ●	C ○	D ○	? Δ		54.	A ○	B ●	C ○	D ○	? Δ
5.	A ○	B ●	C ○	D ○	? Δ		55.	A ○	B ●	C ○	D ○	? Δ
6.	A ○	B ○	C ○	D ○	? Δ		56.	A ○	B ●	C ○	D ○	? Δ
7.	A ○	B ●	C ○	D ○	? Δ		57.	A ○	B ●	C ○	D ○	? Δ
8.	A ○	B ●	C ○	D ○	? Δ		58.	A ○	B ○	C ○	D ○	? Δ
9.	A ○	B ●	C ○	D ○	? Δ		59.	A ○	B ●	C ○	D ○	? Δ
10.	A ○	B ●	C ○	D ○	? Δ		60.	A ○	B ○	C ○	D ○	? Δ
11.	A ○	B ●	C ○	D ○	? Δ		61.	A ○	B ●	C ○	D ○	? Δ
12.	A ○	B ○	C ○	D ○	? Δ		62.	A ○	B ○	C ○	D ○	? Δ
13.	A ○	B ●	C ○	D ○	? Δ		63.	A ○	B ●	C ○	D ○	? Δ
14.	A ○	B ●	C ○	D ○	? Δ		64.	A ○	B ●	C ○	D ○	? Δ
15.	A ○	B ●	C ○	D ○	? Δ		65.	A ○	B ●	C ○	D ○	? Δ
16.	A ○	B ●	C ○	D ○	? Δ		66.	A ○	B ●	C ○	D ○	? Δ
17.	A ○	B ●	C ○	D ○	? Δ		67.	A ○	B ●	C ○	D ○	? Δ
18.	A ○	B ○	C ○	D ○	? Δ		68.	A ○	B ●	C ○	D ○	? Δ
19.	A ○	B ●	C ○	D ○	? Δ		69.	A ○	B ●	C ○	D ○	? Δ
20.	A ○	B ○	C ○	D ○	? Δ		70.	A ○	B ○	C ○	D ○	? Δ
21.	A ○	B ●	C ○	D ○	? Δ		71.	A ○	B ●	C ○	D ○	? Δ
22.	A ○	B ○	C ○	D ○	? Δ		72.	A ○	B ●	C ○	D ○	? Δ
23.	A ○	B ●	C ○	D ○	? Δ		73.	A ○	B ●	C ○	D ○	? Δ
24.	A ○	B ○	C ○	D ○	? Δ		74.	A ○	B ○	C ○	D ○	? Δ
25.	A ○	B ●	C ○	D ○	? Δ		75.	A ○	B ●	C ○	D ○	? Δ
26.	A ○	B ○	C ○	D ○	? Δ		76.	A ○	B ●	C ○	D ○	? Δ
27.	A ○	B ●	C ○	D ○	? Δ		77.	A ○	B ●	C ○	D ○	? Δ
28.	A ○	B ●	C ○	D ○	? Δ		78.	A ○	B ○	C ○	D ○	? Δ
29.	A ○	B ●	C ○	D ○	? Δ		79.	A ○	B ●	C ○	D ○	? Δ
30.	A ○	B ○	C ○	D ○	? Δ		80.	A ○	B ○	C ○	D ○	? Δ
31.	A ○	B ●	C ○	D ○	? Δ		81.	A ○	B ●	C ○	D ○	? Δ
32.	A ○	B ○	C ○	D ○	? Δ		82.	A ○	B ○	C ○	D ○	? Δ
33.	A ○	B ●	C ○	D ○	? Δ		83.	A ○	B ●	C ○	D ○	? Δ
34.	A ○	B ●	C ○	D ○	? Δ		84.	A ○	B ●	C ○	D ○	? Δ
35.	A ○	B ●	C ○	D ○	? Δ		85.	A ○	B ●	C ○	D ○	? Δ
36.	A ○	B ●	C ○	D ○	? Δ		86.	A ○	B ○	C ○	D ○	? Δ
37.	A ○	B ●	C ○	D ○	? Δ		87.	A ○	B ●	C ○	D ○	? Δ
38.	A ○	B ●	C ○	D ○	? Δ		88.	A ○	B ○	C ○	D ○	? Δ
39.	A ○	B ●	C ○	D ○	? Δ		89.	A ○	B ●	C ○	D ○	? Δ
40.	A ○	B ●	C ○	D ○	? Δ		90.	A ○	B ○	C ○	D ○	? Δ
41.	A ○	B ●	C ○	D ○	? Δ		91.	A ○	B ●	C ○	D ○	? Δ
42.	A ○	B ●	C ○	D ○	? Δ		92.	A ○	B ○	C ○	D ○	? Δ
43.	A ○	B ●	C ○	D ○	? Δ		93.	A ○	B ●	C ○	D ○	? Δ
44.	A ○	B ●	C ○	D ○	? Δ		94.	A ○	B ○	C ○	D ○	? Δ
45.	A ○	B ●	C ○	D ○	? Δ		95.	A ○	B ●	C ○	D ○	? Δ
46.	A ○	B ●	C ○	D ○	? Δ		96.	A ○	B ●	C ○	D ○	? Δ
47.	A ○	B ●	C ○	D ○	? Δ		97.	A ○	B ●	C ○	D ○	? Δ
48.	A ○	B ●	C ○	D ○	? Δ		98.	A ○	B ○	C ○	D ○	? Δ
49.	A ○	B ●	C ○	D ○	? Δ		99.	A ○	B ●	C ○	D ○	? Δ
50.	A ○	B ●	C ○	D ○	? Δ		100.	A ○	B ●	C ○	D ○	? Δ

This page left intentionally blank.

©2018 Velociteach. All rights reserved.

#	A	B	C	D	?		#	A	B	C	D	?	
101.	A○	B○	C○	D○	?	Δ	151.	A○	B○	C○	D○	?	Δ
102.	A○	B○	C○	D○	?	Δ	152.	A○	B○	C○	D○	?	Δ
103.	A○	B○	C○	D○	?	Δ	153.	A○	B○	C○	D○	?	Δ
104.	A○	B○	C○	D○	?	Δ	154.	A○	B○	C○	D○	?	Δ
105.	A○	B○	C○	D○	?	Δ	155.	A○	B○	C○	D○	?	Δ
106.	A○	B○	C○	D○	?	Δ	156.	A○	B○	C○	D○	?	Δ
107.	A○	B○	C○	D○	?	Δ	157.	A○	B○	C○	D○	?	Δ
108.	A○	B○	C○	D○	?	Δ	158.	A○	B○	C○	D○	?	Δ
109.	A○	B○	C○	D○	?	Δ	159.	A○	B○	C○	D○	?	Δ
110.	A○	B○	C○	D○	?	Δ	160.	A○	B○	C○	D○	?	Δ
111.	A○	B○	C○	D○	?	Δ	161.	A○	B○	C○	D○	?	Δ
112.	A○	B○	C○	D○	?	Δ	162.	A○	B○	C○	D○	?	Δ
113.	A○	B○	C○	D○	?	Δ	163.	A○	B○	C○	D○	?	Δ
114.	A○	B○	C○	D○	?	Δ	164.	A○	B○	C○	D○	?	Δ
115.	A○	B○	C○	D○	?	Δ	165.	A○	B○	C○	D○	?	Δ
116.	A○	B○	C○	D○	?	Δ	166.	A○	B○	C○	D○	?	Δ
117.	A○	B○	C○	D○	?	Δ	167.	A○	B○	C○	D○	?	Δ
118.	A○	B○	C○	D○	?	Δ	168.	A○	B○	C○	D○	?	Δ
119.	A○	B○	C○	D○	?	Δ	169.	A○	B○	C○	D○	?	Δ
120.	A○	B○	C○	D○	?	Δ	170.	A○	B○	C○	D○	?	Δ
121.	A○	B○	C○	D○	?	Δ	171.	A○	B○	C○	D○	?	Δ
122.	A○	B○	C○	D○	?	Δ	172.	A○	B○	C○	D○	?	Δ
123.	A○	B○	C○	D○	?	Δ	173.	A○	B○	C○	D○	?	Δ
124.	A○	B○	C○	D○	?	Δ	174.	A○	B○	C○	D○	?	Δ
125.	A○	B○	C○	D○	?	Δ	175.	A○	B○	C○	D○	?	Δ
126.	A○	B○	C○	D○	?	Δ	176.	A○	B○	C○	D○	?	Δ
127.	A○	B○	C○	D○	?	Δ	177.	A○	B○	C○	D○	?	Δ
128.	A○	B○	C○	D○	?	Δ	178.	A○	B○	C○	D○	?	Δ
129.	A○	B○	C○	D○	?	Δ	179.	A○	B○	C○	D○	?	Δ
130.	A○	B○	C○	D○	?	Δ	180.	A○	B○	C○	D○	?	Δ
131.	A○	B○	C○	D○	?	Δ	181.	A○	B○	C○	D○	?	Δ
132.	A○	B○	C○	D○	?	Δ	182.	A○	B○	C○	D○	?	Δ
133.	A○	B○	C○	D○	?	Δ	183.	A○	B○	C○	D○	?	Δ
134.	A○	B○	C○	D○	?	Δ	184.	A○	B○	C○	D○	?	Δ
135.	A○	B○	C○	D○	?	Δ	185.	A○	B○	C○	D○	?	Δ
136.	A○	B○	C○	D○	?	Δ	186.	A○	B○	C○	D○	?	Δ
137.	A○	B○	C○	D○	?	Δ	187.	A○	B○	C○	D○	?	Δ
138.	A○	B○	C○	D○	?	Δ	188.	A○	B○	C○	D○	?	Δ
139.	A○	B○	C○	D○	?	Δ	189.	A○	B○	C○	D○	?	Δ
140.	A○	B○	C○	D○	?	Δ	190.	A○	B○	C○	D○	?	Δ
141.	A○	B○	C○	D○	?	Δ	191.	A○	B○	C○	D○	?	Δ
142.	A○	B○	C○	D○	?	Δ	192.	A○	B○	C○	D○	?	Δ
143.	A○	B○	C○	D○	?	Δ	193.	A○	B○	C○	D○	?	Δ
144.	A○	B○	C○	D○	?	Δ	194.	A○	B○	C○	D○	?	Δ
145.	A○	B○	C○	D○	?	Δ	195.	A○	B○	C○	D○	?	Δ
146.	A○	B○	C○	D○	?	Δ	196.	A○	B○	C○	D○	?	Δ
147.	A○	B○	C○	D○	?	Δ	197.	A○	B○	C○	D○	?	Δ
148.	A○	B○	C○	D○	?	Δ	198.	A○	B○	C○	D○	?	Δ
149.	A○	B○	C○	D○	?	Δ	199.	A○	B○	C○	D○	?	Δ
150.	A○	B○	C○	D○	?	Δ	200.	A○	B○	C○	D○	?	Δ

This page left intentionally blank.

©2018 Velociteach. All rights reserved.

ProQuip

Project Plan Pyramid

Stakeholder Engagement Plan
Plan Stakeholder Engagement

Procurement Mgmt. Plan
Plan Procurement Management

Risk Mgmt. Plan
Plan Risk Management

Cost Baseline
Determine Budget

Quality Mgmt. Plan
Plan Quality Management

Resource Mgmt. Plan
Plan Resource Management

Comm. Mgmt. Plan
Plan Communications Management

Scope Mgmt. Plan
Plan Scope Management

Cost Mgmt. Plan
Plan Cost Management

Schedule Baseline
Develop Schedule

Schedule Mgmt. Plan
Plan Schedule Management

Scope Baseline
Create WBS

Configuration Mgmt. Plan
Develop Project Mgmt. Plan

Change Mgmt. Plan
Develop Project Mgmt. Plan

Development Approach
Develop Project Mgmt. Plan

Project Life-Cycle Description
Develop Project Mgmt. Plan

Performance Measurement Baseline
Develop Project Mgmt. Plan

Requirements Mgmt. Plan
Plan Scope Management

© 2018 Velociteach. All rights reserved.

Baseline Exam Answer Key

1. C

By examining the number on a node of the WBS (including the work package which is the bottom node) you can determine to which parent node it belongs.
'A' is incorrect because the numbering system applies to work packages and not to activities (activities are not part of the WBS).
'B' is incorrect because that would be found in the WBS Dictionary – not in the numbering system.
'D' is incorrect because duration estimates take place in a subsequent step, and not as part of the WBS creation.

2. A

PMI advocates direct confrontation in this situation. Notice that the question asked what the project manager should do FIRST. The first step would be to talk with the team member in person.
'B', 'C', and 'D' each might be appropriate at a later time, but they would not be the first step. Ultimately, your best chance of solving the problem rests with a direct discussion with the team member.

3. D

The definition of a project expeditor is someone whose job it is to make sure things happen on time but who has little real authority and usually reports to an executive on the project. This was the scenario described in the question.
'A' is incorrect, since the project manager would be in charge of the project and empowered to handle problems without constantly running to the head of research and development.
'B' is incorrect because the functional manager manages a department and does not typically function in this role.
'C' is incorrect because PMI does not recognize the term "project controller." However, if you read "controller" to mean "coordinator," this is still the incorrect answer; it would almost be correct because the project coordinator and expediter are similar; however, as the coordinator has some authority to make decisions on the project, it would not be the best fit for this question.

4. A

The project charter is a very important document and frequently appears on the PMP® exam. It performs several functions, including formally creating the project, naming the project manager, and giving him authority to use organizational resources against the project.
'B' is incorrect because the budgeting process comes after the charter has been created (do not confuse the statement about applying organizational resources with authorizing budget).
'C' is incorrect because many other planning outputs make up the major input to the project plan – not the project charter.
'D' is incorrect since it is issued by senior management and not the customer.

Baseline Exam Answer Key

5. C

The project management information system (PMIS) supports the project by supporting the gathering and disseminating of the process outputs. The PMIS may be software, meetings, forms, phone calls, etc.

'A' and 'B' are incorrect because they are part of managing communications, which is a separate topic.

'D' is incorrect because that is related to performance measurement, which uses tools other than the PMIS.

6. C

This type of scenario pops up frequently on the exam. In this case, you would not take any action until you had fully evaluated and understood the impact across the entire project.

'A' is incorrect because even if it does not affect schedule or cost, it may well affect risk or quality on the project!

'B' is incorrect for the same reason – the project manager cannot yet say what effect on risk or quality this may have.

'D' is incorrect because involving the change control board is not the first thing you would do. The change control board might be involved later in the process after the project manager has fully evaluated the impact of the change. This answer also requires the test-taker to assume that a CCB exists and is authorized to make decisions, which is not a given. Unless stated otherwise, the project manager decides to approve or reject change requests.

7. D

This would fall under communications management – not scope management. 'A', 'B', and 'C' are all activities performed as part of scope management.

'A' corresponds to Validate Scope, 'B' corresponds to Control Scope, and 'C' corresponds to Create WBS.

8. A

Decomposition is the process of breaking work down into progressively smaller pieces, and it is used during the creation of the WBS as well as in the definition of schedule activities.

'B', 'C', and 'D' are all used as part of activity duration estimating, but are not used in the creation of the WBS or defining activities.

9. B

The first step in answering this question is to draw out the project network diagram, based on the table. Your diagram should look similar to the one depicted below:

The next step is to list out all of the possible paths through the network. They are:

Start-A-B-C-Finish   Start-A-B-E-Finish
Start-A-B-F-Finish   Start-D-B-C-Finish
Start-D-B-E-Finish   Start-D-B-F-Finish

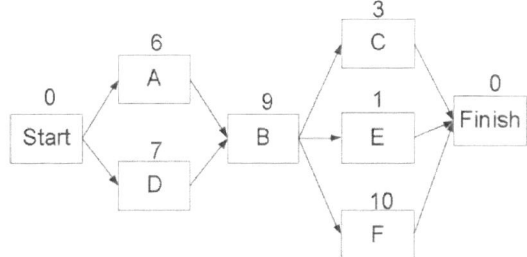

Now, in order to determine the finish date, we
need to determine the critical path. We do this by adding the duration values associated with

©2018 Velociteach. All rights reserved.   Page 371

the activities to determine the duration of each path (the path with the longest duration is the critical path):

Start-A-B-C-Finish = 0+6+9+3+0 = 18   Start-A-B-E-Finish = 0+6+9+1+0 = 16
Start-A-B-F-Finish = 0+6+9+10+0 = 25   Start-D-B-C-Finish = 0+7+9+3+0 = 19
Start-D-B-E-Finish = 0+7+9+1+0 = 17   **Start-D-B-F-Finish = 0+7+9+10+0 = 26**

The critical path emerges as 26 days, and the final step is to add 26 days to the start date. Since the start date itself is a working day, the finish date comes out to January 26 (not January 27).

10. A

Quality actually has several definitions, but the best one in the list of choices was the degree to which a set of characteristics fulfills requirements. When the product, service, or result meets those requirements, it is within the quality limits.
'B' is incorrect, since customer satisfaction may be a result or indication of quality, but it does not define it.
'C' is incorrect since completeness is not the same as quality. That description is more closely aligned with the process of Validate Scope.
'D' is incorrect since the number of defects is only one measure or indication of quality, but not a defining point.

11. C

Histograms are column charts; one form is a Pareto diagram, used to rank defects, and any time specific defects are being examined, it is a Control Quality activity. Histograms fall into the tool category Data Representation.
'A' is a scheduling tool.
'B' is a tool used in Plan Quality Management, but not in Control Quality.
'D' is incorrect because quality audits only show that the process is being followed.

12. C

Progressive elaboration means that a process (or a plan) is not performed only one time and then left alone. For example, a project does not start with initiation, move to planning, then to execution, and so on. Instead, each process may be revisited. Some execution may be performed, and then something may require you to go back and do more planning. Monitoring and controlling may be entered into, and you may then need to go back through parts of planning and execution.
'A' and 'B' are wrong because progressive elaboration is not specifically a part of communications or resource management.
'D' is incorrect because it is the opposite of the meaning of progressive elaboration.

Baseline Exam Answer Key

13. B

   The performance measurement baseline shows what was planned on a project, and is used to help determine any variances by the actual performance.
   'B' is the best answer relative to PMI's process framework.
   'A' is incorrect because it describes quality control measurements.
   'C' is incorrect because it describes performance assessments or appraisals.
   'D' describes creating the WBS, developing the schedule, or determining the budget.

14. C

   Contingency theory states that managers are either relationship-oriented or task-oriented, and the effectiveness of the manager's style is contingent on the situation - whether or not the project is running smoothly.

15. A

   Perform Actuarial Risk Analysis is not a term recognized by PMI.
   'B', 'C', and 'D' are all processes that take place in risk management.

16. A

   This knowledge area of project communications management begins with a planning process. That process results in the communications management plan.
   'B' is a process carried out in project stakeholder management.
   'C' and 'D' are steps that may take place after the communications management plan has been created.

17. B

   With questions that give you the choice of acting swiftly or taking time to fully investigate, you should really lean toward the answer that encourages you to gather all the facts first. This question falls into that category. 'B' is the best answer here because you need to understand the reasoning for the customer request before you affect any changes to your estimates. Remember that the project manager is always supposed to communicate the truth, so 'A' or 'C' do not work, and 'D' is not correct because you should not automatically reject your customer's request without understanding it fully.

18. A

   Make-or-buy analysis is a technique of Plan Procurement Management where you decide whether it makes sense (1) to produce this portion of the project within the organization or (2) to outsource it.

19. C

   The formula for the SPI is EV÷PV. The very first step is to calculate the Budgeted at Completion (BAC) amount. This is given to us as $2,000,000. Next, calculate the Planned Value (PV). To do this, we need to calculate where we had planned to be at this point in the schedule. We are 2 months into an 8 month project, which equates to 25%, and 25% X the BAC of 2,000,000 = $500,000. PV = $500,000. Next we calculate Earned Value, which is where we actually are at this point. We know that the work is 50% complete, and 50% X the

Baseline Exam Answer Key

BAC of \$2,000,000 = \$1,000,000. Now we apply the formula of EV÷PV, which is \$1,000,000 ÷ \$500,000 = 2.   SPI = 2.0

20. B

The formula for channels of communication is: (n (n-1)) ÷ 2.
Applied, that is 8 x7 ÷ 2 = 56 ÷ 2 = 28.

21. D

The work breakdown structure is created during scope management. Then the schedule is assembled during schedule management, and the budget is created during cost management.

22. C

Approximately 90% of an effective project manager's time is spent communicating with the team, the customer, the stakeholders, management, etc.

23. A

You cannot pay bribes, but you are not given enough information to be certain the payment is a bribe. It may be a customary fee. However, to be called at home sounds suspicious. In this case, you should investigate before you act.
'B' is incorrect because the payment could be a bribe and might land you in jail!
'C' is incorrect for the same reason as 'B' is. Customary fees are not usually negotiable!
'D' is incorrect because you do not know that the fee represents a bribe, so this action would not be appropriate.

24. B

The weak matrix organization is most like a functional organization because, similar to a functional organization, power is shifted toward the functional manager.
'A' is incorrect because in a projectized organization, the project manager has complete control.
'C' is incorrect because in a balanced matrix the project manager and functional manager both share power evenly.
'D' is incorrect because the strong matrix shifts power to the project manager.

25. C

The WBS contains all of the work and only the work in the scope of the project. If it isn't in the WBS, it should not be done on the project.
'A' is incorrect because none of the benefit cost analysis is captured in the WBS.
'B' is incorrect because the WBS has *all* of the work packages on the project – not just the ones that are considered critical.
'D' is incorrect because although the WBS may use templates from previous projects, it does not necessarily include every available one.

Exam Scores Summary

Velociteach

Exam	# Correct	Total # Questions	Percentage Correct
Baseline		25	
Integration Management – Chapter 4		25	
Scope Management – Chapter 5		25	
Schedule Management – Chapter 6		25	
Cost Management – Chapter 7		25	
Quality Management – Chapter 8		25	
Resource Management – Chapter 9		25	
Communications Management – Chapter 10		25	
Risk Management – Chapter 11		25	
Procurement Management – Chapter 12		25	
Stakeholder Management – Chapter 13		10	
Final Exam		100 / 200	

This page left intentionally blank.

©2018 Velociteach. All rights reserved.   Page 376